SCOTT, FORESMAN AND COMPANY

EXPLORING MATHEMATICS®

AUTHORS

L. Carey Bolster
Coordinator of Mathematics
Baltimore County Public Schools
Towson, Maryland

Clem Boyer
Coordinator of Mathematics, K-12
District School Board of Seminole County
Sanford, Florida

Thomas Butts
Associate Professor, Mathematics Education
University of Texas at Dallas
Richardson, Texas

Mary Cavanagh
Math/Science Coordinator
Solana Beach School District
Solana Beach, California

Marea W. Channel
Mathematics Resource Teacher
Los Angeles Unified School District
Los Angeles, California

Warren D. Crown
Associate Professor of Mathematics Education
Rutgers, The State University of New Jersey
New Brunswick, New Jersey

Jan Fair
Mathematics Department
Allan Hancock College
Santa Maria, California

Robert Y. Hamada
District Elementary Mathematics Specialist
Los Angeles Unified School District
Los Angeles, California

Margaret G. (Peggy) Kelly
Associate Professor
California State University, Fresno
Fresno, California

Miriam Leiva
Professor of Mathematics
University of North Carolina at Charlotte
Charlotte, North Carolina

Mary Montgomery Lindquist
Callaway Professor of Mathematics Education
Columbus College
Columbus, Georgia

William B. Nibbelink
Professor, Division of Early Childhood and Elementary Education
University of Iowa
Iowa City, Iowa

Linda Proudfit
University Professor of Mathematics and Computer Education
Governors State University
University Park, Illinois

Cathy Rahlfs
Mathematics Coordinator
Humble Independent School District
Humble, Texas

Rosie Ramirez
Assistant Principal
Charles Rice Elementary School
Dallas, Texas

Jeanne F. Ramos
Mathematics Adviser
Los Angeles Unified School District
Los Angeles, California

Gail Robinette
Elementary Mathematics Coordinator
Fresno Unified School District
Fresno, California

David Robitaille
Head, Department of Mathematics and Science Education
University of British Columbia
Vancouver, British Columbia, Canada

James E. Schultz
Associate Professor of Mathematics
The Ohio State University
Columbus, Ohio

Richard Shepardson
Professor, Division of Early Childhood and Elementary Education
University of Iowa
Iowa City, Iowa

Jane Swafford
Professor of Mathematics
Illinois State University
Normal, Illinois

Benny Tucker
Professor of Education; Chairman, Education Department
Union University
Jackson, Tennessee

John Van de Walle
Associate Professor of Education
Virginia Commonwealth University
Richmond, Virginia

David E. Williams
Former Director of Mathematics Education
School District of Philadelphia
Philadelphia, Pennsylvania

Robert J. Wisner
Professor of Mathematics
New Mexico State University
Las Cruces, New Mexico

Editorial Offices: Glenview, Illinois
Regional Offices: Sunnyvale, California • Tucker, Georgia
Glenview, Illinois • Oakland, New Jersey • Dallas, Texas

Contents

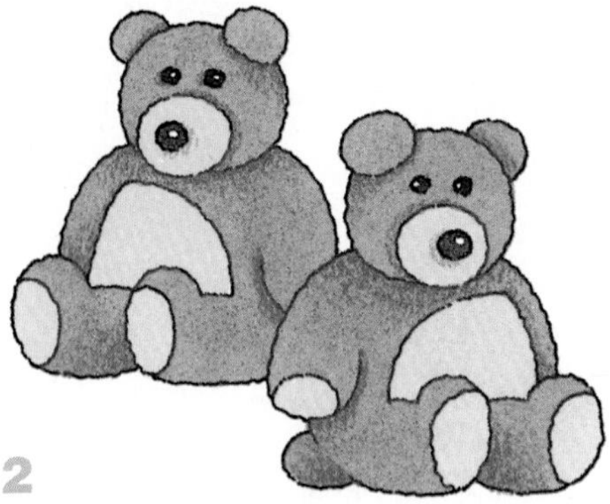

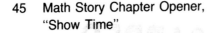

Chapter 3 Addition Through 10

Chapter 4 Understanding Subtraction

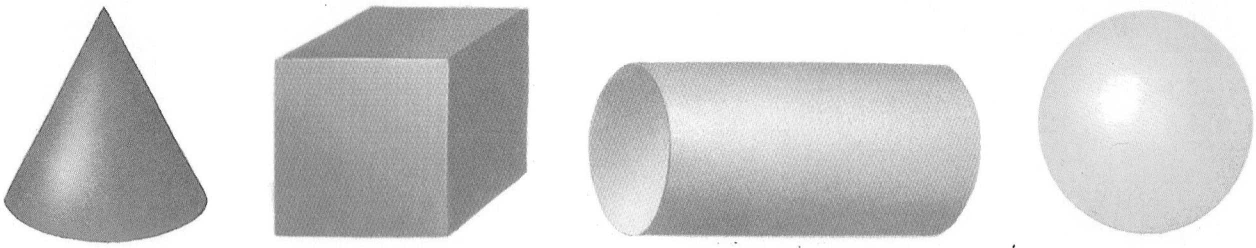

Chapter 5 Subtraction Through 10

Chapter 6 Geometry and Measurement

Chapter 7 Numbers Through 19

Chapter 8 Place Value, Counting, and Number Patterns Through 99

Chapter 9 Money

Chapter 10 Time and Measurement

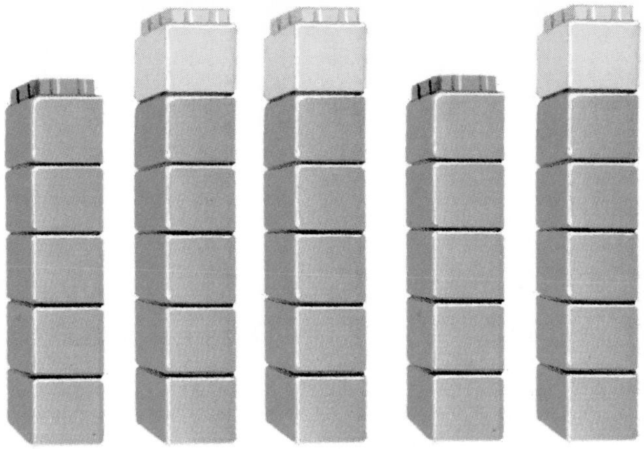

Chapter 11 Addition and Subtraction Through 12

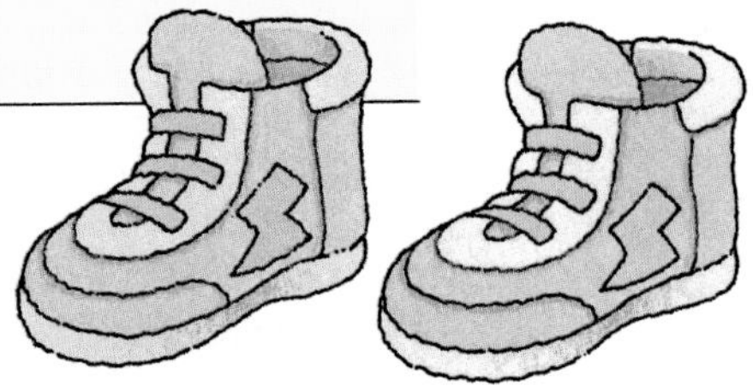

Chapter 12 Fractions and Probability

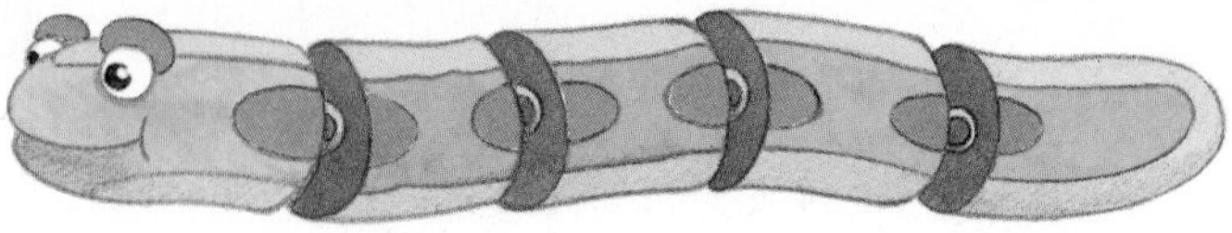

Chapter 13 Addition and Subtraction Through 18

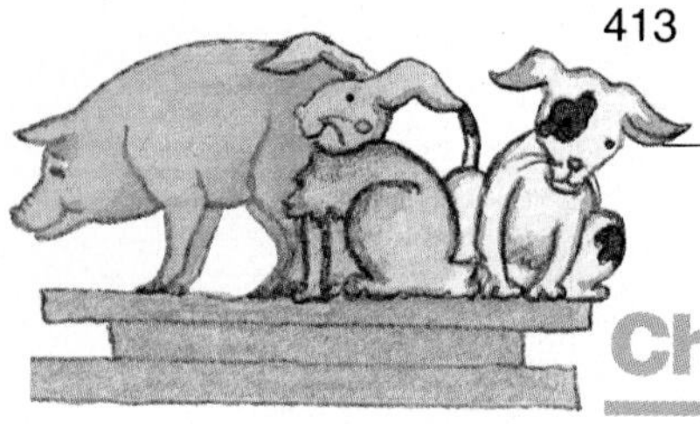

Chapter 14 Exploring Larger Numbers

WELCOME TO EXPLORING MATHEMATICS

We are your new friends.
We will help you learn and have fun with math.

Notes for Home Children become familiar with the animal characters in their math book who will help them learn math concepts.

Name

Fun with Math

We will help you solve problems.
5 + 1 = 6
We will give you clues to help you add and subtract.
We will give you hints to help you measure things.
1
2
We will give you tips to help you learn about shapes.

Notes for Home Children discuss some of the math concepts they will learn this year and ring the picture that shows what they are most interested in.

Name

Look for these children in your book. They will give you clues, hints, and tips.

Notes for Home Children are introduced to the role of the children whose photographs appear in their math book.

Math at School

1.

You will use materials to learn about math.

2.

You will listen to math stories.

3.

You will work with a partner to solve problems.

4.

You will use calculators and computers.

Notes for Home Children learn about some of the activities they will do in their books as they learn about mathematics.

Name

Math at Home

You can add and subtract at home.

You can measure at home.

You can find shapes at home.

You can count coins at home.

Notes for Home Children become aware of opportunities to use mathematics at home.

Dear Family,

There will be many things you can do to help me learn and enjoy math. Math is involved in almost everything we do together. Whenever we measure something, have to do something at a certain time, need to get more of something, fill or empty a container, there is an opportunity to talk about the math concepts we are using.

Every few weeks I will bring home a letter giving suggestions for activities we can do together. This will help me connect at-home math experiences with specific math concepts I'm learning at school.

For instance, this week would be a good time to look for small groups of things at the supermarket, at the mall, or at home. Let's look for groups of 3, 4, 5, or 6. We can count the objects together out loud and write the number on a scrap of paper. Later, we can look at the number and try to recall that we saw 5 pumpkins, 3 backpacks, and 6 lunch boxes.

Love, ______________________________

Chapter

1

Numbers Through 12

Listen to the math story, "In the Snow."
The snowpeople did not look alike.
What did the animals do to make the snowpeople match?

Notes for Home Children listen to a math story introducing chapter concepts and skills. Then they answer a question about the story.

As Many As

Match.

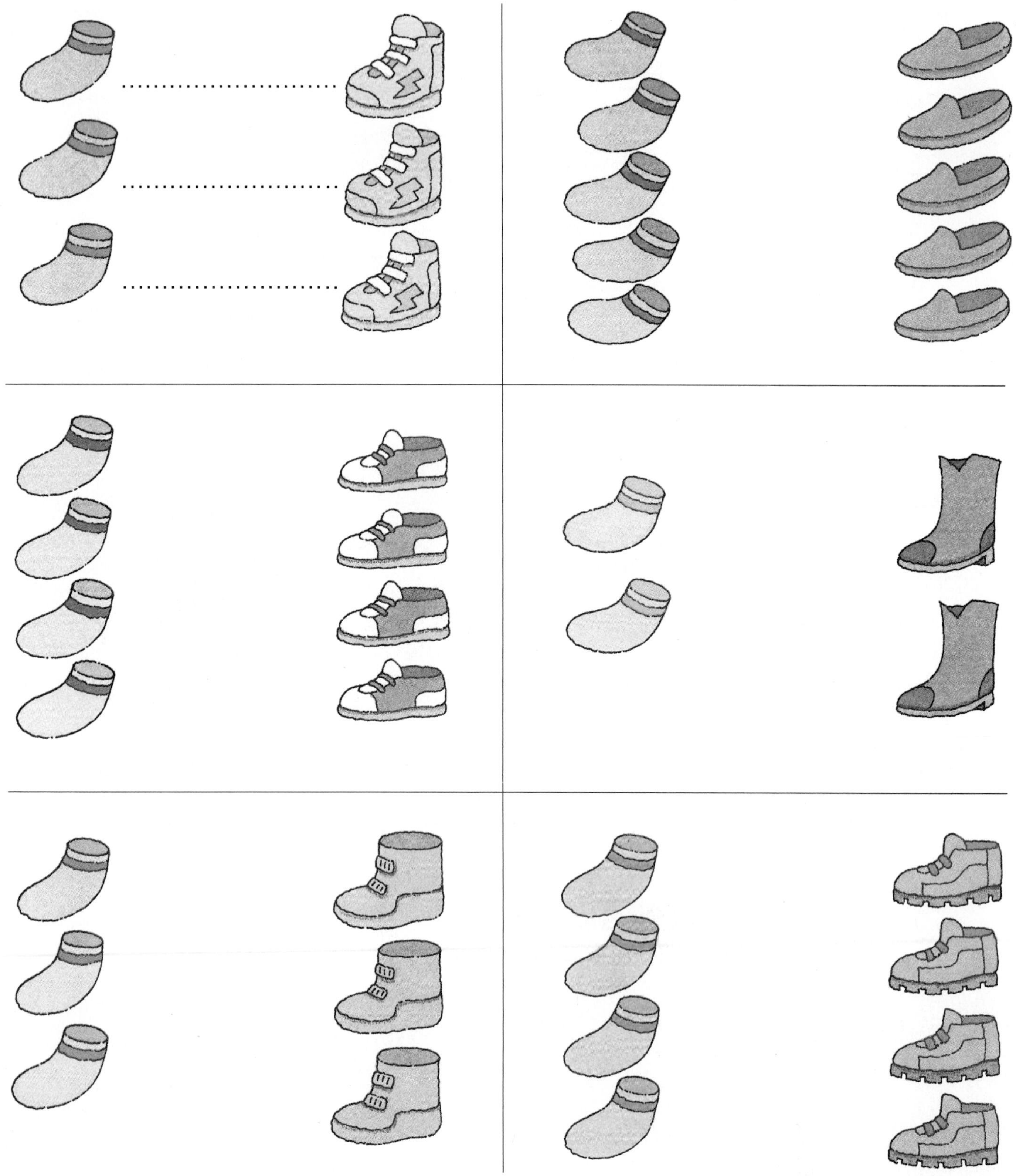

Notes for Home Children use one-to-one matching to determine if there are as many socks as shoes.

Name

One and Two

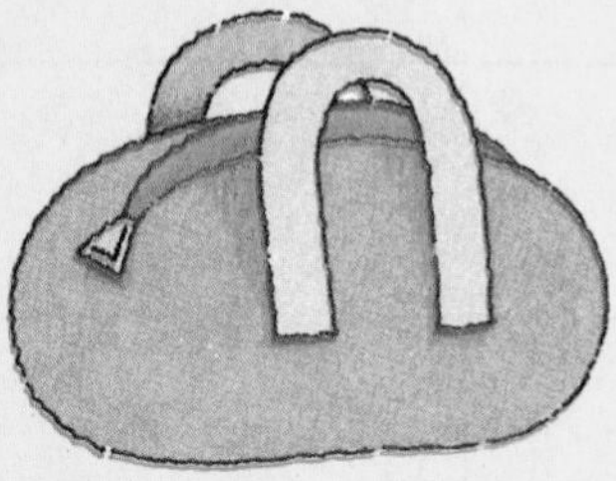

1 one

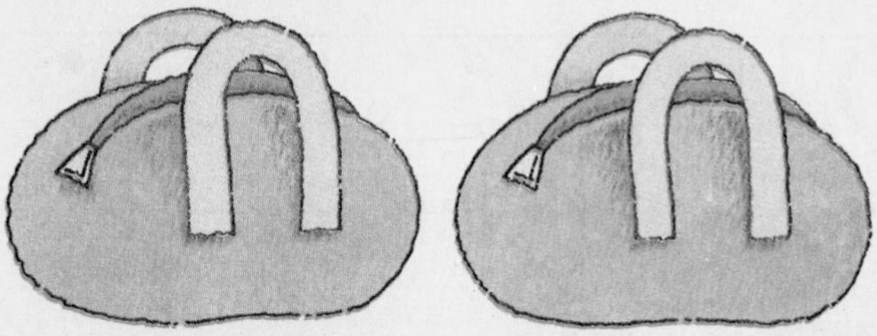

2 two

Ring how many.

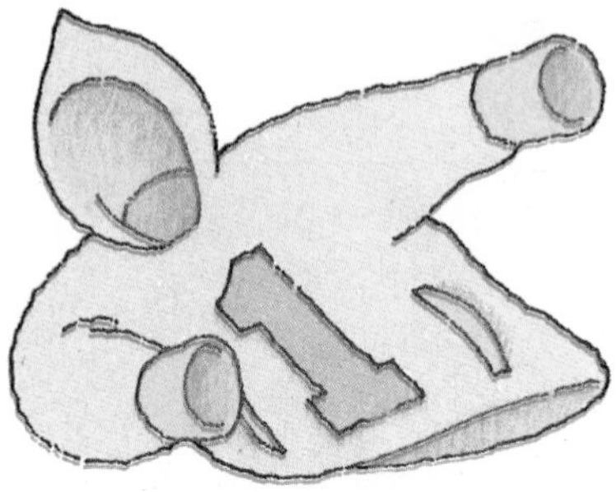

(1) 2

1 2

1 2

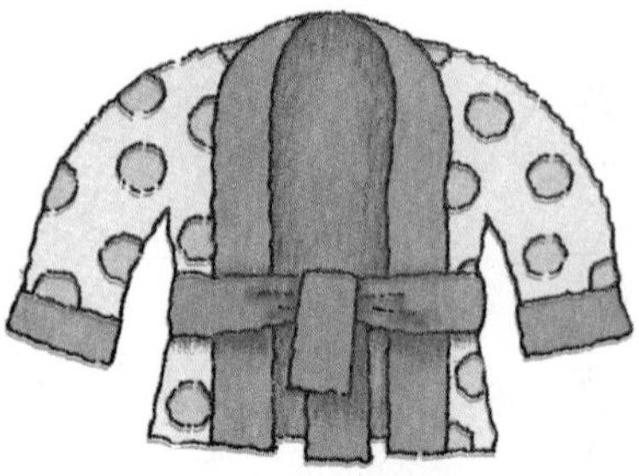

1 2

1 2

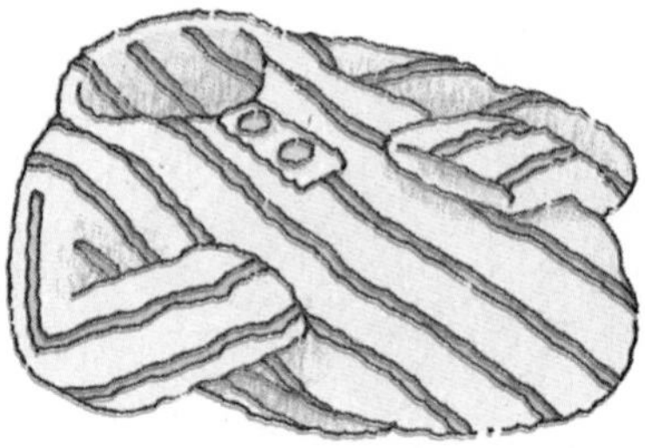

1 2

Notes for Home Children identify groups of 1 and 2.

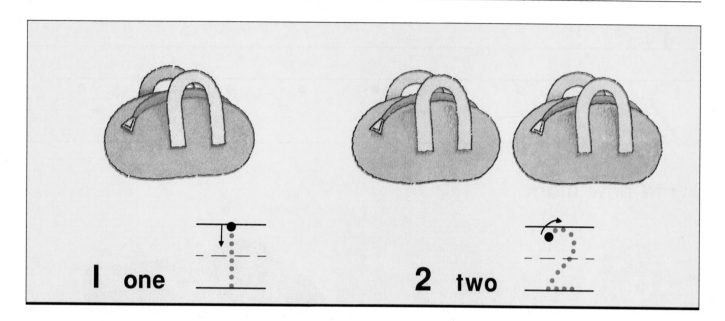

Write 1 and 2.

1

2

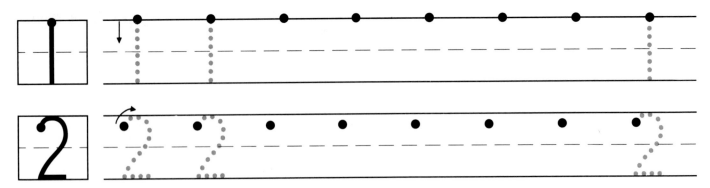

Write how many.

2

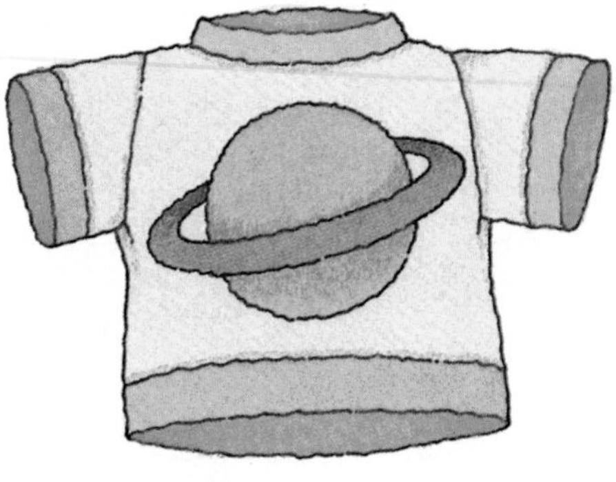

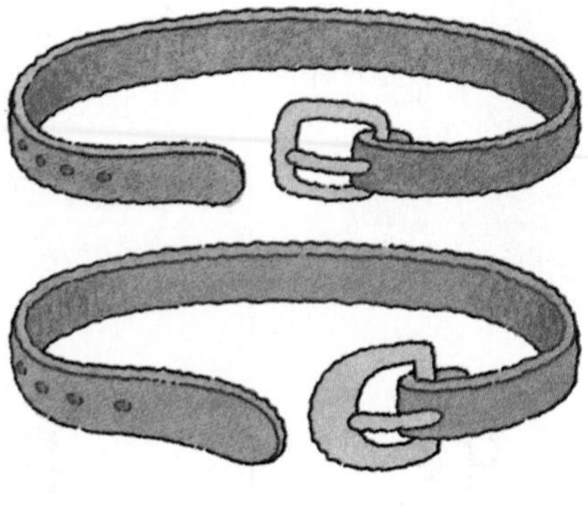

Notes for Home Children write 1 and 2 and identify groups of 1 and 2.

Name

Three and Four

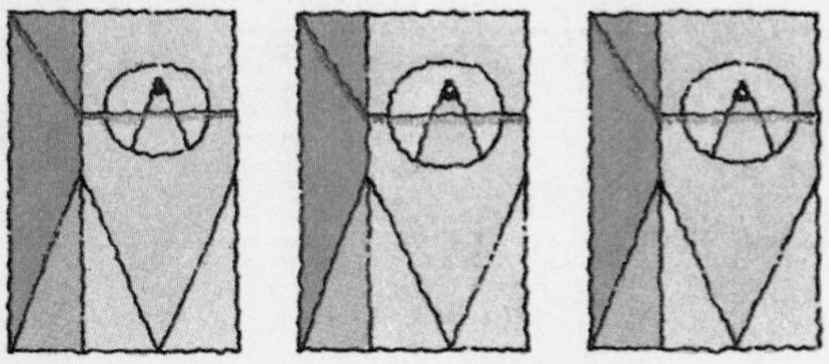

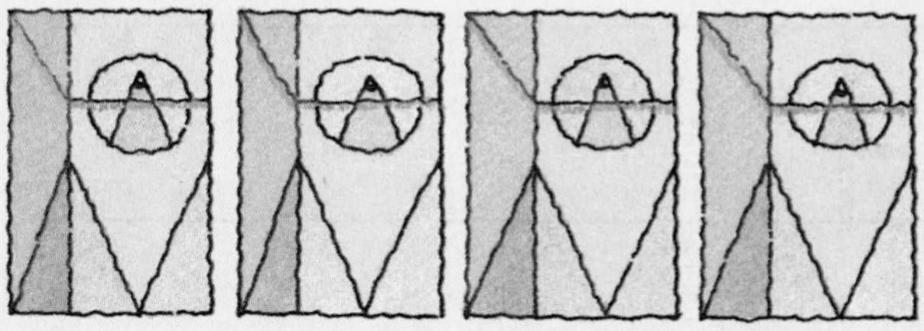

3 **three** 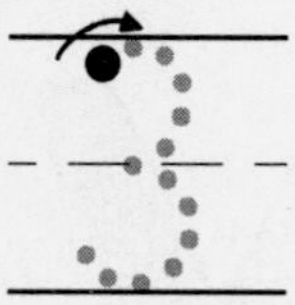

4 **four** 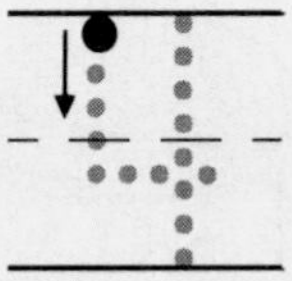

Ring how many.

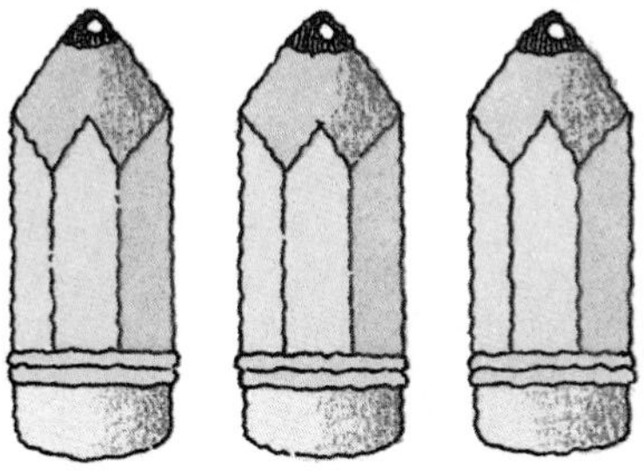

3 4

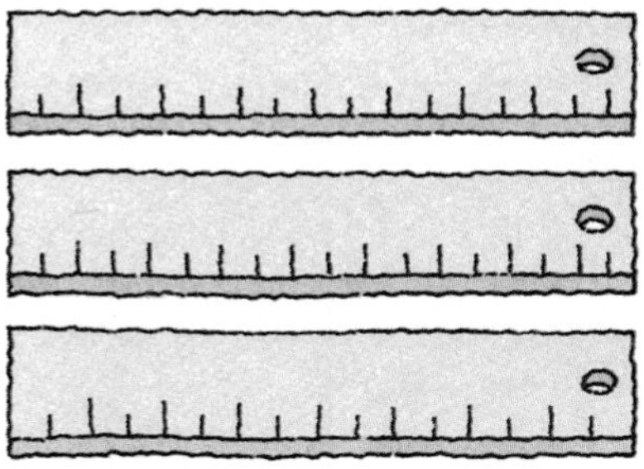

3 4

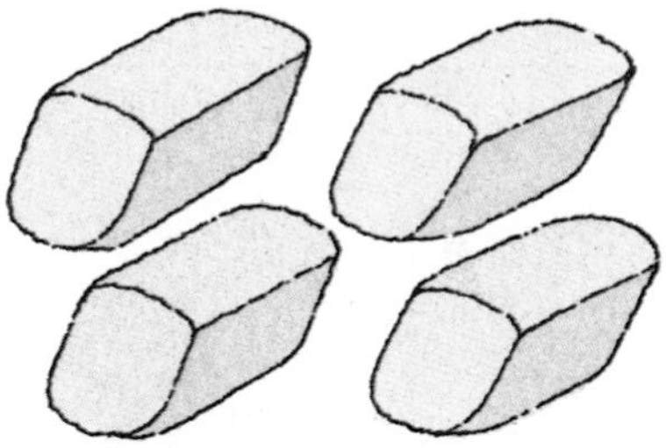

3 4

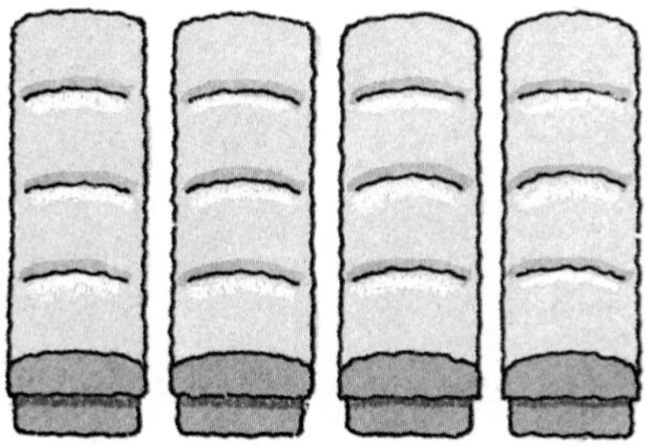

3 4

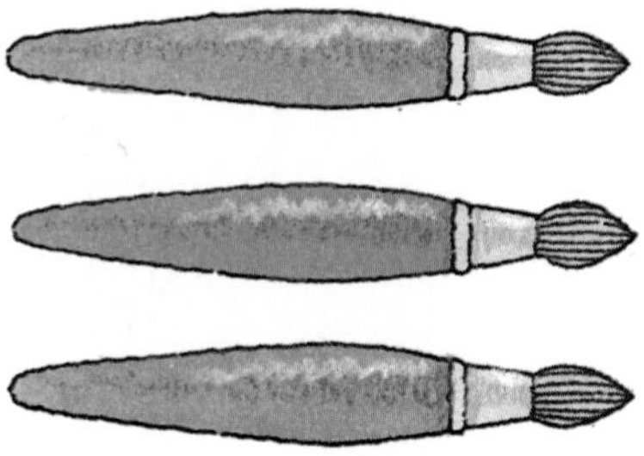

3 4

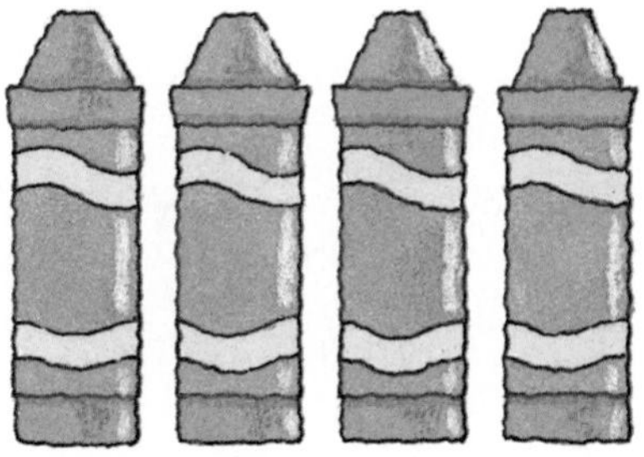

3 4

Notes for Home Children identify groups of 3 and 4.

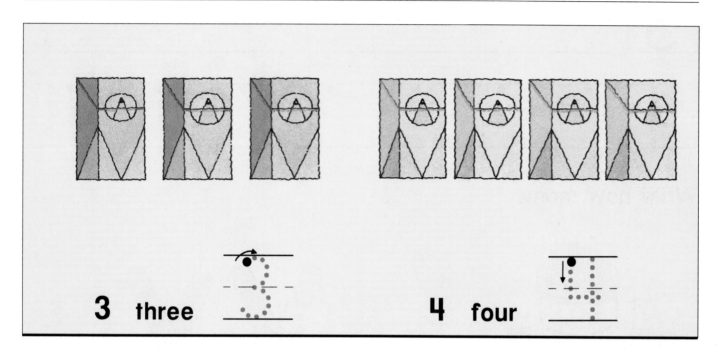

Write 3 and 4.

3 3 3 3

4 4 4 4

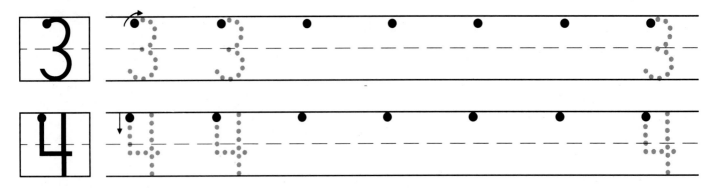

Write how many.

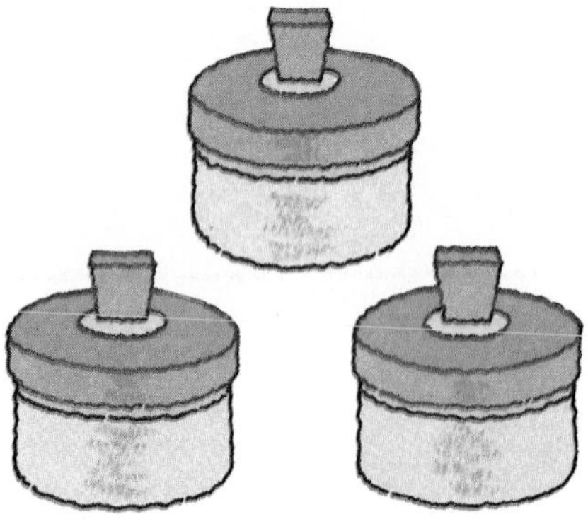

3

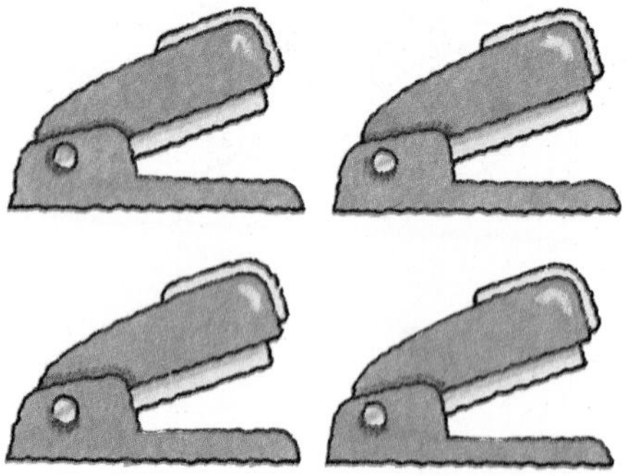

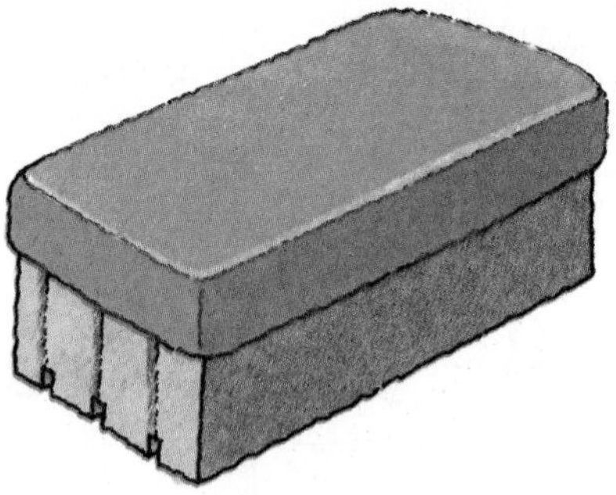

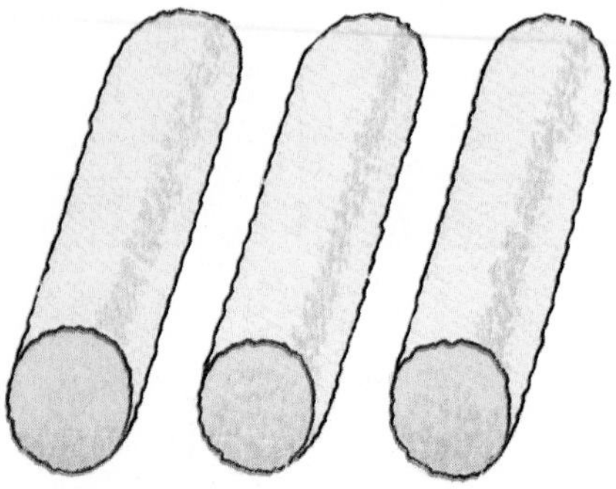

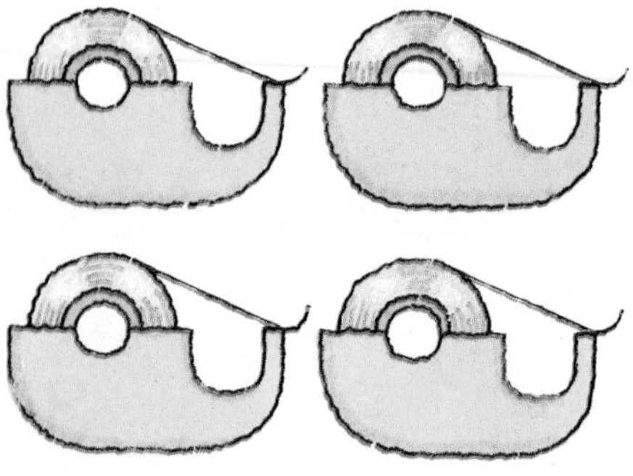

Notes for Home Children write 3 and 4 and identify groups through 4.

Name

Five and Six

5 **five**

6 **six**

Ring how many.

 5 6	 5 6	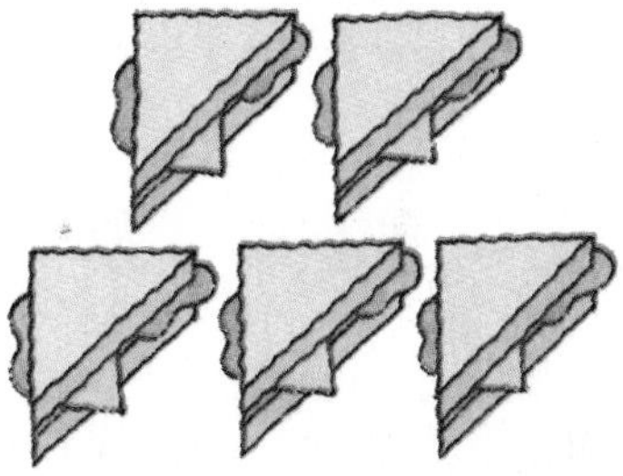 5 6
 5 6	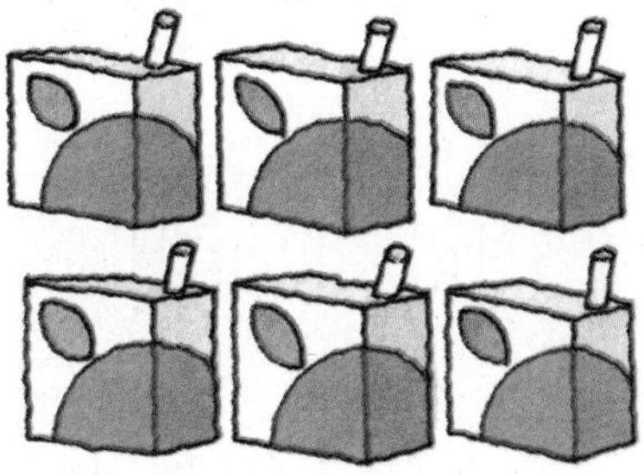 5 6	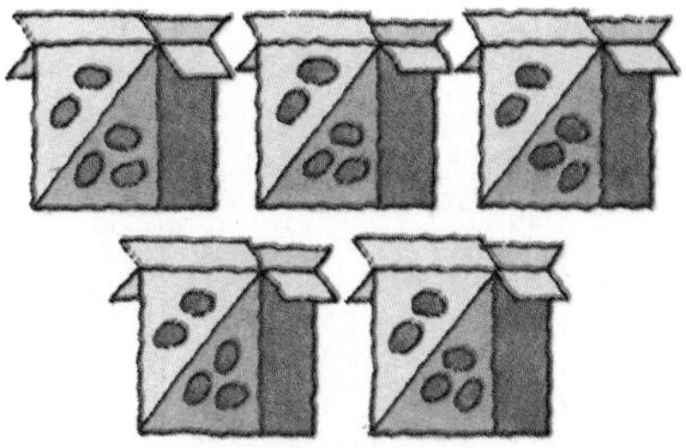 5 6

Notes for Home Children identify groups of 5 and 6.

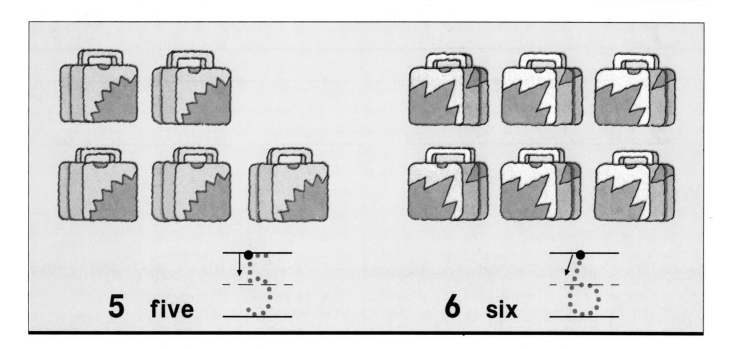

Write 5 and 6.

5 5 5 5

6 6 6 6

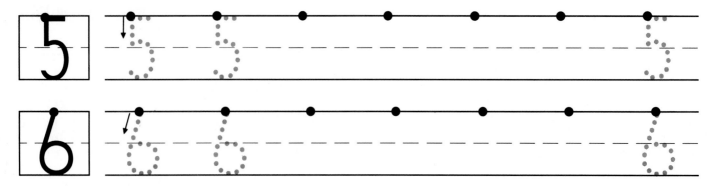

Write how many.

5

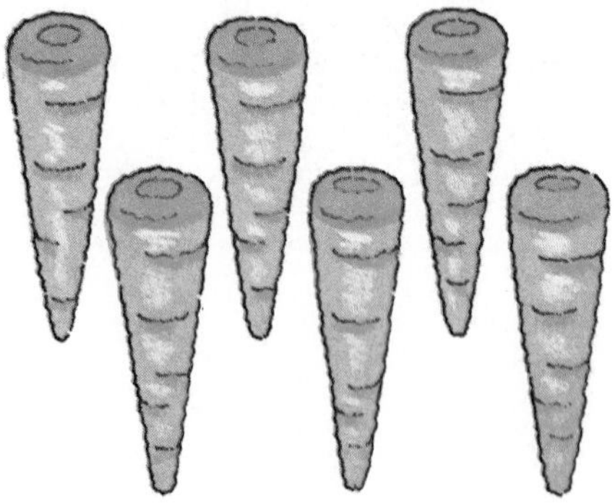

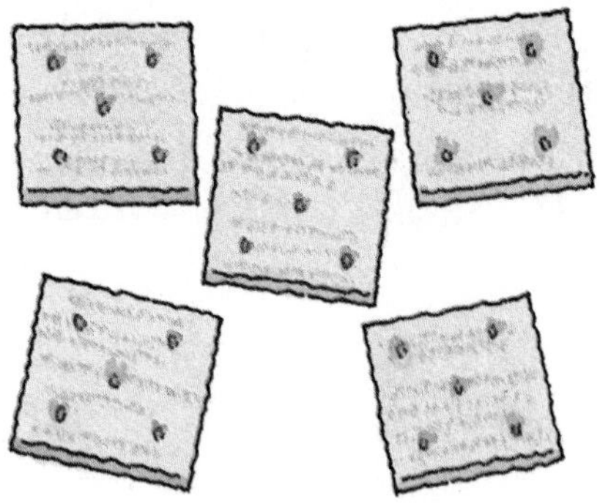

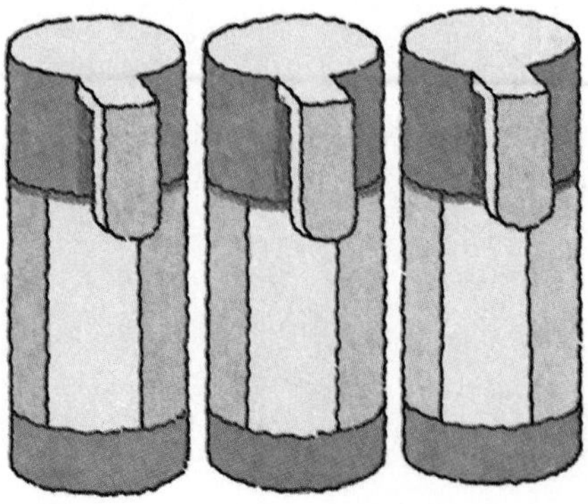

Notes for Home Children write 5 and 6 and identify groups through 6.

Name

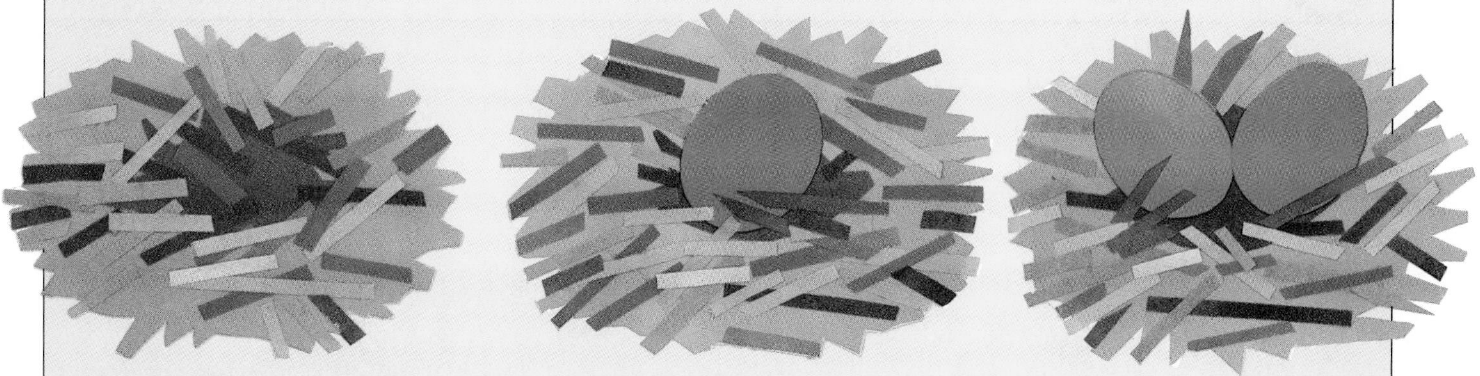

0 zero **1 one** **2 two**

Ring how many.

0 1 2

0 1 2

0 1 2

0 1 2

Notes for Home Children identify 0.

Write 0.

0

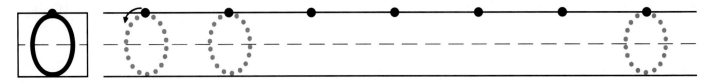

Write how many.

6

Notes for Home Children write 0 and identify groups through 6.

Name

Seven and Eight

7 seven 7

8 eight 8

Ring how many.

7 8

7 8

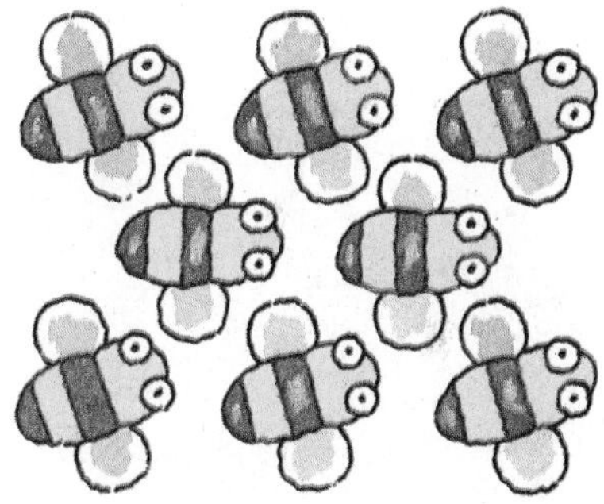

7 8

7 8

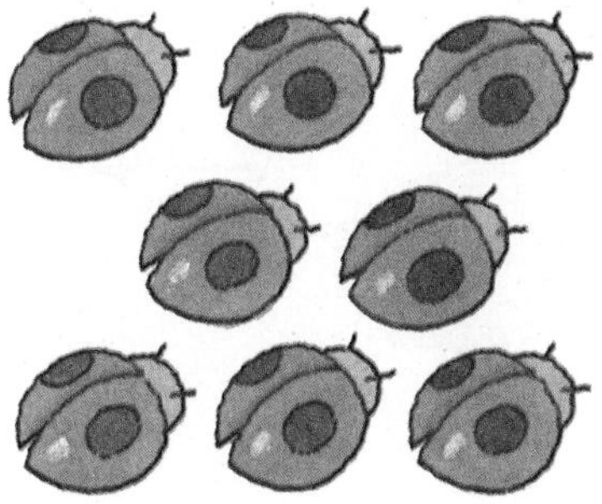

7 8

7 8

Notes for Home Children identify groups of 7 and 8.

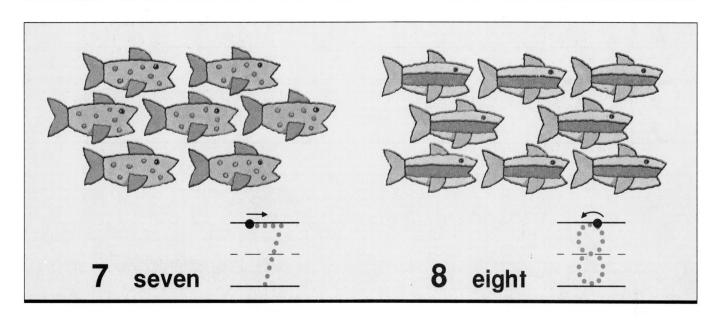

Write 7 and 8.

7

8

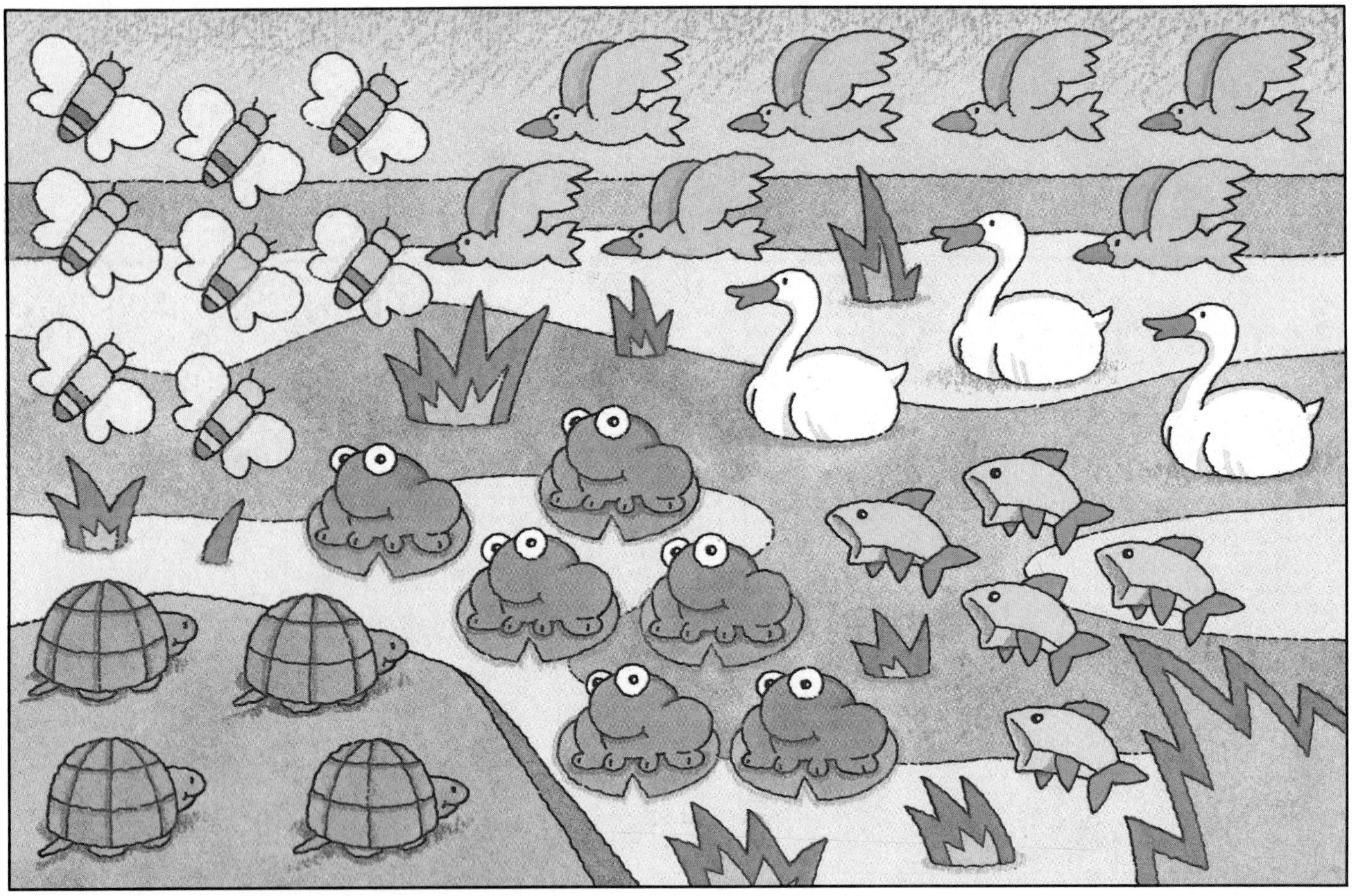

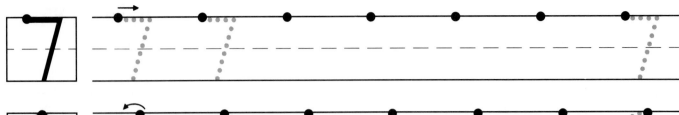

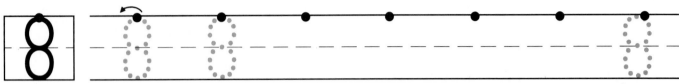

Write how many of each.

 6

Notes for Home Children write 7 and 8 and identify groups through 8.

Name

Nine and Ten

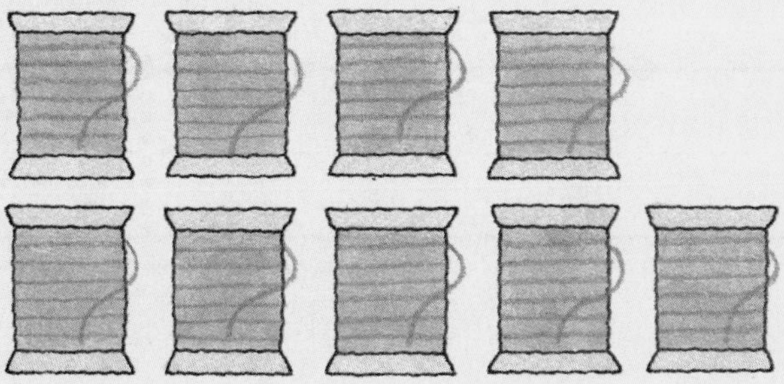

9 nine 9

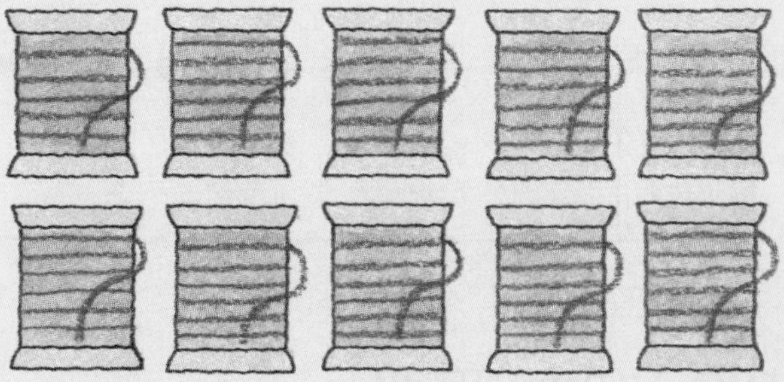

10 ten 10

Ring how many.

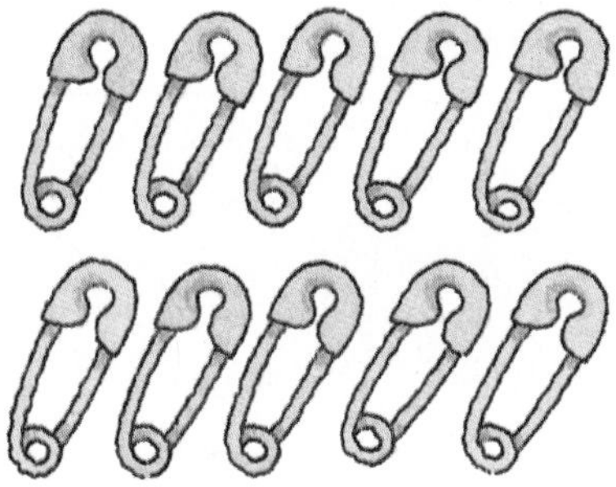

9 (10)

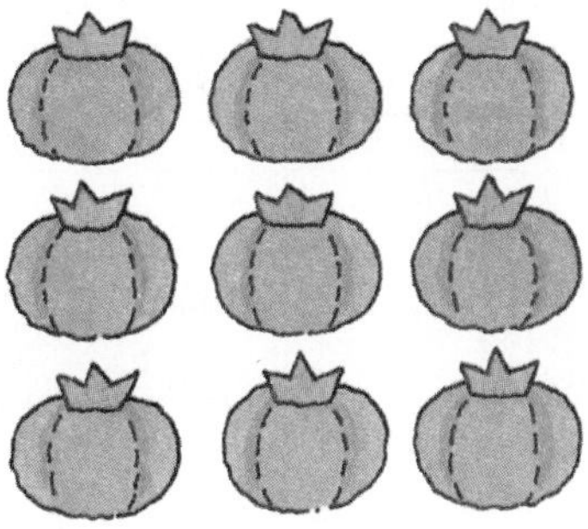

9 10

9 10

9 10

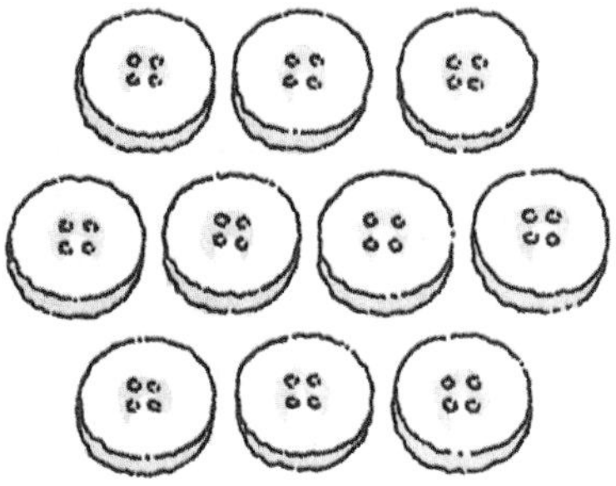

9 10

9 10

Notes for Home Children identify groups of 9 and 10.

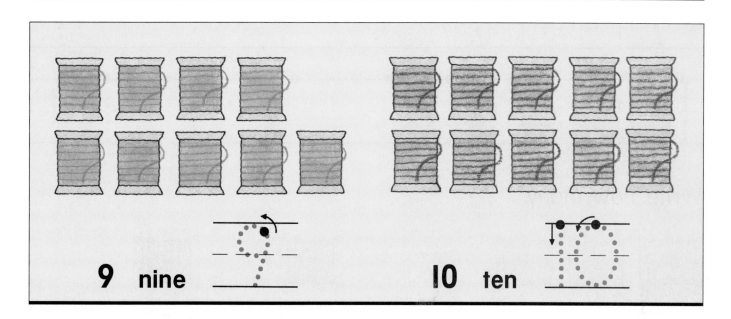

Write 9 and 10.

9

10

Write how many.

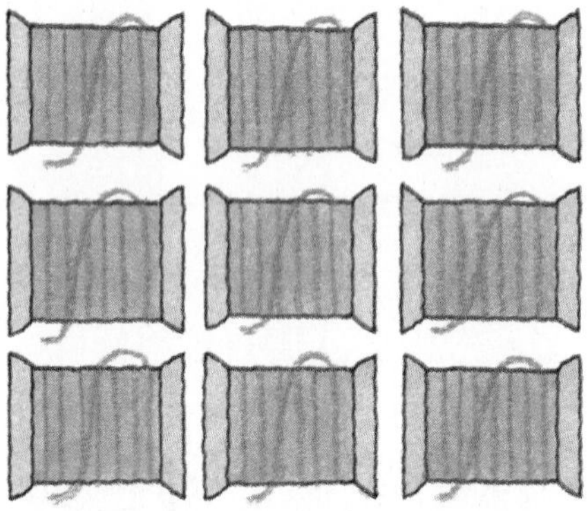

9

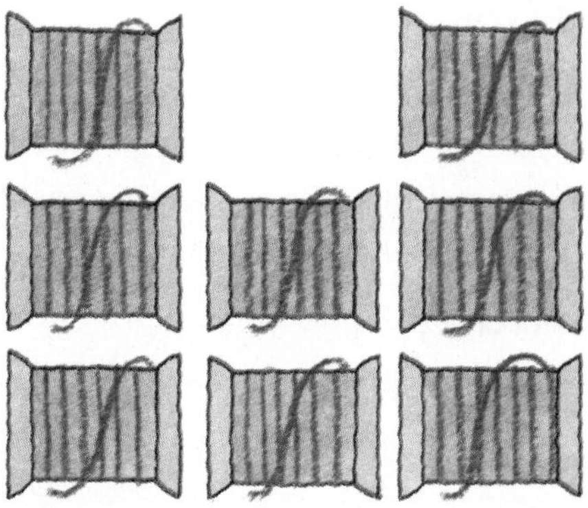

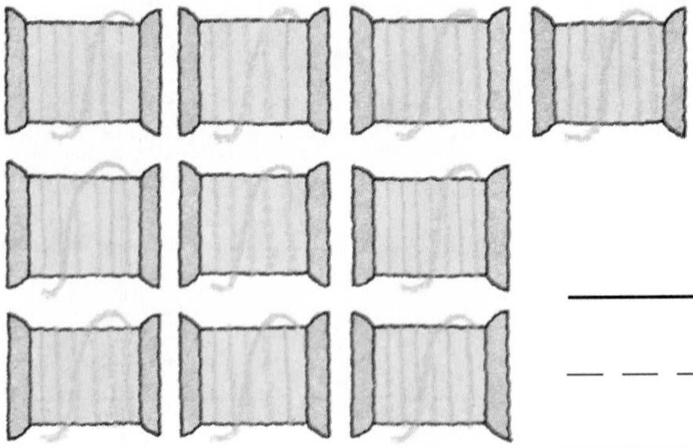

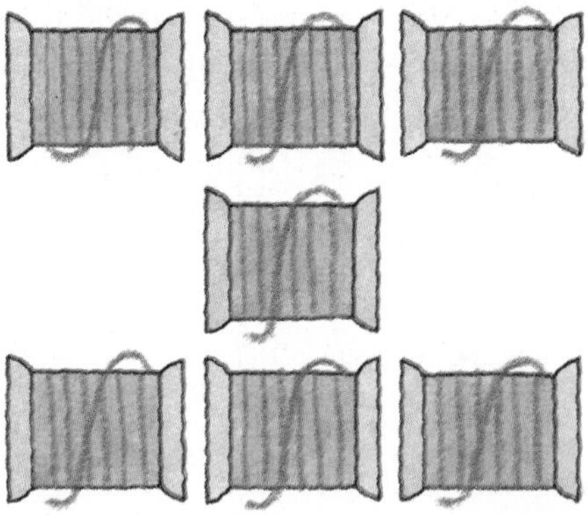

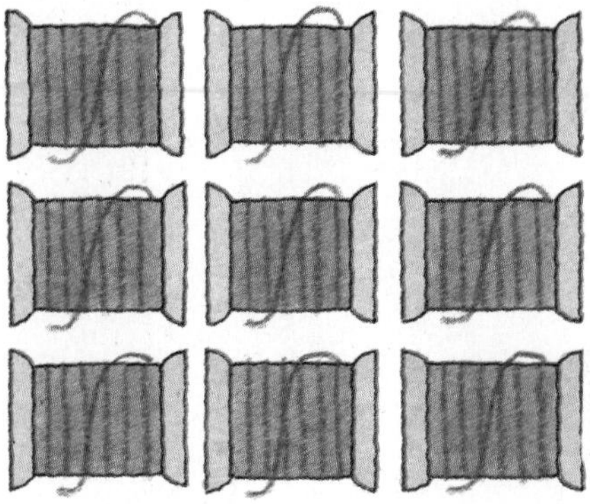

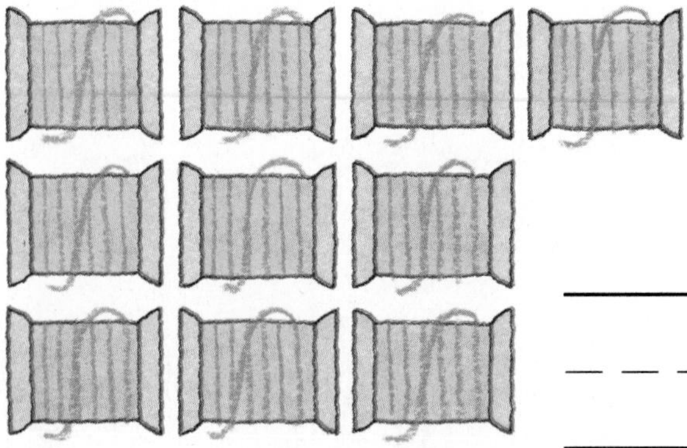

Notes for Home Children write 9 and 10 and identify groups through 10.

See More Practice Set A on page 41.

Name

PROBLEM-SOLVING STRATEGY Activity

Find a Pattern

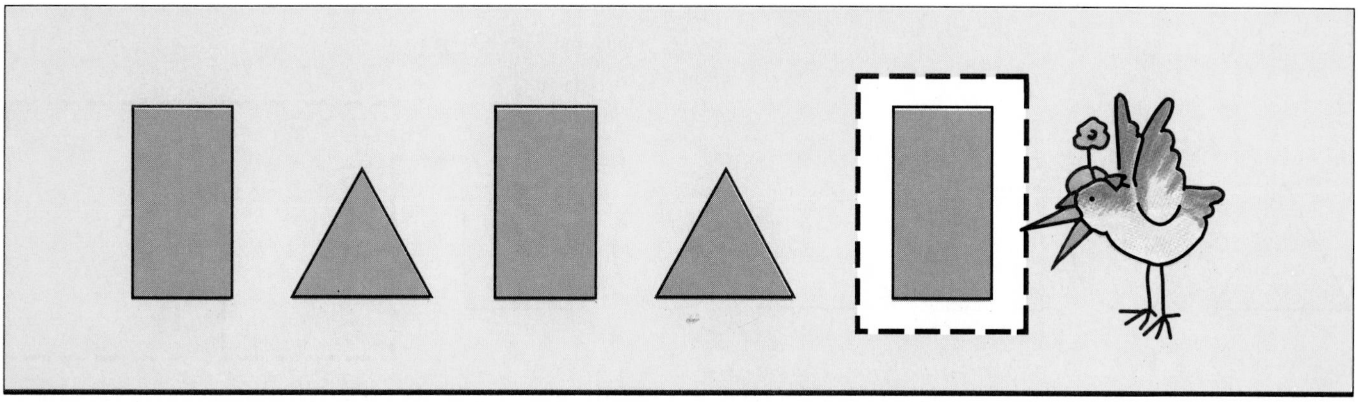

What is the pattern?

Use the shapes on page 23.

Cut and paste the shape that comes next.

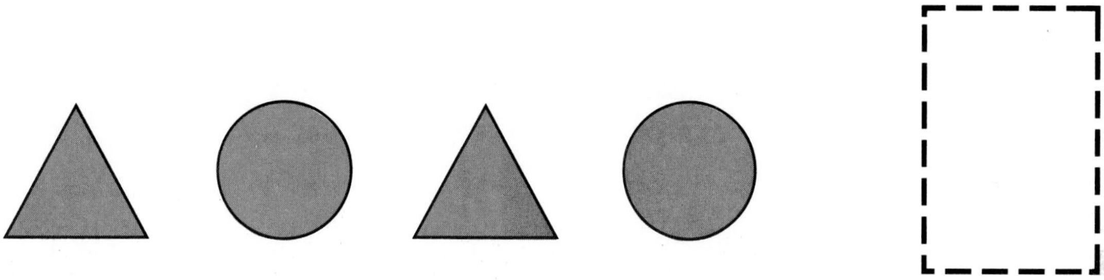

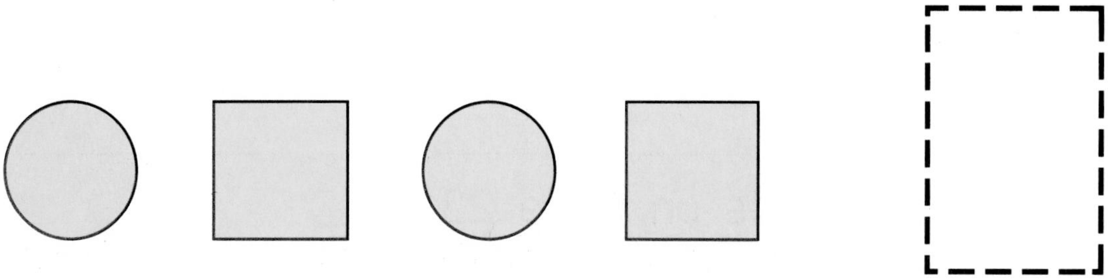

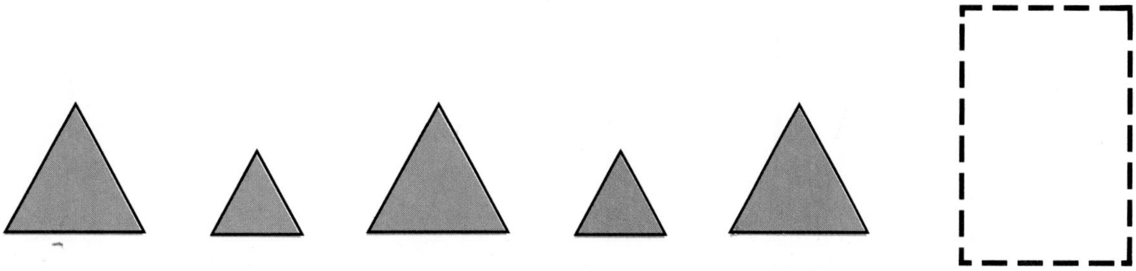

Notes for Home Children explore at the CONCRETE level using cut and paste plane shapes to solve problems by finding patterns.

What is the pattern?
Use the shapes on page 23.
Cut and paste the shapes that come next.

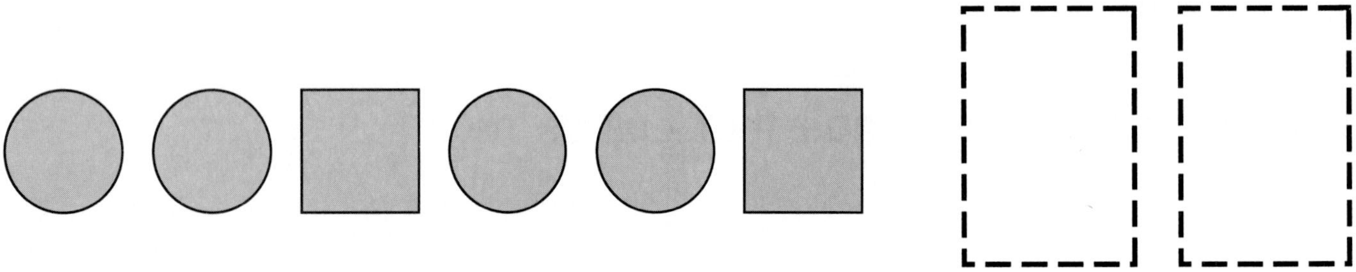

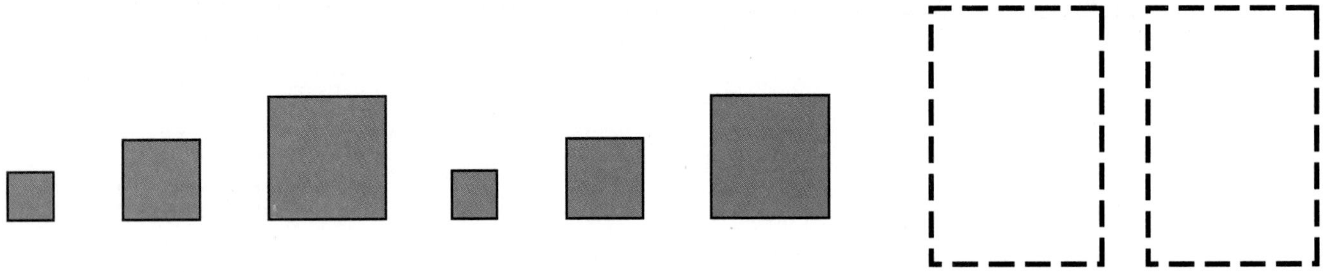

Use the green shapes on page 23.
Make a pattern.

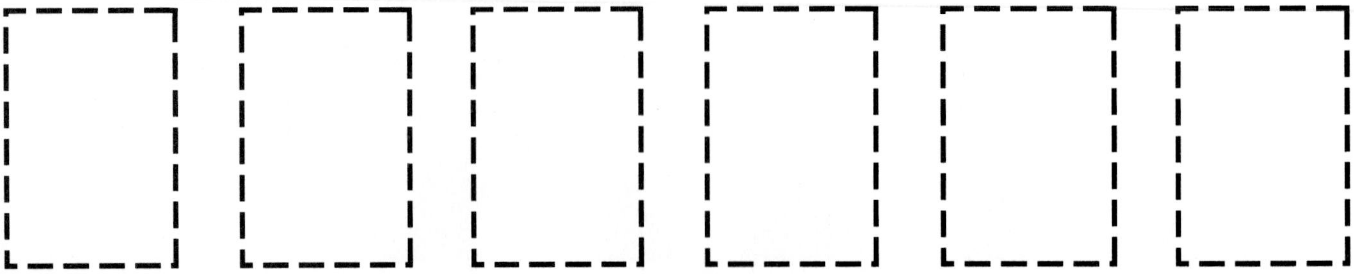

Notes for Home Children explore at the CONCRETE level using cut and paste plane shapes to solve problems by finding patterns.

Use with page 21.

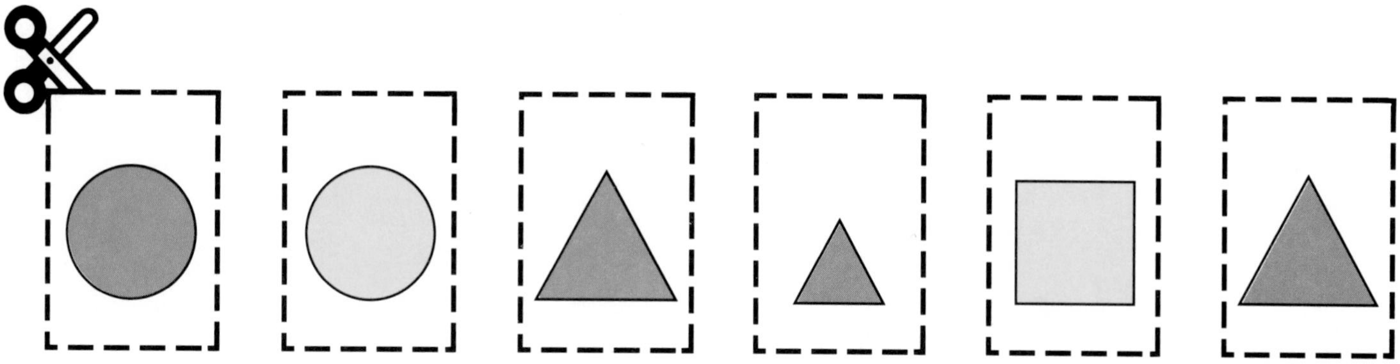

Use with top of page 22.

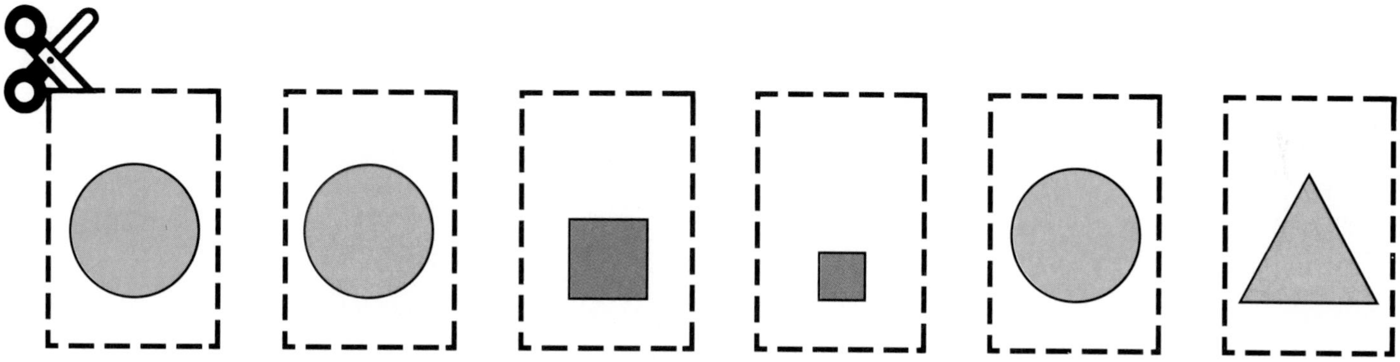

Use with bottom of page 22.

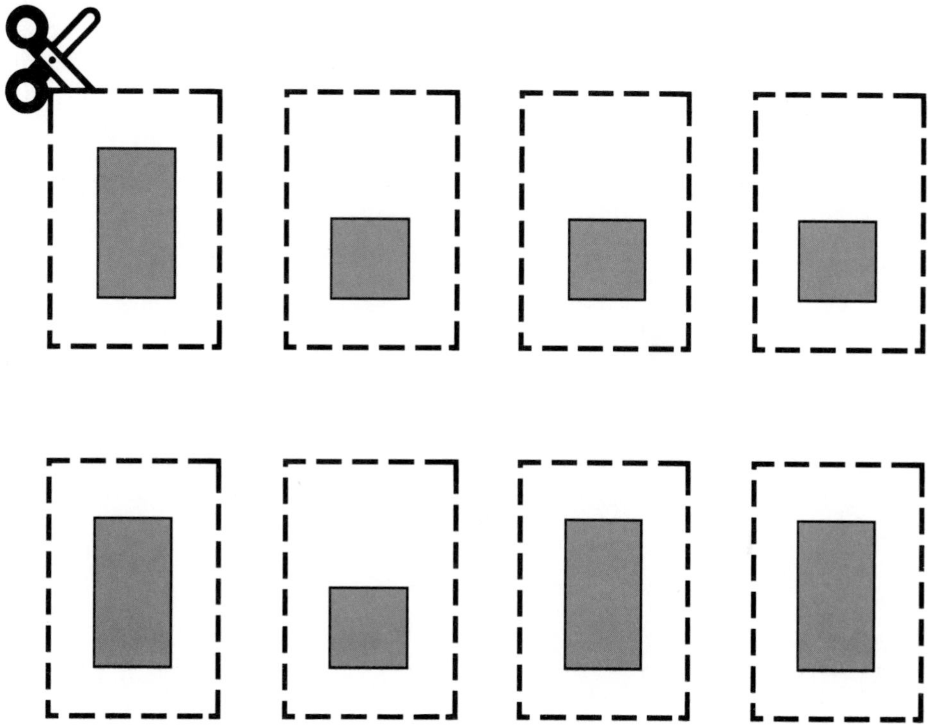

Name ______

Number Sense

Can you name all the groups in the store that are more than 5 and less than 10?

Let's do some more!

Draw a picture of a store.
Show groups of items that are more than 5 and less than 10.
Tell a story about your picture to a friend.

Notes for Home Children develop number understanding by identifying items in the picture that are more than 5, but less than 10.

Skills Review

Fill in the correct ⬭.
How many?

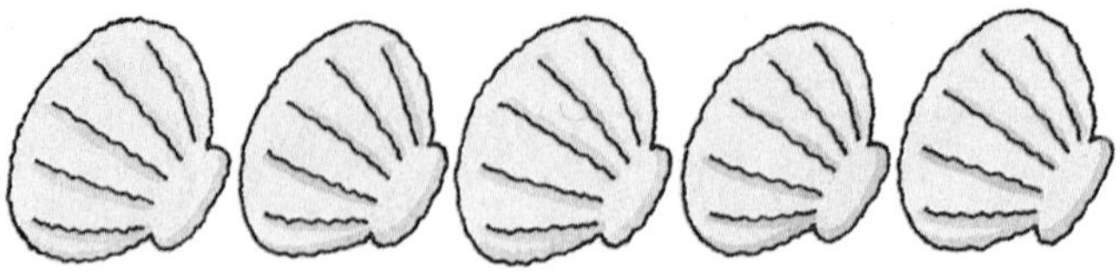

4 Ⓐ   5 Ⓑ

9 Ⓐ   10 Ⓑ

6 Ⓐ   8 Ⓑ

3 Ⓐ   4 Ⓑ

Vocabulary

Match.

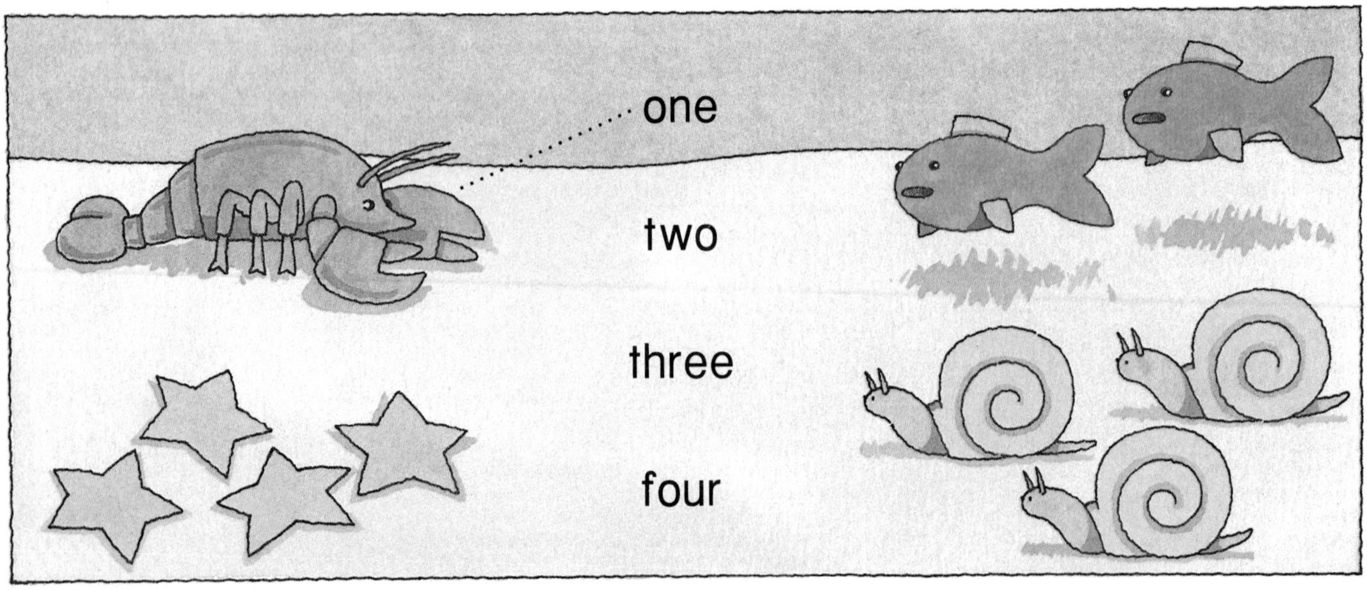

Notes for Home Children review counting objects through 10. Then they review number words.

Name

Pennies

Count to find how much.

3 ¢

____ ¢

____ ¢

____ ¢

____ ¢

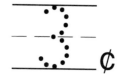

Notes for Home Children identify a penny and count pennies through 10¢.

Ring the pennies needed.

Notes for Home Children ring the number of pennies needed to buy an item.

Name

Eleven and Twelve

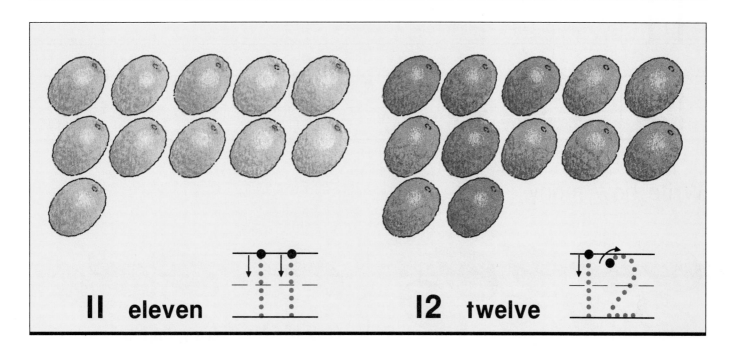

11 **eleven**

12 **twelve**

Ring how many.

11 12

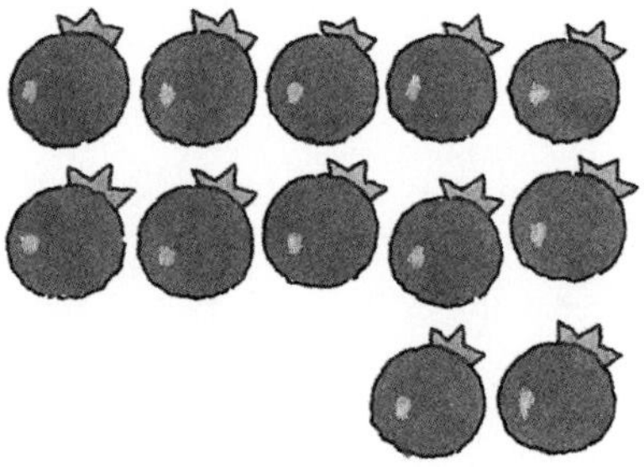

11 12

11 12

11 12

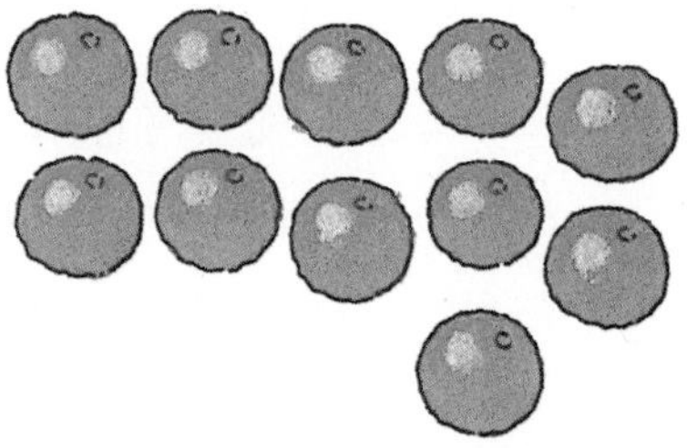

11 12

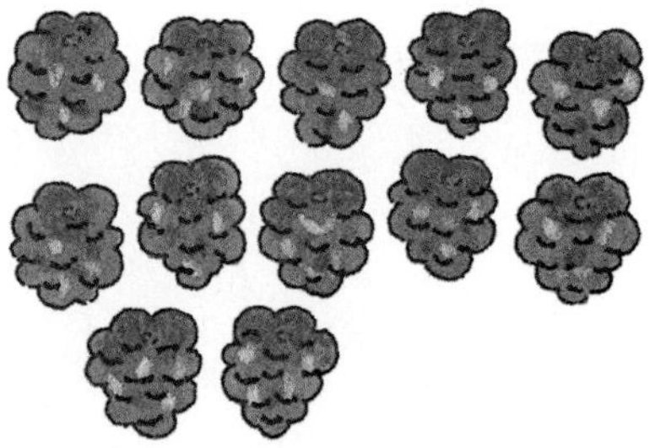

11 12

Notes for Home Children identify groups of 11 and 12.

Write 11 and 12.

11 11 11 11

12 12 12 12

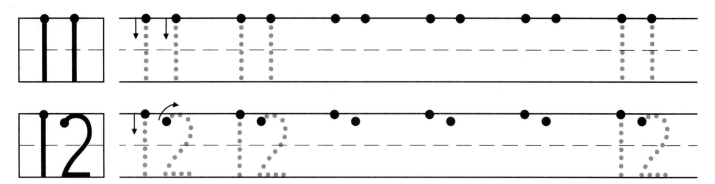

Write how many.

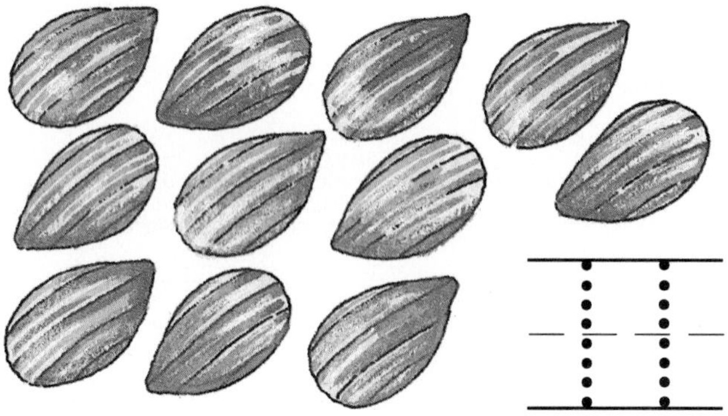

11

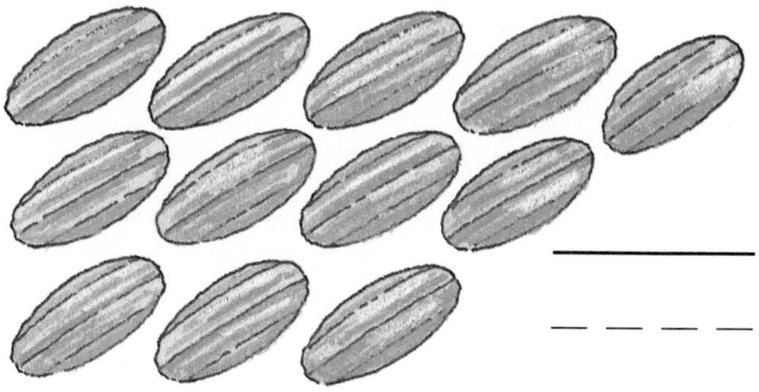

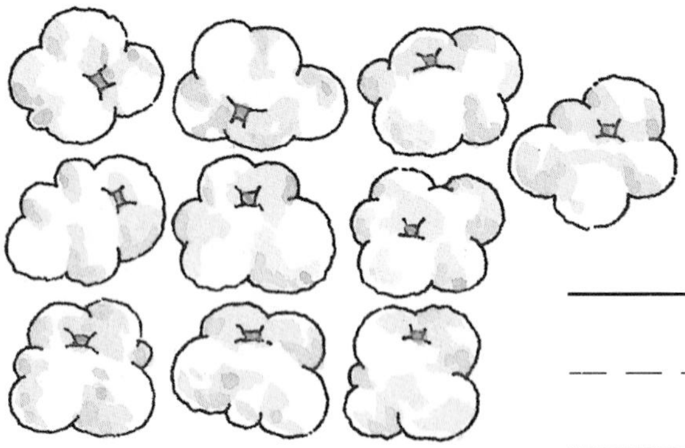

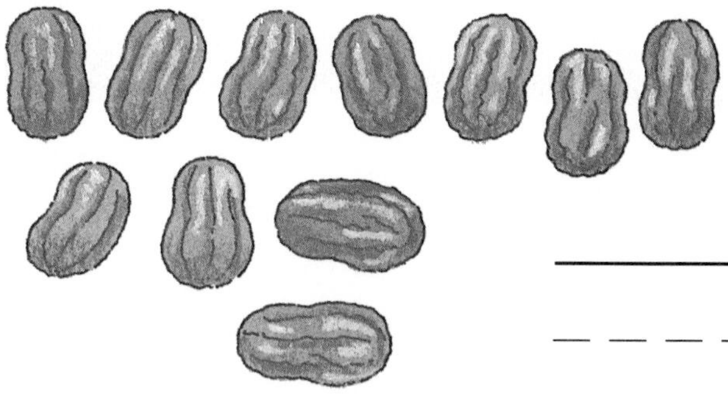

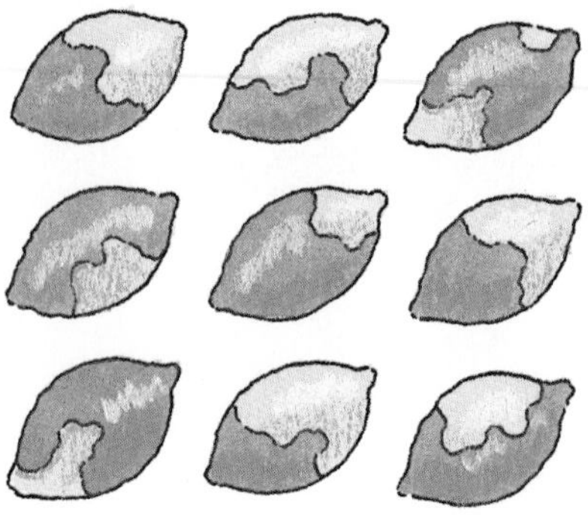

Notes for Home Children write 11 and 12 and identify groups through 12.

Name

Order Through 12

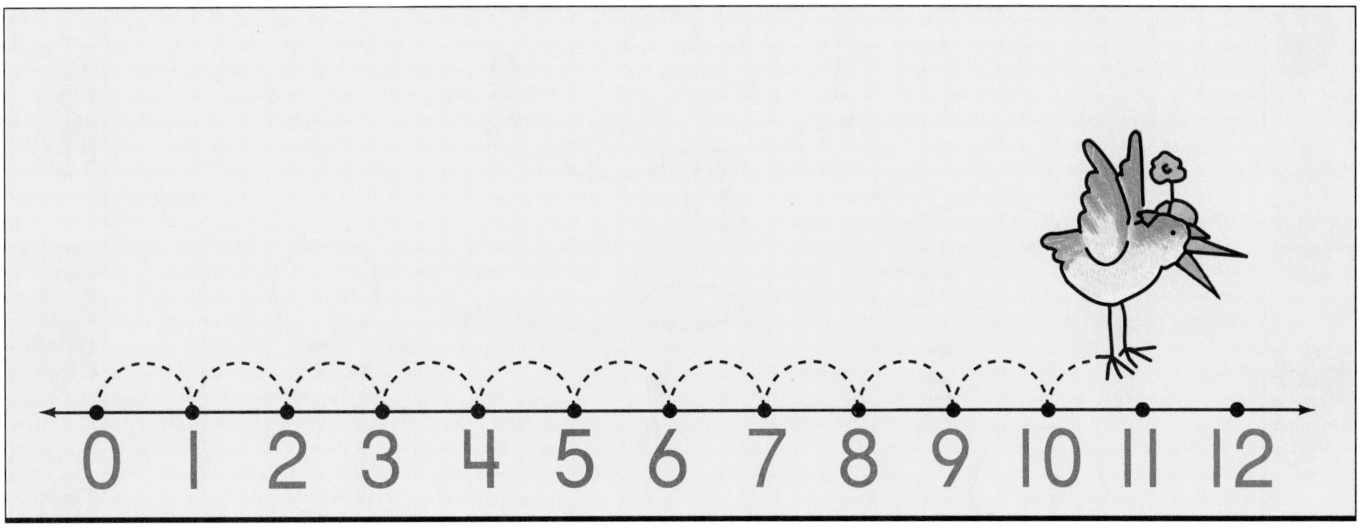

Write the missing numbers.

0 1 2 3 4 5 6

0 1 2 ___ 4 ___ 6

3 4 ___ 6 ___ ___ 9

6 7 ___ ___ 10 ___ 12

Notes for Home Children order numbers through 12.

Connect the dots.

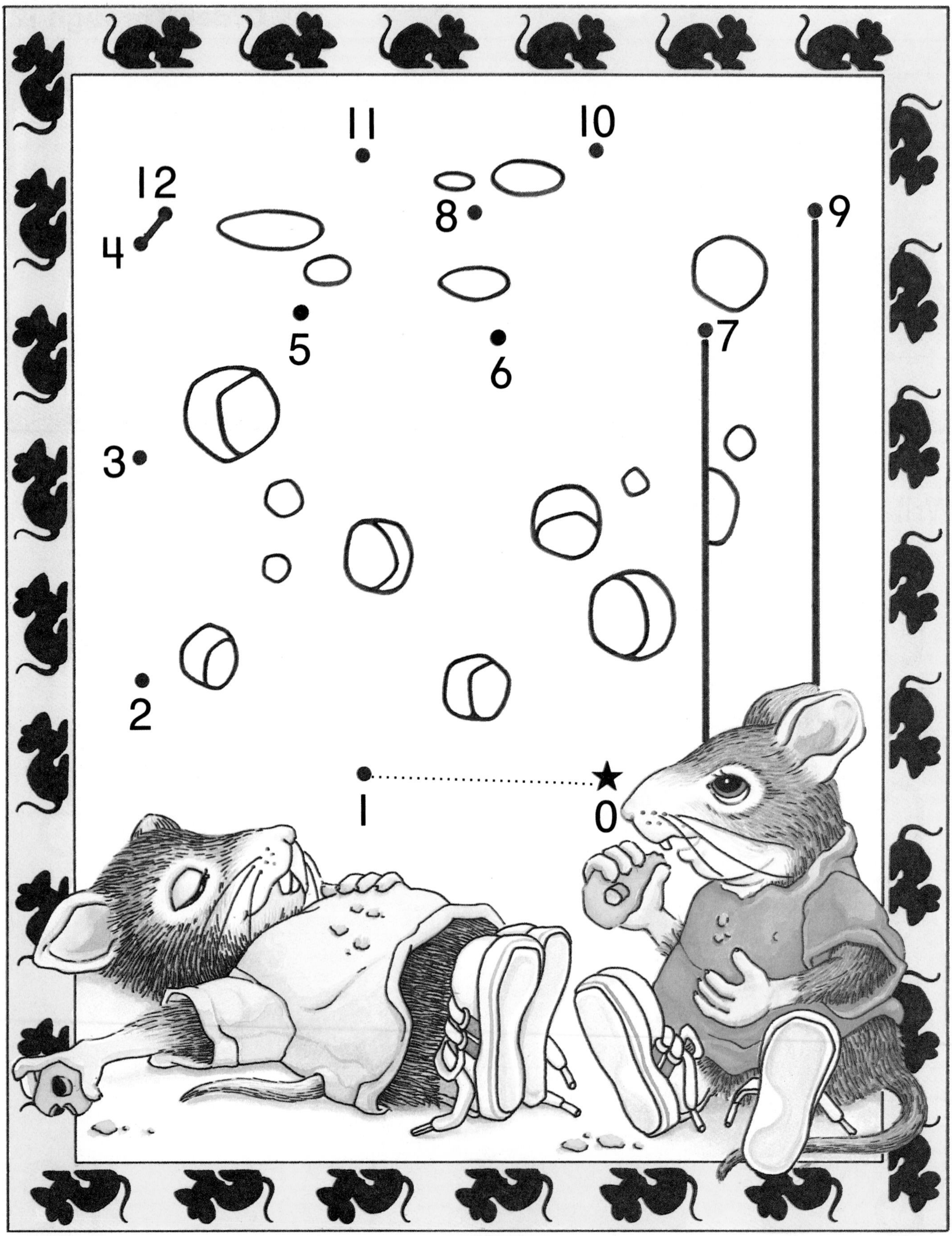

Exploring Mathematics Book One © Scott, Foresman and Company

Notes for Home Children order numbers through 12 by connecting numbers in order.

Name ____________________

Before, After, Between

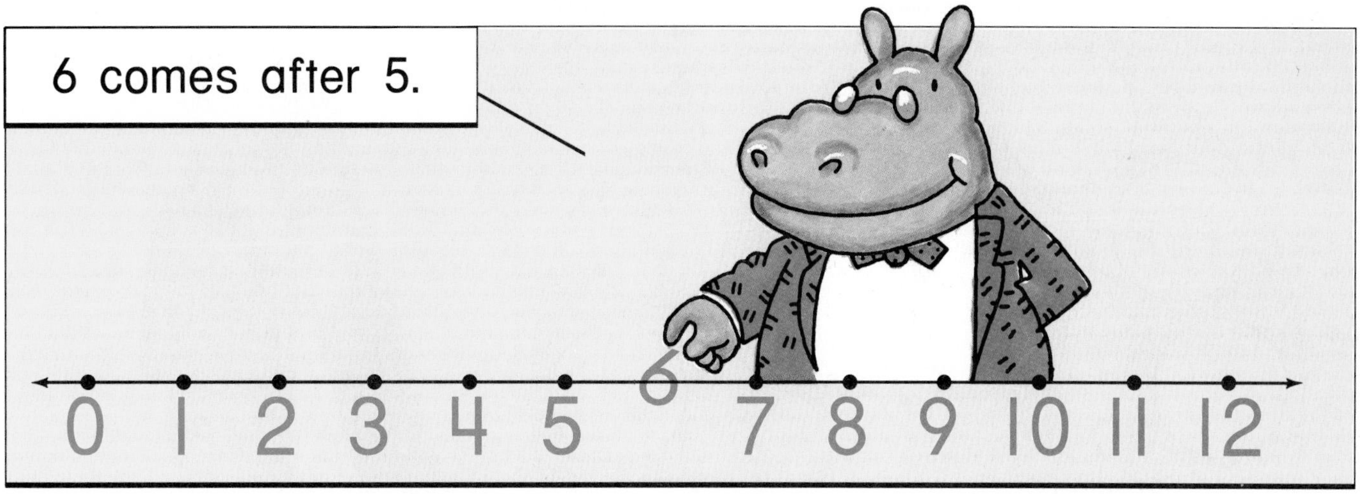

Write the number that comes after.

3 4 5	9 10 ___
5 6 ___	0 1 ___

Write the number that comes before.

2 3 4	___ 11 12
___ 8 9	___ 5 6

Write the number that comes between.

1 2 3	7 ___ 9

Notes for Home Children identify numbers before, after, and between given numbers.

Write the missing numbers on the clock.

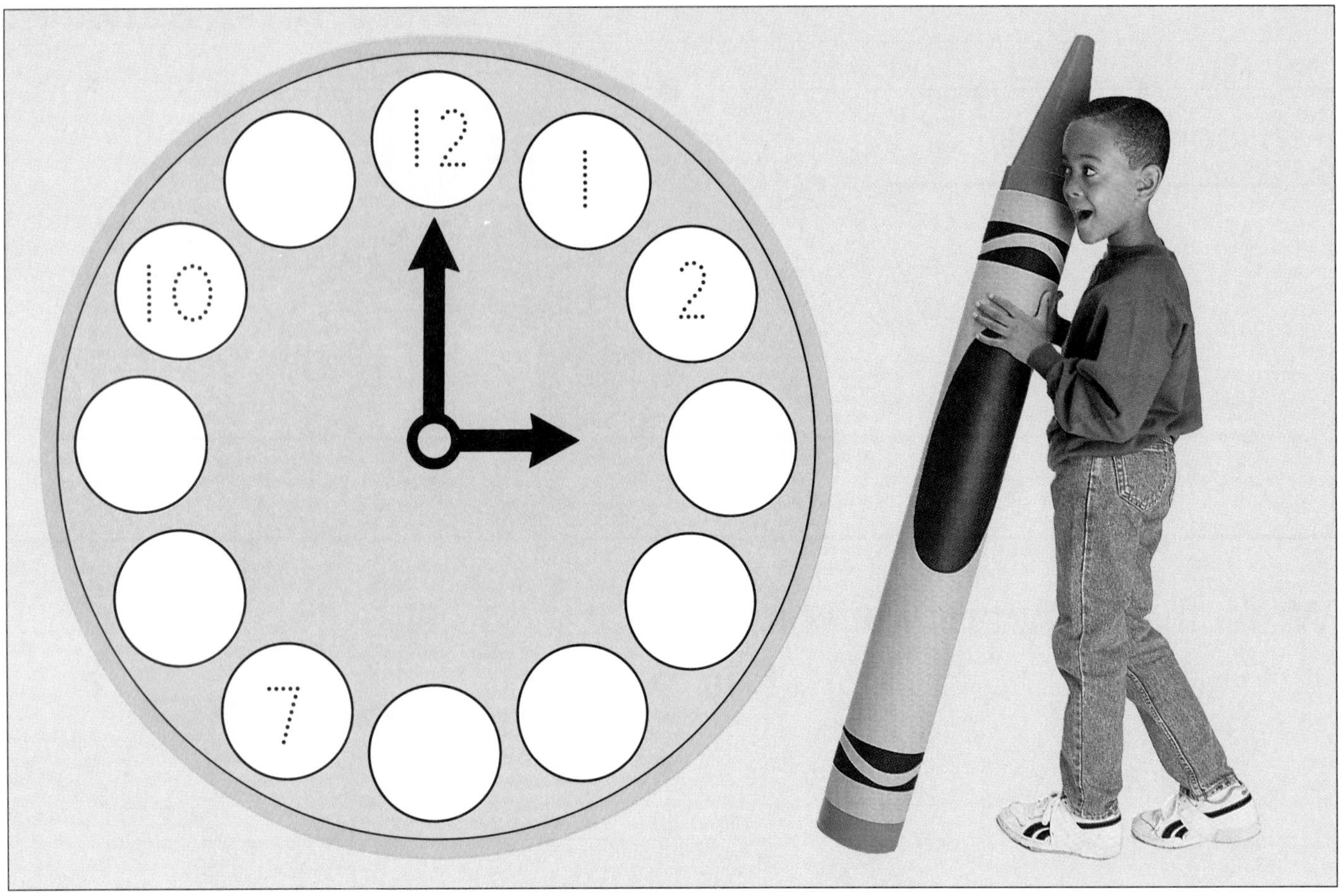

Problem Solving

What number is hidden?

Notes for Home Children order numbers on a clock. Then they solve problems involving number order.

Name ______

Comparing Numbers Through 12

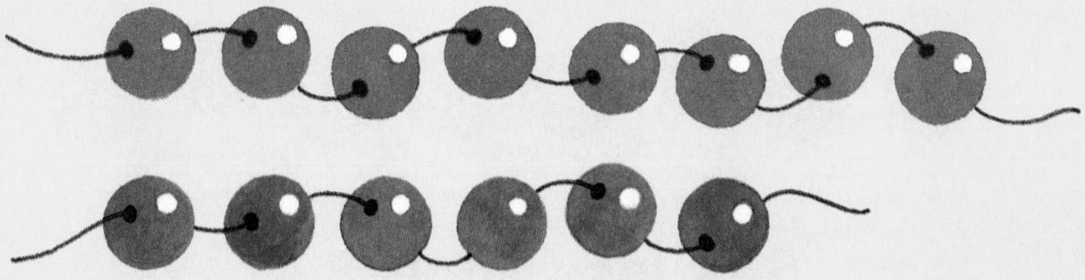

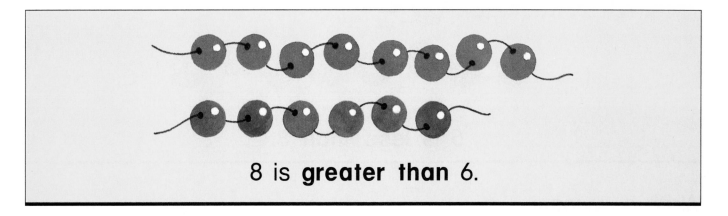

8 is **greater than** 6.

Write how many.
Then ring the greater number.

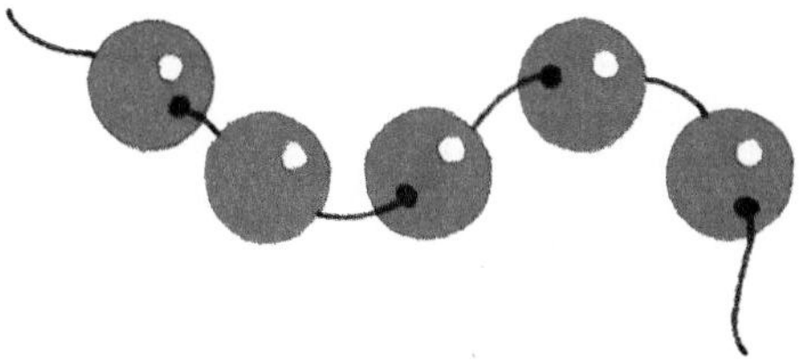

5 ______

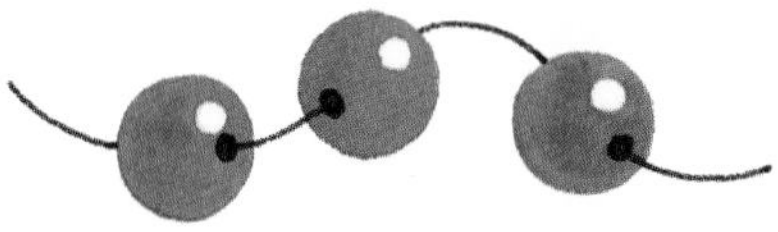

3 ______

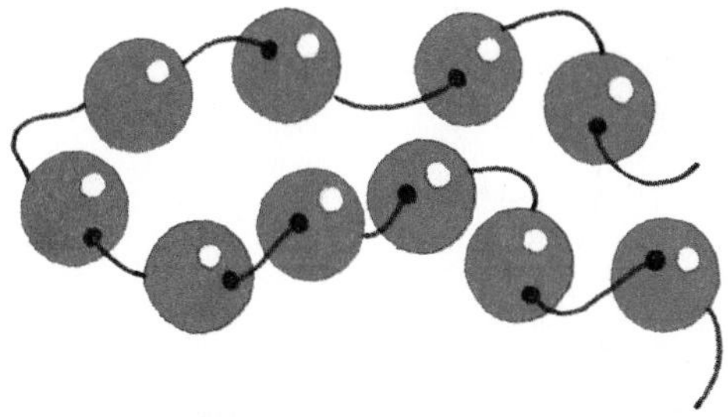

______

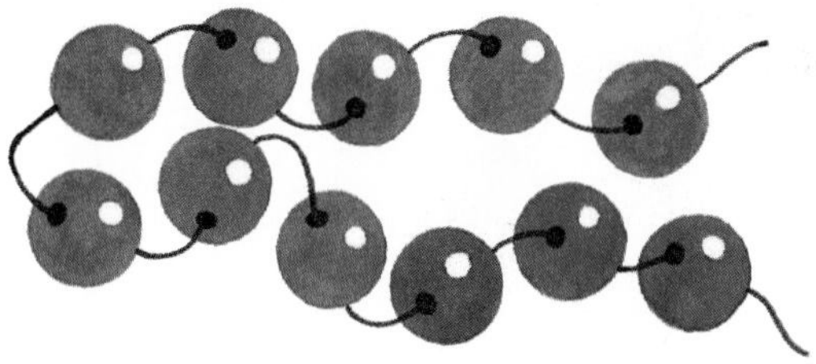

______

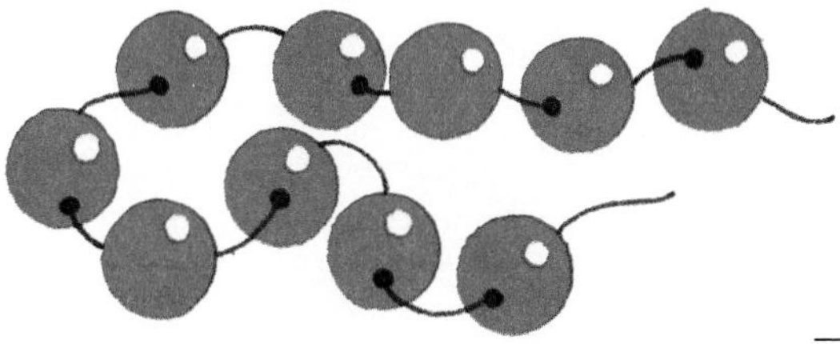

______

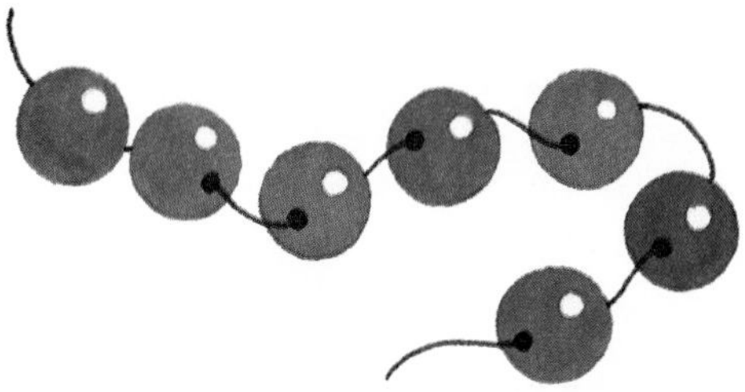

______

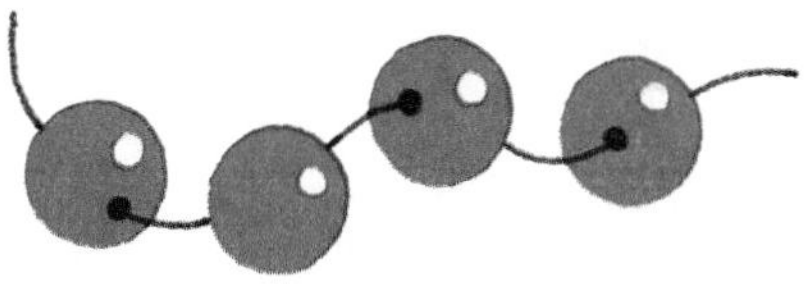

______

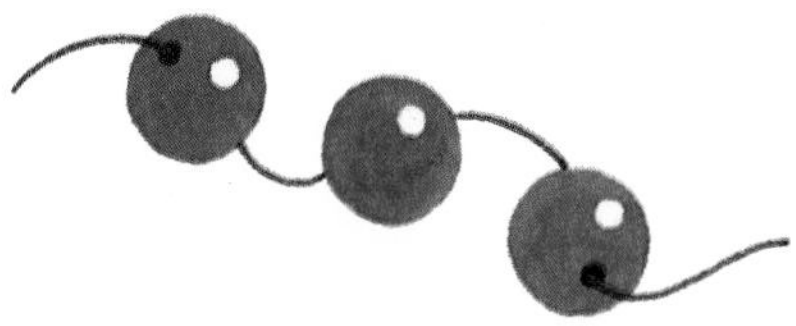

______

Notes for Home Children compare two groups and identify the one that is greater.

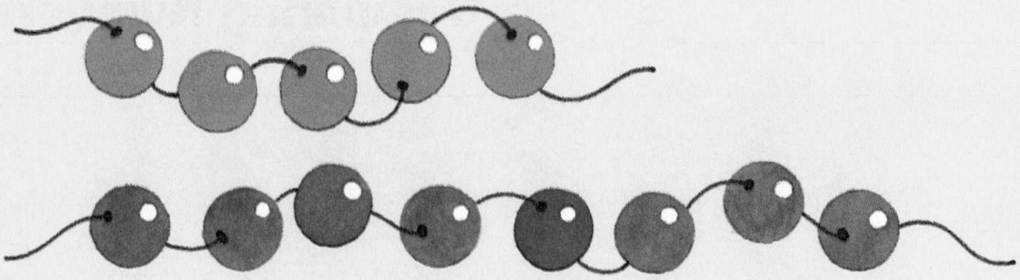

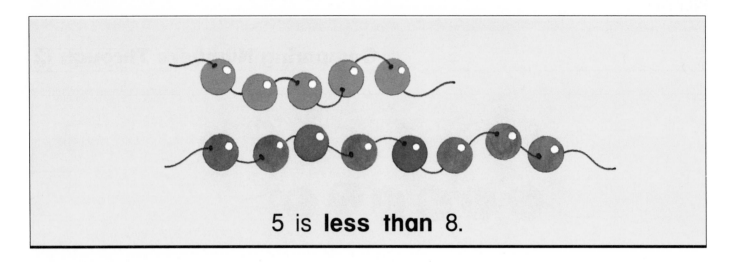

5 is **less than** 8.

Write how many.
Then ring the number that is less.

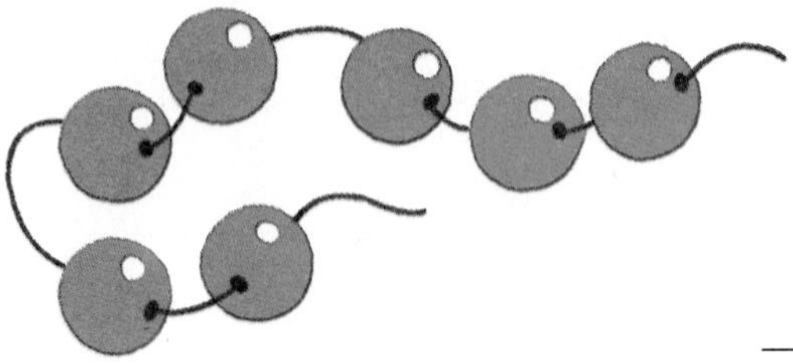

7

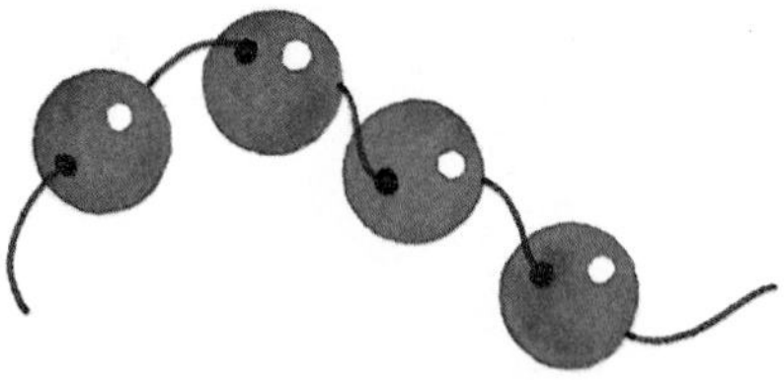

4

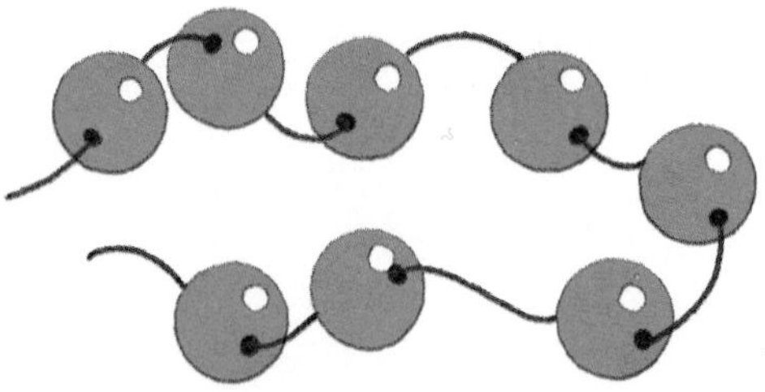

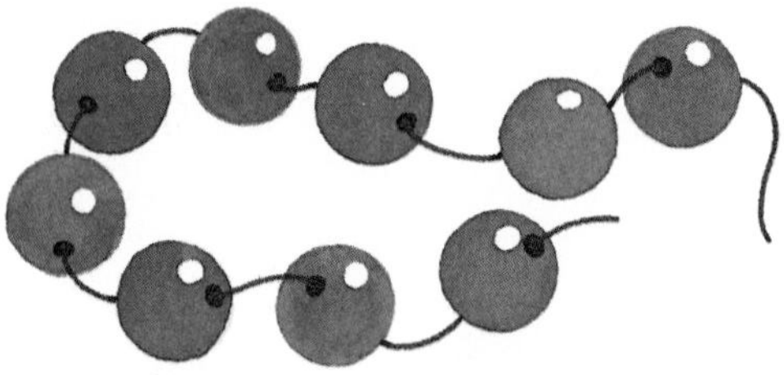

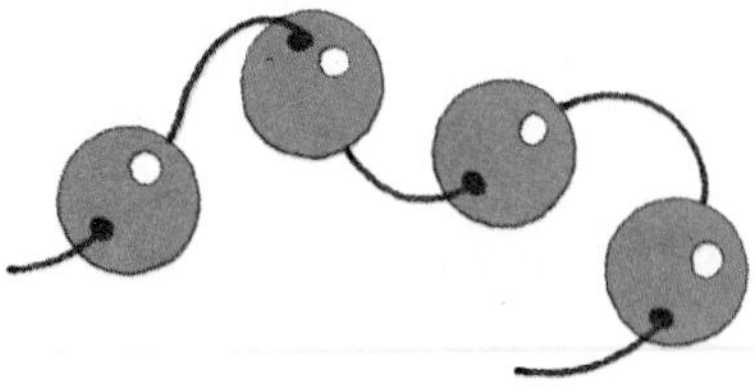

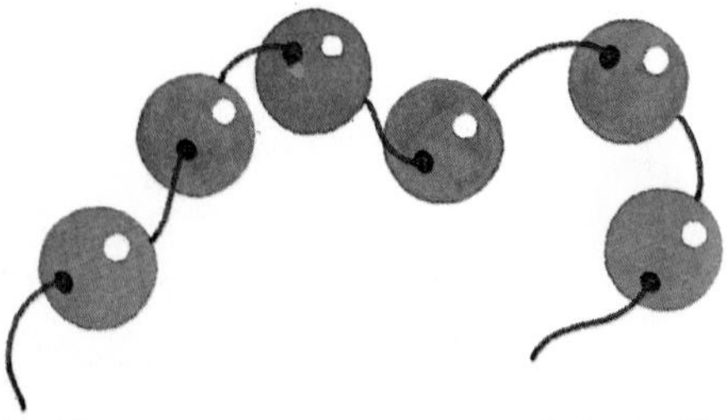

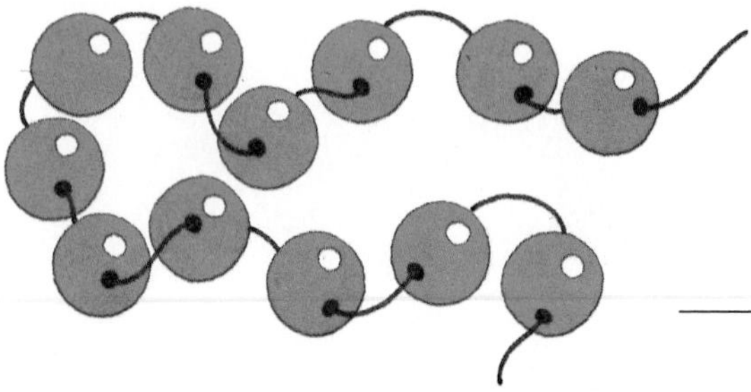

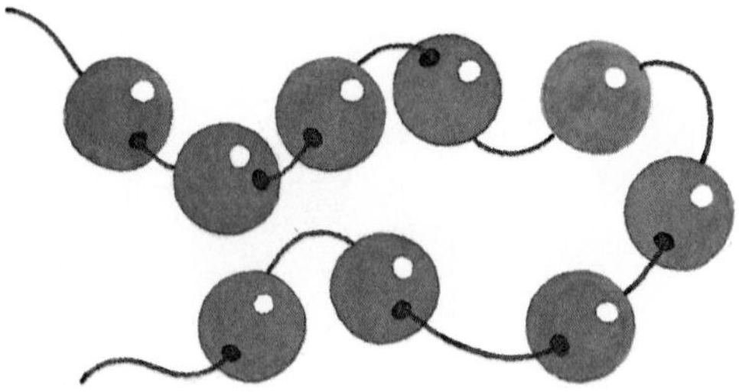

Notes for Home Children compare two groups and identify the one that is less.

See More Practice set B on page 41.

Name ____________________

PROBLEM-SOLVING STRATEGY

Find a Pattern

The pattern is **drum, horn**.
I know what comes next.

What is the pattern?
Ring what comes next.

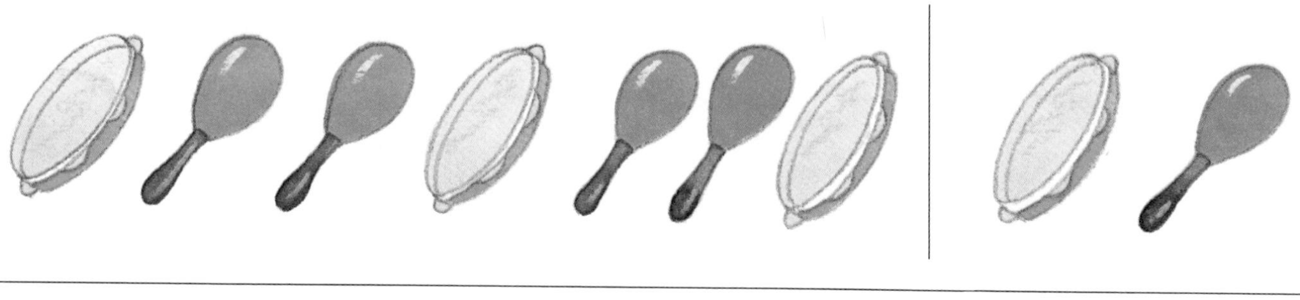

Notes for Home Children learn to solve problems by finding patterns.

What is the pattern?
Ring what comes next.

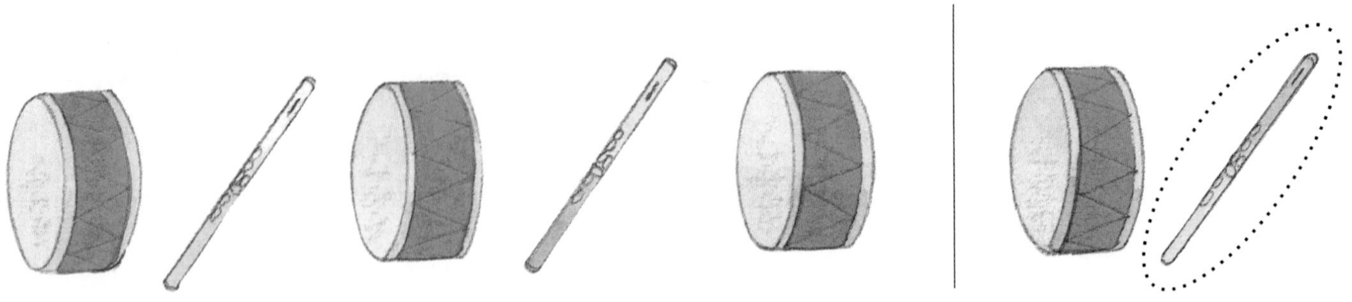

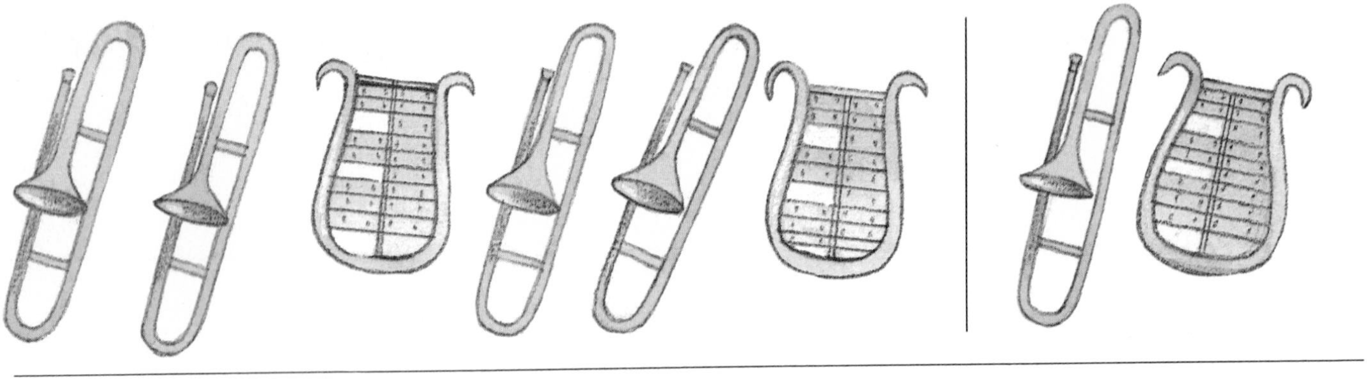

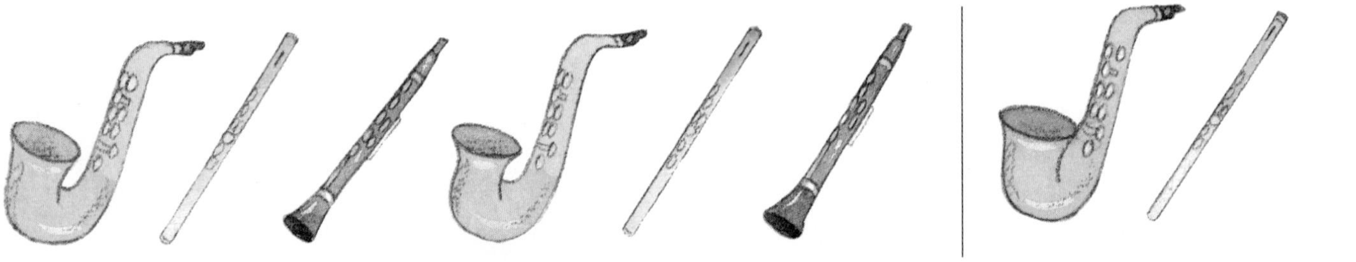

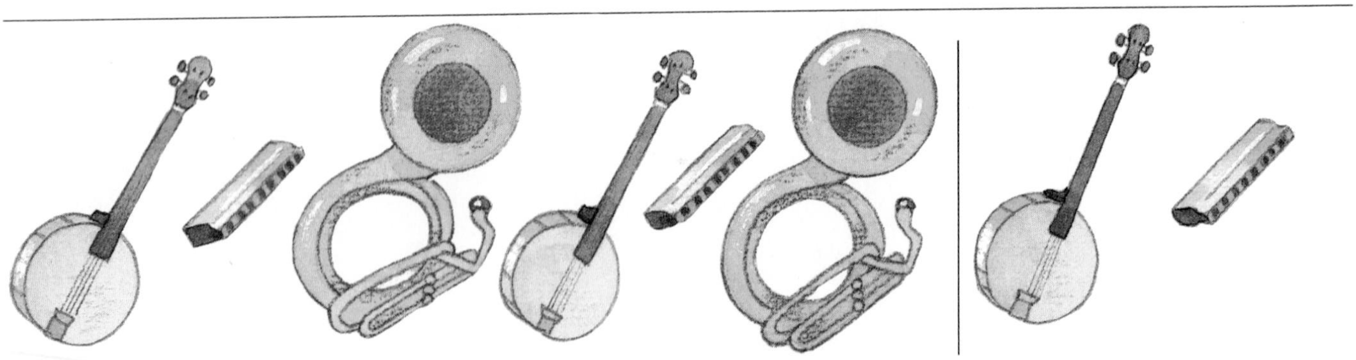

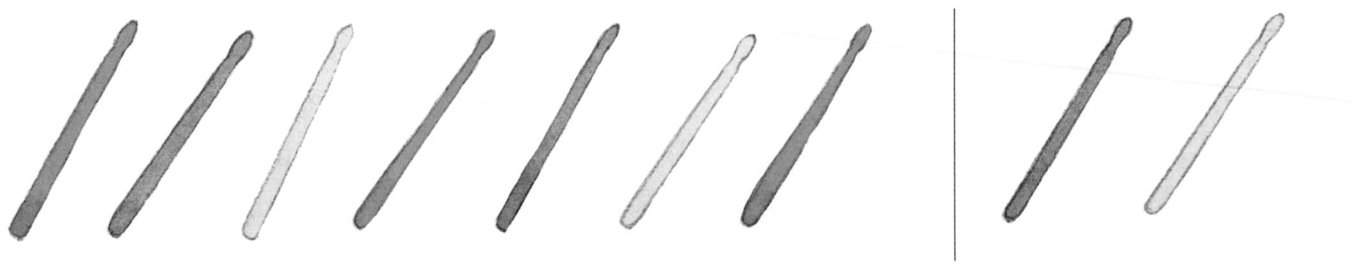

Notes for Home Children solve problems by finding patterns.

Name

Problem-Solving Workshop

Explore as a Team

Work with a partner.
There are three balls.
One is red.
One is blue.
One is yellow.

Pam and Jeff will each choose a ball.
Show the ways they could choose.
Color each ball.

1. 

2. 

3. 

4. 

5. 

6. 

Notes for Home Children explore with a partner to solve a problem. They find different combinations of colors.

Problem-Solving Workshop

Explore with a Calculator

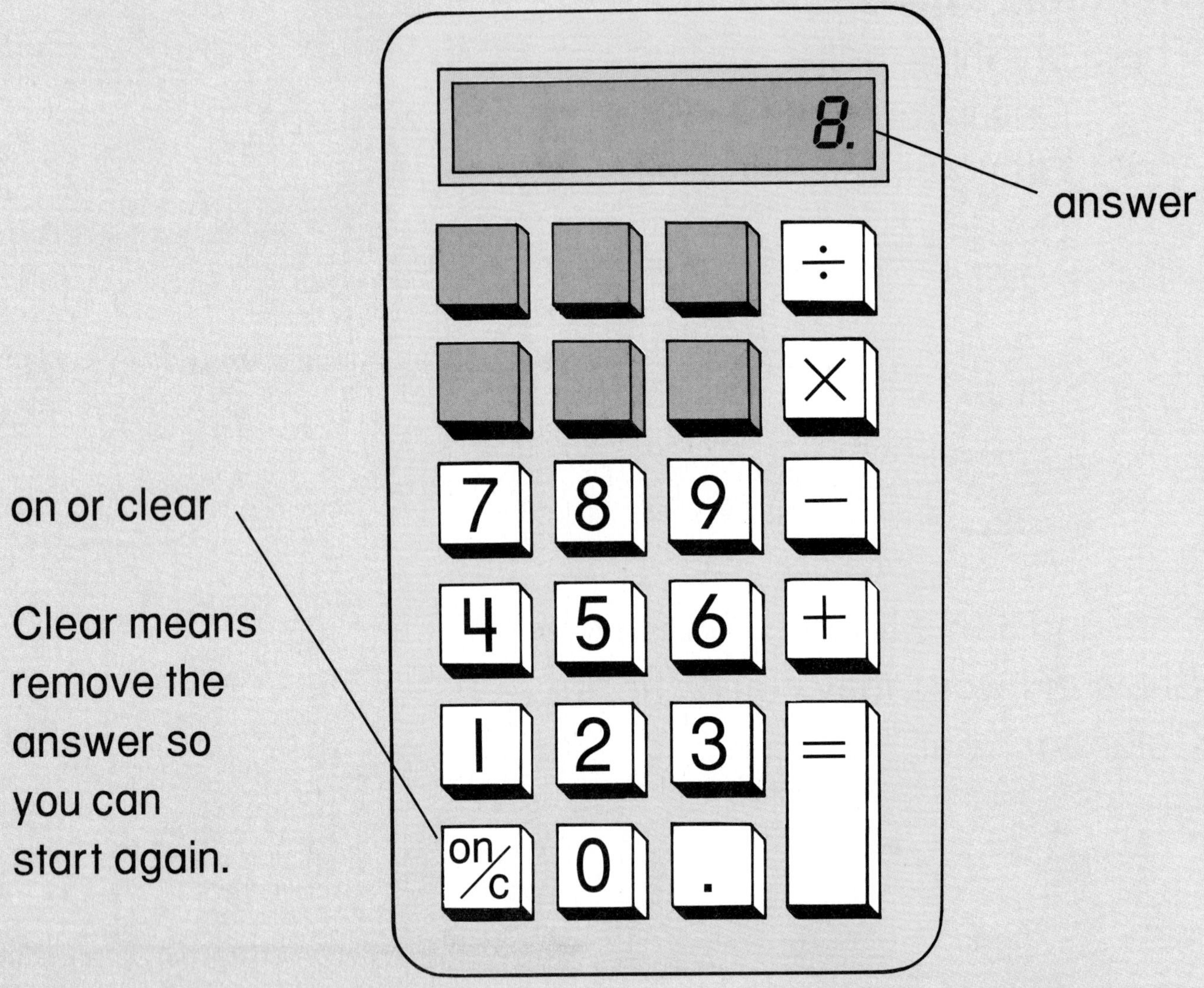

Color 1 red.

Color 2 blue.

Color 3 yellow.

Color 4 green.

Color 5 orange.

Color 6 purple.

Notes for Home Children explore with the calculator. They learn the position of each digit on the calculator.

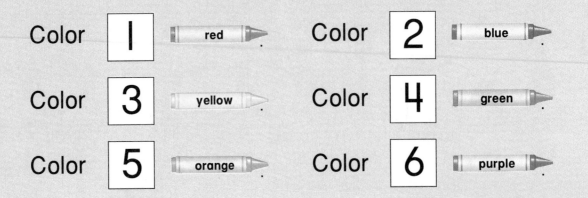

Name ______

More Practice

Set A Use after page 20.

Ring how many.

9 (10)

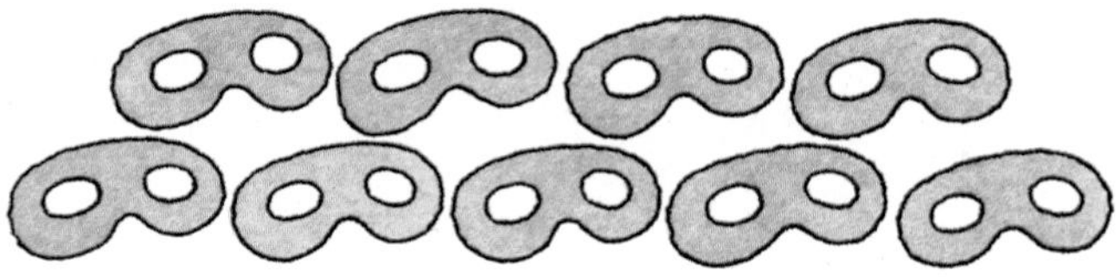

9 10

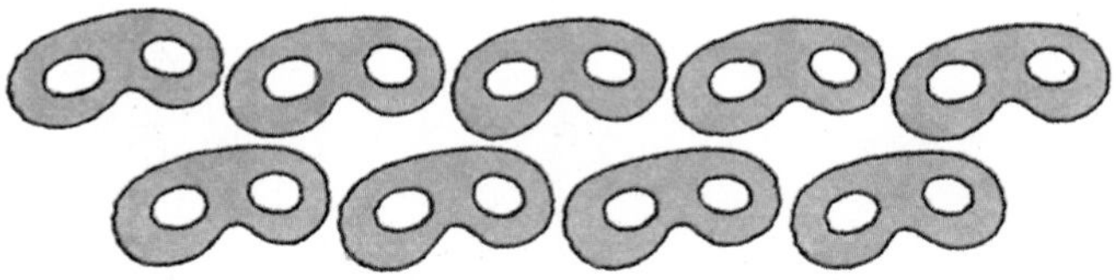

9 10

9 10

Set B Use after page 36.

Write how many.

Then ring the greater number.

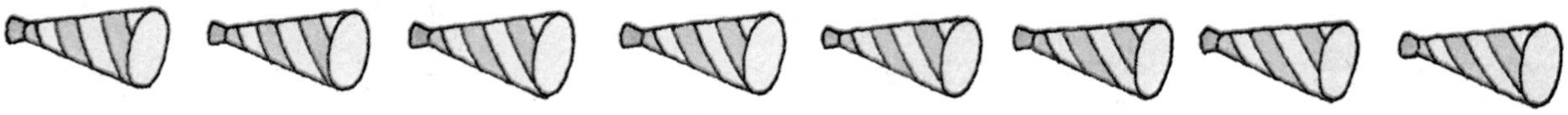

8 ______

______

Write how many.

Then ring the number that is less.

______

______

Notes for Home Set A: Children practice identifying groups of 9 and 10.
Set B: Children practice comparing two groups and identifying the one that is greater or the one that is less.

Enrichment

Write how many.
Then ring the greatest number.

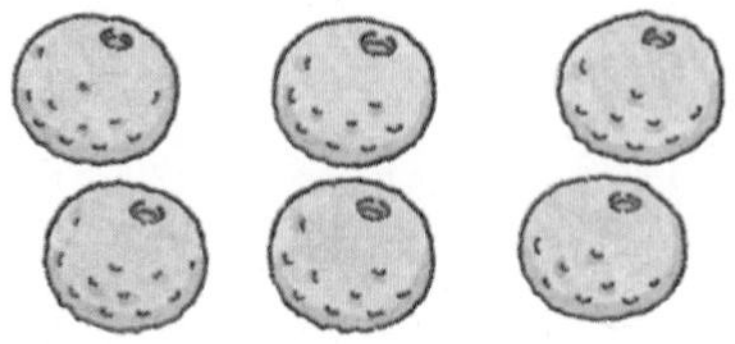
6

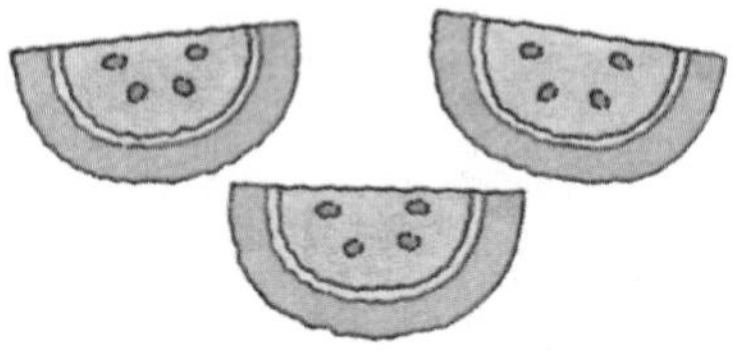
3

(8)

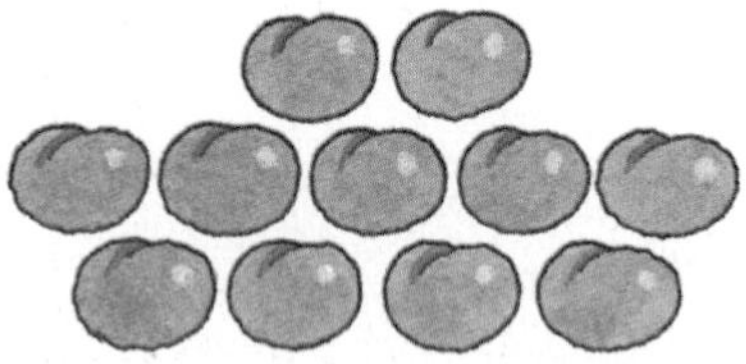
____

____

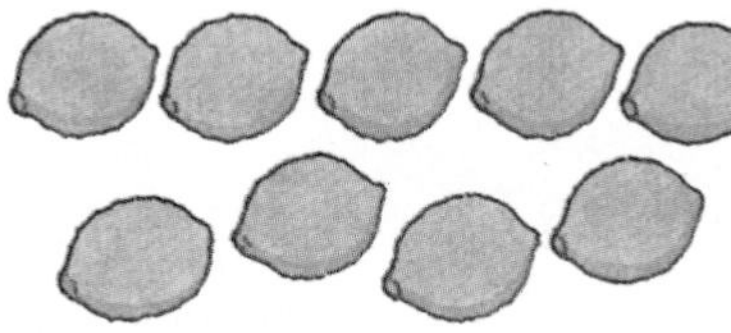
____

Write how many.
Then ring the least number.

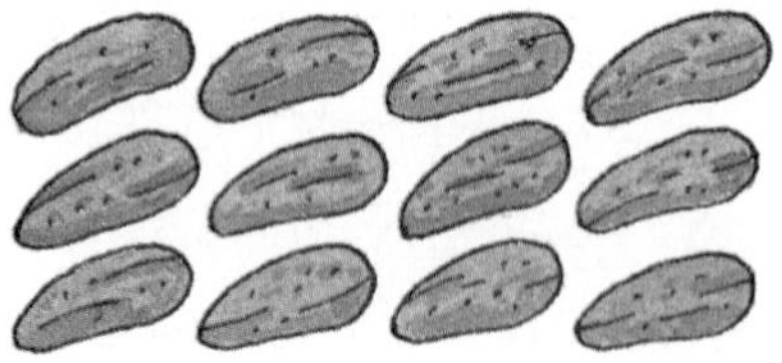
____

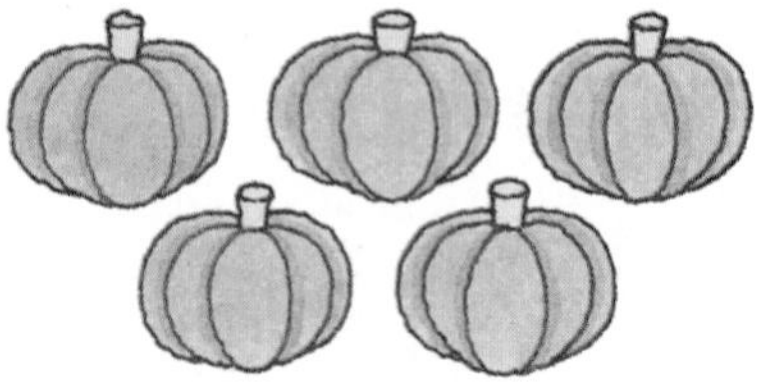
____

____

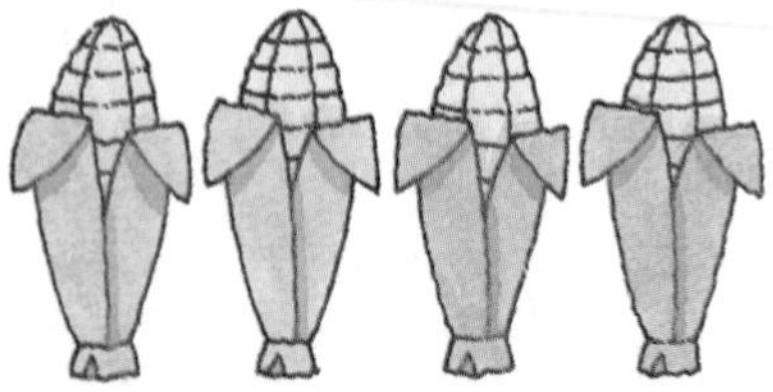
____

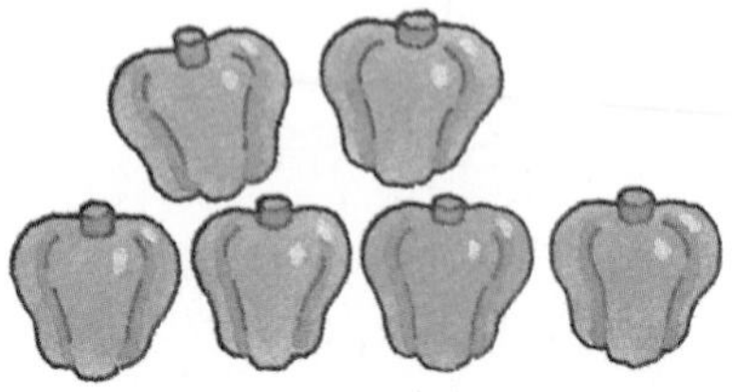
____

____

Notes for Home Children are challenged to find the greatest number or the least number when given a choice of three numbers.

Name ____________________

Chapter 1 Review/Test

Ring how many.

1.

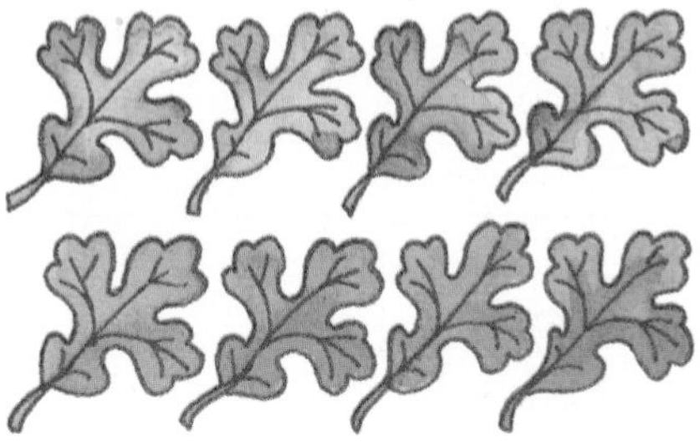

7 8

2.

5 6

3.

11 12

4. How much?

____ ¢

5. Write how many.
Then ring the greater number.

____

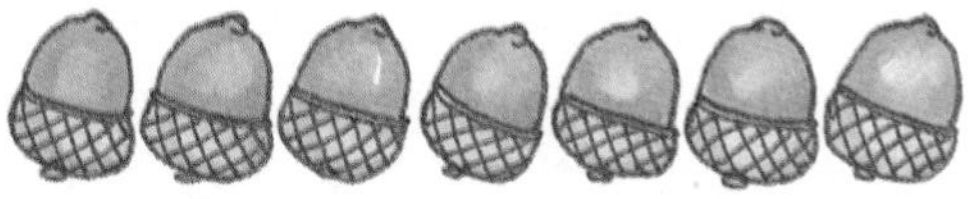

____

6. Write the missing numbers.

6, 7, 8, ____ , ____ , 11, ____

7. What is the pattern?
Ring what comes next.

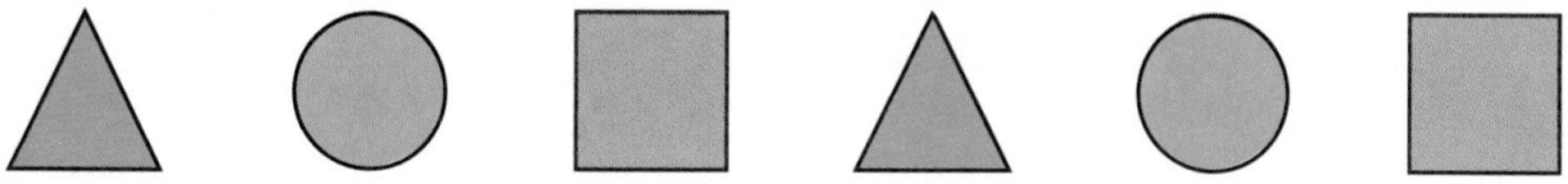

Notes for Home Children are assessed on Chapter 1 concepts, skills, and problem solving.

Exploring Math at Home

Dear Family,

In this chapter I have learned to identify, write, and order numbers 0 through 12. I have also learned to identify pennies and count to 10¢. Please help me with the activities below.

Love, ________________________

Identify pennies among a group of mixed coins and count them.

Tell the missing number when one number is hidden on a clock.

Compare two groups of objects and tell which group has more and which group has less.

Coming Attractions

In the next chapter I will be learning to add through 6 and how to make a graph.

Listen to the math story, "Show Time."
Emma put on a dog act with Sandy.
How many more dogs did she put in her show?

Notes for Home Children listen to a math story introducing chapter concepts and skills. Then they answer a question about the story.

Name

Exploring Addition

2 + 3 = 5

Use 6 counters.
Use the counters to tell an addition story.
Then complete each number sentence.

1. ____ + ____ = ____

2. ____ + ____ = ____

Notes for Home Children explore at the CONCRETE level using counters to create addition stories. They complete number sentences.

Name

Exploring Sums of 4 and 5

2 + 2 = 4

Use 4 counters.
Show different ways to make 4.
Complete each number sentence.

1. ____ + ____ = 4

2. ____ + ____ = 4

3. ____ + ____ = 4

4. ____ + ____ = 4

Notes for Home Children explore at the CONCRETE level using four counters to create addition stories. They complete number sentences.

Use 5 counters.
Show different ways to make 5.
Complete each number sentence.

5. ___ + ___ = 5

6. ___ + ___ = 5

7. ___ + ___ = 5

8. ___ + ___ = 5

9. ___ + ___ = 5

10. ___ + ___ = 5

Notes for Home Children explore at the CONCRETE level using five counters to create addition stories. They complete number sentences.

Name

Exploring Sums of 6

4 + 2 = 6

Use 6 counters.

Show different ways to make 6.

Complete each number sentence.

1. ___ + ___ = 6
2. ___ + ___ = 6
3. ___ + ___ = 6
4. ___ + ___ = 6
5. ___ + ___ = 6
6. ___ + ___ = 6

Notes for Home Children explore at the CONCRETE level using six counters to create addition stories. They complete number sentences.

Use 

and 

.

Show a way to make 6.

Complete each number sentence.

7.

2 + 4 = 6

8.

___ + ___ = 6

9.

___ + ___ = 6

10.

___ + ___ = 6

11.

___ + ___ = 6

Notes for Home Children color some leaves green and some leaves yellow to make sums of 6. They complete number sentences.

Name

Finding Sums Through 6

$1 + 3 = \underline{4}$

Use counters.
Add.

1. $2 + 1 = \_\_\_$
2. $2 + 3 = \_\_\_$
3. $4 + 2 = \_\_\_$
4. $1 + 5 = \_\_\_$

Notes for Home Children explore at the CONCRETE level using counters to find sums.

Use counters.
Add.

5. $1 + 2 = \underline{3}$

6. $1 + 1 = \_\_\_$

7. $1 + 4 = \_\_\_$

8. $4 + 1 = \_\_\_$

9. $2 + 4 = \_\_\_$

10. $5 + 1 = \_\_\_$

11. $3 + 2 = \_\_\_$

12. $2 + 2 = \_\_\_$

13. $3 + 3 = \_\_\_$

14. $3 + 1 = \_\_\_$

Notes for Home Children explore at the CONCRETE level using counters to find sums.

Name ________

Using Pictures to Find Sums

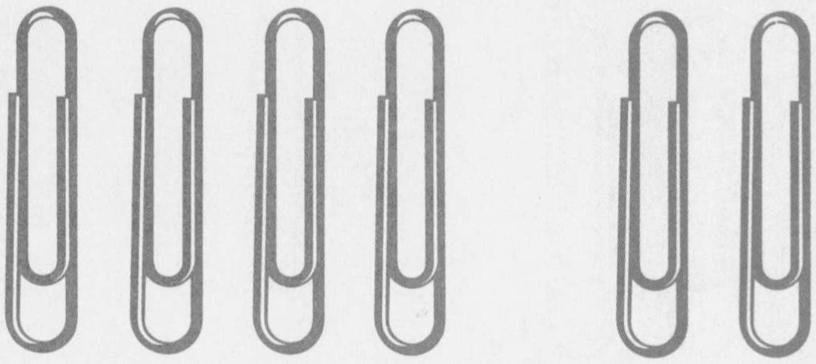

$4 + 2 = \underline{6}$

Add.

1.

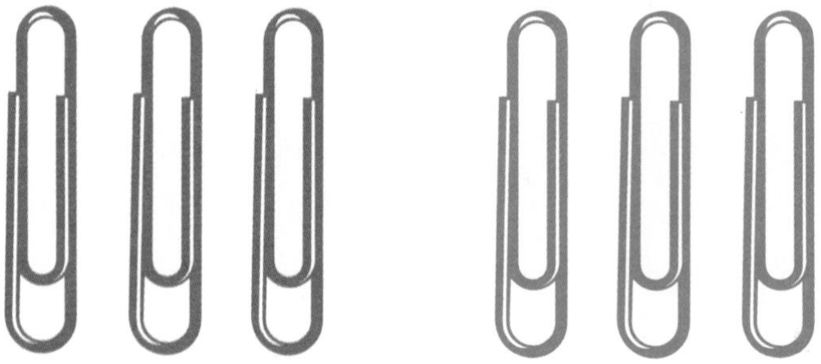

$3 + 3 =$ ____

2.

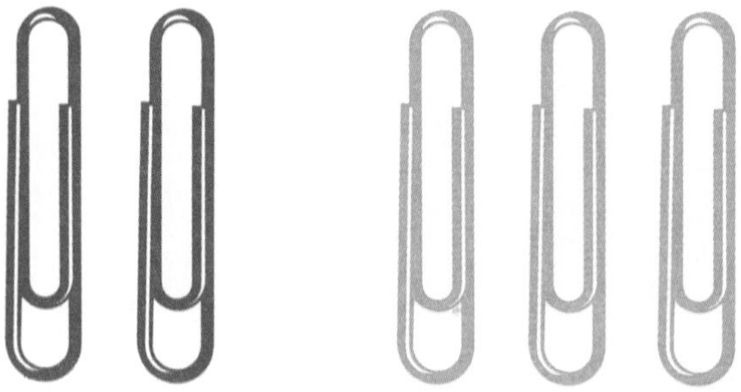

$2 + 3 =$ ____

3.

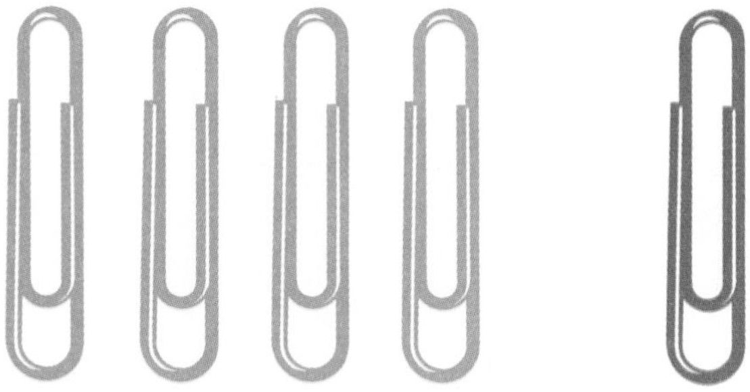

$4 + 1 =$ ____

4.

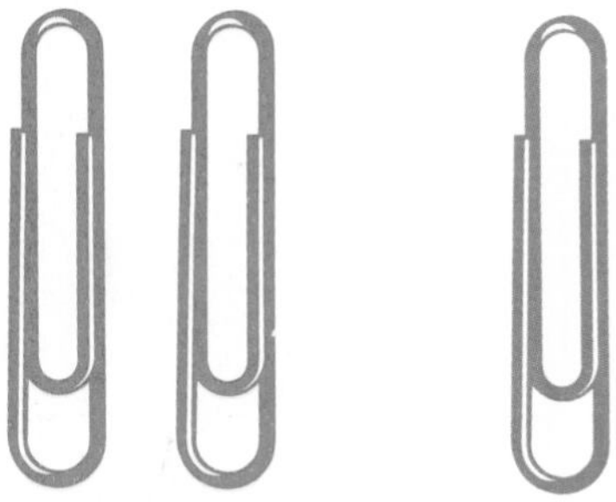

$2 + 1 =$ ____

Notes for Home Children find sums through 6 using pictures of objects.

Add.

5.

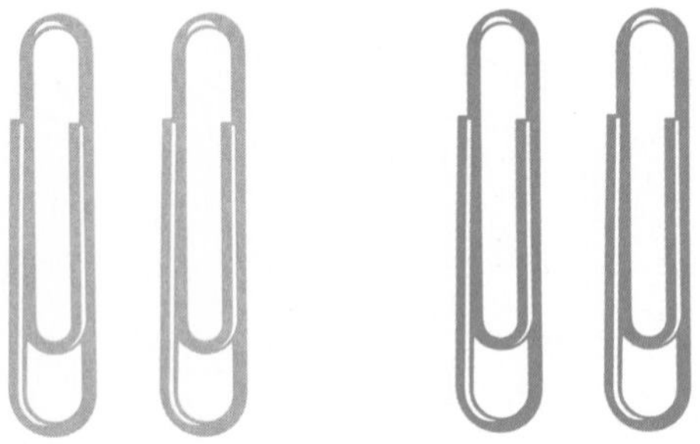

$2 + 2 =$ 4

6.

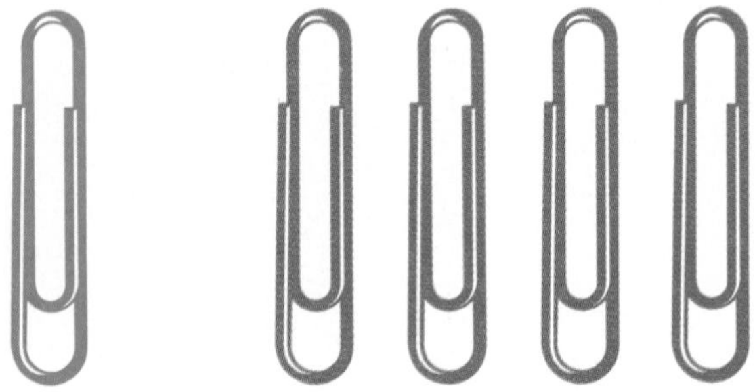

$1 + 4 =$ ____

7.

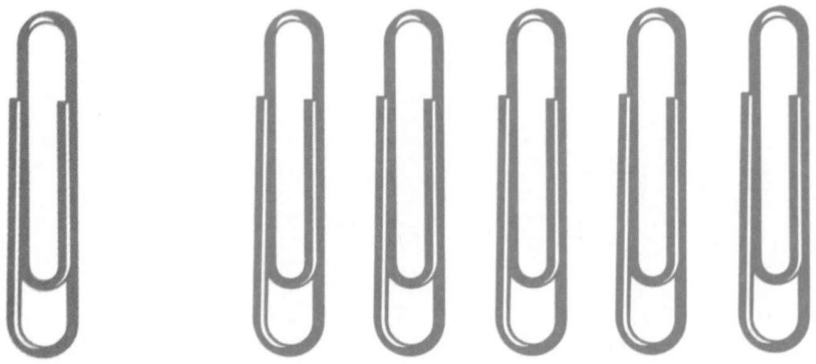

$1 + 5 =$ ____

8.

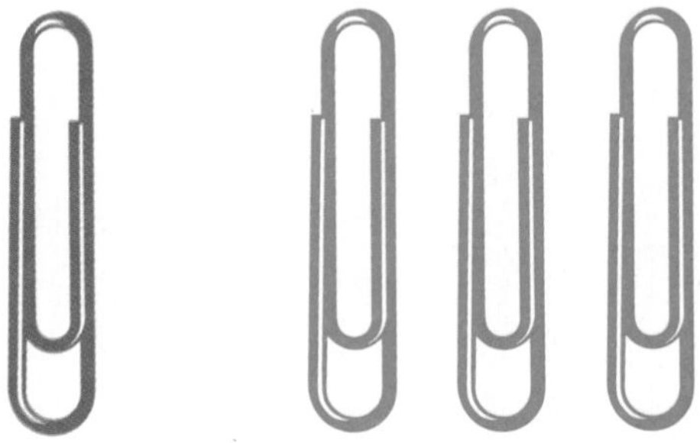

$1 + 3 =$ ____

9.

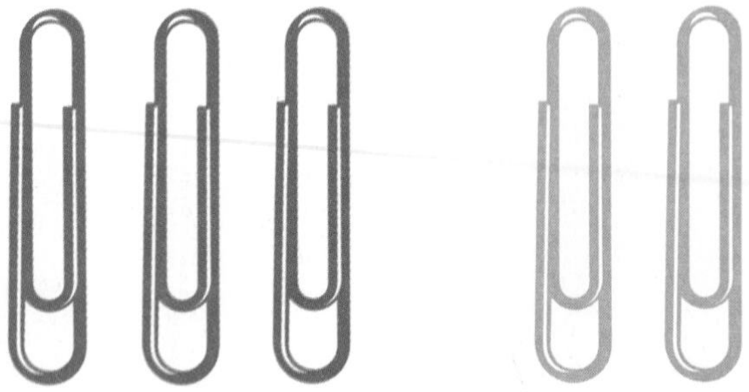

$3 + 2 =$ ____

10.

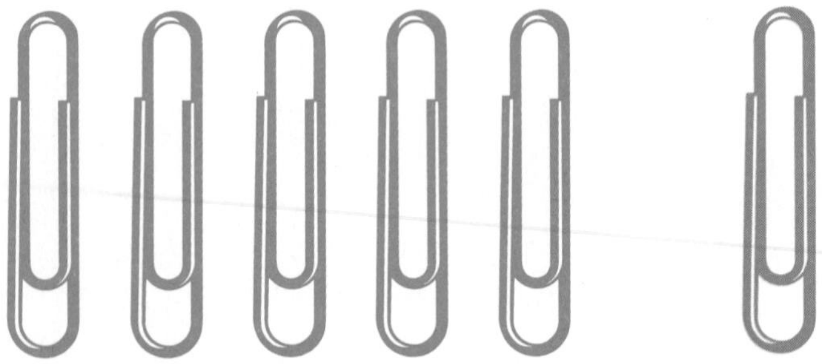

$5 + 1 =$ ____

Notes for Home Children find sums through 6 using pictures of objects.

See More Practice Set A on page 67.

Name

Use Data from a Picture

3 bears in all

Look at the picture.
Tell an addition story.
How many are there in all?

1.

____ deer in all

2.

____ raccoons in all

3.

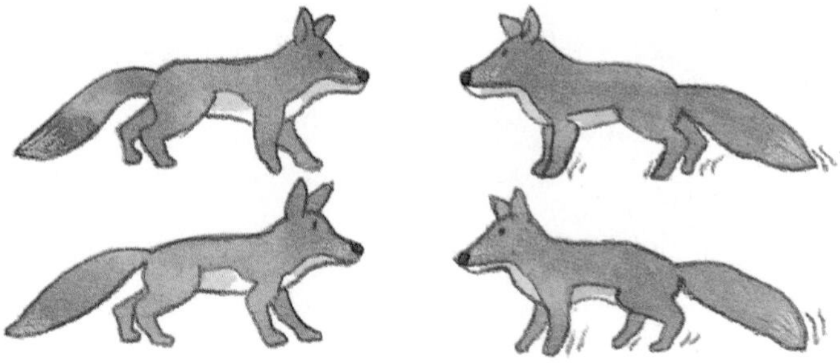

____ foxes in all

4.

____ squirrels in all

Notes for Home Children learn to solve addition problems by using data from pictures.

Look at the picture.
Tell an addition story.
How many are there in all?

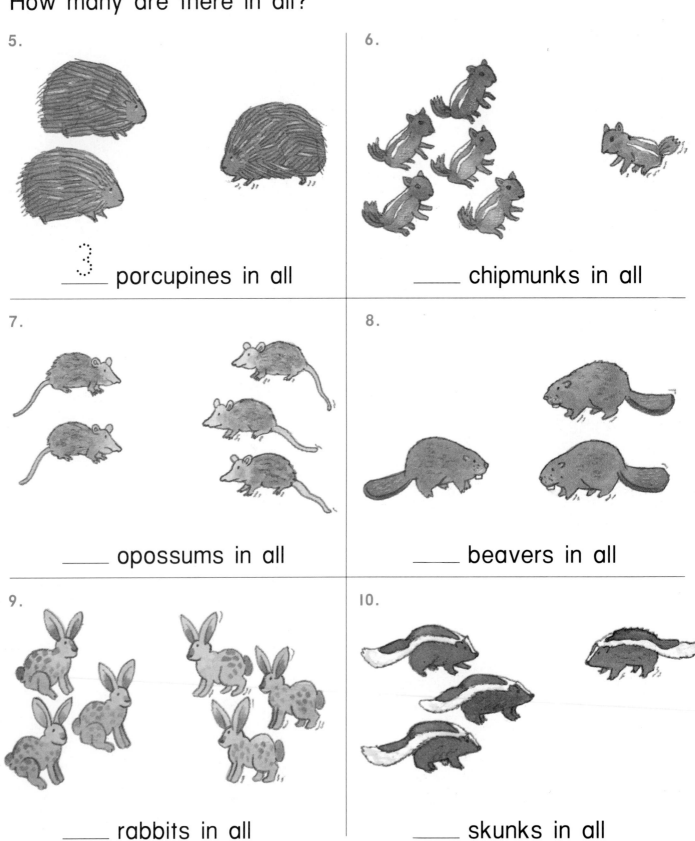

5.

3 porcupines in all

6.

____ chipmunks in all

7.

____ opossums in all

8.

____ beavers in all

9.

____ rabbits in all

10.

____ skunks in all

Notes for Home Children solve addition problems by using data from pictures.

Number Sense

Tell an addition story about each picture.
Can you tell a number sentence that matches each picture?

Let's do some more!

Draw a picture to tell addition stories.
Tell your stories to a friend.

Notes for Home Children develop number understanding by describing addition situations.

SKILLS REVIEW

Skills Review

Fill in the correct ⬭ .

How much?

1.

4¢	5¢	6¢
(A)	(B)	(C)

2.

4¢	5¢	6¢
(A)	(B)	(C)

What number is missing?

3.

4	5	8
(A)	(B)	(C)

4.

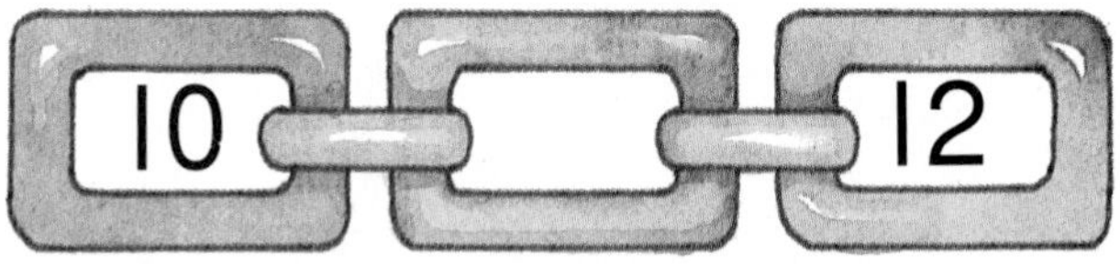

13	11	14
(A)	(B)	(C)

Vocabulary

Read the word.

Ring the number.

5.

one	2	1	7
eight	3	9	8
seven	7	6	1

Notes for Home Children review counting pennies and ordering numbers through 12. Then they review number words.

Name

Addition in Vertical Form

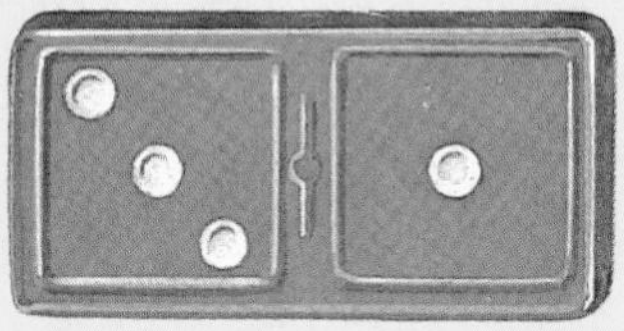

3 + 1 = 4

↑ sum

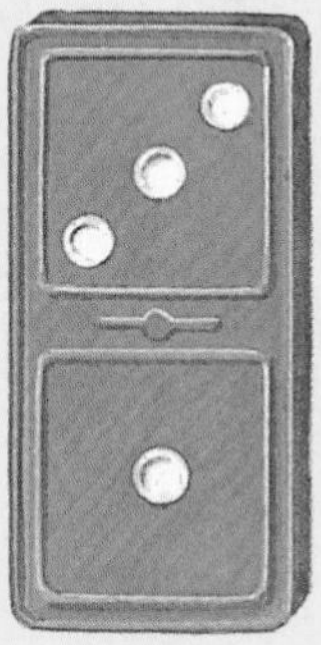

$$\begin{array}{r} 3 \\ +\ 1 \\ \hline 4 \end{array}$$ ← sum

Write the sum.

1.

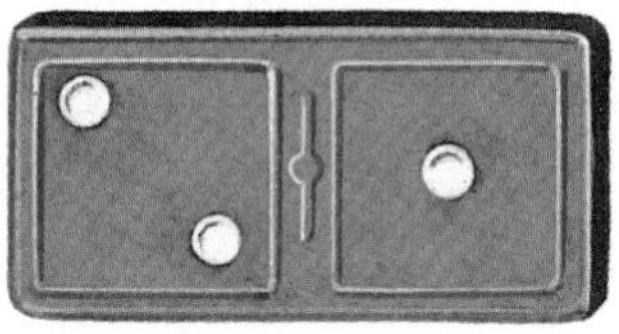

2 + 1 = ____

$$\begin{array}{r} 2 \\ +\ 1 \\ \hline \end{array}$$

2.

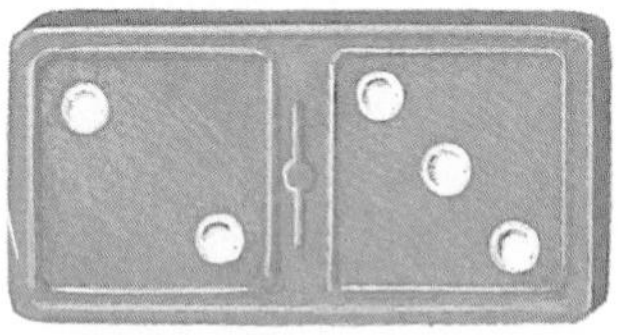

2 + 3 = ____

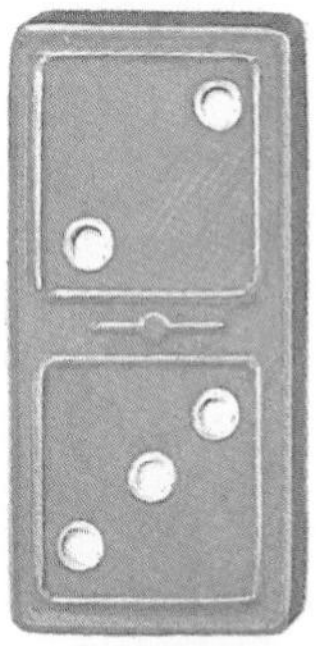

$$\begin{array}{r} 2 \\ +\ 3 \\ \hline \end{array}$$

3.

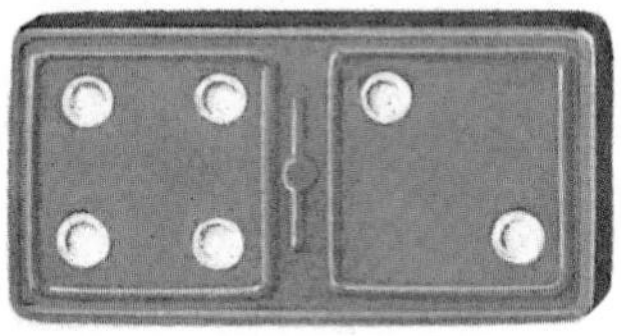

4 + 2 = ____

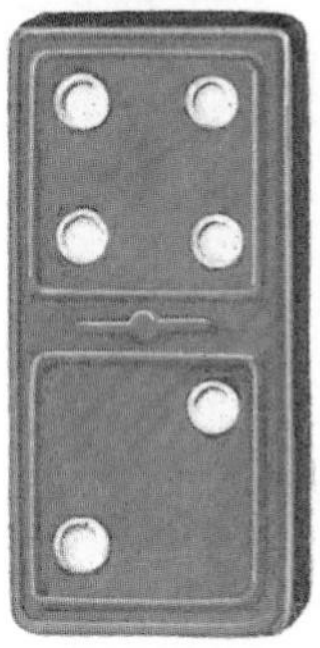

$$\begin{array}{r} 4 \\ +\ 2 \\ \hline \end{array}$$

Notes for Home Children learn to use the vertical form of addition.

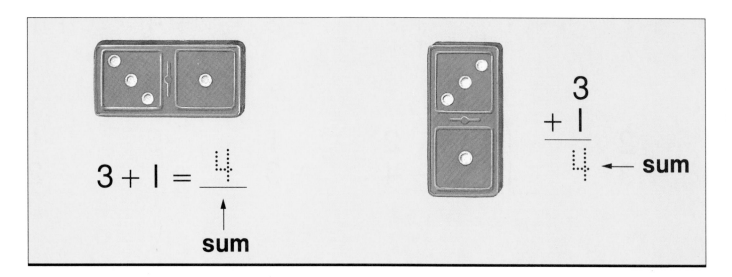

Write the sum.

4. $\begin{array}{r} 2 \\ +\ 1 \\ \hline 3 \end{array}$ $\begin{array}{r} 4 \\ +\ 1 \\ \hline \end{array}$ $\begin{array}{r} 3 \\ +\ 2 \\ \hline \end{array}$ $\begin{array}{r} 3 \\ +\ 3 \\ \hline \end{array}$ $\begin{array}{r} 1 \\ +\ 4 \\ \hline \end{array}$ $\begin{array}{r} 3 \\ +\ 1 \\ \hline \end{array}$

5. $\begin{array}{r} 2 \\ +\ 3 \\ \hline \end{array}$ $\begin{array}{r} 1 \\ +\ 1 \\ \hline \end{array}$ $\begin{array}{r} 2 \\ +\ 4 \\ \hline \end{array}$ $\begin{array}{r} 1 \\ +\ 3 \\ \hline \end{array}$ $\begin{array}{r} 5 \\ +\ 1 \\ \hline \end{array}$ $\begin{array}{r} 1 \\ +\ 2 \\ \hline \end{array}$

6. $\begin{array}{r} 4 \\ +\ 2 \\ \hline \end{array}$ $\begin{array}{r} 1 \\ +\ 3 \\ \hline \end{array}$ $\begin{array}{r} 2 \\ +\ 2 \\ \hline \end{array}$ $\begin{array}{r} 1 \\ +\ 5 \\ \hline \end{array}$ $\begin{array}{r} 1 \\ +\ 1 \\ \hline \end{array}$ $\begin{array}{r} 4 \\ +\ 1 \\ \hline \end{array}$

Problem Solving

Tell an addition story.
How many?

7.

____ rabbits

8.

____ rabbits

Notes for Home Children practice finding sums through 6 using the vertical form. Then they solve problems using addition.

Name

Adding in Any Order

If I know $2 + 3 = 5$,
then I know $3 + 2 = 5$.

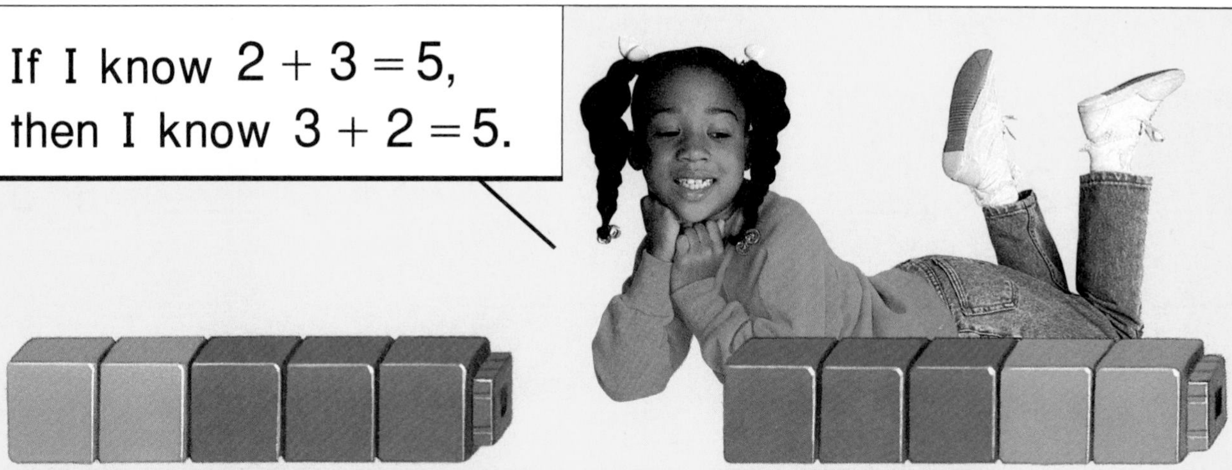

$2 + 3 =$ 5 $\qquad$ $3 + 2 =$ 5

Write the sum.

1.

$4 + 2 =$ ___ $\qquad$ $2 + 4 =$ ___

2.

$1 + 4 =$ ___ $\qquad$ $4 + 1 =$ ___

3.

$5 + 1 =$ ___ $\qquad$ $1 + 5 =$ ___

Notes for Home Children learn to add two numbers in any order.

Write the sum.

4.

$\begin{array}{r} 1 \\ +\ 2 \\ \hline 3 \end{array}$

$\begin{array}{r} 2 \\ +\ 1 \\ \hline \end{array}$

5.

$\begin{array}{r} 3 \\ +\ 1 \\ \hline \end{array}$

$\begin{array}{r} 1 \\ +\ 3 \\ \hline \end{array}$

6. $\begin{array}{r} 3 \\ +\ 2 \\ \hline \end{array}$ $\begin{array}{r} 2 \\ +\ 3 \\ \hline \end{array}$

7. $\begin{array}{r} 2 \\ +\ 4 \\ \hline \end{array}$ $\begin{array}{r} 4 \\ +\ 2 \\ \hline \end{array}$

8. $\begin{array}{r} 1 \\ +\ 2 \\ \hline \end{array}$ $\begin{array}{r} 2 \\ +\ 1 \\ \hline \end{array}$

9. $\begin{array}{r} 1 \\ +\ 4 \\ \hline \end{array}$ $\begin{array}{r} 4 \\ +\ 1 \\ \hline \end{array}$

10. $\begin{array}{r} 5 \\ +\ 1 \\ \hline \end{array}$ $\begin{array}{r} 1 \\ +\ 5 \\ \hline \end{array}$

11. $\begin{array}{r} 4 \\ +\ 2 \\ \hline \end{array}$ $\begin{array}{r} 2 \\ +\ 4 \\ \hline \end{array}$

12. $\begin{array}{r} 1 \\ +\ 3 \\ \hline \end{array}$ $\begin{array}{r} 3 \\ +\ 1 \\ \hline \end{array}$

13. $\begin{array}{r} 2 \\ +\ 3 \\ \hline \end{array}$ $\begin{array}{r} 3 \\ +\ 2 \\ \hline \end{array}$

14. $\begin{array}{r} 1 \\ +\ 5 \\ \hline \end{array}$ $\begin{array}{r} 5 \\ +\ 1 \\ \hline \end{array}$

15. $\begin{array}{r} 2 \\ +\ 4 \\ \hline \end{array}$ $\begin{array}{r} 4 \\ +\ 2 \\ \hline \end{array}$

16. $\begin{array}{r} 2 \\ +\ 1 \\ \hline \end{array}$ $\begin{array}{r} 1 \\ +\ 2 \\ \hline \end{array}$

17. $\begin{array}{r} 4 \\ +\ 1 \\ \hline \end{array}$ $\begin{array}{r} 1 \\ +\ 4 \\ \hline \end{array}$

Notes for Home Children practice finding sums through 6 by adding in any order.

See More Practice Set B on page 67.

Name ____________________

PROBLEM-SOLVING STRATEGY

Make a Graph

1. Make a graph.
Color one picture for each.

2. How many of each are there?

 4

 ____

 ____

Notes for Home Children learn to solve problems by making a graph.

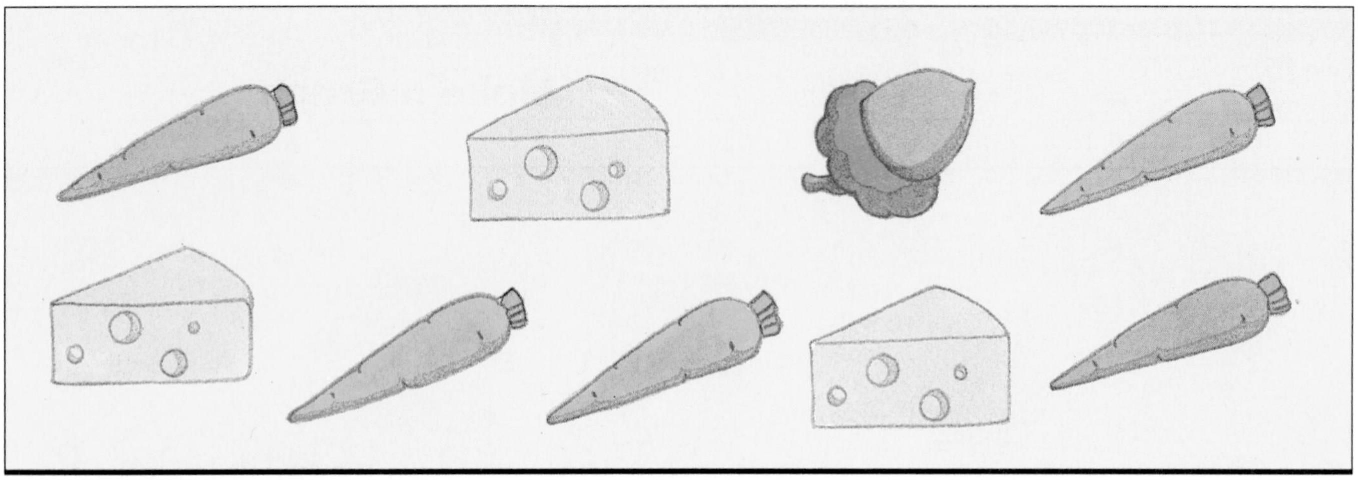

3. Make a graph.
Color one picture for each.

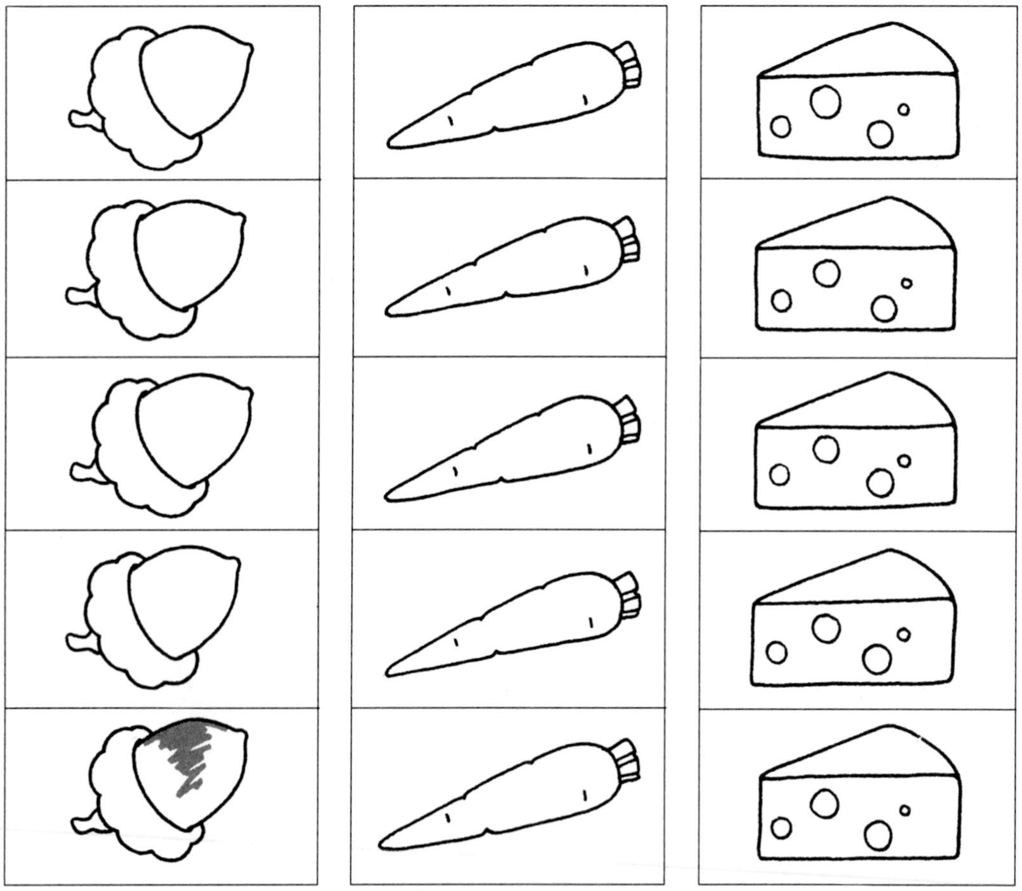

4. How many of each are there?

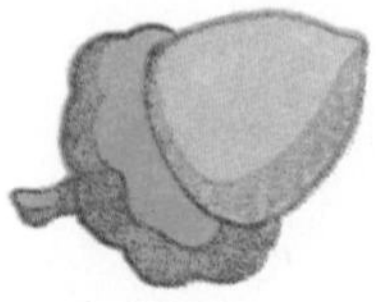 ____ 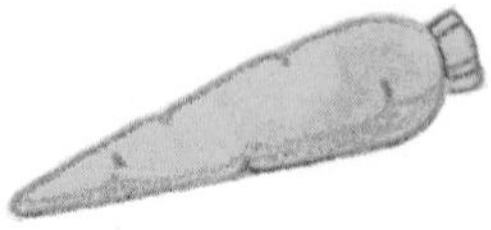 ____ 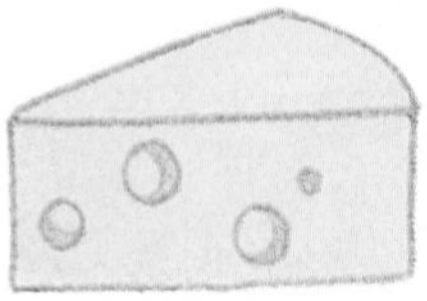 ____

Notes for Home Children solve problems by making a graph.

Name

Problem-Solving Workshop

Explore as a Team

Work with a partner.
Tom has 2 pets.
His pets have 6 legs in all.
What could his two pets be?

Use these pets.

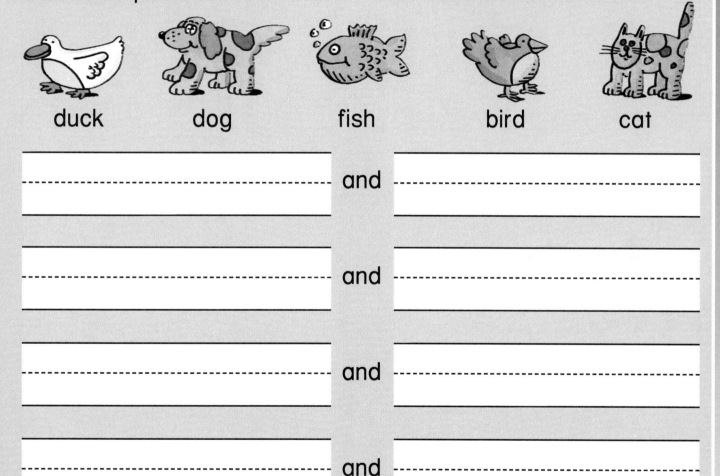

duck dog fish bird cat

________ and ________

________ and ________

________ and ________

________ and ________

Give your partner the name of two pets.
Ask your partner how many legs in all.
Take turns.

Notes for Home Children explore with a partner to solve a problem. They discover which combination of pets have 6 legs.

Problem-Solving Workshop

Explore with a Computer

Primary Graphing and Probability Project

1. Ask 5 people you know which zoo animal they like best. Color one picture for each person.

Zoo Animals Liked Best

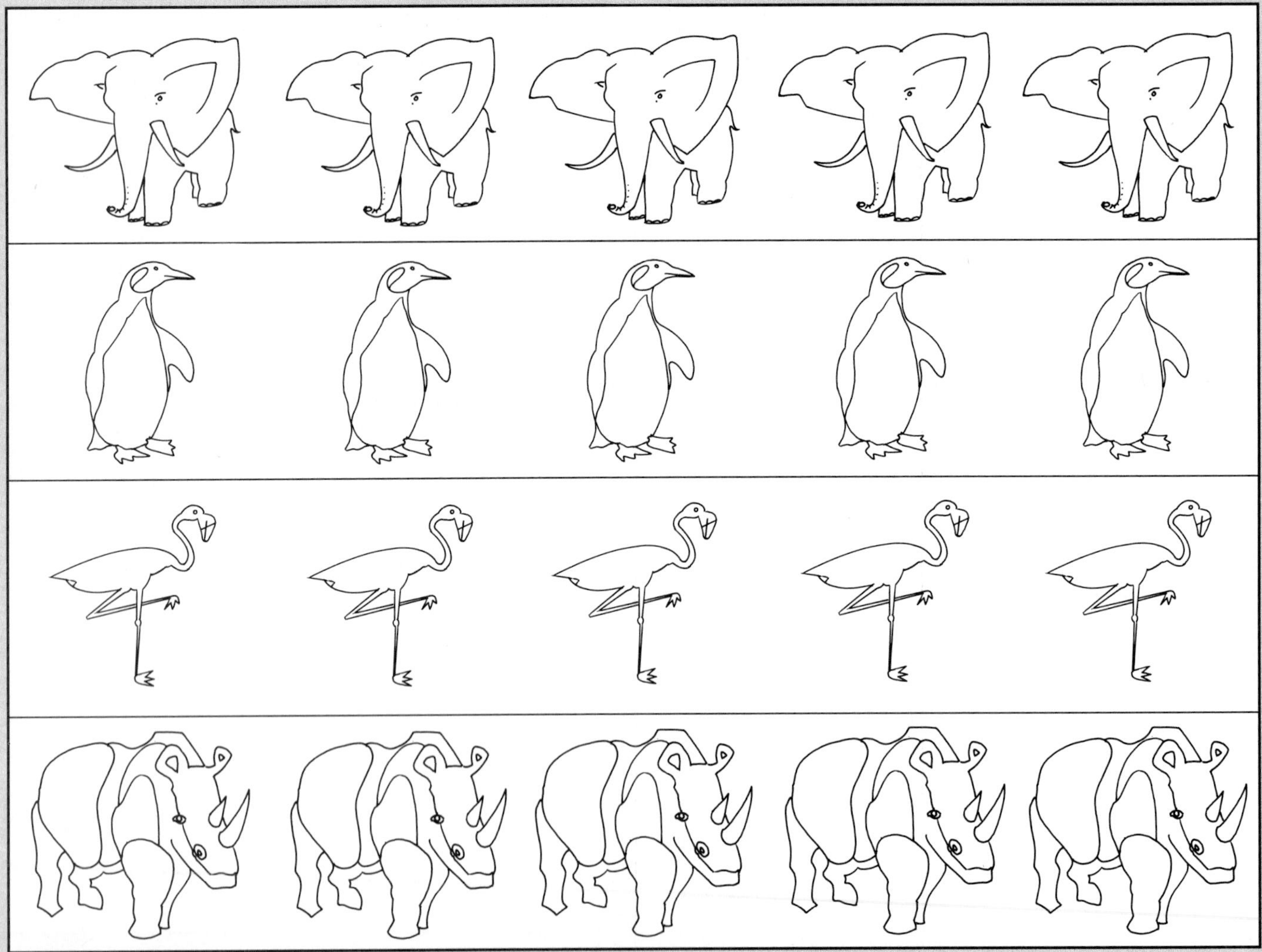

2. Make a picture graph at the computer.

Notes for Home Children take a survey and record the results on a graph. They then use the computer to create a picture of the data they collected.

Name ____________________

More Practice

Set A Use after page 54.

Add.

1. 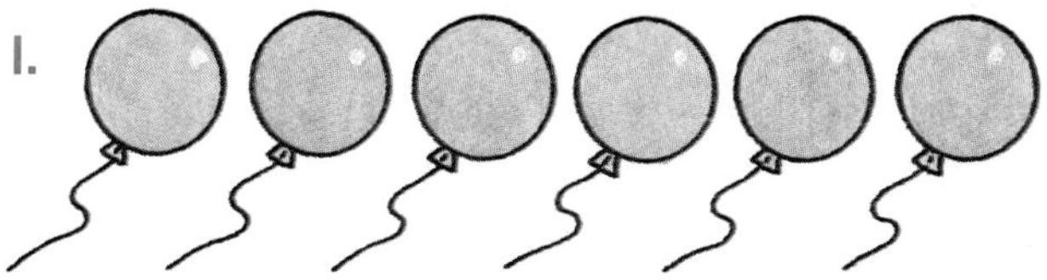

$1 + 5 =$ 6

2. 

$2 + 2 =$ ____

3. 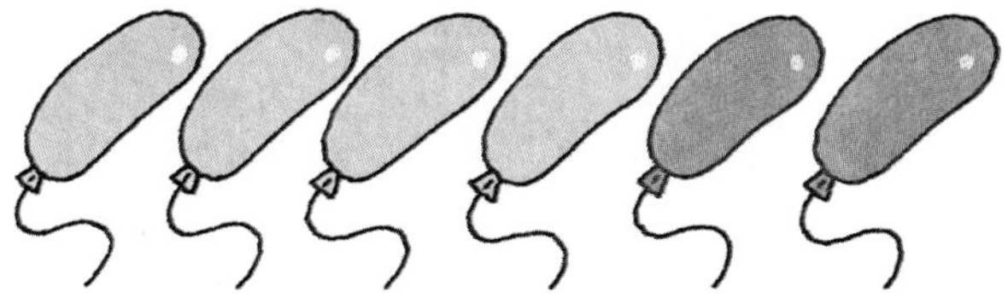

$4 + 2 =$ ____

4. 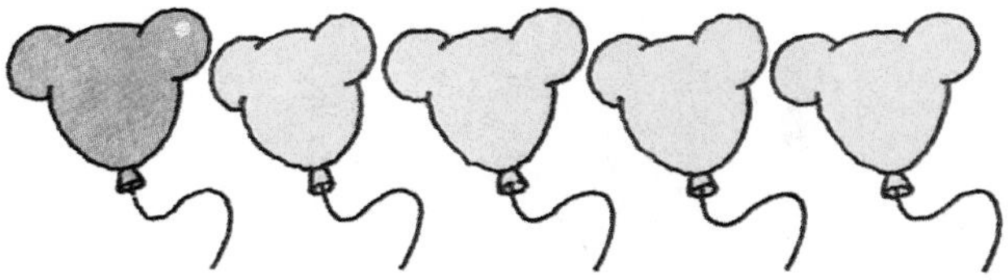

$1 + 4 =$ ____

Set B Use after page 62.

Write the sum.

Use yellow for 4.

Use blue for 5.

Use red for 6.

$$\begin{array}{r} 5 \\ +\,1 \\ \hline \end{array} \qquad \begin{array}{r} 1 \\ +\,5 \\ \hline \end{array}$$

$$\begin{array}{r} 4 \\ +\,1 \\ \hline \end{array} \qquad \begin{array}{r} 1 \\ +\,4 \\ \hline \end{array}$$

$$\begin{array}{r} 3 \\ +\,2 \\ \hline \end{array} \qquad \begin{array}{r} 2 \\ +\,3 \\ \hline \end{array}$$

$$\begin{array}{r} 1 \\ +\,3 \\ \hline 4 \end{array} \qquad \begin{array}{r} 3 \\ +\,1 \\ \hline \end{array}$$

$$\begin{array}{r} 4 \\ +\,2 \\ \hline \end{array} \qquad \begin{array}{r} 2 \\ +\,4 \\ \hline \end{array}$$

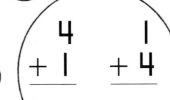

Notes for Home Set A: Children practice using pictures to find sums through 6.
Set B: Children practice adding in any order to find sums through 6.

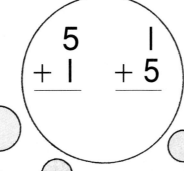

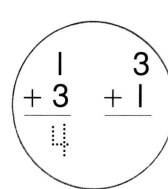

Enrichment

Write the missing numbers.

1.

2 + □ = 3

2.

□ + 3 = 6

3.

□ + 3 = 5

4.

1 + □ = 6

5.

  1
+ □

  5

6.

  □
+ 1

  4

7.

  4
+ □

  6

8.

  □
+ 2

  6

Notes for Home Children are challenged to find missing numbers.

Name ____________________

Chapter 2 Review/Test

1. Look at the picture.
How many are there in all?

____ mice in all

2. Add.

$$\begin{array}{r}2\\+4\\\hline\end{array}\quad\begin{array}{r}4\\+2\\\hline\end{array}\quad\begin{array}{r}2\\+3\\\hline\end{array}\quad\begin{array}{r}3\\+2\\\hline\end{array}$$

3. Color some 

and some 

.

Complete the number sentence.

☐ ☐ ☐ ☐ ☐ ☐

____ + ____ = 6

4. Add.

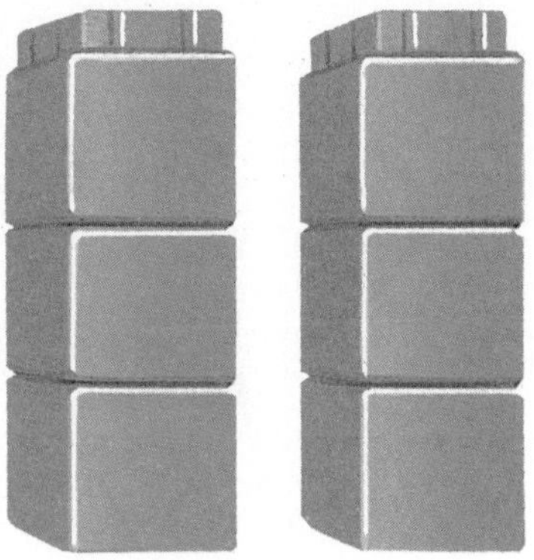

$3 + 3 =$ ____

5. Color one for each.

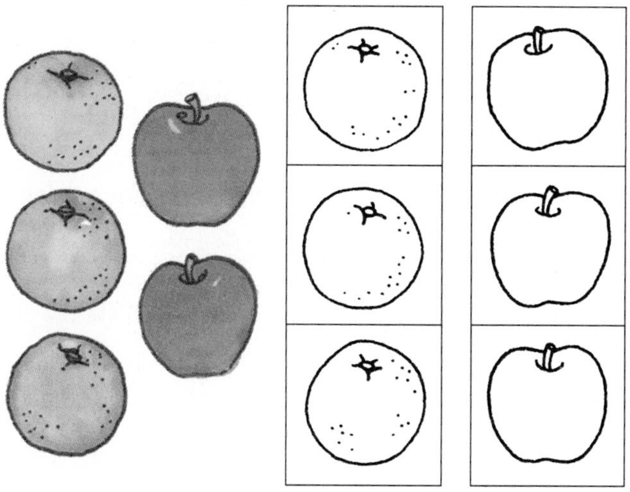

Notes for Home Children are assessed on Chapter 2 concepts, skills, and problem solving.

Exploring Math at Home

Dear Family,

In this chapter I have learned to add through 6 and how to make a graph. Please help me do the activities below.

Love, ____________________

1.

I had 3¢ and found 3¢.
Now I have 6¢.

Use two groups of objects or coins to create addition stories for sums through 6.

2.

Use objects to create addition sentences for numbers through 6.

Coming Attractions

In the next chapter I will be learning to add through 10 and to write addition number sentences.

Chapter

3

Addition Through 10

Listen to the math story, "Hippo Harvest."
Henry worried that he might not have enough chairs.
When did he find out whether he had enough?

Notes for Home Children listen to a math story introducing chapter concepts and skills. Then they answer a question about the story.

Name

Counting On

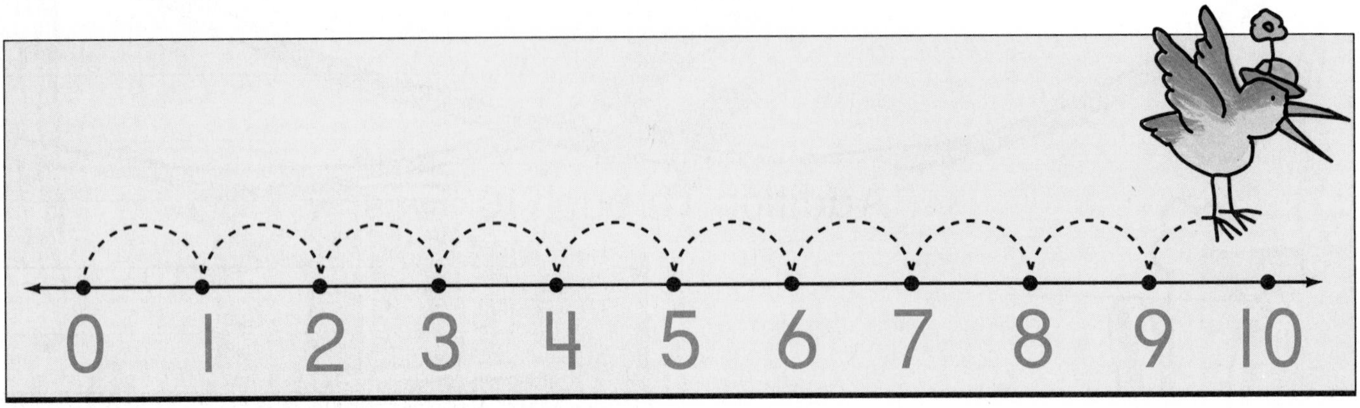

Count on.

1.

6 7

2.

8 ____

3.
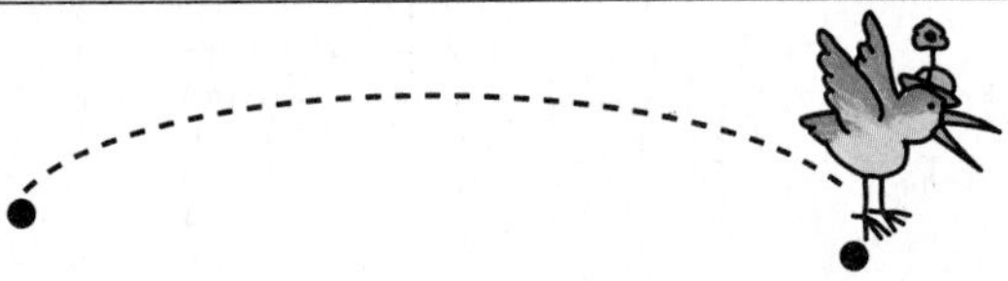
3 ____

4.

1 ____

5.

4 ____ ____

6.
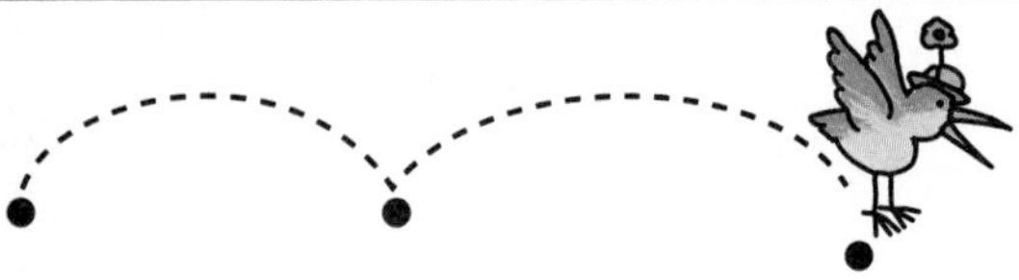
0 ____ ____

7.
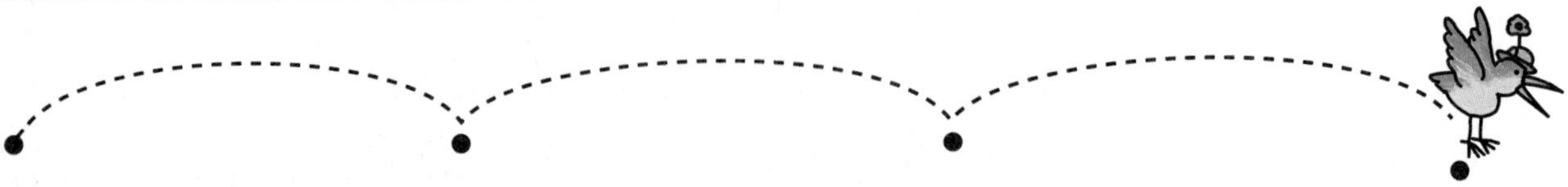
7 ____ ____ ____

Notes for Home Children learn to count on from a given number, using a number line.

Name

Adding 1

First, think 5 .
Then count on 1 more.

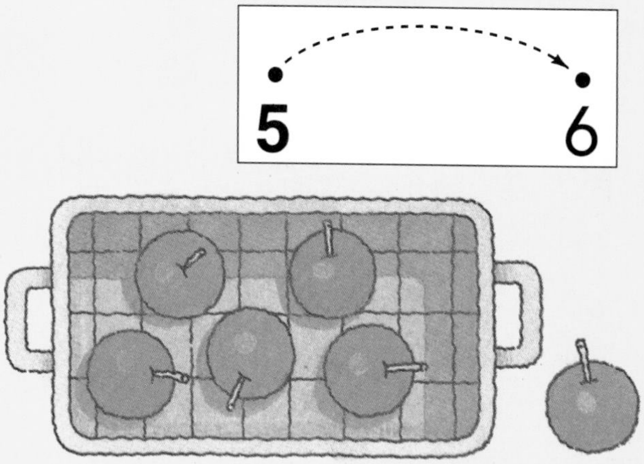
5
6

5 + 1 = 6

Add by counting on.

1.

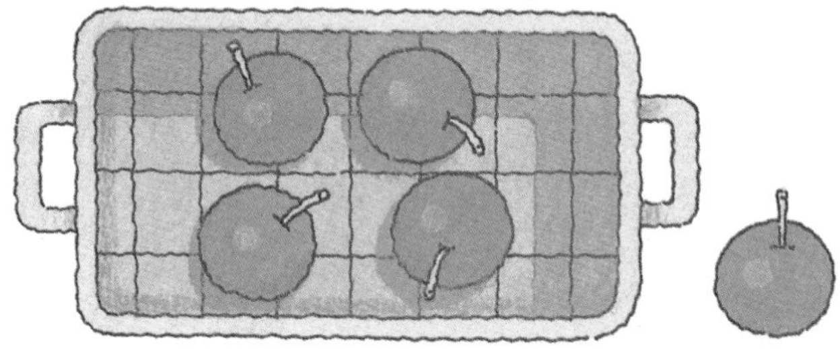

4 + 1 = ____

2.

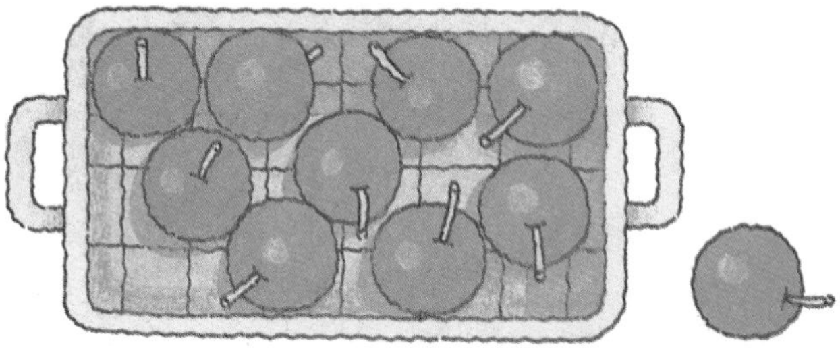

9 + 1 = ____

3.

6

6 + 1 = ____

4.

8

8 + 1 = ____

Notes for Home Children learn to find sums by adding 1 to a given number.

Add by counting on.

5.

$4 + 1 = 5$

6.

$8 + 1 =$

7. $5 + 1 =$ $2 + 1 =$ $6 + 1 =$ $3 + 1 =$ $7 + 1 =$ $9 + 1 =$

8. $8 + 1 =$ $1 + 1 =$ $4 + 1 =$ $6 + 1 =$ $2 + 1 =$ $7 + 1 =$

9. $4 + 1 =$ $3 + 1 =$ $5 + 1 =$ $9 + 1 =$ $7 + 1 =$ $6 + 1 =$

10. $1 + 1 =$ $5 + 1 =$ $8 + 1 =$

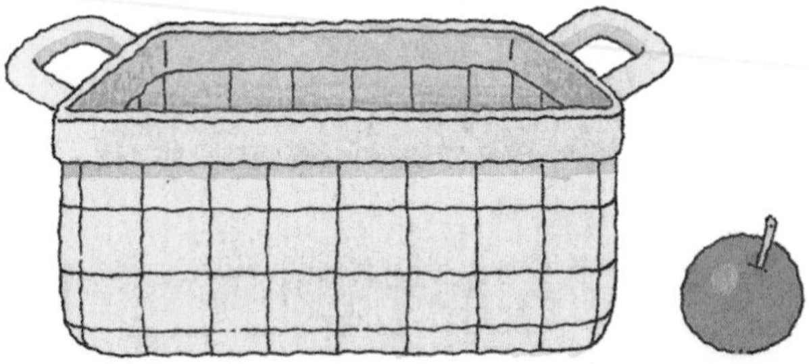

Notes for Home Children practice finding sums by adding 1 to a given number.

Name

Adding 1 or 2

First, think 6 🍓.
Then count on 2 more.

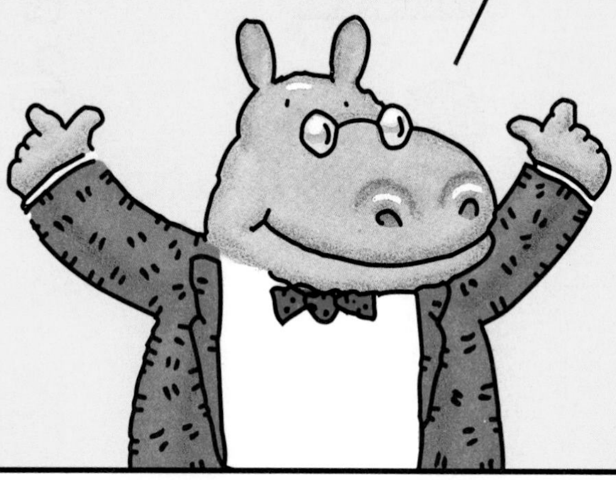

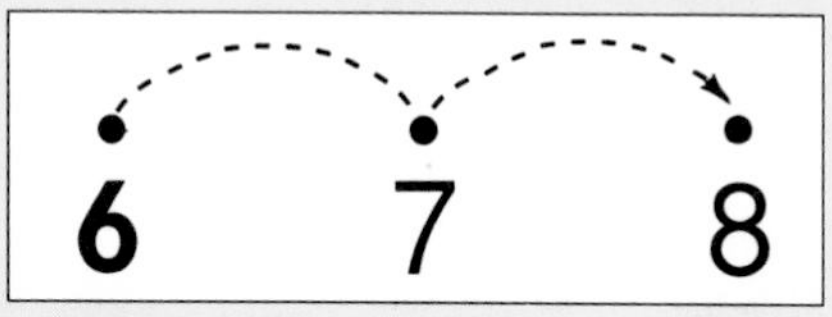

$6 + 2 = 8$

Add by counting on.

1.

$7 + 2 =$ ____

2.

$9 + 1 =$ ____

3.

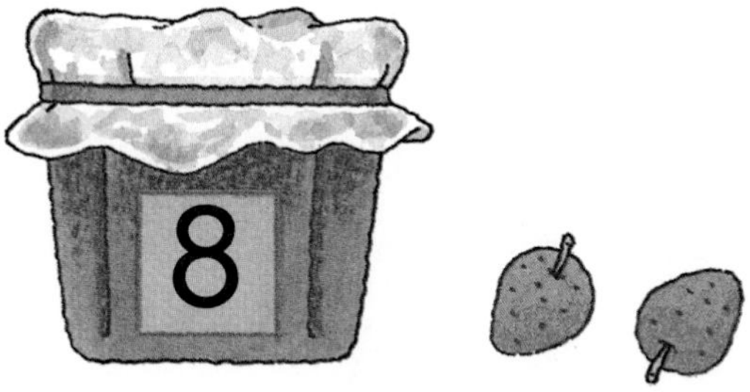

$8 + 2 =$ ____

4.

$7 + 1 =$ ____

Notes for Home Children learn to find sums by adding 1 or 2 to a given number.

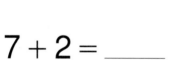

Add by counting on.

5.

$$\begin{array}{r} 5 \\ +\ 2 \\ \hline 7 \end{array}$$

6.

$$\begin{array}{r} 8 \\ +\ 2 \\ \hline \end{array}$$

7. $\begin{array}{r} 4 \\ +\ 2 \\ \hline \end{array}$ $\quad \begin{array}{r} 3 \\ +\ 1 \\ \hline \end{array}$ $\quad \begin{array}{r} 7 \\ +\ 2 \\ \hline \end{array}$ $\quad \begin{array}{r} 9 \\ +\ 1 \\ \hline \end{array}$ $\quad \begin{array}{r} 5 \\ +\ 1 \\ \hline \end{array}$ $\quad \begin{array}{r} 3 \\ +\ 2 \\ \hline \end{array}$

8. $\begin{array}{r} 7 \\ +\ 1 \\ \hline \end{array}$ $\quad \begin{array}{r} 6 \\ +\ 2 \\ \hline \end{array}$ $\quad \begin{array}{r} 4 \\ +\ 1 \\ \hline \end{array}$ $\quad \begin{array}{r} 7 \\ +\ 2 \\ \hline \end{array}$ $\quad \begin{array}{r} 5 \\ +\ 2 \\ \hline \end{array}$ $\quad \begin{array}{r} 2 \\ +\ 1 \\ \hline \end{array}$

9. $\begin{array}{r} 4 \\ +\ 2 \\ \hline \end{array}$ $\quad \begin{array}{r} 3 \\ +\ 2 \\ \hline \end{array}$ $\quad \begin{array}{r} 3 \\ +\ 1 \\ \hline \end{array}$ $\quad \begin{array}{r} 8 \\ +\ 2 \\ \hline \end{array}$ $\quad \begin{array}{r} 6 \\ +\ 1 \\ \hline \end{array}$ $\quad \begin{array}{r} 8 \\ +\ 1 \\ \hline \end{array}$

10. $\begin{array}{r} 1 \\ +\ 1 \\ \hline \end{array}$ $\quad \begin{array}{r} 6 \\ +\ 2 \\ \hline \end{array}$ $\quad \begin{array}{r} 3 \\ +\ 2 \\ \hline \end{array}$

Notes for Home Children practice finding sums by adding 1 or 2 to a given number.

Name

Adding 1, 2, or 3

First, think 5 🍑. Then count on to add.

$5 + 3 = 8$

Add by counting on.

1.

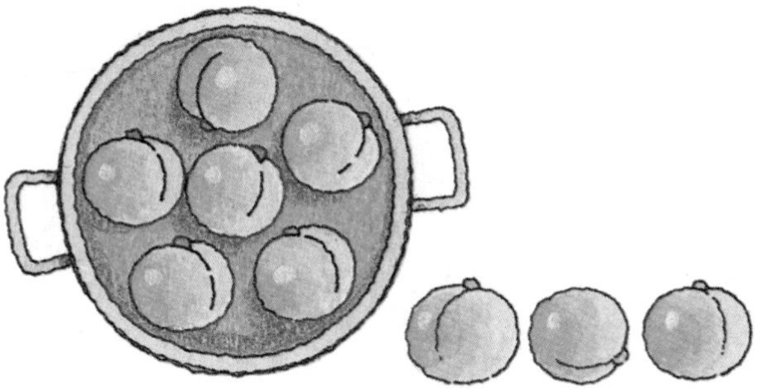

$6 + 3 =$ ____

2.

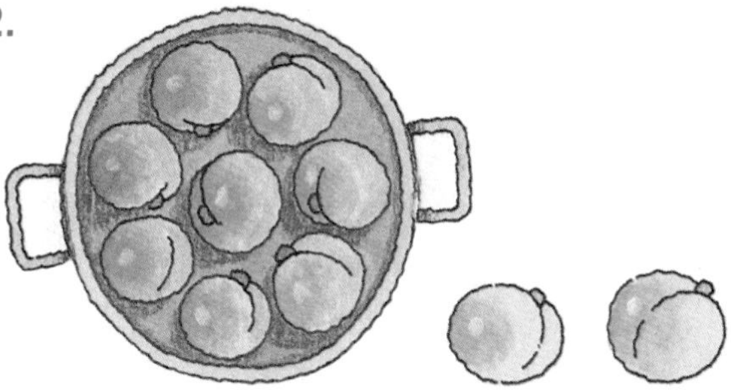

$8 + 2 =$ ____

3.

$4 + 1 =$ ____

4.

$7 + 3 =$ ____

Notes for Home Children learn to find sums by adding 1, 2, or 3 to a given number.

Add by counting on.

5.

$$\begin{array}{r} 4 \\ +\ 3 \\ \hline 7 \end{array}$$

6.

$$\begin{array}{r} 7 \\ +\ 2 \\ \hline \end{array}$$

7.	8 + 2	2 + 1	6 + 3	4 + 1	9 + 1	3 + 2
8.	6 + 1	7 + 3	8 + 1	5 + 2	4 + 2	3 + 1
9.	5 + 3	7 + 1	4 + 3	7 + 2	5 + 1	6 + 2
10.	7 + 3	4 + 2	9 + 1			

Notes for Home Children practice finding sums by adding 1, 2, or 3 to a given number.

Name ____________________

Adding from Any Number

Think of the greater number.
Then count on.

$5 + 3 = 8$ $\qquad$ $3 + 5 = 8$

Add by counting on.

1.

 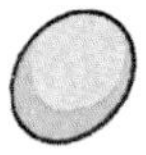

$4 + 1 =$ ____ $\qquad$ $1 + 4 =$ ____

2.

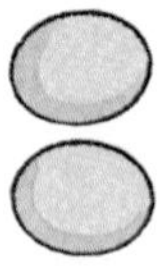 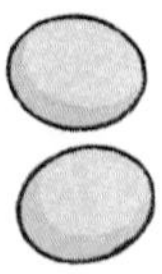

$6 + 2 =$ ____ $\qquad$ $2 + 6 =$ ____

3.

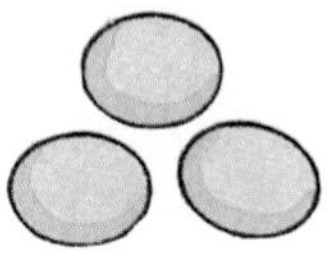 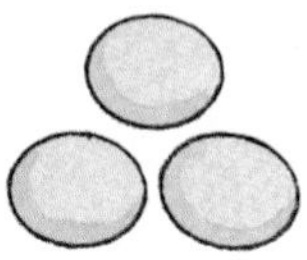

$7 + 3 =$ ____ $\qquad$ $3 + 7 =$ ____

Notes for Home Children identify the greater of two numbers. Then they add 1, 2, or 3 to find the sum.

Think of the greater number.
Then add by counting on.

4. $\begin{array}{r} 2 \\ +\ 6 \\ \hline 8 \end{array}$ 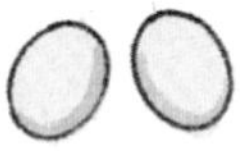 $\begin{array}{r} 6 \\ +\ 2 \\ \hline \end{array}$ 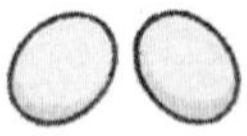

5. $\begin{array}{r} 4 \\ +\ 3 \\ \hline \end{array}$ 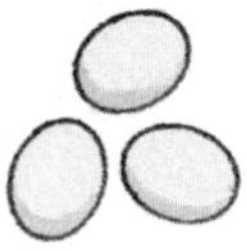 $\begin{array}{r} 3 \\ +\ 4 \\ \hline \end{array}$ 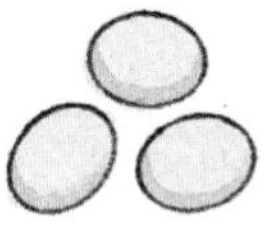

6. $\begin{array}{r} 3 \\ +\ 1 \\ \hline \end{array}$ $\begin{array}{r} 1 \\ +\ 3 \\ \hline \end{array}$

7. $\begin{array}{r} 3 \\ +\ 6 \\ \hline \end{array}$ $\begin{array}{r} 6 \\ +\ 3 \\ \hline \end{array}$

8. $\begin{array}{r} 1 \\ +\ 7 \\ \hline \end{array}$ $\begin{array}{r} 7 \\ +\ 1 \\ \hline \end{array}$

9. $\begin{array}{r} 8 \\ +\ 2 \\ \hline \end{array}$ $\begin{array}{r} 2 \\ +\ 8 \\ \hline \end{array}$

10. $\begin{array}{r} 6 \\ +\ 1 \\ \hline \end{array}$ $\begin{array}{r} 1 \\ +\ 6 \\ \hline \end{array}$

11. $\begin{array}{r} 2 \\ +\ 4 \\ \hline \end{array}$ $\begin{array}{r} 4 \\ +\ 2 \\ \hline \end{array}$

12. $\begin{array}{r} 5 \\ +\ 2 \\ \hline \end{array}$ $\begin{array}{r} 2 \\ +\ 6 \\ \hline \end{array}$ $\begin{array}{r} 9 \\ +\ 1 \\ \hline \end{array}$ $\begin{array}{r} 2 \\ +\ 7 \\ \hline \end{array}$ $\begin{array}{r} 4 \\ +\ 1 \\ \hline \end{array}$ $\begin{array}{r} 7 \\ +\ 3 \\ \hline \end{array}$

13. $\begin{array}{r} 8 \\ +\ 1 \\ \hline \end{array}$ $\begin{array}{r} 3 \\ +\ 5 \\ \hline \end{array}$ $\begin{array}{r} 7 \\ +\ 2 \\ \hline \end{array}$

Notes for Home Children practice finding sums by adding 1, 2, or 3 to the greater number.

See More Practice Set A on page 99.

Name ____________________

PROBLEM-SOLVING STRATEGY

Write a Number Sentence

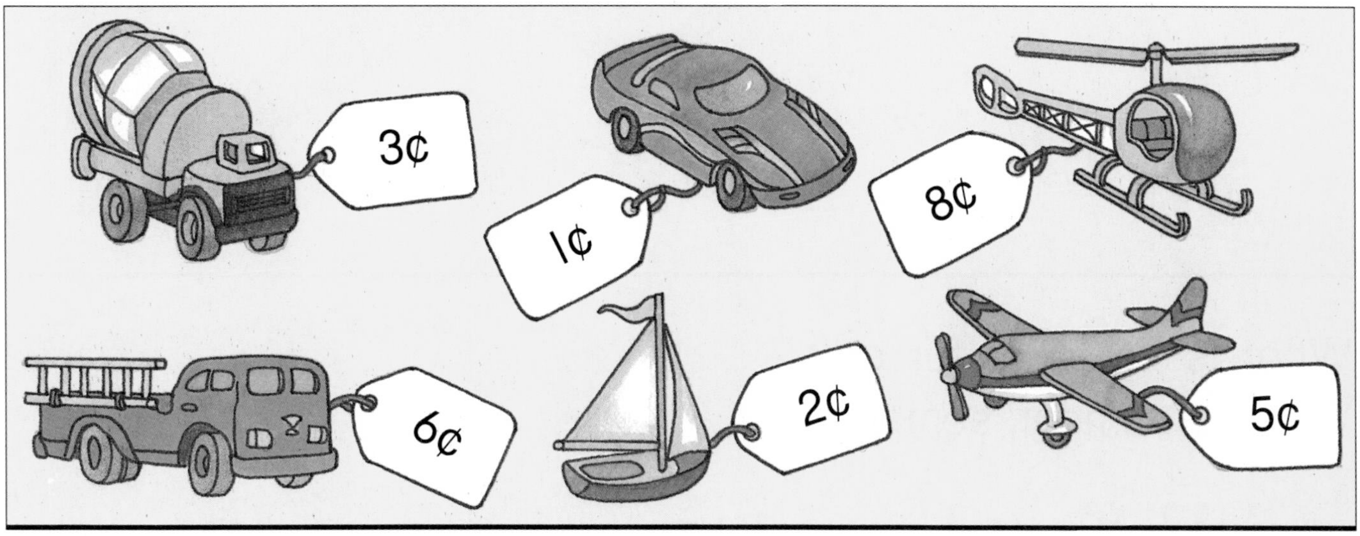

What is the cost for both?
Write a number sentence.

1.

6 ¢ + 2 ¢ = 8 ¢

2.

____ ¢ + ____ ¢ = ____ ¢

3.

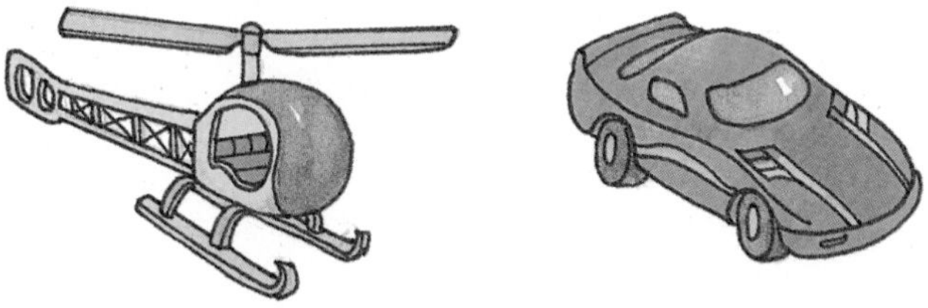

____ ¢ + ____ ¢ = ____ ¢

4.

____ ¢ + ____ ¢ = ____ ¢

Notes for Home Children learn to solve problems involving money by writing number sentences.

What is the cost for both?
Write a number sentence.

5.

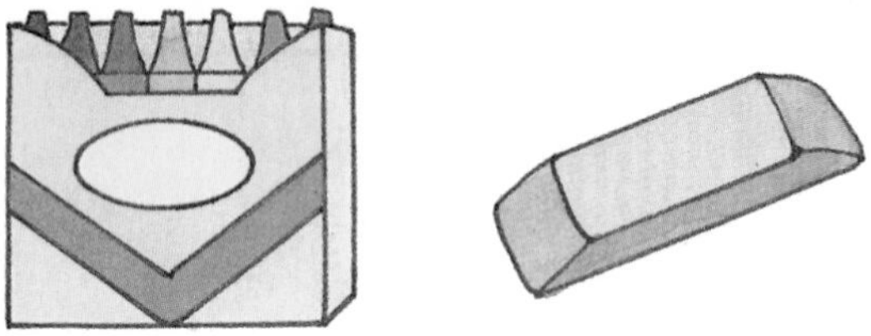

5 ¢ + 2 ¢ = 7 ¢

6.

___ ¢ + ___ ¢ = ___ ¢

7.

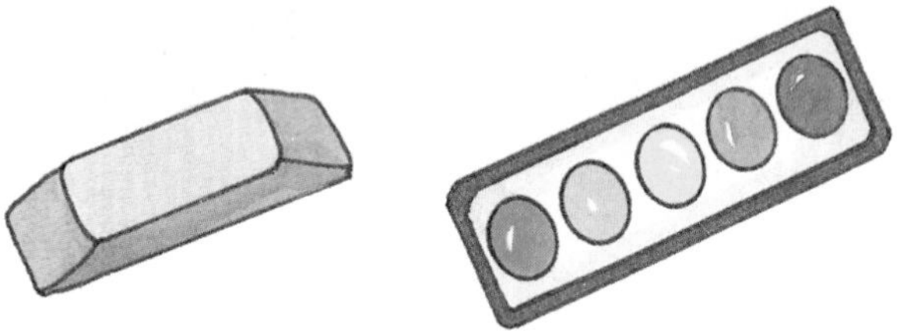

___ ¢ + ___ ¢ = ___ ¢

8.

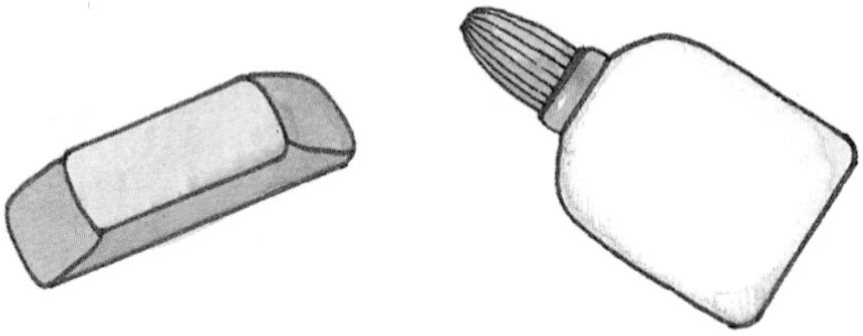

___ ¢ + ___ ¢ = ___ ¢

9.

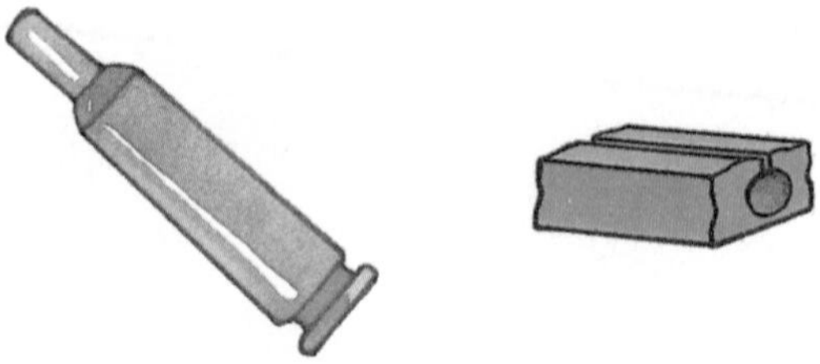

___ ¢ + ___ ¢ = ___ ¢

10.

___ ¢ + ___ ¢ = ___ ¢

Notes for Home Children solve problems involving money by writing number sentences.

Name

Number Sense

Tell an addition story for $5 + 2 = 7$ that each child could be thinking.

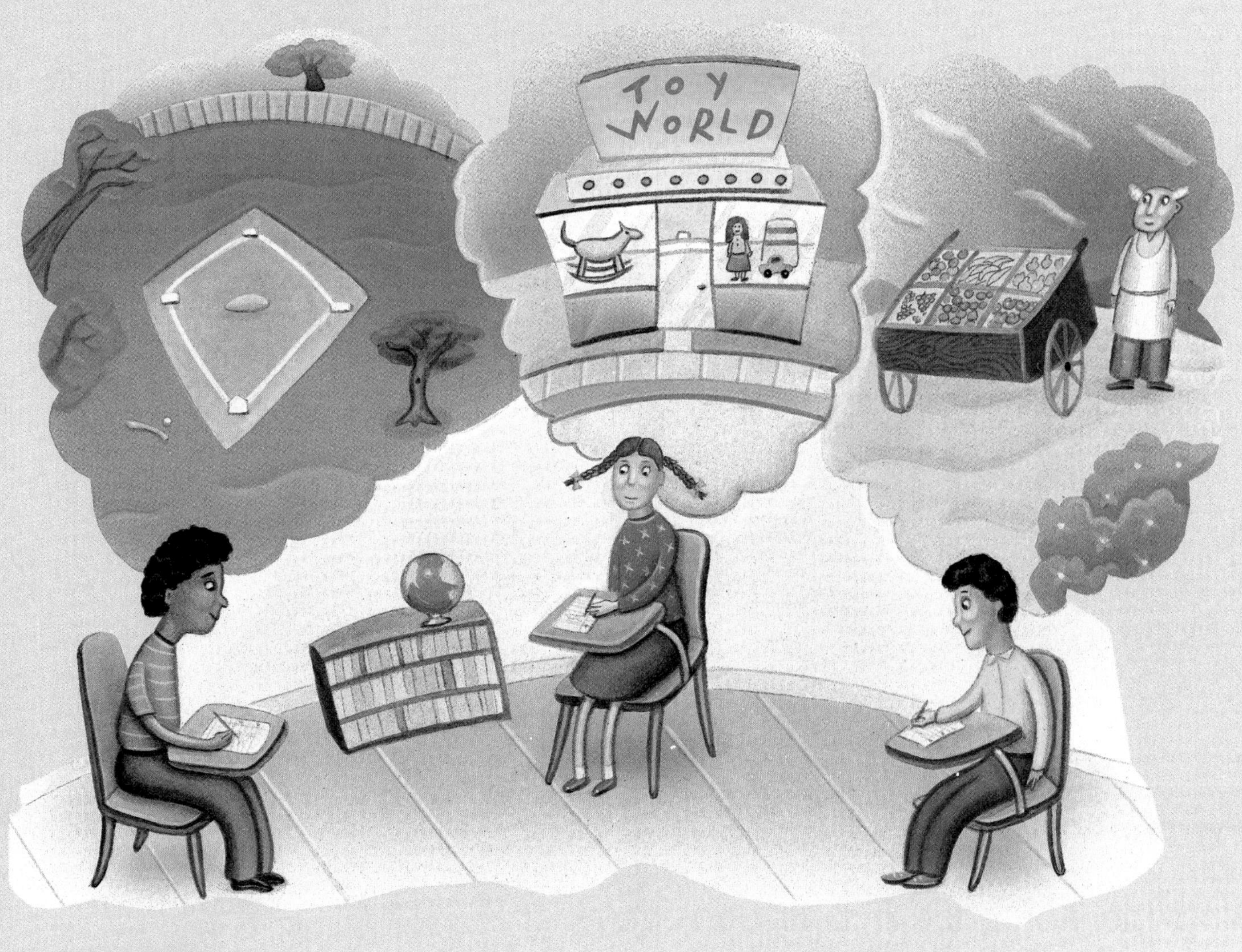

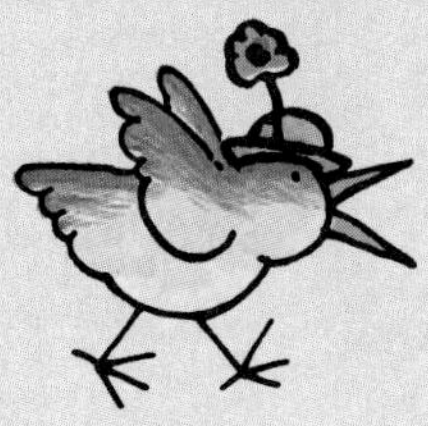

Let's do some more!

Think of stories to show $6 + 3 = 9$.
Tell your stories to a friend.

Notes for Home Children develop number understanding by creating stories for a given number sentence.

Skills Review

Fill in the correct ⬭.

Which is greater?

1.		2.	
9	7	10	11
Ⓐ	Ⓑ	Ⓐ	Ⓑ

Which is less?

3.		4.	
4	6	12	8
Ⓐ	Ⓑ	Ⓐ	Ⓑ

Find the sum.

5. $\begin{array}{r} 2 \\ +3 \\ \hline \end{array}$ $\begin{array}{r} 3 \\ +2 \\ \hline \end{array}$

Ⓐ 3
Ⓑ 4
Ⓒ 5

6. $\begin{array}{r} 2 \\ +4 \\ \hline \end{array}$ $\begin{array}{r} 4 \\ +2 \\ \hline \end{array}$

Ⓐ 4
Ⓑ 6
Ⓒ 2

Vocabulary

Ring the sentence if it is correct.

7. I cent is the same as I penny.
8. 8 is less than 5.
9. 4 is greater than 3.

Notes for Home Children review which of two numbers is greater or less. Then they review adding in any order. Children review math terms.

Name

Adding Zero

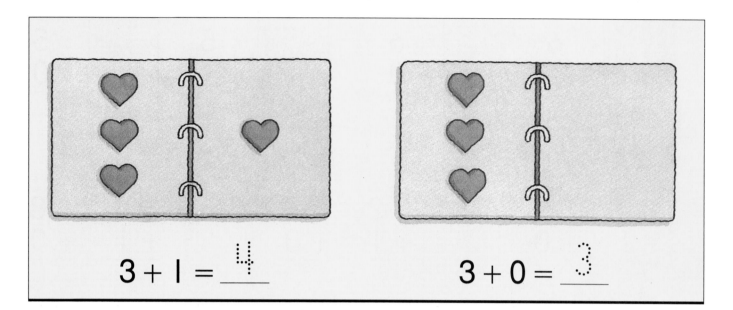

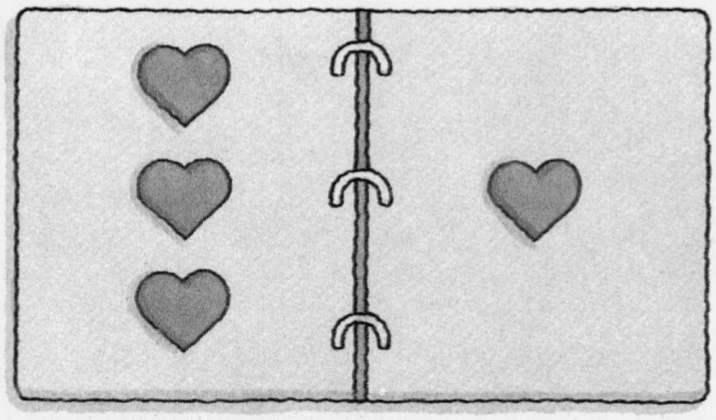

$3 + 1 =$ 4

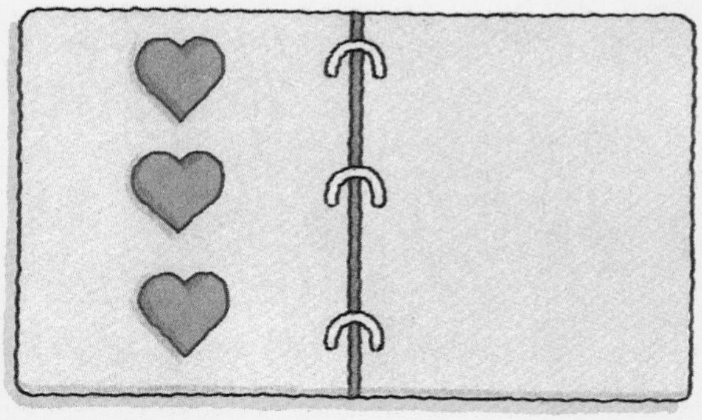

$3 + 0 =$ 3

Add.

1\.

$7 + 1 =$ ____

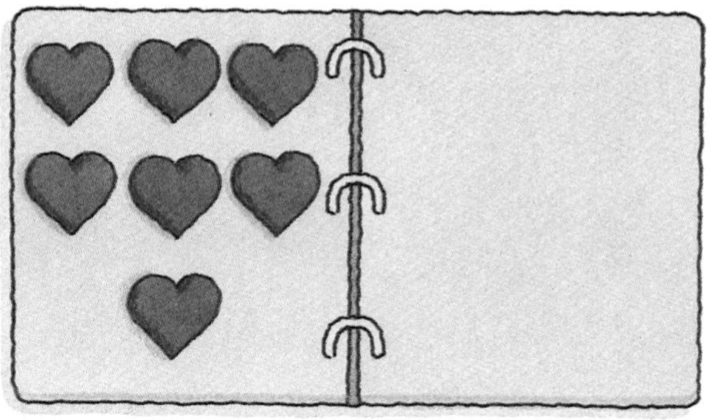

$7 + 0 =$ ____

2\.

$9 + 1 =$ ____

$9 + 0 =$ ____

Notes for Home Children add 0 to find sums. They discover that when 0 is added to a number, the sum is the number itself.

Add.

3.  $\begin{array}{r} 6 \\ +\ 1 \\ \hline 7 \end{array}$  $\begin{array}{r} 6 \\ +\ 0 \\ \hline \end{array}$

4. 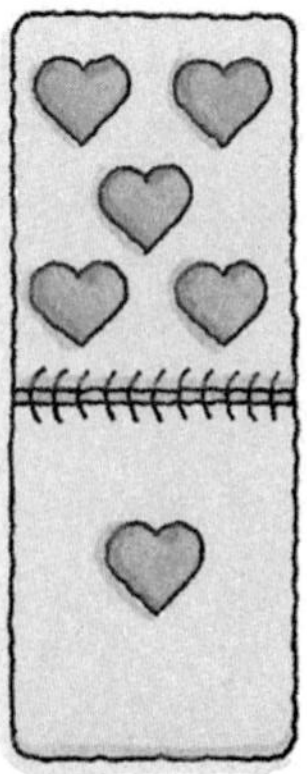 $\begin{array}{r} 5 \\ +\ 1 \\ \hline \end{array}$  $\begin{array}{r} 5 \\ +\ 0 \\ \hline \end{array}$

5. $\begin{array}{r} 4 \\ +\ 1 \\ \hline \end{array}$ $\begin{array}{r} 4 \\ +\ 0 \\ \hline \end{array}$

6. $\begin{array}{r} 2 \\ +\ 1 \\ \hline \end{array}$ $\begin{array}{r} 2 \\ +\ 0 \\ \hline \end{array}$

7. $\begin{array}{r} 8 \\ +\ 1 \\ \hline \end{array}$ $\begin{array}{r} 8 \\ +\ 0 \\ \hline \end{array}$

8. $\begin{array}{r} 7 \\ +\ 1 \\ \hline \end{array}$ $\begin{array}{r} 7 \\ +\ 0 \\ \hline \end{array}$

9. $\begin{array}{r} 3 \\ +\ 1 \\ \hline \end{array}$ $\begin{array}{r} 3 \\ +\ 0 \\ \hline \end{array}$

10. $\begin{array}{r} 9 \\ +\ 1 \\ \hline \end{array}$ $\begin{array}{r} 9 \\ +\ 0 \\ \hline \end{array}$

11. $\begin{array}{r} 3 \\ +\ 6 \\ \hline \end{array}$ $\begin{array}{r} 5 \\ +\ 2 \\ \hline \end{array}$ $\begin{array}{r} 2 \\ +\ 0 \\ \hline \end{array}$ $\begin{array}{r} 3 \\ +\ 5 \\ \hline \end{array}$ $\begin{array}{r} 0 \\ +\ 1 \\ \hline \end{array}$ $\begin{array}{r} 2 \\ +\ 7 \\ \hline \end{array}$

12. $\begin{array}{r} 3 \\ +\ 0 \\ \hline \end{array}$ $\begin{array}{r} 1 \\ +\ 7 \\ \hline \end{array}$ $\begin{array}{r} 0 \\ +\ 0 \\ \hline \end{array}$ $\begin{array}{r} 1 \\ +\ 8 \\ \hline \end{array}$ $\begin{array}{r} 4 \\ +\ 3 \\ \hline \end{array}$ $\begin{array}{r} 0 \\ +\ 4 \\ \hline \end{array}$

Notes for Home Children practice finding sums through 10.

Name

Adding with Doubles

These are doubles.

$3 + 3 = 6$ $4 + 4 = 8$

Write the sum.

1.

$2 + 2 =$ ____

2.

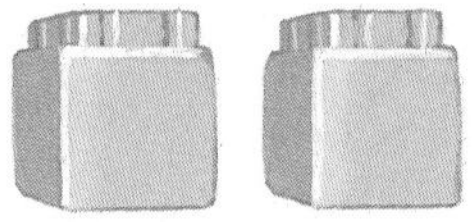

$1 + 1 =$ ____

3.

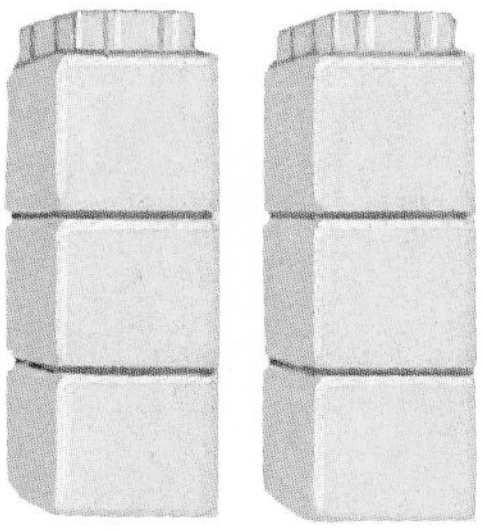

$3 + 3 =$ ____

4.

$5 + 5 =$ ____

Notes for Home Children learn to use doubles to find sums through 10.

Write the sum.
Ring the doubles.

5.	2	4	7	1	3	2
	+ 2	+ 3	+ 2	+ 4	+ 3	+ 6
	4					

6.	5	1	4	1	5	7
	+ 5	+ 9	+ 2	+ 1	+ 1	+ 3

7.	3	0	1	5	4	6
	+ 5	+ 0	+ 3	+ 2	+ 4	+ 1

Problem Solving

How many in all?
Write a number sentence.

8.

___ + ___ = ___

9.

___ + ___ = ___

Notes for Home Children practice addition facts through 10 and identify facts that are doubles. Then they write number sentences to solve problems.

Name

Adding with Doubles and I More

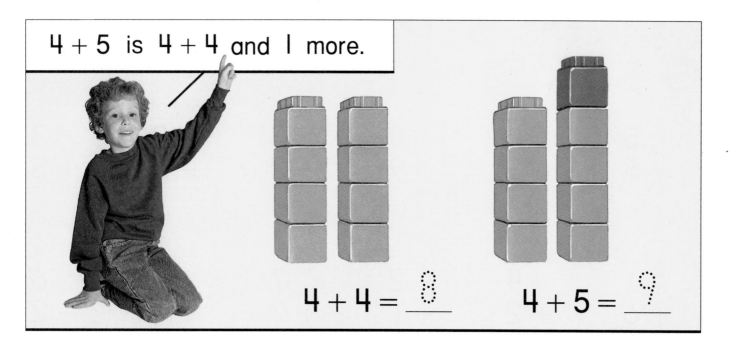

4 + 5 is 4 + 4 and I more.

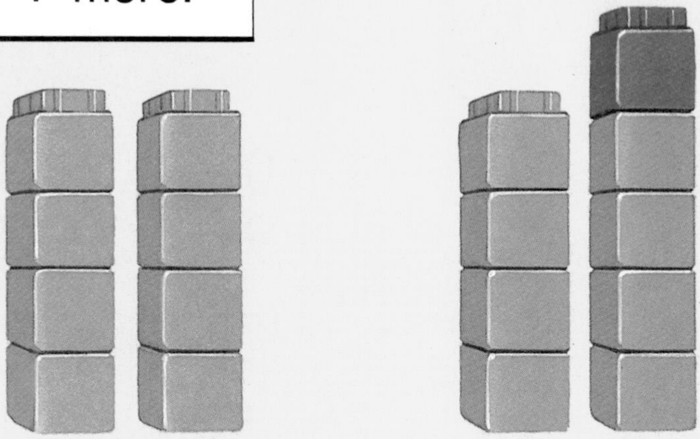

4 + 4 = 8   4 + 5 = 9

Write the sum.

I.

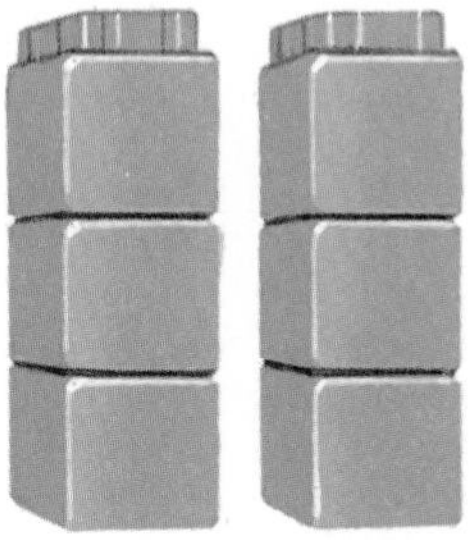

3 + 3 = ____

3 + 4 = ____

2.

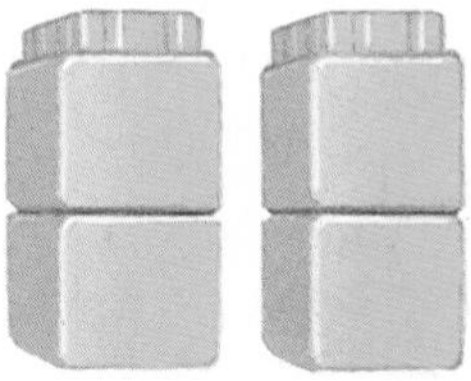

2 + 2 = ____

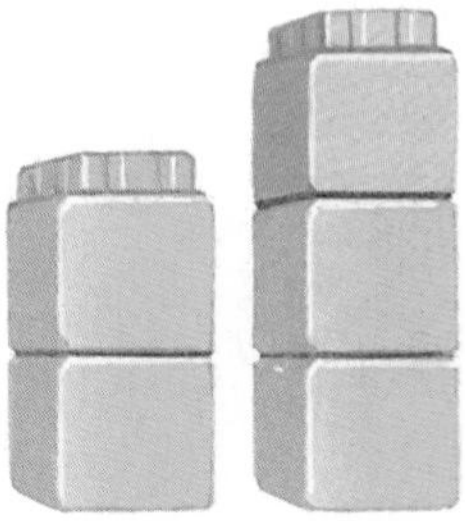

2 + 3 = ____

Notes for Home Children learn to use doubles facts to find sums of doubles and I more.

Write the sum.

3. $\begin{array}{r} 3 \\ +\,3 \\ \hline 6 \end{array}$ $\begin{array}{r} 3 \\ +\,4 \\ \hline \end{array}$

4. $\begin{array}{r} 4 \\ +\,4 \\ \hline \end{array}$ $\begin{array}{r} 4 \\ +\,5 \\ \hline \end{array}$

5. $\begin{array}{r} 2 \\ +\,2 \\ \hline \end{array}$ $\begin{array}{r} 2 \\ +\,3 \\ \hline \end{array}$

6. $\begin{array}{r} 5 \\ +\,5 \\ \hline \end{array}$ $\begin{array}{r} 4 \\ +\,3 \\ \hline \end{array}$ $\begin{array}{r} 0 \\ +\,9 \\ \hline \end{array}$ $\begin{array}{r} 3 \\ +\,2 \\ \hline \end{array}$ $\begin{array}{r} 2 \\ +\,7 \\ \hline \end{array}$ $\begin{array}{r} 3 \\ +\,5 \\ \hline \end{array}$

7. $\begin{array}{r} 1 \\ +\,6 \\ \hline \end{array}$ $\begin{array}{r} 4 \\ +\,2 \\ \hline \end{array}$ $\begin{array}{r} 2 \\ +\,1 \\ \hline \end{array}$ $\begin{array}{r} 7 \\ +\,3 \\ \hline \end{array}$ $\begin{array}{r} 5 \\ +\,4 \\ \hline \end{array}$ $\begin{array}{r} 6 \\ +\,2 \\ \hline \end{array}$

Problem Solving

How many?
Write the numbers.
Then add.

8.

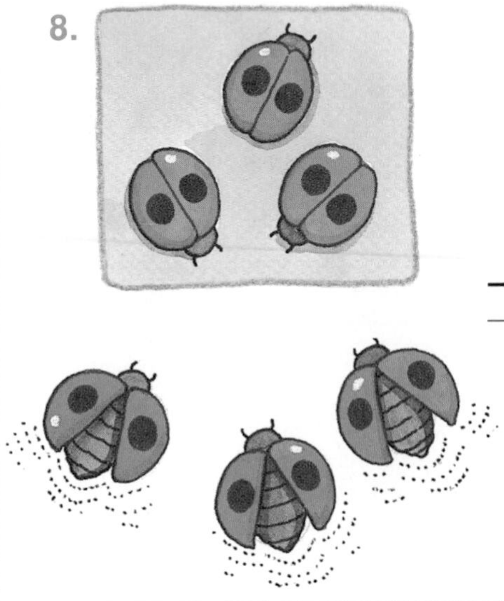

□ + □ = □

9.

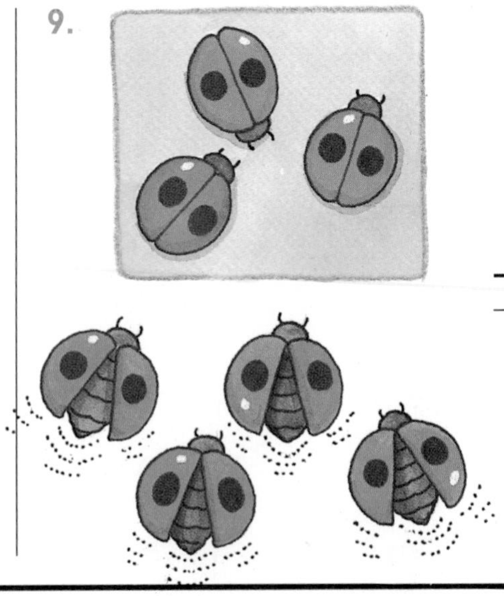

□ + □ = □

Notes for Home Children practice finding sums through 10. Then they solve problems using addition.

Name

Combinations of 10

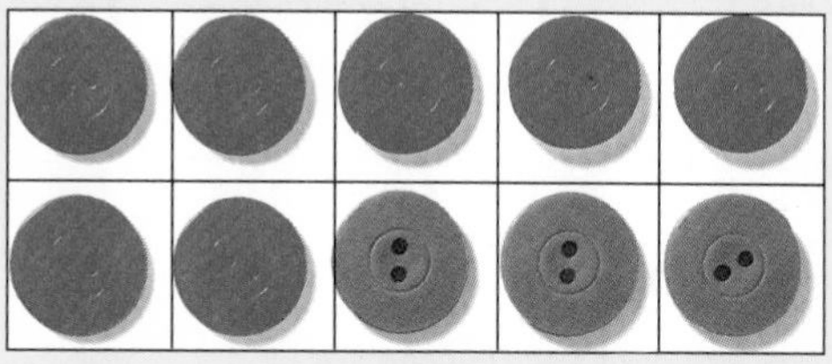

7 + 3 = 10

Complete the number sentence.

1.

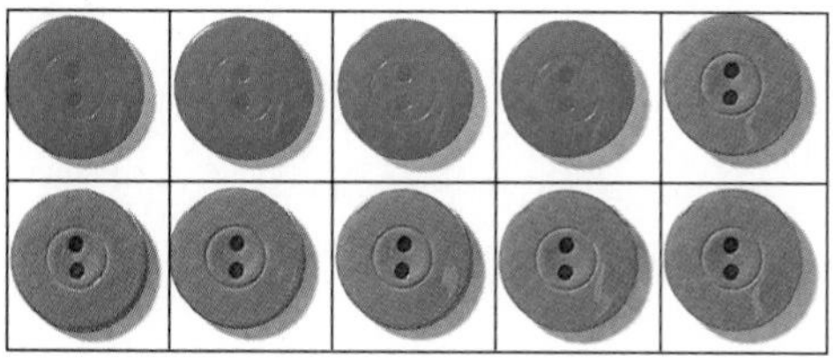

____ + ____ = 10

2.

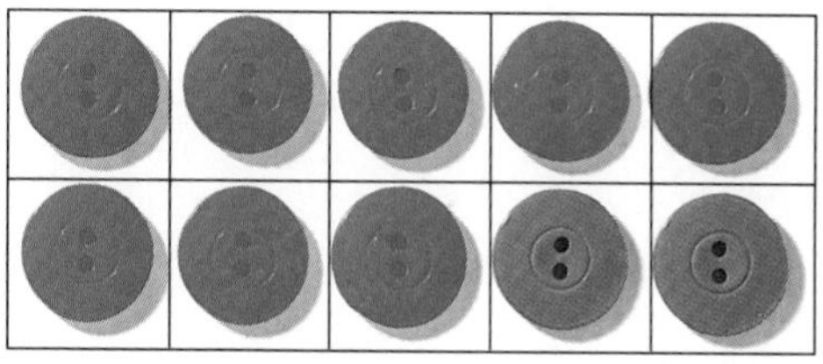

____ + ____ = 10

3.

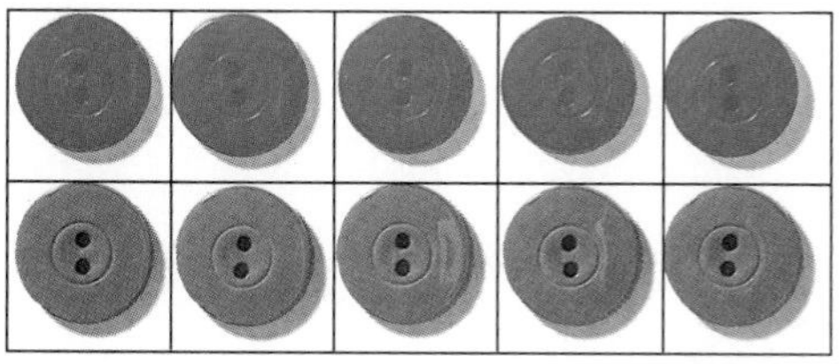

____ + ____ = 10

4.

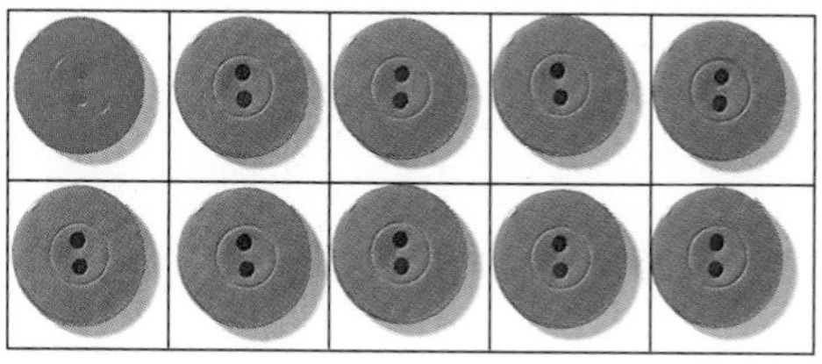

____ + ____ = 10

5.

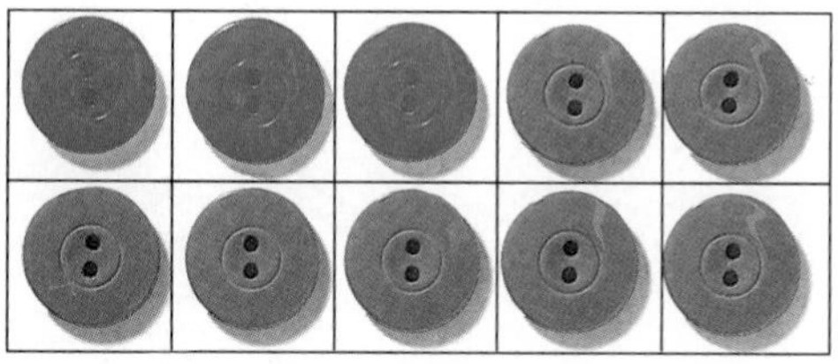

____ + ____ = 10

6.

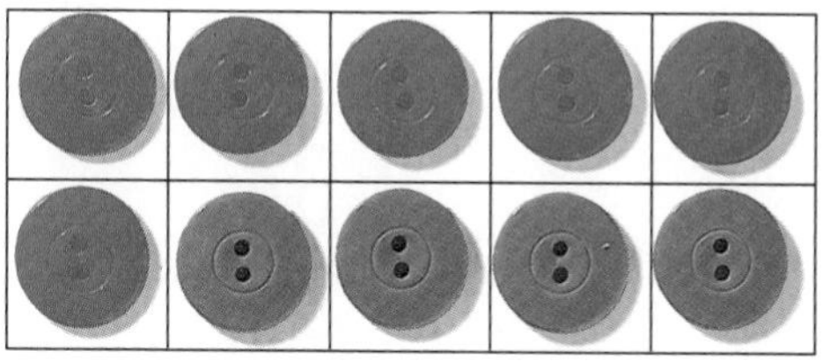

____ + ____ = 10

Notes for Home Children complete number sentences for sums of 10.

Add.

Ring the sums of 10.

7.	4 + 3 = 7	8 + 2 = 10	6 + 4	7 + 1	4 + 5	1 + 9
8.	3 + 7	5 + 3	1 + 8	4 + 4	7 + 3	2 + 5
9.	5 + 4	6 + 2	4 + 6	2 + 7	3 + 3	2 + 8
10.	9 + 1	7 + 2	3 + 6	5 + 5	3 + 5	6 + 3
11.	3 + 4	2 + 6	5 + 1			
12.	1 + 7	8 + 2	7 + 2			

Notes for Home Children practice addition facts through 10 and identify sums of 10.

Addition Through 10

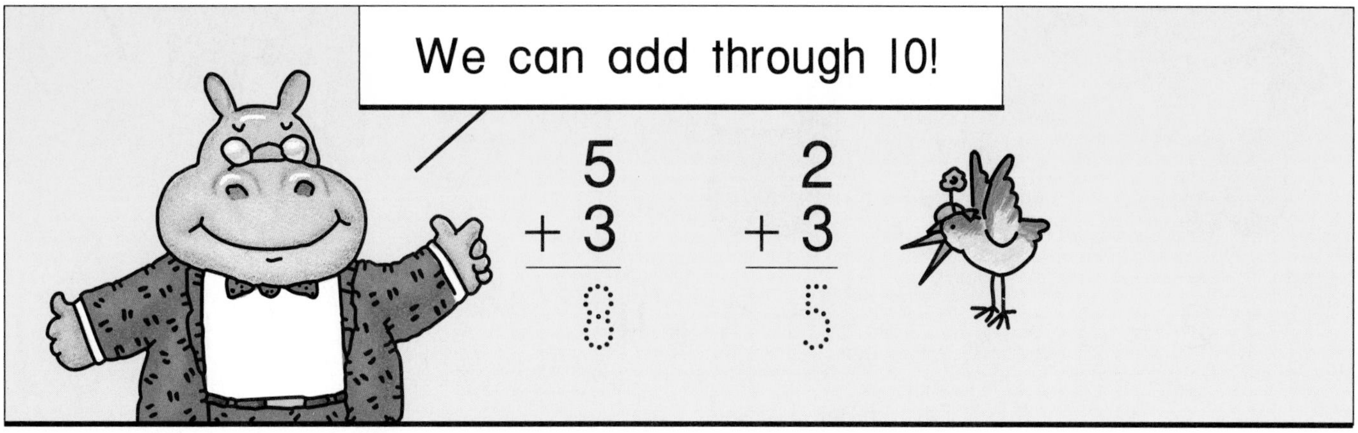

We can add through 10!

$$\begin{array}{r} 5 \\ + 3 \\ \hline 8 \end{array} \qquad \begin{array}{r} 2 \\ + 3 \\ \hline 5 \end{array}$$

Add.

1.
$$\begin{array}{r} 8 \\ +1 \\ \hline \end{array} \quad \begin{array}{r} 3 \\ +4 \\ \hline \end{array} \quad \begin{array}{r} 6 \\ +3 \\ \hline \end{array} \quad \begin{array}{r} 2 \\ +1 \\ \hline \end{array} \quad \begin{array}{r} 3 \\ +2 \\ \hline \end{array} \quad \begin{array}{r} 6 \\ +4 \\ \hline \end{array}$$

2.
$$\begin{array}{r} 5 \\ +4 \\ \hline \end{array} \quad \begin{array}{r} 1 \\ +3 \\ \hline \end{array} \quad \begin{array}{r} 6 \\ +2 \\ \hline \end{array} \quad \begin{array}{r} 0 \\ +2 \\ \hline \end{array} \quad \begin{array}{r} 2 \\ +6 \\ \hline \end{array} \quad \begin{array}{r} 7 \\ +3 \\ \hline \end{array}$$

3.
$$\begin{array}{r} 2 \\ +8 \\ \hline \end{array} \quad \begin{array}{r} 1 \\ +7 \\ \hline \end{array} \quad \begin{array}{r} 5 \\ +2 \\ \hline \end{array} \quad \begin{array}{r} 9 \\ +1 \\ \hline \end{array} \quad \begin{array}{r} 4 \\ +5 \\ \hline \end{array} \quad \begin{array}{r} 1 \\ +2 \\ \hline \end{array}$$

4.
$$\begin{array}{r} 7 \\ +2 \\ \hline \end{array} \quad \begin{array}{r} 5 \\ +5 \\ \hline \end{array} \quad \begin{array}{r} 8 \\ +0 \\ \hline \end{array} \quad \begin{array}{r} 6 \\ +1 \\ \hline \end{array} \quad \begin{array}{r} 4 \\ +6 \\ \hline \end{array} \quad \begin{array}{r} 1 \\ +8 \\ \hline \end{array}$$

Notes for Home Children find sums through 10.

Ring the facts for each number.

5.

2 + 3

2 + 2

4 + 1

5 + 0

6.

3 + 4

3 + 3

0 + 6

2 + 4

7.

4 + 3

1 + 6

3 + 5

5 + 2

8.

5 + 3

4 + 4

1 + 7

6 + 2

9.

6 + 3

4 + 5

3 + 5

2 + 7

10.

0 + 9

2 + 8

5 + 5

3 + 7

Notes for Home Children identify facts for a given number.

See More Practice Set B on page 99.

Use Data from a Picture

Look at the picture.
Ring each thing you could buy.

1. You have 7¢.

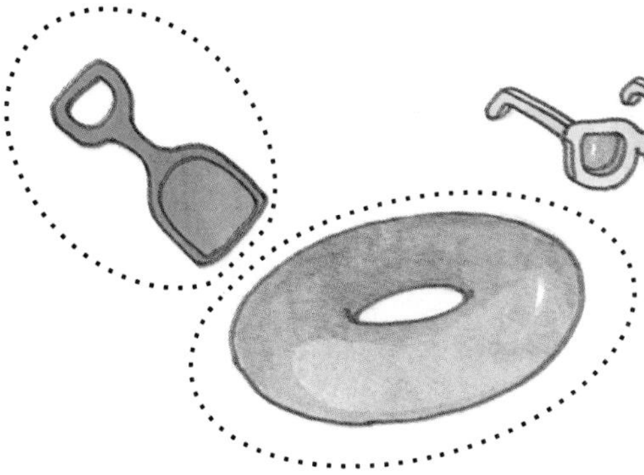

2. You have 5¢.

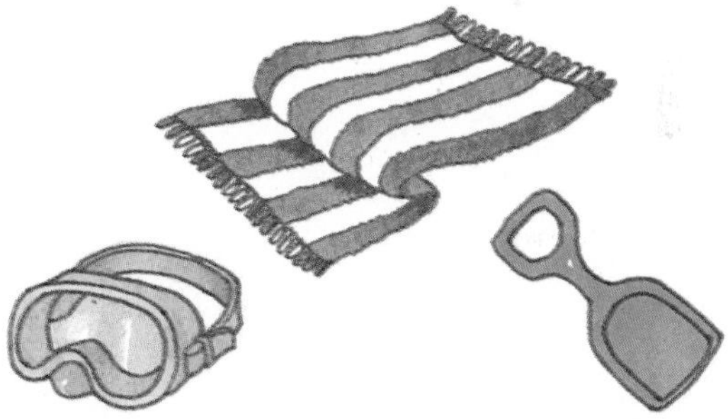

3. You have 8¢.

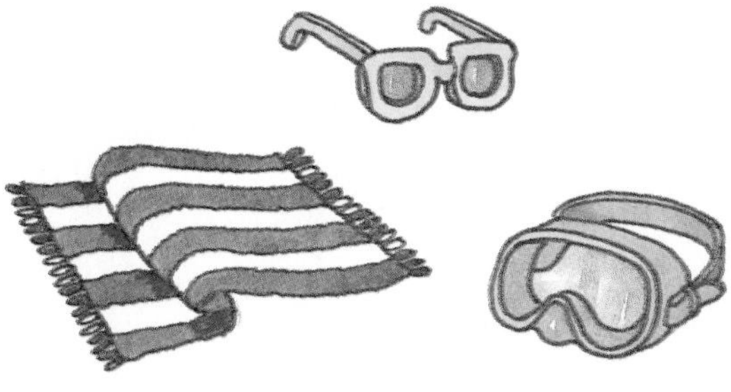

4. You have 10¢.

Notes for Home Children learn to solve problems involving money by using data from pictures.

Look at the picture.
Ring each shell you could buy.

5. You have 6¢.

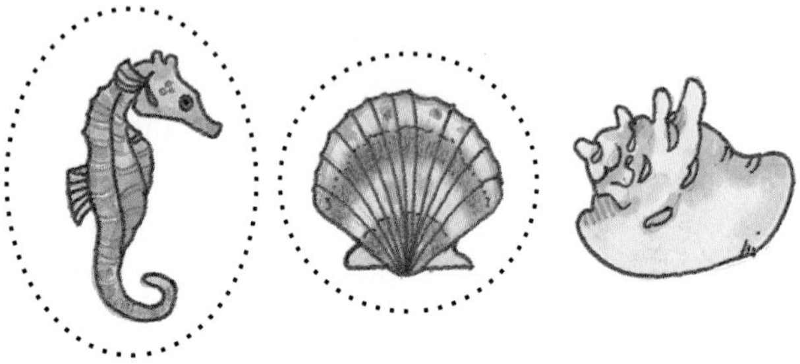

6. You have 5¢.

7. You have 8¢.

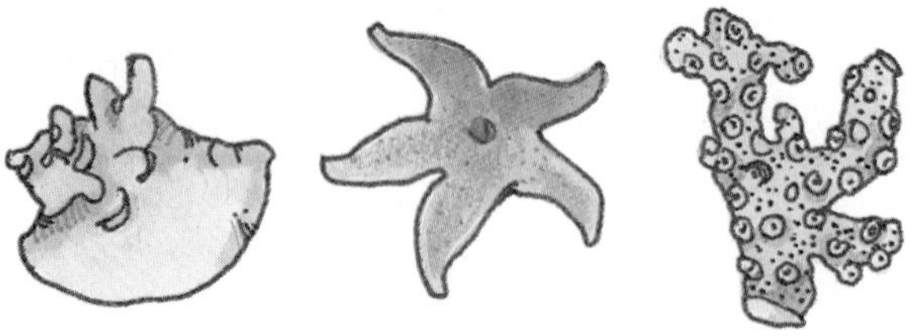

8. You have 4¢.

9. You have 10¢.

10. You have 7¢.

Notes for Home Children solve problems involving money by using data from pictures.

Name

Problem-Solving Workshop

Explore as a Team

Work with a partner.
Use 10 counters.
Use 2 bags.
Take turns doing this activity.

1. Put some counters in each bag.

2. One partner counts the counters in one bag.

3. The other partner guesses how many counters are in the other bag.

4. Count to see if your guess was right.

Work with a partner.
Use 9 counters.
Do this activity again.

Let's do some more!

Notes for Home Children explore with a partner to solve problems. They discover combinations of 10.

Problem-Solving Workshop

Explore with a Calculator

Use a calculator to solve. Write what the calculator will show.

1.

3 + 4 = 7

2.

2 + 3 = ___

3.

4 + 2 = ___

4.

5 + 5 = ___

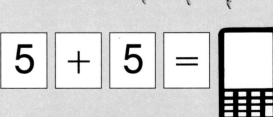

Notes for Home Children explore with a calculator to solve addition problems.

Name ______________________________

More Practice

Set A Use after page 80.

Add by counting on.

1. $4 + 1 = 5$ $5 + 2 =$ ___ $3 + 6 =$ ___ $2 + 4 =$ ___ $7 + 2 =$ ___ $5 + 1 =$ ___

2. $2 + 8 =$ ___ $9 + 1 =$ ___ $1 + 3 =$ ___ $2 + 6 =$ ___ $5 + 3 =$ ___ $3 + 7 =$ ___

Set B Use after page 94.

Add.

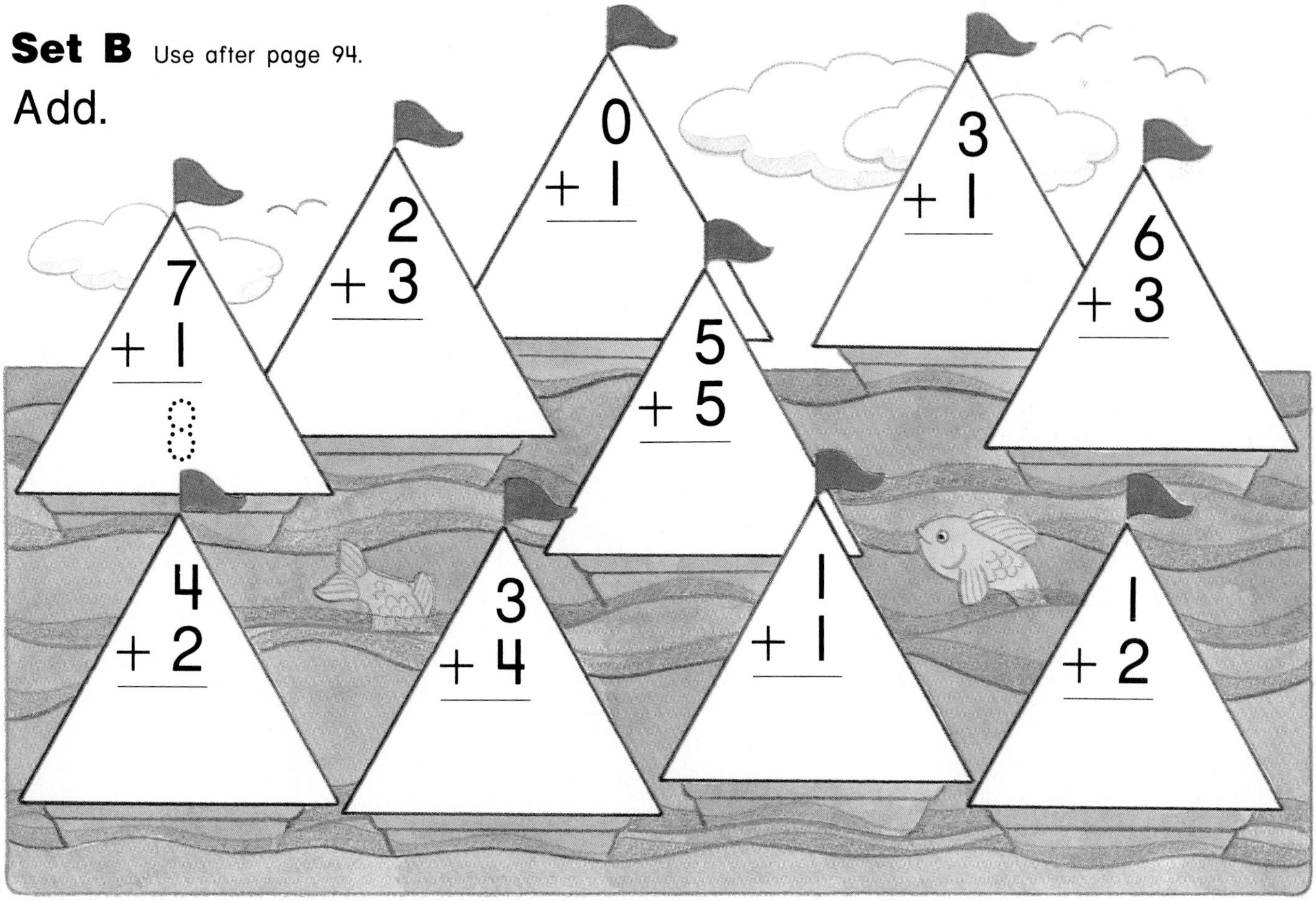

Notes for Home Set A: Children practice finding sums by adding 1, 2, or 3 to a given number.
Set B: Children practice finding sums through 10.

Enrichment

Add.

Complete the table.

+	0	1	2	3	4	5	6	7	8	9
0	0	1								
1	1	2								
2										
3										
4										
5										
6										
7										
8										
9										

Notes for Home Children are challenged to complete an addition table.

Name ______________________________

Chapter 3 Review/Test

Add.

1.

6	7	5	1	3	2
+ 1	+ 2	+ 3	+ 4	+ 6	+ 5

2.

0	3	4	0	5	3
+ 0	+ 3	+ 5	+ 4	+ 5	+ 4

3.

6	2	6	5	2	3
+ 4	+ 3	+ 2	+ 4	+ 8	+ 7

4. Use the picture above.
What is the cost for both?
Write a number sentence.

____¢ + ____¢ = ____¢

5. Use the picture above.
You have 4¢.
Ring each of the toys
you could buy.

Notes for Home Children are assessed on Chapter 3 concepts, skills, and problem solving.

Exploring Math at Home

Dear Family,

In this chapter I have learned to add through 10. I have learned to count on from a given number and to use doubles to find sums through 10. Please help me do the activities below.

Love, ______________________

1.

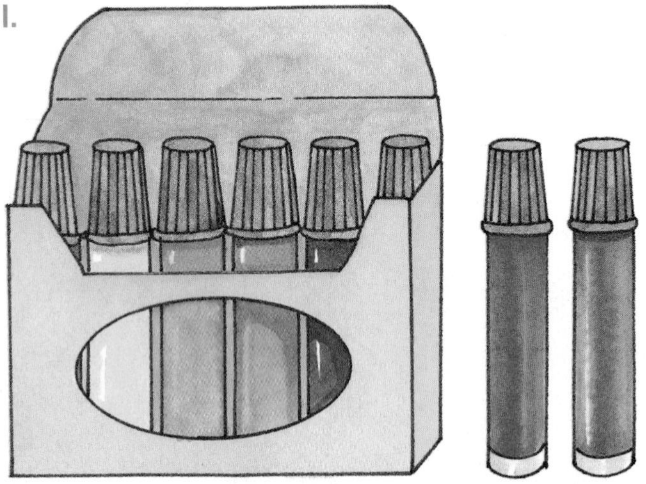

Use two groups of objects to create addition stories through 10.

2.

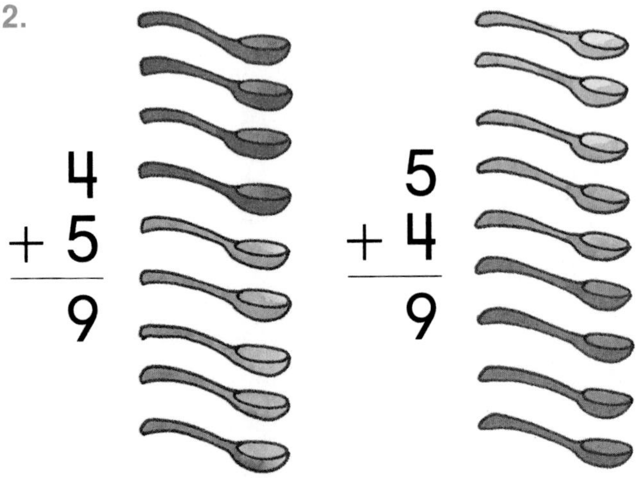

Use two groups of objects through 10 to show that numbers can be added in any order.

3.

Start with a given number. Count on 1, 2, or 3 to find the sum.

Coming Attractions

In the next chapter I will be learning to subtract through 6 and to solve problems when I have to choose between addition and subtraction.

Name ______________________

Cumulative Review/Test

Fill in the correct ⬭.
How many?

1.

1 Ⓐ 2 Ⓑ 3 Ⓒ

2.

9 Ⓐ 10 Ⓑ 11 Ⓒ

3.

7 Ⓐ 8 Ⓑ 9 Ⓒ

4.

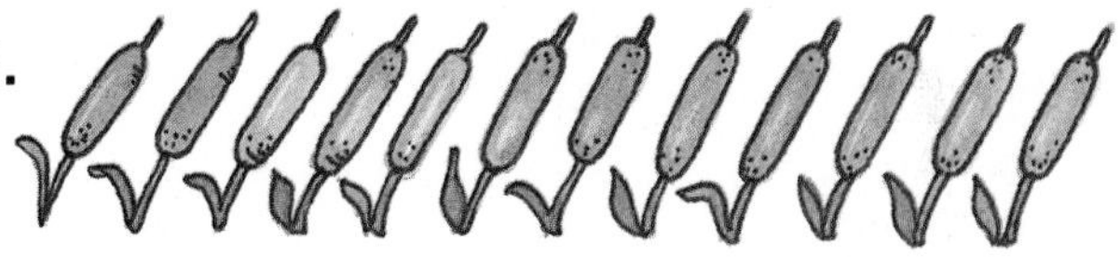

10 Ⓐ 11 Ⓑ 12 Ⓒ

What number is missing?

5.

8, 9, 10, ____

7 Ⓐ 11 Ⓑ 12 Ⓒ

Which is more?

6.

5 Ⓐ 6 Ⓑ

Add.

7.

$$\begin{array}{r} 3 \\ +\ 1 \\ \hline \end{array}$$

3 Ⓐ 4 Ⓑ 5 Ⓒ

8.

$5 + 5 =$ ____

8 Ⓐ 9 Ⓑ 10 Ⓒ

Notes for Home Children are assessed on Chapters 1-3 concepts, skills, and problem solving using a multiple-choice format.

Fill in the correct ◯.

Add.

9.

$$\begin{array}{r} 7 \\ +\ 0 \\ \hline \end{array}$$

6 (A) 7 (B) 8 (C)

10.

$$\begin{array}{r} 6 \\ +\ 2 \\ \hline \end{array}$$

4 (A) 6 (B) 8 (C)

11.

$$\begin{array}{r} 2 \\ +\ 2 \\ \hline \end{array}$$

4 (A) 5 (B) 7 (C)

12.

$$\begin{array}{r} 5 \\ +\ 4 \\ \hline \end{array}$$

3 (A) 9 (B) 10 (C)

How many in all?

13.

6 (A) 8 (B) 10 (C)

14.

5 (A) 7 (B) 9 (C)

What comes next?

15.

 (A)

 (B)

 (C)

Notes for Home Children are assessed on Chapters 1-3 concepts, skills, and problem solving using a multiple-choice format.

Chapter 4

Understanding Subtraction

Listen to the math story, "A New Nest is Best."
Two birds left to find new nests.
How do you think the other bird felt?

Notes for Home Children listen to a math story introducing chapter concepts and skills. Then they answer a question about the story.

Name

Exploring Subtraction

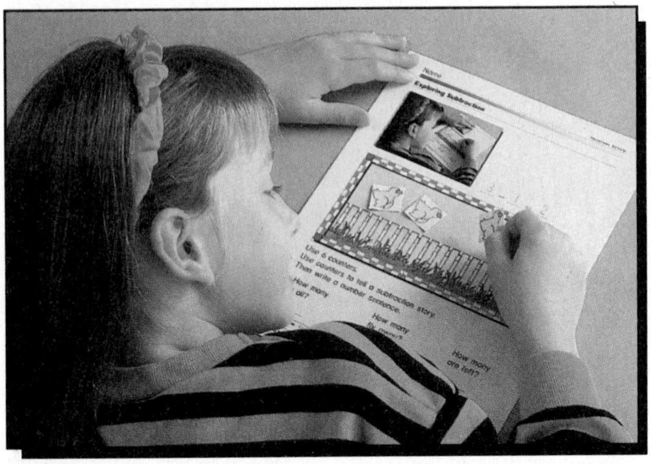

3 − 1 = 2

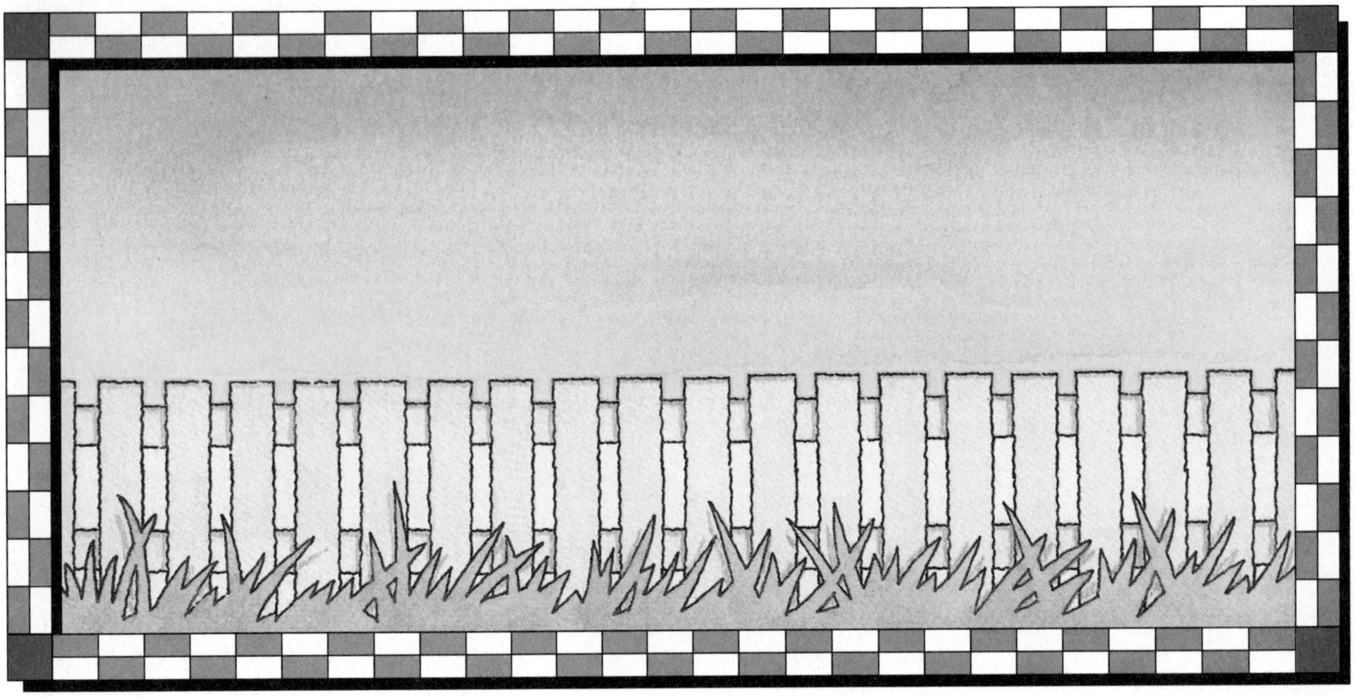

Use 6 counters.
Use counters to tell a subtraction story.
Then write a number sentence.

How many in all?	How many fly away?	How many are left?

____ − ____ = ____

Notes for Home Children explore at the CONCRETE level using counters of birds to create subtraction stories. They write a number sentence.

Name

Exploring Subtraction from 4 and 5

4 − 3 = 1

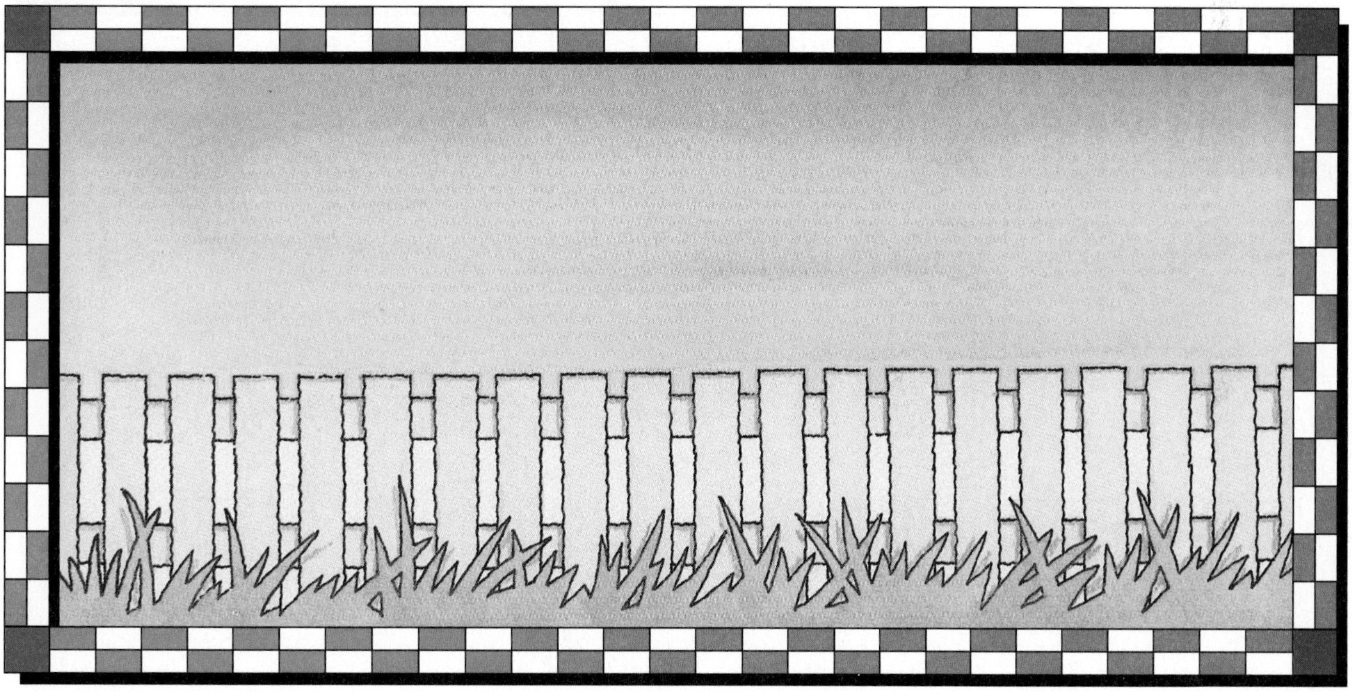

Use 4 counters.
Show different ways to subtract from 4.
Complete each number sentence.

1. 4 − ___ = ___

2. 4 − ___ = ___

3. 4 − ___ = ___

4. 4 − ___ = ___

Notes for Home Children explore at the CONCRETE level using four counters to create subtraction stories. They complete number sentences.

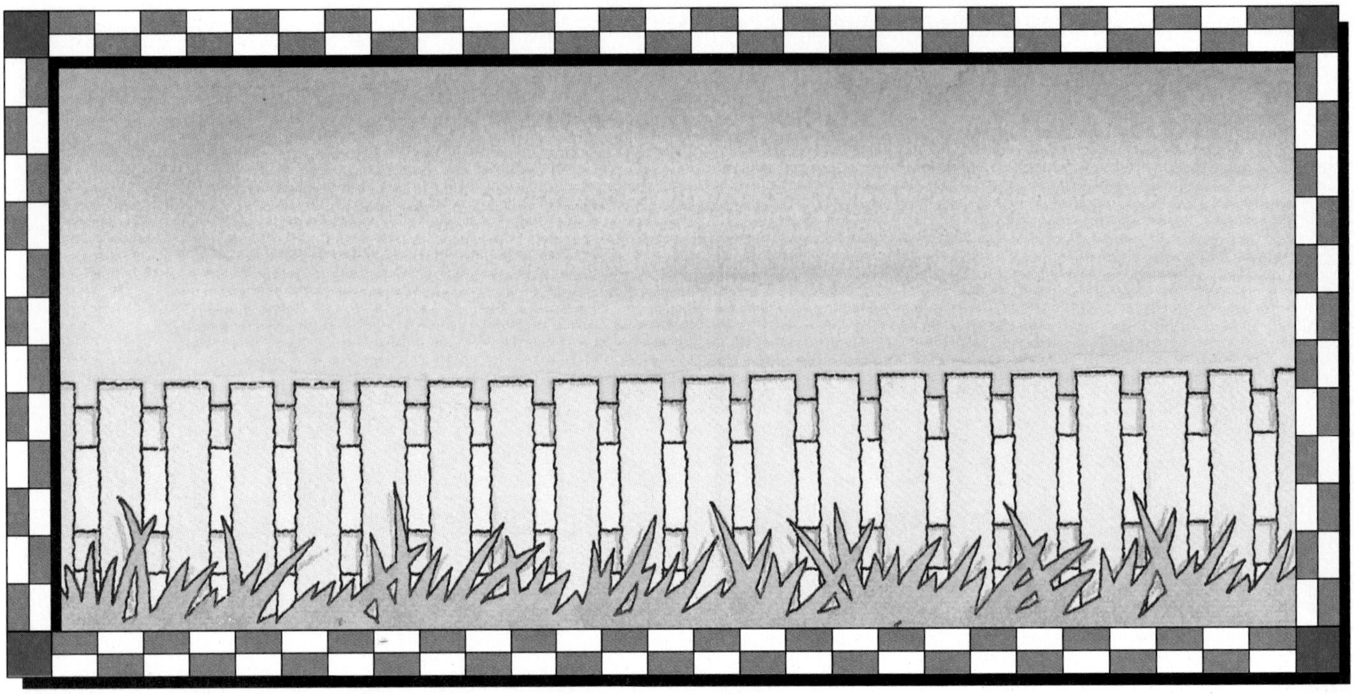

Use 5 counters.
Show different ways to subtract from 5.
Complete each number sentence.

5. 5 – ___ = ___

6. 5 – ___ = ___

7. 5 – ___ = ___

8. 5 – ___ = ___

9. 5 – ___ = ___

10. 5 – ___ = ___

Notes for Home Children explore at the CONCRETE level using five counters to create subtraction stories. They complete number sentences.

Name Activity

Exploring Subtraction from 6

6 – 5 = 1

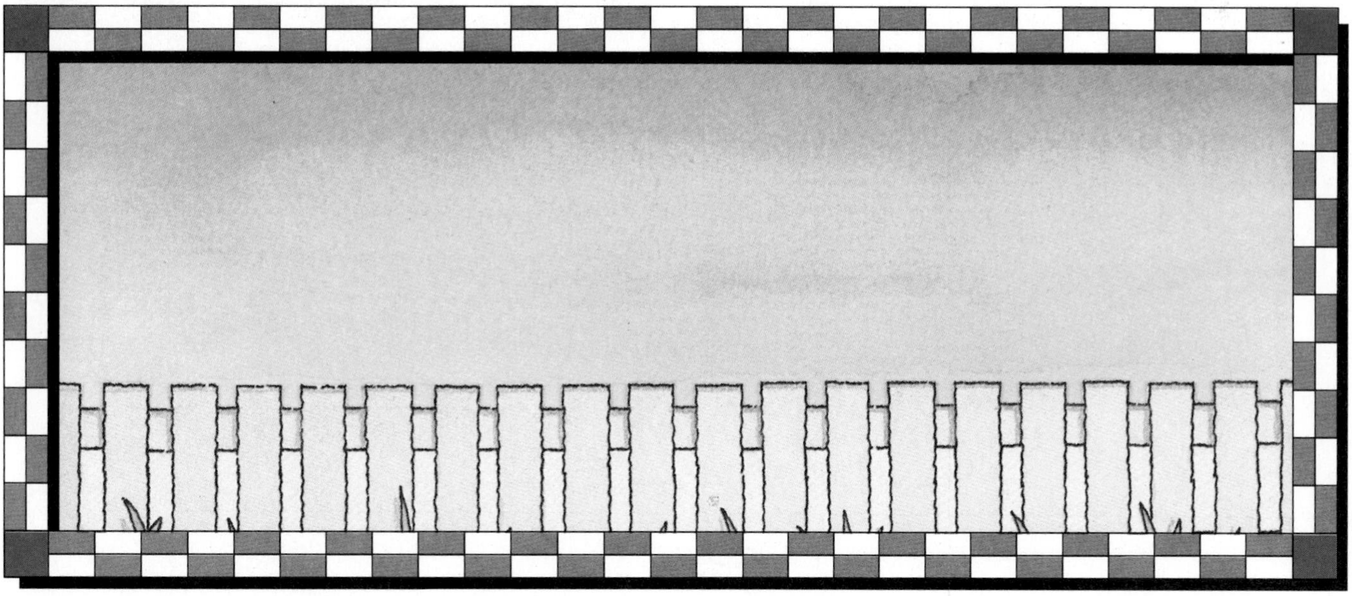

Use 6 counters.
Show different ways to subtract from 6.
Complete each number sentence.

1. 6 – ___ = ___
2. 6 – ___ = ___
3. 6 – ___ = ___
4. 6 – ___ = ___
5. 6 – ___ = ___
6. 6 – ___ = ___

Notes for Home Children explore at the CONCRETE level using six counters to create subtraction stories. They complete number sentences.

Start with 6.

Cross out some.

Complete each number sentence.

7.

6 − 1 = 5

8.

6 − ___ = ___

9.

6 − ___ = ___

10.

6 − ___ = ___

11.

6 − ___ = ___

Notes for Home Children cross out some objects to subtract from 6. They complete number sentences.

Finding Differences Through 6

$4 - 2 = \underline{2}$

Use counters.
Subtract.

1. $5 - 1 =$ ____
2. $6 - 2 =$ ____
3. $6 - 5 =$ ____
4. $4 - 3 =$ ____

Notes for Home Children explore at the CONCRETE level using counters to find differences.

Use counters.
Subtract.

5. 4 − 1 = 3

6. 6 − 4 = ___

7. 3 − 1 = ___

8. 5 − 3 = ___

9. 5 − 2 = ___

10. 6 − 1 = ___

11. 6 − 3 = ___

12. 3 − 2 = ___

13. 5 − 4 = ___

14. 6 − 5 = ___

15. 4 − 3 = ___

16. 3 − 2 = ___

17. 5 − 1 = ___

18. 4 − 2 = ___

Notes for Home Children work at the CONCRETE level using counters to find differences.

Name

Using Pictures to Find Differences

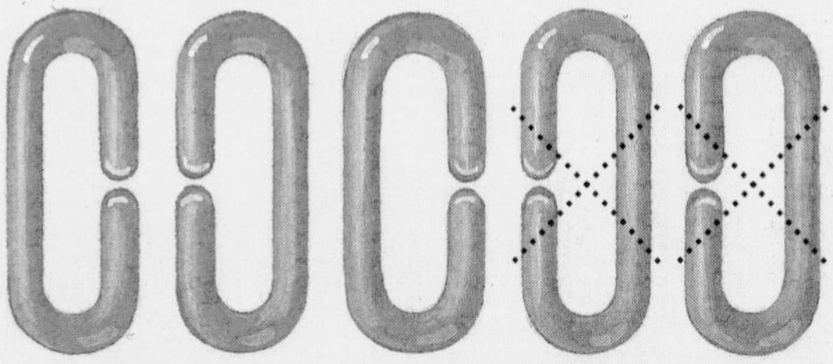

$5 - 2 =$ 3

Make an X to subtract.
Write how many are left.

1.

$3 - 2 =$ ___

2.

$6 - 4 =$ ___

3.

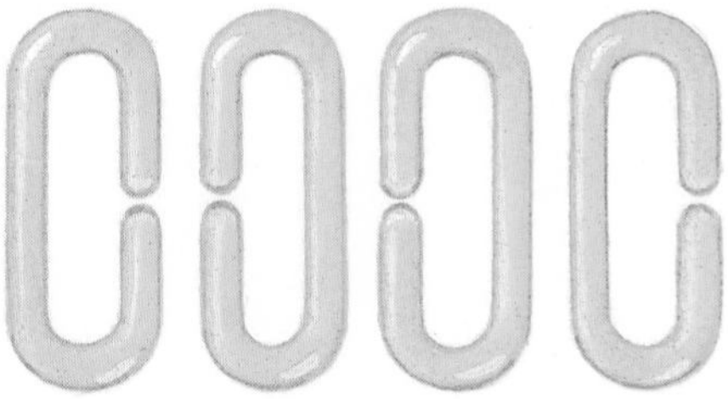

$4 - 1 =$ ___

4.

$2 - 1 =$ ___

Notes for Home Children find differences from 6 or less using pictures of objects.

Make an X to subtract.
Write how many are left.

5.

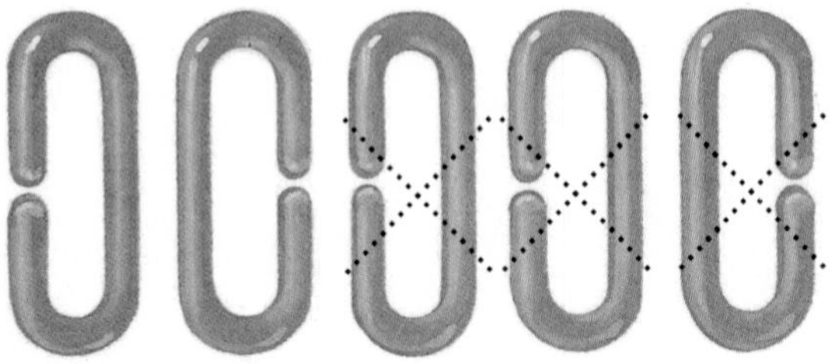

$5 - 3 = \underline{2}$

6.

$4 - 2 = \_\_\_$

7.

$6 - 1 = \_\_\_$

8.

$5 - 4 = \_\_\_$

9.

$3 - 1 = \_\_\_$

10.

$6 - 3 = \_\_\_$

Notes for Home Children find differences from 6 or less using pictures of objects.

See More Practice Set A on page 125.

Name

Use Data from a Picture

3 birds are left.

Look at the picture.
Tell a subtraction story.
How many are left?

1.

____ bird is left.

2.

____ birds are left.

3.

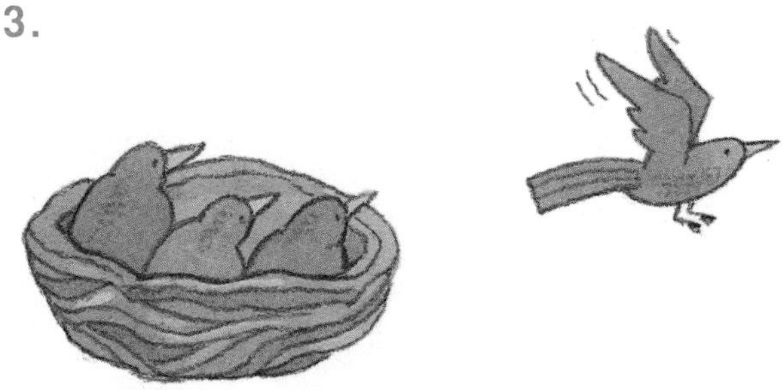

____ birds are left.

4.

____ bird is left.

Notes for Home Children learn to solve subtraction problems by using data from pictures.

Look at the picture.
Tell a subtraction story.
How many are left?

5.

2 birds are left.

6.

____ birds are left.

7.

____ birds are left.

8.

____ birds are left.

9.

____ bird is left.

10.

____ birds are left.

Notes for Home Children solve subtraction problems by using data from pictures.

Name

Number Sense

Find subtraction stories in the picture.
Tell a number sentence about each story.

Let's do some more!

Draw a picture to show subtraction stories.
Tell your stories to a friend.

Notes for Home Children develop number understanding by describing subtraction situations.

Skills Review

Fill in the correct ⬭.
Add.

1. $\begin{array}{r} 1 \\ +2 \\ \hline \end{array}$	Ⓐ 1 Ⓑ 2 Ⓒ 3	2. $3 + 6 =$	Ⓐ 9 Ⓑ 6 Ⓒ 3	3. $\begin{array}{r} 7 \\ +1 \\ \hline \end{array}$	Ⓐ 7 Ⓑ 1 Ⓒ 8
4. $8 + 2 =$	Ⓐ 10 Ⓑ 8 Ⓒ 2	5. $4 + 0 =$	Ⓐ 0 Ⓑ 3 Ⓒ 4	6. $\begin{array}{r} 5 \\ +4 \\ \hline \end{array}$	Ⓐ 5 Ⓑ 4 Ⓒ 9

Vocabulary

Fill in the correct word.

less greater

7. 9 is less than 10.

8. 8 is ________ than 6.

9. 4 is ________ than 7.

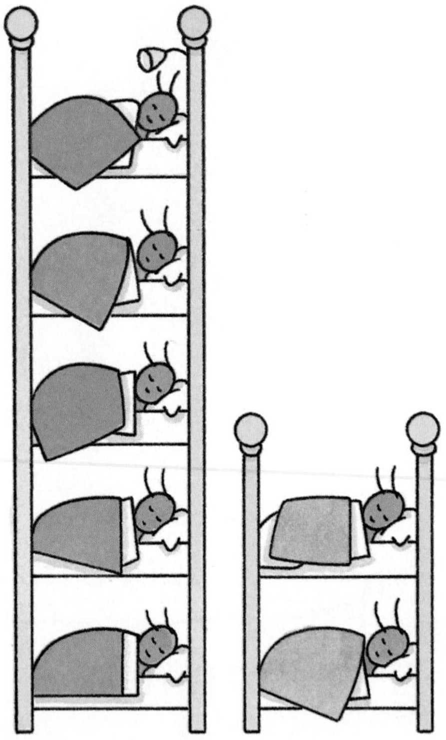

Notes for Home Children review addition facts through 10. Then they review greater than and less than.

Name

Subtraction in Vertical Form

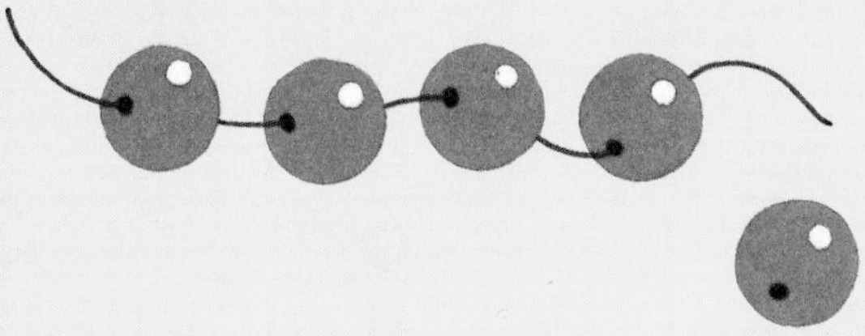

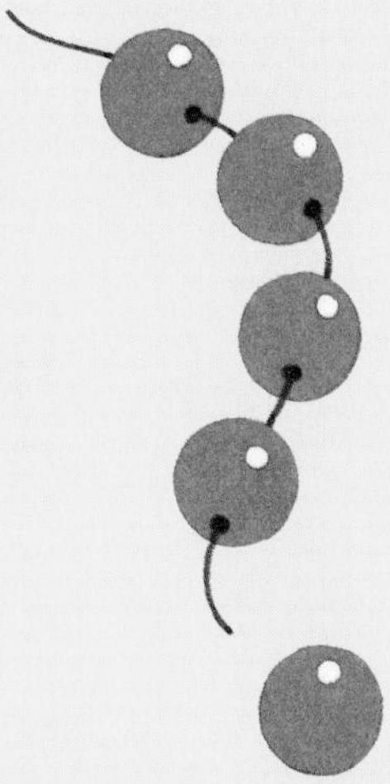

$$\begin{array}{r} 5 \\ -\ 1 \\ \hline 4 \end{array}$$

↑
difference

5 − 1 = 4

↑
difference

Write the difference.

1.

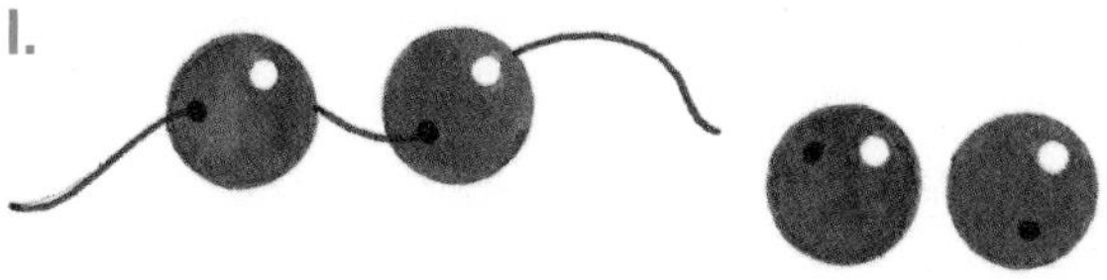

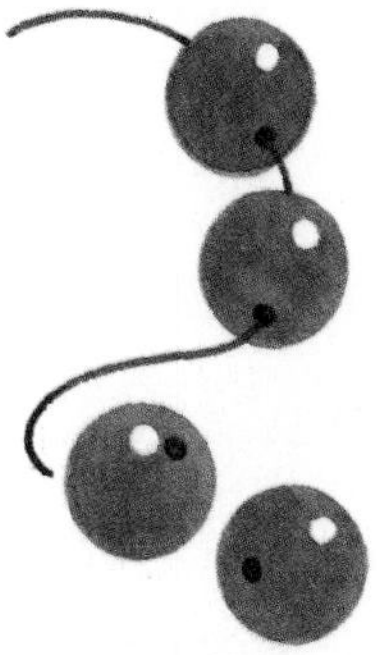

$$\begin{array}{r} 4 \\ -\ 2 \\ \hline \end{array}$$

4 − 2 = ____

2.

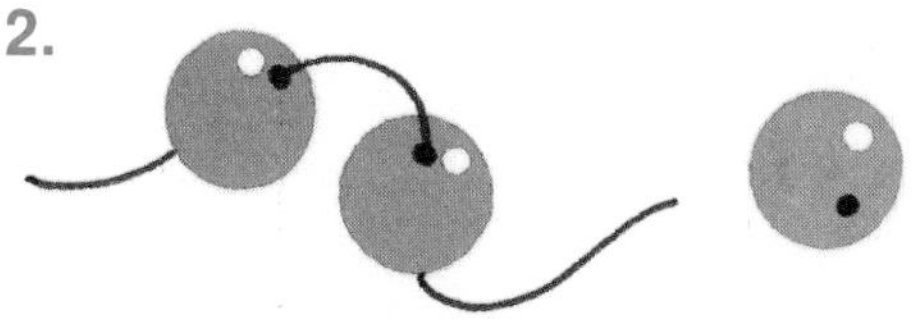

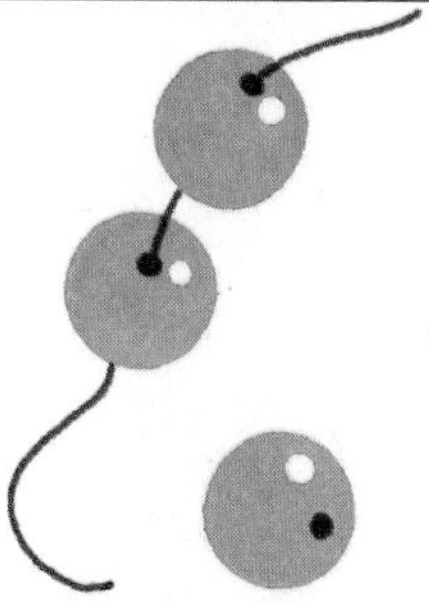

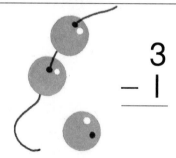

$$\begin{array}{r} 3 \\ -\ 1 \\ \hline \end{array}$$

3 − 1 = ____

3.

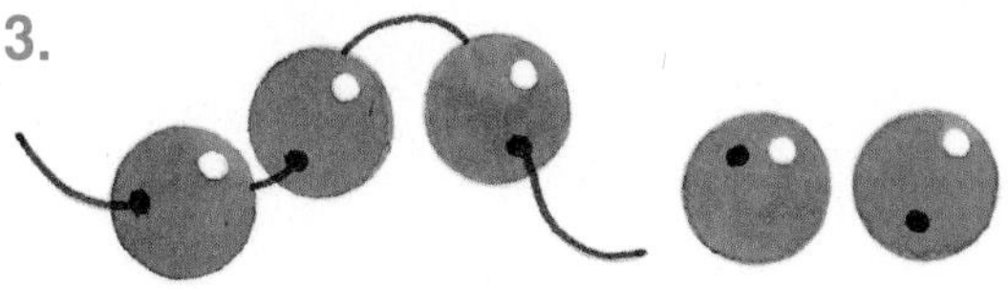

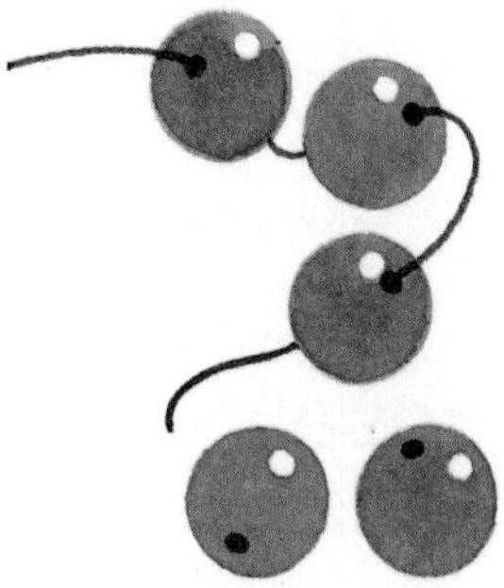

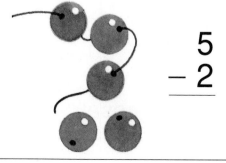

$$\begin{array}{r} 5 \\ -\ 2 \\ \hline \end{array}$$

5 − 2 = ____

Notes for Home Children learn to use vertical form for subtraction.

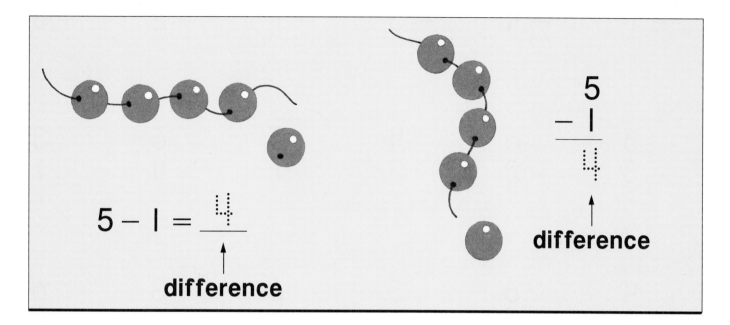

Write the difference.

4.	$\begin{array}{r} 2 \\ -\ 1 \\ \hline \end{array}$	$\begin{array}{r} 5 \\ -\ 4 \\ \hline \end{array}$	$\begin{array}{r} 6 \\ -\ 3 \\ \hline \end{array}$	$\begin{array}{r} 4 \\ -\ 1 \\ \hline \end{array}$	$\begin{array}{r} 3 \\ -\ 2 \\ \hline \end{array}$	$\begin{array}{r} 6 \\ -\ 5 \\ \hline \end{array}$
5.	$\begin{array}{r} 5 \\ -\ 3 \\ \hline \end{array}$	$\begin{array}{r} 6 \\ -\ 2 \\ \hline \end{array}$	$\begin{array}{r} 4 \\ -\ 3 \\ \hline \end{array}$	$\begin{array}{r} 5 \\ -\ 1 \\ \hline \end{array}$	$\begin{array}{r} 6 \\ -\ 4 \\ \hline \end{array}$	$\begin{array}{r} 3 \\ -\ 1 \\ \hline \end{array}$
6.	$\begin{array}{r} 4 \\ -\ 2 \\ \hline \end{array}$	$\begin{array}{r} 6 \\ -\ 1 \\ \hline \end{array}$	$\begin{array}{r} 5 \\ -\ 2 \\ \hline \end{array}$	$\begin{array}{r} 6 \\ -\ 4 \\ \hline \end{array}$	$\begin{array}{r} 3 \\ -\ 2 \\ \hline \end{array}$	$\begin{array}{r} 6 \\ -\ 2 \\ \hline \end{array}$

Problem Solving

Tell a subtraction story.
How many are left?

7.

____ goose

8.

____ chicks

Notes for Home Children subtract from 6 or less using vertical form. Then they solve problems using subtraction.

See More Practice Set B on page 125.

Name

Choose an Operation

Do you add or subtract to solve?
Ring the correct number sentence.

1. How many are left?

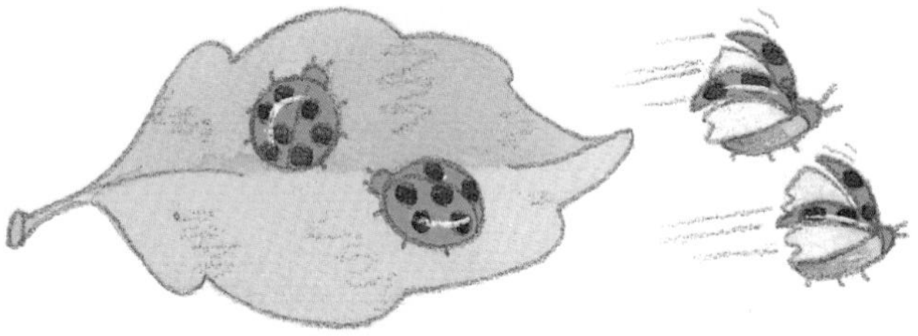

4 + 2 = 6   4 − 2 = 2

2. How many in all?

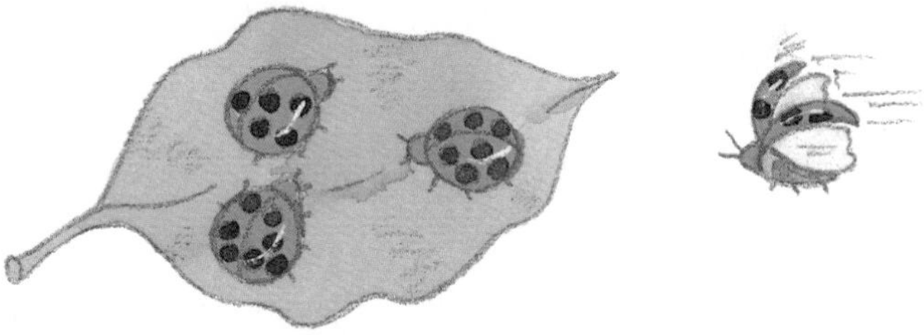

3 + 1 = 4   3 − 1 = 2

3. How many are left?

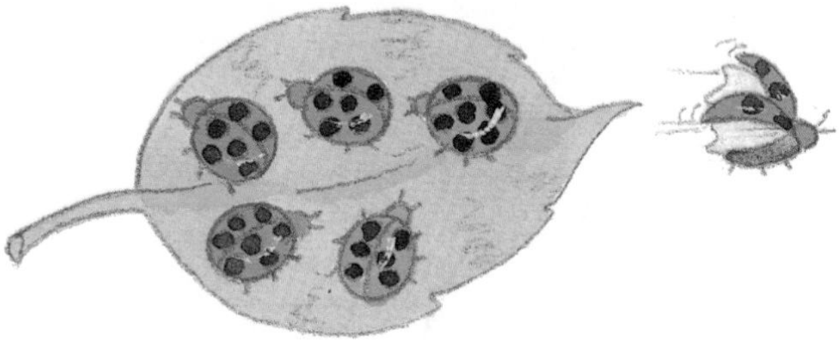

6 + 1 = 7   6 − 1 = 5

4. How many in all?

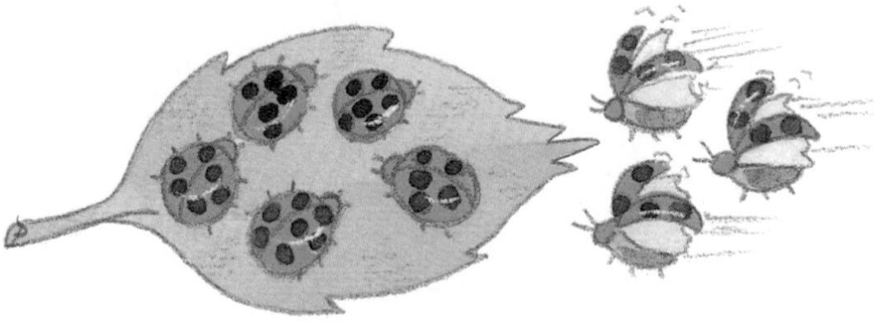

5 + 3 = 8   5 − 3 = 2

Notes for Home Children learn to solve addition and subtraction problems by choosing the operation.

Do you add or subtract to solve?
Ring the correct number sentence.

5. How many are left?

6 + 4 = 10   (6 − 4 = 2)

6. How many in all?

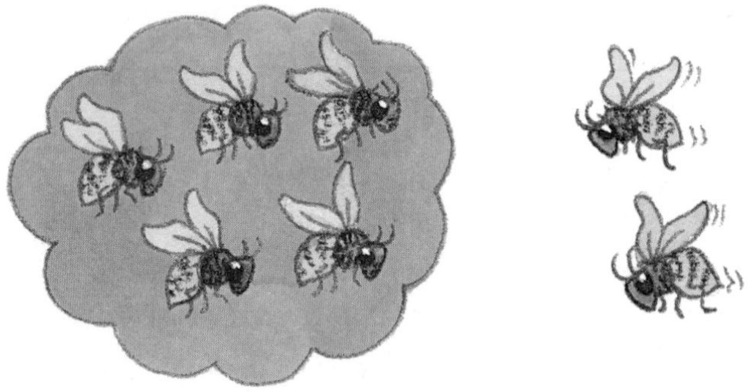

5 + 2 = 7   5 − 2 = 3

7. How many in all?

5 + 4 = 9   5 − 4 = 1

8. How many are left?

6 + 2 = 8   6 − 2 = 4

9. How many are left?

4 + 1 = 5   4 − 1 = 3

10. How many in all?

6 + 3 = 9   6 − 3 = 3

Notes for Home Children solve addition and subtraction problems by choosing the operation.

Name

Problem-Solving Workshop

Explore as a Team

Work with a partner.
Use 6 counters.
Use a bowl.

1. Partner A shows some counters.

2. Partner B counts how many counters, then covers his eyes.

3. Partner A covers some of the counters with a bowl.

4. Partner B guesses how many counters are covered, then checks his guess.

Notes for Home Children explore with a partner to solve problems involving missing numbers.

Problem-Solving Workshop

Explore with a Computer

Money and Time Project

1. Use coins at the computer.
Add a nickel to one sack.
Add pennies to the other sack to show the same amount.

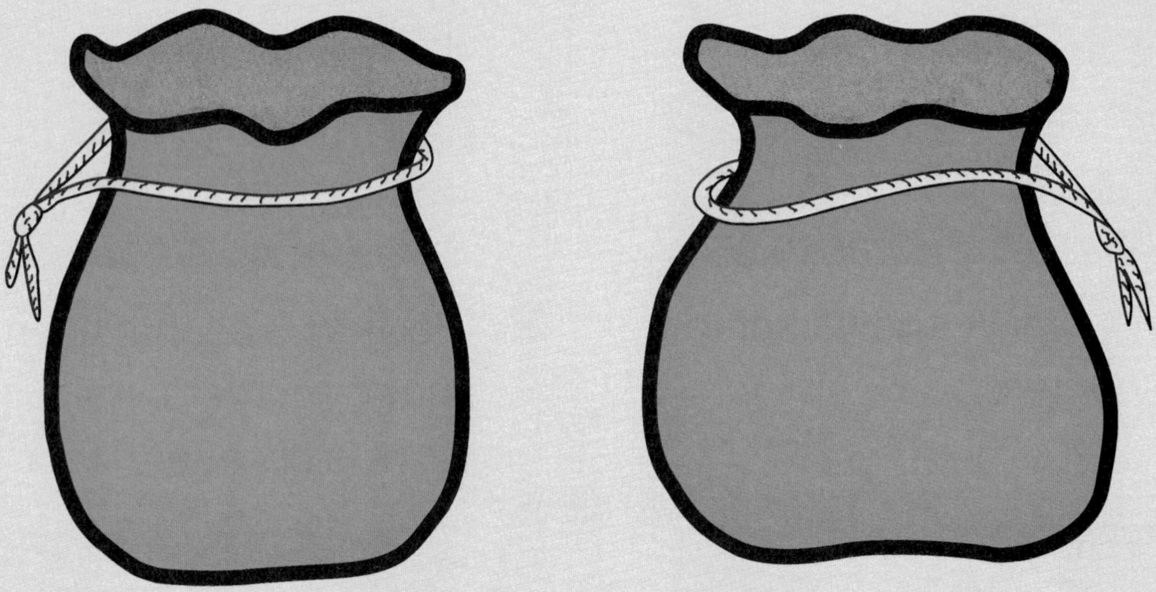

2. Add more nickels and pennies to each sack.
Write the amount.

nickels ______ pennies ______

3. Ring the sack that has the greater amount.

nickels pennies

Notes for Home Children learn how many pennies it takes to equal one nickel. Then they use the computer to make comparisons between different amounts of nickels and pennies.

Name ______________________

More Practice

Set A Use after page 114.

Make an X to subtract.
Write how many are left.

1.

5 − 1 = 4

2.

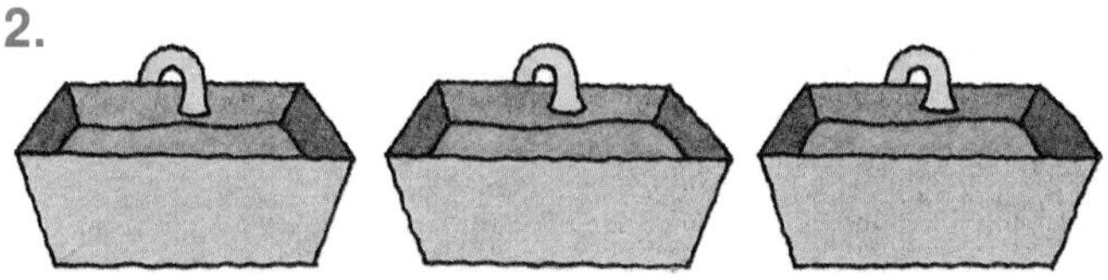

3 − 2 = ____

3.

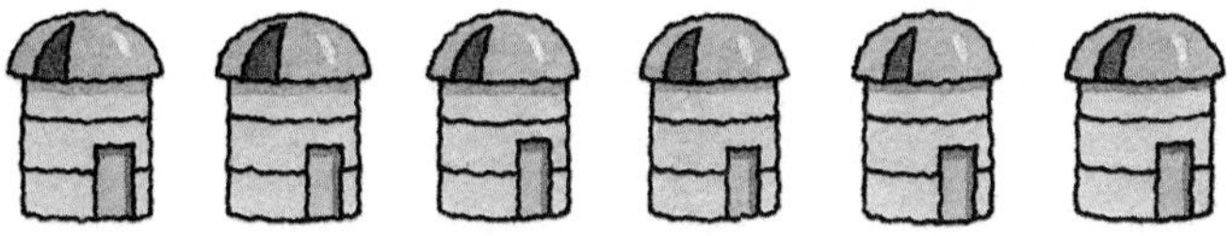

6 − 3 = ____

4.

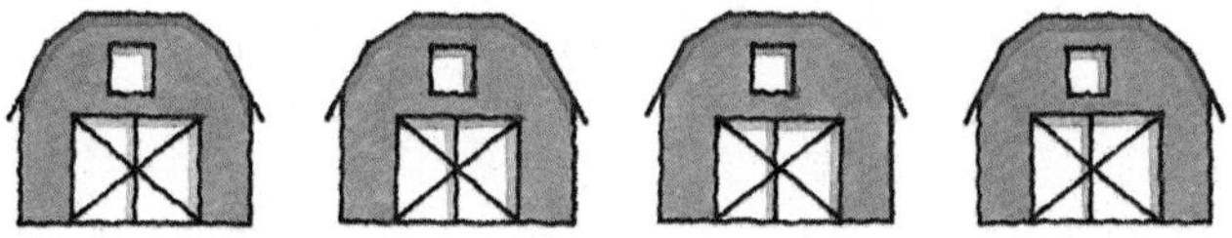

4 − 1 = ____

Set B Use after page 120.

Write the difference.

1. $\begin{array}{r} 5 \\ -4 \\ \hline \end{array}$ $\begin{array}{r} 3 \\ -1 \\ \hline \end{array}$ $\begin{array}{r} 6 \\ -2 \\ \hline \end{array}$ $\begin{array}{r} 3 \\ -2 \\ \hline \end{array}$ $\begin{array}{r} 5 \\ -2 \\ \hline \end{array}$ $\begin{array}{r} 6 \\ -1 \\ \hline \end{array}$

2. $\begin{array}{r} 4 \\ -2 \\ \hline \end{array}$ $\begin{array}{r} 6 \\ -5 \\ \hline \end{array}$ $\begin{array}{r} 5 \\ -3 \\ \hline \end{array}$ $\begin{array}{r} 4 \\ -1 \\ \hline \end{array}$ $\begin{array}{r} 6 \\ -4 \\ \hline \end{array}$ $\begin{array}{r} 4 \\ -3 \\ \hline \end{array}$

Notes for Home Set A: Children practice finding differences from 6 or less using pictures of objects.
Set B: Children practice subtracting from 6 or less using vertical form.

Independent Study ENRICHMENT

Enrichment

Write the missing numbers.

1\.

$6 - \square = 5$

2\.

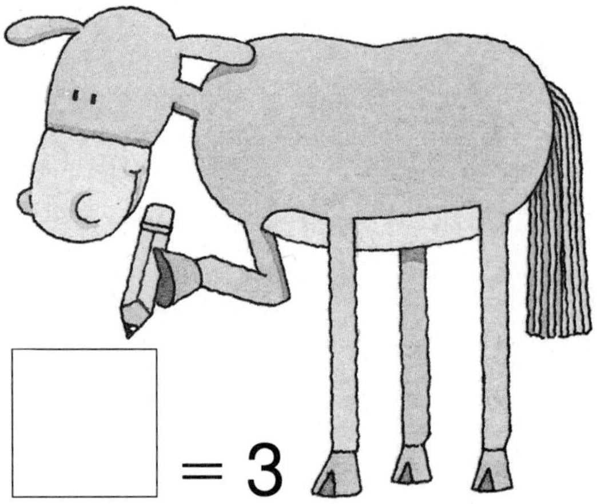

$5 - \square = 3$

3\.

$4 - \square = 1$

4\.

$6 - \square = 3$

5\.

$$\begin{array}{r} 5 \\ - \square \\ \hline 2 \end{array}$$

6\.

$$\begin{array}{r} 4 \\ - \square \\ \hline 2 \end{array}$$

7\.

$$\begin{array}{r} 6 \\ - \square \\ \hline 4 \end{array}$$

8\.

$$\begin{array}{r} 6 \\ - \square \\ \hline 2 \end{array}$$

Notes for Home Children are challenged to find missing numbers.

Name

Chapter 4 Review/Test

1. Make an X to subtract.
Write the difference.

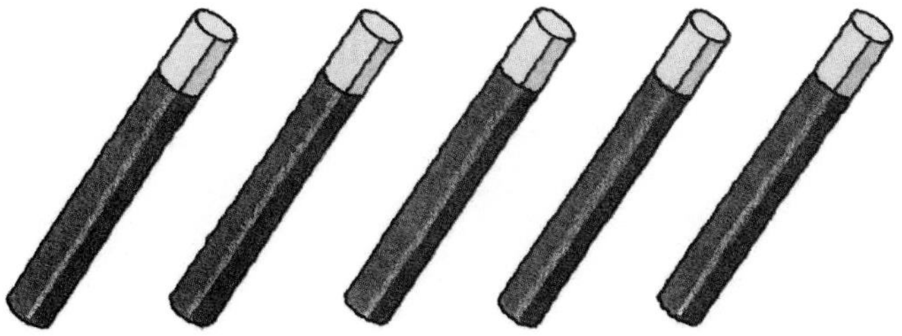

$5 - 3 =$ ___

2. Write the difference.

6	4	5	3
− 4	− 1	− 2	− 1

3. Cross out some.
Complete the number sentence.

$6 -$ ___ $=$ ___

4. How many rabbits are left?

___ rabbits are left.

5. Do you add or subtract?
Ring the correct number sentence.

How many in all?

$3 + 1 = 4$ $3 - 1 = 2$

Notes for Home Children are assessed in Chapter 4 concepts, skills, and problem solving.

Exploring Math at Home

Dear Family,

In this chapter I have learned subtraction facts through 6. Please help me with the activities below.

Love, ______________________________

1.

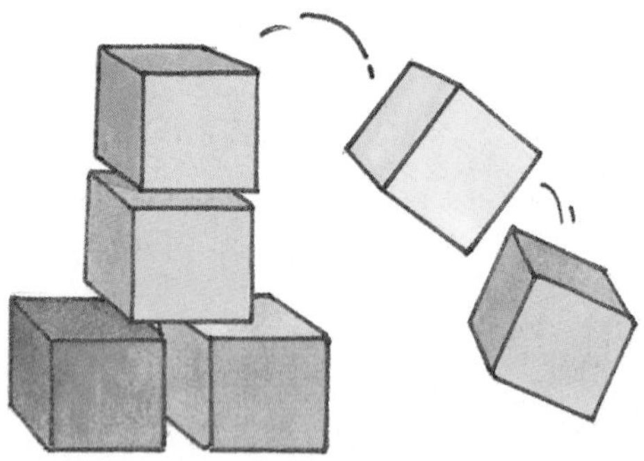

$6 - 2 = 4$

Use small objects through 6 to create subtraction stories.

2.

$6 - 1 = 5$

Use a picture book to tell subtraction stories.

3.

$5 - 3 = 2$

Play a game. Find a number of objects through 6. Hide some of the objects. Ask how many are hidden. Repeat the activity with a different number of objects hidden each time.

Coming Attractions

In the next chapter I will be learning subtraction facts through 10 and how to count back from a given number. I also will learn to solve problems using a graph.

Chapter

5

Subtraction Through 10

Listen to the math story, "The Lime Line."
The flamingo put limes along the path.
How did the limes help her find her way?

Notes for Home Children listen to a math story introducing chapter concepts and skills. Then they answer a question about the story.

Name

Counting Back

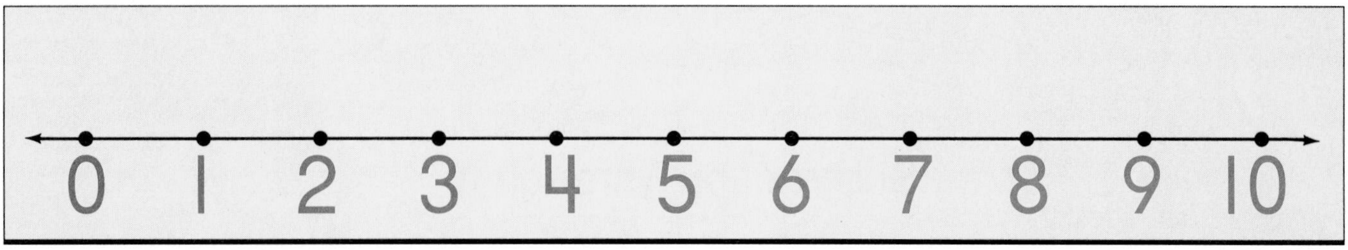

Write the number.

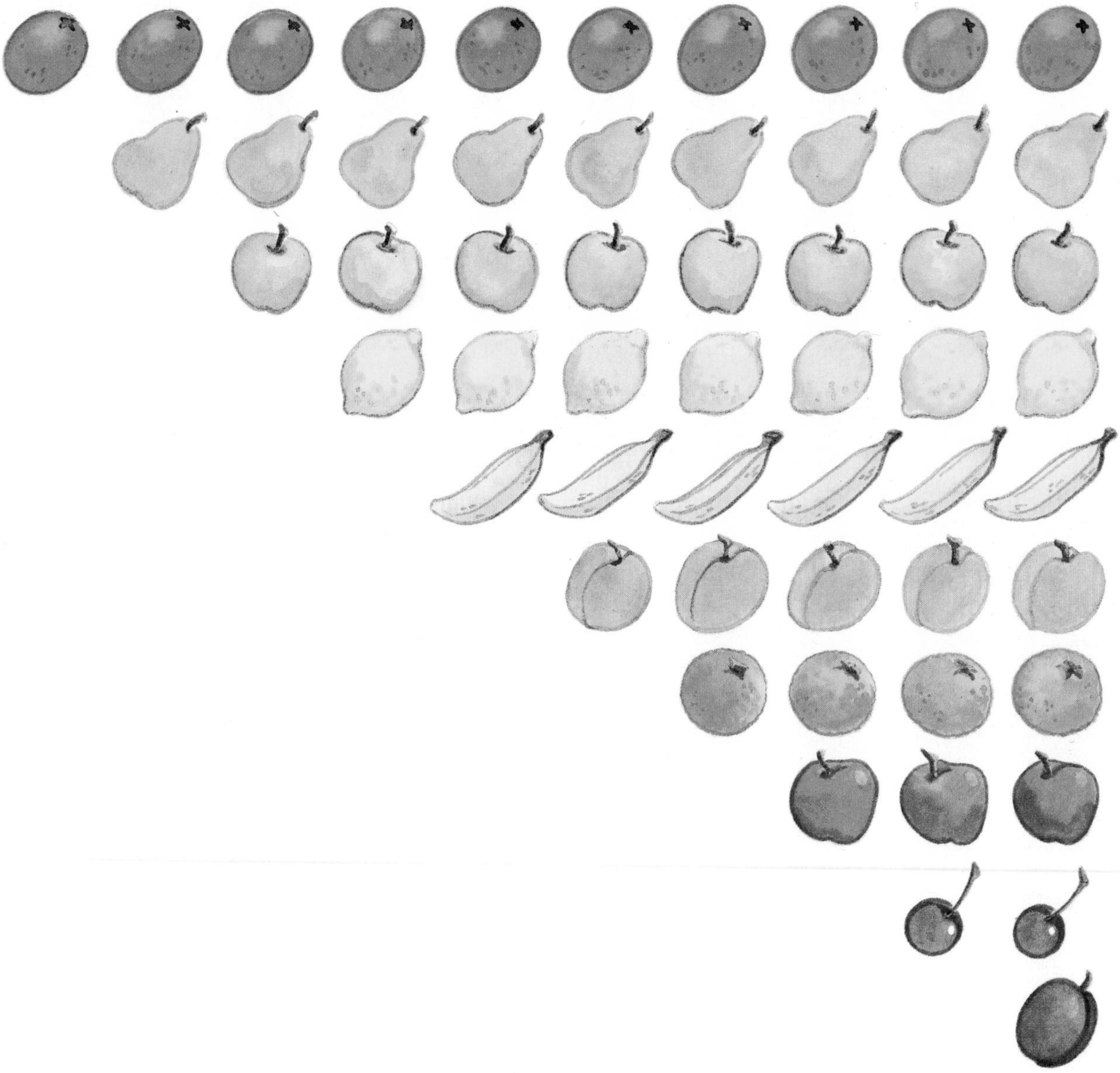

10

Notes for Home Children learn to count back using a number line.

Name

Counting Back 1, 2, or 3

Count back 1.

1. 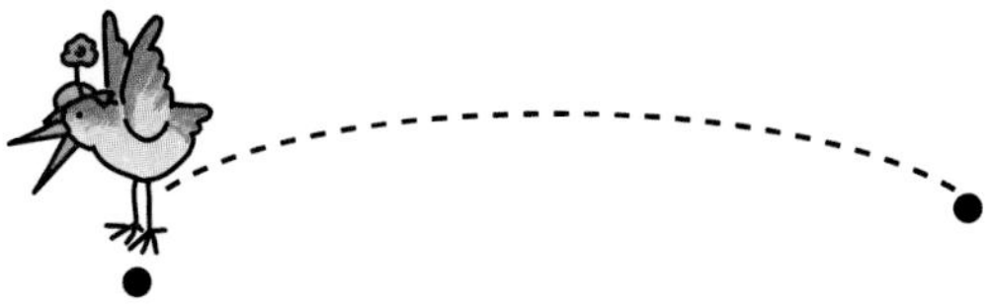

3 4

2. 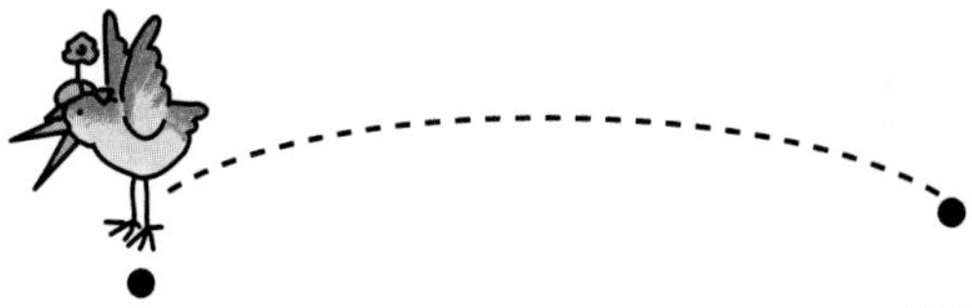

7

3. 

8

4. 

10

5. 

6

6. 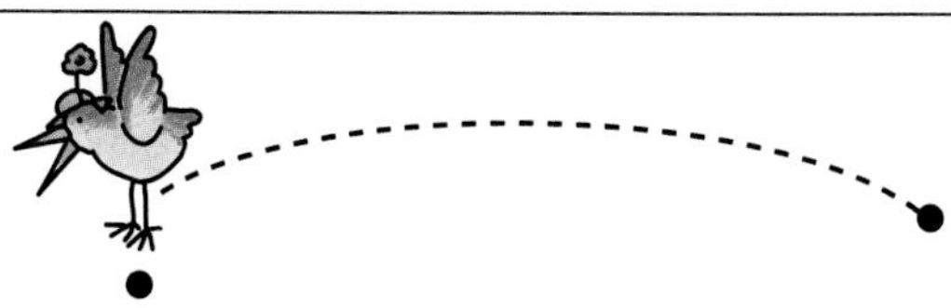

2

7. 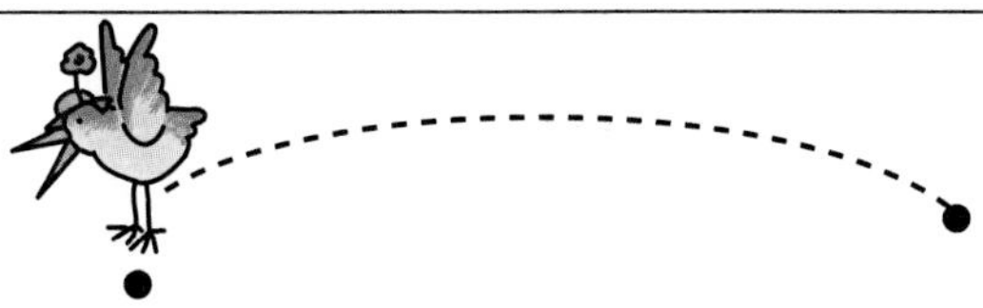

1

8. 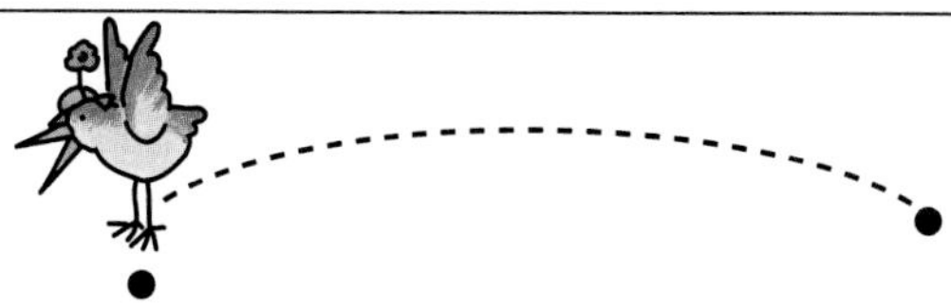

9

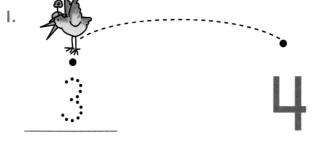

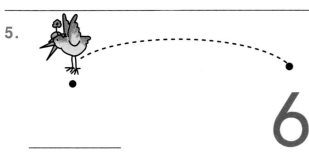

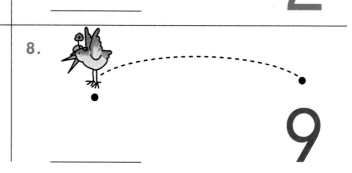

Notes for Home Children learn to count back 1 from a given number using a number line.

Count back 2.

9.

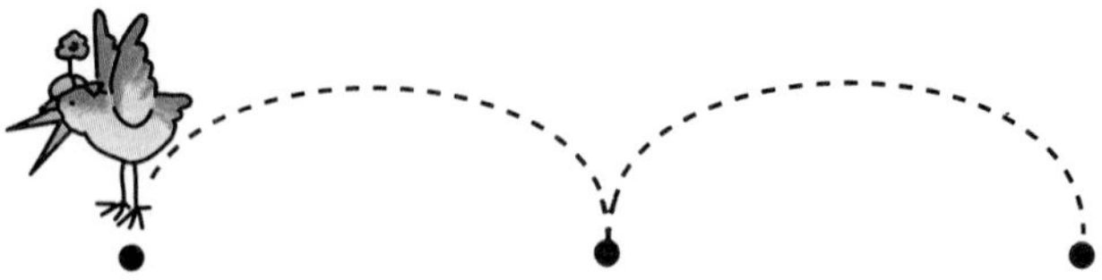

6 7 8

10.

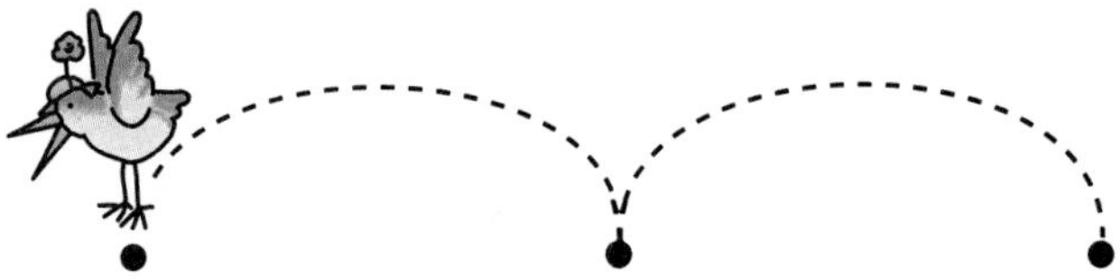

___ ___ 10

Count back 3.

11.

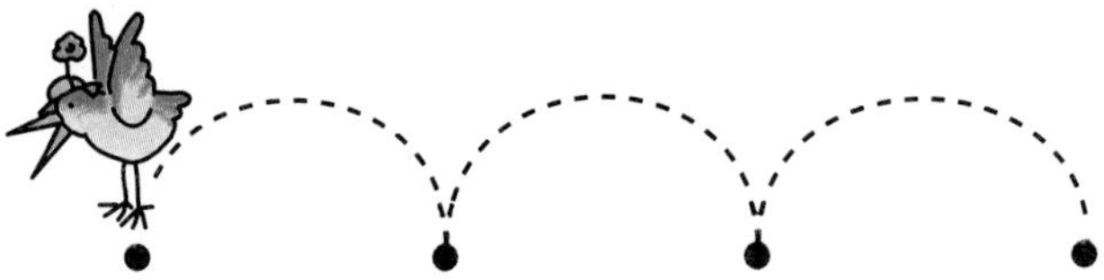

___ ___ ___ 9

12.

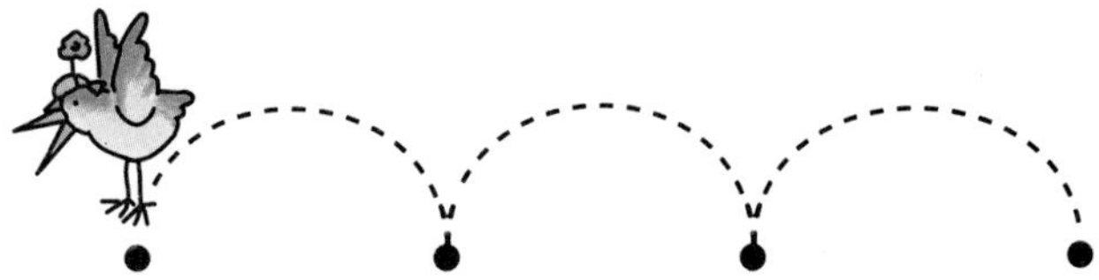

___ ___ ___ 5

13.

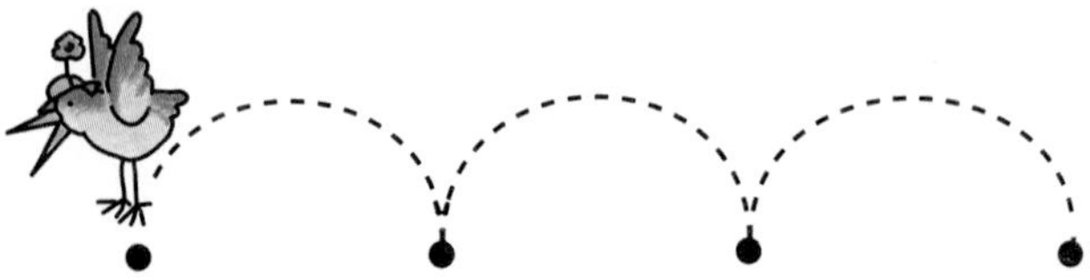

___ ___ ___ 8

14.

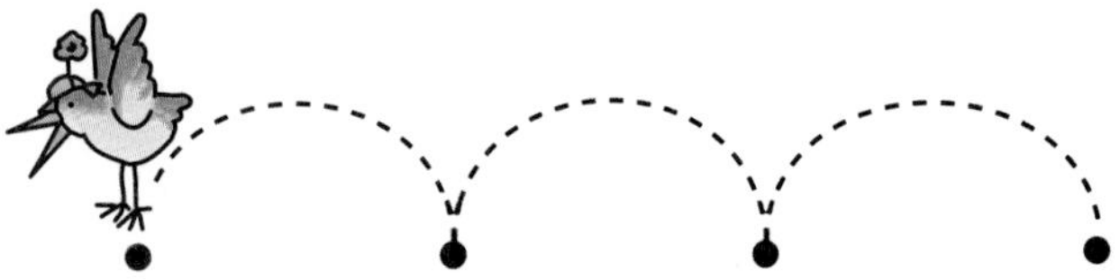

___ ___ ___ 6

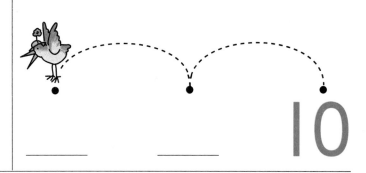

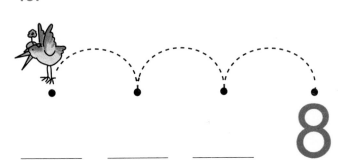

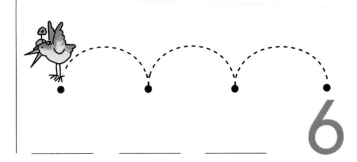

Notes for Home Children learn to count back 2 or 3 from a given number using a number line.

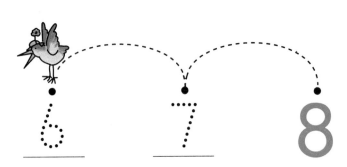

Name

Subtracting 1

Subtract by counting back.

1.

7 − 1 = ___

2.

9 − 1 = ___

3.

4 − 1 = ___

4.

5 − 1 = ___

Notes for Home Children learn to find differences by subtracting 1 from a given number.

Subtract by counting back.

5. 

$$\begin{array}{r} 10 \\ -\ 1 \\ \hline 9 \end{array}$$

6. 

$$\begin{array}{r} 8 \\ -\ 1 \\ \hline \end{array}$$

7. $\begin{array}{r} 7 \\ -\ 1 \\ \hline \end{array}$ $\begin{array}{r} 8 \\ -\ 1 \\ \hline \end{array}$ $\begin{array}{r} 4 \\ -\ 1 \\ \hline \end{array}$ $\begin{array}{r} 6 \\ -\ 1 \\ \hline \end{array}$ $\begin{array}{r} 10 \\ -\ 1 \\ \hline \end{array}$ $\begin{array}{r} 3 \\ -\ 1 \\ \hline \end{array}$

8. $\begin{array}{r} 2 \\ -\ 1 \\ \hline \end{array}$ $\begin{array}{r} 5 \\ -\ 1 \\ \hline \end{array}$ $\begin{array}{r} 9 \\ -\ 1 \\ \hline \end{array}$ $\begin{array}{r} 3 \\ -\ 1 \\ \hline \end{array}$ $\begin{array}{r} 8 \\ -\ 1 \\ \hline \end{array}$ $\begin{array}{r} 6 \\ -\ 1 \\ \hline \end{array}$

9. $\begin{array}{r} 4 \\ -\ 1 \\ \hline \end{array}$ $\begin{array}{r} 7 \\ -\ 1 \\ \hline \end{array}$ $\begin{array}{r} 10 \\ -\ 1 \\ \hline \end{array}$ $\begin{array}{r} 2 \\ -\ 1 \\ \hline \end{array}$ $\begin{array}{r} 5 \\ -\ 1 \\ \hline \end{array}$ $\begin{array}{r} 9 \\ -\ 1 \\ \hline \end{array}$

10. $\begin{array}{r} 2 \\ -\ 1 \\ \hline \end{array}$ $\begin{array}{r} 7 \\ -\ 1 \\ \hline \end{array}$ $\begin{array}{r} 3 \\ -\ 1 \\ \hline \end{array}$

Notes for Home Children practice finding differences by subtracting 1 from a given number.

Name

Subtracting 1 or 2

Subtract by counting back.

1.

6 − 2 = ____

2.

4 − 1 = ____

3.

10 − 2 = ____

4.

8 − 1 = ____

Notes for Home Children learn to find differences by subtracting 1 or 2 from a given number.

Subtract by counting back.

5.

$$\begin{array}{r} 4 \\ -\ 2 \\ \hline 2 \end{array}$$

6.

$$\begin{array}{r} 9 \\ -\ 1 \\ \hline \end{array}$$

7. $7 - 1 =$ ___ $4 - 1 =$ ___ $9 - 2 =$ ___ $2 - 1 =$ ___ $10 - 1 =$ ___ $6 - 2 =$ ___

8. $8 - 1 =$ ___ $10 - 2 =$ ___ $5 - 1 =$ ___ $3 - 2 =$ ___ $7 - 2 =$ ___ $3 - 1 =$ ___

9. $10 - 1 =$ ___ $5 - 2 =$ ___ $9 - 1 =$ ___ $7 - 1 =$ ___ $4 - 2 =$ ___ $3 - 2 =$ ___

10. $9 - 2 =$ ___ $8 - 2 =$ ___ $6 - 1 =$ ___

Notes for Home Children practice finding differences by subtracting 1 or 2 from a given number.

Name

Subtract by counting back.

1.

$7 - 3 =$ ____

2.

$8 - 2 =$ ____

3.

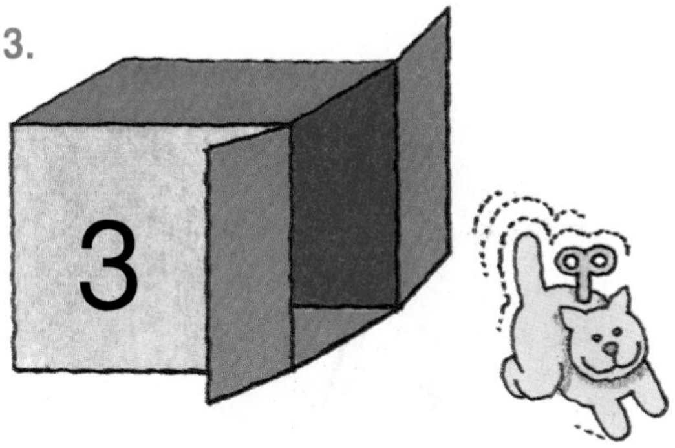

$3 - 1 =$ ____

4.

$9 - 3 =$ ____

Notes for Home Children learn to find differences by subtracting 1, 2, or 3 from a given number.

Subtract by counting back.

5.

$$\begin{array}{r} 9 \\ -\ 2 \\ \hline 7 \end{array}$$

6.

$$\begin{array}{r} 5 \\ -\ 3 \\ \hline \end{array}$$

7.	$6 - 1$	$8 - 3$	$4 - 2$	$7 - 3$	$9 - 1$	$3 - 2$
8.	$9 - 3$	$5 - 1$	$6 - 2$	$8 - 1$	$6 - 3$	$9 - 2$
9.	$8 - 2$	$10 - 3$	$7 - 1$	$4 - 3$	$5 - 2$	$3 - 1$
10.	$7 - 2$	$2 - 1$	$8 - 3$			

Notes for Home Children practice finding differences by subtracting 1, 2, or 3 from a given number.

Name

Related Subtraction Facts

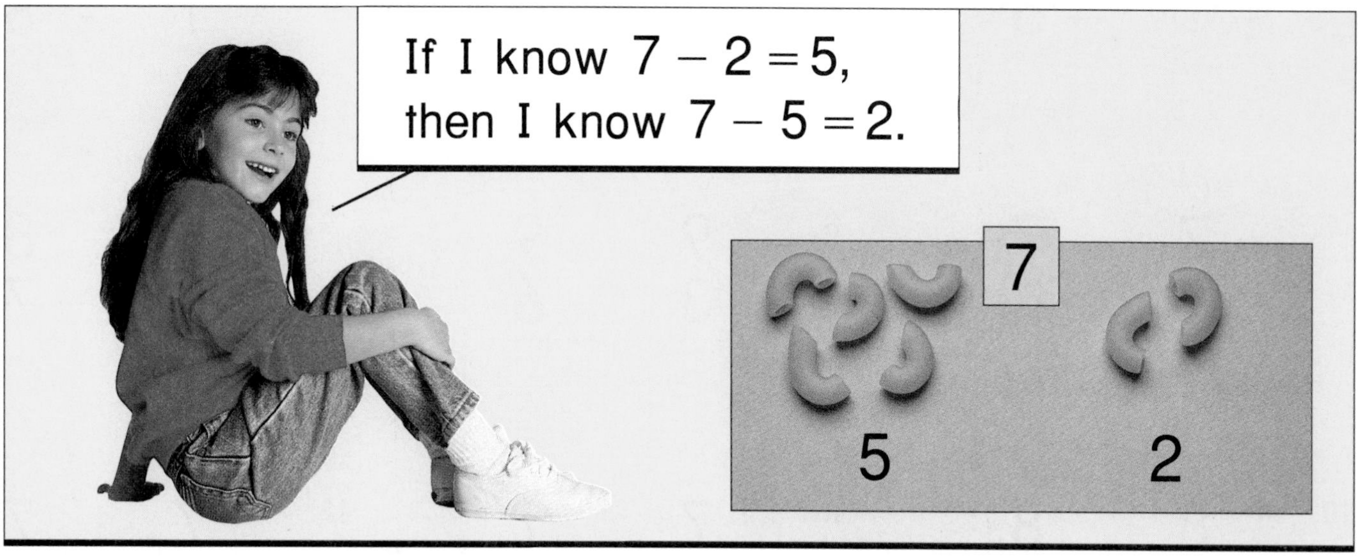

Subtract.

1.

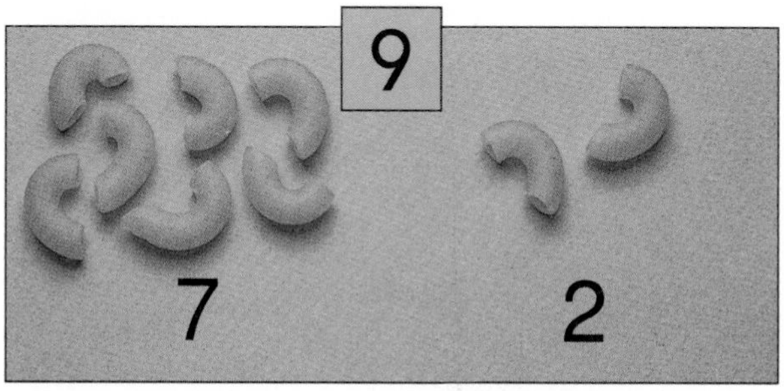

$9 - 2 =$ 7

$9 - 7 =$ ____

2.

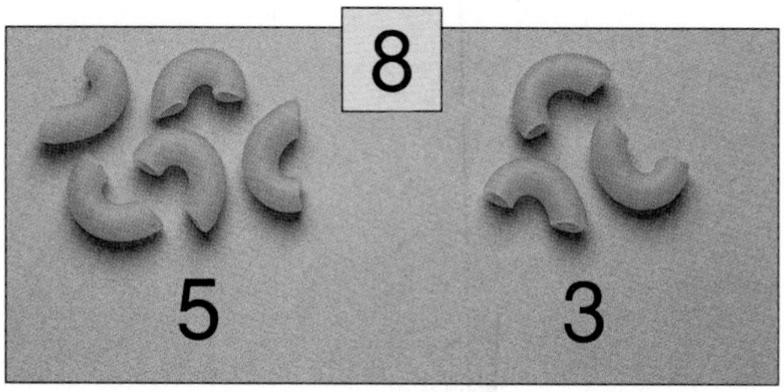

$8 - 3 =$ ____

$8 - 5 =$ ____

3.

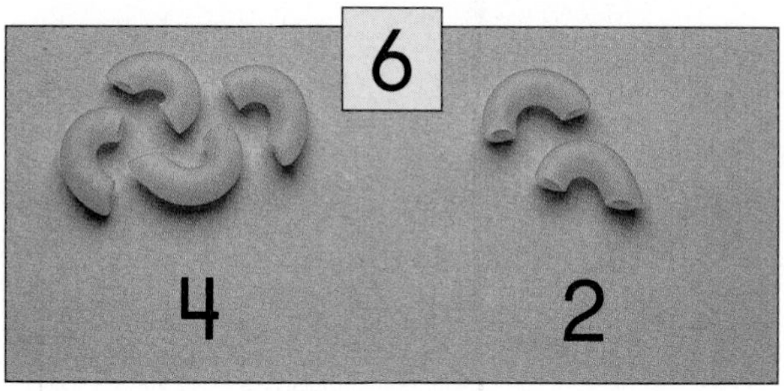

$6 - 2 =$ ____

$6 - 4 =$ ____

Notes for Home Children learn to use a known subtraction fact to solve a related subtraction fact.

Subtract.

4. $\begin{array}{r} 6 \\ -1 \\ \hline 5 \end{array}$ $\begin{array}{r} 6 \\ -5 \\ \hline \end{array}$

5. $\begin{array}{r} 5 \\ -1 \\ \hline \end{array}$ $\begin{array}{r} 5 \\ -4 \\ \hline \end{array}$

6. $\begin{array}{r} 9 \\ -1 \\ \hline \end{array}$ $\begin{array}{r} 9 \\ -8 \\ \hline \end{array}$

7. $\begin{array}{r} 7 \\ -3 \\ \hline \end{array}$ $\begin{array}{r} 7 \\ -4 \\ \hline \end{array}$

8. $\begin{array}{r} 9 \\ -3 \\ \hline \end{array}$ $\begin{array}{r} 9 \\ -6 \\ \hline \end{array}$

9. $\begin{array}{r} 8 \\ -1 \\ \hline \end{array}$ $\begin{array}{r} 8 \\ -7 \\ \hline \end{array}$

10. $\begin{array}{r} 8 \\ -2 \\ \hline \end{array}$ $\begin{array}{r} 8 \\ -6 \\ \hline \end{array}$

11. $\begin{array}{r} 7 \\ -6 \\ \hline \end{array}$ $\begin{array}{r} 7 \\ -1 \\ \hline \end{array}$

12. $\begin{array}{r} 7 \\ -2 \\ \hline \end{array}$ $\begin{array}{r} 7 \\ -5 \\ \hline \end{array}$

13. $\begin{array}{r} 10 \\ -1 \\ \hline \end{array}$ $\begin{array}{r} 10 \\ -9 \\ \hline \end{array}$

14. $\begin{array}{r} 5 \\ -2 \\ \hline \end{array}$ $\begin{array}{r} 5 \\ -3 \\ \hline \end{array}$

15. $\begin{array}{r} 10 \\ -3 \\ \hline \end{array}$ $\begin{array}{r} 10 \\ -7 \\ \hline \end{array}$

16. $\begin{array}{r} 4 \\ -1 \\ \hline \end{array}$ $\begin{array}{r} 4 \\ -3 \\ \hline \end{array}$

17. $\begin{array}{r} 10 \\ -2 \\ \hline \end{array}$ $\begin{array}{r} 10 \\ -8 \\ \hline \end{array}$

18. $\begin{array}{r} 3 \\ -1 \\ \hline \end{array}$ $\begin{array}{r} 3 \\ -2 \\ \hline \end{array}$

19. $\begin{array}{r} 9 \\ -2 \\ \hline \end{array}$ $\begin{array}{r} 9 \\ -7 \\ \hline \end{array}$

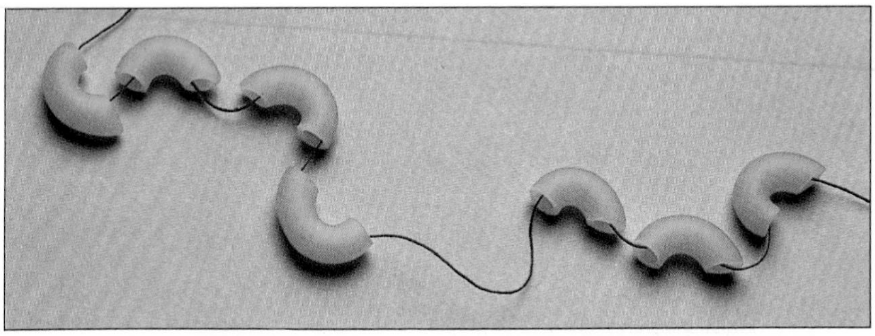

Notes for Home Children practice related subtraction facts through 10.

See More Practice Set A on page 159.

Name

PROBLEM-SOLVING STRATEGY

Make a Graph

1. Make a graph.
Color one box for each.

Number of Fruit

	apple	peach	orange	banana
5				
4				
3				
2				
1	■			

2. How many of each are there?

apples 4   bananas ____

oranges ____   peaches ____

Notes for Home Children solve a problem by making a graph.

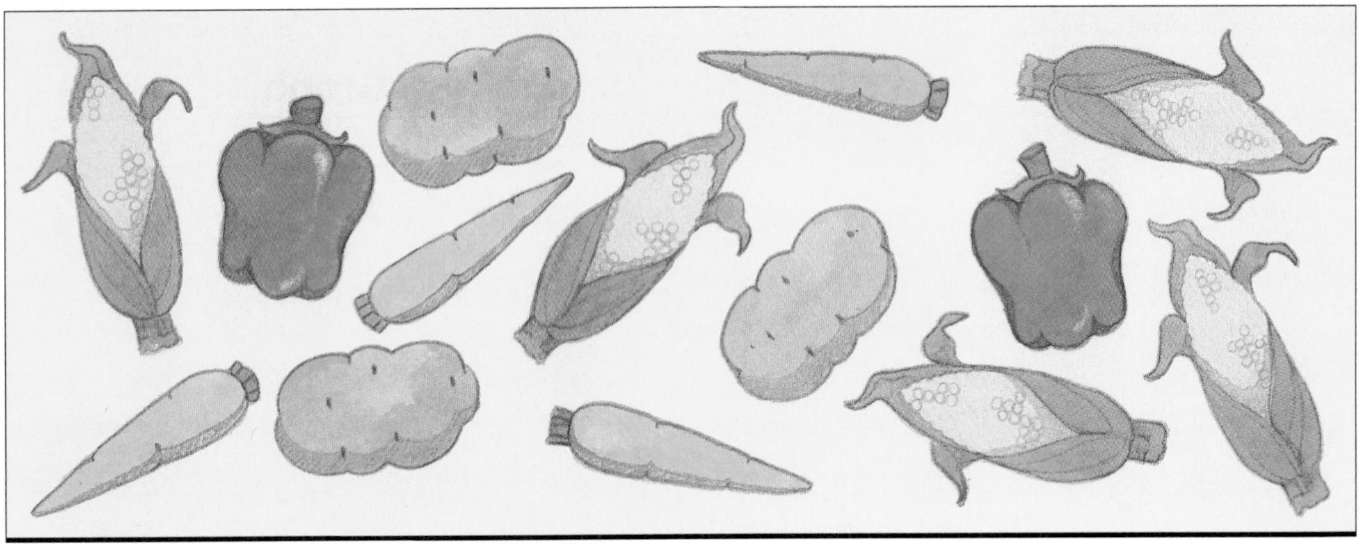

3. Make a graph.
Color one box for each.

Number of Vegetables

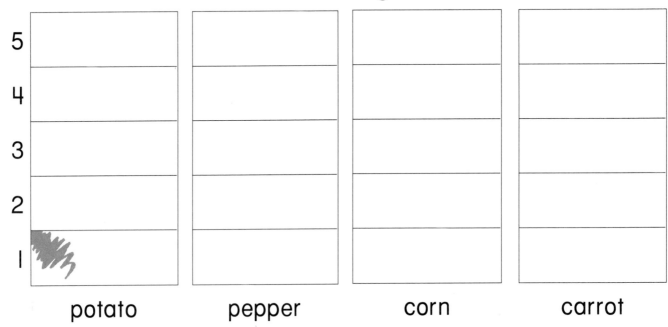

	potato	pepper	corn	carrot
5				
4				
3				
2				
1				

4. How many of each are there?

ears of corn 5 carrots ____

potatoes ____ peppers ____

Notes for Home Children solve a problem by making a graph.

Name

Number Sense

Tell a subtraction story for $8 - 2 = 6$ that each child could be thinking.

Let's do some more!

Think of subtraction stories.
Tell your stories to a friend.

Notes for Home Children develop number understanding by creating stories for a given number sentence.

Skills Review

Fill in the correct ⬭.
Subtract.

1. $\begin{array}{r} 4 \\ -\ 1 \\ \hline \end{array}$
   - (A) 1
   - (B) 2
   - (C) 3

2. $6 - 2 =$
   - (A) 4
   - (B) 5
   - (C) 6

3. $5 - 3 =$
   - (A) 2
   - (B) 3
   - (C) 4

4. $3 - 2 =$
   - (A) 3
   - (B) 2
   - (C) 1

5. $\begin{array}{r} 4 \\ -\ 3 \\ \hline \end{array}$
   - (A) 4
   - (B) 1
   - (C) 2

6. $\begin{array}{r} 6 \\ -\ 4 \\ \hline \end{array}$
   - (A) 0
   - (B) 1
   - (C) 2

Vocabulary

Fill in the correct word.

add	minus	cent

7. A + is the sign to ____add____.

8. The ¢ is the sign for ________.

9. The − is the ________ sign.

Notes for Home Children review subtracting from 6 or less. Then they review math symbols and terms.

Name ______________________________

Subtracting Zero

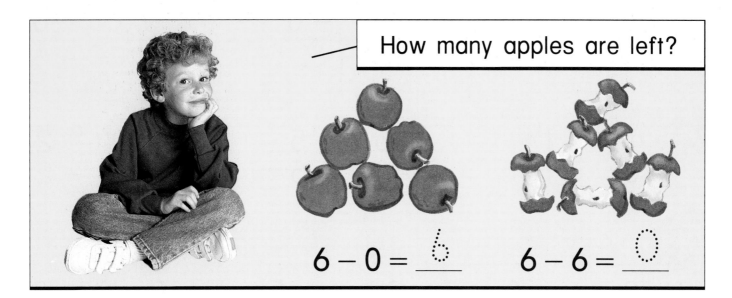

How many apples are left?

$6 - 0 = \underline{6}$ $6 - 6 = \underline{0}$

Subtract.

1.

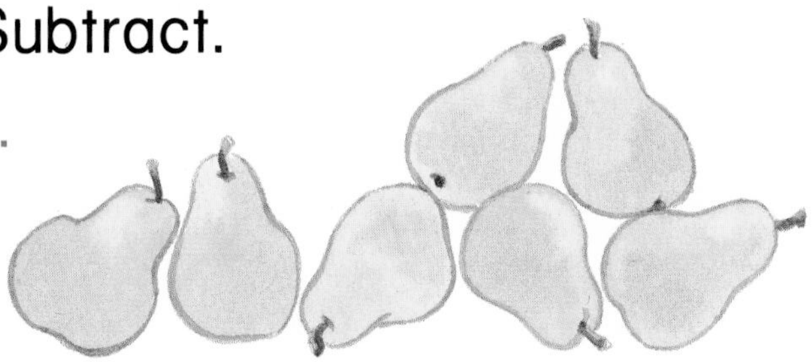

$7 - 0 =$ ____ $7 - 7 =$ ____

2.

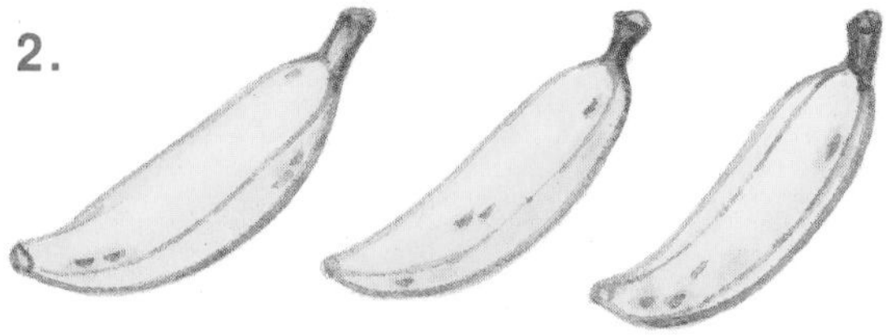

$3 - 0 =$ ____ $3 - 3 =$ ____

3.

$4 - 0 =$ ____ $4 - 4 =$ ____

Notes for Home Children learn to subtract using 0.

Subtract.

4. $\begin{array}{r}7\\-\ 0\\\hline 7\end{array}$ $\begin{array}{r}7\\-\ 7\\\hline\end{array}$ 5. $\begin{array}{r}9\\-\ 9\\\hline\end{array}$ $\begin{array}{r}9\\-\ 0\\\hline\end{array}$ 6. $\begin{array}{r}8\\-\ 0\\\hline\end{array}$ $\begin{array}{r}8\\-\ 8\\\hline\end{array}$

7. $\begin{array}{r}1\\-\ 0\\\hline\end{array}$ $\begin{array}{r}1\\-\ 1\\\hline\end{array}$ 8. $\begin{array}{r}5\\-\ 0\\\hline\end{array}$ $\begin{array}{r}5\\-\ 5\\\hline\end{array}$ 9. $\begin{array}{r}2\\-\ 0\\\hline\end{array}$ $\begin{array}{r}2\\-\ 2\\\hline\end{array}$

10. $\begin{array}{r}8\\-\ 6\\\hline\end{array}$ $\begin{array}{r}0\\-\ 0\\\hline\end{array}$ $\begin{array}{r}8\\-\ 0\\\hline\end{array}$ $\begin{array}{r}5\\-\ 0\\\hline\end{array}$ $\begin{array}{r}9\\-\ 7\\\hline\end{array}$ $\begin{array}{r}2\\-\ 2\\\hline\end{array}$

11. $\begin{array}{r}9\\-\ 0\\\hline\end{array}$ $\begin{array}{r}7\\-\ 5\\\hline\end{array}$ $\begin{array}{r}3\\-\ 0\\\hline\end{array}$ $\begin{array}{r}5\\-\ 5\\\hline\end{array}$ $\begin{array}{r}3\\-\ 1\\\hline\end{array}$ $\begin{array}{r}2\\-\ 0\\\hline\end{array}$

Problem Solving

Solve.

12. Jim had 5 .
He ate 2 .
How many were left?

_____ 

13. Ann had 6 .
She ate 6 .
How many were left?

_____ 

Notes for Home Children practice subtraction facts through 10. Then they solve problems using subtraction.

Name ________________

Subtracting with Doubles

4 + 4 helps me know 8 – 4.

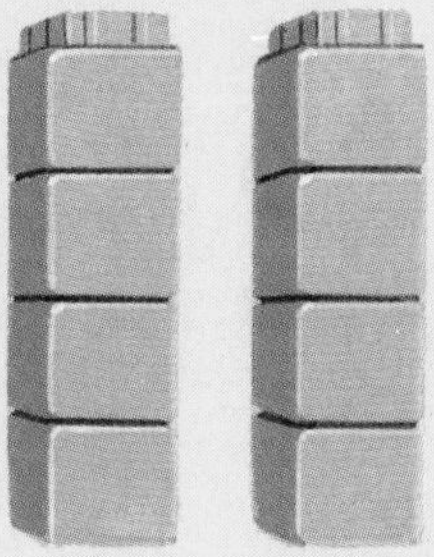
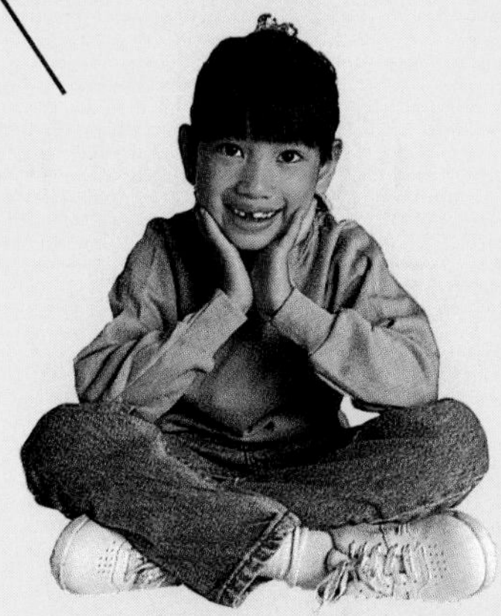
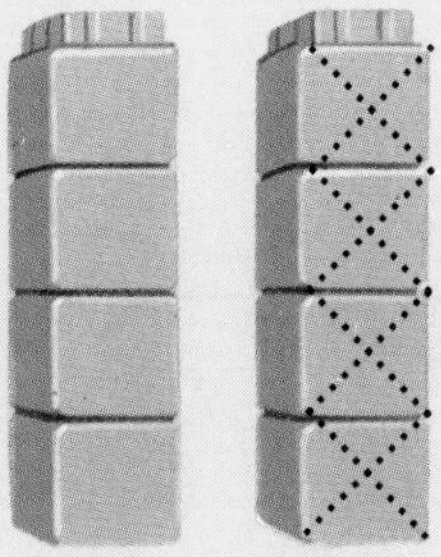

$4 + 4 =$ 8 $8 - 4 =$ 4

Add or subtract.
Cross out when subtracting.

1.

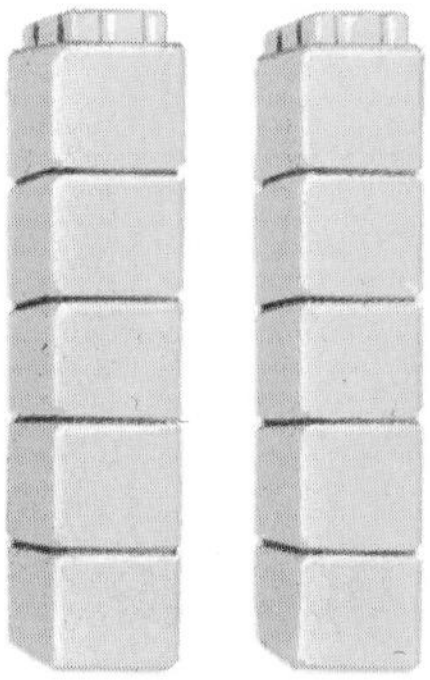

$5 + 5 =$ ____

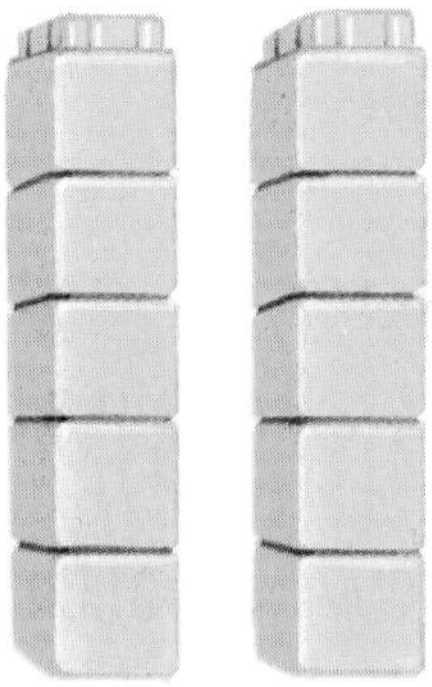

$10 - 5 =$ ____

2.

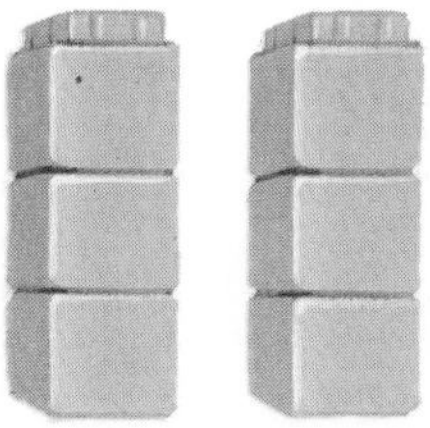

$3 + 3 =$ ____

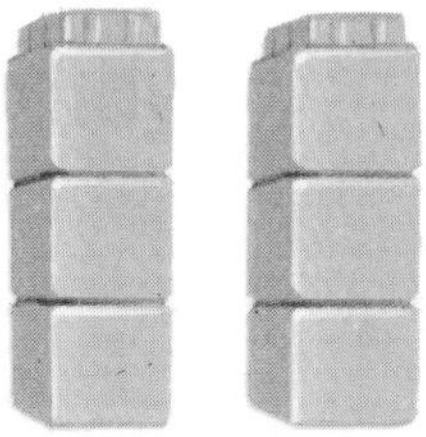

$6 - 3 =$ ____

Notes for Home Children learn subtraction double facts by using addition doubles.

Add or subtract.

3. $\begin{array}{r} 5 \\ +5 \\ \hline 10 \end{array}$ $\begin{array}{r} 10 \\ -5 \\ \hline \end{array}$

4. $\begin{array}{r} 4 \\ +4 \\ \hline \end{array}$ $\begin{array}{r} 8 \\ -4 \\ \hline \end{array}$

5. $\begin{array}{r} 3 \\ +3 \\ \hline \end{array}$ $\begin{array}{r} 6 \\ -3 \\ \hline \end{array}$

6. $\begin{array}{r} 6 \\ -0 \\ \hline \end{array}$ $\begin{array}{r} 8 \\ -5 \\ \hline \end{array}$ $\begin{array}{r} 10 \\ -8 \\ \hline \end{array}$ $\begin{array}{r} 10 \\ -5 \\ \hline \end{array}$ $\begin{array}{r} 6 \\ -6 \\ \hline \end{array}$ $\begin{array}{r} 2 \\ -1 \\ \hline \end{array}$

7. $\begin{array}{r} 4 \\ -2 \\ \hline \end{array}$ $\begin{array}{r} 2 \\ -0 \\ \hline \end{array}$ $\begin{array}{r} 8 \\ -4 \\ \hline \end{array}$ $\begin{array}{r} 1 \\ -0 \\ \hline \end{array}$ $\begin{array}{r} 9 \\ -6 \\ \hline \end{array}$ $\begin{array}{r} 4 \\ -4 \\ \hline \end{array}$

Problem Solving

Do you add or subtract?
Ring the correct word.

8. Sue had 3 oranges.
She got 3 more.
How many oranges did she have in all?

add subtract

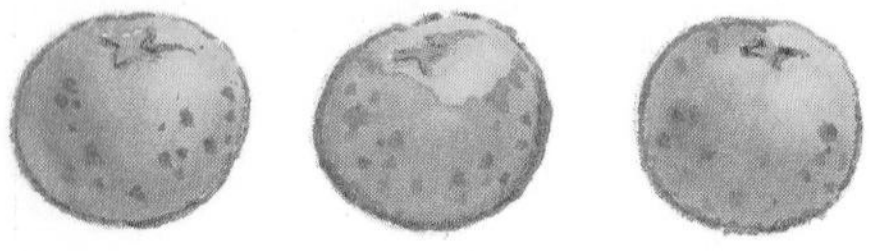

9. Tom had 8 apples.
He gave 4 away.
How many apples were left?

add subtract

Notes for Home Children practice subtraction facts. Then they solve problems involving addition and subtraction.

Name

Subtracting from 10

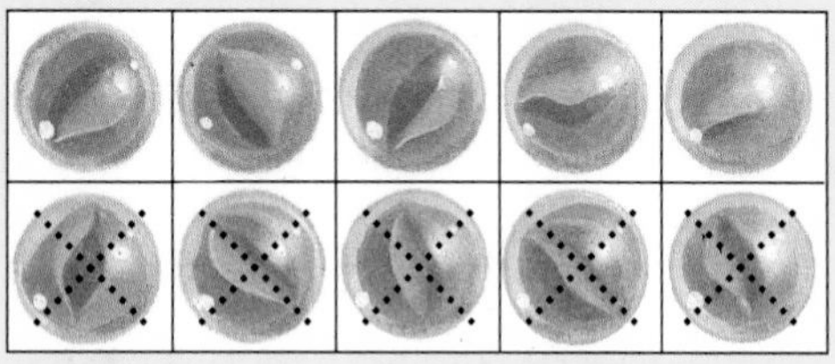

10 − 5 = 5

Cross out to subtract.
Write the difference.

1.

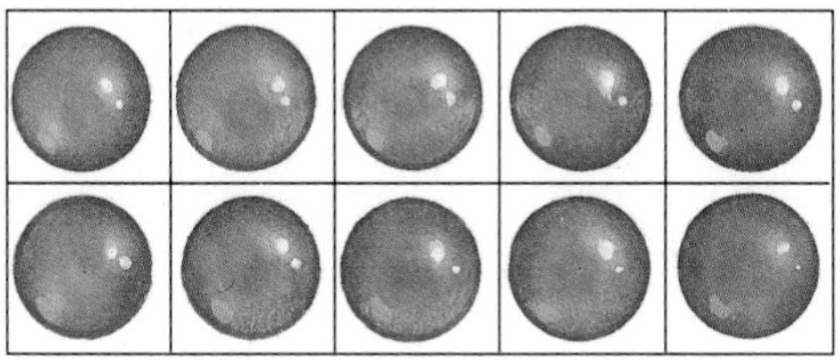

10 − 3 = ____

2.

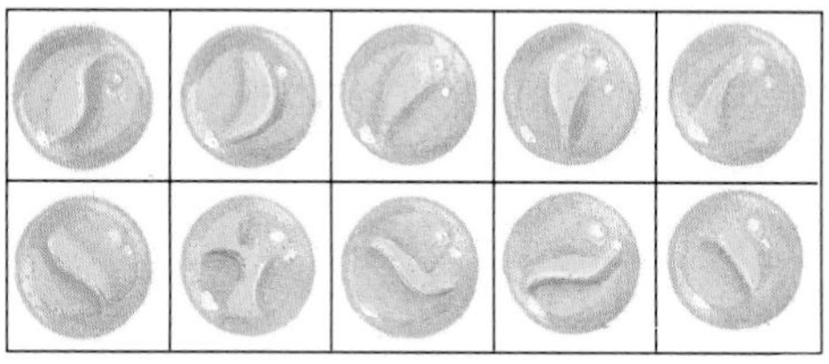

10 − 8 = ____

3.

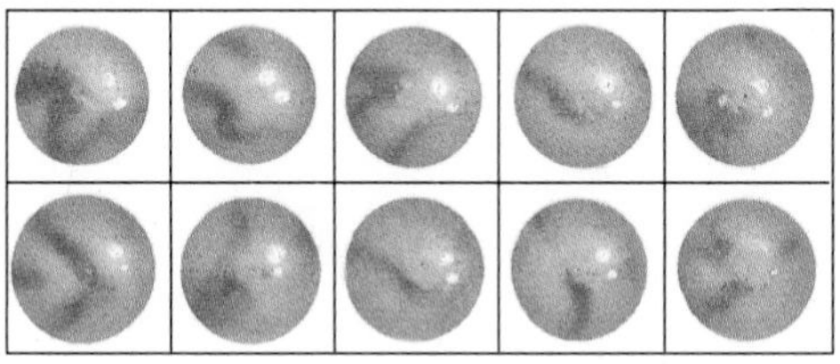

10 − 2 = ____

4.

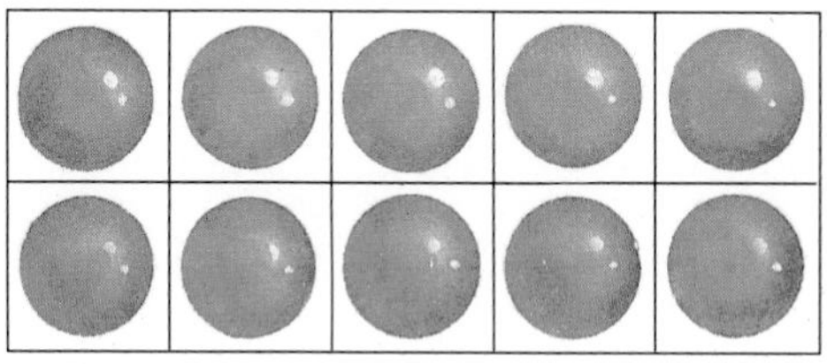

10 − 6 = ____

5.

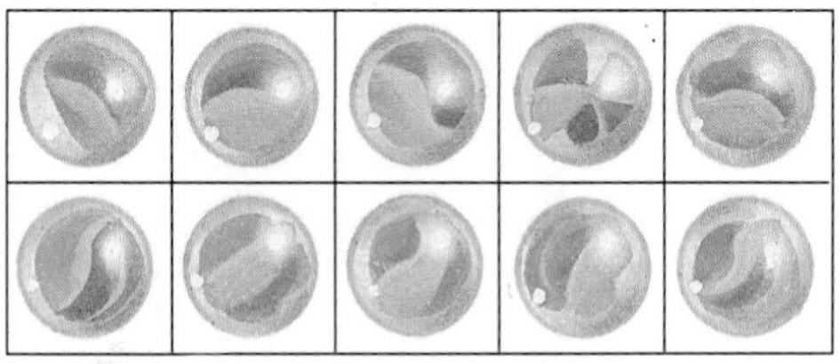

10 − 4 = ____

6.

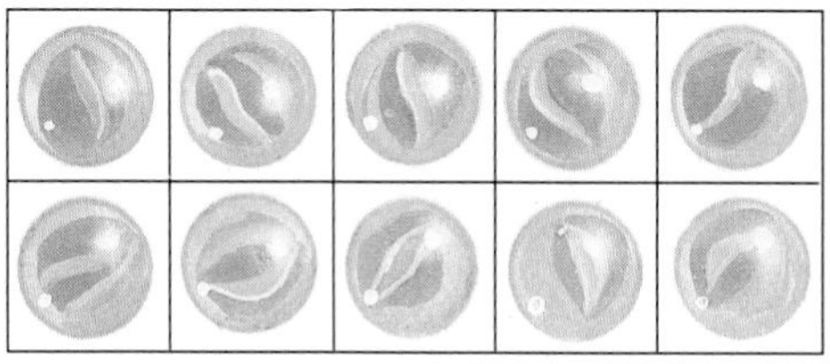

10 − 7 = ____

Notes for Home Children learn to subtract from 10.

Write the difference.

7.	$10 - 4 = 6$	$10 - 2$	$10 - 9$	$10 - 7$	$10 - 1$	$10 - 8$
8.	$10 - 6$	$10 - 3$	$10 - 5$	$10 - 9$	$10 - 4$	$10 - 3$
9.	$6 - 5$	$9 - 7$	$7 - 4$	$10 - 6$	$6 - 4$	$10 - 5$
10.	$10 - 2$	$8 - 5$	$10 - 4$	$7 - 5$	$9 - 0$	$5 - 4$
11.	$5 - 3$	$10 - 1$	$4 - 3$			
12.	$10 - 8$	$7 - 7$	$9 - 4$			

Notes for Home Children practice subtraction facts through 10.

Finding Families of Facts

This is a family of facts.

$3 + 4 = 7$ $7 - 4 = 3$

$4 + 3 = 7$ $7 - 3 = 4$

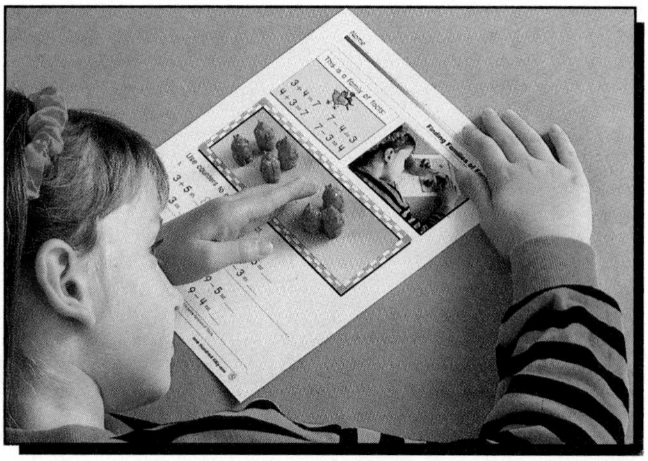

Use counters to add or subtract.

1.

$3 + 5 =$ 8 $8 - 5 =$ ____

$5 + 3 =$ ____ $8 - 3 =$ ____

2.

$4 + 5 =$ ____ $9 - 5 =$ ____

$5 + 4 =$ ____ $9 - 4 =$ ____

Notes for Home Children work at the CONCRETE level using counters to solve families of facts.

Use counters to add or subtract.

3.

$2 + 4 = \underline{6}$ $6 - 4 =$ ___

$4 + 2 =$ ___ $6 - 2 =$ ___

4.

$3 + 6 =$ ___ $9 - 6 =$ ___

$6 + 3 =$ ___ $9 - 3 =$ ___

5.

$3 + 4 =$ ___ $7 - 4 =$ ___

$4 + 3 =$ ___ $7 - 3 =$ ___

6.

$2 + 6 =$ ___ $8 - 6 =$ ___

$6 + 2 =$ ___ $8 - 2 =$ ___

Notes for Home Children work at the CONCRETE level using counters to solve families of facts.

Name

Addition and Subtraction Through 10

Add or subtract.

1.

Add 1	
2	3
8	9
9	
6	

2.

Add 2	
5	
7	
6	
8	

3.

Add 3	
2	
5	
6	
4	

4.

Subtract 1	
9	8
6	5
10	
8	

5.

Subtract 2	
7	
9	
8	
10	

6.

Subtract 3	
6	
10	
9	
3	

Notes for Home Children practice addition and subtraction facts through 10.

Add or subtract.

7.	$4 - 3$	$10 - 6$	$4 + 5$	$8 - 3$	$3 + 7$	$0 + 8$
8.	$2 + 5$	$9 - 4$	$1 + 7$	$4 + 6$	$10 - 7$	$5 - 5$
9.	$9 - 5$	$2 + 8$	$10 - 4$	$2 + 7$	$5 + 4$	$6 + 4$

Find the sum or difference.

10. Use red for 5.

Use yellow for 6.

Use blue for 7.

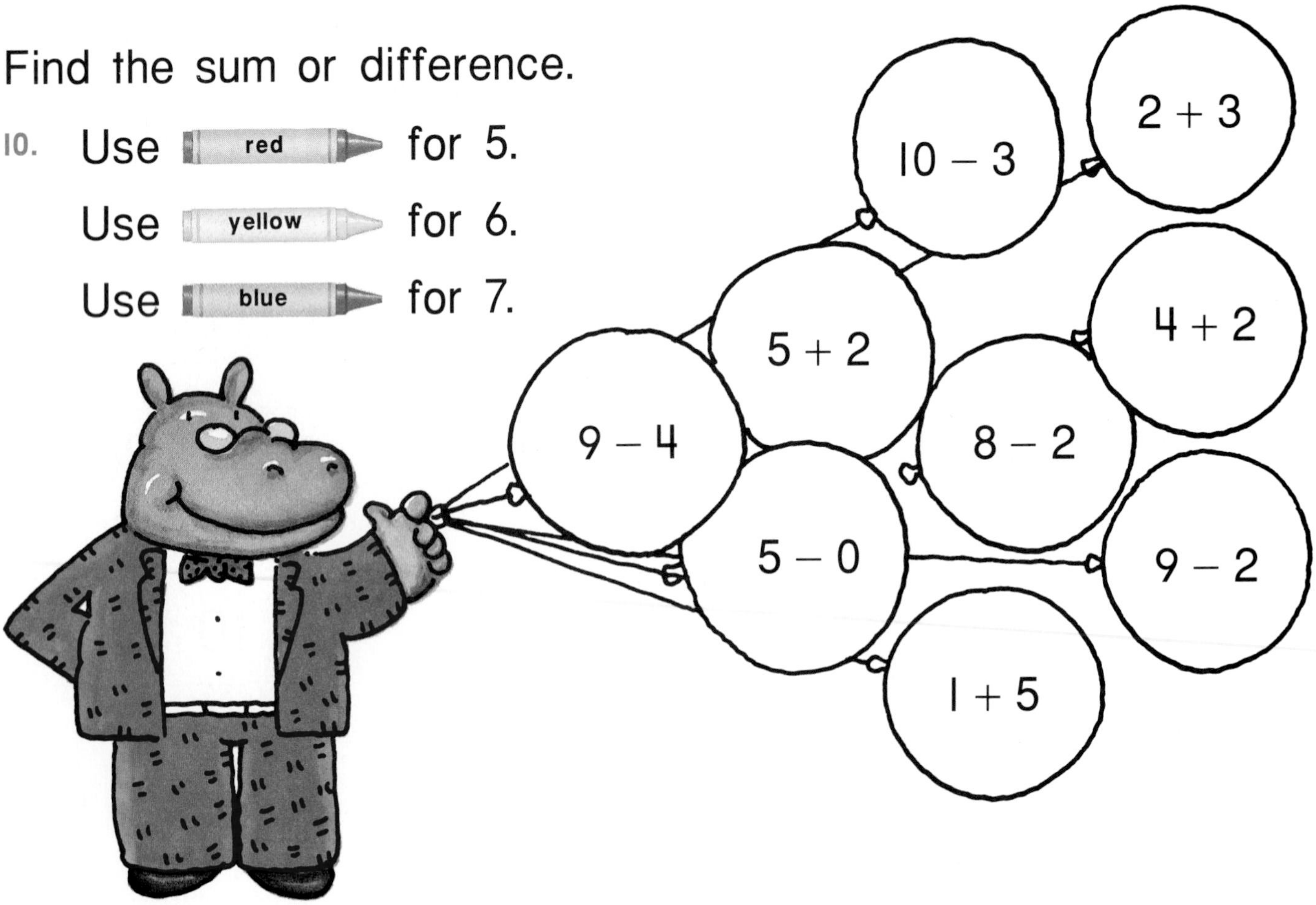

Notes for Home Children practice addition and subtraction facts through 10.

See More Practice Set B on page 159.

Name ____________________

PROBLEM-SOLVING STRATEGY

Choose an Operation

Stephanie had 8¢.
She spent 3¢.
How much does she have?

$$\begin{array}{r} 8¢ \\ - \; 3¢ \\ \hline 5¢ \end{array}$$

Write + or − in the □.
Then solve.

1. Antonio had 6¢.
He saved 2¢ more.
How much does he have?

$$\begin{array}{r} 6¢ \\ \square \; 2¢ \\ \hline ¢ \end{array}$$

2. Sarah had 10¢.
She spent 4¢.
How much does she have?

$$\begin{array}{r} 10¢ \\ \square \; 4¢ \\ \hline ¢ \end{array}$$

3. Harley had 8¢.
He earned 2¢.
How much does he have?

$$\begin{array}{r} 8¢ \\ \square \; 2¢ \\ \hline ¢ \end{array}$$

Notes for Home Children learn to solve problems involving addition or subtraction of money by choosing the operation.

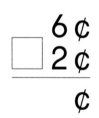

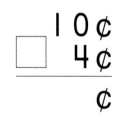

Write + or − in the □.
Then solve.

4. Rita had 4¢.
She found 5¢.
How much does she have?

   4¢
[+] 5¢
   9¢

5. Jason had 9¢.
He spent 6¢.
How much does he have?

   9¢
□ 6¢
   ¢

6. Sumi had 6¢.
She saved 4¢ more.
How much does she have?

   6¢
□ 4¢
   ¢

7. Keith had 5¢.
He gave Alice 3¢.
How much does he have?

   5¢
□ 3¢
   ¢

Notes for Home Children solve problems involving addition or subtraction of money by choosing the operation.

Name

Problem-Solving Workshop

Explore as a Team

Work with a partner.
Use these numbers to solve the riddle.

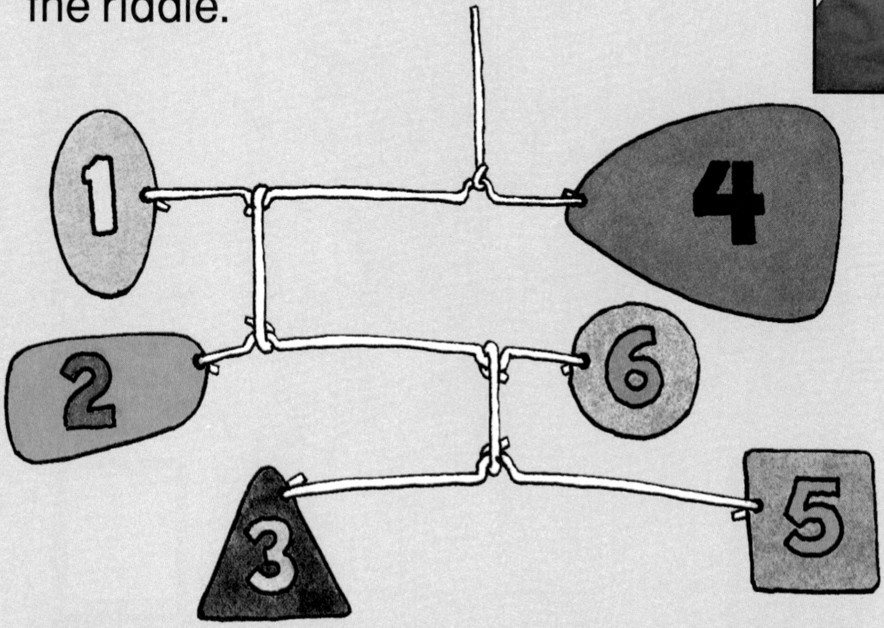

When you add these numbers you get 7.

When you subtract these numbers you get 5.

What are the two numbers? ☐ ☐

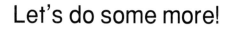

Let's do some more!

Make up a riddle for your partner.
Use the numbers above for your riddle.
Take turns.

Notes for Home Children explore with a partner to solve problems involving addition and subtraction.

Problem-Solving Workshop

Explore with a Calculator

Use a calculator to solve. Write what the calculator will show.

1.

7 − 3 = 4

2.

6 − 1 =

3.

4 − 2 =

4.

9 − 3 =

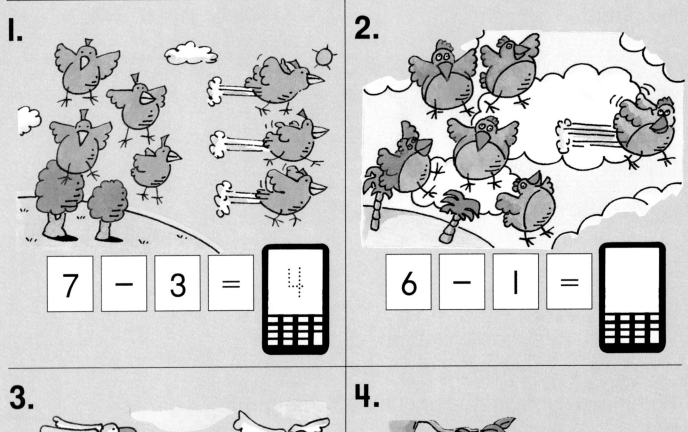

Notes for Home Children explore with a calculator to solve subtraction problems.

Name

More Practice

Set A Use after page 140.

Subtract.

1.	6 − 2 = 4	6 − 4 =	2.	8 − 3 =	8 − 5 =	3.	7 − 2 =	7 − 5 =
4.	9 − 1 =	9 − 8 =	5.	10 − 3 =	10 − 7 =	6.	5 − 1 =	5 − 4 =

Set B Use after page 154.

Find the sum or difference.

Use blue for 5.

Use red for 6.

Use yellow for 7.

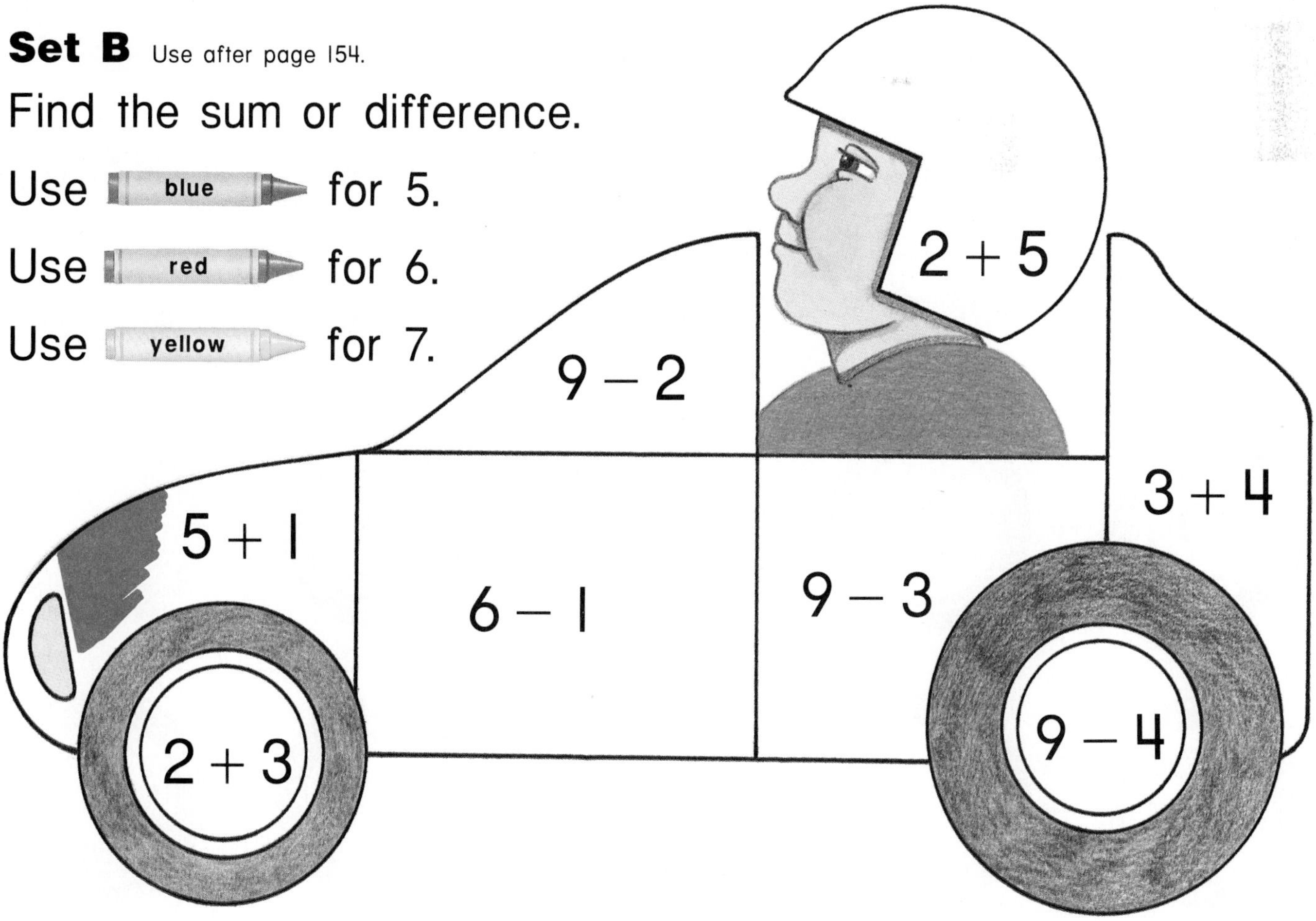

Notes for Home Set A: Children practice subtraction facts through 10.
Set B: Children practice addition and subtraction facts through 10.

Enrichment

Add or subtract.

1. 6 + 2 − 3 + 2 = 7

2. 7 − 6 + 2 + 4 = ___

3. 4 + 2 + 1 − 3 = ___

4. 5 − 4 + 6 − 2 = ___

5. 10 − 3 − 2 + 4 = ___

6. 9 + 1 − 6 + 3 = ___

Notes for Home Children are challenged to complete addition and subtraction chains.

Name

Chapter 5 Review/Test

Add or subtract.

1.

9	7	8	6	9	9
− 1	− 3	− 2	− 6	− 2	− 7

2.

5	10	10	8	10	5
+ 5	− 5	− 7	+ 2	− 6	+ 4

3. Count back 2.

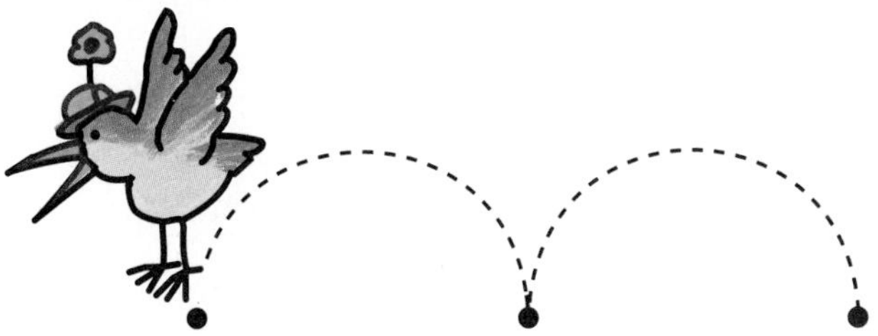

____ ____ 10

4. Add or subtract.

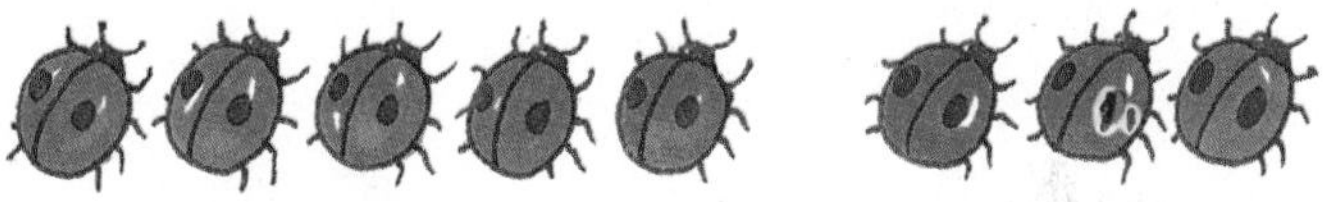

5 + 3 = ____ 8 − 3 = ____

3 + 5 = ____ 8 − 5 = ____

5. Write + or − in the □.
Then solve.

Robert had 9¢.
He spent 6¢.
How much does
he have now?

9¢
□ 6¢
¢

6. Color one box for each.

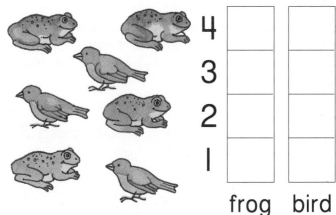

	frog	bird
4		
3		
2		
1		

Notes for Home Children are assessed on Chapter 5 concepts, skills, and problem solving.

Exploring Math at Home

Dear Family,

In this chapter I have learned how to count back from a given number. I have also learned subtraction facts through 10 and how to make a graph. Please help me with the activities below.

Love, ______________________________

1.

Recite the "Ten Little Indians" song.

2.

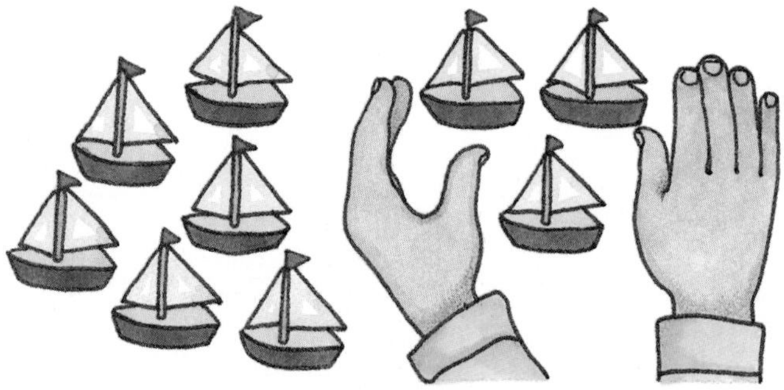

$$9 - 3 = 6$$

Use objects to create subtraction stories through 10.

3.

$$7 - 4 = 3$$

Play the "Shell Game" with a cup. Start with a given number of dried beans. Close your eyes. Have your partner cover some beans with the cup. Open your eyes. Tell how many beans are covered with the cup.

Coming Attractions

In the next chapter I will be learning about shapes. I will also compare and measure lengths and heights of objects.

Chapter 6

Geometry and Measurement

Listen to the math story, "Professor Guesser." The hunter saw some tracks in the sand. What was strange about the tracks?

Notes for Home Children listen to a math story introducing chapter concepts and skills. Then they answer a question about the story.

Name

Plane Shapes

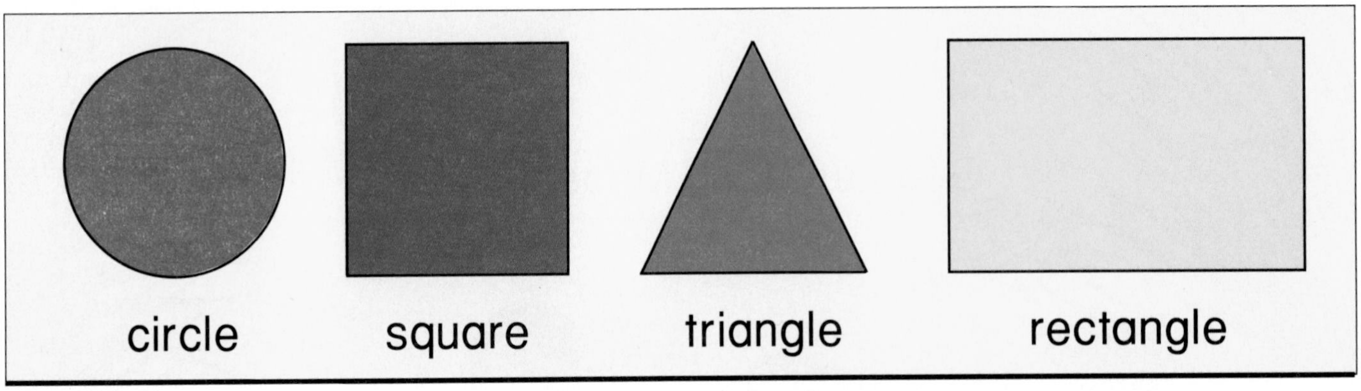

Color circles red and squares blue.

Color triangles green and rectangles yellow.

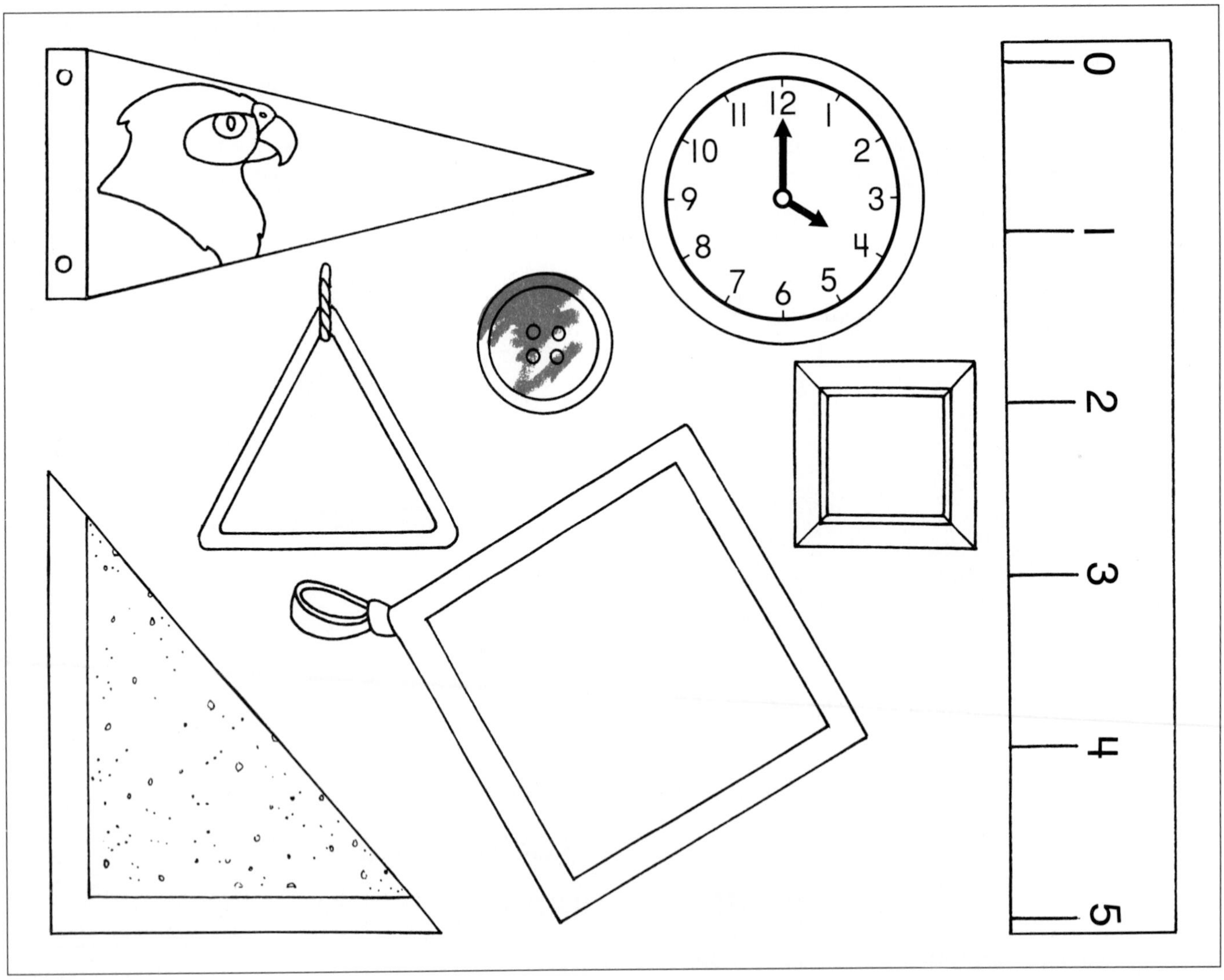

Notes for Home Children identify circles, squares, triangles, and rectangles.

Name

Attributes of Plane Shapes

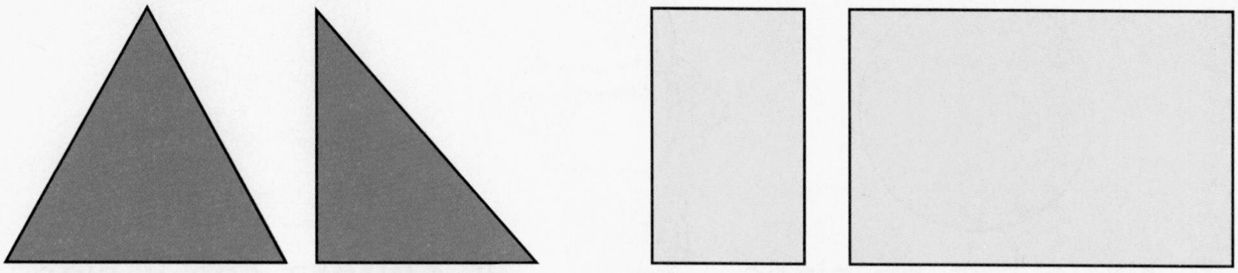

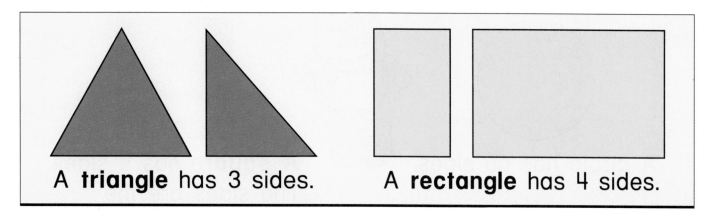

A **triangle** has 3 sides. A **rectangle** has 4 sides.

1. Color triangles 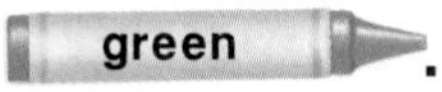

.

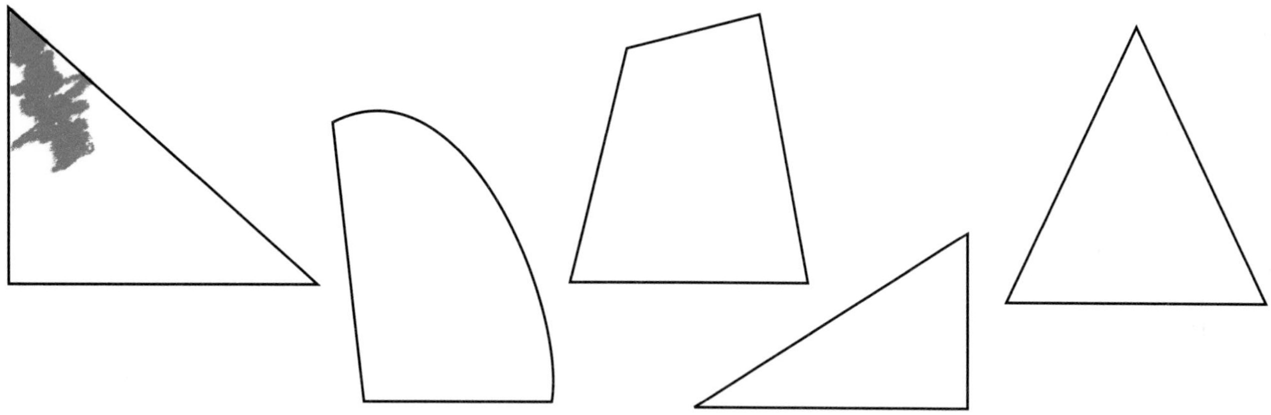

2. Color rectangles 

.

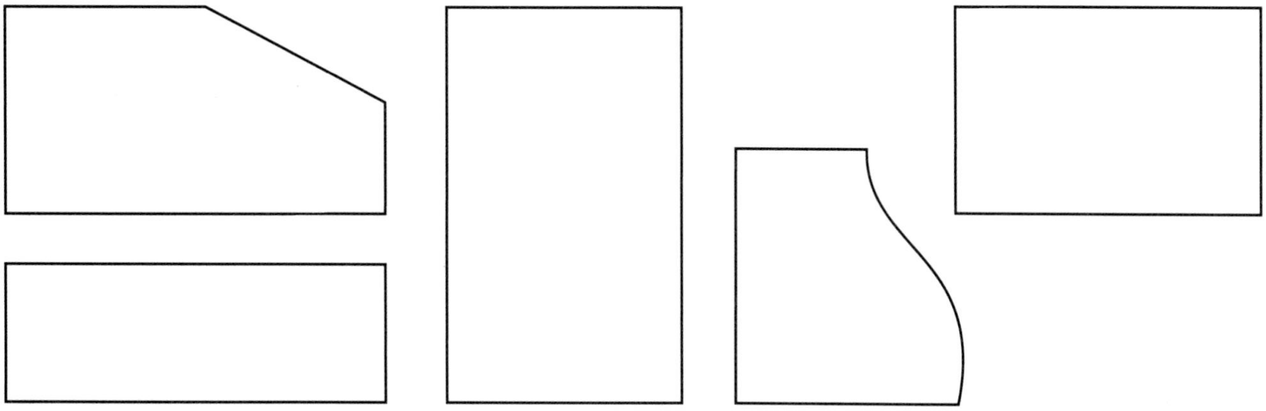

Notes for Home Children use attributes of triangles and rectangles to classify these shapes.

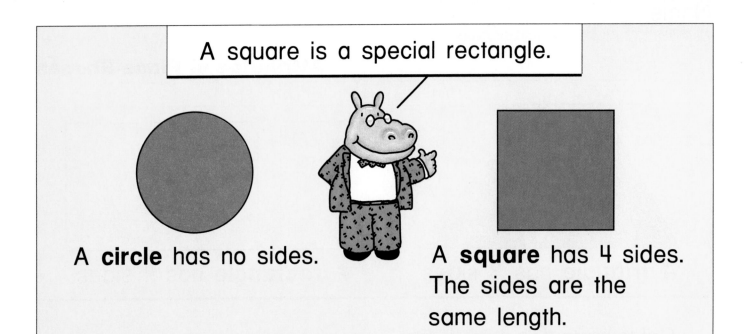

A square is a special rectangle.

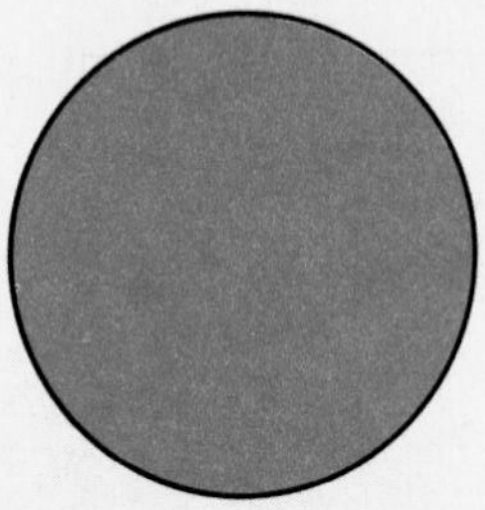

A **circle** has no sides.

A **square** has 4 sides. The sides are the same length.

3. Color circles red.

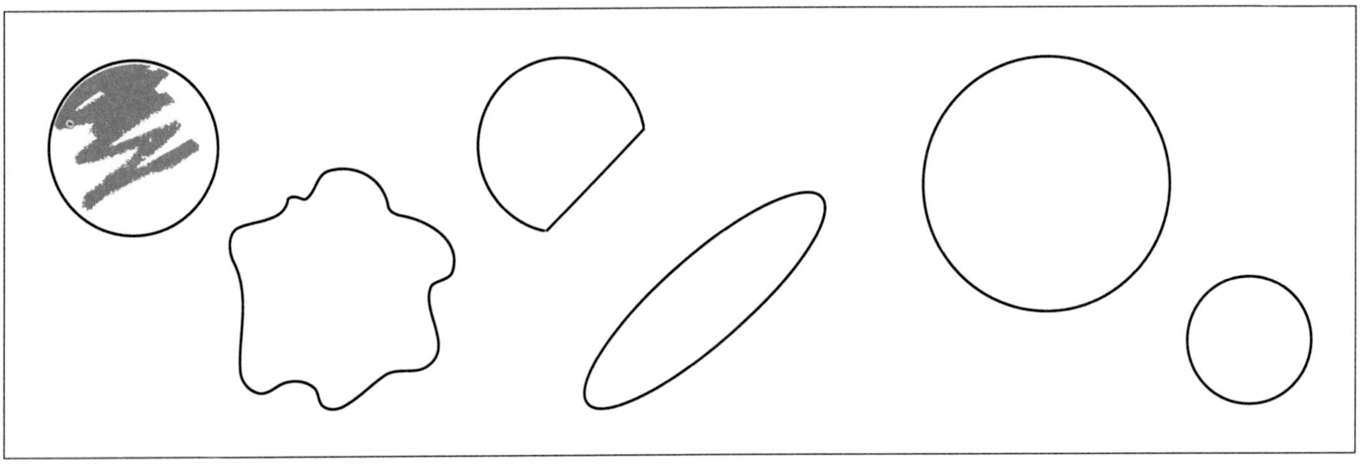

4. Color squares blue.

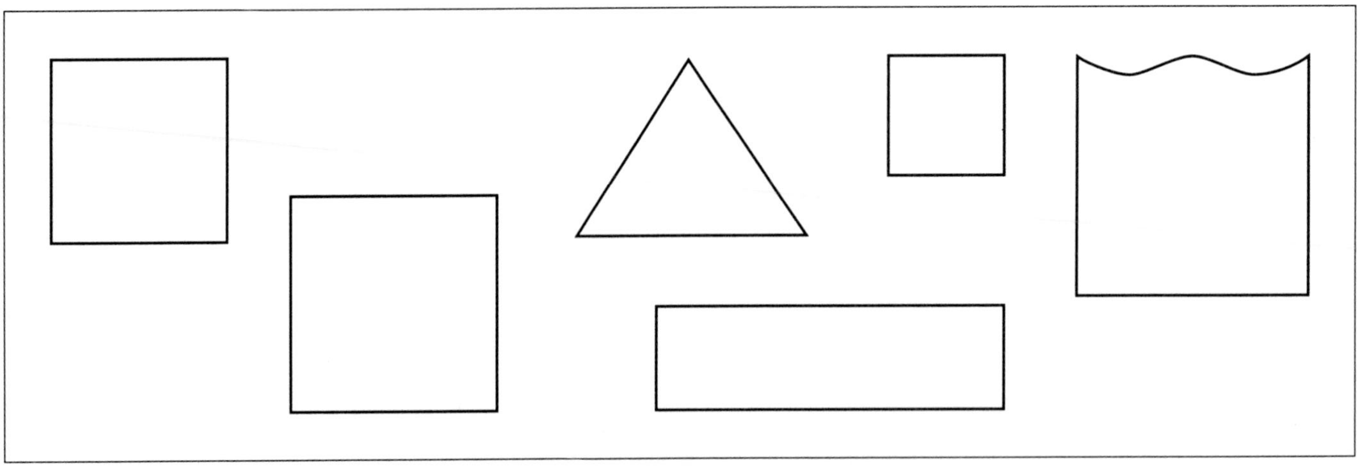

Notes for Home Children use attributes of circles and squares to classify these shapes.

Name

Copying and Naming Shapes

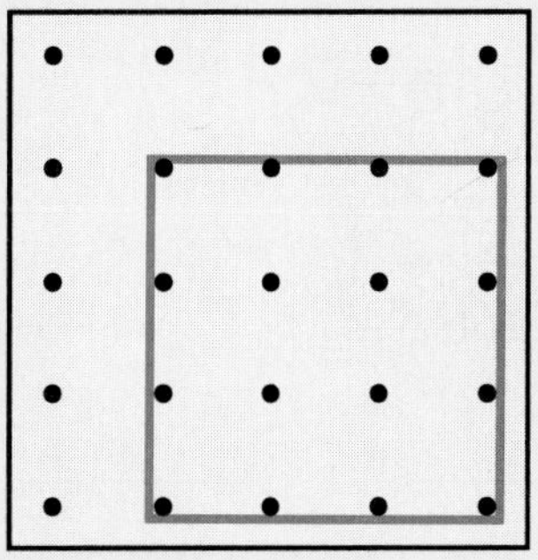
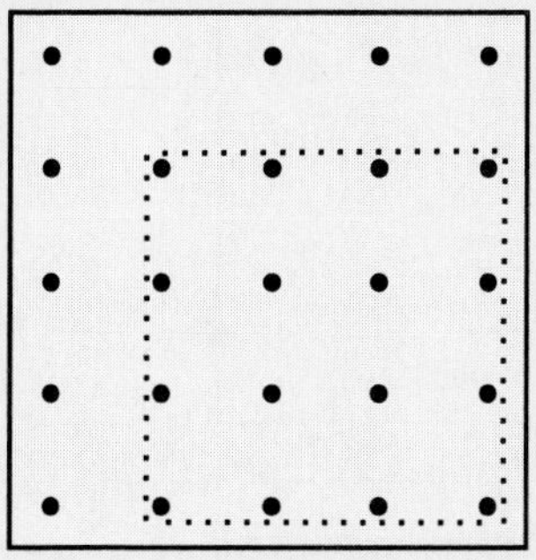

square

triangle

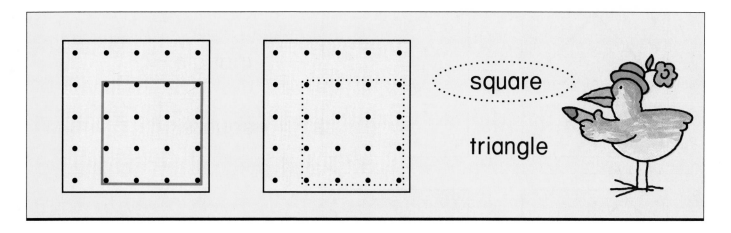

Copy the shape.
Then ring the name.

1.

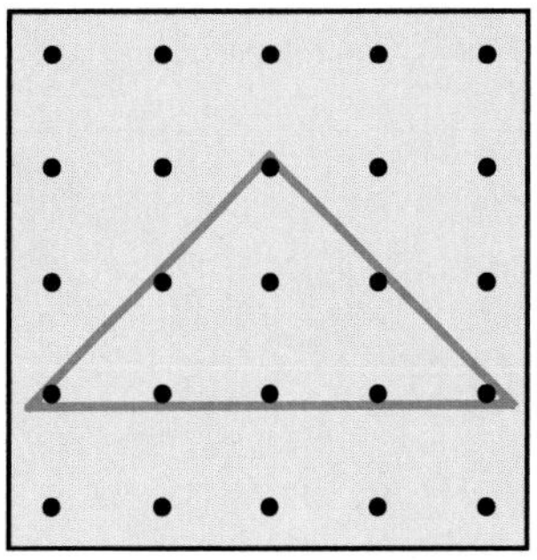
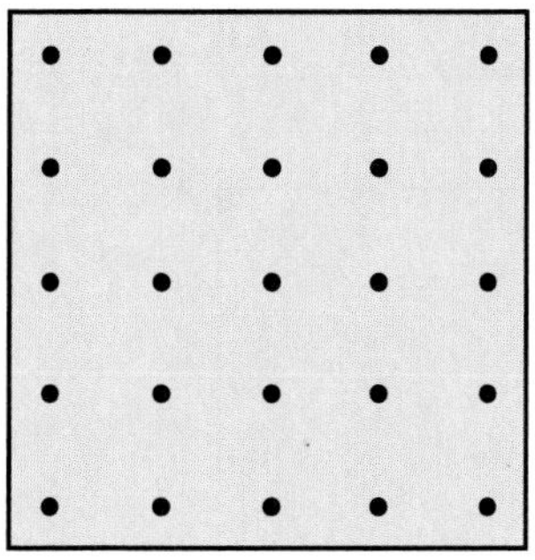

triangle

rectangle

2.

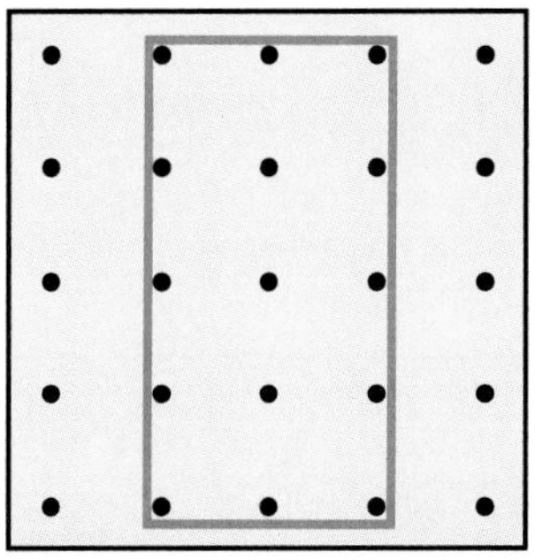
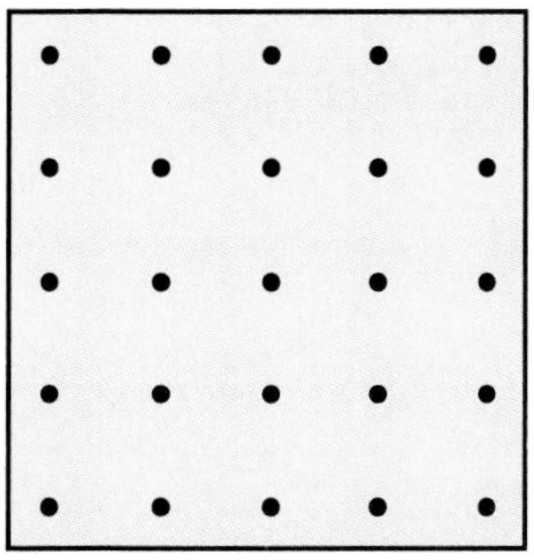

triangle

rectangle

3.

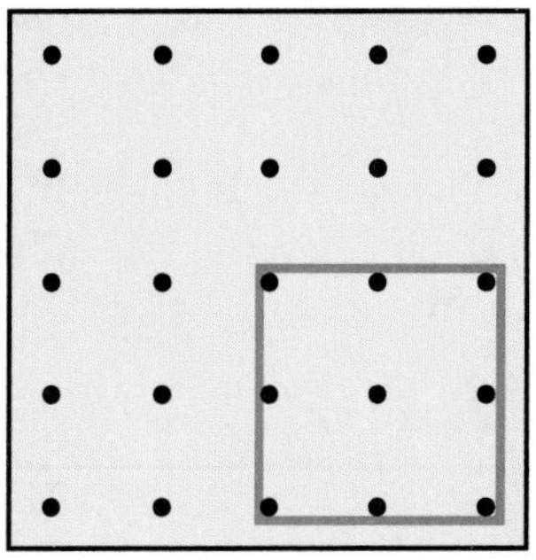
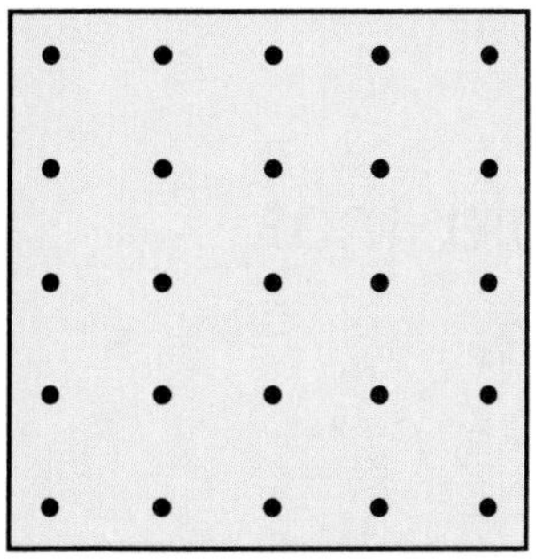

triangle

square

Notes for Home Children copy plane shapes on pictures of geoboards. Then they identify the shapes.

Copy the shape.
Then ring the name.

4.

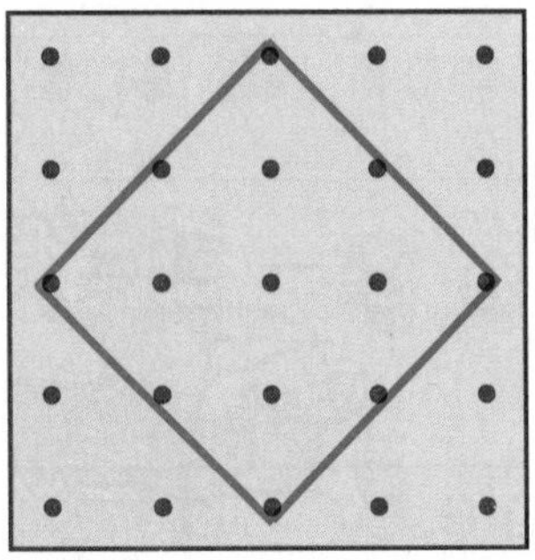

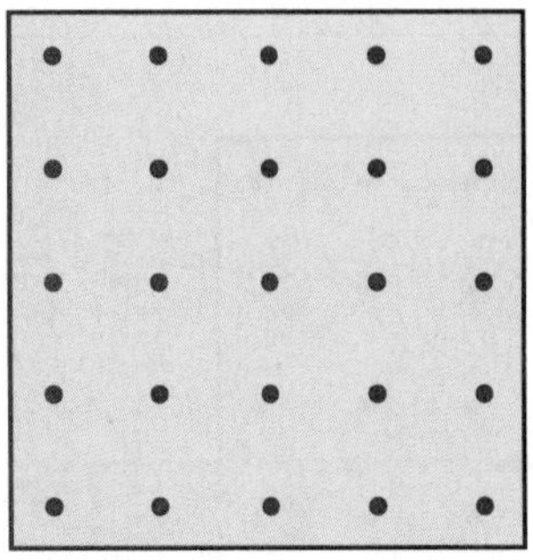

triangle

square

5.

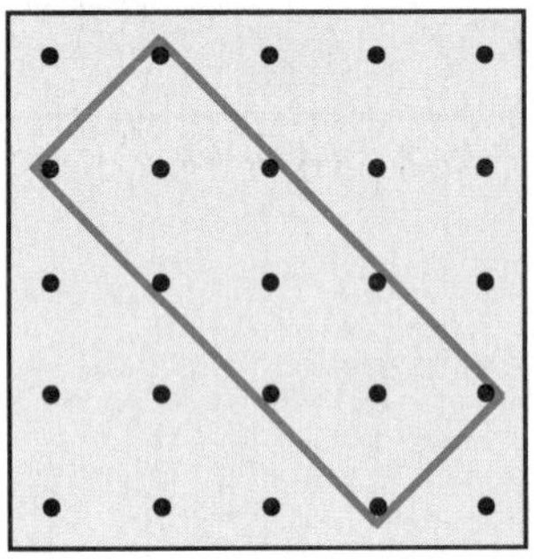

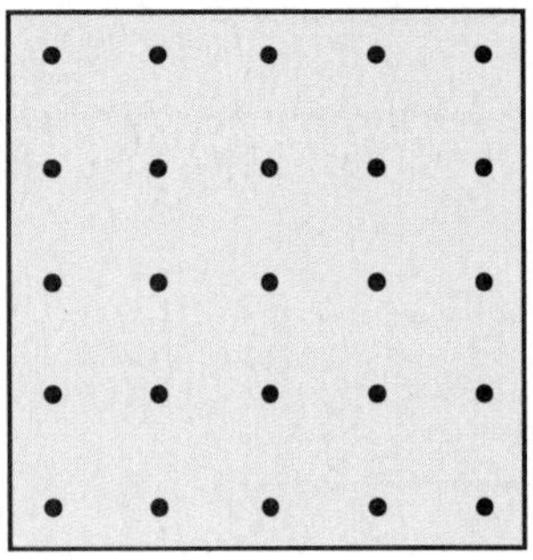

triangle

rectangle

6.

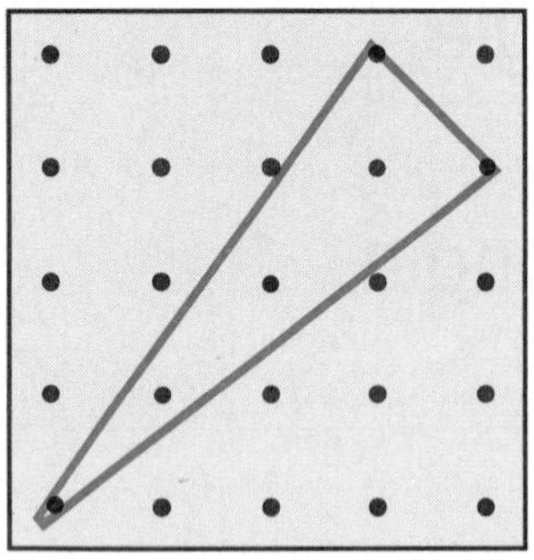

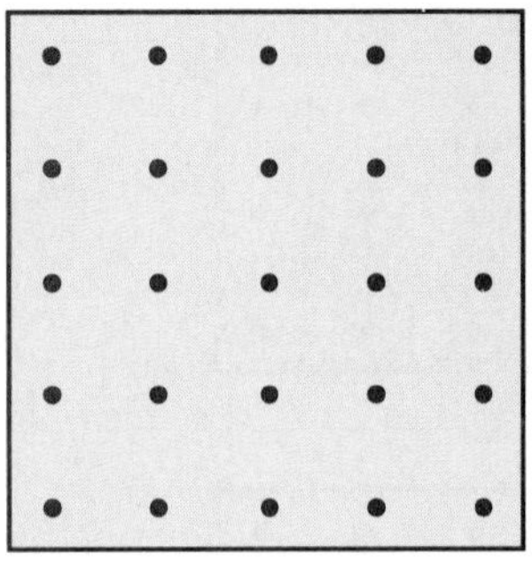

triangle

square

Problem Solving

Solve.

7. Ring the marble that is **inside** the triangle.

8. Put an X on the marble that is **outside** the triangle.

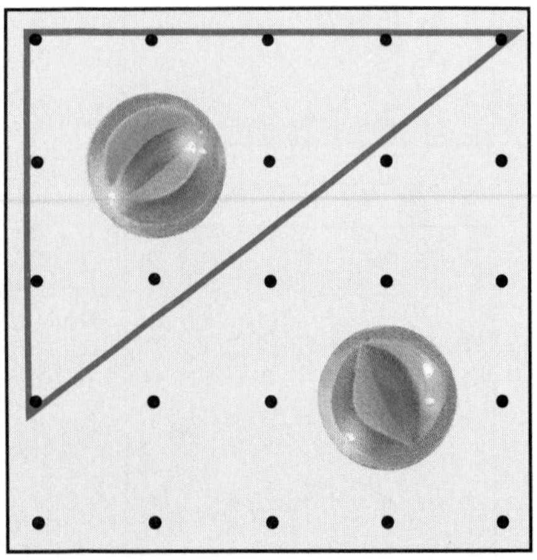

Notes for Home Children copy and identify shapes on pictures of geoboards. Then they solve problems involving the interior and exterior of a shape.

Name

Making Shapes

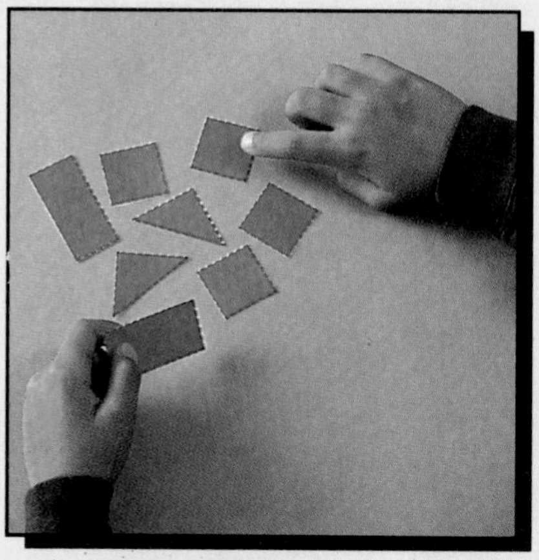

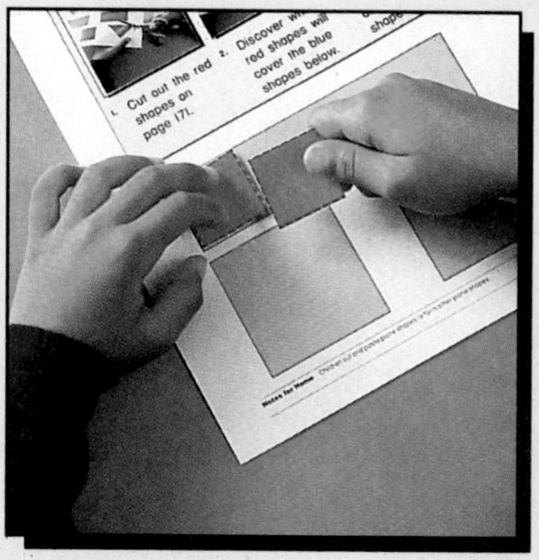

1. Cut out the red shapes on page 171.
2. Discover which red shapes will cover the blue shapes below.
3. Paste the red shapes to cover each blue shape below.

1.

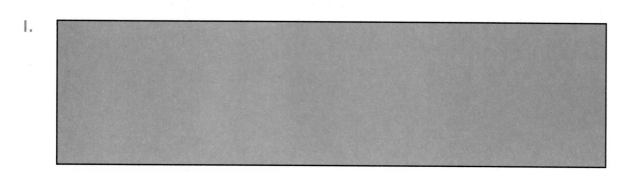

2.

3.

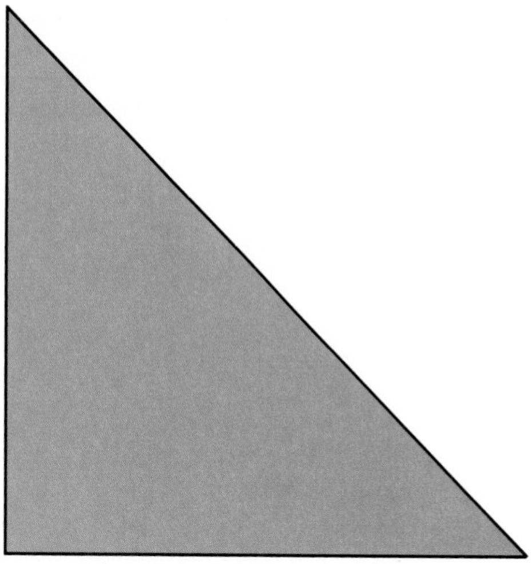

Notes for Home Children cut and paste plane shapes to form other plane shapes.

4. Use shapes on page 171.
Cut and paste the shapes to make a design.

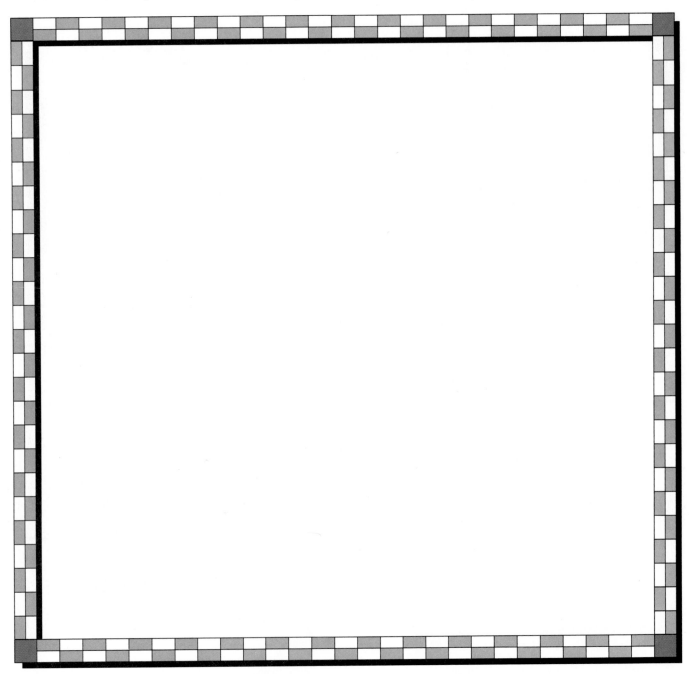

How many did you use?

5. triangles ____

6. squares ____

7. circles ____

8. rectangles ____

Notes for Home Children cut and paste plane shapes to create a geometric design.

Use with page 169.

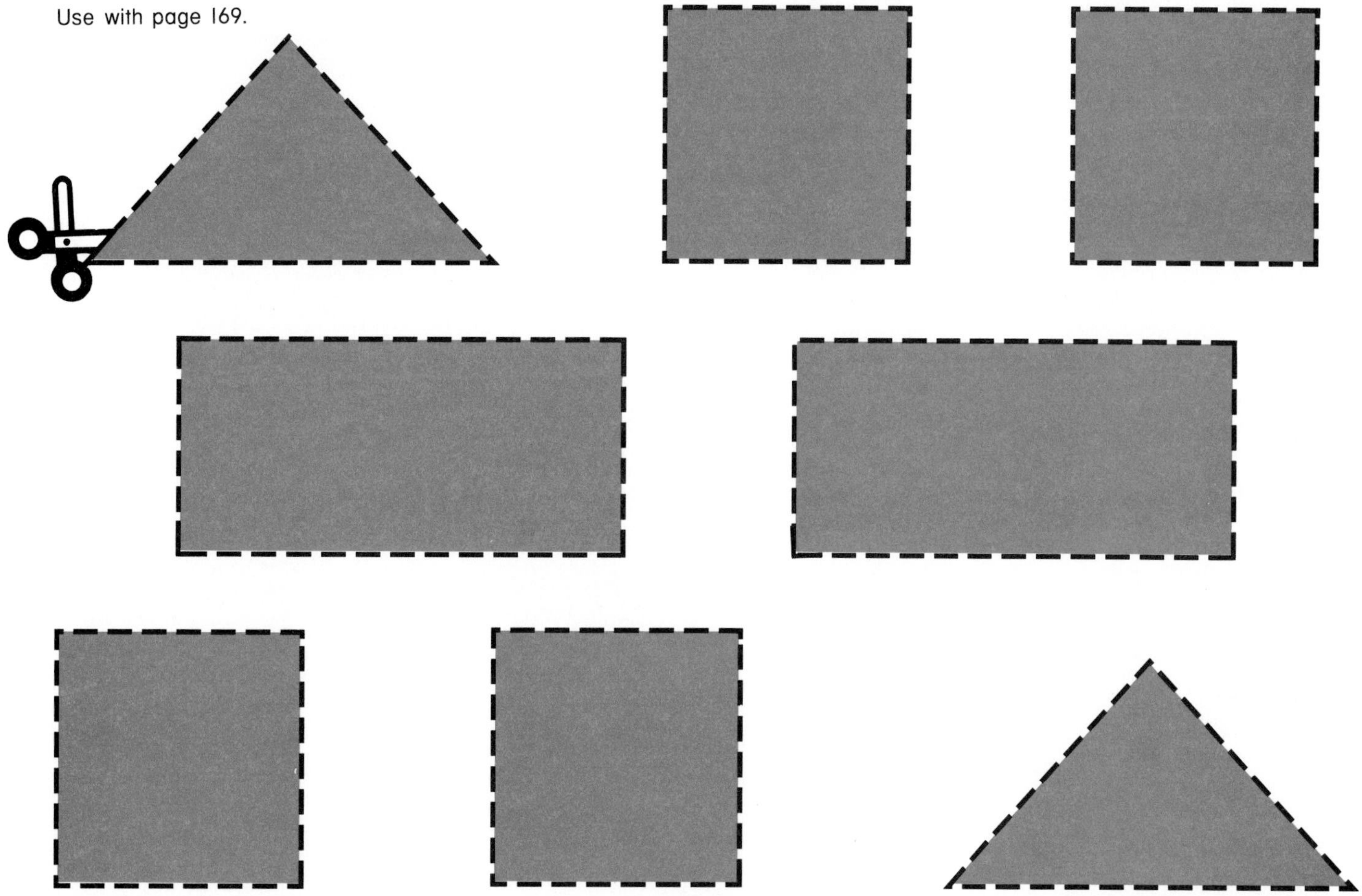

Use with page 170.

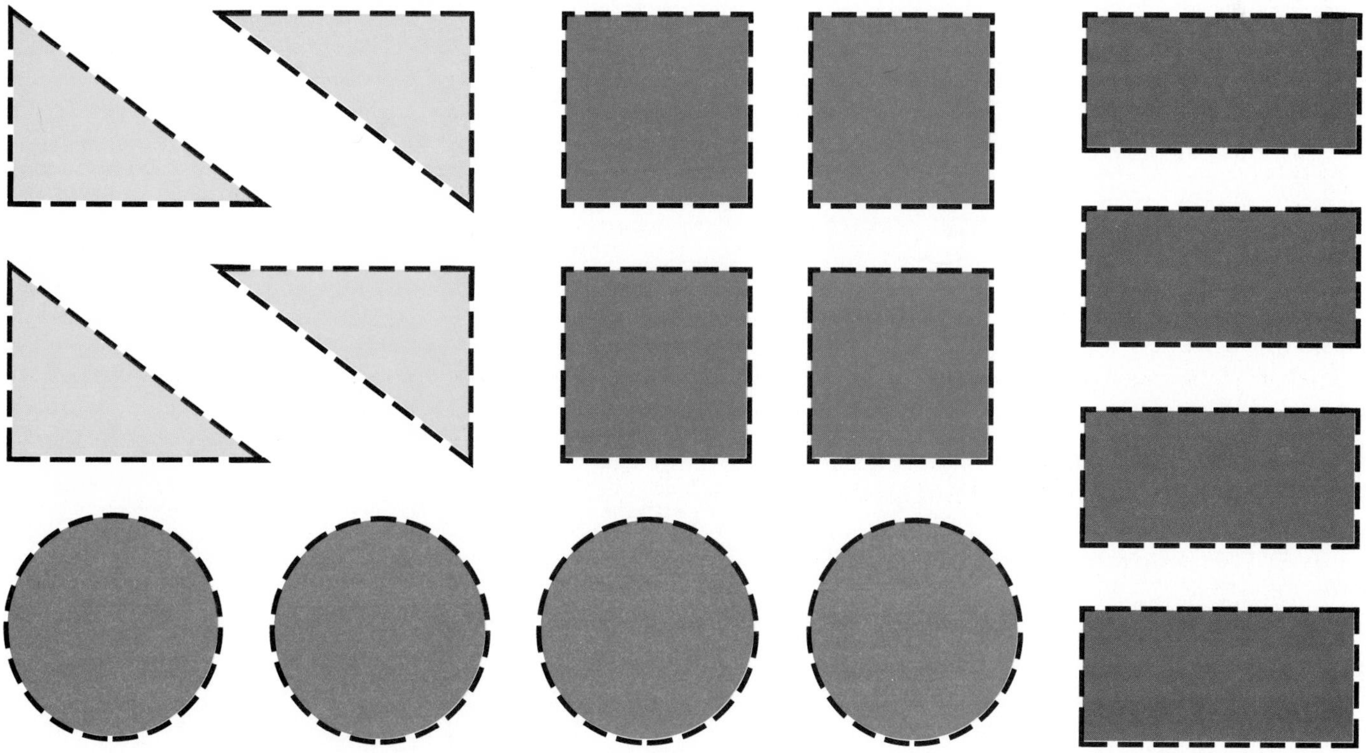

Name

Solids

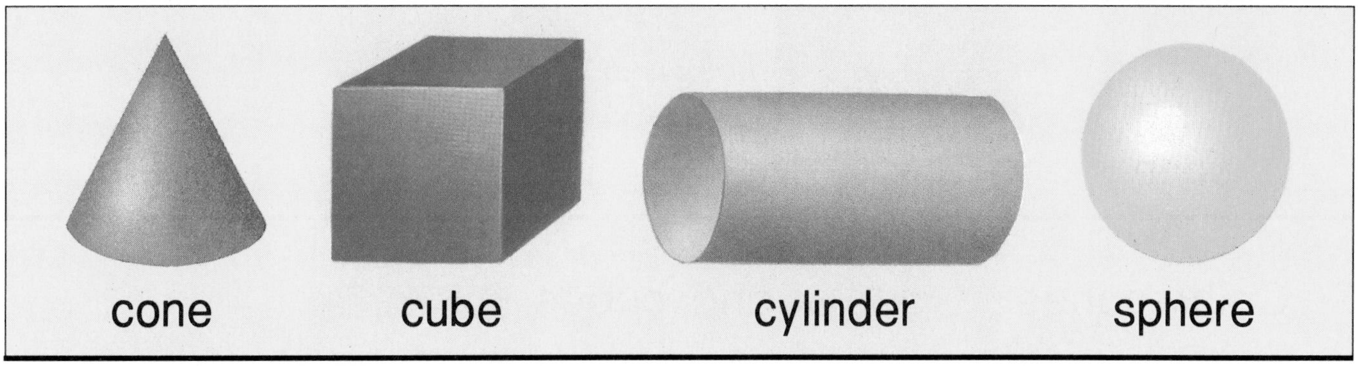

1. Color cones  and cubes .

Color cylinders  and spheres .

Notes for Home Children identify cones, cubes, cylinders, and spheres.

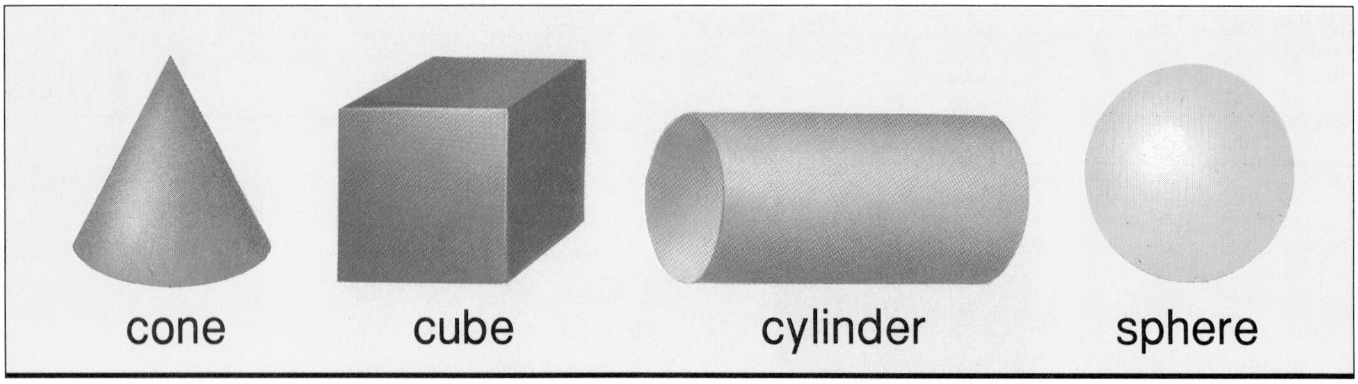

| cone | cube | cylinder | sphere |

2. Color cones 

and cubes 

.
Color cylinders blue 

and spheres yellow.

.

Notes for Home Children identify cones, cubes, cylinders, and spheres.

See More Practice Set A on page 195.

Name

Use Logical Reasoning

Think about the shape being traced.
Ring the correct shape.

1.
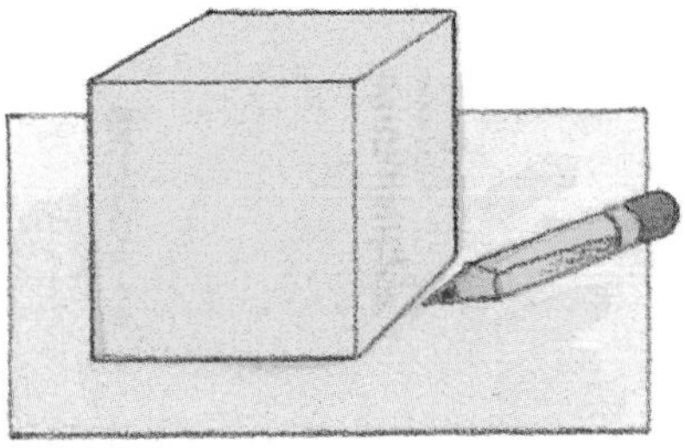
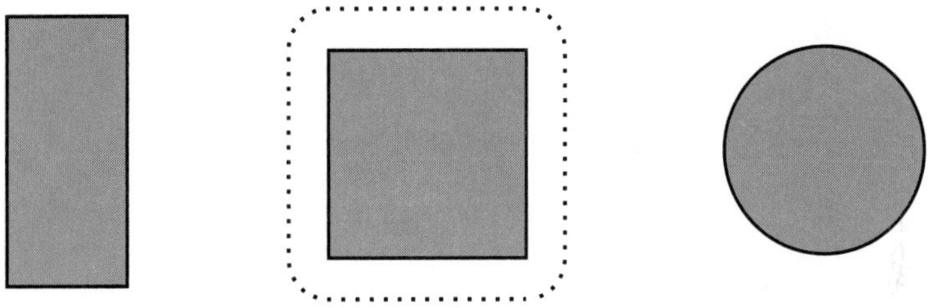

2.
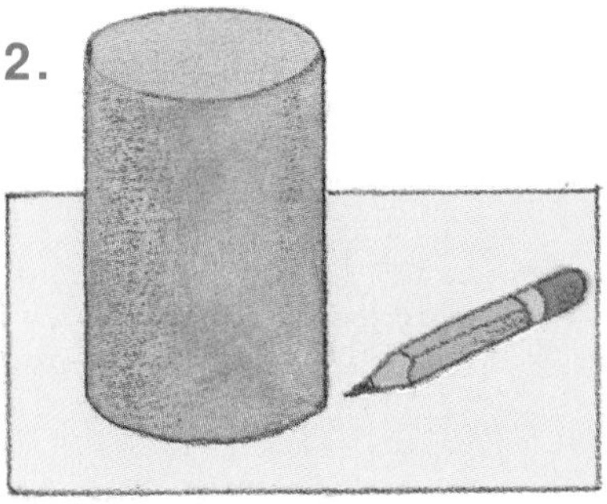
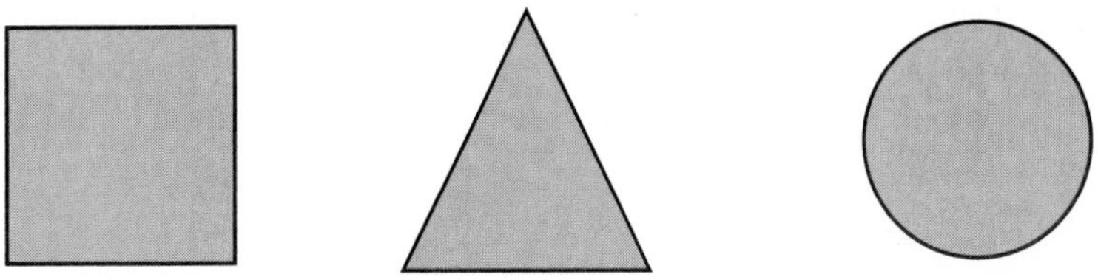

3.
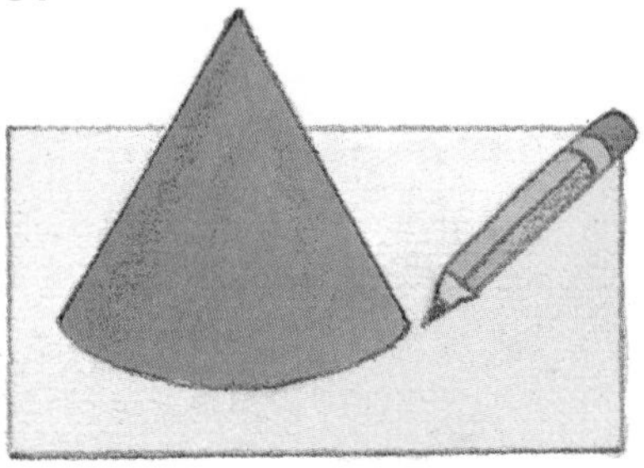
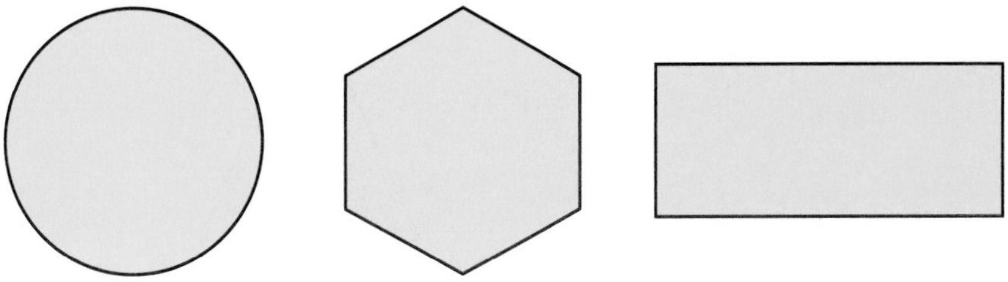

Notes for Home Children learn to solve problems involving solid shapes by using logical reasoning.

What shape can be traced?
Ring the correct shape.

4.

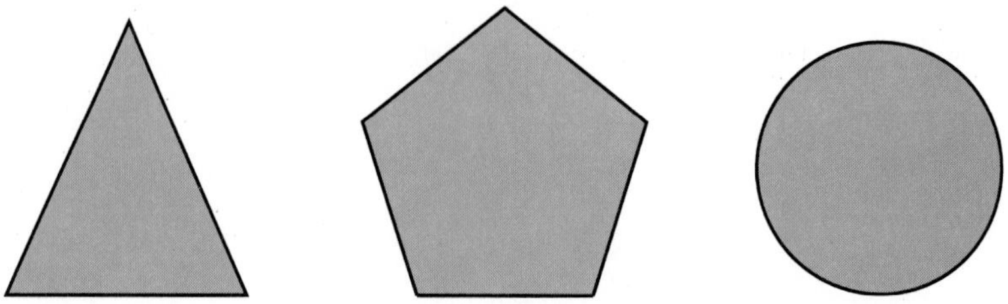

5.

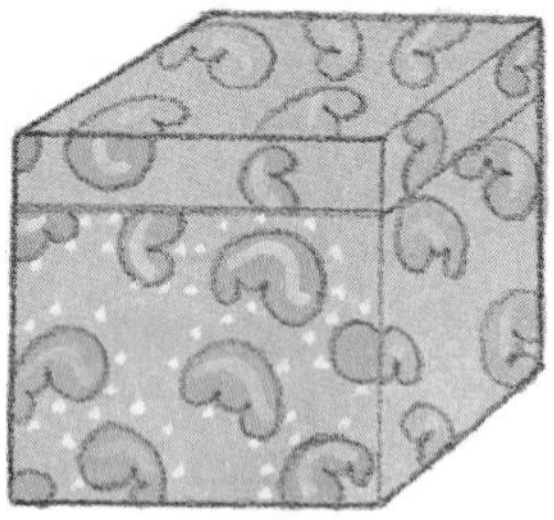

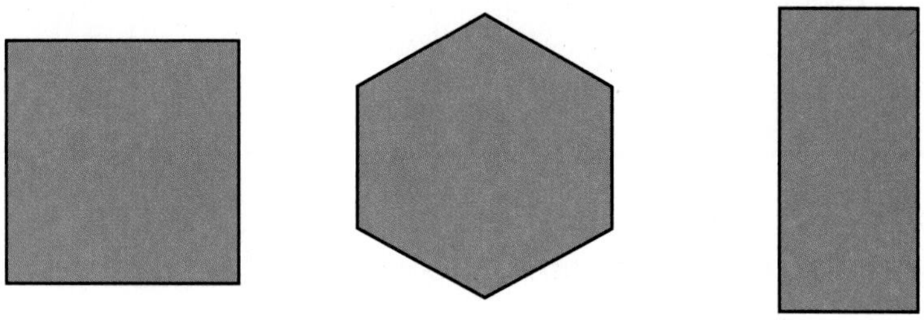

6.

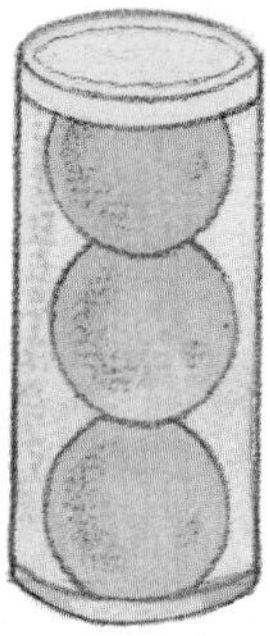

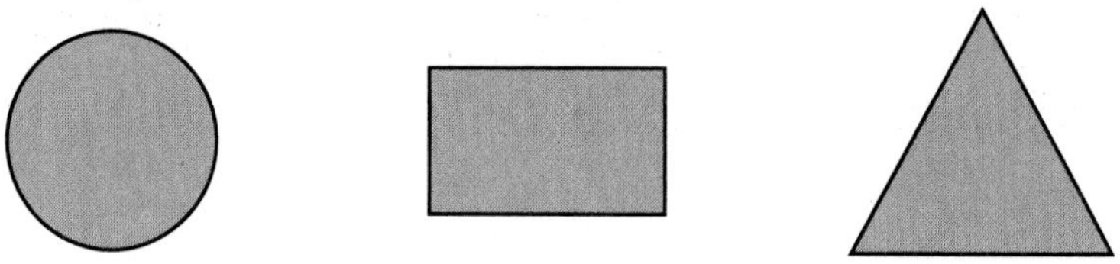

7.

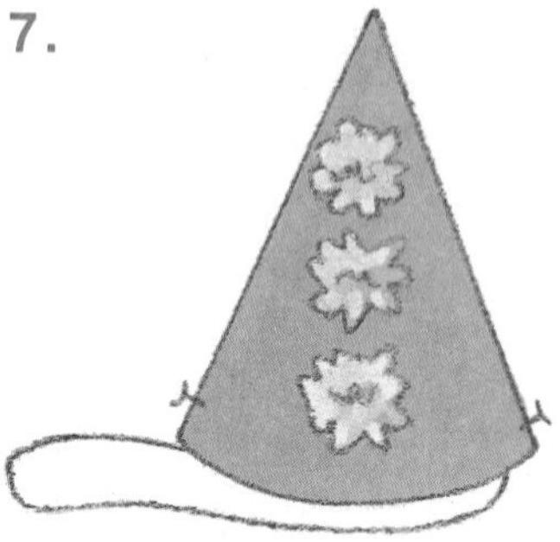

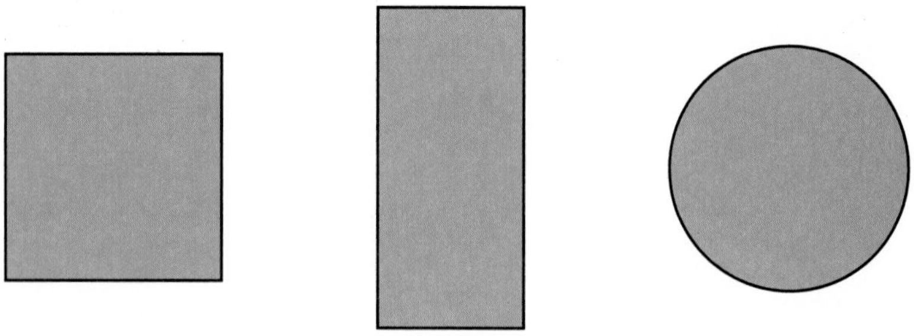

8.

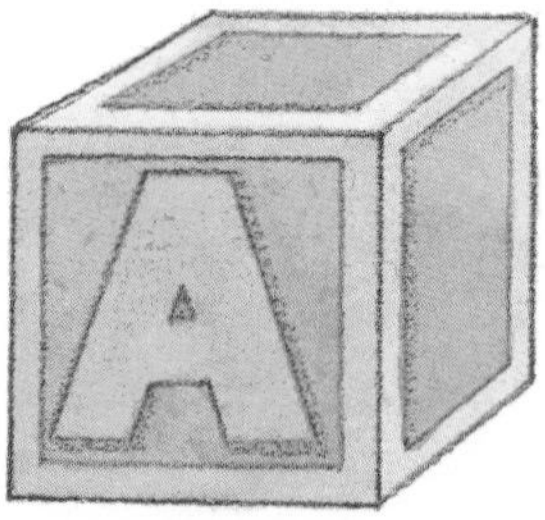

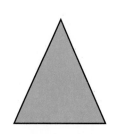

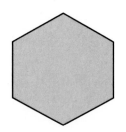

Notes for Home Children solve problems involving solid shapes by using logical reasoning.

Name

Number Sense

Name as many things as you can find in the classroom that are shaped like a rectangle.

Let's do some more!

Draw a picture of a grocery store with objects shaped like rectangles.

Notes for Home Children develop an understanding of mathematics by exploring the shapes of objects found in the classroom.

SKILLS REVIEW

Skills Review

Fill in the correct ◯.

Subtract.

1. $\begin{array}{r} 10 \\ -\ 9 \\ \hline \end{array}$ Ⓐ 1 Ⓑ 2 Ⓒ 3	2. $8 - 6 =$ Ⓐ 4 Ⓑ 3 Ⓒ 2	3. $\begin{array}{r} 7 \\ -\ 2 \\ \hline \end{array}$ Ⓐ 7 Ⓑ 5 Ⓒ 6
4. $9 - 8 =$ Ⓐ 5 Ⓑ 3 Ⓒ 1	5. $\begin{array}{r} 7 \\ -\ 3 \\ \hline \end{array}$ Ⓐ 4 Ⓑ 6 Ⓒ 8	6. $6 - 5 =$ Ⓐ 0 Ⓑ 1 Ⓒ 2

Add or subtract.

7. $2 + 7 =$	8. $\begin{array}{r} 10 \\ -\ 4 \\ \hline \end{array}$	9. $\begin{array}{r} 5 \\ +\ 5 \\ \hline \end{array}$
8 Ⓐ 9 Ⓑ 10 Ⓒ	2 Ⓐ 4 Ⓑ 6 Ⓒ	0 Ⓐ 5 Ⓑ 10 Ⓒ

Vocabulary

Match.

10. penny •	• $3 - 1 =$ 2
sum •	• $2 + 3 =$ 5
difference •	• 1 cent

Notes for Home Children review addition and subtraction facts through 10. Then they review math terms.

Name

Comparing Lengths

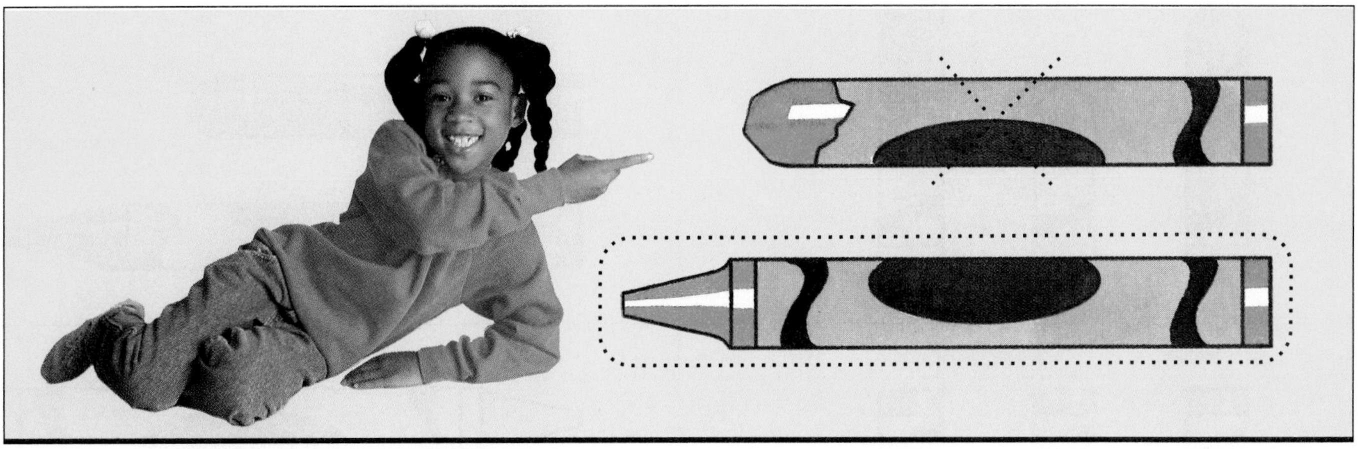

Ring the longer.
Put an X on the shorter.

1.

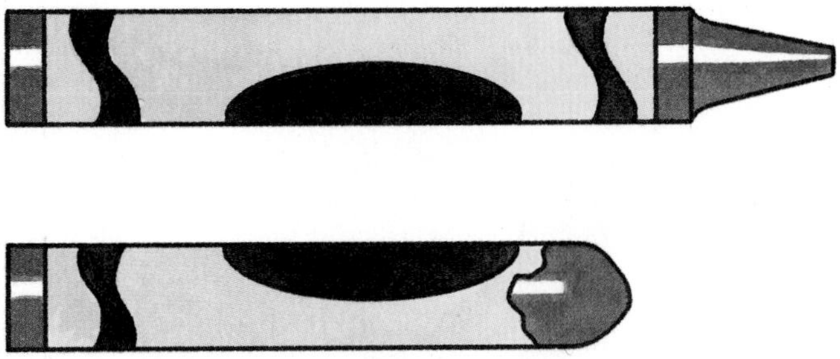

2.

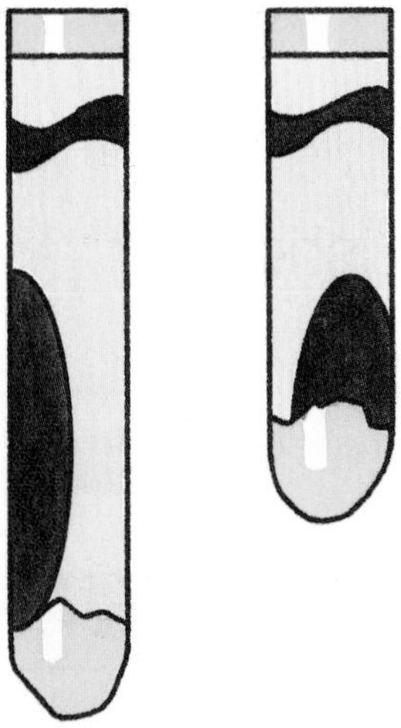

3.

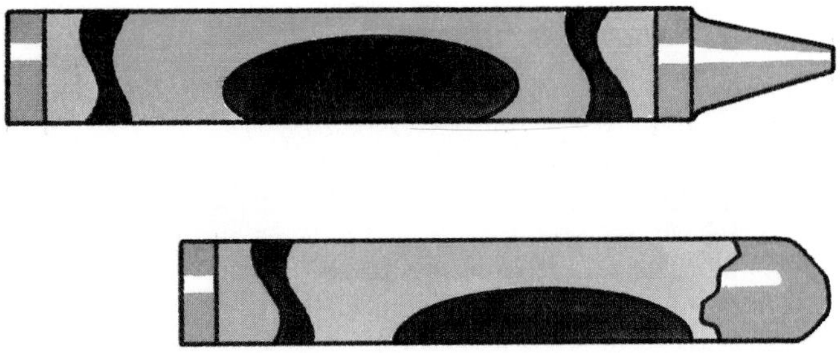

4.

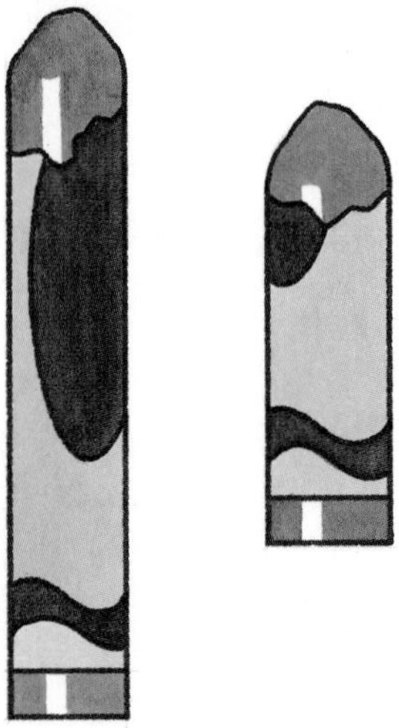

Notes for Home Children compare two objects and identify the longer one.

Ring the longest.

5.

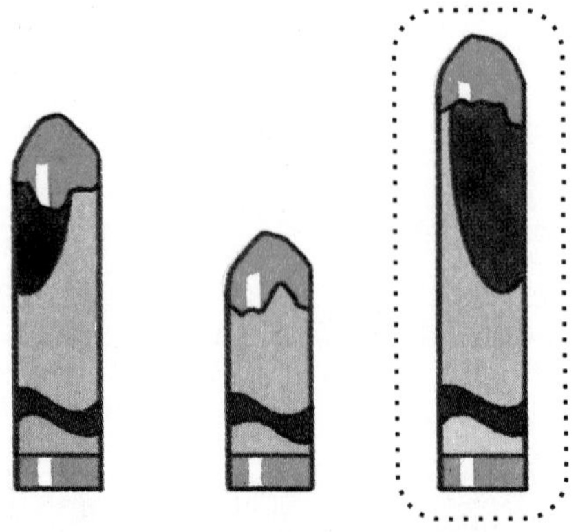

6.

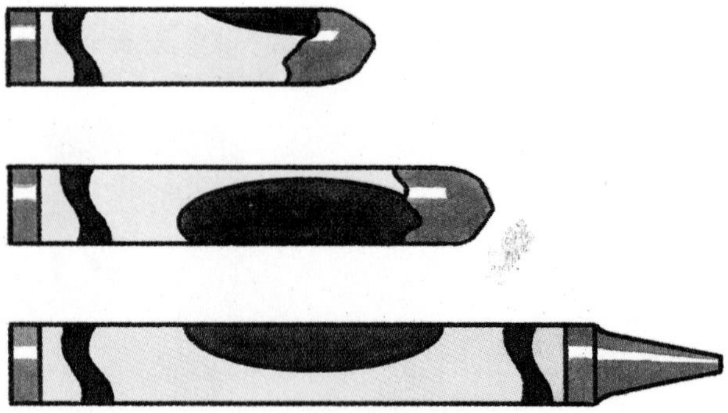

7.

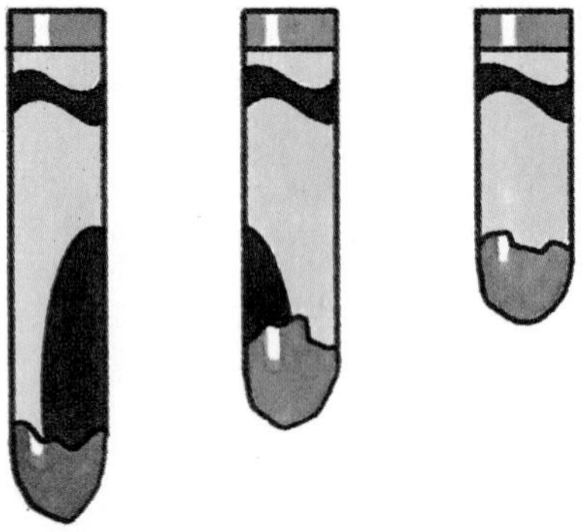

8.

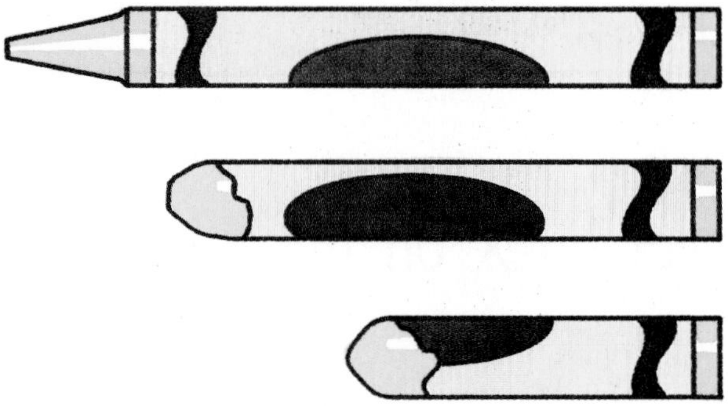

Ring the shortest.

9.

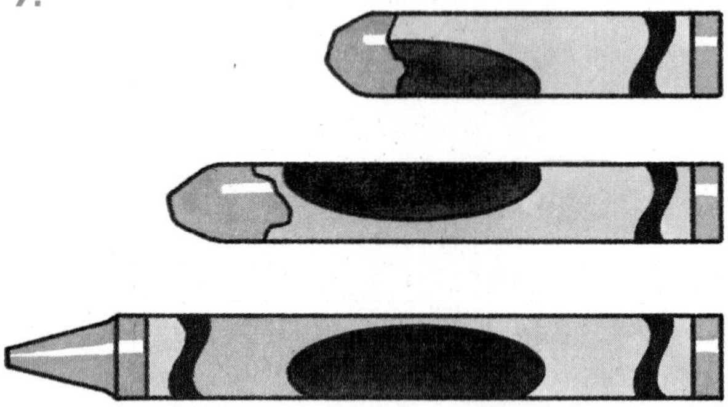

10.

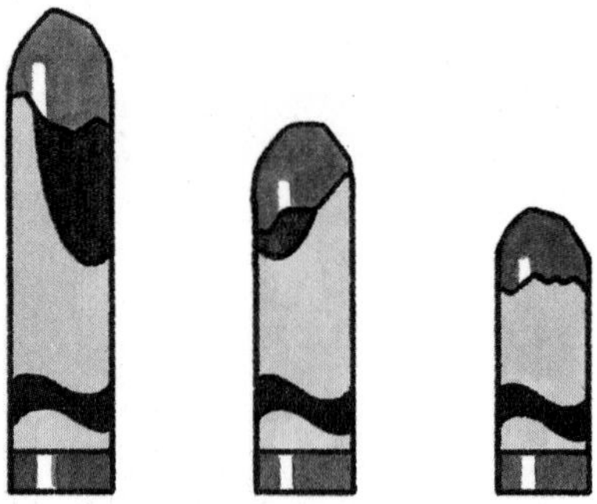

11.

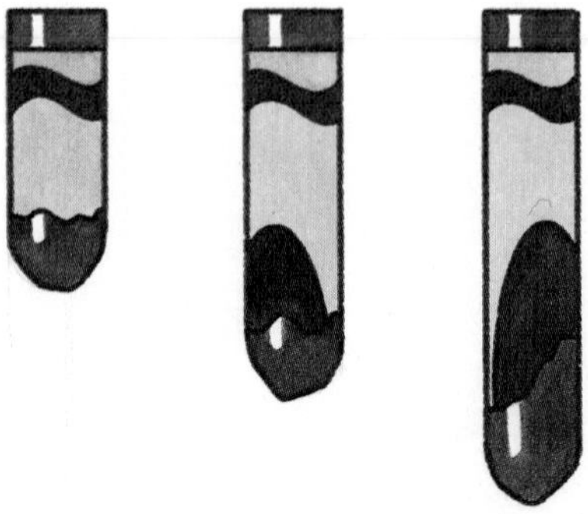

12.

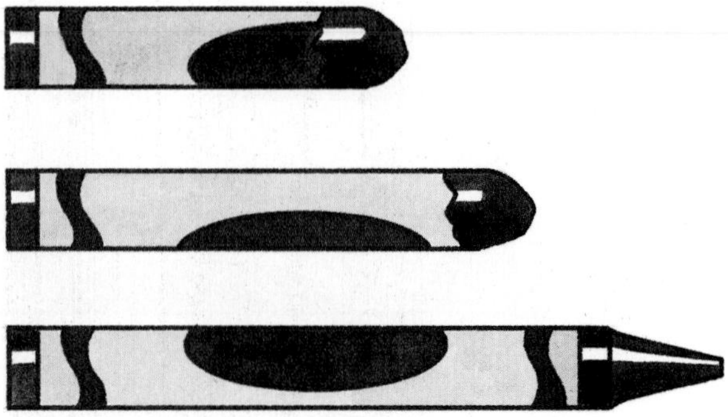

Notes for Home Children compare three objects and identify the longest or the shortest.

Name

Measuring Length

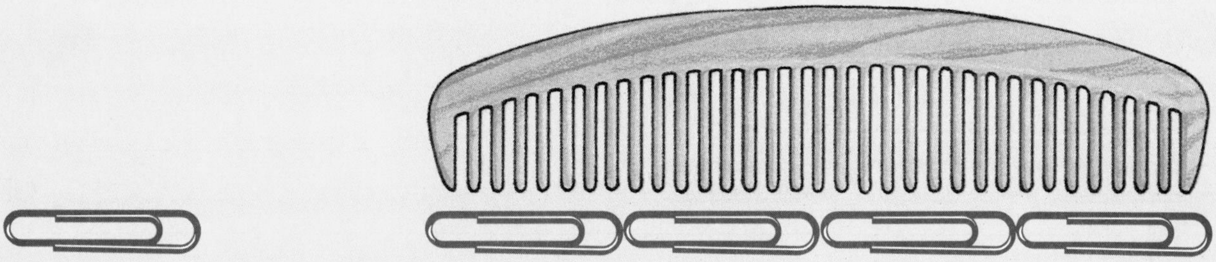

1 **unit** about __4__ **units** long

About how long is each object?

1.

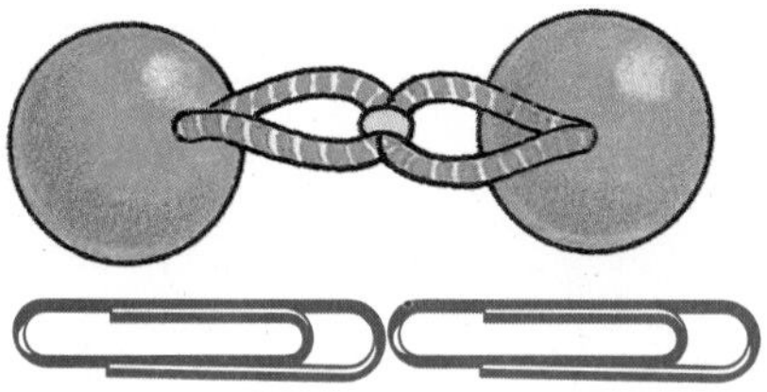

____ units

2.

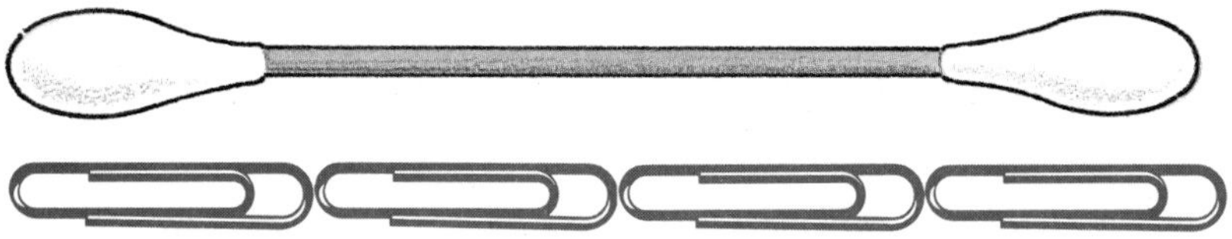

____ units

3.

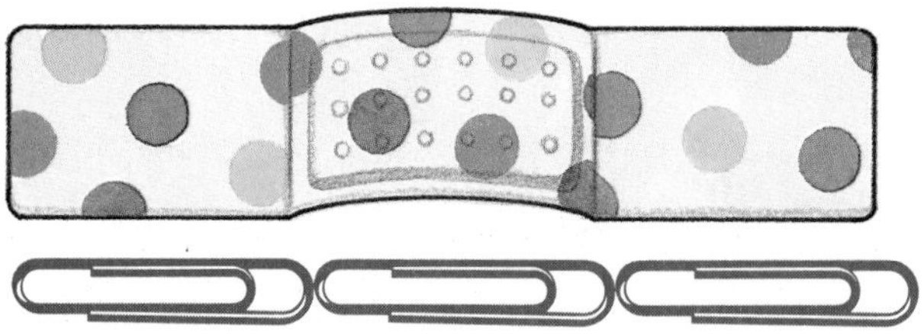

____ units

4.

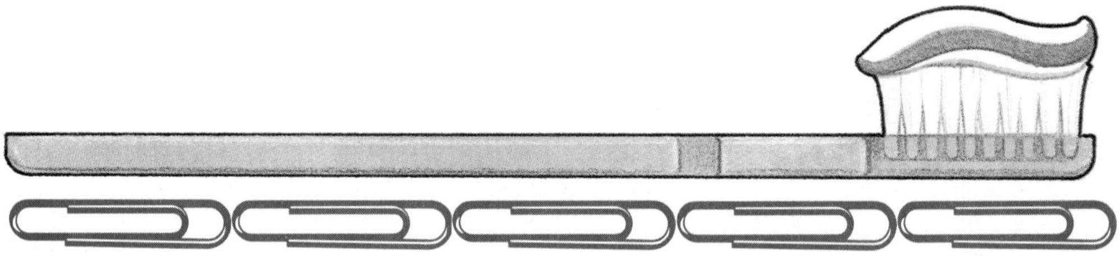

____ units

Notes for Home Children measure lengths of objects using nonstandard units of measure.

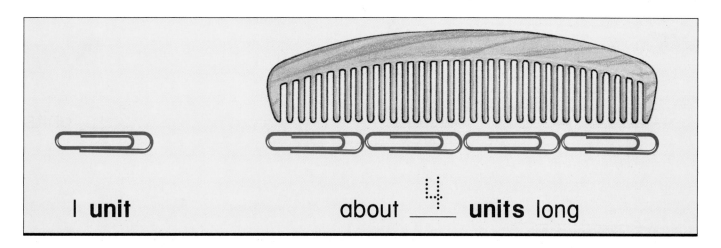

About how long is each object?

5.

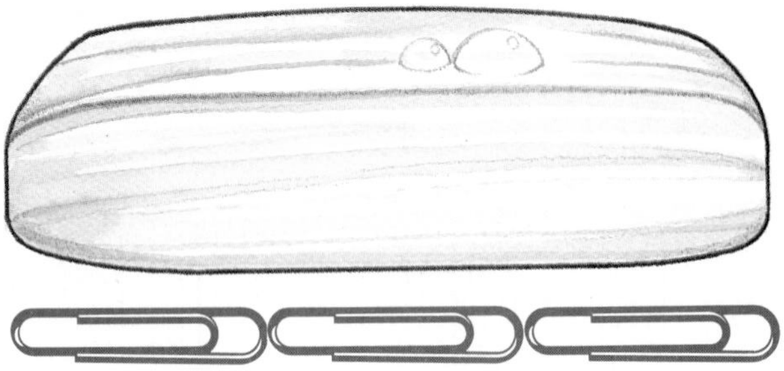

3 units

6.

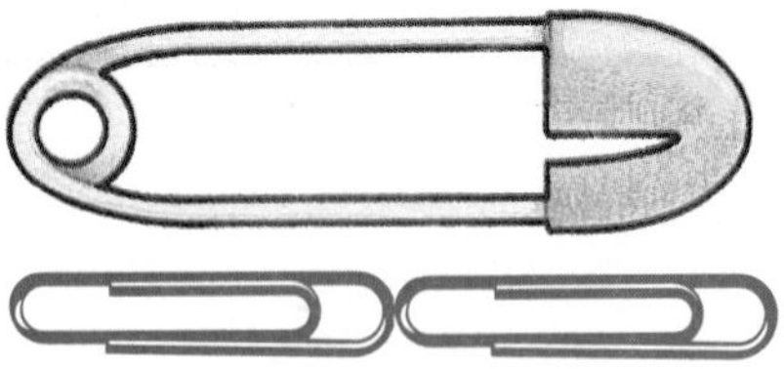

____ units

7.

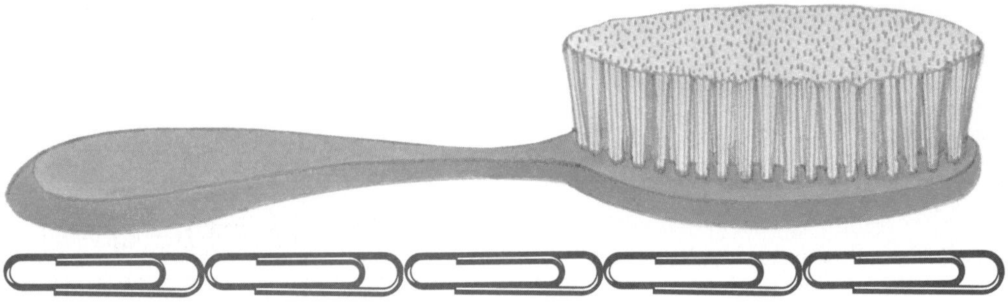

____ units

8.

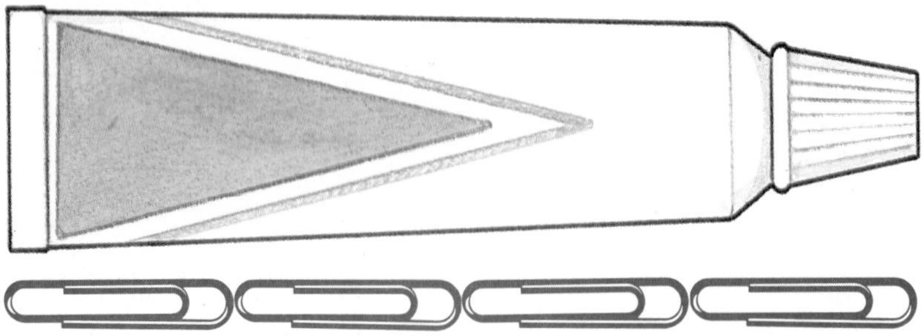

____ units

9.

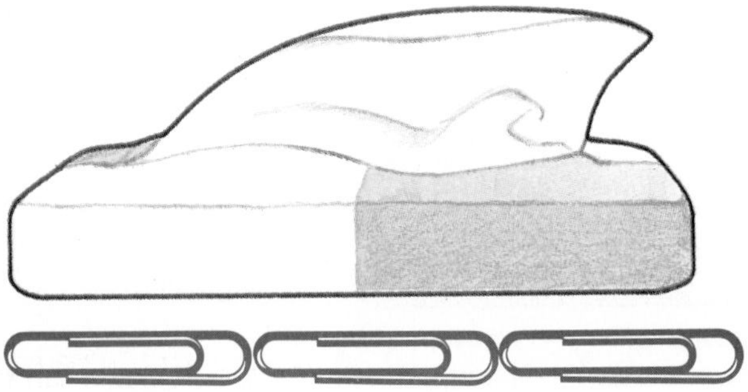

____ units

Notes for Home Children measure lengths of objects using nonstandard units of measure.

Name ____________________

Comparing Units of Measure

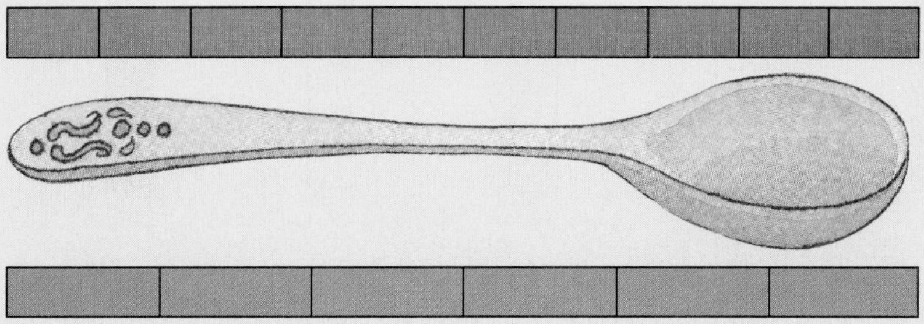

10 red units

6 blue units

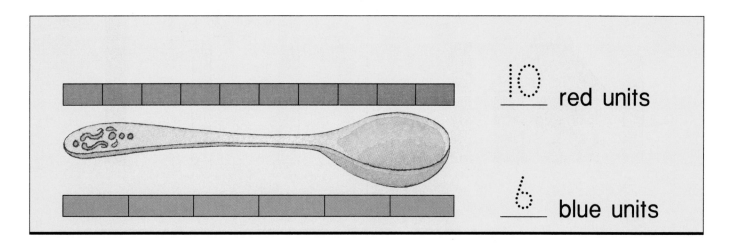

About how long is each object?

1.

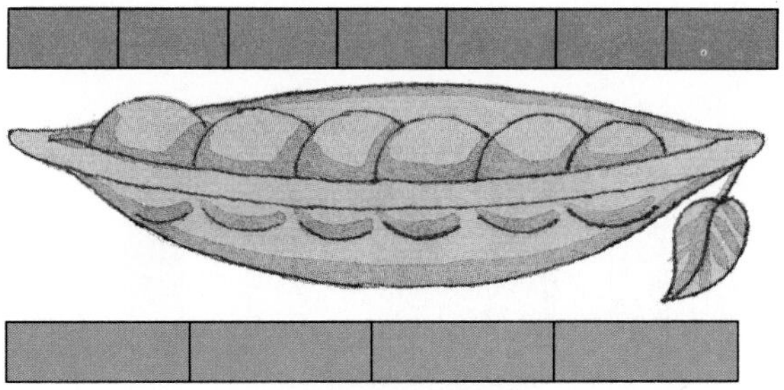

____ red units

____ blue units

2.

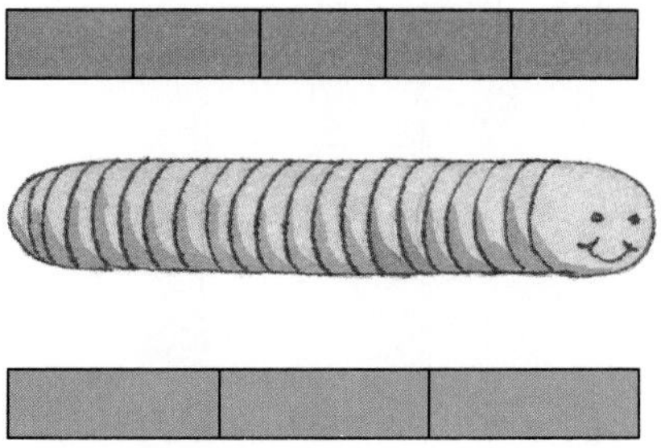

____ red units

____ blue units

3.

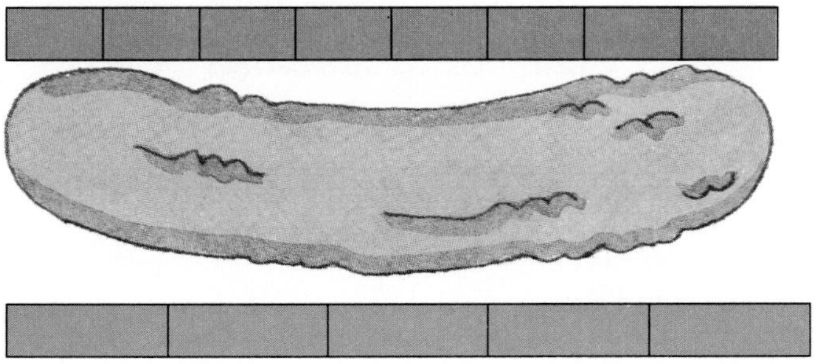

____ red units

____ blue units

Notes for Home Children measure and compare the lengths of objects using two different nonstandard units of measure.

About how tall is each object?

4.

3 red units ___ blue units

5.

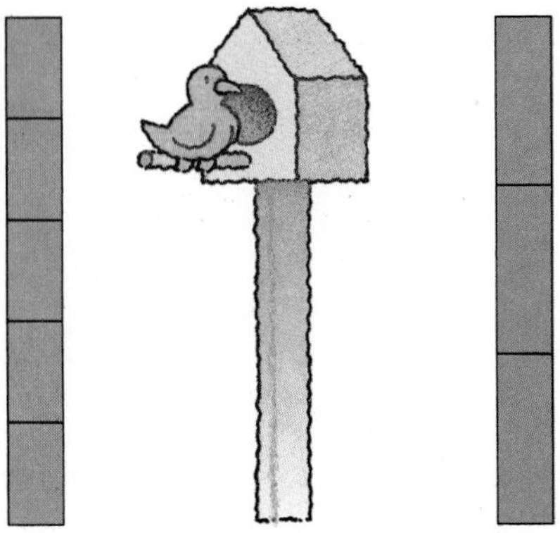

___ red units ___ blue units

6.

___ red units ___ blue units

7.

___ red units ___ blue units

Notes for Home Children measure and compare the heights of objects using two different nonstandard units of measure.

Name

Using a Ruler

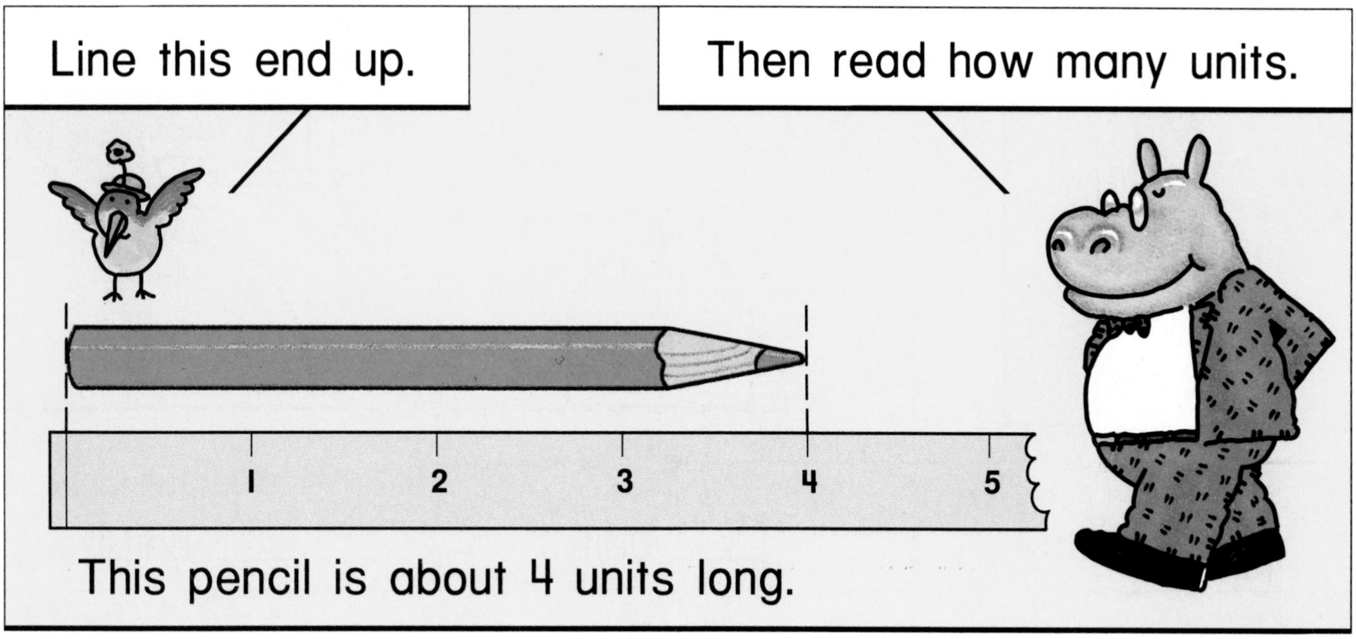

This pencil is about 4 units long.

Use a ruler.
About how long is each pencil?

1. 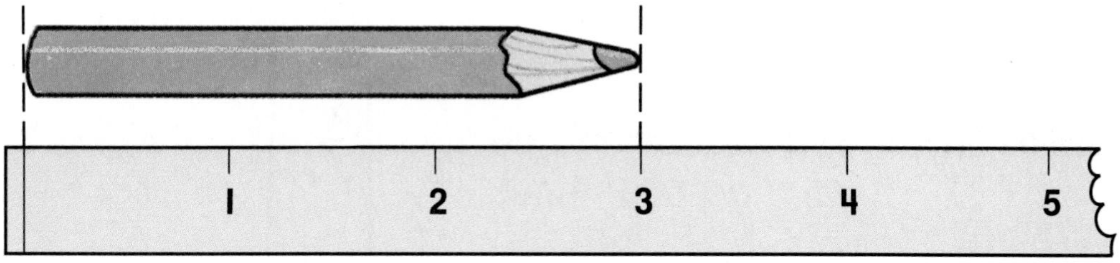

3 units

2. 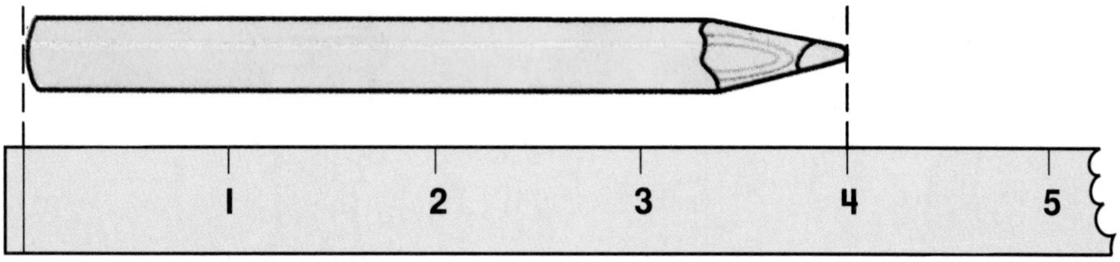

_____ units

3. 

_____ units

4. 

_____ units

Notes for Home Children explore at the CONCRETE level using a ruler with nonstandard units to measure length.

Use a ruler.
About how tall is each object?

5.

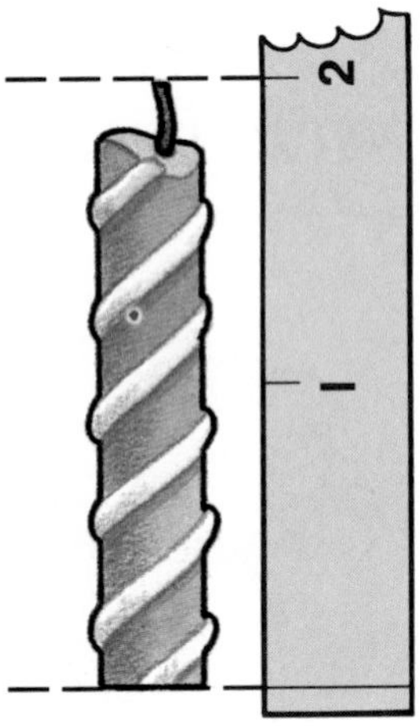

2 units

6.

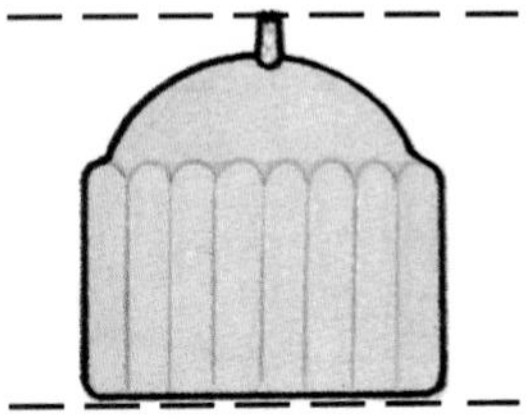

____ unit

7.

____ units

8.

____ units

9.

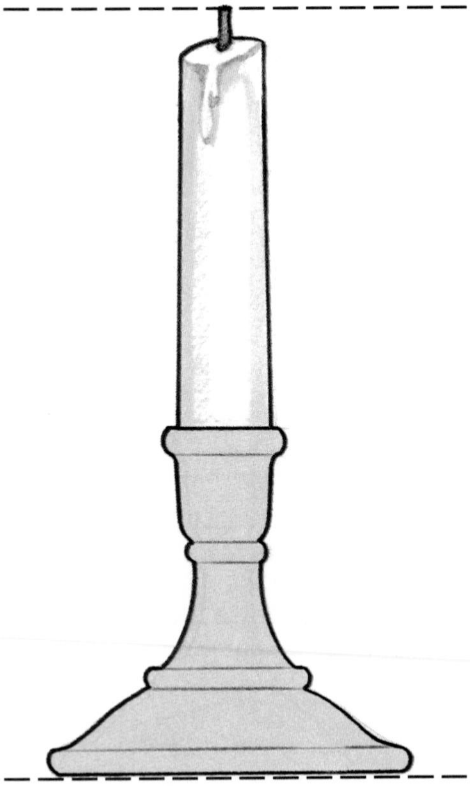

____ units

Notes for Home Children explore at the CONCRETE level using a ruler with nonstandard units to measure height.

Name

Measuring Inches

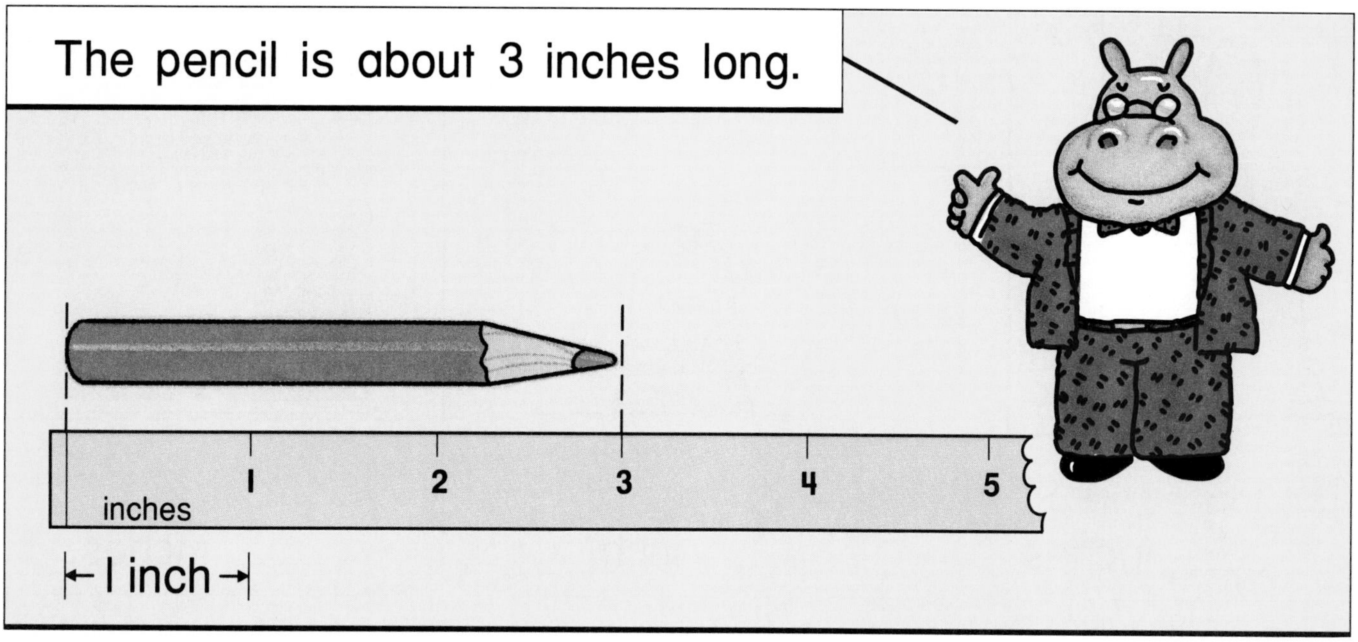

Use an inch ruler.
About how long is each pencil?

1. 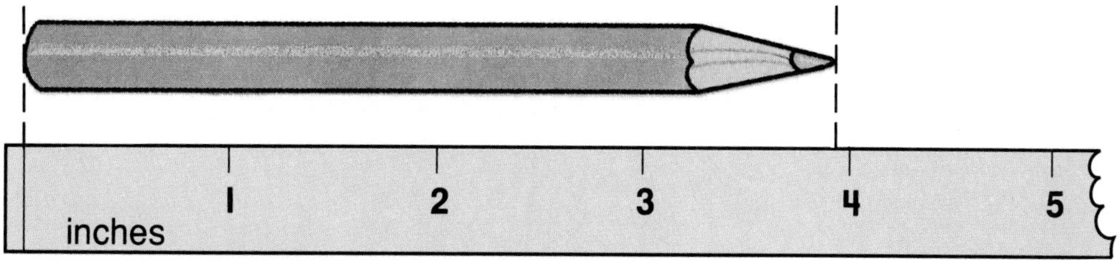

__4__ inches

2. 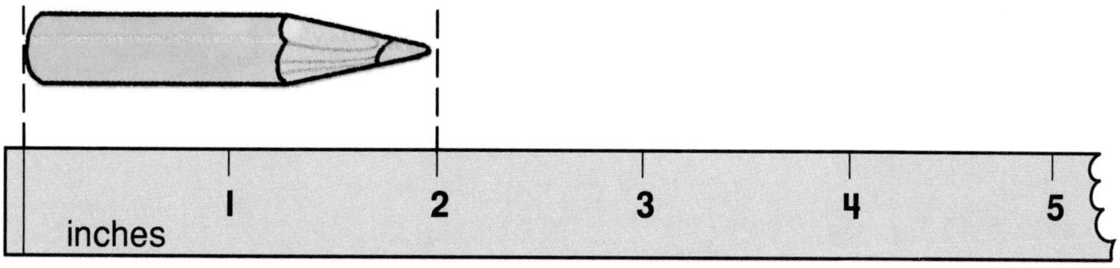

____ inches

3. 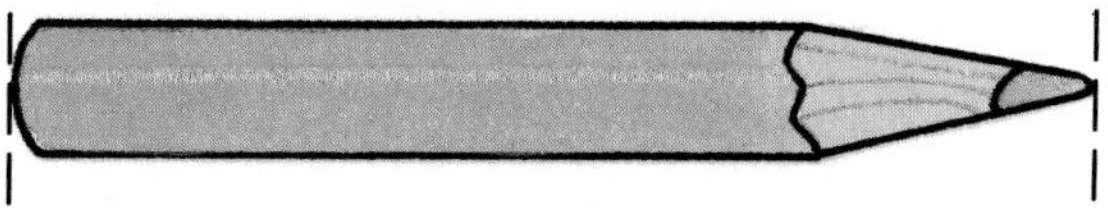

____ inches

4. 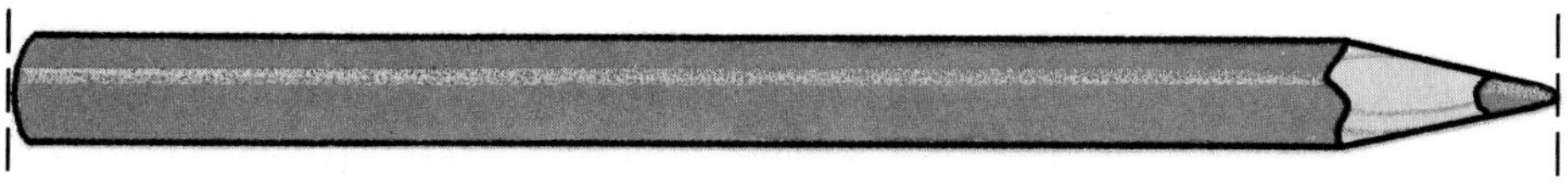

____ inches

Notes for Home Children explore at the CONCRETE level using an inch ruler to measure length.

Use an inch ruler.
About how tall is each object?

5.

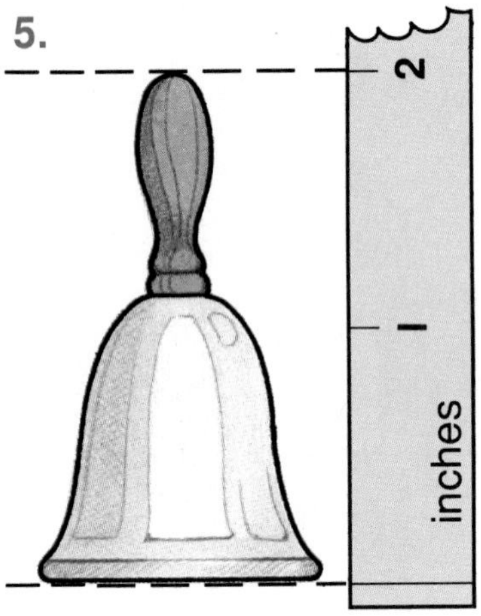

2 inches

6.

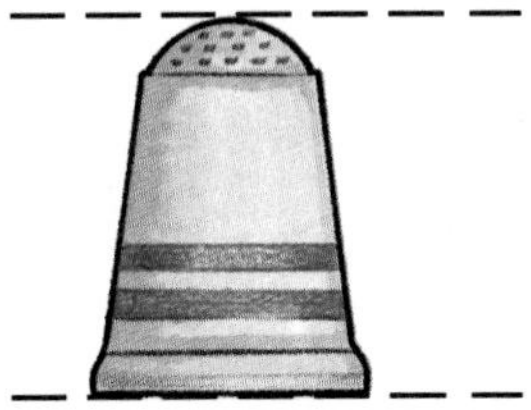

____ inch

7.

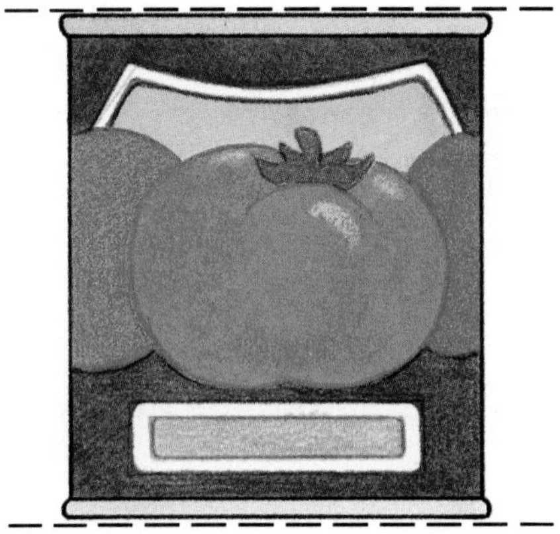

____ inches

8.

____ inches

9.

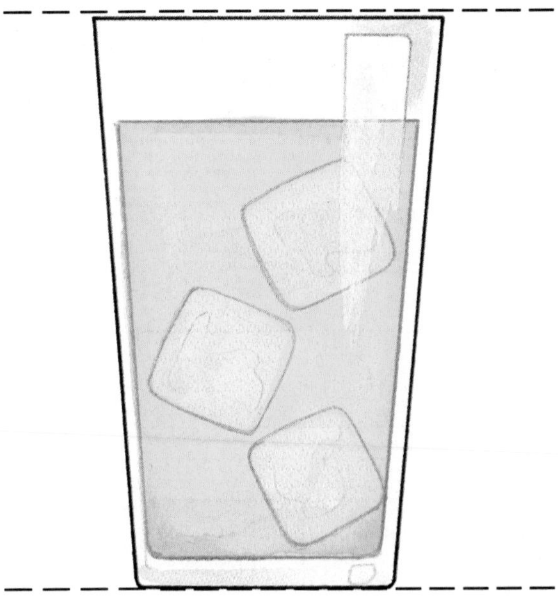

____ inches

Notes for Home Children explore at the CONCRETE level using an inch ruler to measure height.

See More Practice Set B on page 195.

Name _______________ **Activity**

Measuring Centimeters

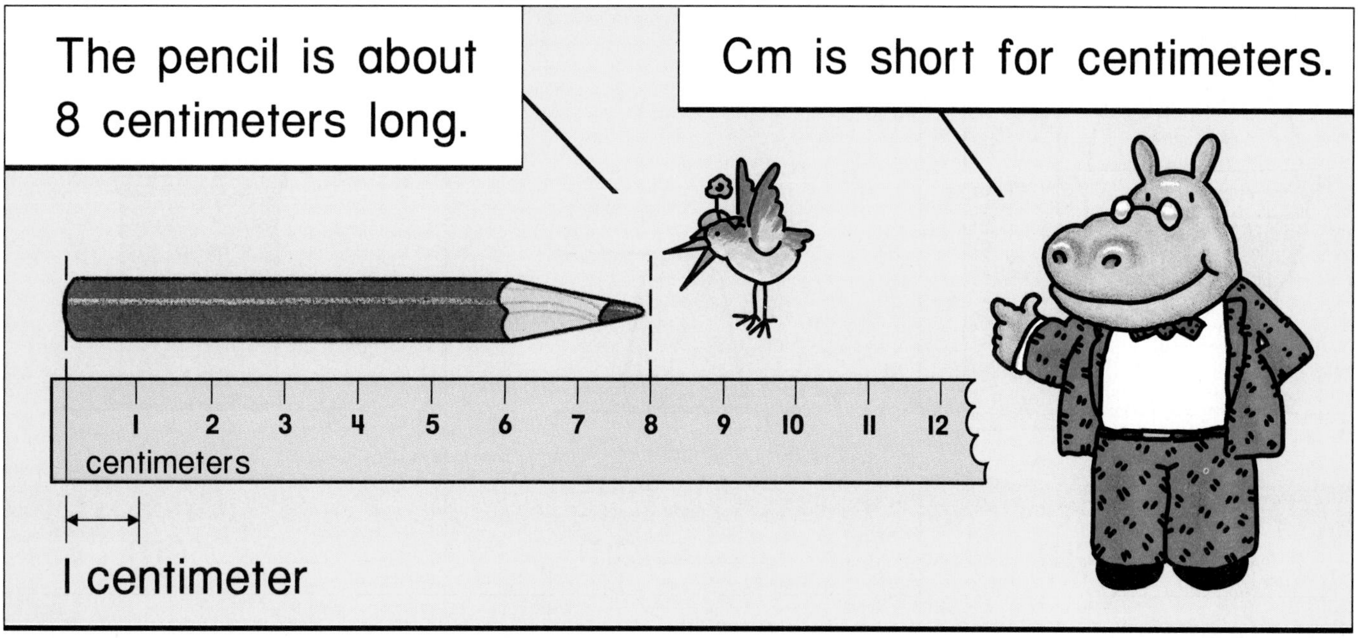

Use a centimeter ruler.
About how long is each pencil?

1.

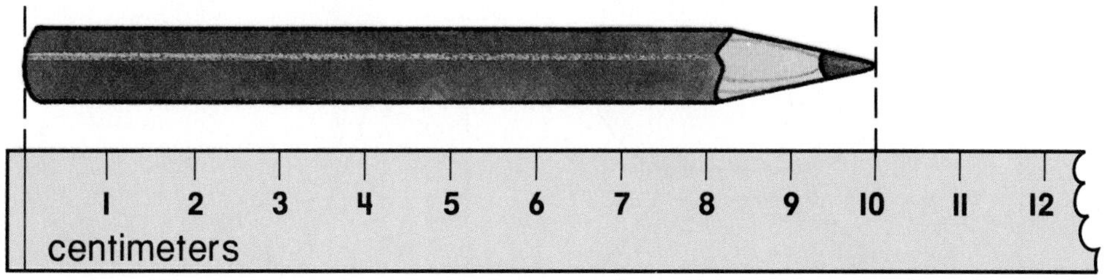

10 cm

2.

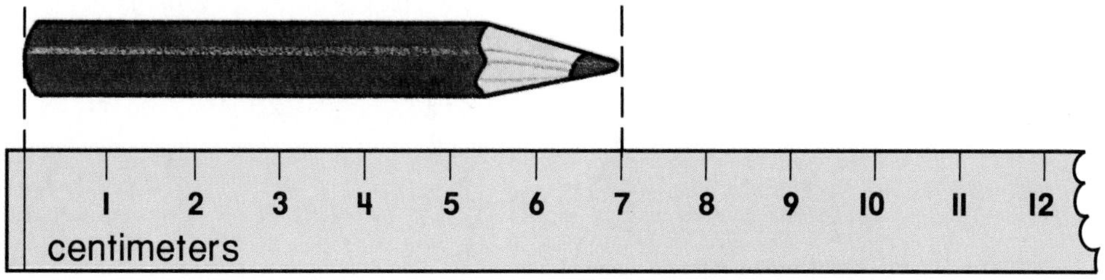

_____ cm

3.

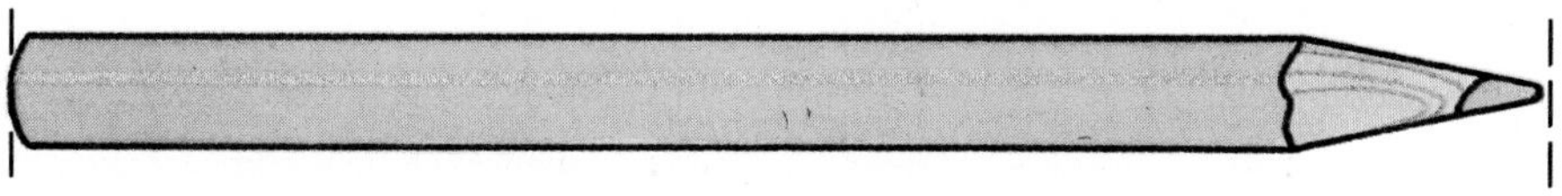

_____ cm

4.

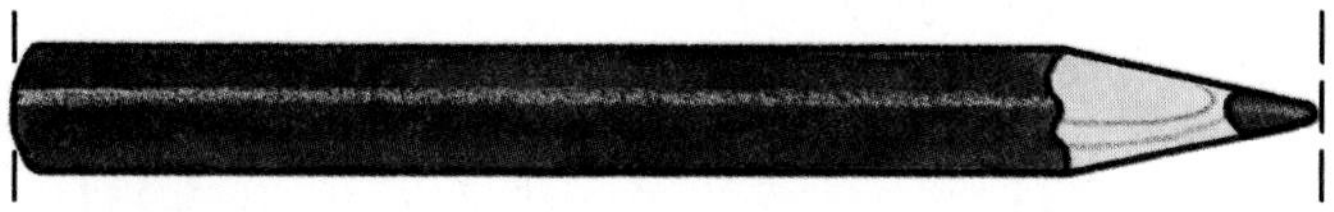

_____ cm

Notes for Home Children explore at the CONCRETE level using a centimeter ruler to measure length.

Use a centimeter ruler.
About how tall is each object?

5.

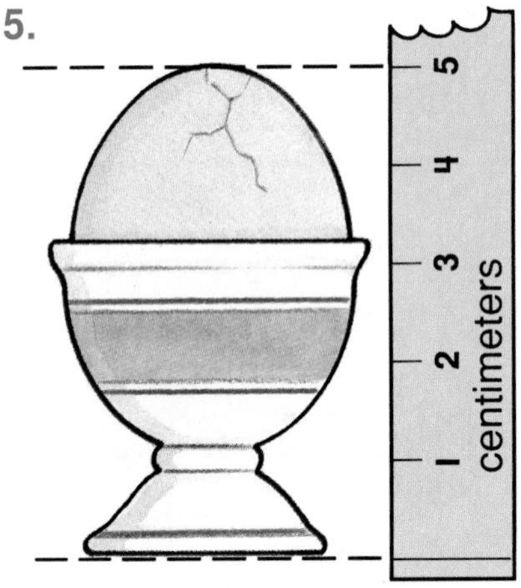

5 ___ cm

6.

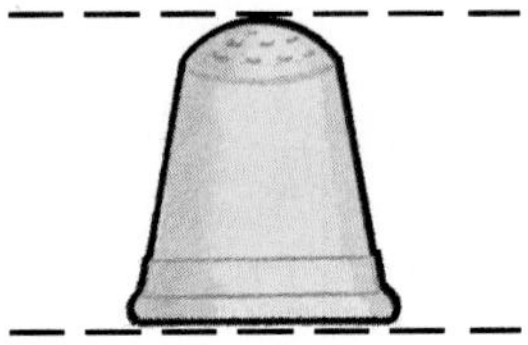

___ cm

7.

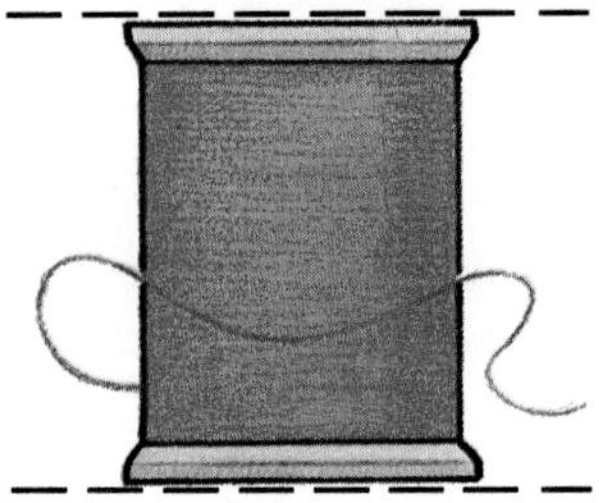

___ cm

8.

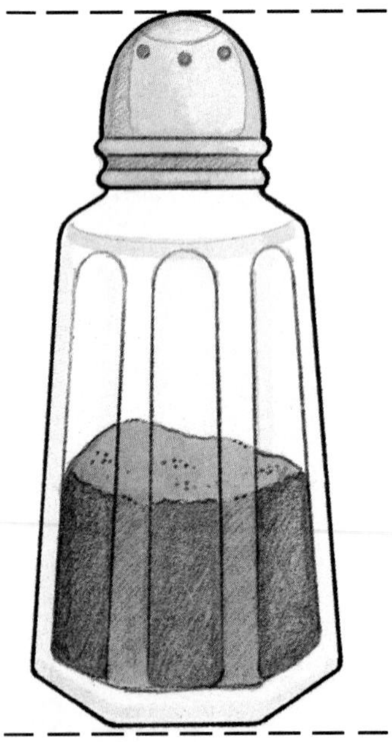

___ cm

9.

___ cm

10.

___ cm

Notes for Home Children explore at the CONCRETE level using a centimeter ruler to measure height.

Name ______________________

PROBLEM-SOLVING STRATEGY Activity

Try and Check

I guess that the crayon is 4 inches long.
I measured the crayon. It is 3 inches long.

Guess about how many inches long.
Check with an inch ruler to measure.

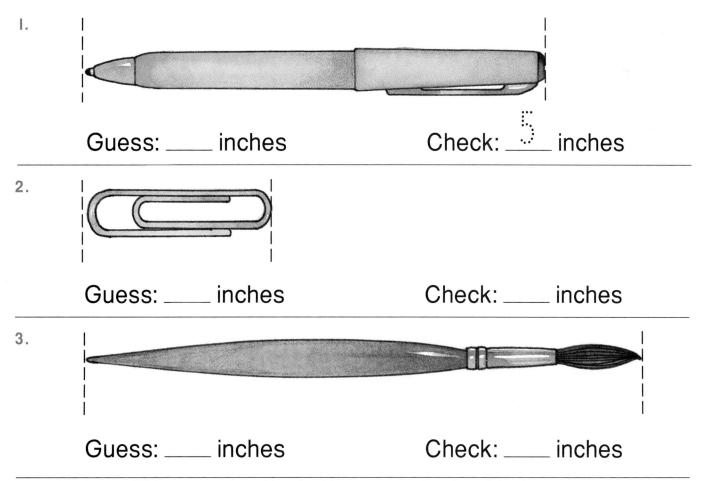

1.

Guess: ____ inches   Check: 5 inches

2.

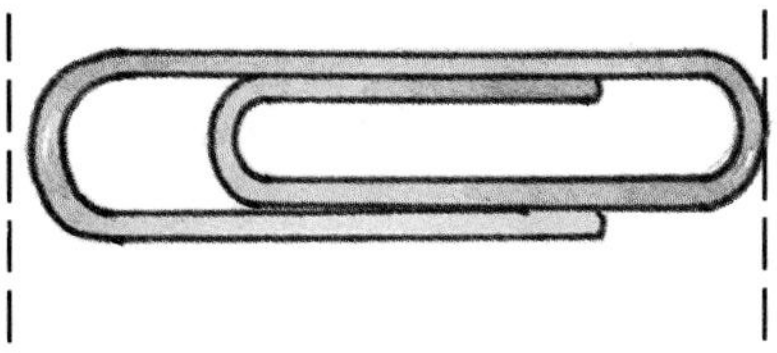

Guess: ____ inches   Check: ____ inches

3.

Guess: ____ inches   Check: ____ inches

Notes for Home Children learn to solve problems involving measurement by trying and checking.

Guess about how many inches long.
Check with an inch ruler to measure.

	Guess	Check
4. your pencil 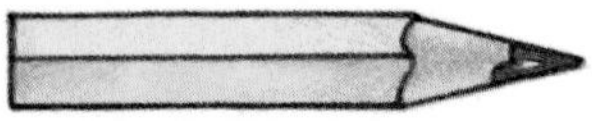	____ inches	____ inches
5. your book 	____ inches	____ inches
6. your shoe 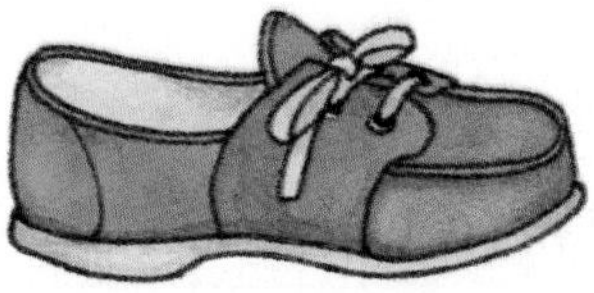	____ inches	____ inches
7. your crayon 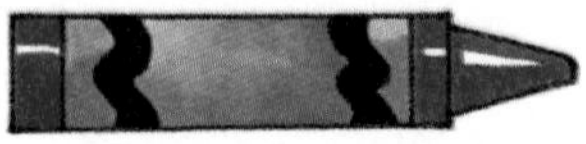	____ inches	____ inches
8. your hand 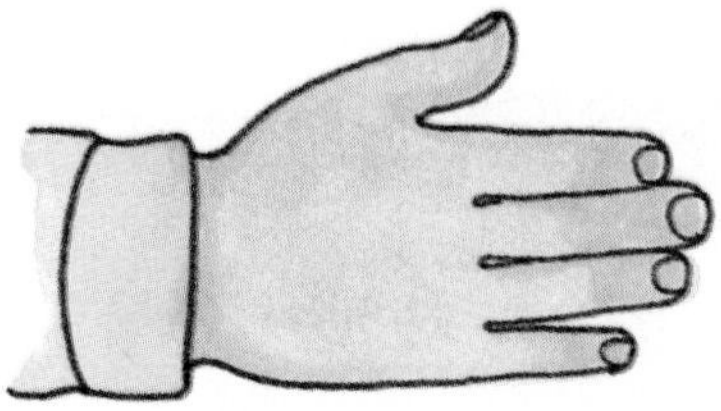	____ inches	____ inches

Notes for Home Children solve problems involving measurement by trying and checking.

Name

Problem-Solving Workshop

Explore as a Team

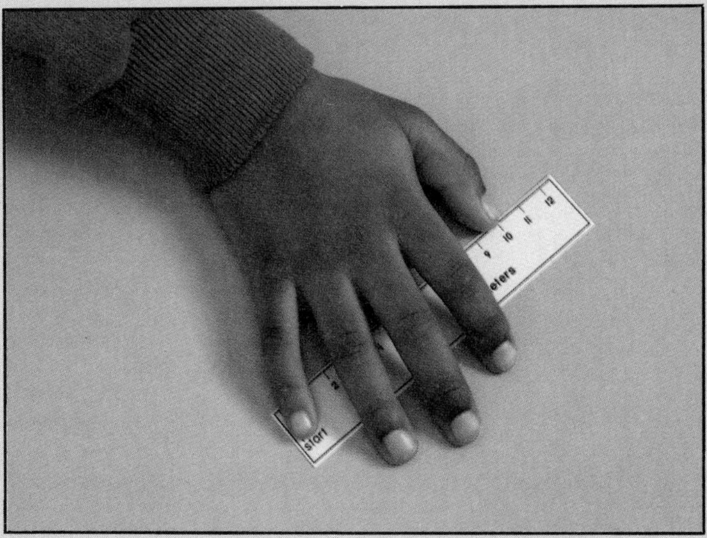

Work with a partner.
Spread your fingers out.
Use your centimeter ruler.
Measure the distance between the tip of your little finger and the tip of your thumb.

The hand in the picture measures 10 centimeters.
Ten **centimeters** is one **decimeter**.

1. Name objects in your classroom that are about one decimeter long.

2. About how many decimeters high is this page? Check your measure by using your hand.

3. About how many decimeters wide is your desk? Check your measure by using your hand.

Notes for Home Children explore with a partner at the CONCRETE level using their hands as a decimeter ruler.

Problem-Solving Workshop

Explore with a Computer

Primary Geometry Project

1. The rectangles make a ruler.
About how long is the hose?

☐ units

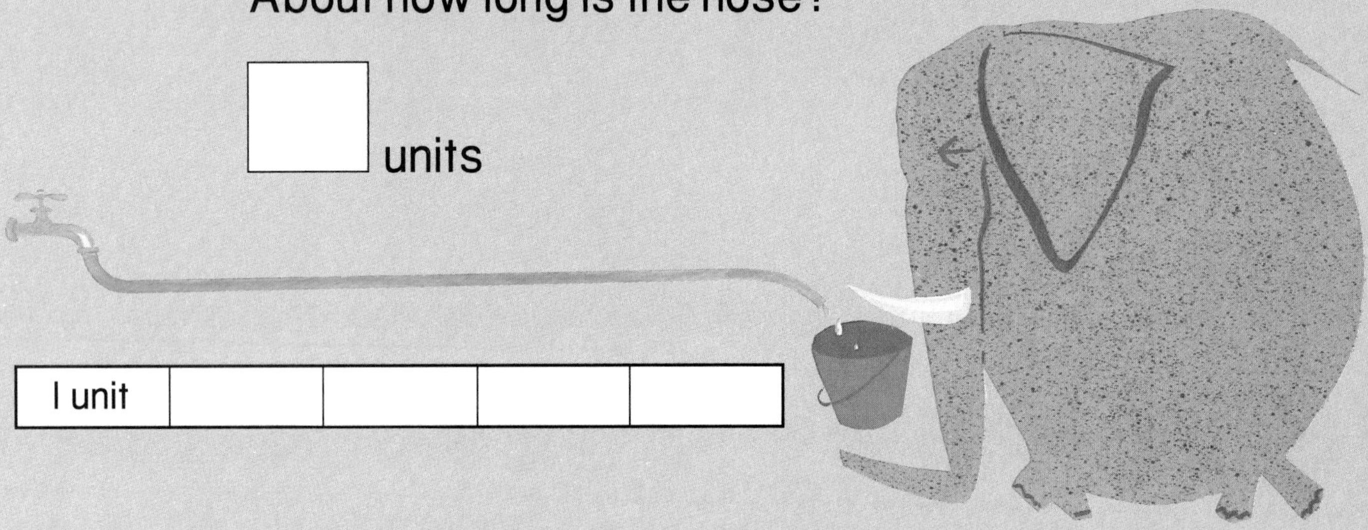

2. At the computer, get these shapes.

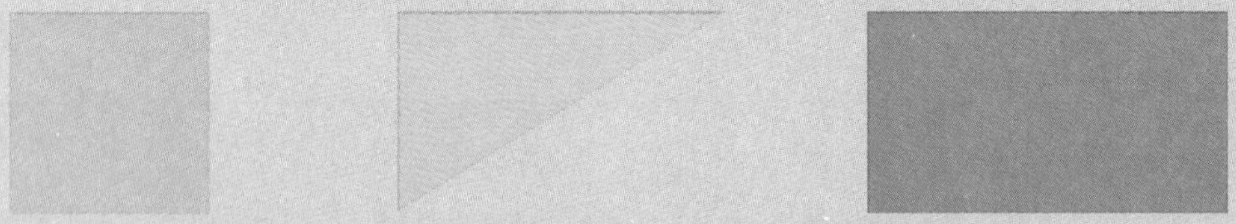

3. About how long is one side of each shape?
Measure the side.
Mark the side you measure.

square ☐ units triangle ☐ units

rectangle ☐ units

Notes for Home Children learn to measure items to determine lengths in units. Then they measure a side of a square, a triangle, and a rectangle at the computer and record the length of each in units.

Name

More Practice

Set A Use after page 174.

Match.

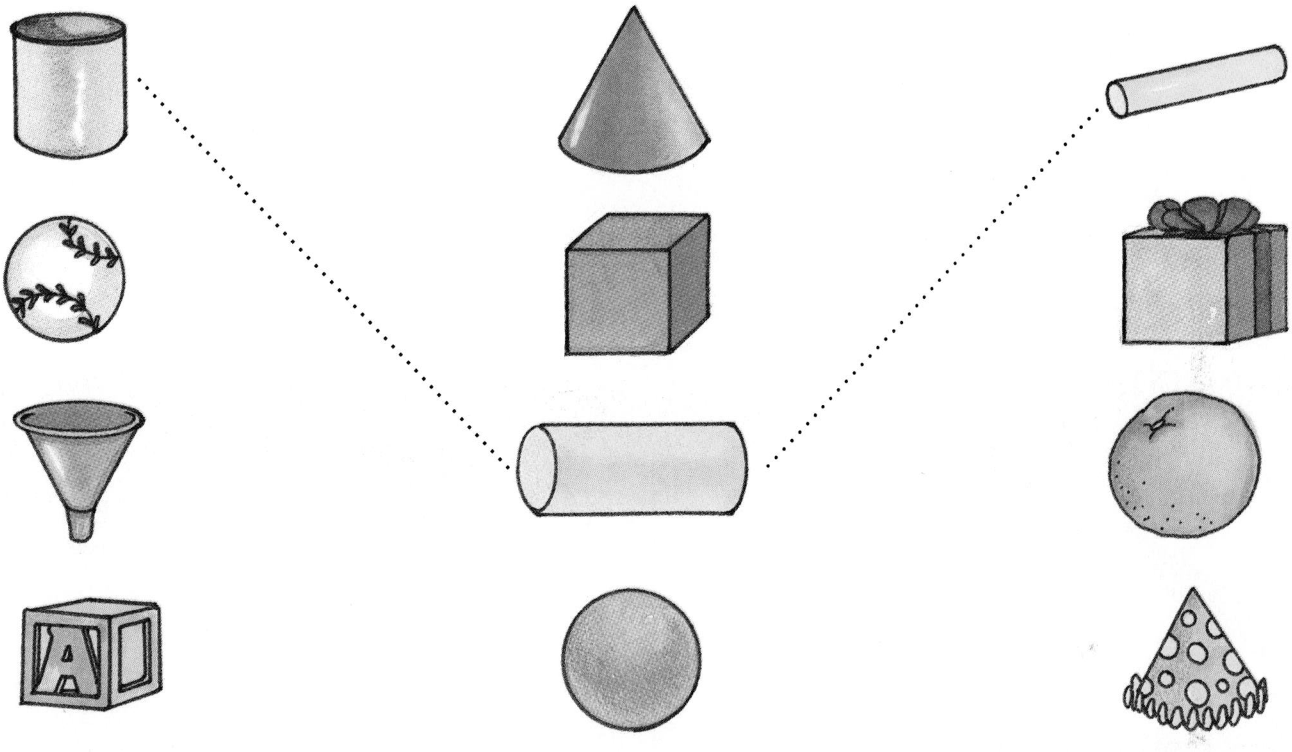

Set B Use after page 188.

About how long or tall is each object?

1.

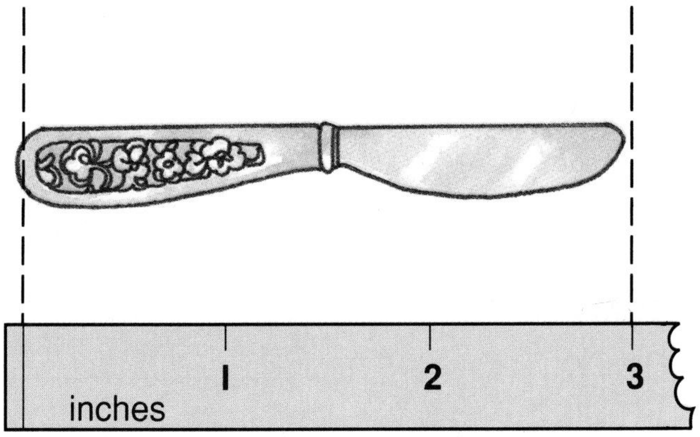

3 inches

2.

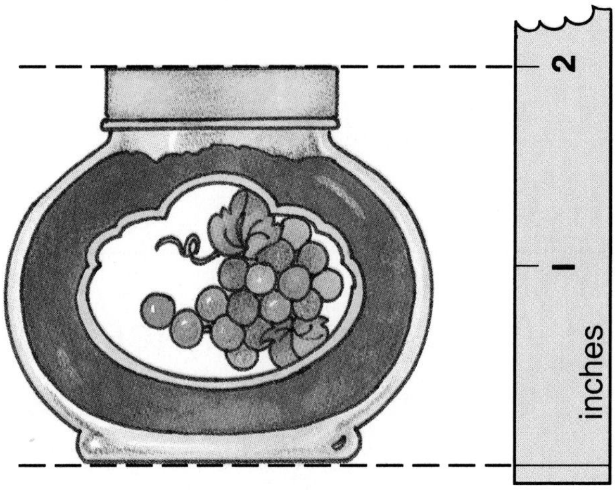

____ inches

Notes for Home Set A: Children match cones, cubes, cylinders, and spheres.
Set B: Children use an inch ruler to practice measuring lengths or heights of objects.

Enrichment

A **foot** is 12 **inches**.
The longer edge of this page is about 1 foot.

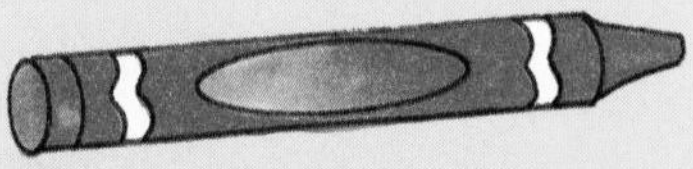

You use **inches** to measure small objects.

You use **feet** to measure large objects.

Which is the better measure to use?
Ring inches or feet.

1. 

inches

feet

2. 

inches

feet

3. 

inches

feet

4. 

inches

feet

5. Name some things in your room that are about one foot long.

____

6. About how many feet wide is your desk?
Use the edge of this page to check. ____________

7. About how many feet wide is your teacher's desk? Use the edge of this page to check. ____________

Notes for Home Children are challenged to find the better unit of measure to use for measuring different lengths and explore the concept of foot at a **CONCRETE** level.

Name

Chapter 6 Review/Test

1. Ring the longer pencil.

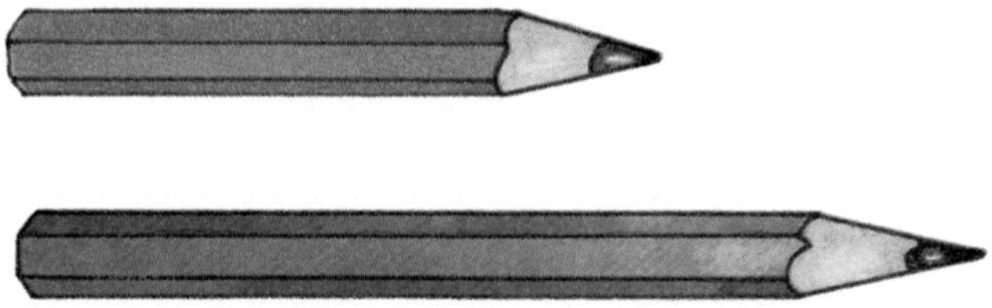

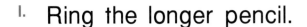

2. Use a centimeter ruler. About how long is the crayon?

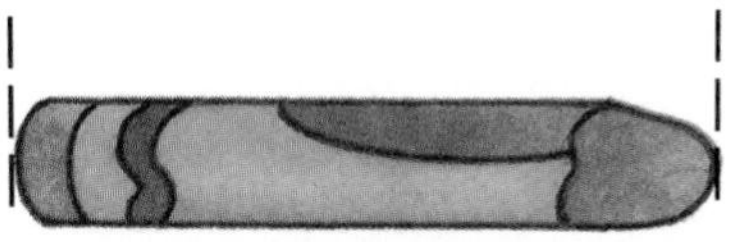

____ cm

3. How many triangles?

____ triangles

4. About how long is the pencil?

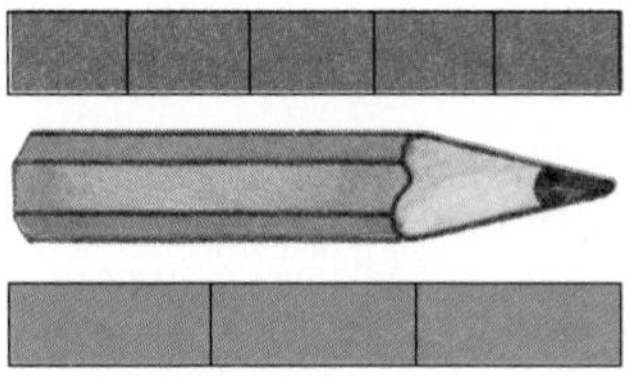

____ red units

____ blue units

5. What shape can be traced? Ring the shape.

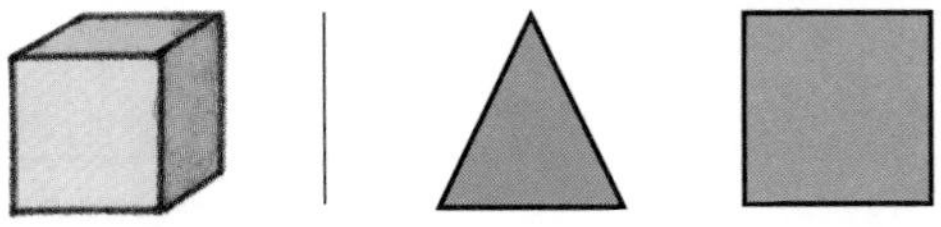

6. Ring the cone.

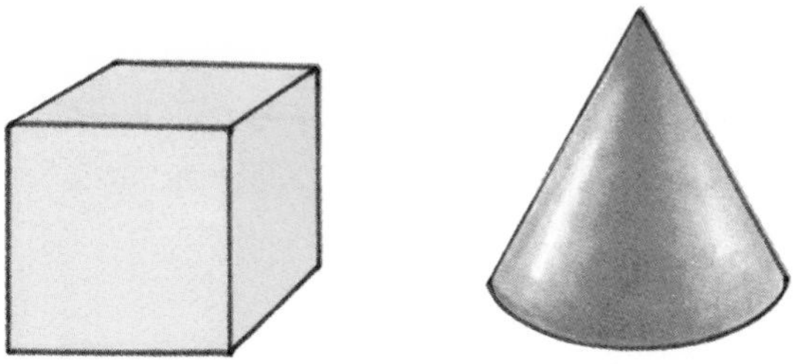

7. Copy the shape. Then ring the name.

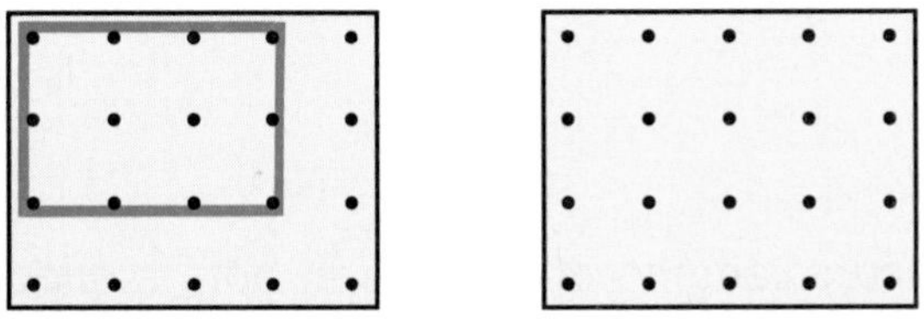

triangle

rectangle

8. Guess how many inches long. Then measure with the inch ruler.

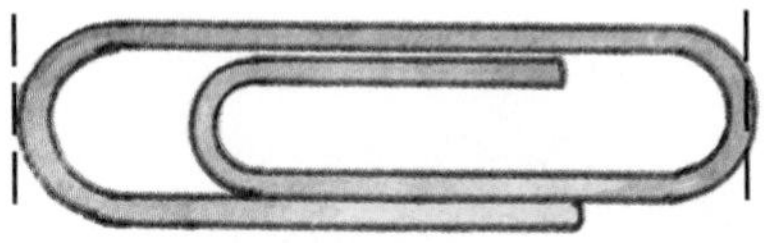

Guess: ____ inches Measure: ____ inches

Notes for Home Children are assessed on Chapter 6 concepts, skills, and problem solving.

Exploring MATH AT HOME

Exploring Math at Home

Dear Family,

In this chapter I have learned to identify shapes. I can also compare objects and measure them. Please help me with the activities below.

Love, ______________________________

1.

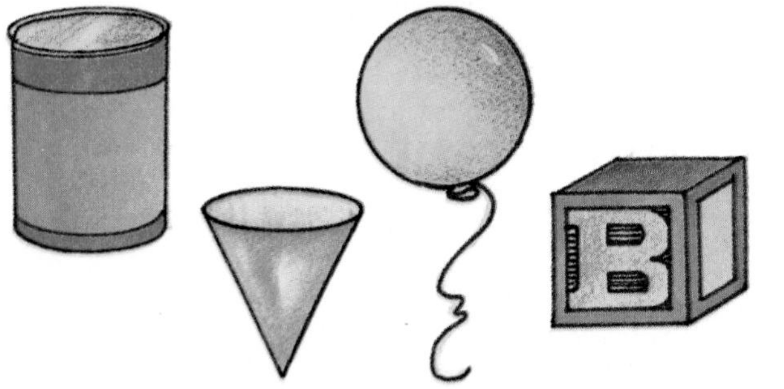

Identify the shapes of common objects.

2.

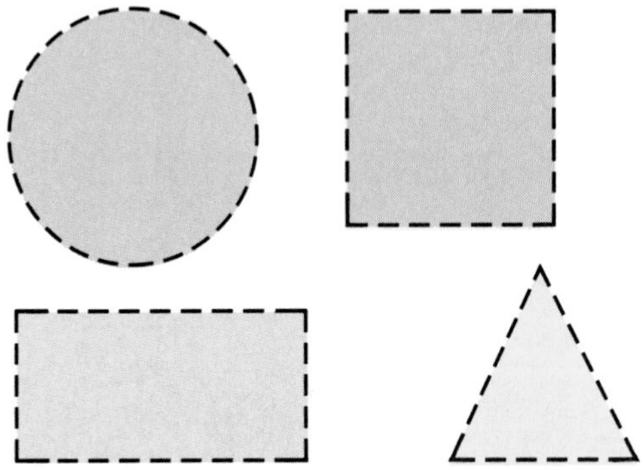

Draw a circle, square, rectangle, and triangle. Tell how many sides each has.

3.

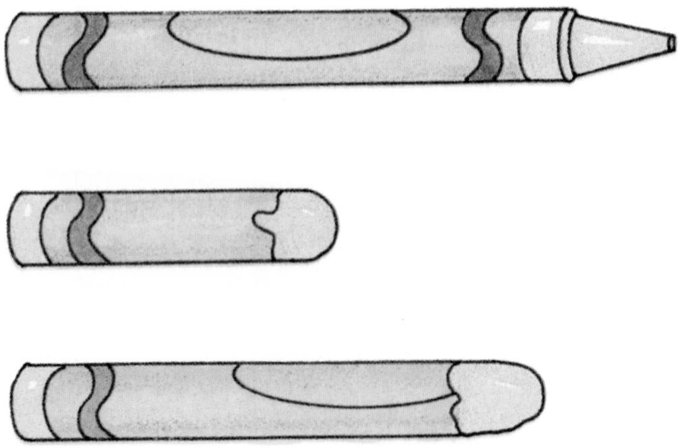

Compare the lengths of three objects and identify the longest and the shortest.

4.

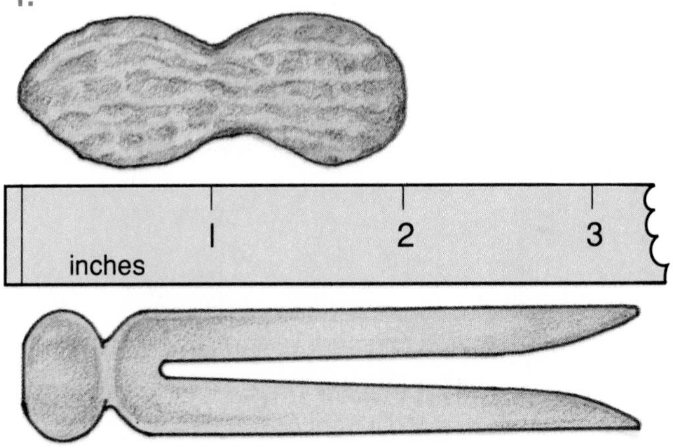

Measure lengths of objects in both standard and nonstandard units.

Coming Attractions

In the next chapter I will learn about ordinals through tenth and numbers through 19. I will also learn the value of a nickel and a dime.

Chapter

7

Numbers Through 19

Listen to the math story, "The Fifth Frog."
The frog won first place in the singing contest.
Do you think he will sing more songs?

Notes for Home Children listen to a math story introducing chapter concepts and skills. Then they answer a question about the story.

Name

Ordinals Through Fifth

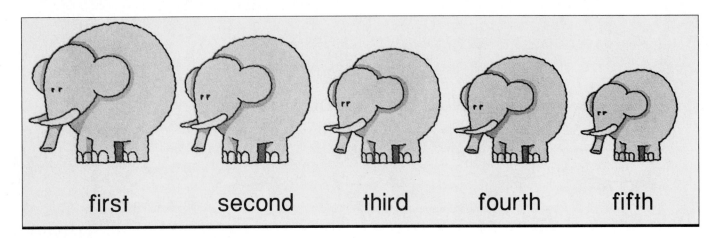

first second third fourth fifth

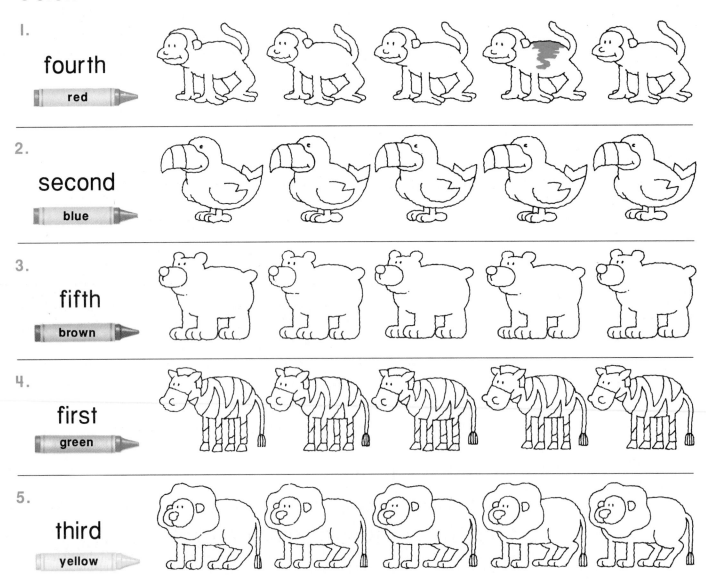

Color.

1. fourth

red

2. second

blue

3. fifth

brown

4. first

green

5. third

yellow

Notes for Home Children use ordinal number words through fifth to identify position.

Name

Ordinals Through Tenth

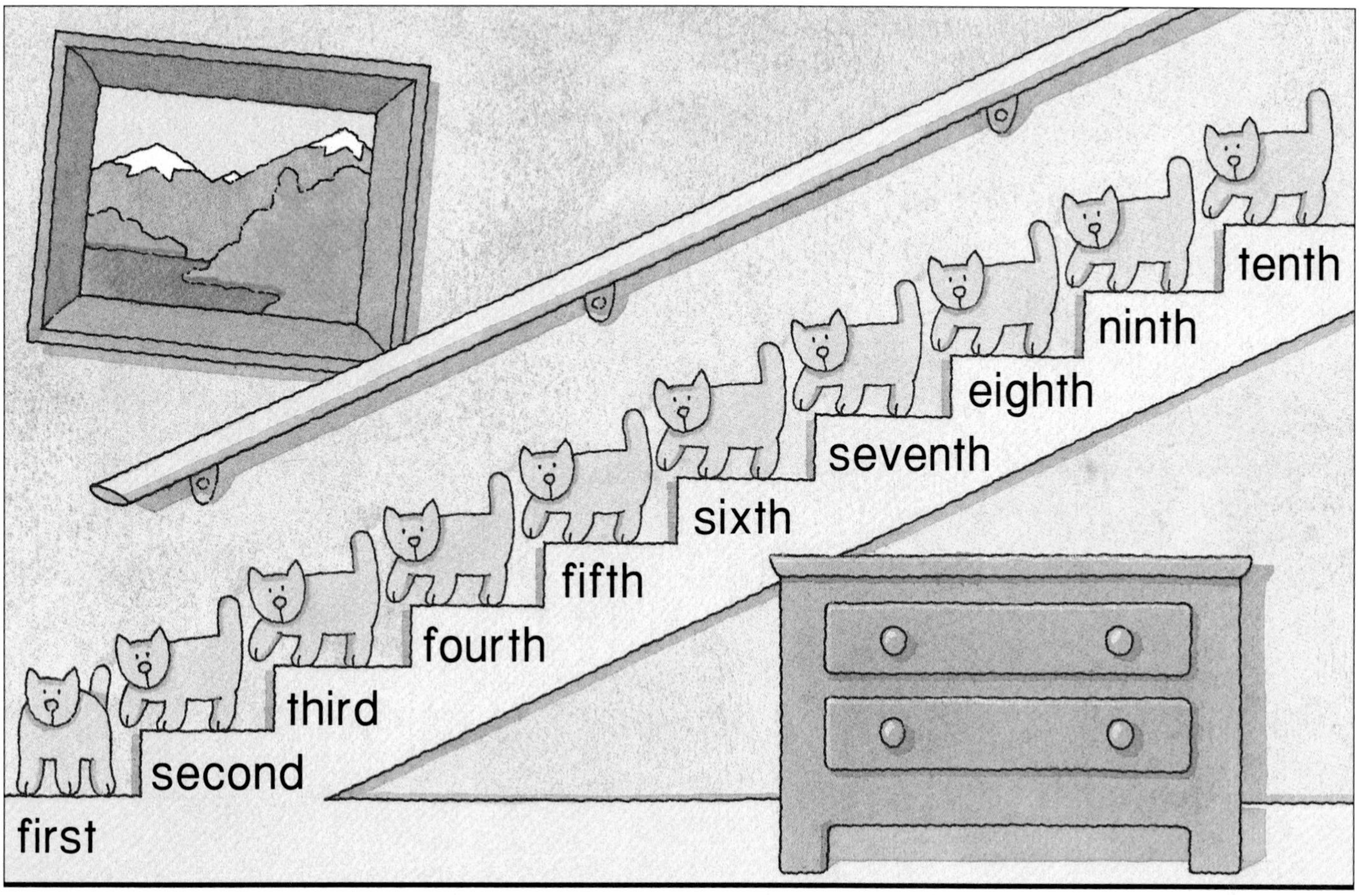

Match.

1.

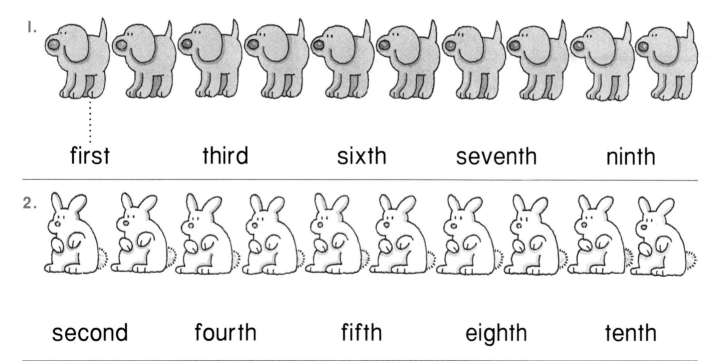

first third sixth seventh ninth

2.

second fourth fifth eighth tenth

Notes for Home Children learn to use ordinal number words through tenth to identify position.

Match.

3.

first second fifth seventh ninth

4.

tenth eighth sixth fourth third

5.

eighth seventh fifth fourth first

6.

second third sixth ninth tenth

Notes for Home Children use ordinal number words through tenth to identify position.

Name

Numbers Through 19

10	ten
11	eleven
12	twelve
13	thirteen
14	fourteen
15	fifteen
16	sixteen
17	seventeen
18	eighteen
19	nineteen

How many?

1.

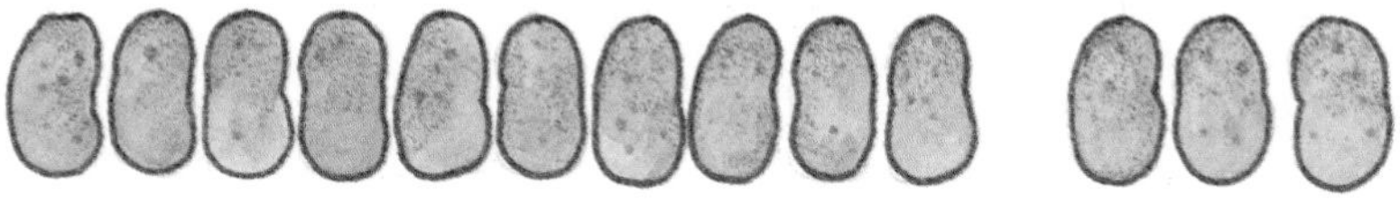

13 in all

2.

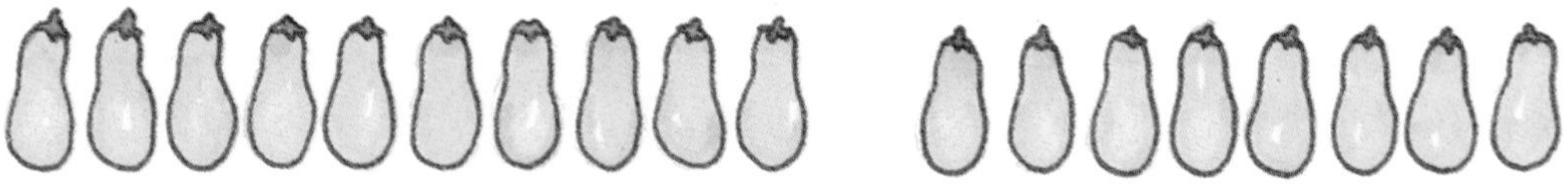

_____ in all

3.

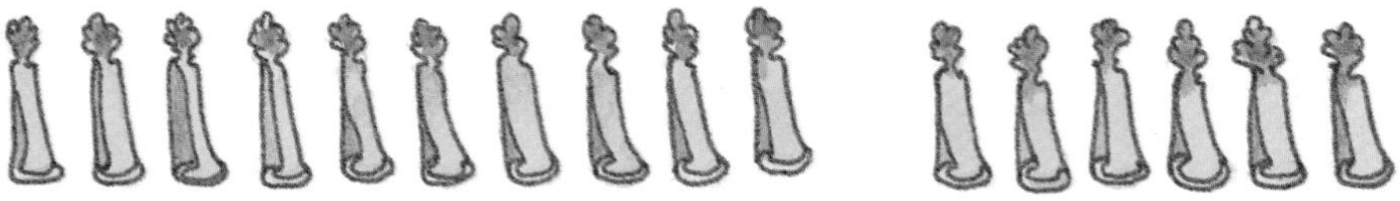

_____ in all

4.

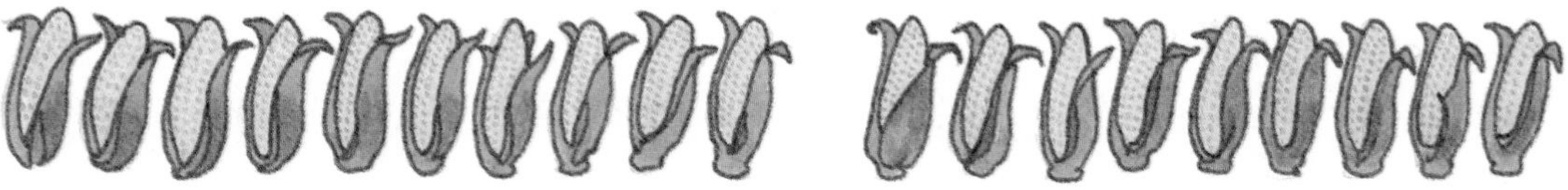

_____ in all

Notes for Home Children learn about numbers through 19 by writing how many in all.

How many?

5.

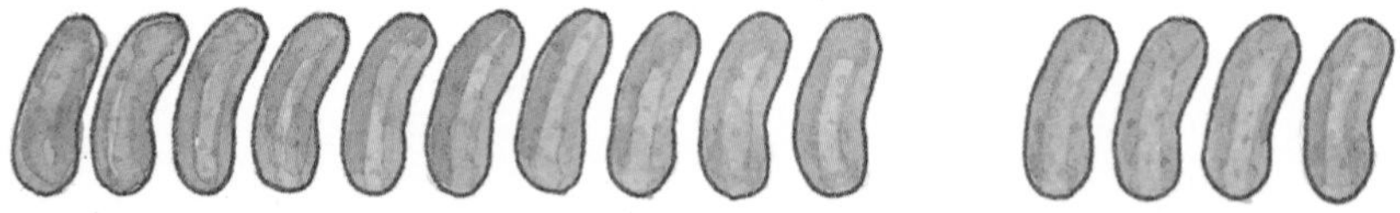

14 in all

6.

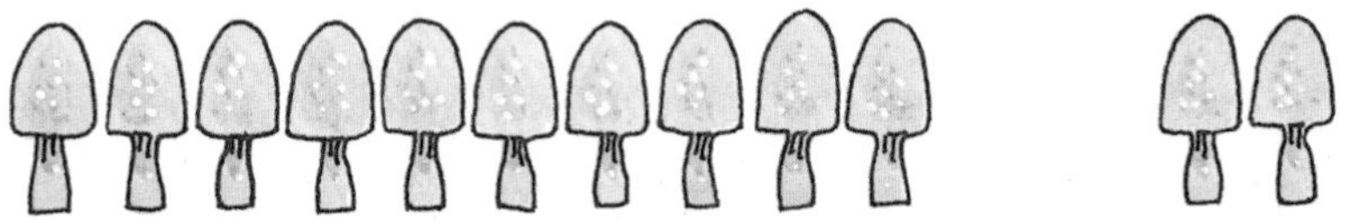

____ in all

7.

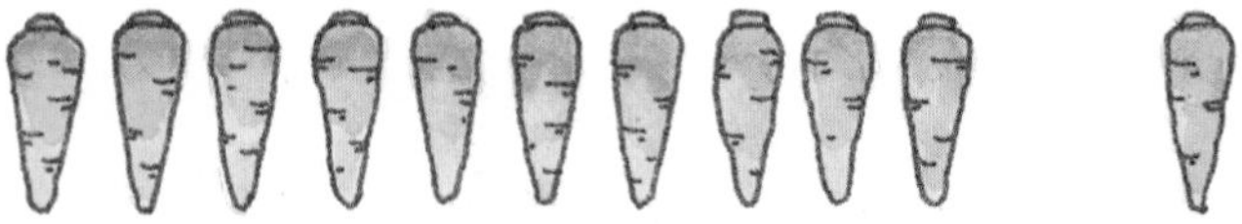

____ in all

8.

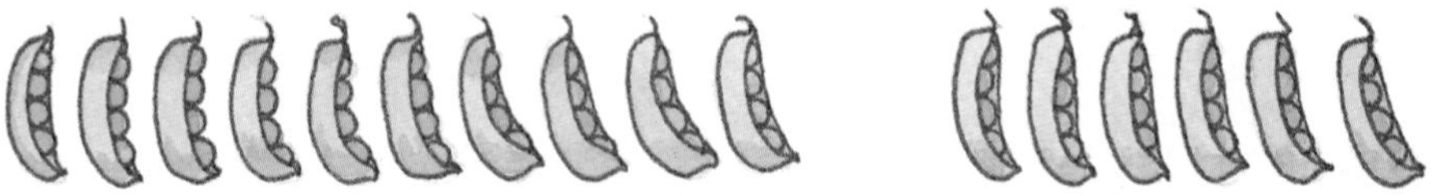

____ in all

9.

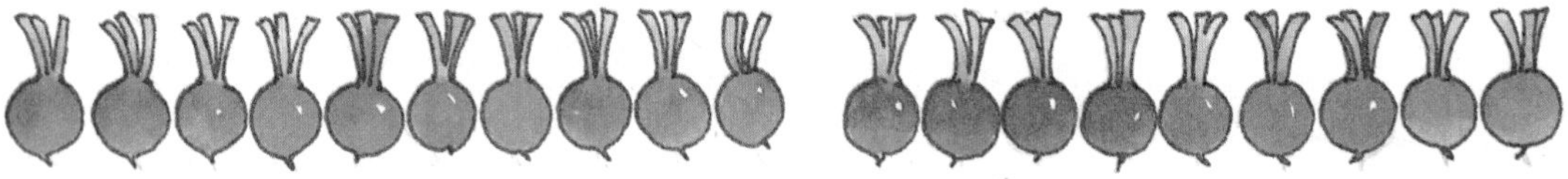

____ in all

10.

____ in all

11.

____ in all

12.

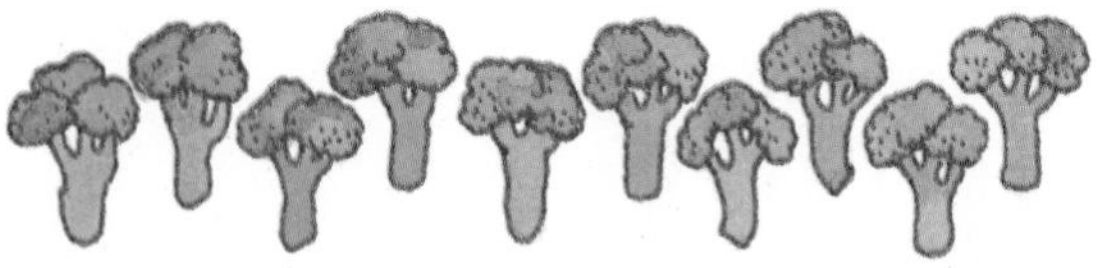

____ in all

Notes for Home Children practice identifying numbers through 19 by writing how many in all.

Name

Making a Group of Ten

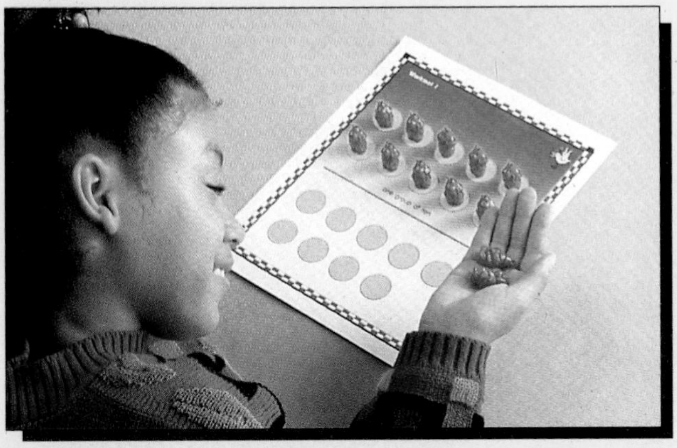

1. Use counters to make a group of ten.

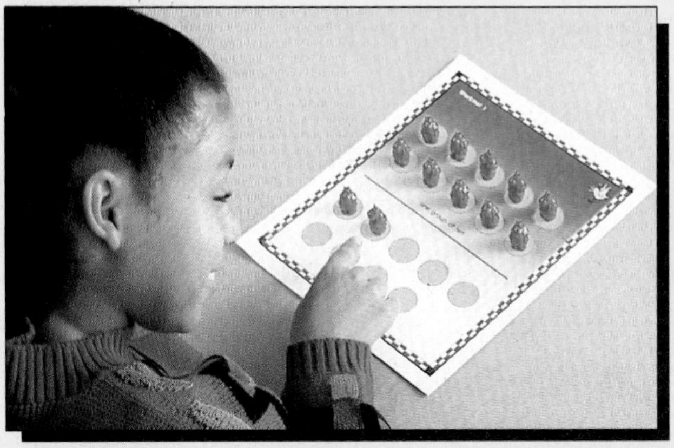

2. Then count how many ones.

Use Workmat 1.
Use counters.

	Show this many.	How many groups of ten?	How many ones?
1.	12	1 ten	2 ones
2.	15	____ ten	____ ones
3.	11	____ ten	____ one
4.	14	____ ten	____ ones

Notes for Home Children explore numbers through 19 at the CONCRETE level using counters and a workmat to make a group of ten. They record how many.

Use Workmat I.
Use counters.

	Show this many.	How many groups of ten?	How many ones?
5.	15	1 ten	5 ones
6.	12	____ ten	____ ones
7.	18	____ ten	____ ones
8.	13	____ ten	____ ones
9.	16	____ ten	____ ones
10.	10	____ ten	____ ones
11.	17	____ ten	____ ones

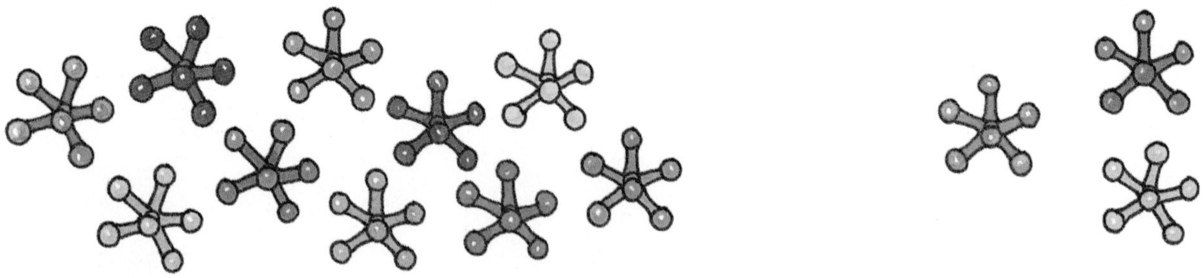

Notes for Home Children work at the CONCRETE level using counters and a workmat to make a group of ten. They record how many.

Name ______________________________

Order Through 19

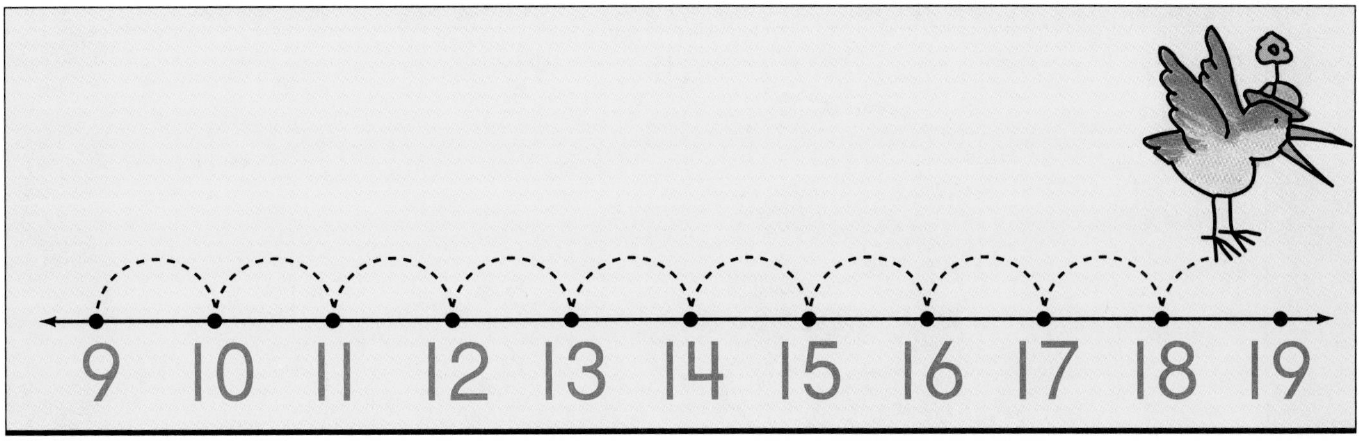

Write the missing numbers.

1. 12 13 14 ____ 16 ____

2. 14 ____ ____ ____ 18 ____

3. 7 8 ____ ____ ____ ____

4. 13 ____ ____ ____ ____ 18

5. 11 ____ ____ ____ 15 ____

Notes for Home Children learn to order numbers through 19.

6. Connect the dots.

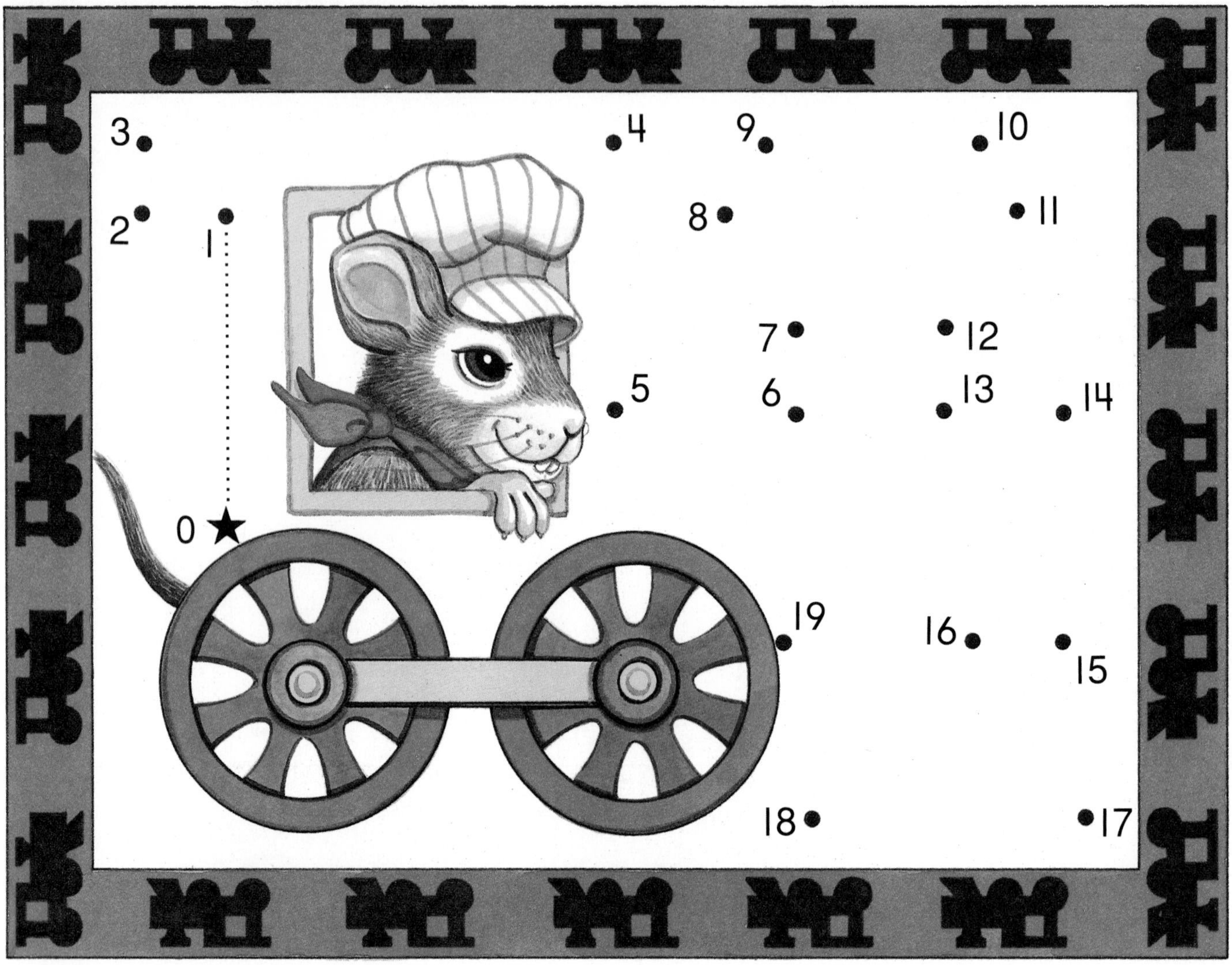

Problem Solving

What number is one more?
Solve.

7. Jan had

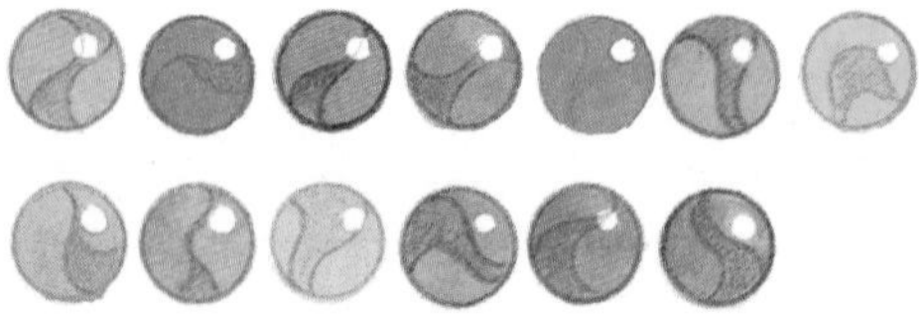

One more is ____.

8. Tom had

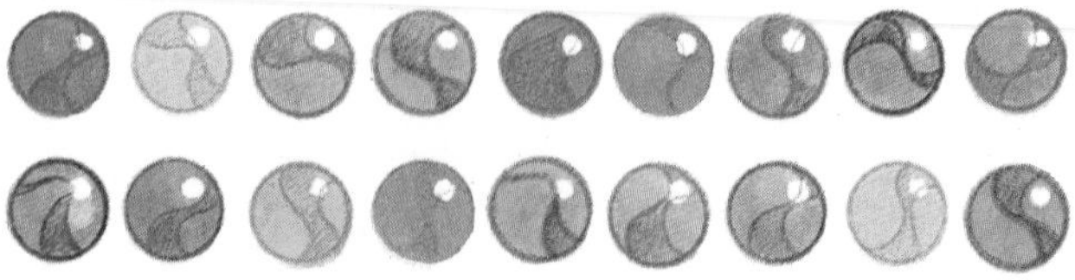

One more is ____.

Notes for Home Children practice ordering numbers through 19 by completing a dot-to-dot picture. Then they solve problems involving one more than a given number.

Name ______________________

Write the number that comes after.

1. 15 16 17

2. 10 11 ___

3. 17 18 ___

4. 13 14 ___

Write the number that comes before.

5. 11 12 13

6. ___ 17 18

7. ___ 15 16

8. ___ 11 12

Write the number that comes between.

9. 12 13 14

10. 17 ___ 19

Notes for Home Children identify numbers before, after, and between given numbers.

Write the missing numbers.

11. 14 ___ 16 ___ 18 ___

12. ___ 11 12 ___ ___ 15

13. 9 ___ ___ 12 ___ ___

14. ___ 7 ___ ___ 10 ___

15. 11 ___ ___ ___ 15 ___

16. ___ ___ 14 ___ ___ ___

Problem Solving

Solve.

17. Jack had cards for the numbers 10 through 19. Now he has these cards left. Which cards did he lose?

___ ___ ___ ___

Notes for Home Children identify missing numbers. Then they solve a problem involving missing numbers.

Name ______

Comparing Numbers Through 19

15 is **greater than** 13.
15
13

Write how many.
Then ring the greater number.

1. (16) 12

2. ______ ______

3. ______ ______

4. ______ ______

Notes for Home Children compare two numbers and identify the one that is greater.

Write how many.
Then ring the number that is less.

5.

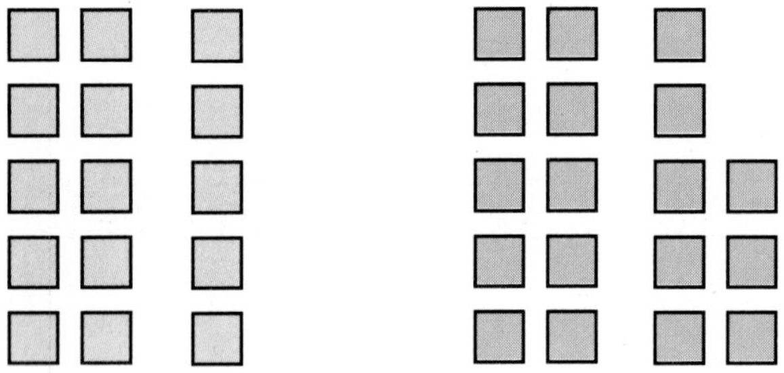

(15) 18

6.

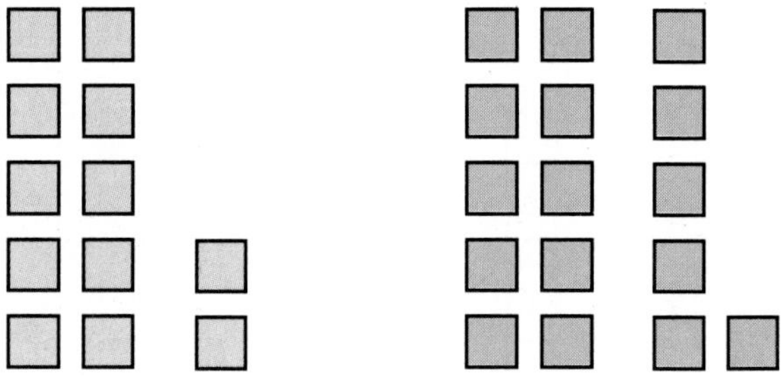

____ ____

7.

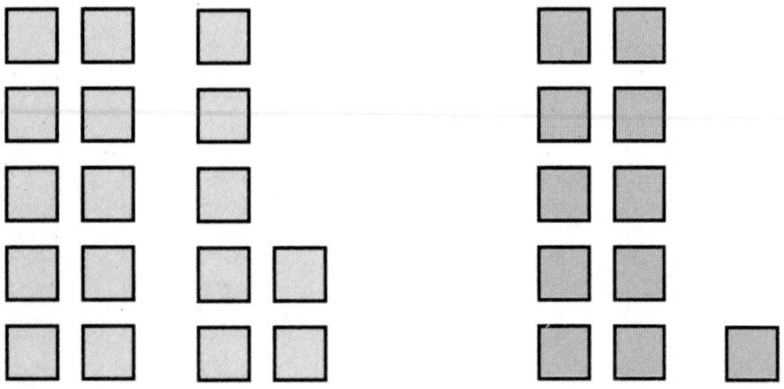

____ ____

8.

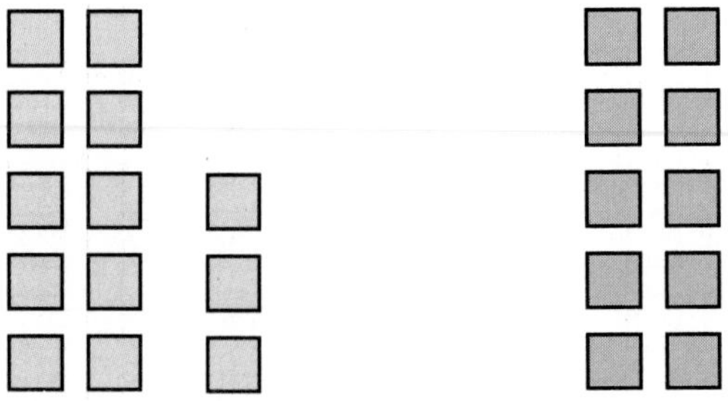

____ ____

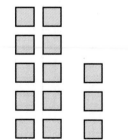

Notes for Home Children compare two numbers and identify the one that is less.

See More Practice Set A on Page 225.

Name ______________________________

PROBLEM-SOLVING STRATEGY

Make a Table

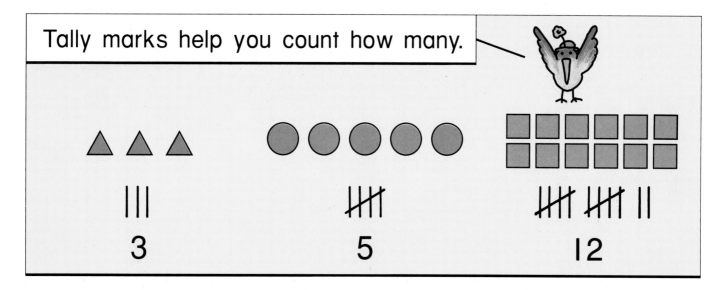

Tally marks help you count how many.

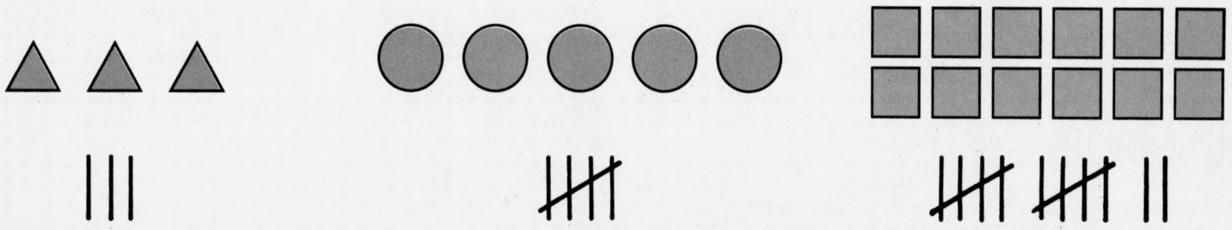

3 5 12

I. Make a tally mark for each shape.
Write how many.

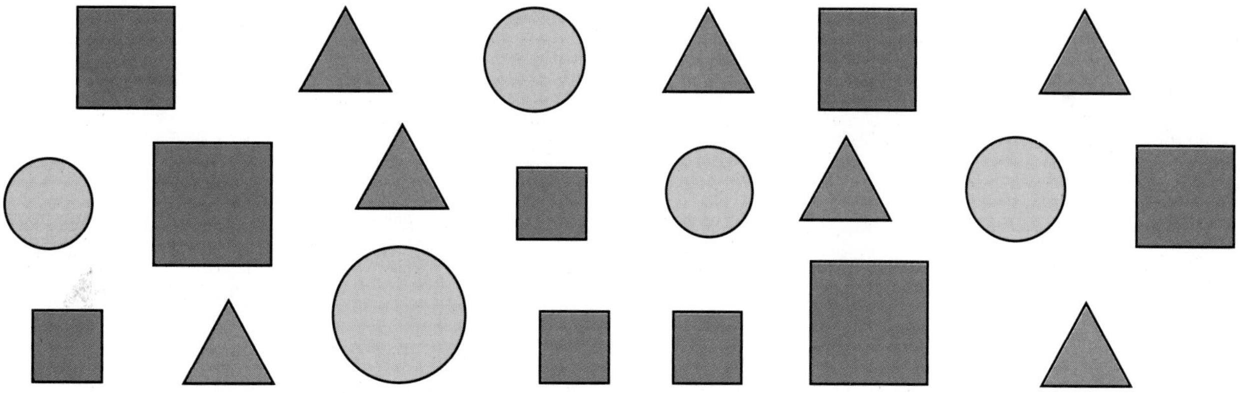

Shape	Tallies	Total

Notes for Home Children solve a problem by making tally marks.

2. Make a tally mark for each.
Write how many.

Fish	Tallies	Total
	卌 |	

Notes for Home Children solve a problem by making tally marks.

Name

Number Sense

First guess how many vowels in the sentence below. Then count to check.

When the door opened, the space creatures walked out.

Guess ☐ Check ☐

Let's do some more!

Write your own sentence.
Have a friend guess how many vowels.

Notes for Home Children develop an understanding of numbers by guessing and then checking a certain number of things.

Skills Review

Fill in the correct ⬭.
How many sides?

1.

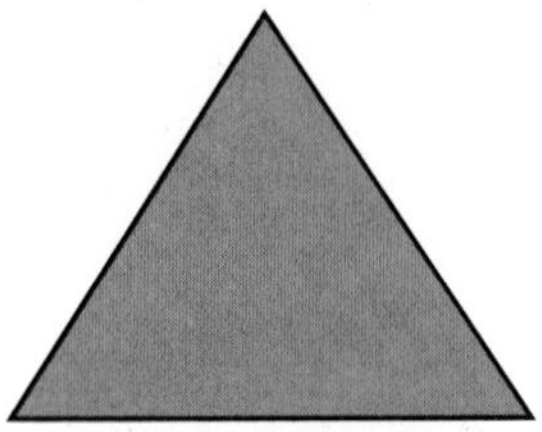

(A) 1
(B) 2
(C) 3

2.

(A) 2
(B) 4
(C) 6

Find the shape that matches.

3.

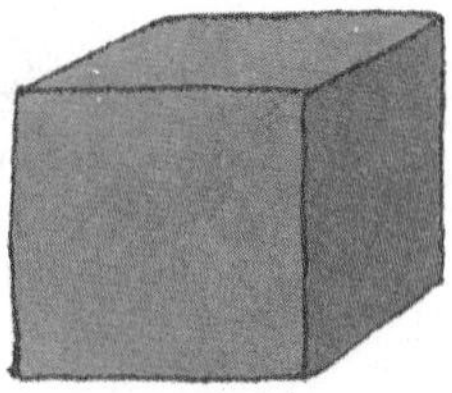

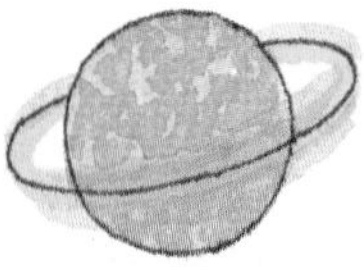

(A)

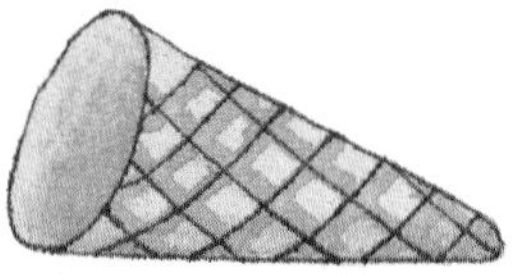

(B)

(C)

4.

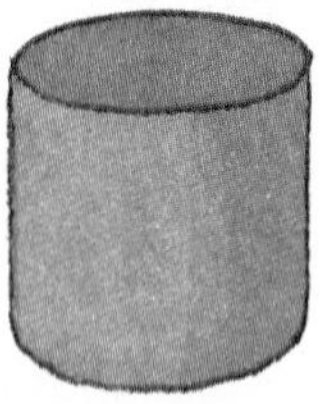

(A)

(B)

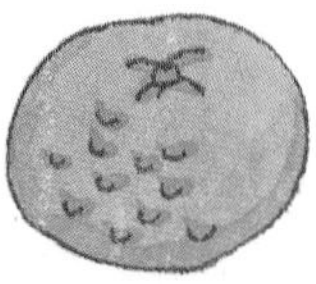

(C)

Vocabulary

5. Draw a circle for a face.

6. Draw a square for the body.

7. Draw four rectangles for arms and legs.

8. Draw a triangle for a hat.

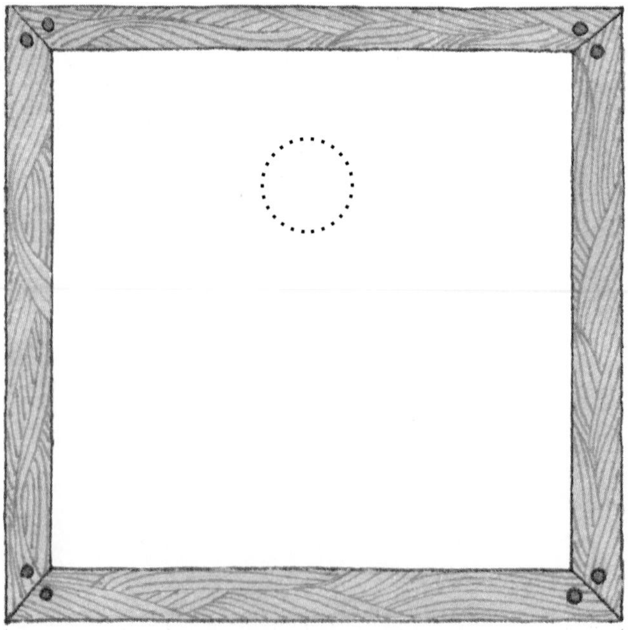

Notes for Home Children review attributes of plane shapes. Then they identify solid shapes. Children review terms for shapes in order to make a drawing.

Name ______

Nickels

Count on to find how much.

1.

5 ¢ 6 ¢ 7 ¢

7 ¢ in all

2.

____ ¢ ____ ¢ ____ ¢ ____ ¢ ____ ¢

____ ¢ in all

3.

____ ¢ ____ ¢ ____ ¢ ____ ¢

____ ¢ in all

Notes for Home Children learn the value of a nickel. They count a nickel and some pennies.

Count on to find how much in all.

4.

6 ¢

5.

____ ¢

6.

____ ¢

7.

____ ¢

8.

____ ¢

9.

____ ¢

Notes for Home Children practice counting a nickel and some pennies.

Name ______________________

Dimes

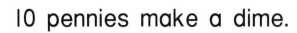

10 pennies make a dime.

 or 

dime

10 cents

10¢

Count on to find how much.

1. 

10 ¢ 11 ¢ 12 ¢ 13 ¢

13 ¢ in all

2. 

____¢ ____¢ ____¢ ____¢ ____¢

____¢ in all

3. 

____¢ ____¢ ____¢

____¢ in all

Notes for Home Children learn the value of a dime. They count a dime and some pennies.

Count on to find how much in all.

4.

12 ¢

5.

_____ ¢

6.

_____ ¢

7.

_____ ¢

8.

_____ ¢

9.

_____ ¢

Notes for Home Children practice counting a dime and some pennies.

See More Practice Set B on page 225.

Use Data from a Graph

This pictograph shows how many animals the children saw at the zoo.

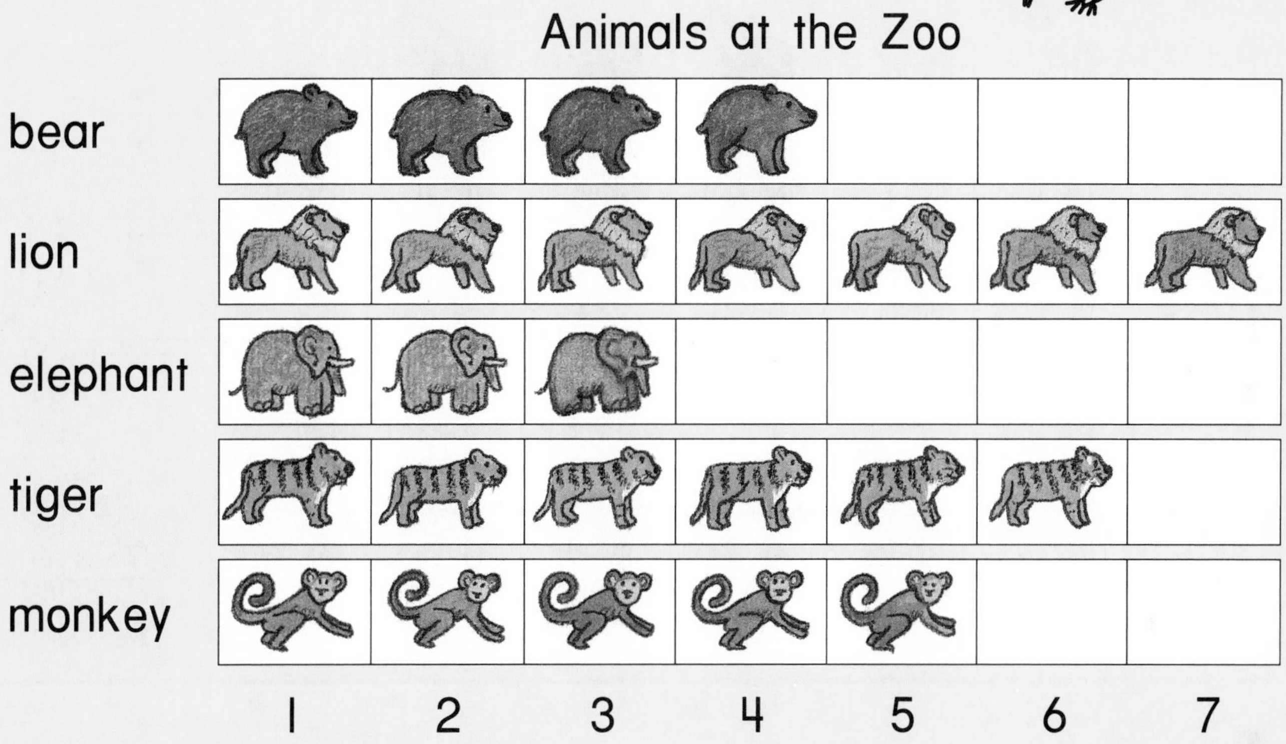

Look at the graph.

1. How many of each animal did the children see?

bears 4 ____ elephants ____ tigers ____

monkeys ____ lions ____

2. Ring the animal they saw more often.

monkeys or elephants   tigers or lions

Notes for Home Children learn to solve problems by using a graph.

This pictograph shows how many animals the children saw at the Children's Zoo.

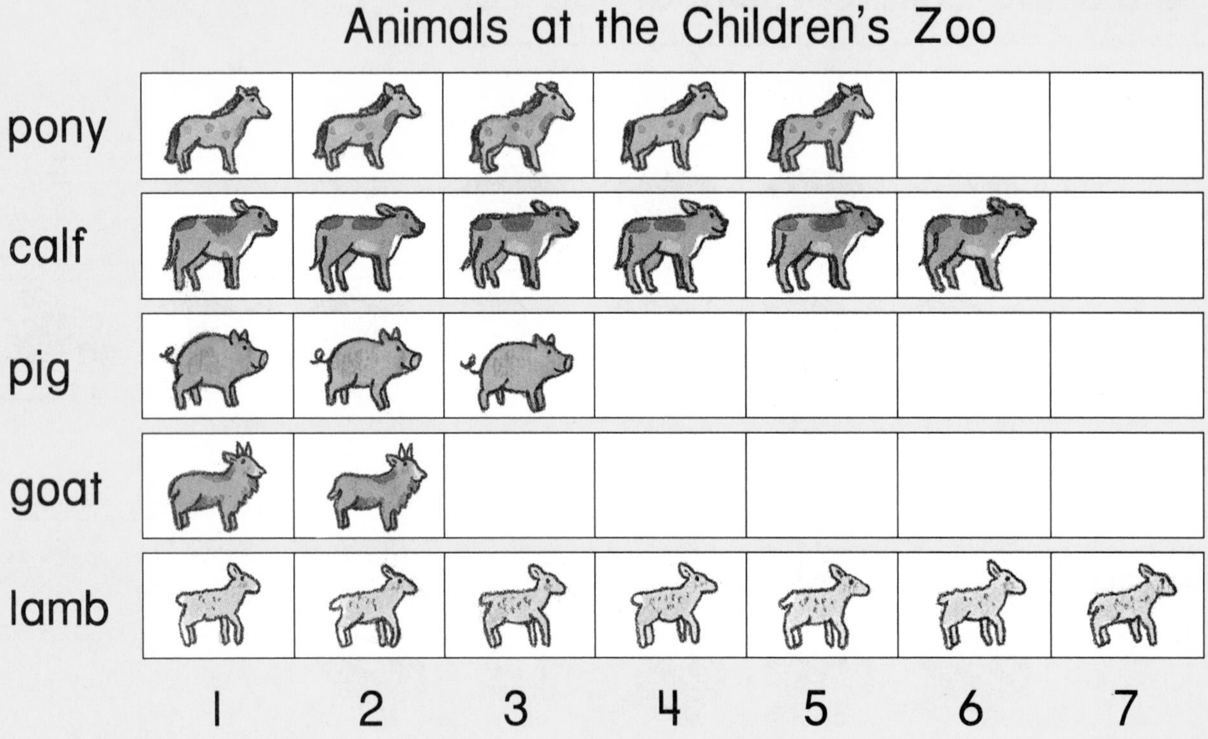

Look at the graph.

3. How many of each animal did the children see?

pigs 3 ____ lambs ____ goats ____

calves ____ ponies ____

4. Ring the animal they saw less often.

goats or lambs pigs or ponies

Notes for Home Children solve problems by using a graph.

Name

Problem-Solving Workshop

Explore as a Team

Work with a partner.
Solve the problem.
Write how many in each bowl.

1. 12 cherries in all.
3 are in the red bowl.
Yellow has more than blue.

red bowl ____
blue bowl ____
yellow bowl ____

2. 16 cherries in all.
8 are in the blue bowl.
Yellow has 2 more than red.

red bowl ____
blue bowl ____
yellow bowl ____

Notes for Home Children explore with a partner to solve a problem involving logical reasoning.

Problem-Solving Workshop

Explore with a Computer

Primary Graphing and Probability Project

1. Count how many of each animal.
Then write the number.

Forest Animals

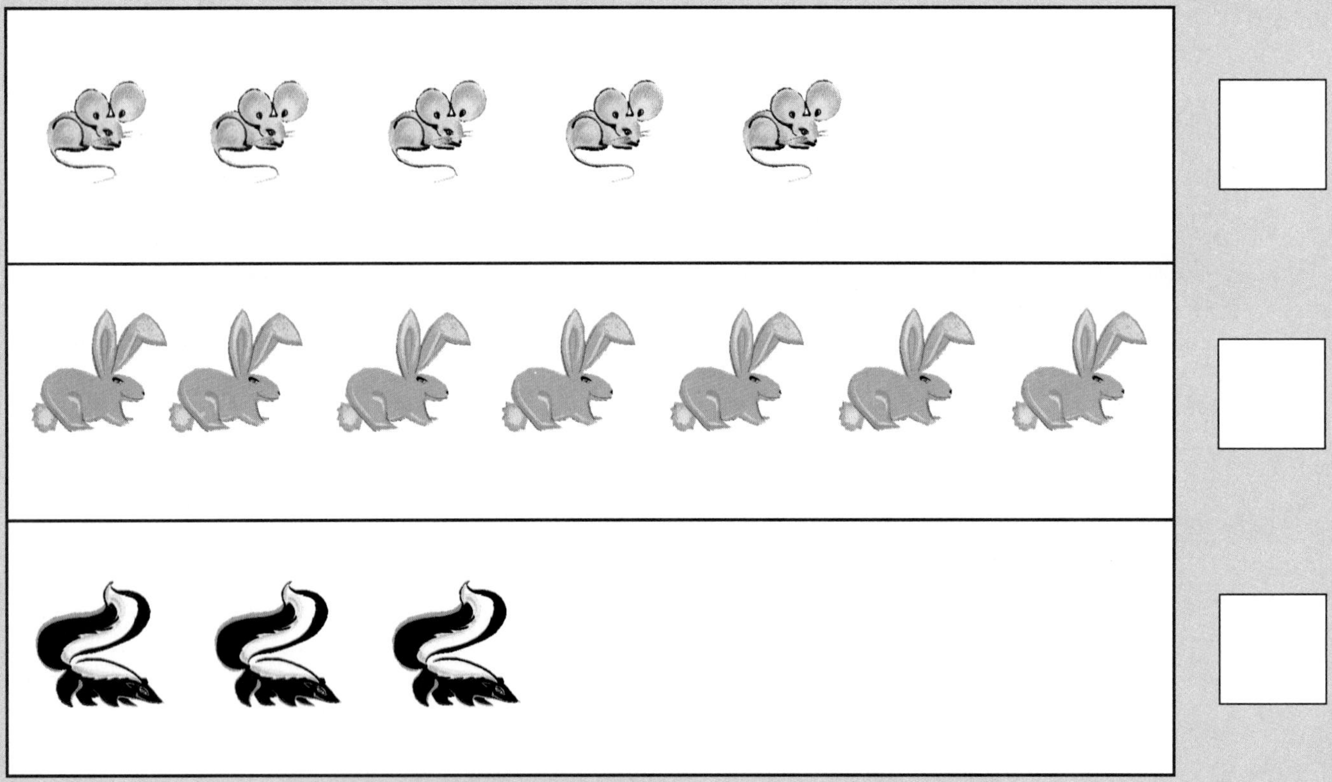

2. At the computer, make a graph to show how many animals there are.

Notes for Home Children add items to match a given number. Then they use the computer to create picture graphs of numerical information.

Name ______________________________

More Practice

Set A Use after page 212.

Write how many.
Ring the greater number.

1.

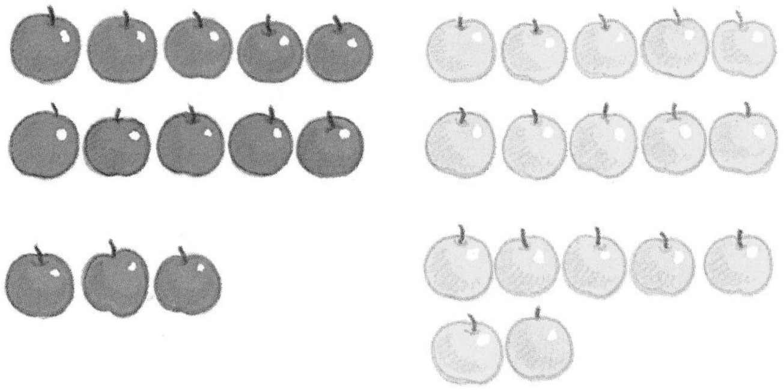

13 ______ (17) ______

Write how many.
Ring the number that is less.

2.

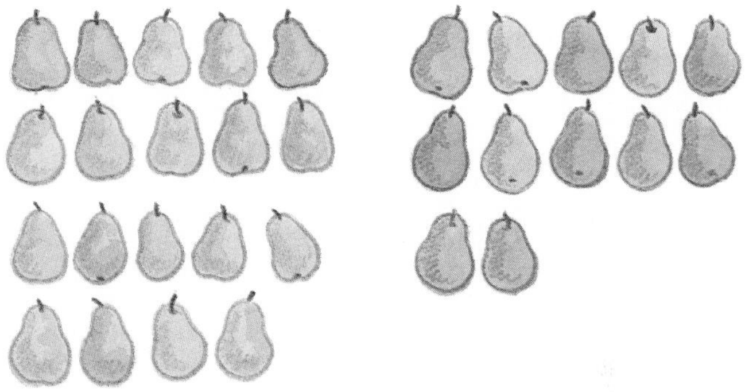

______ ______

Set B Use after page 220.

Count the money.
Write the amount.

1.

5 ¢ ______¢ ______¢ ______¢ ______¢

______¢
in all

2.

______¢ ______¢ ______¢ ______¢ ______¢

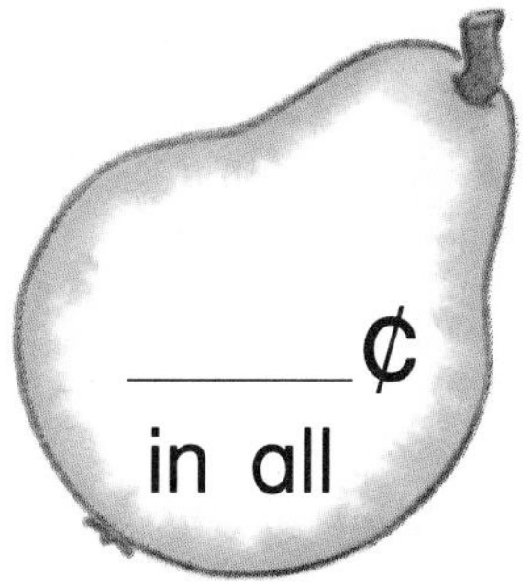

______¢
in all

Notes for Home Set A: Children practice comparing two numbers and identifying the one that is greater or the one that is less.
Set B: Children practice counting a nickel and pennies and a dime and pennies through 19¢.

Enrichment

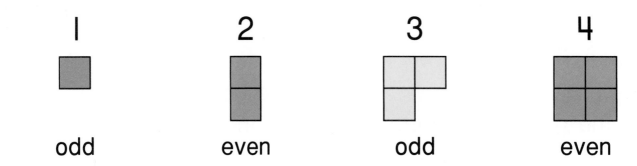

1	2	3	4
	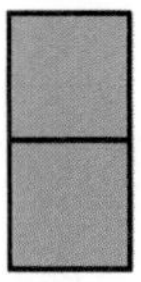	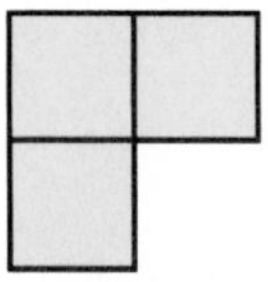	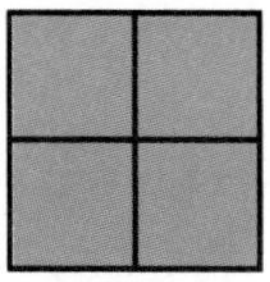
odd	even	odd	even

Even numbers can be grouped in pairs.
Odd numbers always have an extra.

Decide if the number is odd or even.
Ring odd or even.

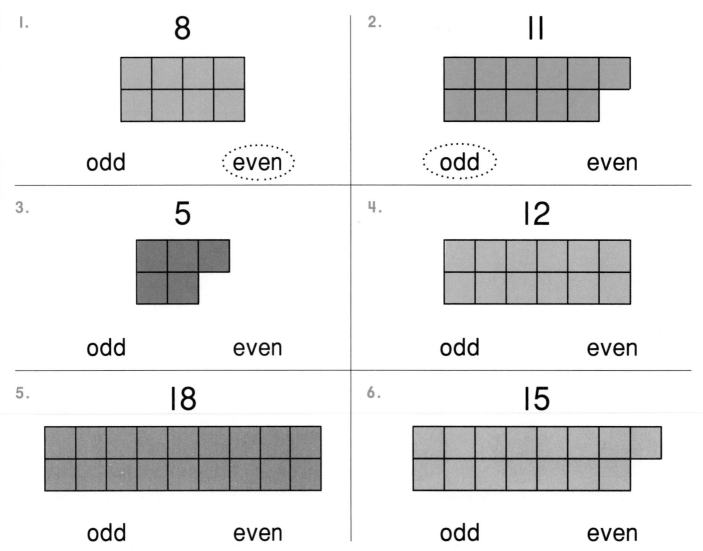

1. 8

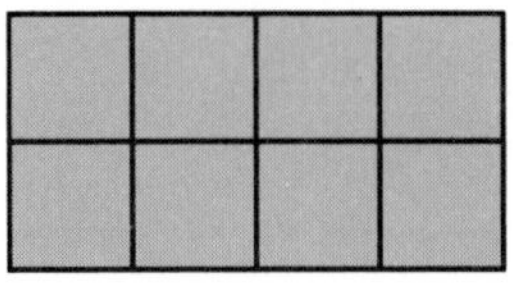

odd even [ringed: even]

2. 11

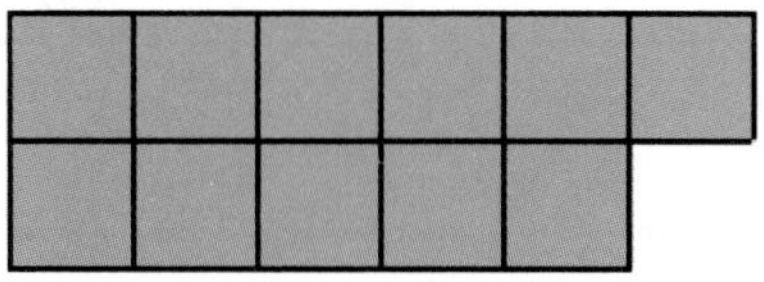

odd [ringed: odd] even

3. 5

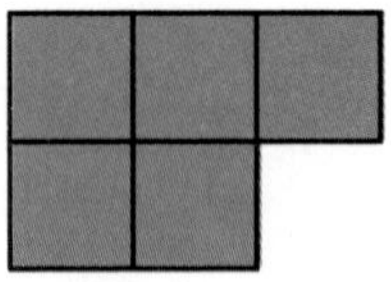

odd even

4. 12

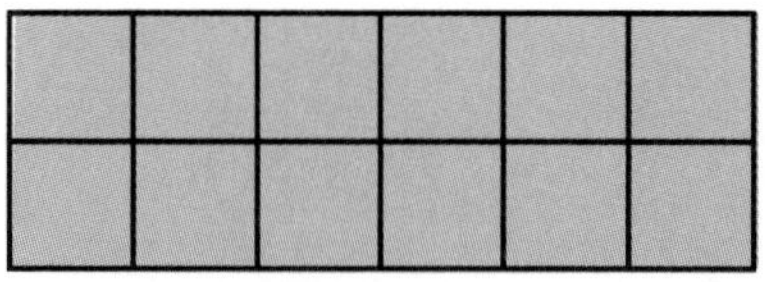

odd even

5. 18

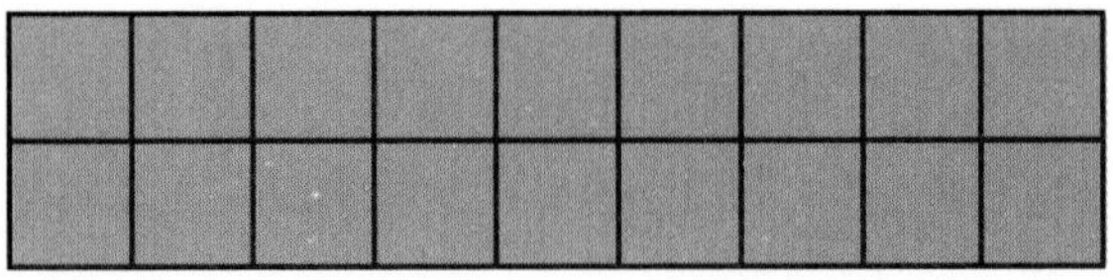

odd even

6. 15

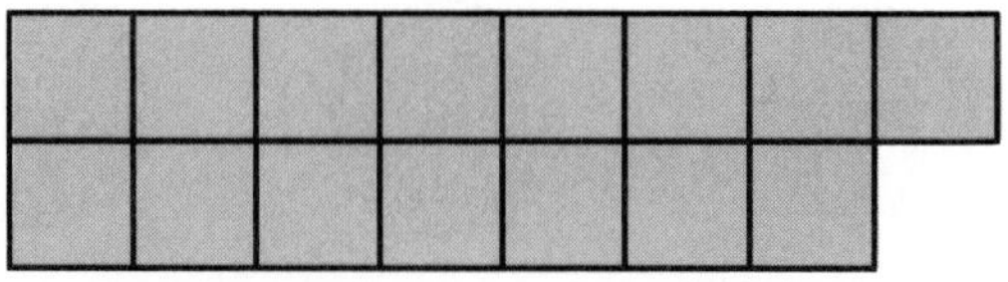

odd even

Notes for Home Children are challenged to identify odd and even numbers.

Name

Chapter 7 Review/Test

1. Match.

sixth third

2. Write the missing numbers.

____, 17, 18, ____

3. Ring a group of 10.
Write how many.

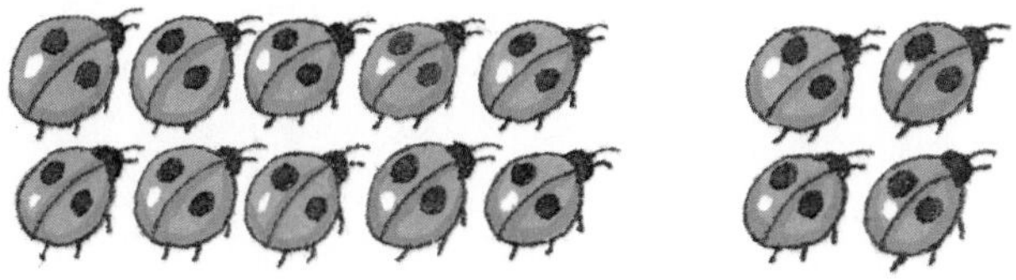

____ ten ____ ones

4. Write how many. Then ring the number that is less.

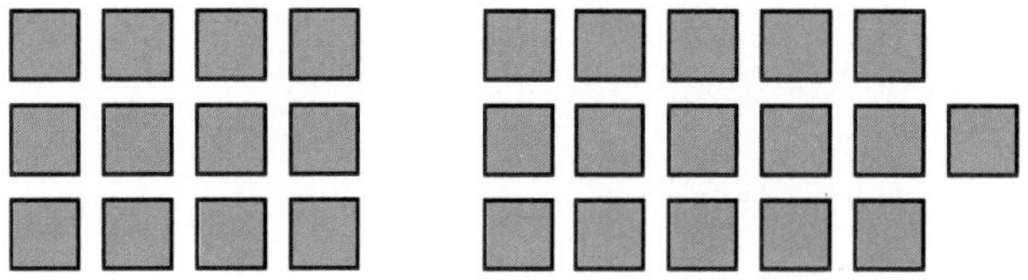

____ ____

Count on to find how much in all.

5. 

____¢

6. 

____¢

7. Make a tally mark for each shape.

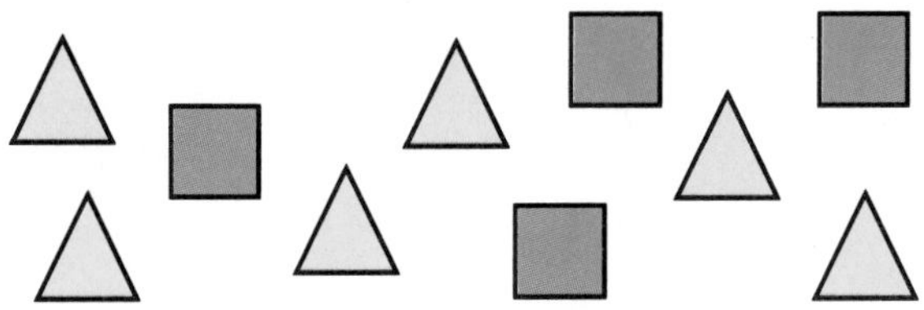

Shape	Tallies

8. Look at the graph.

1 2 3 4 5

How many of each pet?

dog ____ cat ____

Notes for Home Children are assessed on Chapter 7 concepts, skills, and problem solving.

Exploring Math at Home

Dear Family,

In this chapter I have learned about numbers through 19 and ordinal numbers through tenth. I also learned about the value of a nickel and a dime. Please help me with the activities below.

Love, ______________________________

1.

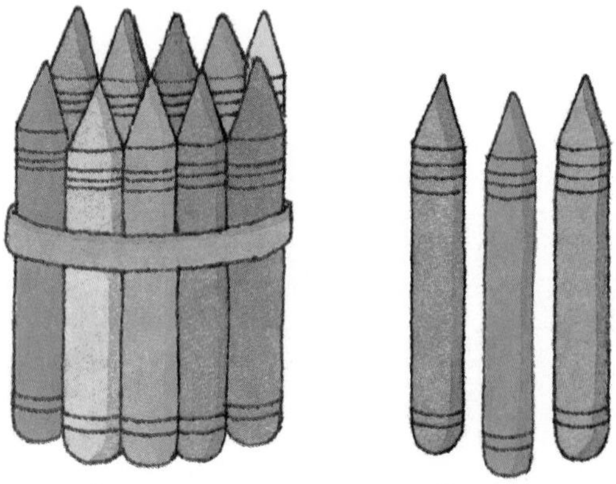

1 ten   3 ones = 13

Use counters to make a group of ten and a group of ones for numbers through 19. Tell how many in all.

2.

first

Line up objects and tell the ordinal number position of each.

3.

Practice counting a nickel and pennies to 19¢. Repeat the activity with different amounts.

4.

Practice counting a dime and pennies to 19¢. Repeat the activity with different amounts.

Coming Attractions

In the next chapter I will learn about tens and ones through 99. I will also count by twos, fives, and tens and learn to read a graph and a table.

Name

Fill in the correct ◯.
Add or subtract.

1. $\begin{array}{r} 10 \\ -\ 6 \\ \hline \end{array}$

2 ◯ 4 ◯ 7 ◯

2. $\begin{array}{r} 7 \\ +\ 2 \\ \hline \end{array}$

6 ◯ 8 ◯ 9 ◯

3. $\begin{array}{r} 8 \\ -\ 5 \\ \hline \end{array}$

3 ◯ 5 ◯ 6 ◯

4. $3 + 4 =$

7 ◯ 9 ◯ 10 ◯

5. $8 - 4 =$

1 ◯ 3 ◯ 4 ◯

6. $9 - 3 =$

6 ◯ 8 ◯ 9 ◯

7. $\begin{array}{r} 10 \\ -\ 3 \\ \hline \end{array}$

6 ◯ 7 ◯ 8 ◯

8. $\begin{array}{r} 2 \\ +\ 6 \\ \hline \end{array}$

8 ◯ 9 ◯ 10 ◯

9. $\begin{array}{r} 6 \\ +\ 4 \\ \hline \end{array}$

7 ◯ 8 ◯ 10 ◯

What shape is it?

10.

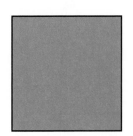

circle ◯
triangle ◯
square ◯

11.

cone ◯
cube ◯
cylinder ◯

Notes for Home Children are assessed on Chapters 1-7 concepts, skills, and problem solving using a multiple-choice format.

12. How many?

14 16 17

13. Which is less?

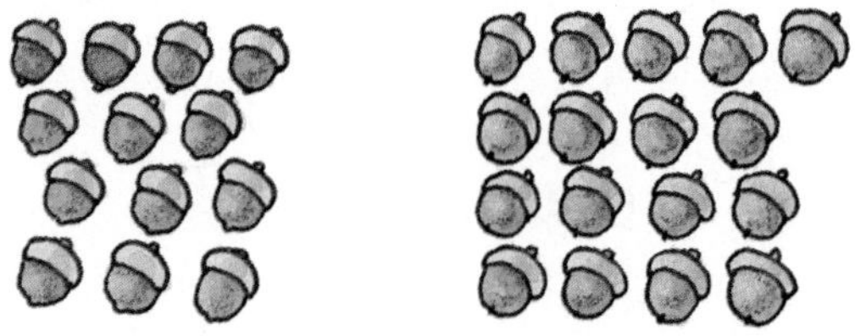

13 17

14. What number is missing?

14, ____, 16, 17

13 15 18

15. About how many inches long?

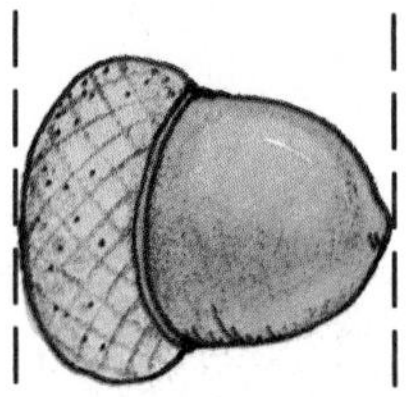

1 inch

2 inches

3 inches

Choose the correct number sentence.

16. Jeff had 8¢.
He earned 2¢ more.
How much does he have now?

8¢ + 2¢ = 10¢

8¢ − 2¢ = 6¢

17. How many are left?

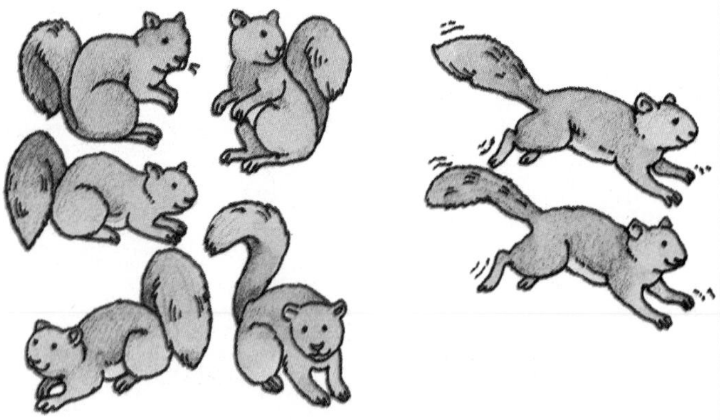

3 5 7

18. Use the graph.

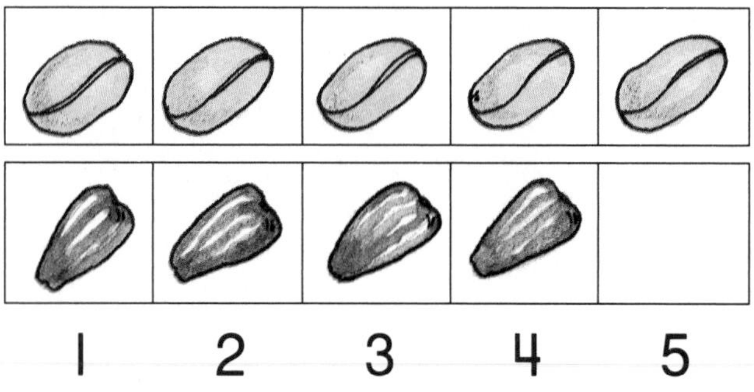

How many peanuts?

4 5 6

Notes for Home Children are assessed on Chapters 1-7 concepts, skills, and problem solving using a multiple-choice format.

Chapter

8

Place Value, Counting, Number Patterns Through 99

Listen to the math story, "Nicholas and the Penny Jar."
Nicholas put his pennies in rows of ten.
How did this help him count the pennies?

Notes for Home Children listen to a math story introducing chapter concepts and skills. Then they answer a question about the story.

Name

Grouping Tens

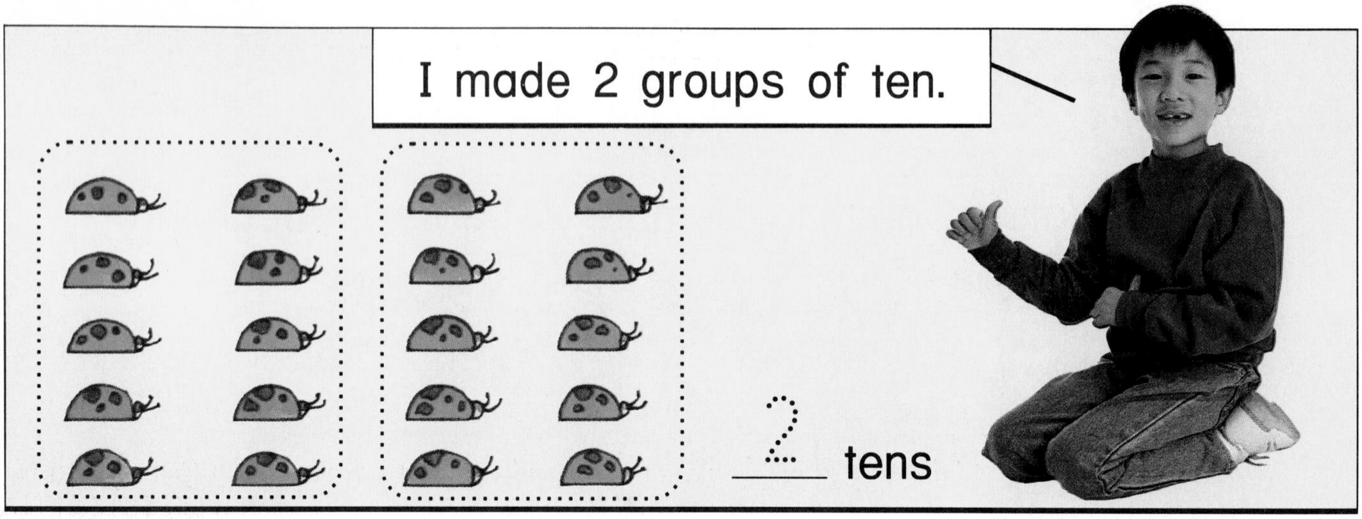

Ring groups of ten.
Then write the number of tens.

1.

____ tens

2.

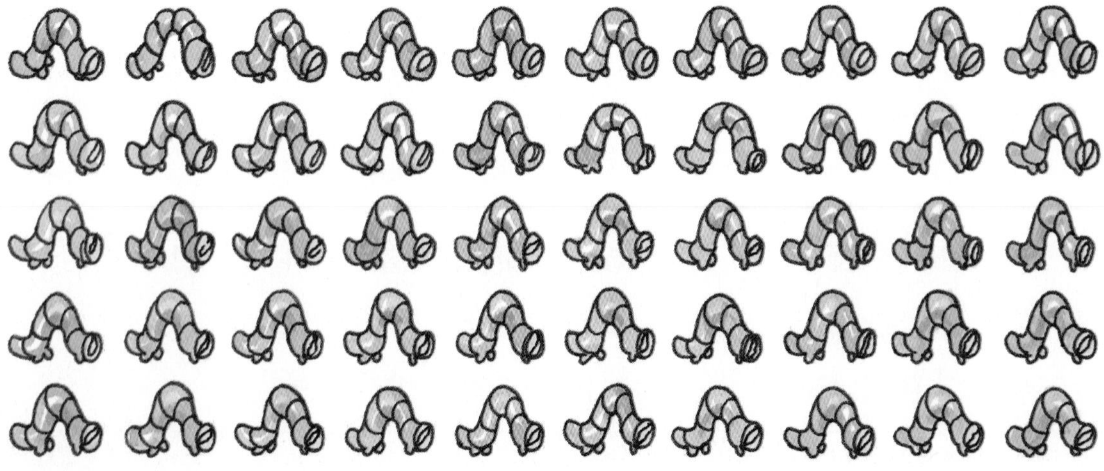

____ tens

Notes for Home Children ring groups of ten objects. They write the number of tens.

Name

Decade Numbers

ten	10	
twenty	20	
thirty	30	
forty	40	
fifty	50	
sixty	60	
seventy	70	
eighty	80	
ninety	90	

4 tens
40
forty

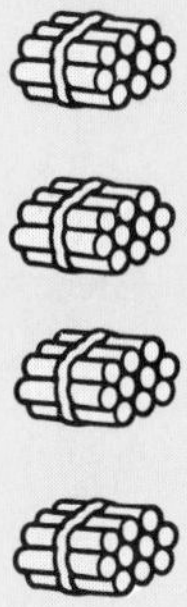

Write the number of tens.
Then write the number.

1.

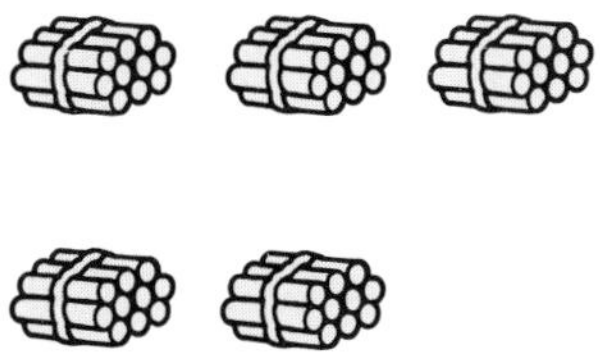

5 tens

50

2.

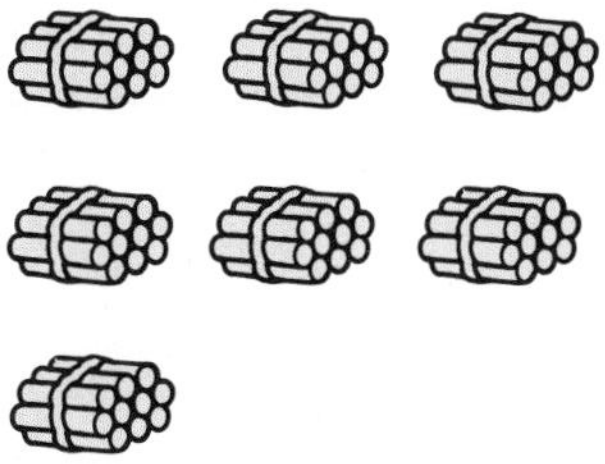

_____ tens

_____

3.

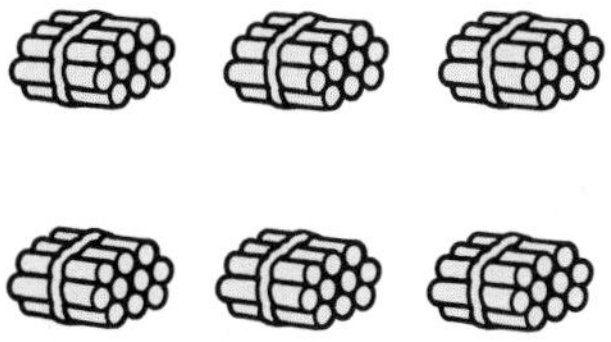

_____ tens

_____

4.

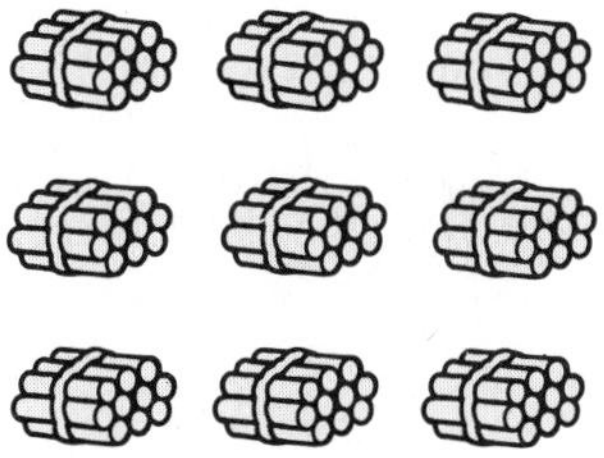

_____ tens

_____

Notes for Home Children count groups of tens and write the corresponding decade number.

Ring the number of tens.

5. 30

6. 70

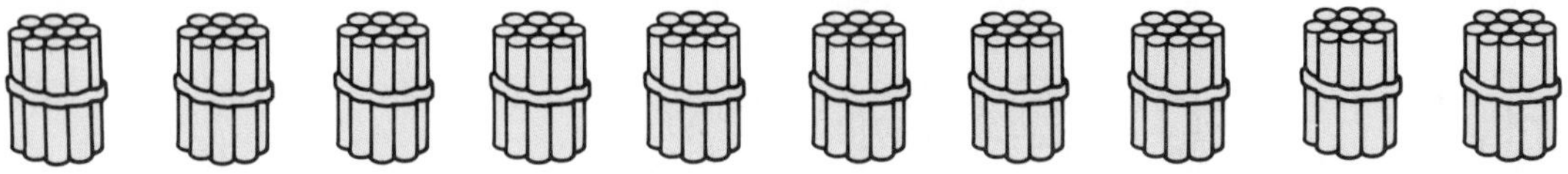

7. 40

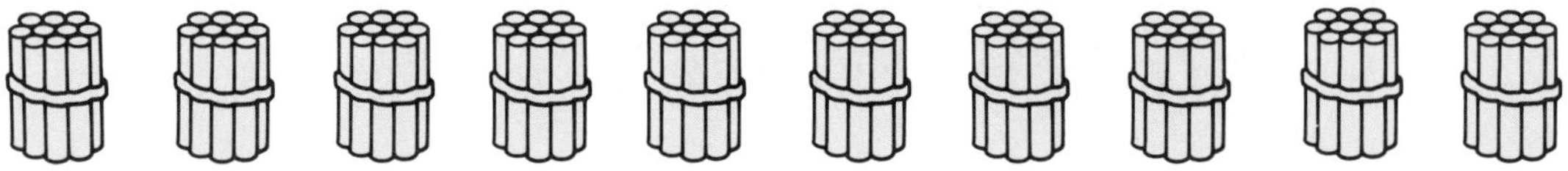

8. 60

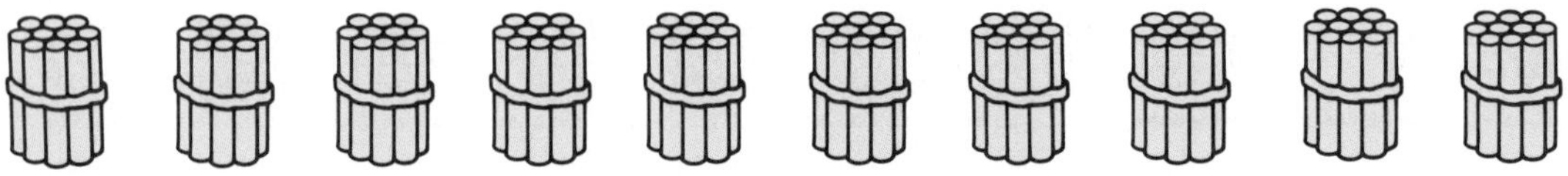

9. 90

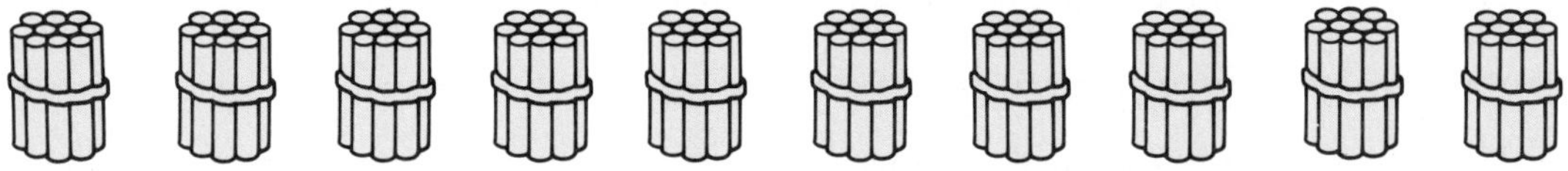

10. 80

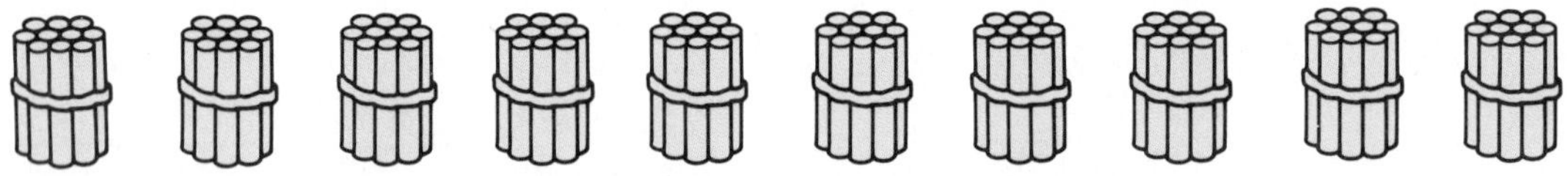

Count by tens.
Write the missing numbers.

11. 10 20 30 ___ ___ 60 ___ 80 90

12. ___ 20 ___ ___ 50 ___ ___ ___ ___

Notes for Home Children practice identifying groups of tens for a given decade number. They skip count by tens.

Name **Activity**

Understanding Tens and Ones

1. Use ones counters. Show the number.

2. Show one more.

3. Trade when you have 10 ones.

Use Workmat 2.
Use tens and ones counters.
Write the number of tens and ones.

1.

Show 6 ones. →

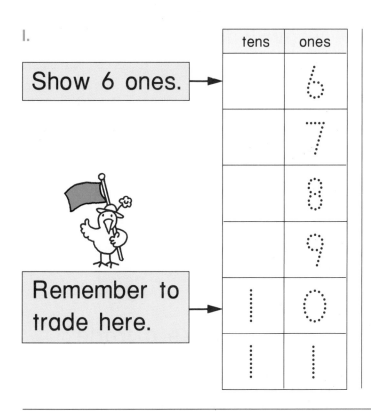

tens	ones
	6
	7
	8
	9
1	0
1	1

Remember to trade here. →

2.

Show 1 ten 2 ones. →

tens	ones
1	2

Notes for Home Children explore at the CONCRETE level using tens and ones counters and a workmat to show a given number of tens and ones. They count by ones and trade 10 ones for 1 ten when necessary.

Use tens and ones counters and Workmat 2.
Show one more. Write the number of tens and ones.

3.

Show 1 ten
8 ones.

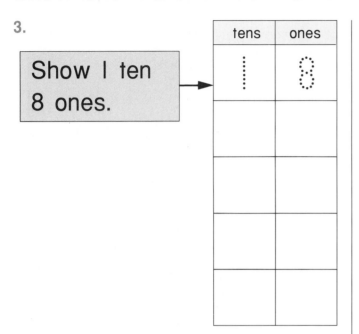

tens	ones
1	8

Did you make a trade?

yes   no

4.

Show 2 tens
3 ones.

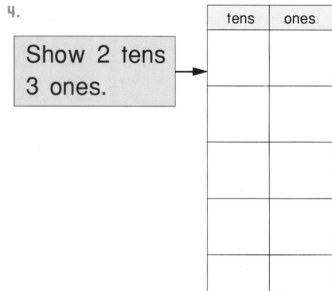

tens	ones

Did you make a trade?

yes   no

5.

Show 2 tens
8 ones.

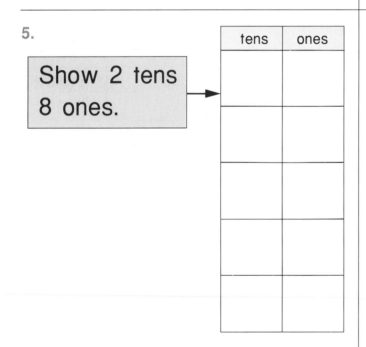

tens	ones

Did you make a trade?

yes   no

6.

Show 3 tens
3 ones.

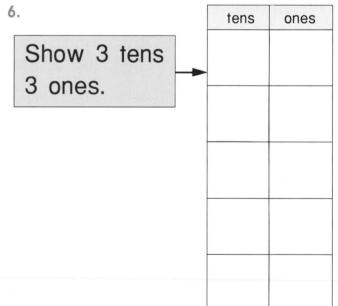

tens	ones

Did you make a trade?

yes   no

Notes for Home Children explore at the CONCRETE level using tens and ones counters and a workmat to show a given number of tens and ones. They count by ones and trade 10 ones for 1 ten when necessary.

Name

Understanding Tens and Ones

I need to make a trade when I have 10 ones.

Use Workmat 2.
Use tens and ones counters.

Show this many.	Show 1 more. Do you need to make a trade?	Write the number of tens and ones.
1. 3 tens 9 ones	(yes) no	tens 4, ones 0
2. 2 tens 4 ones	yes no	tens ___, ones ___
3. 9 ones	yes no	tens ___, ones ___

Notes for Home Children work at the CONCRETE level using tens and ones counters and a workmat to show a given number of tens and ones. They add one more and determine if a trade of 10 ones for 1 ten is required.

Use Workmat 2.
Use tens and ones counters.

Show this many.	Show 2 more. Do you need to make a trade?	Write the number of tens and ones.
4. 2 tens 4 ones	yes / no	tens: 2, ones: 6
5. 3 tens 8 ones	yes / no	tens: ___, ones: ___
6. 1 ten 9 ones	yes / no	tens: ___, ones: ___
7. 4 tens 3 ones	yes / no	tens: ___, ones: ___
8. 2 tens 8 ones	yes / no	tens: ___, ones: ___

Notes for Home Children work at the CONCRETE level using tens and ones counters and a workmat to show a given number of tens and ones. They add two more and determine if a trade of 10 ones for 1 ten is required.

Name

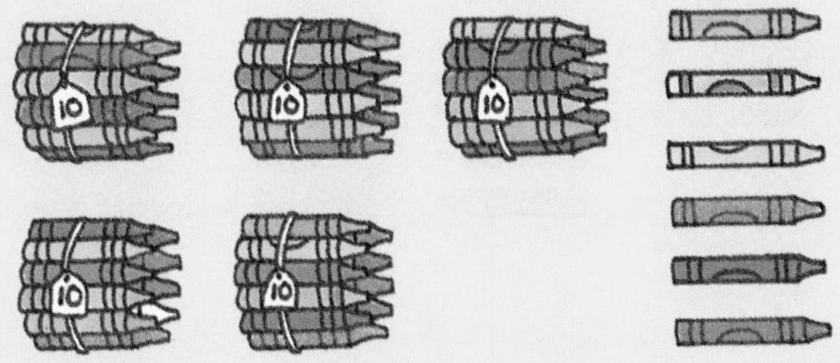

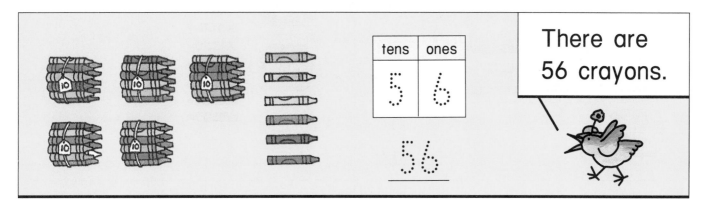

tens	ones
5	6

56

Write the number of tens and ones.
Then write the number.

1.

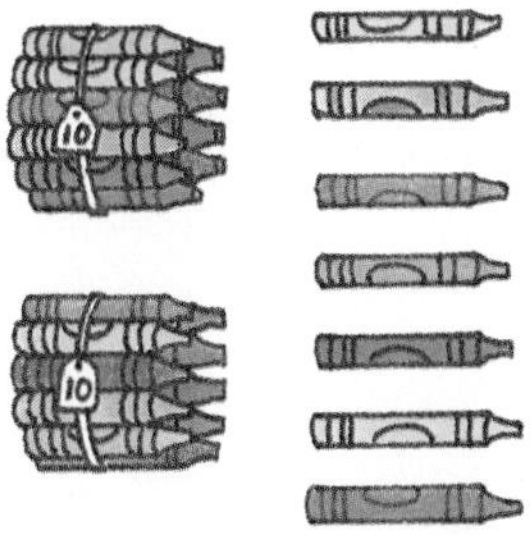

tens	ones

______

2.

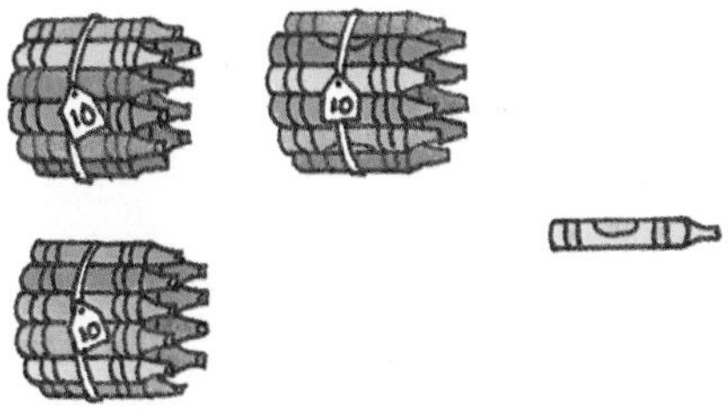

tens	ones

______

3.

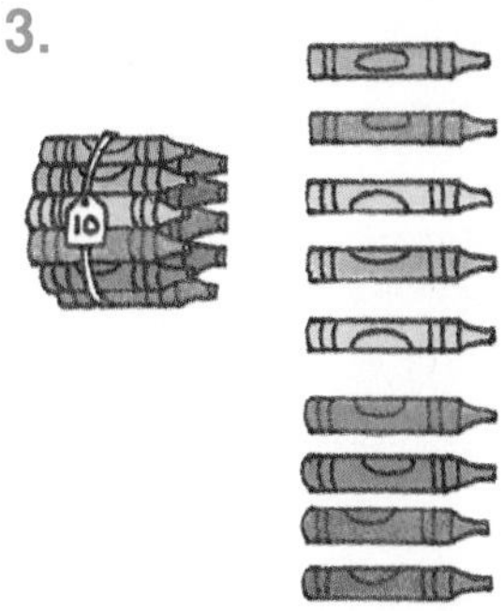

tens	ones

______

4.

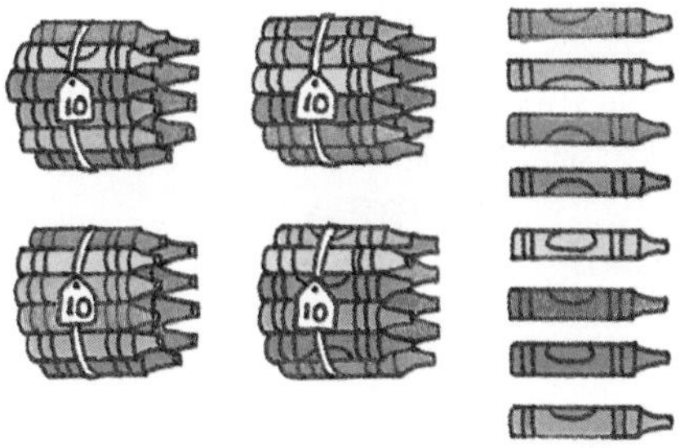

tens	ones

______

5.

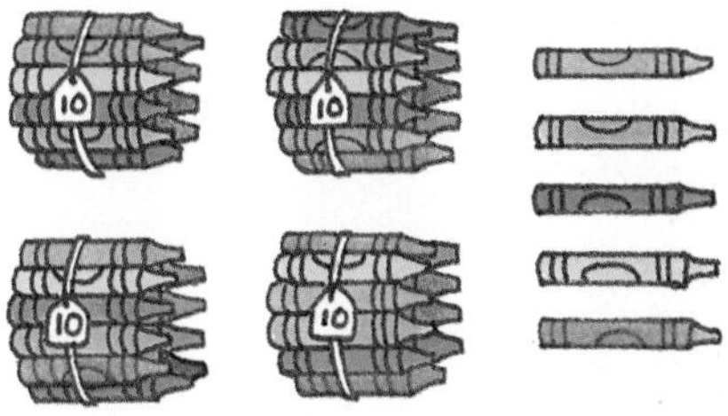

tens	ones

______

6.

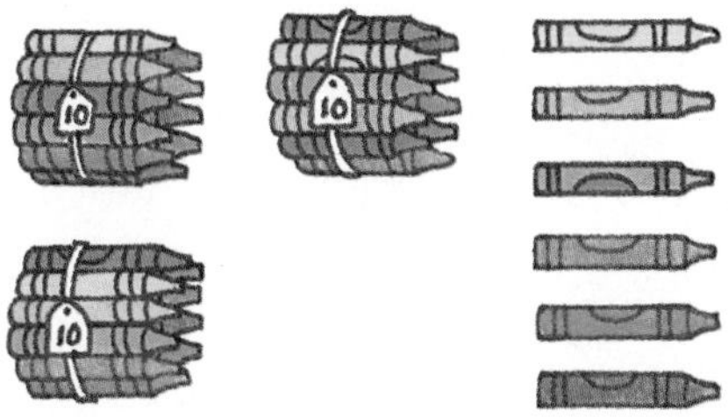

tens	ones

______

Notes for Home Children learn to identify tens and ones for numbers through 99.

Write the number.

7.

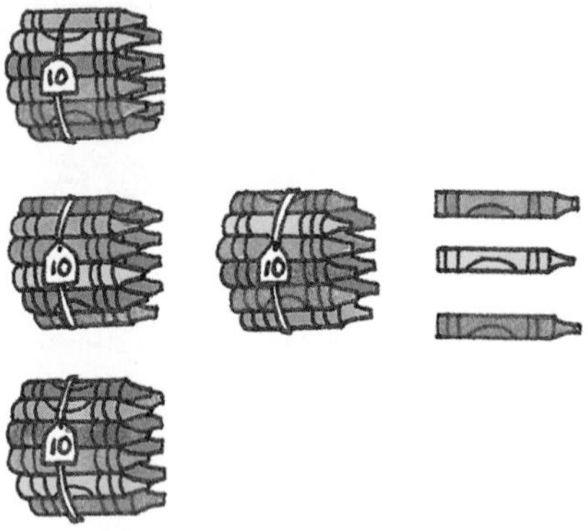

43

8.

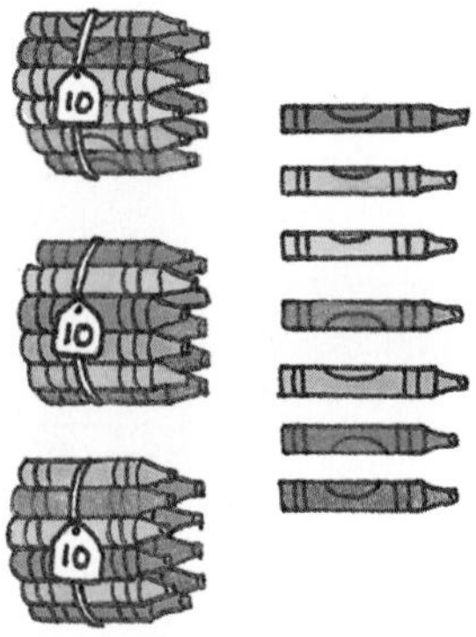

9.

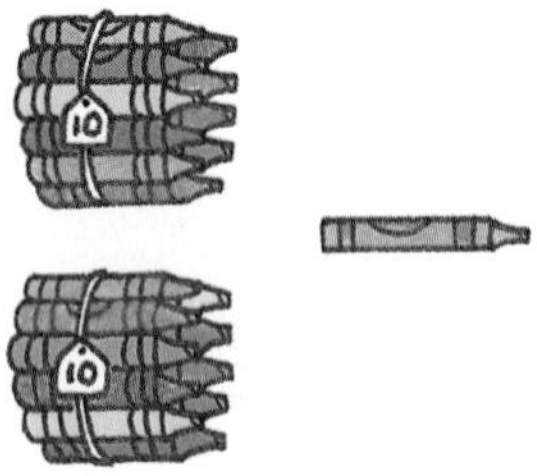

10.

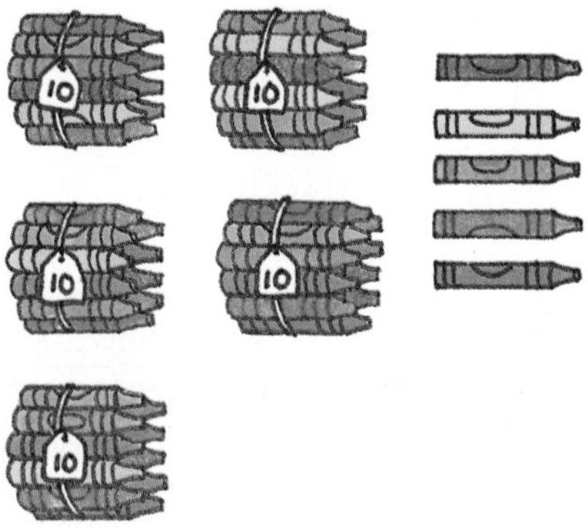

11.

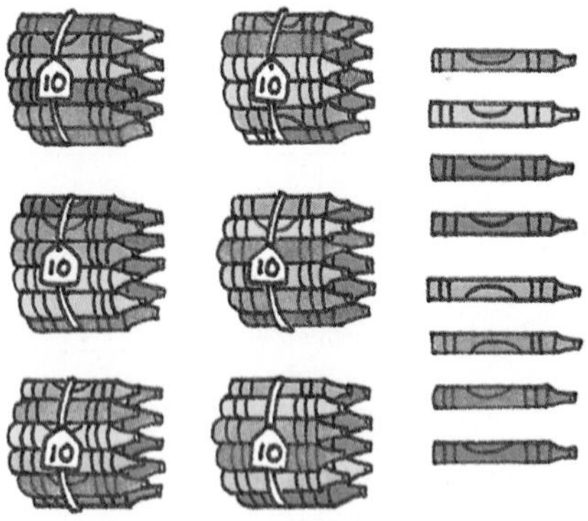

12.

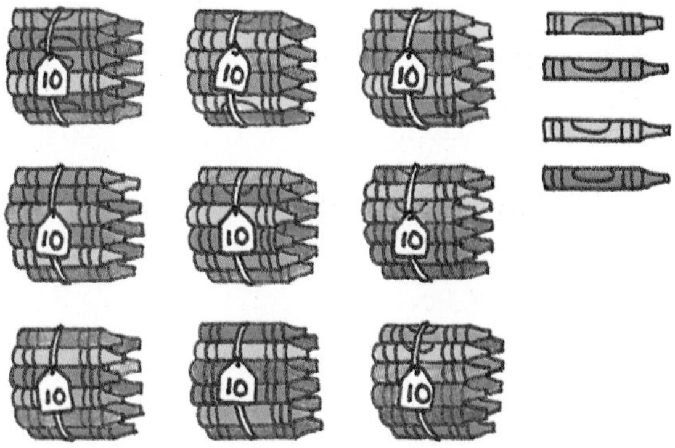

13.

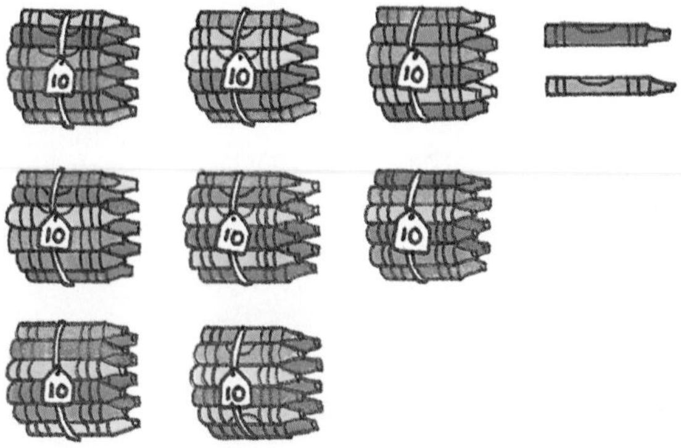

14.

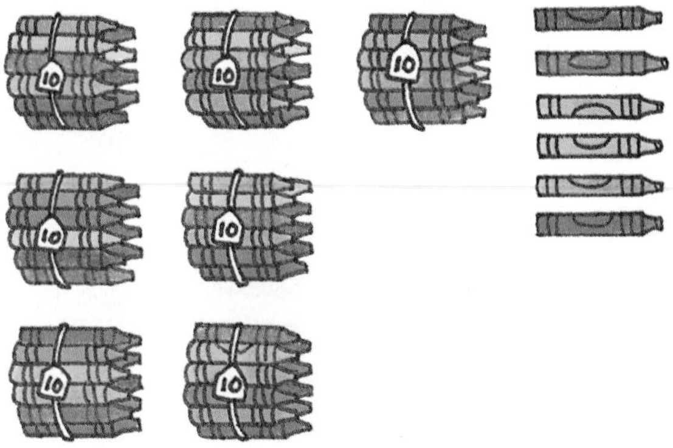

Notes for Home Children practice identifying tens and ones for numbers through 99.

Name

Tens and Ones Through 99

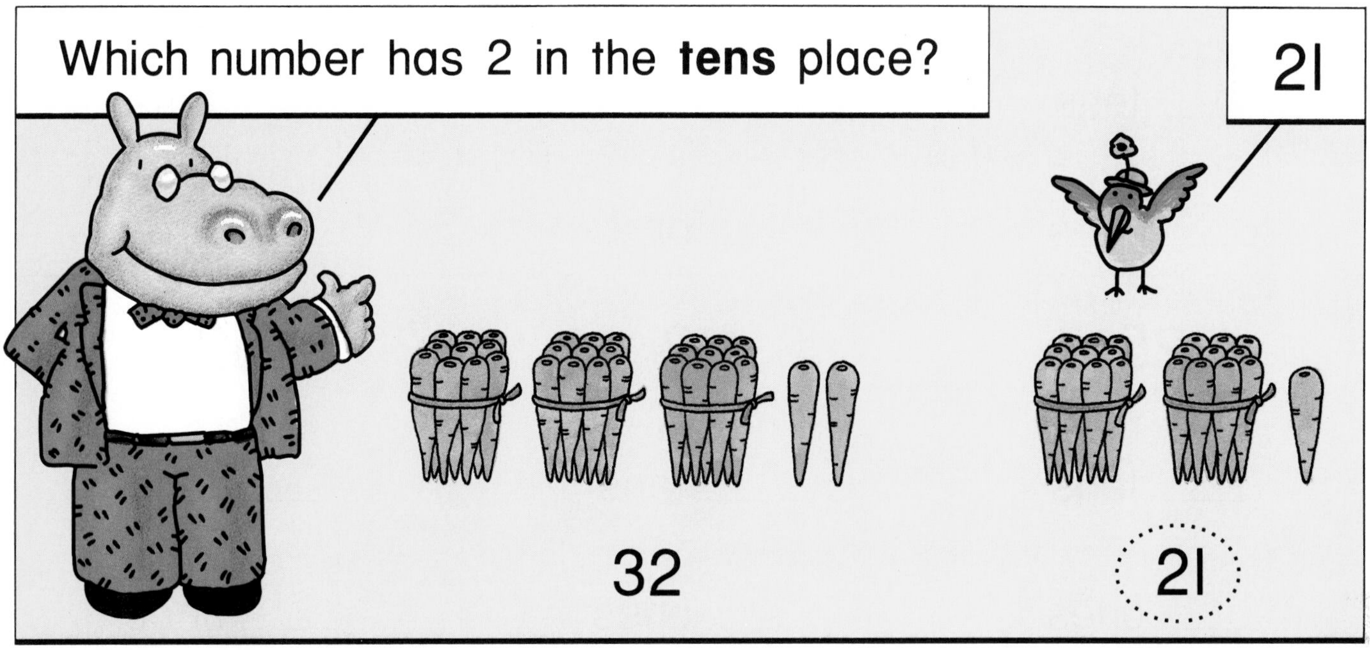

Which number has 2 in the **tens** place?
21
32
21

Ring the number that has

1\. 8 in the **ones** place.

28 82

2\. 4 in the **tens** place.

64 49

3\. 5 in the **tens** place.

95 51

4\. 7 in the **ones** place.

74 57

5\. 6 in the **ones** place.

26 65

6\. 9 in the **tens** place.

79 97

Notes for Home Children demonstrate their understanding of place value by identifying the position of a given digit for numbers through 99.

Write how many tens and ones.

7. 87 8 tens 7 ones	8. 68 ____ tens ____ ones	9. 93 ____ tens ____ ones
10. 25 ____ tens ____ ones	11. 49 ____ tens ____ ones	12. 52 ____ tens ____ ones
13. 76 ____ tens ____ ones	14. 34 ____ tens ____ ones	15. 60 ____ tens ____ ones

16. Color all the numbers with 4 in the **tens** place.

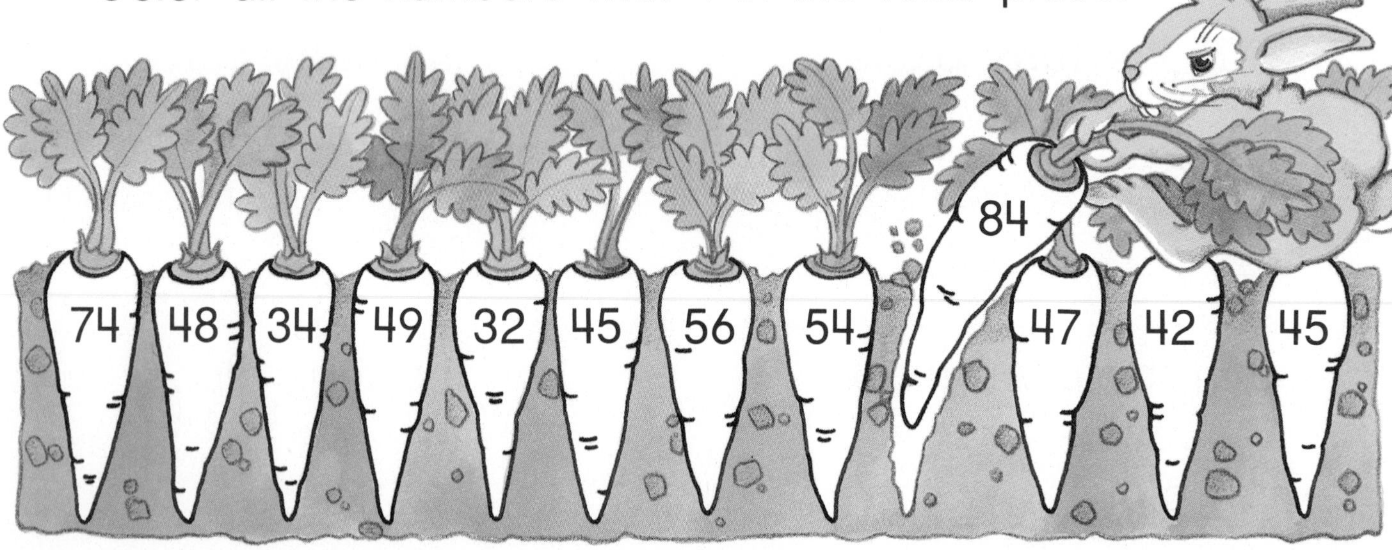

Notes for Home Children demonstrate their understanding of place value by identifying tens and ones for numbers through 99.

See More Practice Set A on page 259.

Name

Use Data from a Table

March						
Sunday	Monday	Tuesday	Wednesday	Thursday	Friday	Saturday
		1	2	3	4	5
6	7	8	9	10	11	12
13	14	15	16	17	18	19
20	21	22	23	24	25	26
27	28	29	30	31		

Use the calendar above.

1. How many days are in this month? 31

2. How many days are in one week? ____

3. On what day does this month begin? ____________

Ring the day that comes just after.

4. Monday	Sunday	Tuesday	Thursday
5. Saturday	Friday	Monday	Sunday
6. Wednesday	Thursday	Tuesday	Saturday

Notes for Home Children learn to solve problems by using data from a table.

7. Write the missing numbers.

April						
Sunday	Monday	Tuesday	Wednesday	Thursday	Friday	Saturday
					1	2
3	4		6	7		
10		12			15	
	18			21		23
24			27			30

Use the calendar above.

8. How many days are in this month? ______

9. How many Saturdays are in this month? ______

10. How many Tuesdays are in this month? ______

Ring the correct day.

11. April 4	Sunday	Monday
12. April 14	Thursday	Friday
13. April 24	Saturday	Sunday

Notes for Home Children solve problems by using data from a table.

Number Sense

Can you tell different ways to count how many children?

Let's do some more!

Guess how many children are in your class.

Notes for Home Children develop an understanding of numbers by counting a group different ways.

SKILLS REVIEW

Skills Review

Fill in the correct ⬭.

About how long?

1.

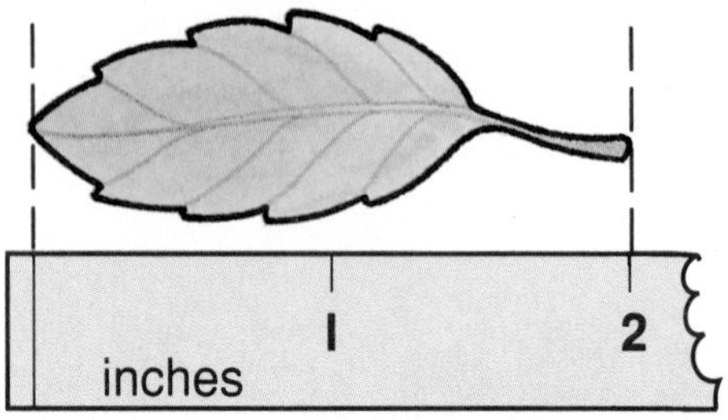

I inch	2 inches	3 inches
(A)	(B)	(C)

2.

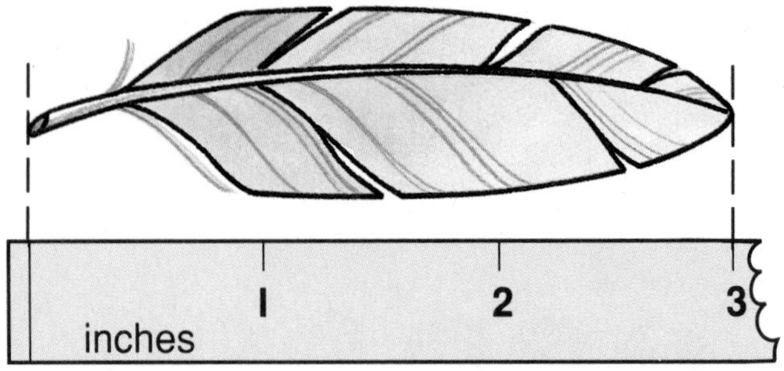

I inch	2 inches	3 inches
(A)	(B)	(C)

About how tall?

3.

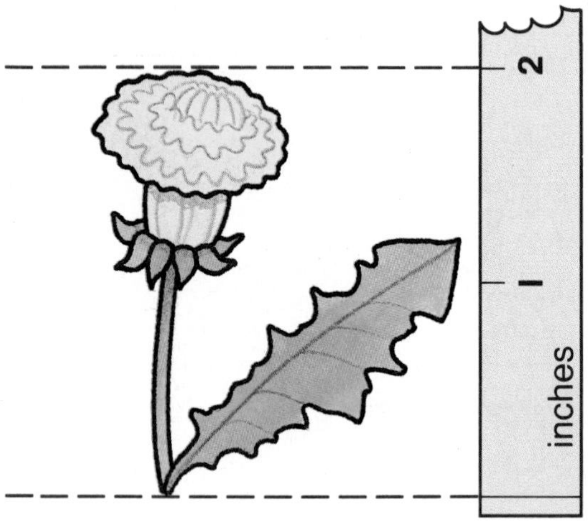

I inch	2 inches	3 inches
(A)	(B)	(C)

4.

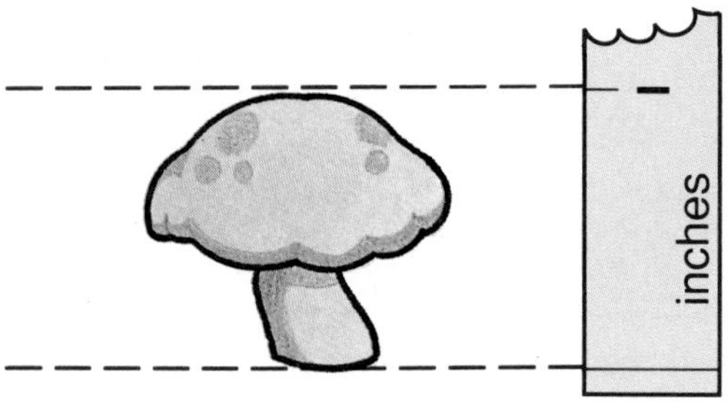

I inch	2 inches	3 inches
(A)	(B)	(C)

Vocabulary

Ring the sentence if it is correct.

5. I9 is I ten and 9 ones.

6. I4 is one more than I5.

7. I8 is less than I9.

8. I5 is I ten and 4 ones.

Notes for Home Children review using a ruler to measure lengths and heights of objects. Then they review math terms.

Name

Order Through 99

1. Complete the chart.

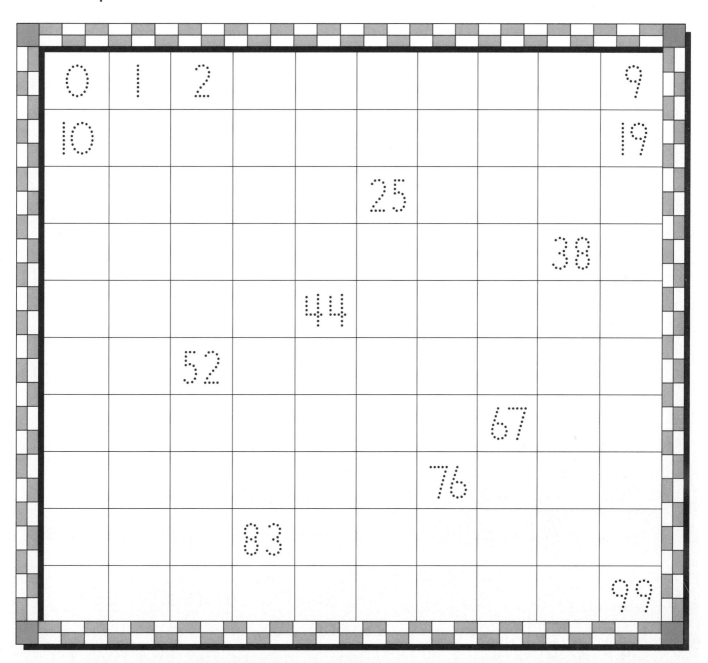

0	1	2							9
10									19
					25				
								38	
				44					
		52							
							67		
						76			
			83						
									99

2. Color the numbers with 4 in the ones place red.

3. Color the numbers with 9 in the tens place blue.

4. Which number has two colors? ______

Notes for Home Children learn to order numbers through 99.

Write the missing numbers.

5. 22 23 ___ 25	6. ___ 78 79 ___
7. 54 55 ___ ___	8. ___ ___ 40 41
9. ___ 61 ___ 63	10. 94 ___ ___ 97
11. 48 ___ ___ 51	12. ___ ___ 89 90
13. ___ 65 ___ ___	14. ___ ___ ___ 30

Problem Solving

Solve.

15. Karen had some number cards.
She picked three cards.
The numbers were between 29 and 33.
What numbers did she pick?

___ ___ ___

Notes for Home Children identify numbers before, after, and between given numbers. Then they solve a problem involving number order.

Name

Comparing Numbers Through 99

32   24

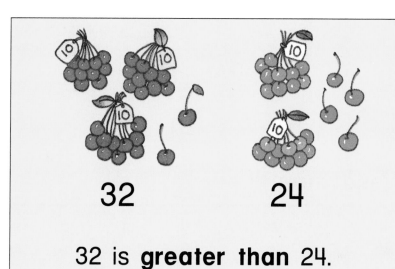

I know 32 is greater than 24 because there are more tens.

32 is **greater than** 24.

Ring the number that is greater.

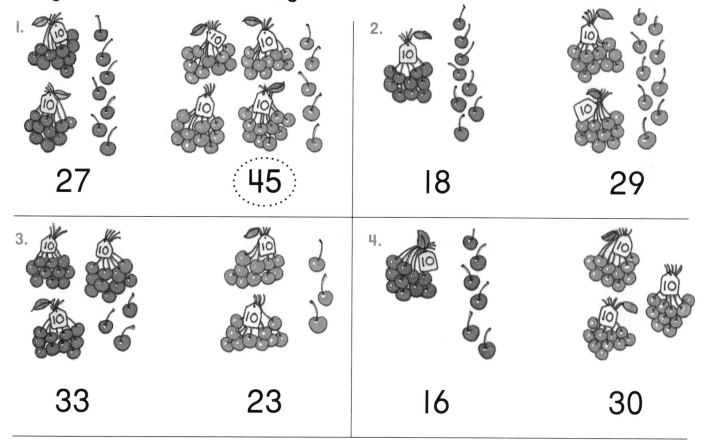

1.

27   45

2.

18   29

3.

33   23

4.

16   30

Which is greater?

5. 84   96

6. 99   94

7. 82   28

Notes for Home Children compare two numbers and identify the one that is greater.

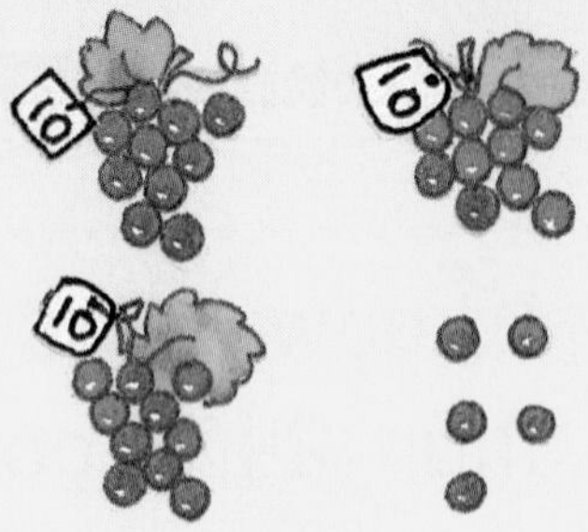

35

41

35 is **less than** 41.

Ring the number that is less.

8.

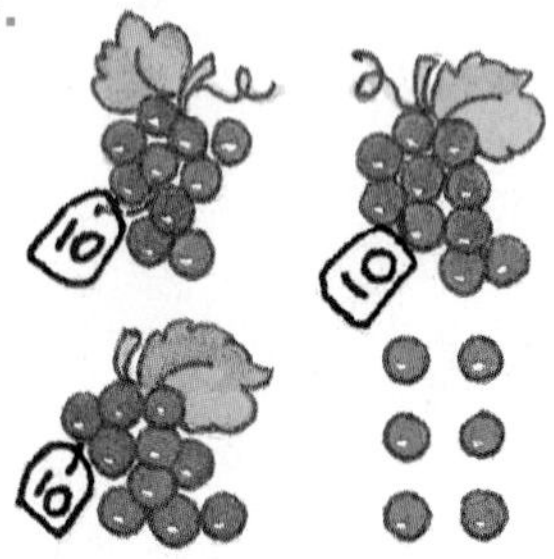

36 21

9.

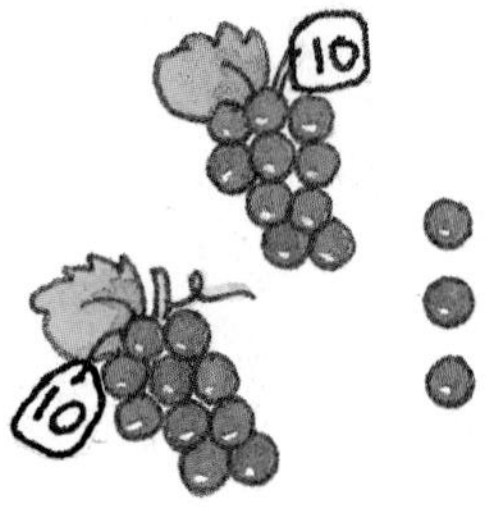

23 37

10.

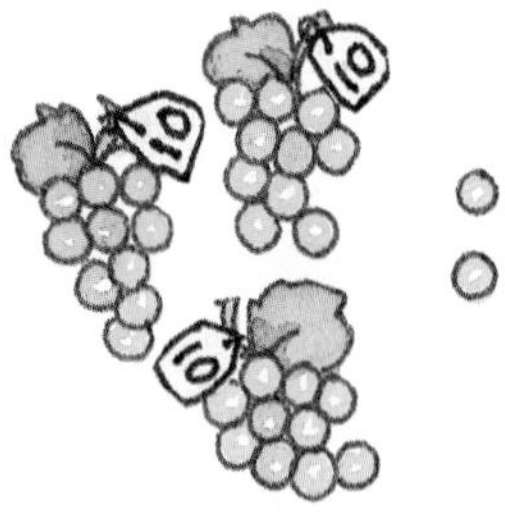

29 32

11.

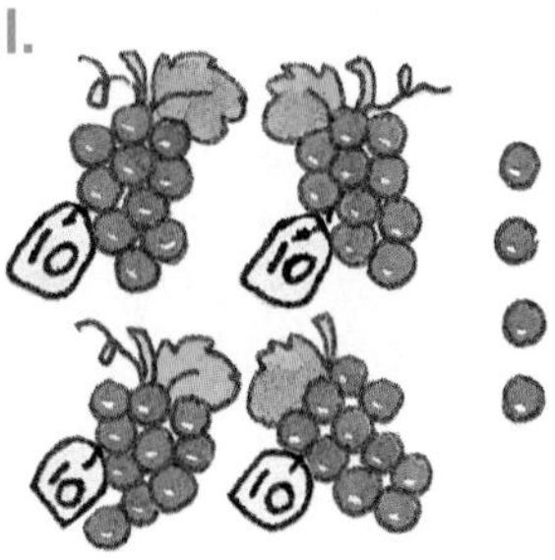

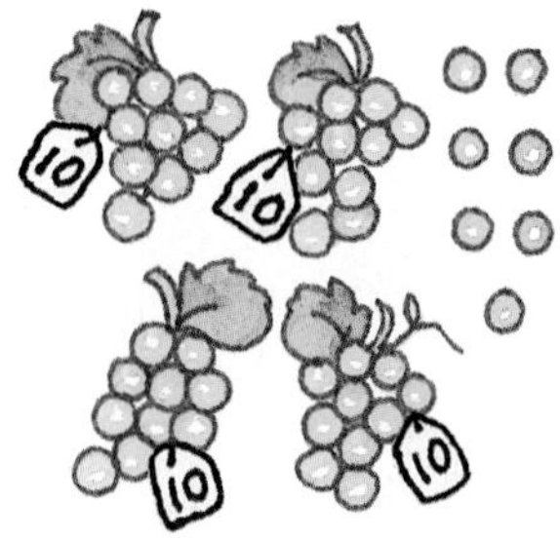

44 47

Which is less?

12. 65 59 13. 84 91 14. 72 28

Notes for Home Children compare two numbers and identify the one that is less.

 See More Practice Set B on page 259.

Name

Counting by Twos, Fives, and Tens

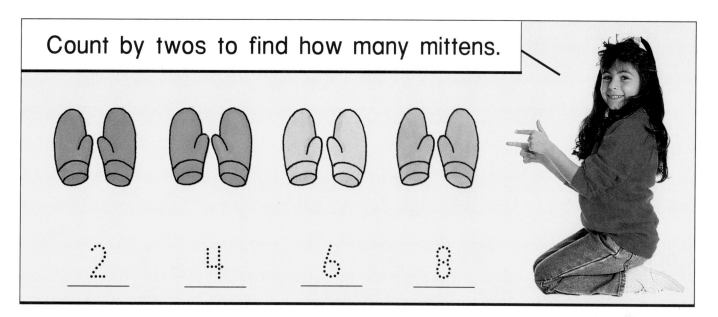

Count by twos to find how many mittens.

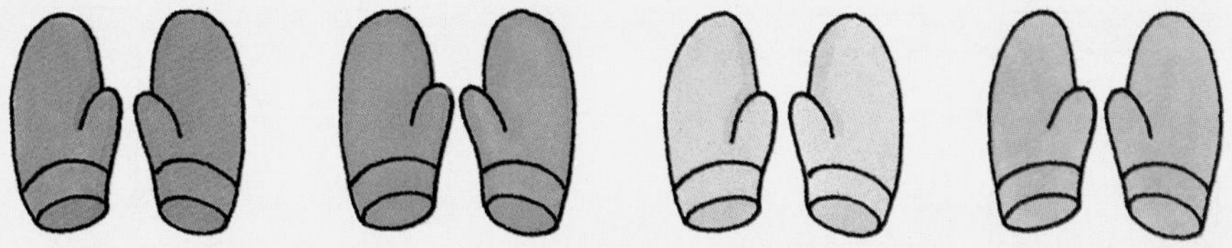

2 4 6 8

1. How many shoes? Count by twos.

2. How many fingers? Count by fives.

5

3. How many toes? Count by fives.

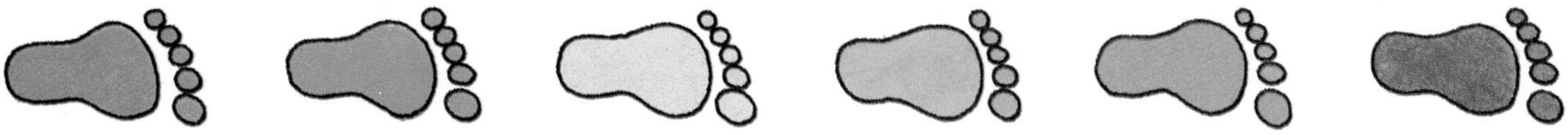

Notes for Home Children learn to skip count by twos and fives.

Count by twos.

4.

5.

Count by fives.

6.

7.

Count by tens.

8.

9.

Notes for Home Children practice skip counting by twos, fives, and tens.

Name ______________________________

Counting on with Nickels or Dimes

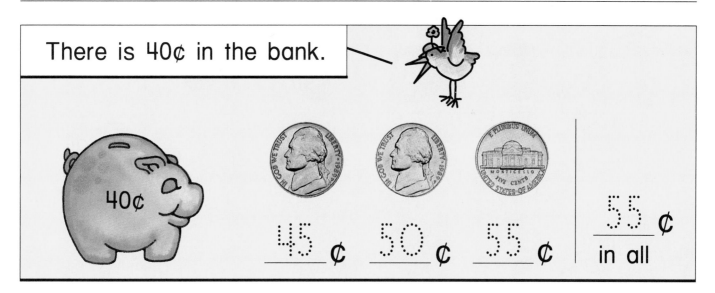

There is 40¢ in the bank.

45 ¢ 50 ¢ 55 ¢

55 ¢ in all

Count by fives.
Write how much.

1.

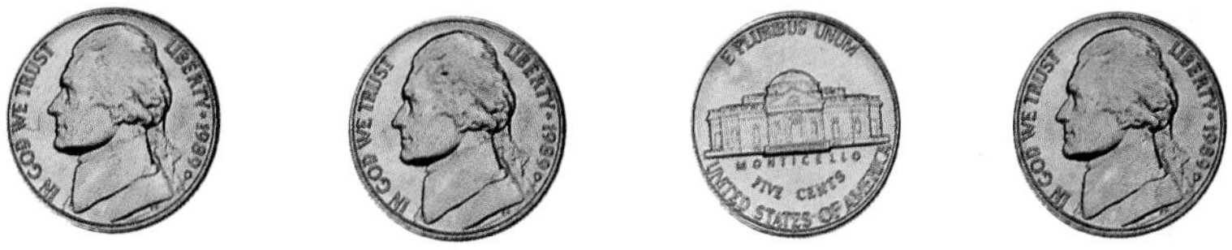

____¢ ____¢ ____¢ ____¢

____¢ in all

2.

____¢ ____¢ ____¢

____¢ in all

3.

____¢ ____¢ ____¢ ____¢

____¢ in all

Notes for Home Children skip count by fives by counting on with nickels from a given amount.

Count by tens.
Write how much.

4.

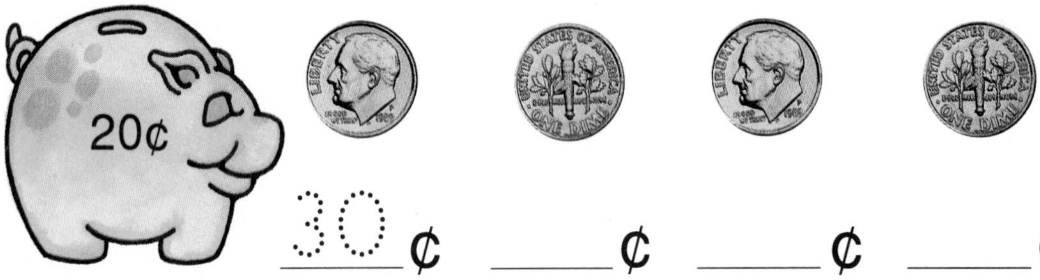

30 ¢ ____ ¢ ____ ¢ ____ ¢

____ ¢ in all

5.

____ ¢ ____ ¢ ____ ¢

____ ¢ in all

6.

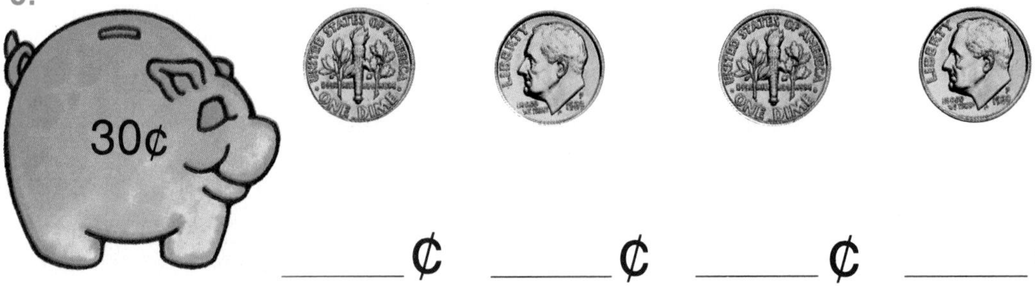

____ ¢ ____ ¢ ____ ¢ ____ ¢

____ ¢ in all

Problem Solving

Solve.

7. Ann has 30¢.
Dad gives her 6 nickels.
How much does she have now?

____ ¢

8. Cliff has 50¢.
Mom gives him 4 dimes.
How much does he have now?

____ ¢

Notes for Home Children skip count by tens by counting on with dimes from a given amount. Then they solve problems involving money.

Name ______________________

PROBLEM-SOLVING STRATEGY

Find a Pattern

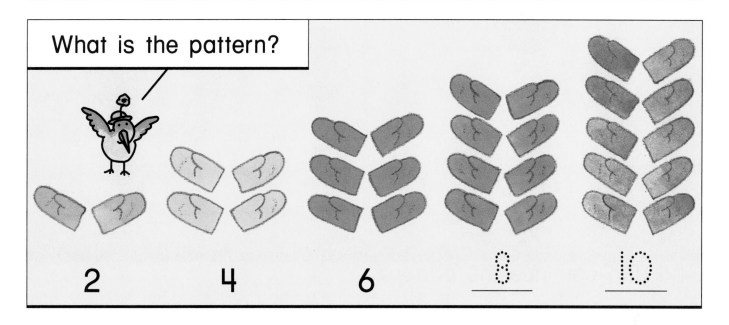

What is the pattern?

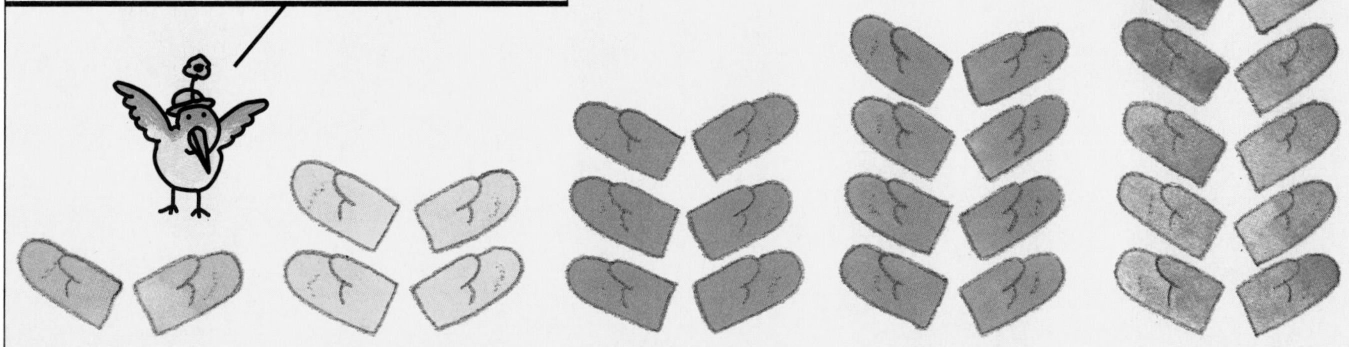

2 4 6 8 10

Find and continue the pattern.

1.

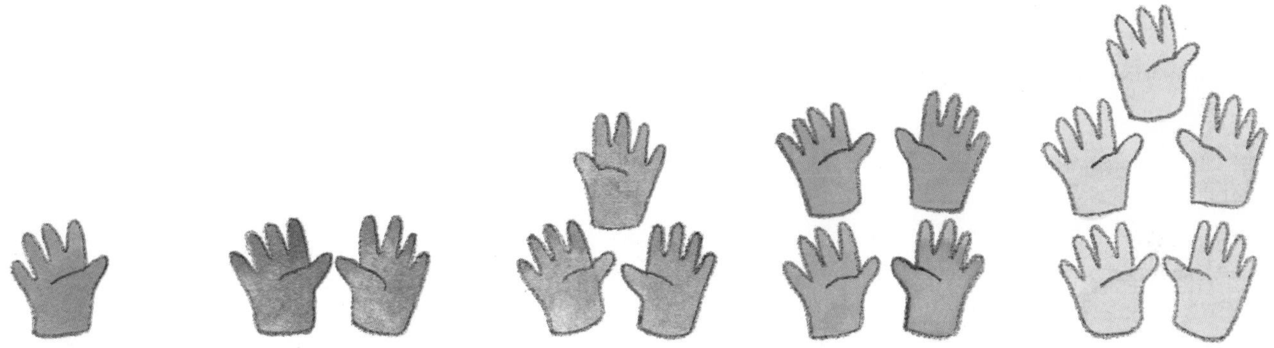

5 10 15 ____ ____

2.

2 3 2 3 ____ ____

Notes for Home Children solve number problems by finding patterns.

Find and continue the pattern.

3.

2 5 6 2 5 6 2 5 ___ ___

4.

6 6 8 6 6 8 ___ ___ ___ ___

5.

M N O M N O ___ ___ ___ ___

6.

4 7 7 4 7 7 ___ ___ ___ ___

7.

3 5 7 9 3 5 7 9 ___ ___ ___ ___

8.

W X Y Z W X Y Z ___ ___ ___ ___

Notes for Home Children solve number and letter problems by finding patterns.

Name

Problem-Solving Workshop

Explore as a Team

Work with a partner.
Help Gina find her classroom door.
The number on her door has 2 digits.
The digits are always different.
The sum of the digits is 12.
Write what the number could be.

Now write the numbers in order.

The third number is the right number.
Write the number on the door.

Notes for Home Children explore with a partner to solve a problem finding different combinations of 12.

Problem-Solving Workshop

Explore with a Calculator

Use a  to solve.

	Start at	Press	Write the pattern
1.	2	+ 2 = = =	4 6 8
2.	2 4	+ 2 = = =	
3.	6 8	+ 2 = = =	
4.	5	+ 5 = = =	
5.	7 5	+ 5 = = =	
6.	1 0	+ 1 0 = = =	
7.	5 0	+ 1 0 = = =	

Notes for Home Children explore with a calculator to solve problems involving counting by twos, fives, and tens.

Name

Set A Use after page 242.

Color all the numbers with 6 in the **tens** place.

Set B Use after page 250.

Which is greater?

1. 66 43 2. 82 54 3. 37 77

Which is less?

4. 32 34 5. 89 98 6. 49 50

Notes for Home Set A: Children practice identifying tens and ones for numbers through 99.
Set B: Children practice comparing two numbers and identifying the one that is greater or the one that is less.

Enrichment

The alligator's mouth is always open to the greater number.

21 72

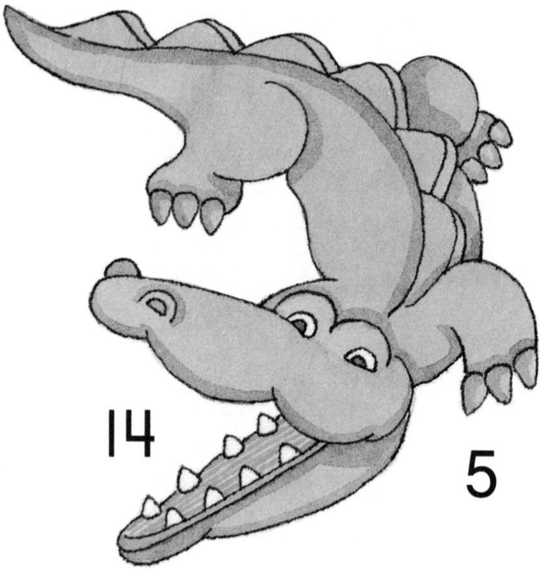

14 5

21 < 72 14 > 5

Which number is greater? Which number is less?
Write < or >.

1. 62 > 12	2. 7 < 9
3. 49 ◯ 81	4. 75 ◯ 29
5. 52 ◯ 50	6. 98 ◯ 99
7. 36 ◯ 63	8. 87 ◯ 78

Notes for Home Children are challenged to use greater than or less than symbols when comparing numbers.

Name

Chapter 8 Review/Test

Write the number.

1. 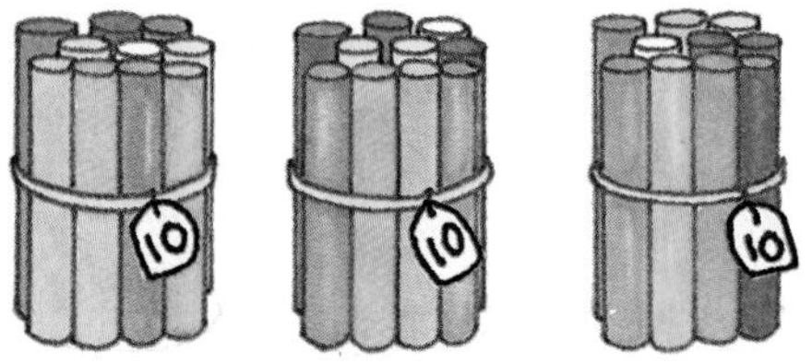

____

2. 

____

3. Which is greater?

78 96

4. Write the missing numbers.

58, ____, ____, 61

5. Ring the number that has 6 in the ones place.

36 68

6. Write the number of tens and ones.

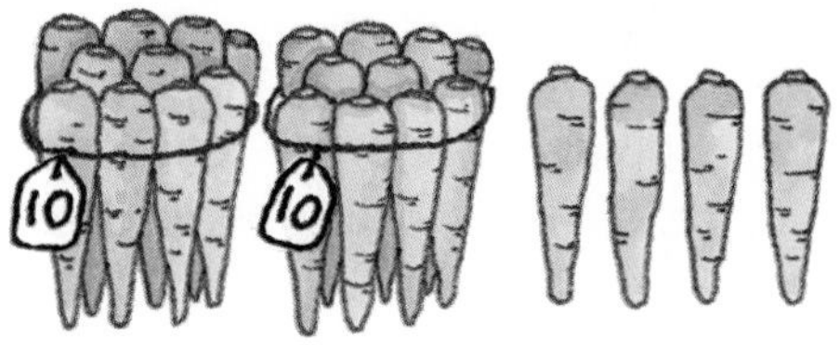

tens	ones

7. Write how much in all.

____¢

8. Find and complete the pattern.

25, 30, 35, 40, ____, ____, ____, ____, ____

June		
Sunday	Monday	Tuesday
	1	2
7	8	9

Ring the correct day.

9. June 2 Monday Tuesday

10. June 8 Sunday Monday

Notes for Home Children are assessed on Chapter 8 concepts, skills, and problem solving.

Exploring Math at Home

Dear Family,

In this chapter I have learned about tens and ones through 99. I have also learned to count by twos, fives, and tens and how to count on with nickels and dimes. Please help me do the activities below.

Love, ____________________

1.

Use straws. Show a given number of tens and ones. Place one more straw into the ones pile. Decide if a trade is needed.

2.

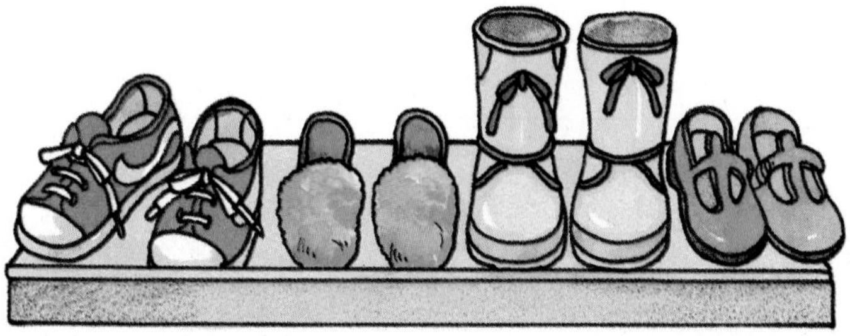

Count by twos by counting pairs of shoes, gloves, or boots.

3.

Count by fives. Count on by using hands of each family member in the house.

Coming Attractions

In the next chapter I will be learning to count coins to 99¢. I will also learn about money amounts.

Chapter 9

Money

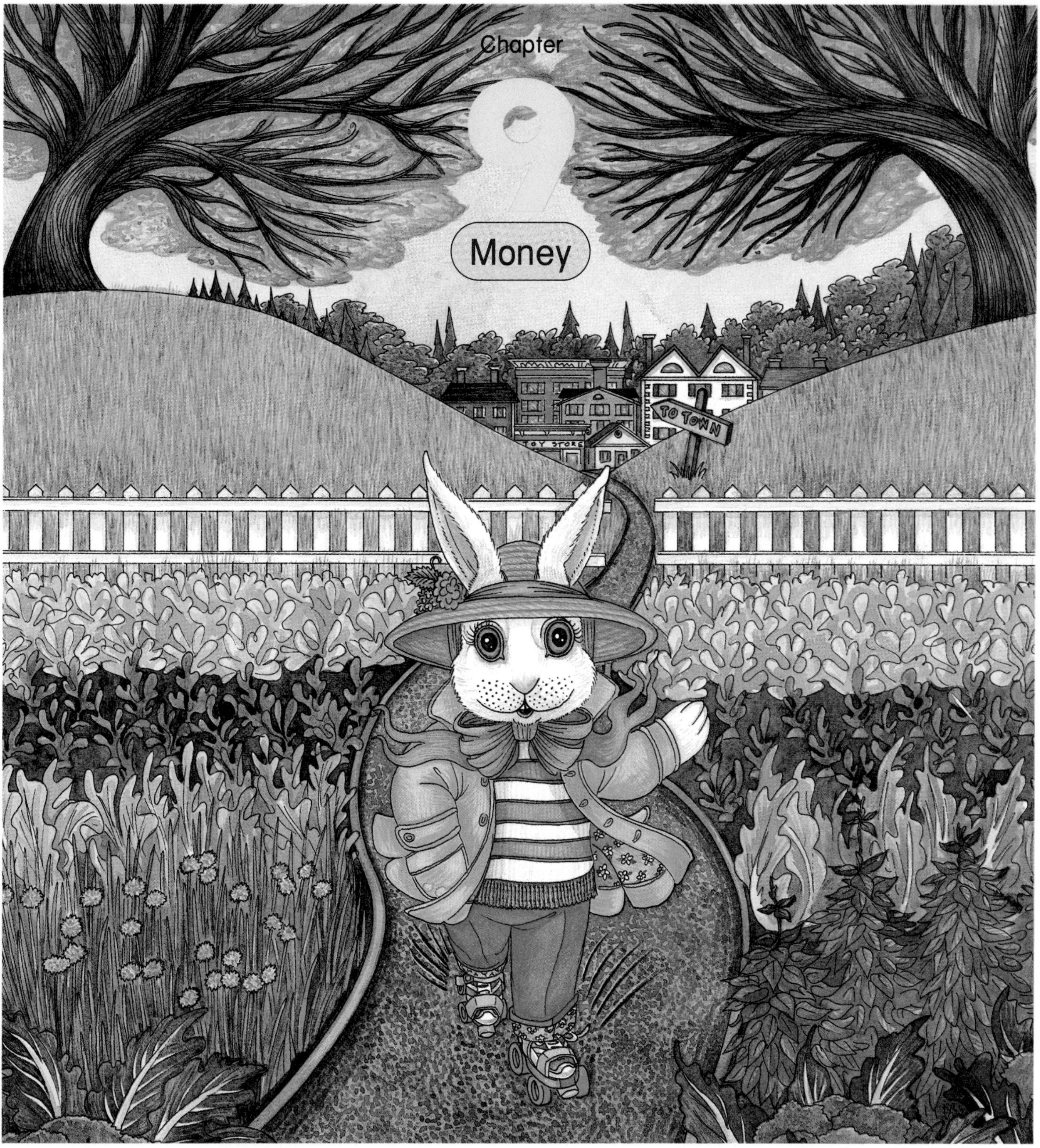

Listen to the math story, "Bunny Money."
Pat had enough money to buy one toy.
How do you think she decided which toy to buy?

Notes for Home Children listen to a math story introducing chapter concepts and skills. Then they answer a question about the story.

Name

Pennies, Nickels, and Dimes

penny
1¢

nickel
5¢

dime
10¢

Write how much in all.

1.

5 ¢

2.

____ ¢

3.

____ ¢

4.

____ ¢

5.

____ ¢

6.

____ ¢

Notes for Home Children review pennies, nickels, and dimes.

Name ______________________

Counting Nickels and Dimes

Start with the coin of greater value.
Count on by tens and fives.

10 ¢ 20 ¢ 25 ¢ 30 ¢ 35 ¢

35 ¢ in all

Count on to find how much.

1.

____ ¢ ____ ¢ ____ ¢ ____ ¢

____ ¢ in all

2.

____ ¢ ____ ¢ ____ ¢ ____ ¢

____ ¢ in all

3.

____ ¢ ____ ¢ ____ ¢ ____ ¢ ____ ¢

____ ¢ in all

Notes for Home Children learn to count dimes and nickels. They start with the coin of greater value and count on to find the amount.

Count on to find how much in all.

4.

40 ¢

5.

_____ ¢

6.

_____ ¢

7.

_____ ¢

8.

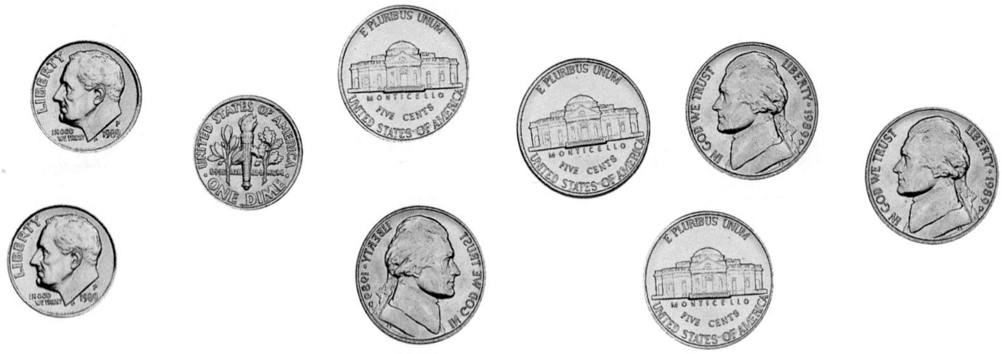

_____ ¢

9.

_____ ¢

Notes for Home Children count dimes and nickels to find how much money in all.

Name ______________________________

Counting Pennies, Nickels, and Dimes

Start with the coin of greatest value.
Count on by tens, fives, and ones.

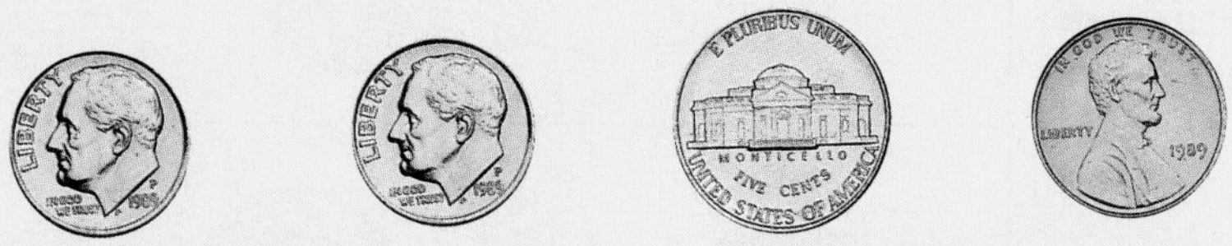

10 ¢ 20 ¢ 25 ¢ 26 ¢

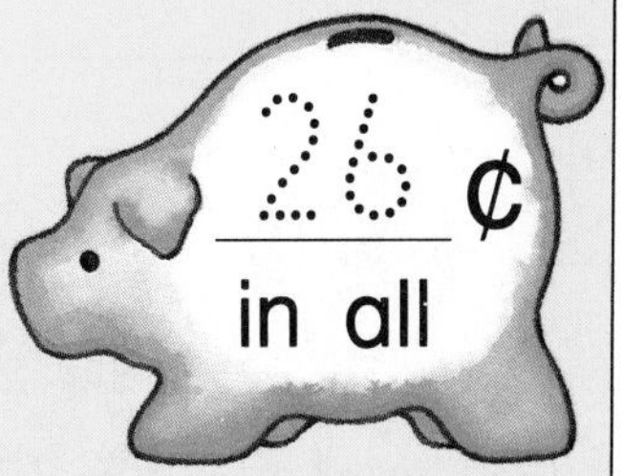

26 ¢ in all

Count on to find how much.

1.

____ ¢ ____ ¢ ____ ¢ ____ ¢ ____ ¢

____ ¢ in all

2.

____ ¢ ____ ¢ ____ ¢ ____ ¢ ____ ¢

____ ¢ in all

3.

____ ¢ ____ ¢ ____ ¢ ____ ¢ ____ ¢

____ ¢ in all

Notes for Home Children count on to find the value of pennies, nickels, and dimes.

Count on to find how much in all.

4.

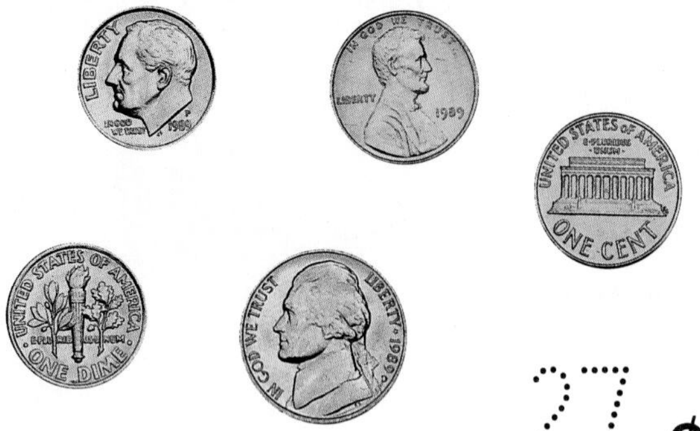

27 ¢

5.

____ ¢

6.

____ ¢

7.

____ ¢

8.

____ ¢

Problem Solving

How much money does each have?

9.

____ ¢

10.

____ ¢

Notes for Home Children count on to find the value of pennies, nickels, and dimes. Then they solve problems involving money.

Name **Activity**

Finding the Value of a Quarter

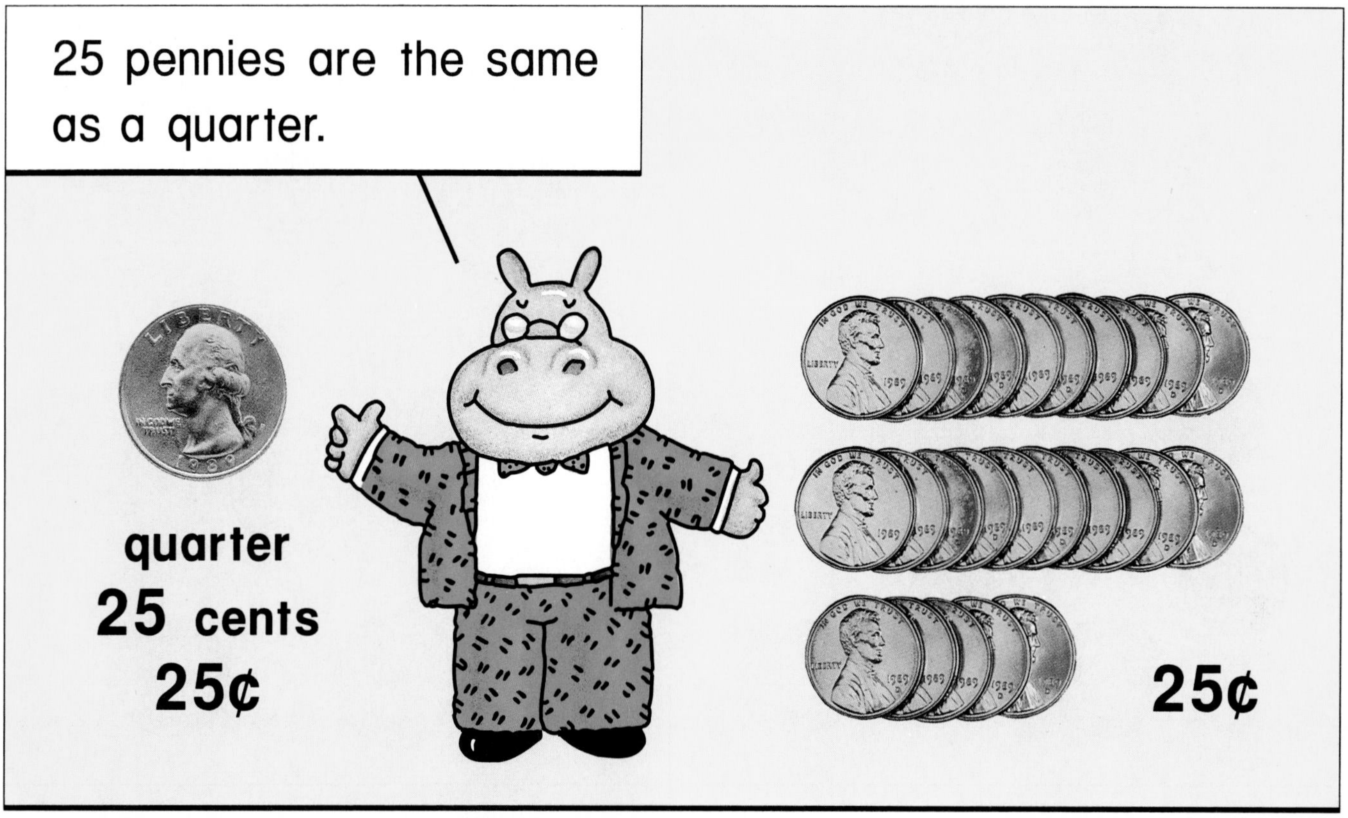

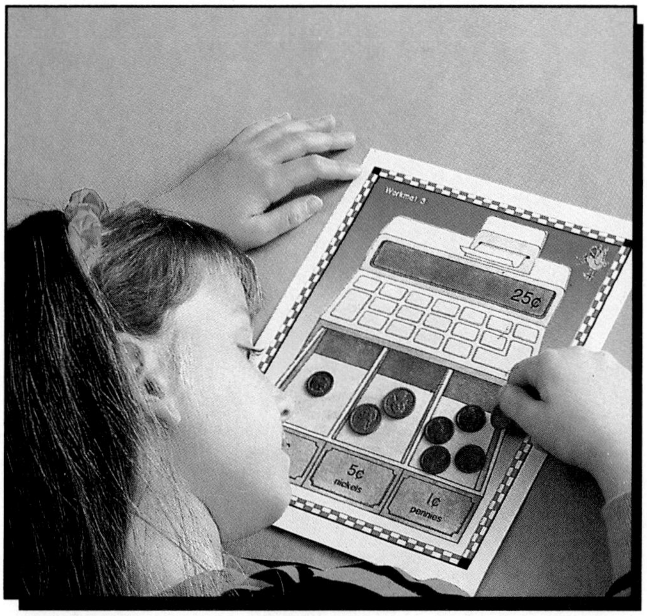

Use coins and Workmat 3. Show four different ways to make 25¢.

1.	1	2	5
2.			
3.			
4.			

Notes for Home Children explore at the CONCRETE level using coins to find different combinations that make 25¢.

Ring the coins needed to make 25¢.

5.

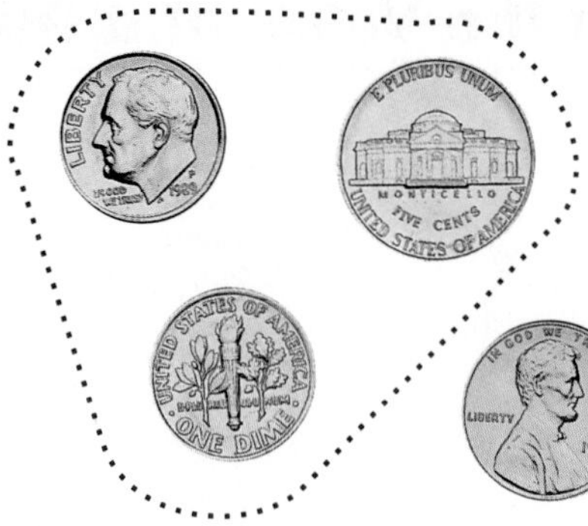

6.

7.

8.

9.

10.

Notes for Home Children identify coins that make 25¢.

Name ____________________

Counting On from a Quarter

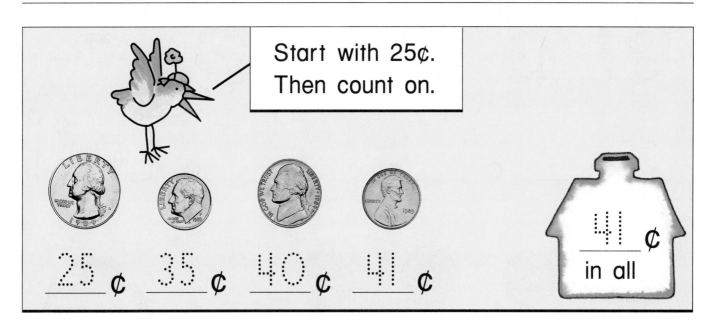

Start with 25¢.
Then count on.

25 ¢ 35 ¢ 40 ¢ 41 ¢

41 ¢ in all

Count on to find how much.

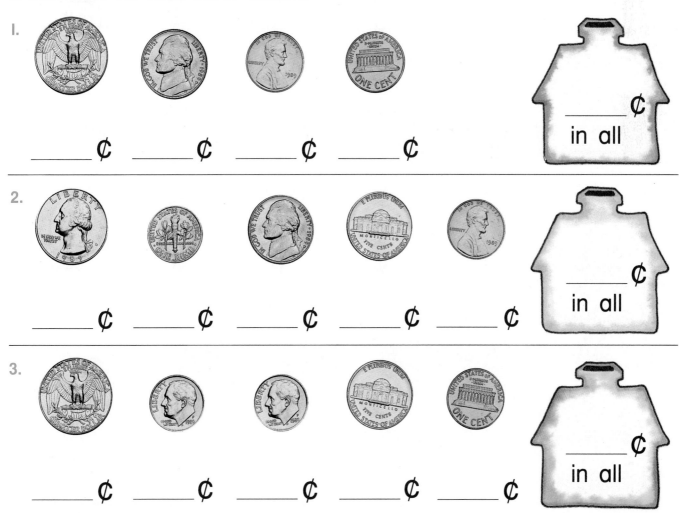

1.

____¢ ____¢ ____¢ ____¢

____¢ in all

2.

____¢ ____¢ ____¢ ____¢ ____¢

____¢ in all

3.

____¢ ____¢ ____¢ ____¢ ____¢

____¢ in all

Notes for Home Children count on to find the value of quarters, dimes, nickels, and pennies.

Count on to find how much.

4.

25 ¢ ___ ¢ ___ ¢ ___ ¢ ___ ¢

___ ¢ in all

5.

___ ¢ ___ ¢ ___ ¢ ___ ¢

___ ¢ in all

6.

___ ¢ ___ ¢ ___ ¢ ___ ¢ ___ ¢

___ ¢ in all

7.

___ ¢ ___ ¢ ___ ¢ ___ ¢ ___ ¢

___ ¢ in all

Notes for Home Children count on to find the value of quarters, dimes, nickels, and pennies.

Name

Counting Coins Through 99¢

Please help me count my money.
You can count on me!
62 ¢

Count on to find how much in all.

1.

_____ ¢

2.

_____ ¢

3.

_____ ¢

Notes for Home Children count on to find the value of coins through 99¢.

Count on to find how much in all.

4.

5.

6.

7.

Notes for Home Children count on to find the value of coins through 99¢.

See More Practice Set A on 287.

Name

Use Data from a Table

Look at the price list.
Use all the coins.
Which drink do you buy?

1. 

milk

apple juice

2. 

grape juice

orange juice

3. 

milk

apple juice

4. 

grape juice

orange juice

Notes for Home Children solve problems involving money by using data from a table.

School Item	Price
paint	46¢
notebook	51¢
scissors	62¢
crayons	67¢

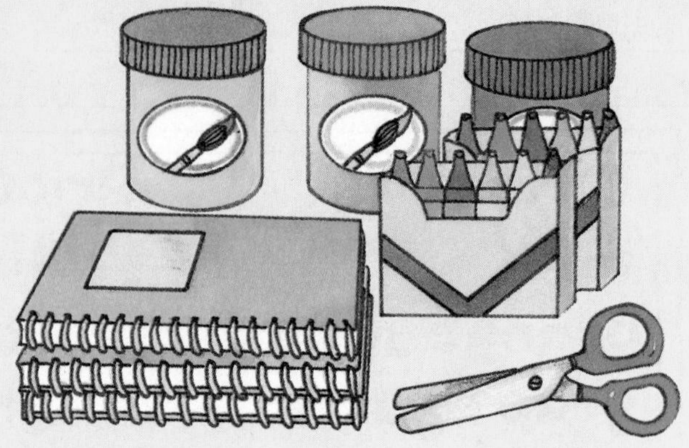

Look at the price list.
Use all the coins.
Which school item do you buy?

5.

crayons

scissors

6.

notebook

paint

7.

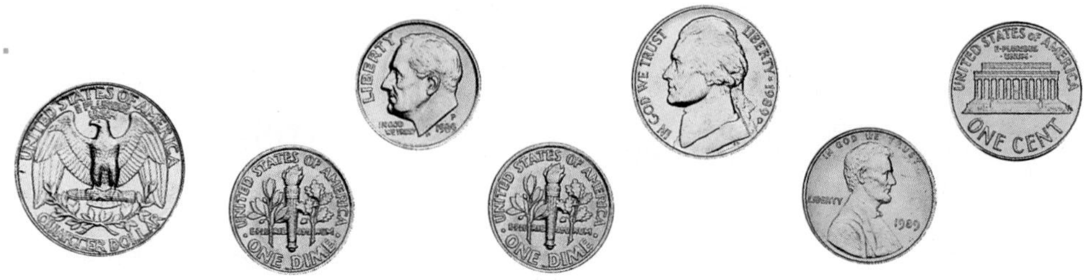

crayons

scissors

8.

paint

notebook

Notes for Home Children solve problems involving money by using data from a table.

Name

Number Sense

Create a new coin.
Give your coin a name.
Tell how much it is worth.

front   back

Let's do some more!

What would you buy with your coin?
How much are two of your coins worth?

Notes for Home Children develop an understanding of money by describing the creation of a new coin.

Skills Review

Fill in the correct ⬭.

About how long?

1.

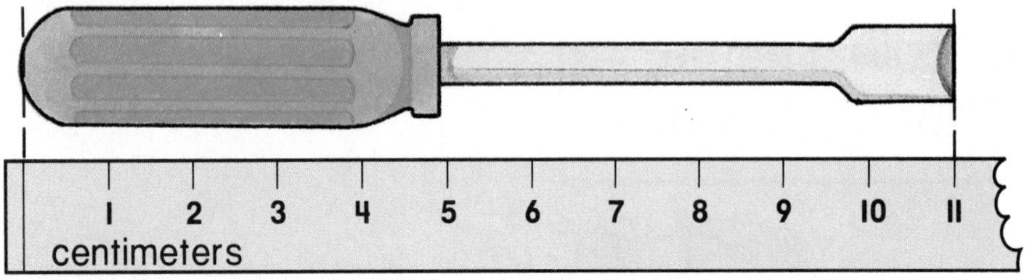

Ⓐ 9 cm
Ⓑ 10 cm
Ⓒ 11 cm

2.

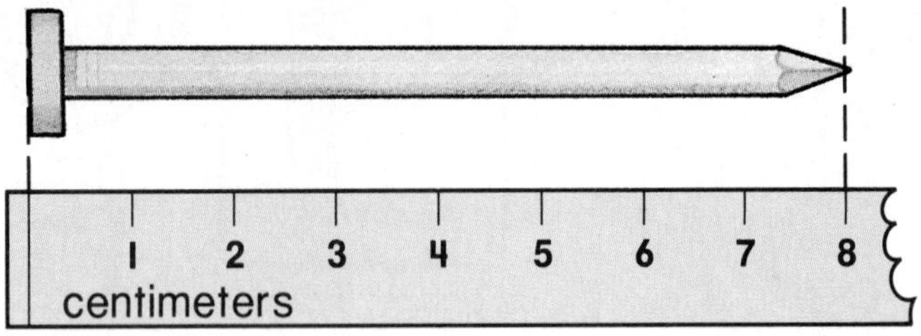

Ⓐ 4 cm
Ⓑ 6 cm
Ⓒ 8 cm

Which is greater?

3. 83 Ⓐ 51 Ⓑ

4. 67 Ⓐ 76 Ⓑ

5. 94 Ⓐ 95 Ⓑ

Vocabulary

Read the sentences.

6. Color the **first** bear red.

7. Color the **fourth** bear yellow.

8. Color the **sixth** bear blue.

Notes for Home Children review measuring with a centimeter ruler. Then they compare two numbers and identify the one that is greater. Children review ordinal numbers.

Name

Finding Equivalent Amounts

You can buy the apple with different groups of coins.
15¢
15¢
15¢

Ring the coins to show the amount.

1.

2.
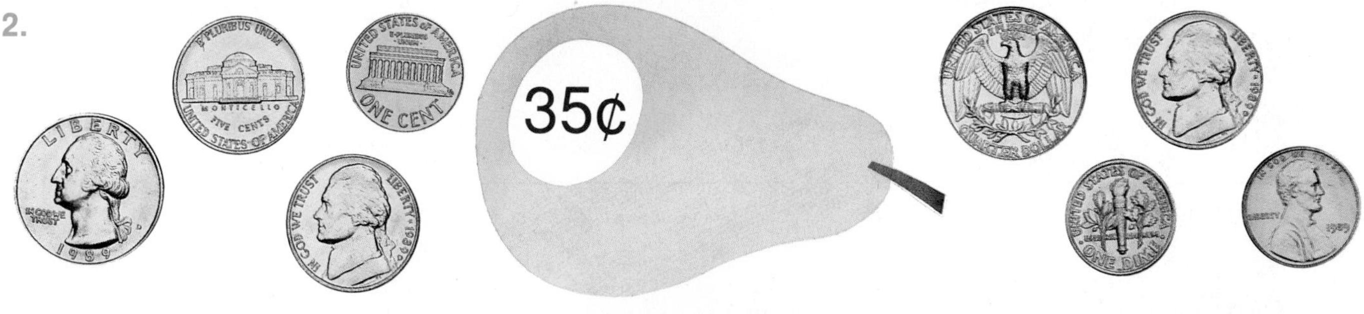

3.

Notes for Home Children identify equivalent values of coins.

Ring the coins to show the amount.

4.

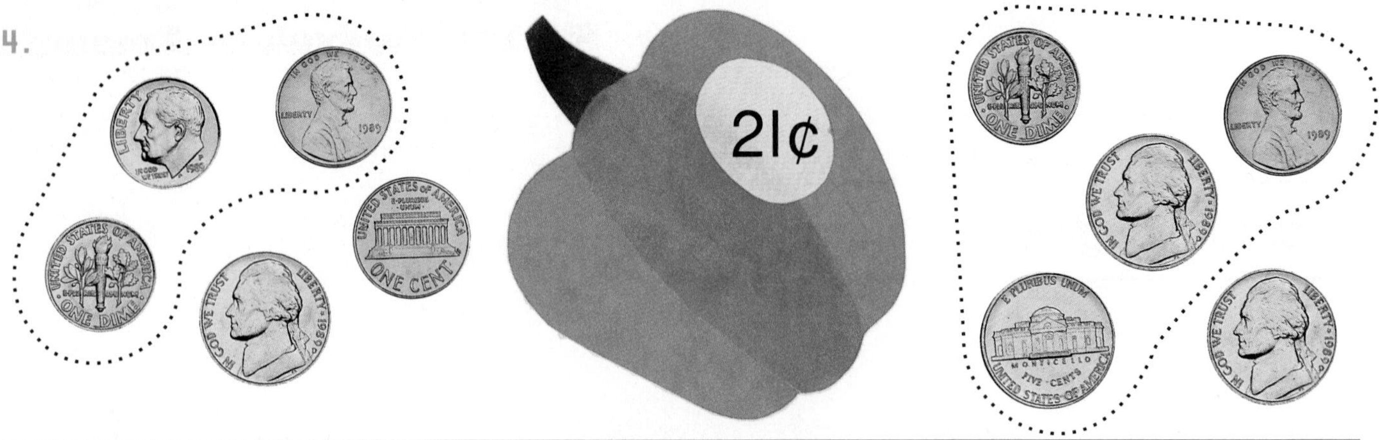

5.

6.

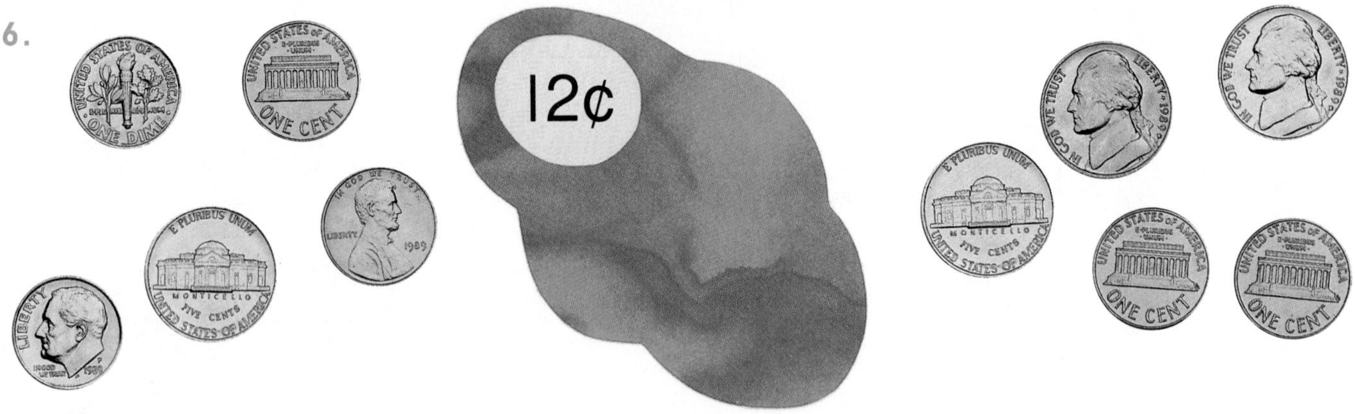

7.

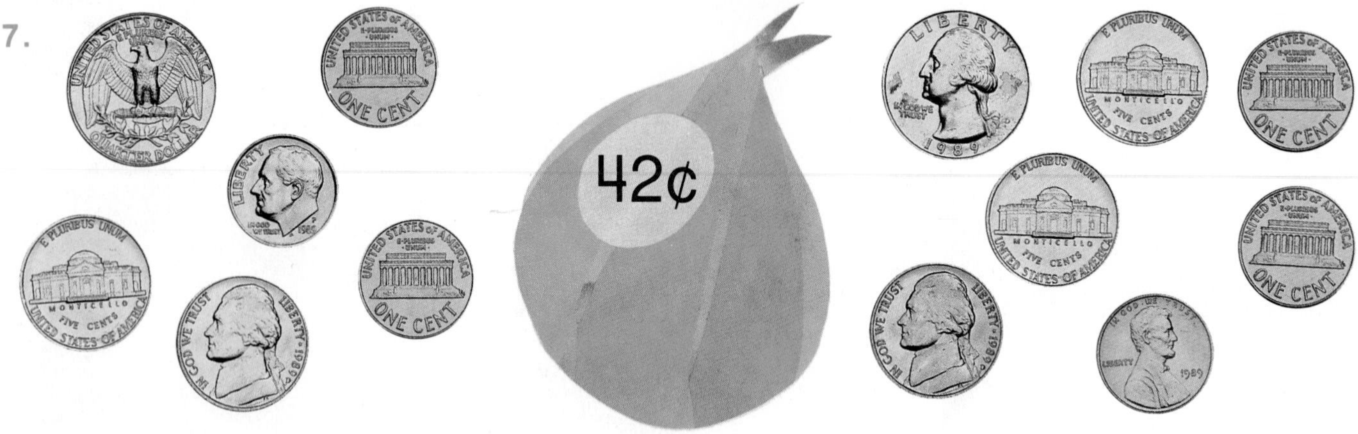

Notes for Home Children identify equivalent values of coins.

Name ______________________________

Comparing Money Amounts

Write each amount.
Ring the amount that is more.

1.

20 ¢

22 ¢

2.

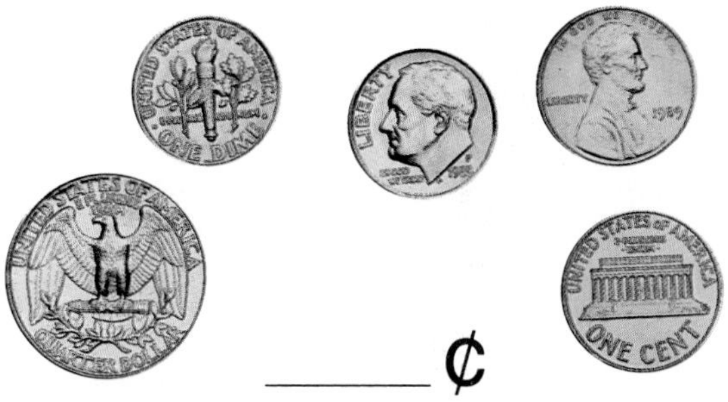

____ ¢

____ ¢

3.

____ ¢

____ ¢

Notes for Home Children compare two money amounts. They identify the greater amount.

Write each amount.
Ring the amount that is less.

4.

40 ¢

32 ¢

5.

____ ¢

____ ¢

6.

____ ¢

____ ¢

Problem Solving

7. Who has more money?
Ring the name.

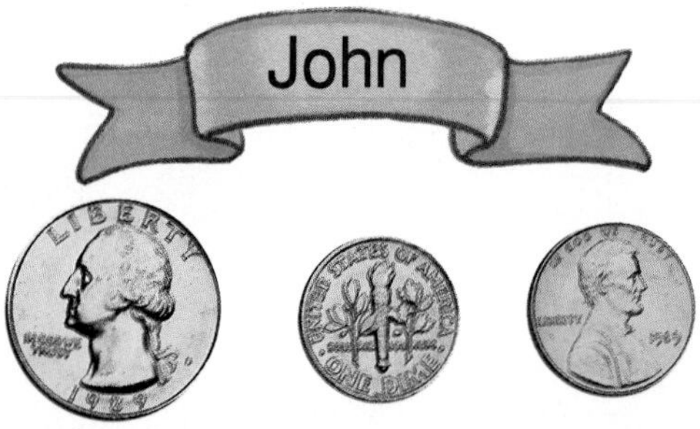

Notes for Home Children compare two money amounts. They identify the amount that is less. Then they solve a problem involving money.

See More Practice Set B on page 287.

Give Sensible Answers

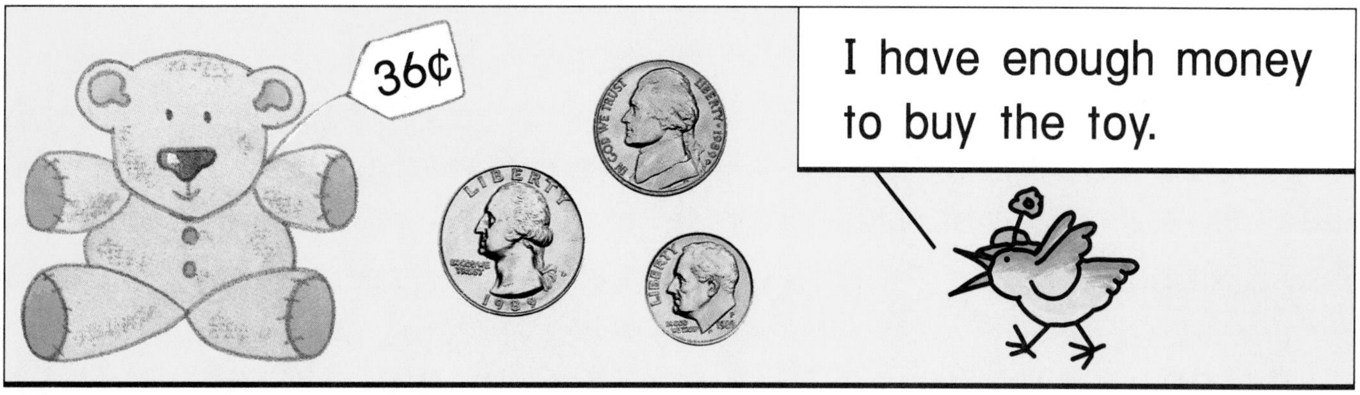

Look at the price of the toy.
Is there enough money to buy the toy?
Ring yes or no.

1.

yes

no

2.

yes

no

3.

yes

no

Notes for Home Children solve problems involving money by choosing sensible answers.

Look at the price of the toy.
Is there enough money to buy the toy?
Ring yes or no.

4.

yes no

5.

yes no

6.

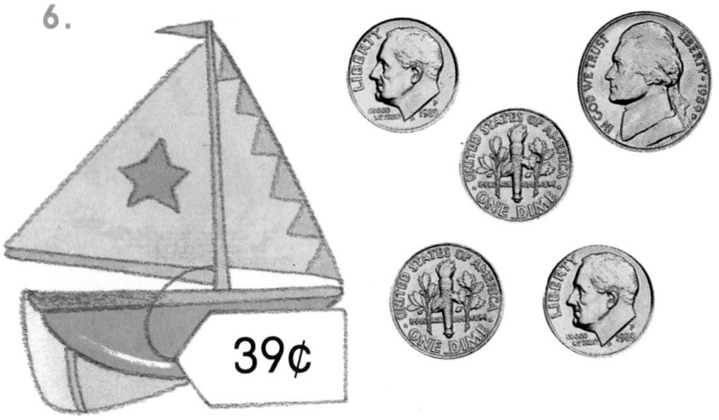

yes no

7.

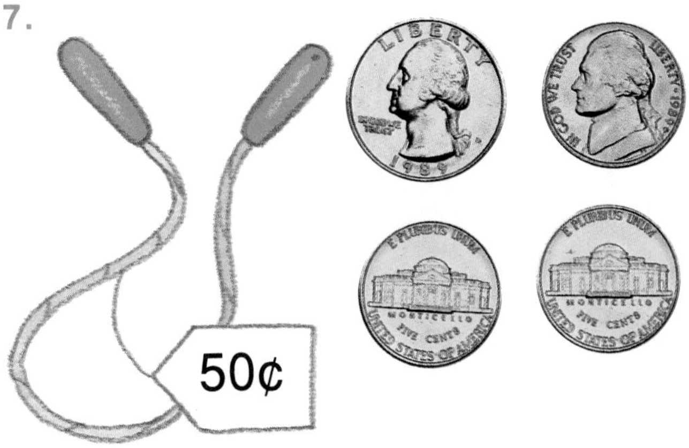

yes no

8.

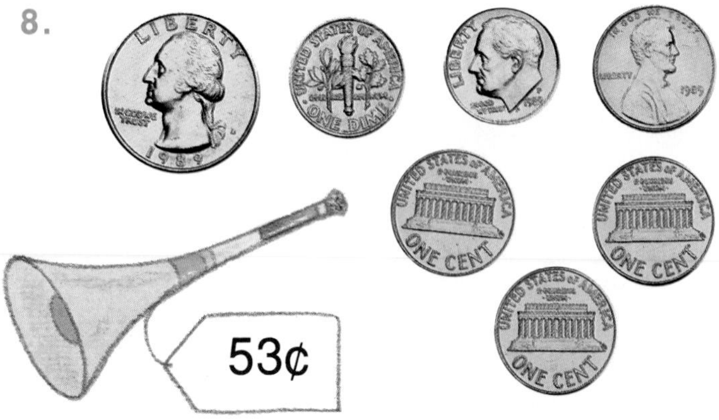

yes no

9.

yes no

Notes for Home Children solve problems involving money by choosing sensible answers.

Name

Problem-Solving Workshop

Explore as a Team

Work with a partner.
Each bank has some dimes.
There is 90¢ in all.

Find 3 different ways to show 90¢.

The  is not empty.

The  has less than the .

The  has less than the .

The  has less than the .

¢	¢	¢
¢	¢	¢
¢	¢	¢

Notes for Home Children explore with a partner to solve a problem finding different ways to show 90¢.

Problem-Solving Workshop

Explore with a Computer

Money and Time Project

You have saved these coins.

1. Ring the fruit you would buy.

28¢

34¢

65¢

2. At the computer, put the coins in the sack to buy the fruit.

3. Have the computer count the coins to check your work.

Notes for Home Children identify the item they have enough money to buy. At the computer, they put the coins into the sack on the screen, and have the computer count the coins to check their work.

Name

More Practice

Set A Use after page 274.

Count on to find how much in all.

1.

62 ¢

2.

____ ¢

3.

____ ¢

Set B Use after page 282.

Write each amount.

Ring the amount that is more.

1.

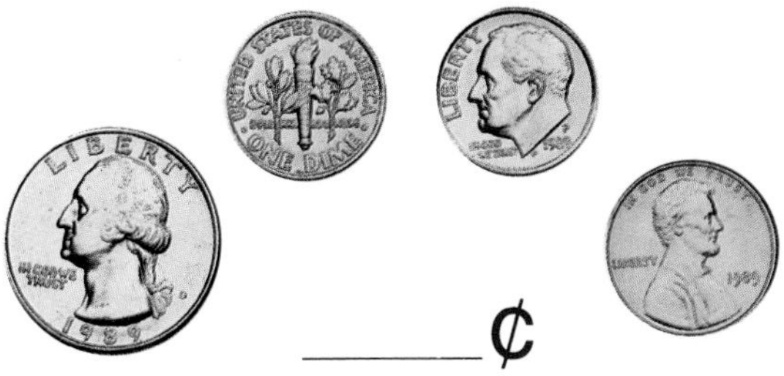

____ ¢

____ ¢

Ring the amount that is less.

2.

____ ¢

____ ¢

Notes for Home Set A: Children practice counting on to find the value of coins through 99¢.
Set B: Children practice comparing two money amounts and identifying the amount that is greater or less.

Enrichment

You buy.	Cross out what you spend.	How much is left?
1. 		7 ¢
2. 		____ ¢
3. 		____ ¢
4. 		____ ¢

Notes for Home Children are challenged to find how much is left after a toy has been bought.

Name

Chapter 9 Review/Test

Count on to find how much in all.

1\.

_____¢

2\.

_____¢

3\. Write each amount.
Ring the amount that is less.

_____¢

_____¢

4\. Ring the coins to show the amount.

20¢

5\. Do you have enough to buy the toy? Ring yes or no.

yes

no

Fruit	Price
apple	15¢
orange	17¢

6\. Which would you buy? Use all the coins.

apple

orange

Notes for Home Children are assessed on Chapter 9 concepts, skills, and problem solving.

Exploring MATH AT HOME

Exploring Math at Home

Dear Family,

In this chapter I have learned to count coins to 99¢. I also learned about money amounts by using a table. Please help me with the activities below.

Love, ______________________________

1.

Count on from the coin of greatest value. Identify the value of a group of coins. Include pennies, nickels, dimes, and not more than one quarter.

2.

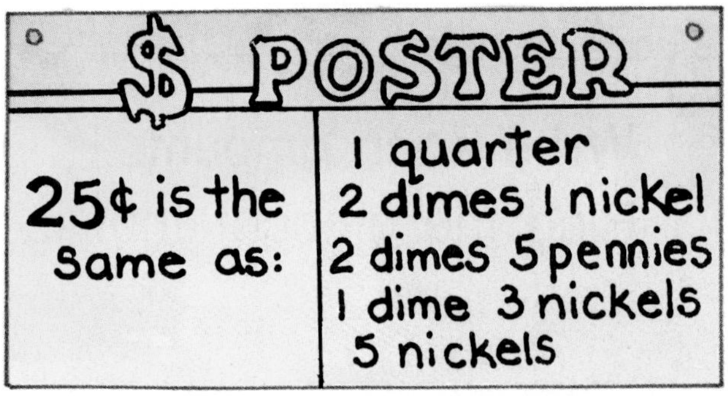

On a poster show different combinations of coins that total the same amount. Make a list.

3.

Go to a store. Compare the cost of two items less than 99¢. Tell which costs more. Can you buy the item with a given amount of coins you have in your hand?

Coming Attractions

In the next chapter I will be learning about telling time. I will also learn about measuring capacity.

Chapter

10

Time and Measurement

Listen to the math story, “Bob and Jay.”
Bob and Jay were each paid to do 3 jobs.
Which fox was paid more money?

Notes for Home Children listen to a math story introducing chapter concepts and skills. Then they answer a question about the story.

Name

Time Duration

This takes **more** time.
This takes **less** time.

Which takes more time? Ring.

1.

2.

3.

Notes for Home Children compare the duration of two activities and identify the one that takes more time.

Name

More or Less Than 1 Minute

This takes **less** than 1 minute.	This takes about 1 minute.	This takes **more** than 1 minute.

Does it take about 1 minute?
Ring yes or no.

1\.

yes (ringed)   no

2\.

yes   no

3\.

yes   no

4\.

yes   no

Notes for Home Children identify activities that take about 1 minute.

Does it take more or less than 1 minute?
Ring more or less.

5.

more less

6.

more less

7.

more less

8.

more less

9.

more less

10.

more less

Notes for Home Children identify activities that take more or less than 1 minute.

Name ______ **Activity**

Telling Time to the Hour

The short hand is the hour hand.
The long hand is the minute hand.

The hour hand points to 3.

It is __3__ o'clock.

Use a clock.
Show the time. Write the time.

1.

______ o'clock

2.

______ o'clock

3.

______ o'clock

4.

______ o'clock

5.

______ o'clock

6.

______ o'clock

Notes for Home Children explore at the CONCRETE level using manipulative clocks to learn to tell time to the hour.

Write the time.

7.

12 o'clock

8.

_____ o'clock

9.

_____ o'clock

10.

_____ o'clock

11.

_____ o'clock

12.

_____ o'clock

13.

_____ o'clock

14.

_____ o'clock

Notes for Home Children practice telling time to the hour.

Name

Telling Time to the Hour

Both clocks show the same time.

9 o'clock

9:00

What time is it?

1.

_____ o'clock

_____ : _____

2.

_____ o'clock

_____ : _____

3.

_____ o'clock

_____ : _____

4.

_____ o'clock

_____ : _____

5.

_____ o'clock

_____ : _____

6.

_____ o'clock

_____ : _____

Notes for Home Children learn to tell time to the hour using both standard and digital clocks.

Draw the hands to show the time.

7.

8.

9.

10.

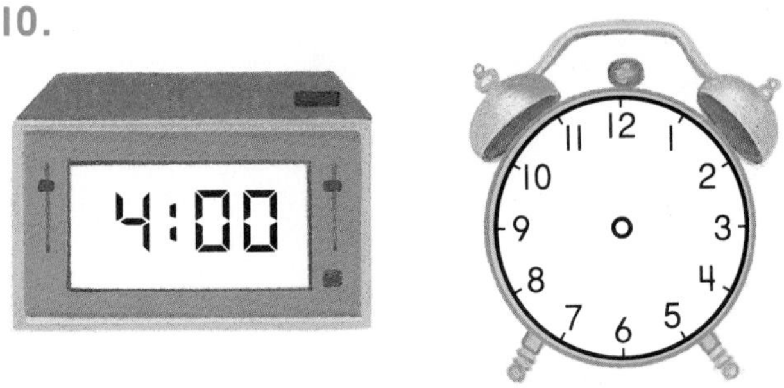

11.

12.

Problem Solving

13. Mary went to school at 8 o'clock. Show the time on the clock.

Notes for Home Children draw clock hands to show time to the hour. Then they solve a problem involving time.

Name **Activity**

Telling Time to the Half Hour

This clock shows 1:00.

This clock shows 1:30.

1:30 means 30 minutes after 1 o'clock.

Use a clock.
Show the time. Write the time.

1.

7:00

7:30

2.

___:___

___:___

3.

___:___

___:___

Notes for Home Children explore at the CONCRETE level using manipulative clocks to learn to tell time to the half hour.

Write the time.

4.

2:30

5.

___ : ___

6.

___ : ___

7.

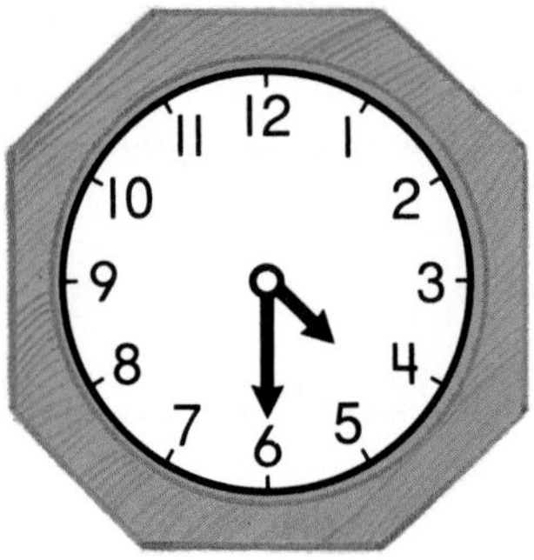

___ : ___

8.

___ : ___

9.

___ : ___

10.

___ : ___

11.

___ : ___

Notes for Home Children practice telling time to the half hour.

Name

Telling Time to the Half Hour

Both clocks show 30 minutes after 3 o'clock.

3:30

Write the time.

1.

:

2.

:

3.

:

4.

:

5.

:

6.

:

Notes for Home Children learn to tell time to the half hour using both standard and digital clocks.

Ring the clock that shows the same time.

7.

8.

9.

10.

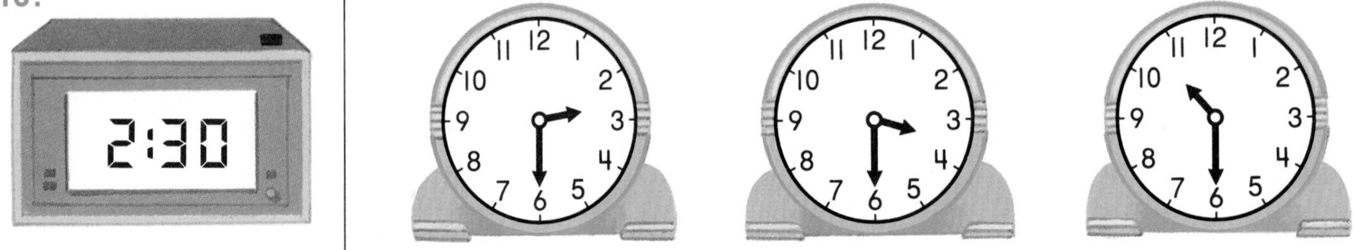

11.

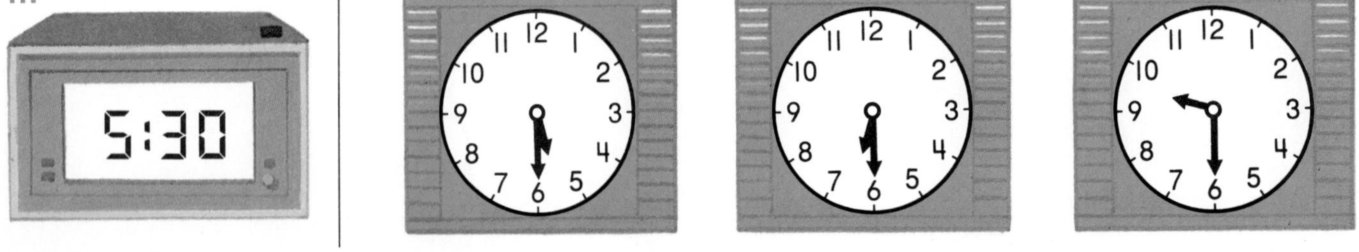

Notes for Home Children practice telling time to the half hour.

Name

Telling Time to the Hour and Half Hour

7:00

Write the time.

1.

___ : ___

___ : ___

___ : ___

2.

___ : ___

___ : ___

___ : ___

3.

___ : ___

___ : ___

___ : ___

Notes for Home Children tell time to the hour and the half hour.

4. Match the clocks that show the same time.

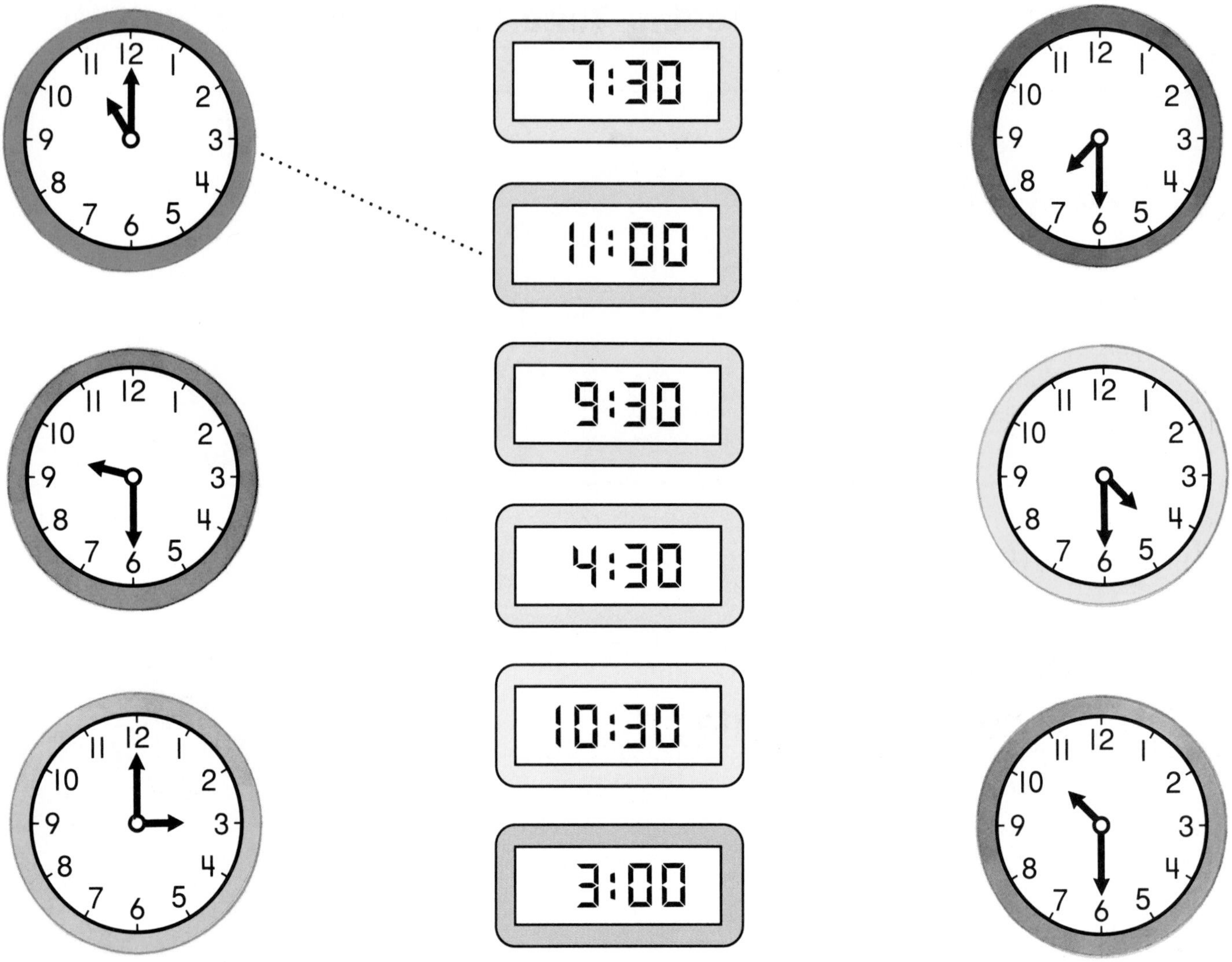

Problem Solving

5. What time did Jeff start reading?

___ : ___

6. What time did Jeff stop reading?

___ : ___

Notes for Home Children practice telling time to the hour and the half hour. Then they solve problems involving time.

See More Practice Set A on page 327.

Name ______________________

Use Logical Reasoning

PROBLEM-SOLVING STRATEGY

Betty started reading at 6:00.
She read for 2 hours.
What time did she stop?

8 o'clock

Solve.

1. Ken left school at 3:00.
He got home 1 hour later.
What time did he get home?

____ o'clock

2. Thomas started playing football at 2:00.
He played for 3 hours.
What time did he stop?

____ o'clock

3. Susan left to visit a friend at 9:00.
She returned 2 hours later.
What time did she return?

____ o'clock

Notes for Home Children solve problems involving elapsed time by using logical reasoning.

Solve.

4. Richard began riding his bike at 4:00.
He stopped riding 1 hour later.
What time did he stop?

5 o'clock

5. Lynn went to the park at 3:00.
She returned home 3 hours later.
What time did she return home?

____ o'clock

6. Jack began his homework at 5:00.
He finished 2 hours later.
What time did he finish?

____ o'clock

7. Diane left for a picnic at 10:00.
She returned home 4 hours later.
What time did she return home?

____ o'clock

Notes for Home Children solve problems involving elapsed time by using logical reasoning.

Name

Number Sense

How many of your classmates can you name in one minute? First guess, then check.

Guess ☐ Check ☐

Let's do some more!

How many numbers can you write in one minute?
How can you find out?

Notes for Home Children develop an understanding of time by guessing and checking what they can do in one minute.

Skills Review

Fill in the correct ⬭.
Count on to find how much.

1.

(A) 53¢
(B) 63¢
(C) 65¢

Which is the greater amount?

2.

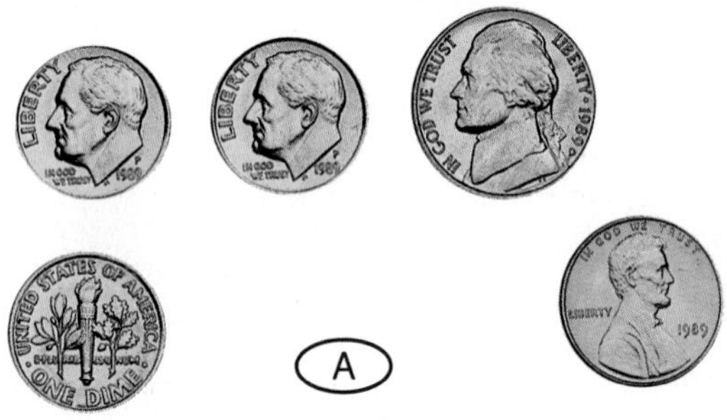

(A)

or

(B)

Vocabulary

Match the word with the coin.
Match the coin with the amount.

3. quarter •
4. penny •
5. dime •
6. nickel •

• one cent
• twenty-five cents
• five cents
• ten cents

Notes for Home Children review counting on to find the value of coins through 99¢. Then they compare two money amounts. Children review money terms.

Name

Comparing Capacity

This holds **more** water.
This holds **less** water.

Which holds more? Ring.

1.

2.

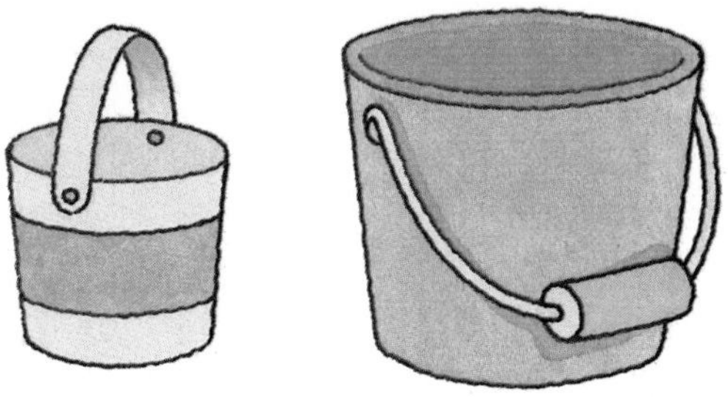

3.

4.

Notes for Home Children compare the capacities of two containers and identify the one that holds more.

Which holds less? Ring.

5.

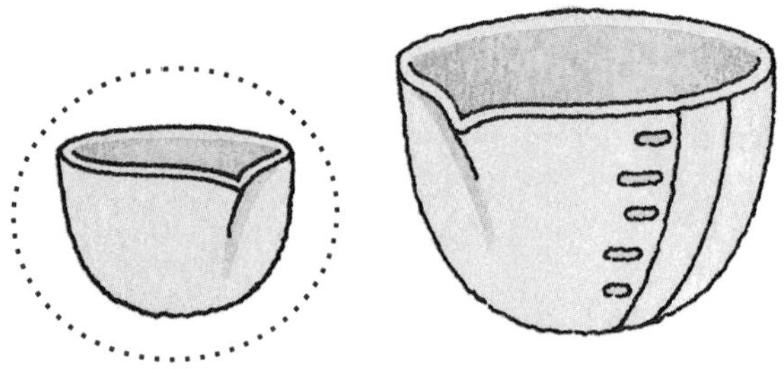

6.

7.

8.

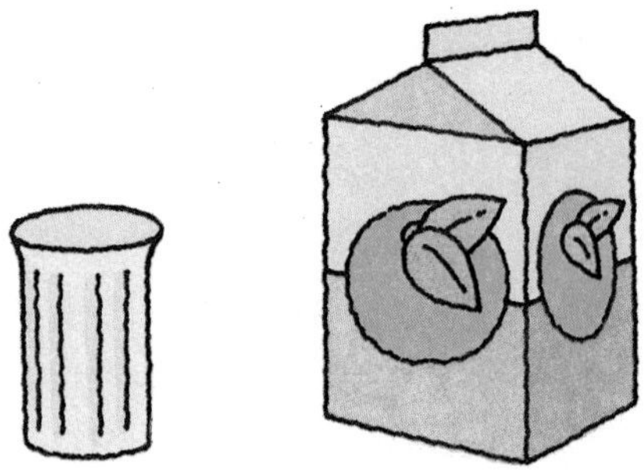

9.

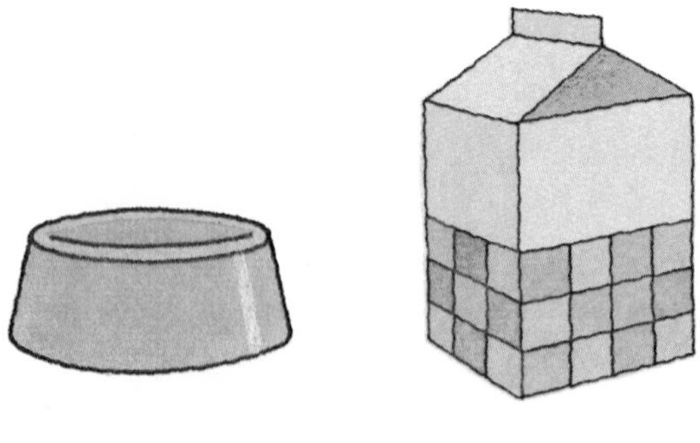

10.

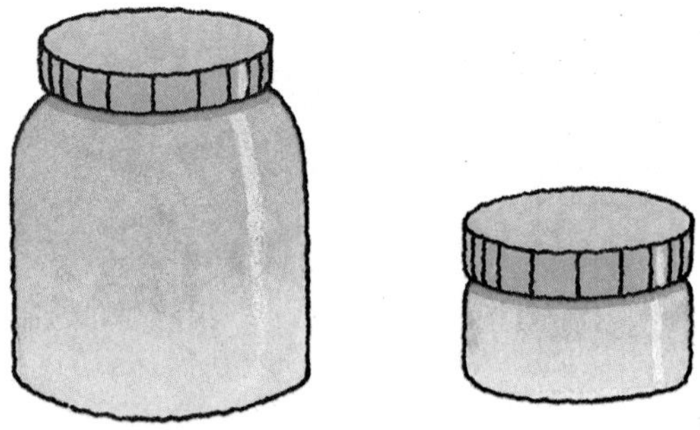

11.

12.

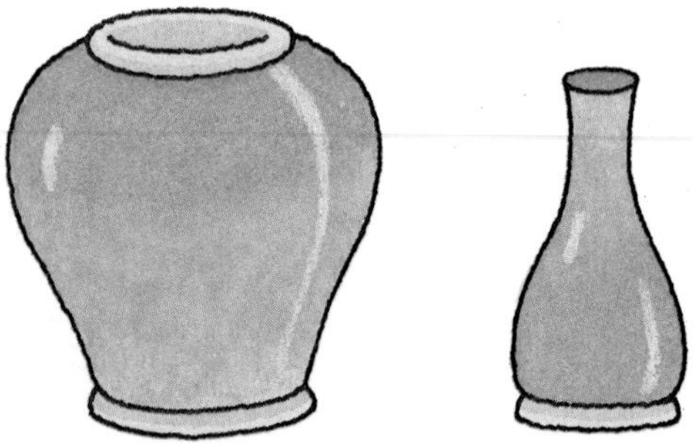

Notes for Home Children compare the capacities of two containers and identify the one that holds less.

Name

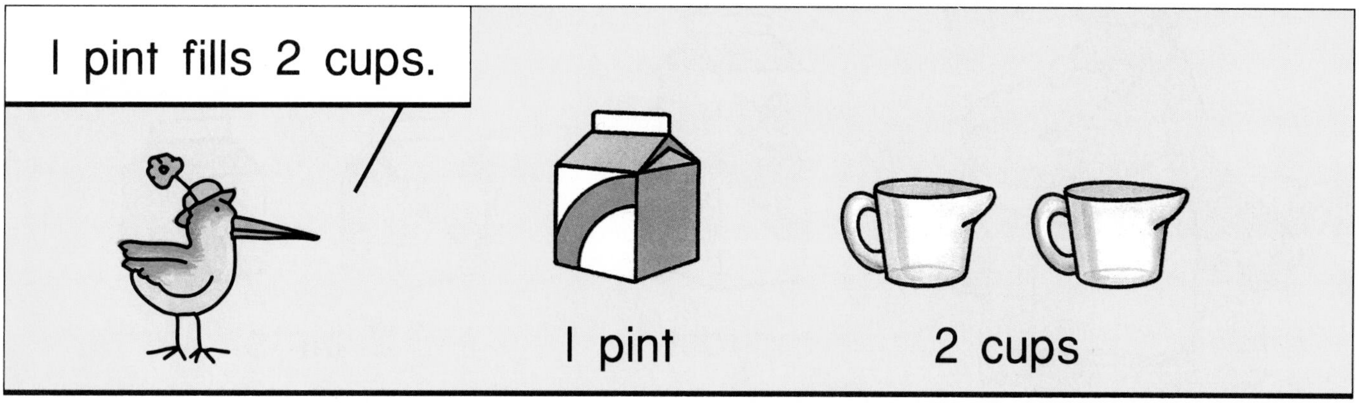

Color the cups you can fill.

1.

1 pint

2.

2 pints

3.

3 pints

Notes for Home Children identify how many cups a given number of pints will fill.

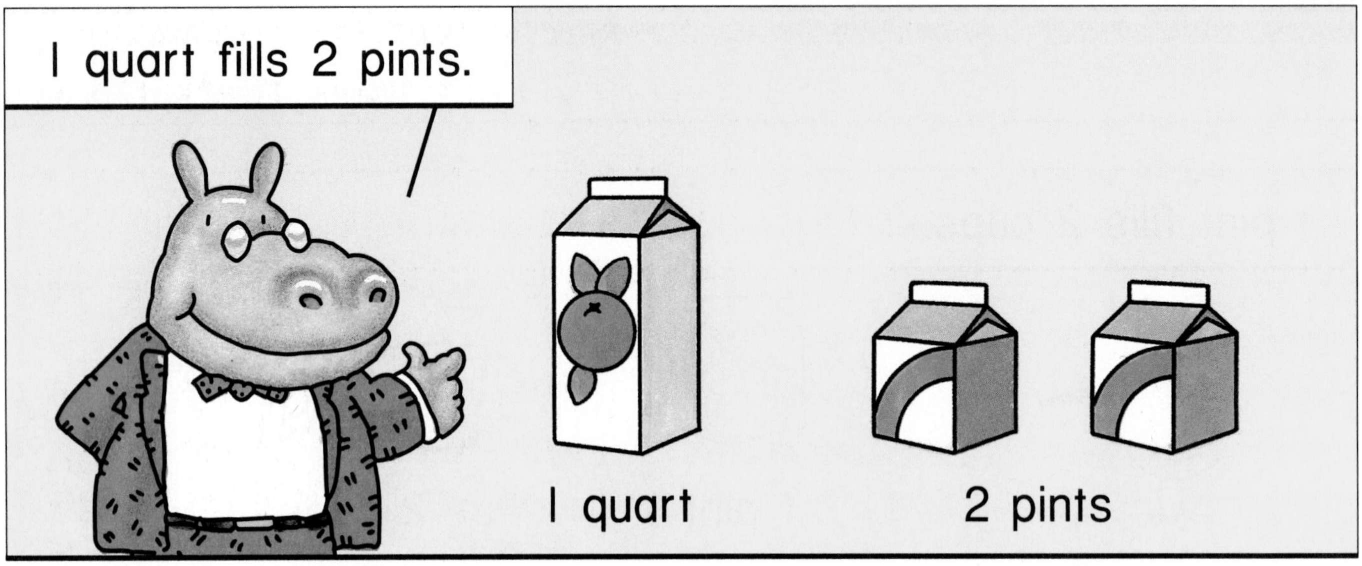

Color the pints you can fill.

4.

I quart

5.

2 quarts

6.

3 quarts

Notes for Home Children identify how many pints a given number of quarts will fill.

Name

I liter fills about 4 large glasses.
I liter

1. Which holds more than I liter? Ring.

Notes for Home Children identify containers that hold more than I liter.

2. Which holds less than I liter? Ring.

Notes for Home Children identify containers that hold less than I liter.

Name

Comparing Weight

Which is heavier? Ring.

1.

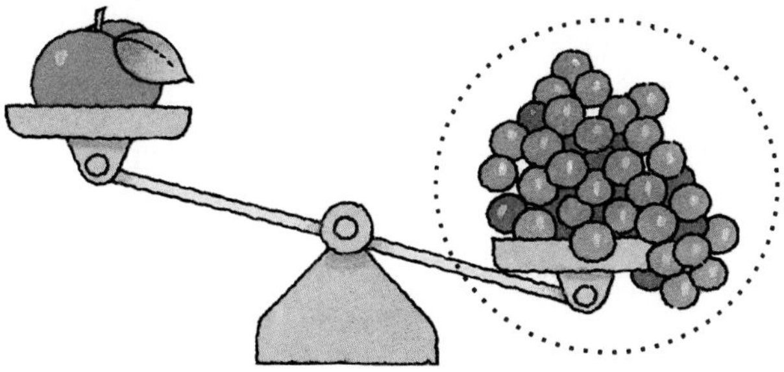

2.

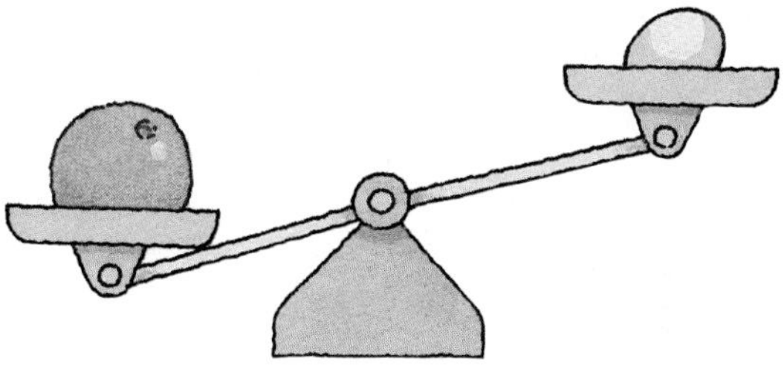

3.

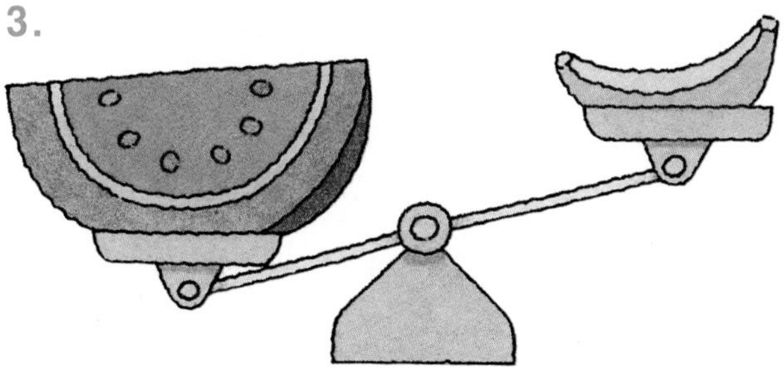

4.

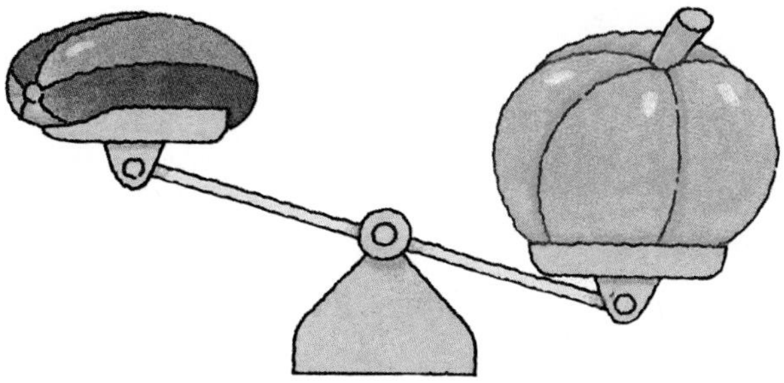

5.

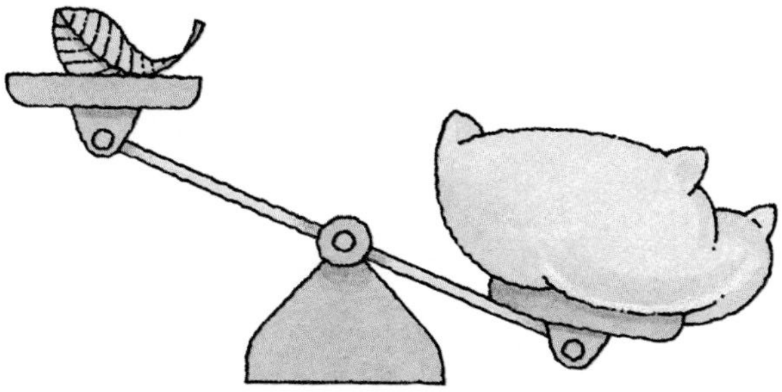

6.

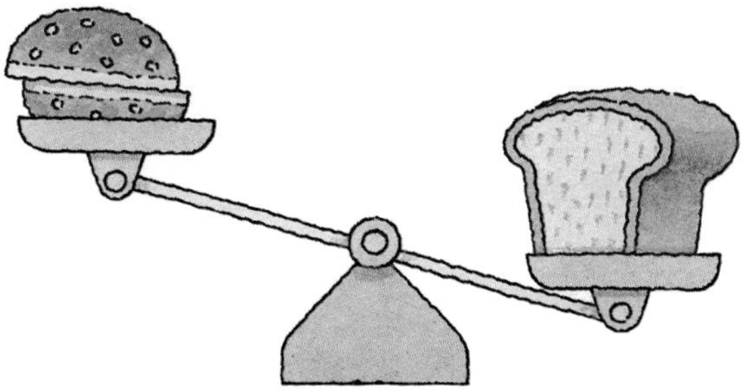

Notes for Home Children compare the weights of two objects and identify the one that is heavier.

Which is lighter? Ring.

7.
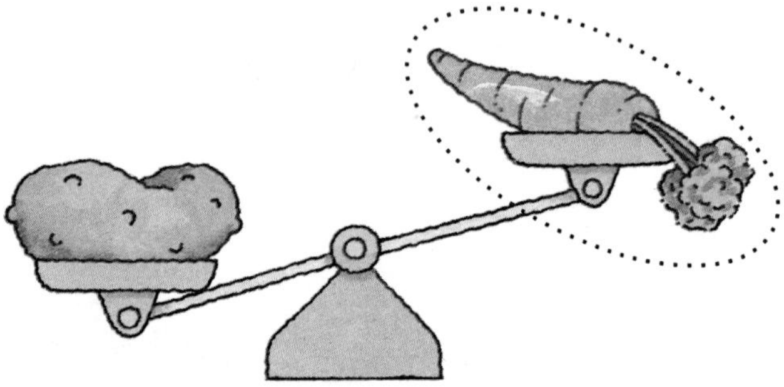

8.
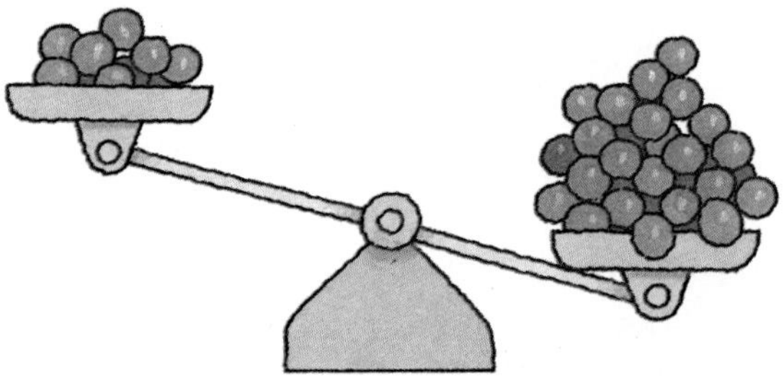

9.
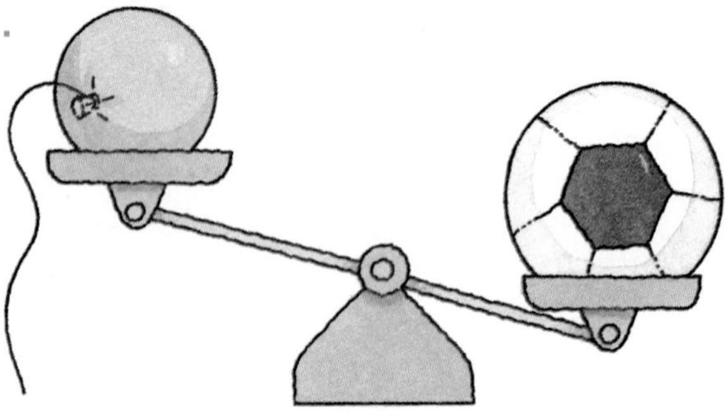

10.

11.
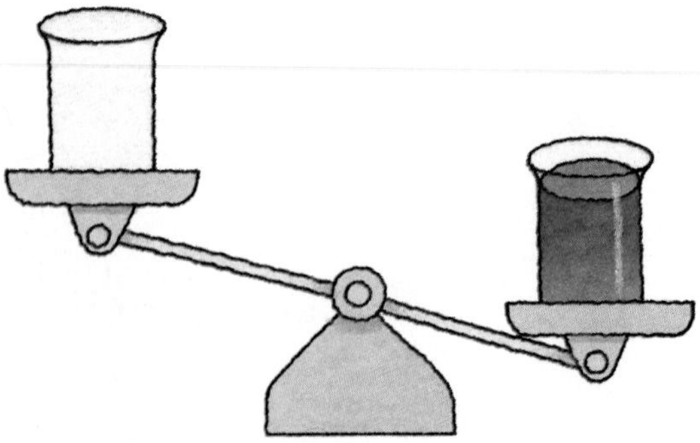

12.
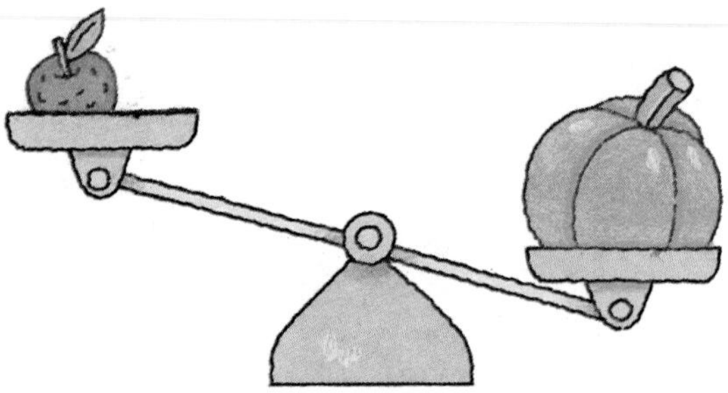

Notes for Home Children compare the weights of two objects and identify the one that is lighter.

Name ______

Pounds

This weighs about 1 pound.
1

1. Which weighs more than 1 pound? Ring.

Notes for Home Children identify objects that weigh more than 1 pound.

2. Which weighs less than I pound? Ring.

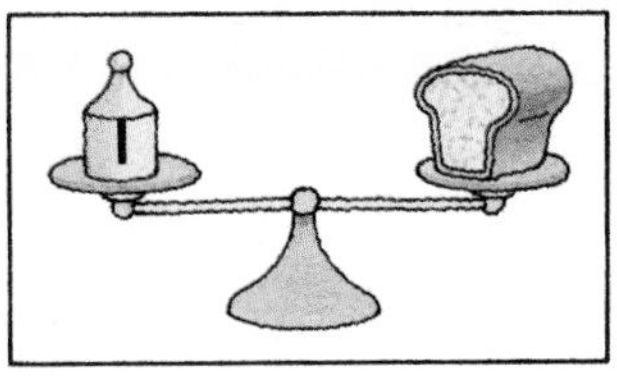

Problem Solving

Does it weigh more than or less than I pound?
Ring more or less.

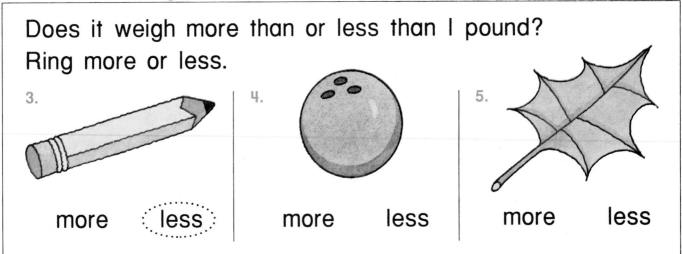

3.

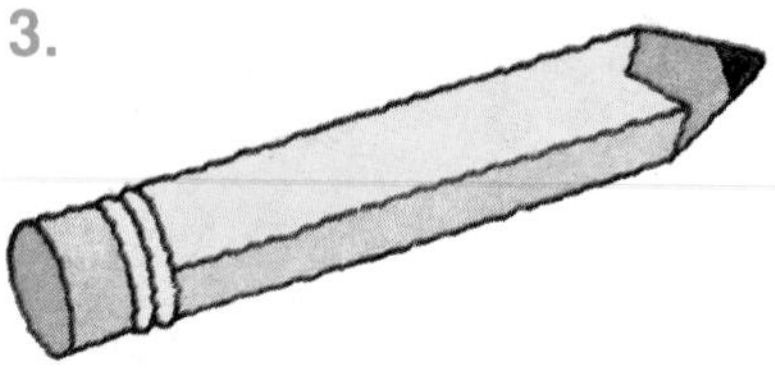

more less

4.

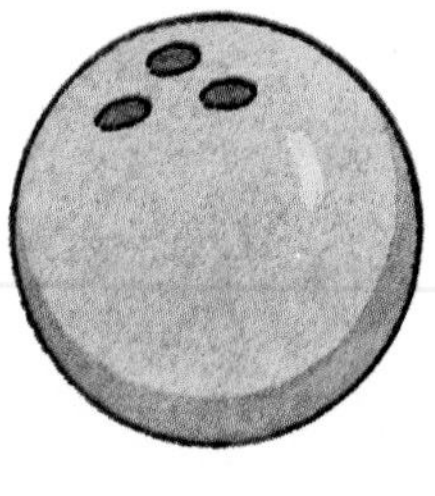

more less

5.

more less

Notes for Home Children identify objects that weigh less than I pound. Then they solve problems involving weight.

See More Practice Set B on page 327.

Name

Kilograms

This is about as heavy as 1 kilogram.

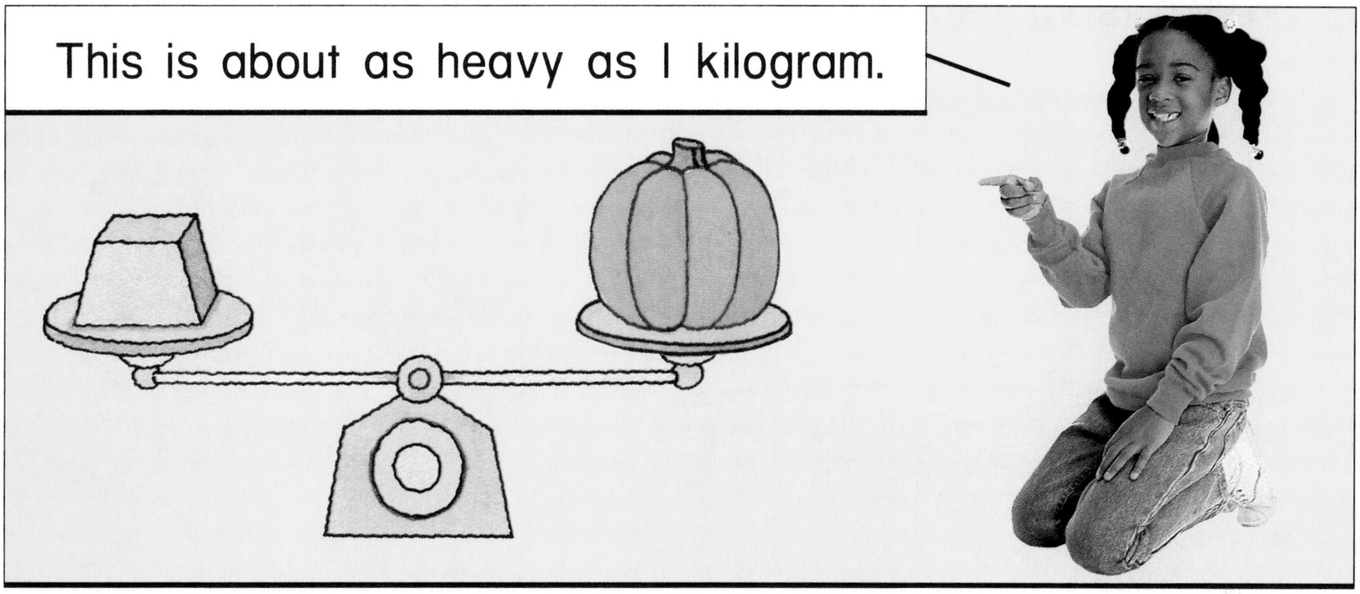

1. Which is heavier than 1 kilogram? Ring.

Notes for Home Children identify objects that are heavier than 1 kilogram.

2. Which is lighter than I kilogram? Ring.

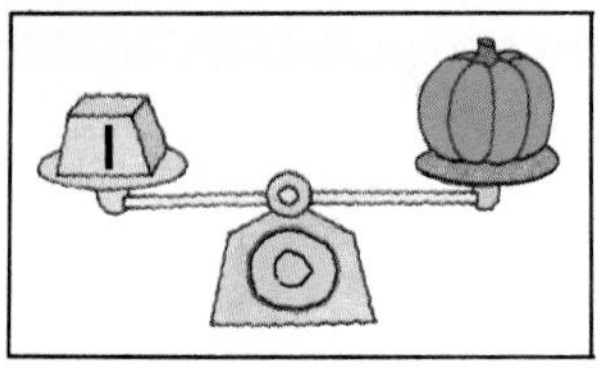

Notes for Home Children identify objects that are lighter than I kilogram.

Name

Find a Pattern

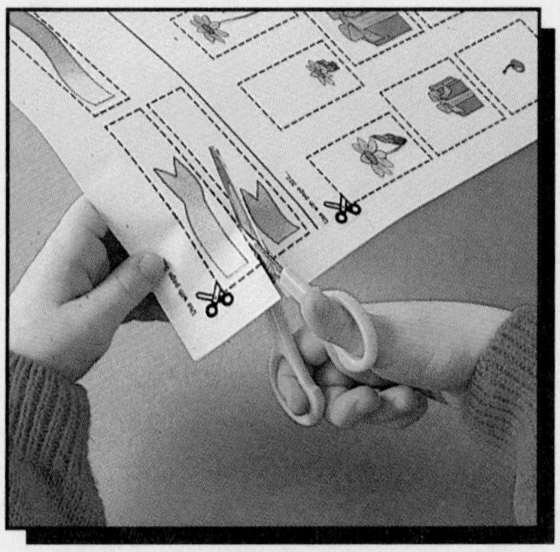

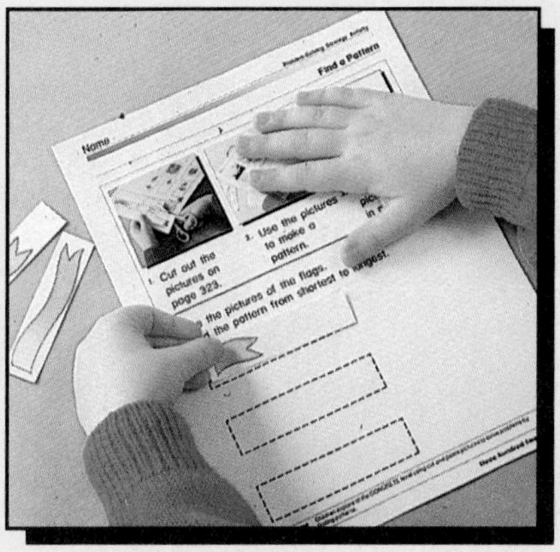

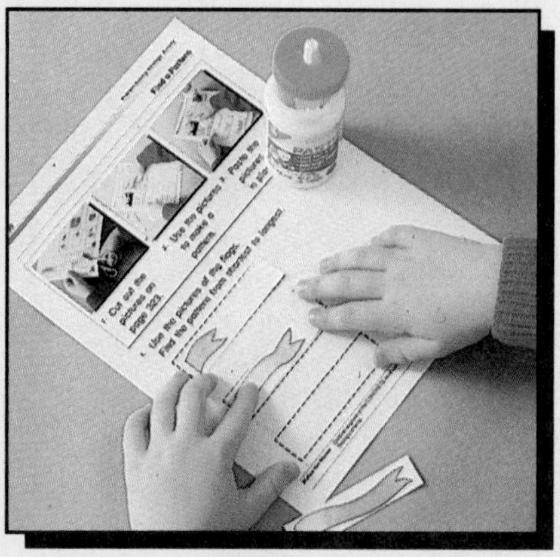

1. Cut out the pictures on page 323.

2. Use the pictures to make a pattern.

3. Paste the pictures in place.

1. Use the pictures of the flags.
Find the pattern from shortest to longest.

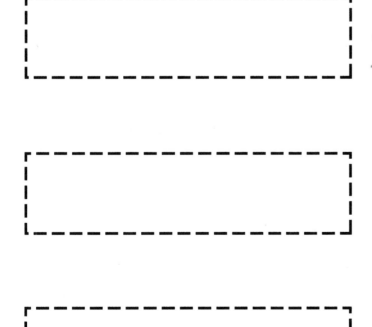

Notes for Home Children explore at the CONCRETE level using cut and paste pictures to solve problems by finding patterns.

2. Use the pictures of the flowers.
Find the pattern from shortest to tallest.

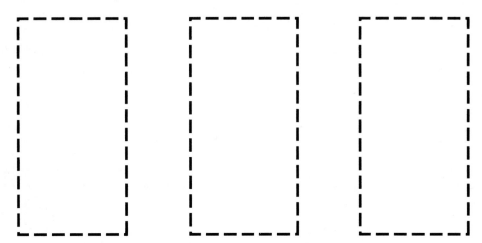

3. Use the pictures of the gifts.
Find the pattern from smallest to largest.

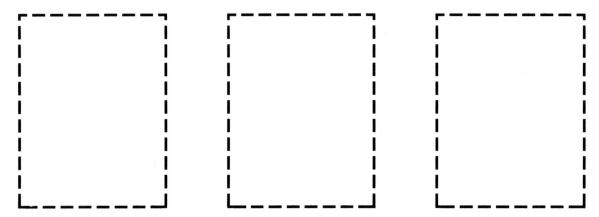

4. Use the pictures of the fruit.
Find the pattern from lightest to heaviest.

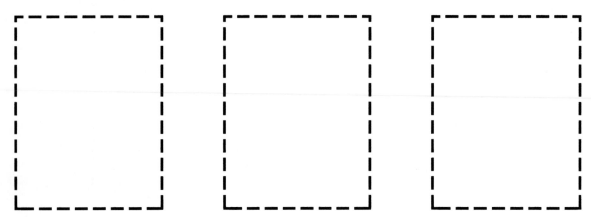

Notes for Home Children explore at the CONCRETE level using cut and paste pictures to solve problems by finding patterns.

Use with page 321.

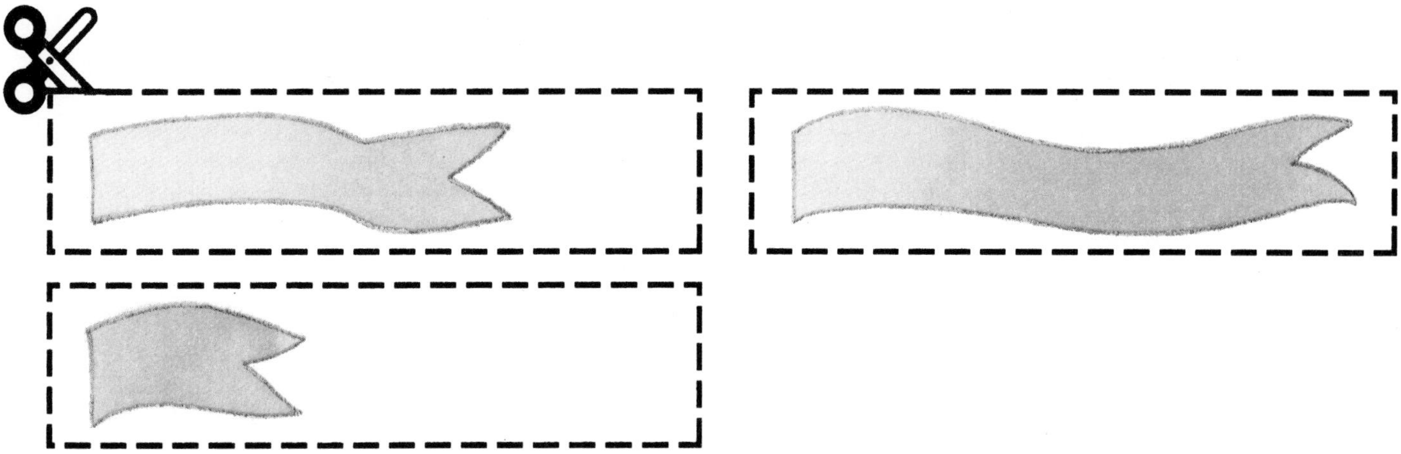

Use with page 322.

Name

Problem-Solving Workshop

Explore as a Team

Work with a partner.
Take turns pretending you are a balance scale.

1. Give your partner two objects.

2. Have your partner put one object in each hand.

3. Your partner shows which is heavier by acting like a balance scale.

4. Write which two objects were weighed. Ring the heavier.

Notes for Home Children explore with a partner to compare the weight of objects.

Problem-Solving Workshop

Explore with a Computer

Money and Time Project

1. Sara's birthday party begins at 3 o'clock
Draw the hands to show the time on the clock.

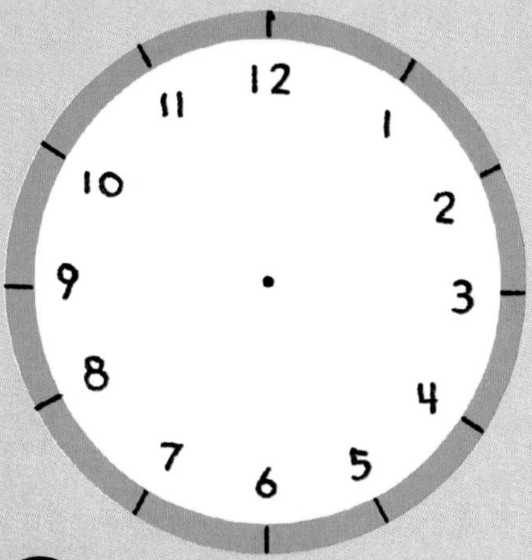

2. At the computer, set the first clock for 3 o'clock.

3. This clock tells when Sara's party ended.
Set the second clock to show this time.

4. How long did Sara's party last?
Ring the time.

30 minutes　　1 hour　　1 hour and 30 minutes

Notes for Home Children draw clock hands to show time to the hour. Then they set times on the computer to show time to the hour and half hour.

Name ______________________________

More Practice

Set A Use after page 304.

What time is it?

1\.

11:00

2\.

___ : ___

3\.

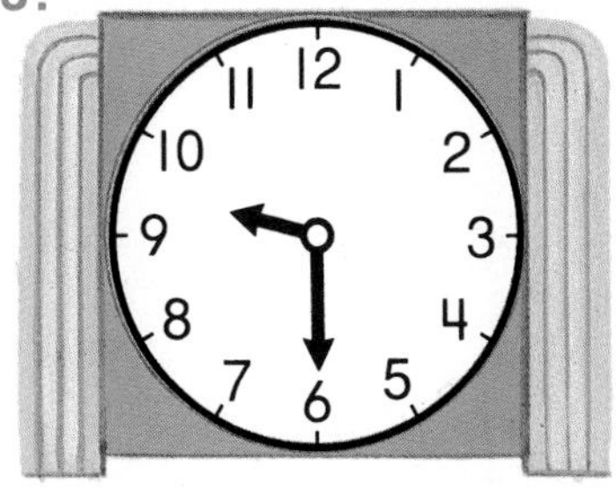

___ : ___

4\.

___ : ___

Set B Use after page 318.

About how much does it weigh?

Use 

for objects that weigh more than 1 pound.

Use 

for objects that weigh less than 1 pound.

Notes for Home Set A: Children practice telling time to the hour and the half hour.
Set B: Children color objects that weigh more than or less than 1 pound.

Enrichment

Write the time.

1.

It is 3:00.

2 hours later it will be ____:____.

2 hours earlier it was ____:____.

2.

It is ____:____.

1 hour later it will be ____:____.

1 hour earlier it was ____:____.

3.

It is ____:____.

4 hours later it will be ____:____.

4 hours earlier it was ____:____.

4.

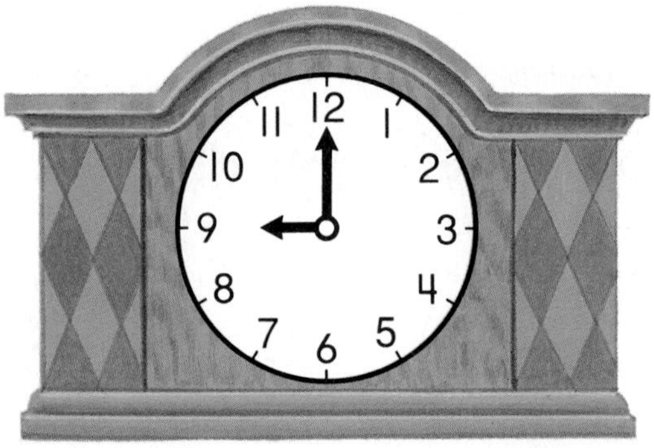

It is ____:____.

3 hours later it will be ____:____.

3 hours earlier it was ____:____.

Notes for Home Children are challenged to write the time after and before the time shown on a clock.

Name

Chapter 10 Review/Test

1. Write the time.

___ : ___   ___ : ___

2. Does it take about 1 minute?

yes

no

3. Color the cups you can fill.

1 pint

4. Which holds less than 1 liter?

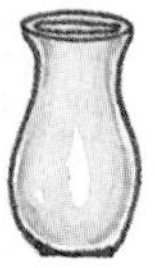

5. Which is heavier than 1 pound?

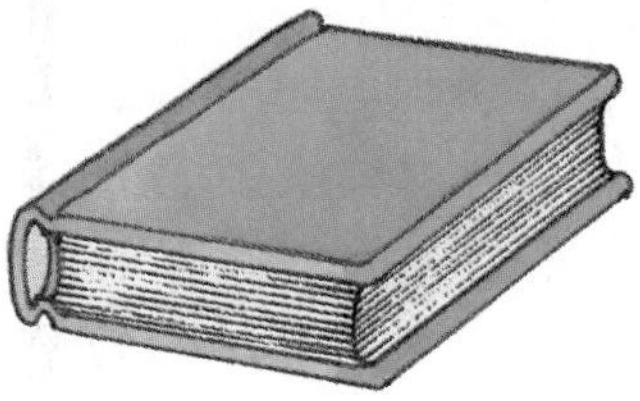

6. Which is heavier than 1 kilogram?

7. Solve.
Al started painting at 2:00.
He painted for 2 hours.
What time did he stop?

_____ o'clock

8. Are the flowers in order from shortest to tallest?

yes

no

Notes for Home Children are assessed on Chapter 10 concepts, skills, and problem solving.

Exploring MATH AT HOME

Exploring Math at Home

Dear Family,

In this chapter I have learned to tell time to the hour and half hour. I have also learned about cups, pints, quarts, and liters as well as pounds and kilograms. Please help me with the activities below.

Love, ______________________

1.

Talk about activities that take about a minute, a half hour, or an hour. Set a timer to check estimates.

2.

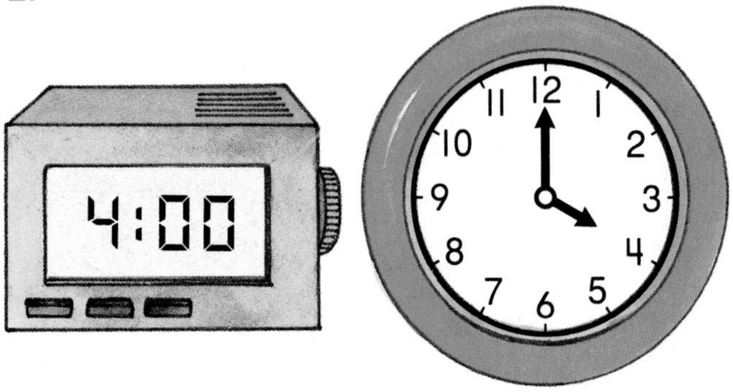

Use both standard and digital clocks to tell time to the hour and half hour.

3.

Fill bottles, pitchers, and jars with a measuring cup. Compare capacities of various containers.

4.

Go to the market. Find things that are heavier or lighter than 1 pound or 1 kilogram. Use a scale.

Coming Attractions

In the next chapter I will learn addition and subtraction facts through 12. I will also add three numbers.

Chapter

11

Addition and Subtraction Through 12

Listen to the math story, "The Ladybug Ball."
Lucinda counted 5 ladybugs.
Which ladybug did she forget to count?

Notes for Home Children listen to a math story introducing chapter concepts and skills. Then they answer a question about the story.

Name

Addition and Subtraction Through 10

Let's review facts through 10.

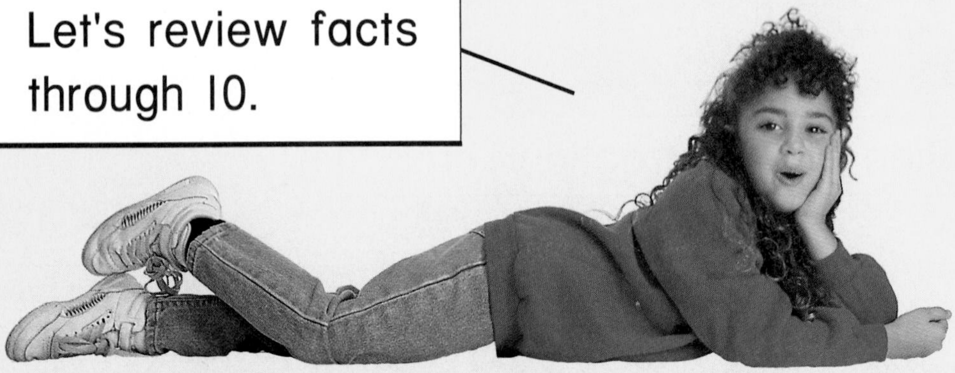

$$\begin{array}{r} 8 \\ +2 \\ \hline 10 \end{array} \qquad \begin{array}{r} 7 \\ -2 \\ \hline 5 \end{array}$$

Add or subtract.

1.

10	4	5	6	4	9	1
− 8	+ 3	+ 0	− 2	+ 6	− 7	+ 5

2.

3	8	1	4	5	10	8
+ 5	− 2	+ 6	− 0	+ 4	− 6	− 7

3.

6	3	8	2	10	0	9
− 6	+ 6	− 5	+ 2	− 3	+ 8	− 5

4.

7	5	6	9	2	7	1
+ 3	− 3	+ 2	− 3	+ 4	− 4	+ 9

Notes for Home Children review addition and subtraction facts through 10 as readiness for facts through 12.

Name ______

Adding 2 or 3

First, think of the greater number.
Then count on to add.

8 9 10 11

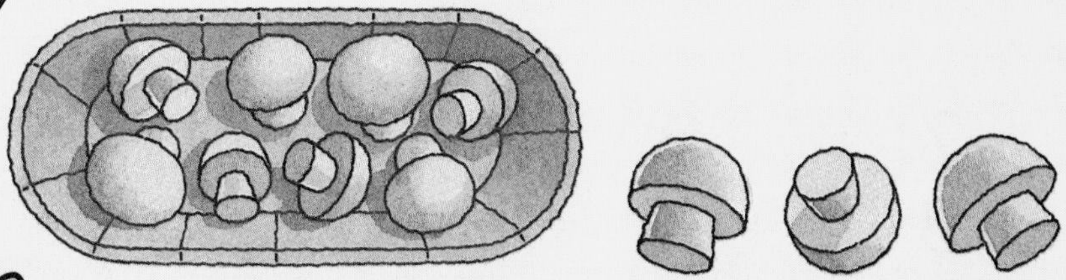

$8 + 3 = 11$

$3 + 8 = 11$

Think of the greater number.
Then add by counting on.

1.

$9 + 2 =$ ______

$2 + 9 =$ ______

2.

$9 + 3 =$ ______

$3 + 9 =$ ______

3. $3 + 8 =$ ______

$8 + 3 =$ ______

4. $2 + 9 =$ ______

$9 + 2 =$ ______

5. $3 + 9 =$ ______

$9 + 3 =$ ______

Notes for Home Children learn to find sums through 12 by adding 2 or 3 to a given number.

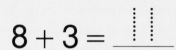

Think of the greater number.
Then add by counting on.

6.	$3 + 8$	$8 + 3$	7.	$3 + 9$	$9 + 3$	8.	$2 + 9$	$9 + 2$

9.	$7 + 3$	$2 + 9$	$3 + 5$	$8 + 2$	$3 + 9$	$2 + 7$	$1 + 9$
10.	$2 + 5$	$3 + 8$	$6 + 3$	$9 + 2$	$2 + 6$	$5 + 3$	$6 + 4$
11.	$9 + 3$	$7 + 2$	$2 + 8$	$8 + 3$	$3 + 7$	$6 + 2$	$4 + 5$
12.	$3 + 4$	$5 + 2$	$3 + 6$				

Notes for Home Children practice finding sums by adding 2 or 3 to the greater number.

Name ______________________________

Using Doubles to Add

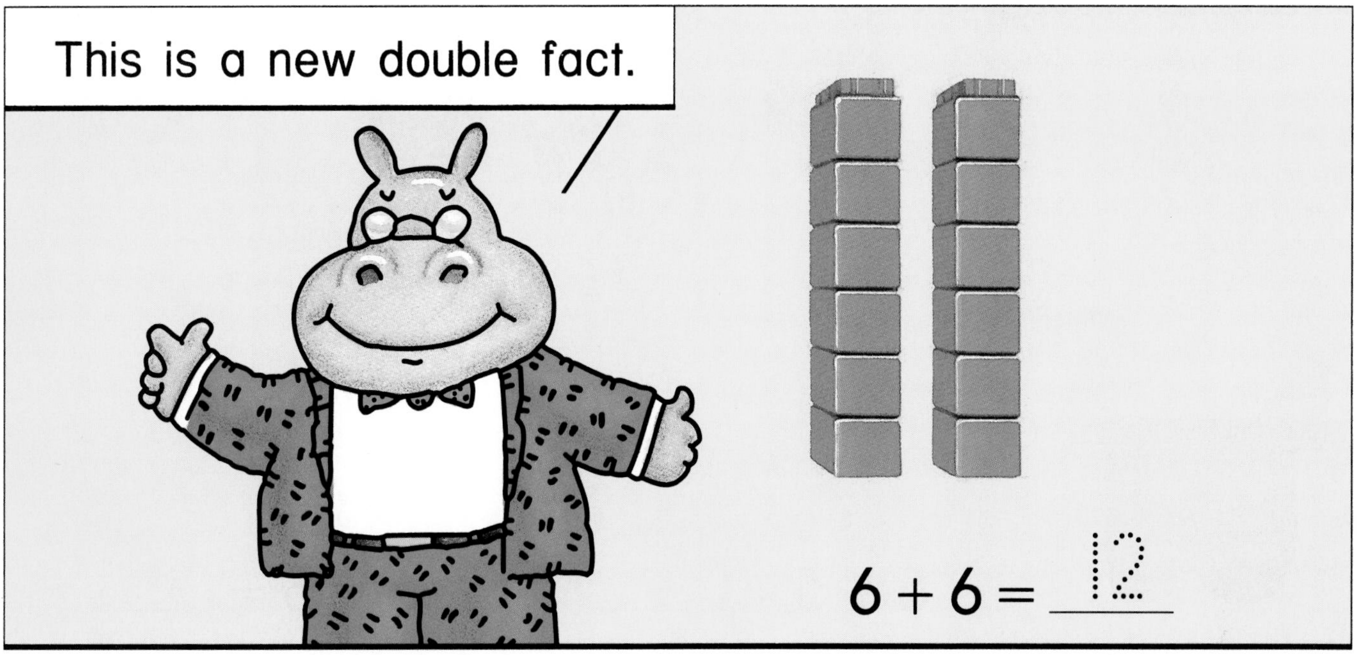

$6 + 6 = $ 12

Add.

1.

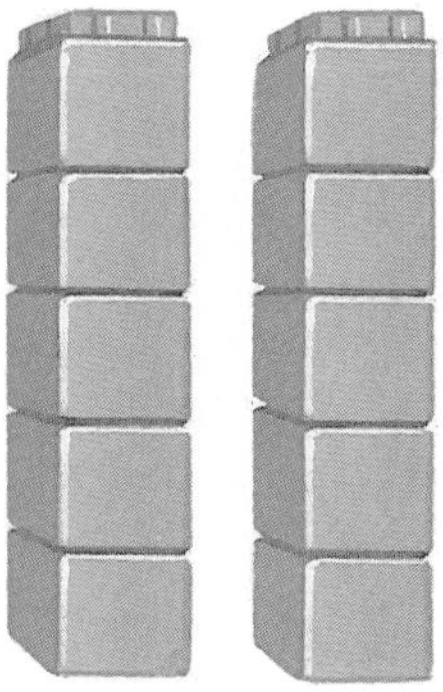

$5 + 5 = $ ____

2.

$6 + 6 = $ ____

3.

$\begin{array}{r} 3 \\ +\ 3 \\ \hline \end{array}$	$\begin{array}{r} 5 \\ +\ 5 \\ \hline \end{array}$	$\begin{array}{r} 4 \\ +\ 4 \\ \hline \end{array}$	$\begin{array}{r} 6 \\ +\ 6 \\ \hline \end{array}$	$\begin{array}{r} 2 \\ +\ 2 \\ \hline \end{array}$	$\begin{array}{r} 6 \\ +\ 6 \\ \hline \end{array}$

Notes for Home Children learn a new doubles fact, 6 + 6.

How do you solve these facts?
First, I think of the double. Then I add 1 more.

$5 + 6 =$ 11 $\qquad 6 + 5 =$ 11

Add.

4.

$5 + 5 =$ ____ $\qquad 5 + 6 =$ ____ $\qquad 6 + 5 =$ ____

5.

5	4	5	6	3	6
+ 6	+ 4	+ 5	+ 5	+ 3	+ 6
____	____	____	____	____	____

Notes for Home Children learn to solve doubles and 1 more, 6 + 5 and 5 + 6, by thinking of 5 + 5.

Name

Adding Three Numbers

First, add two numbers.
Then add the last number.

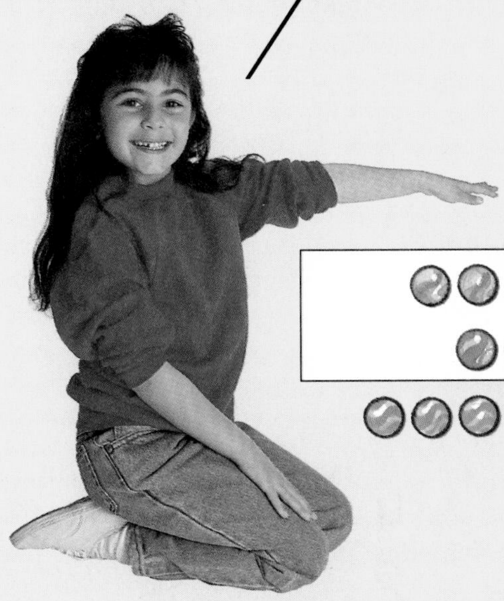

$$\begin{array}{r} 3 \\ 2 \\ +\ 4 \\ \hline 9 \end{array}$$

3 + 2 = 5

Add.

1.

$$\begin{array}{r} 4 \\ 2 \\ +\ 5 \\ \hline \end{array}$$

4 + 2 = 6

2.

$$\begin{array}{r} 2 \\ 5 \\ +\ 3 \\ \hline \end{array}$$

2 + 5 = 7

3.

$$\begin{array}{r} 5 \\ 0 \\ +\ 3 \\ \hline \end{array}$$

5 + 0 = 5

4.

$$\begin{array}{r} 3 \\ 5 \\ +\ 3 \\ \hline \end{array}$$

3 + 5 = 8

Notes for Home Children learn to add three numbers.

Add.

5.	3	2	4	2	1	5	7
	3	3	0	2	7	1	2
	+ 1	+ 2	+ 5	+ 1	+ 1	+ 3	+ 1
	7						

6.	2	2	3	4	2	4	1
	1	2	0	1	2	4	5
	+ 3	+ 2	+ 4	+ 5	+ 4	+ 3	+ 1

7.	3	6	2	4	1	2	5
	1	3	9	2	3	6	3
	+ 6	+ 3	+ 0	+ 4	+ 4	+ 3	+ 2

8.	5	0	2
	3	4	1
	+ 4	+ 6	+ 5

Notes for Home Children practice adding three numbers.

Using 10 to Add

1. To add 7 + 5, first show 7.

2. Then add to make 10.

3. Then add to find the sum.

7 + 5 = 12

Use counters. First, add to 10.
Then find how many in all.

1. 7 + 4 = ____ 2. 8 + 4 = ____ 3. 7 + 5 = ____

4 + 7 = ____ 4 + 8 = ____ 5 + 7 = ____

Notes for Home Children explore at the CONCRETE level using counters to first add to 10 and then to count the remaining group to find how many in all.

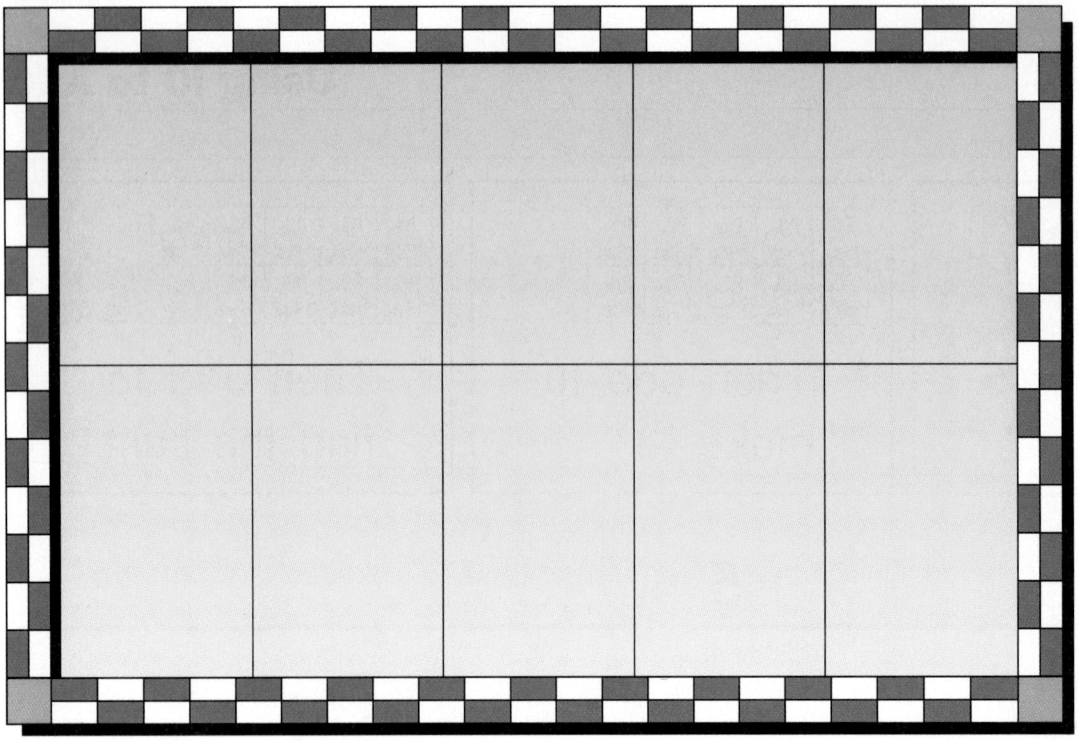

Use counters. First, add to 10.
Then find how many in all.

4.	4 + 8 = 12	8 + 4	5.	2 + 9	9 + 2	
6.	5 + 7	7 + 5				

7.	3 + 9	5 + 7	4 + 7	9 + 3	8 + 4	7 + 4	7 + 5
8.	9 + 2	3 + 8	7 + 5	8 + 3	3 + 9	4 + 8	2 + 9

Notes for Home Children explore at the CONCRETE level using counters to first add to 10 and then to count the remaining group to find how many in all.

See More Practice Set A on page 359.

Name

Use Data from a Graph

Use the graph.

1. How many books were read?

Heidi 4____ Larry ____ Rod ____

Tracy ____ Helen ____

2. Who read the most books? ____________________

3. Who read the fewest books? ____________________

Notes for Home Children learn to solve problems by using a graph.

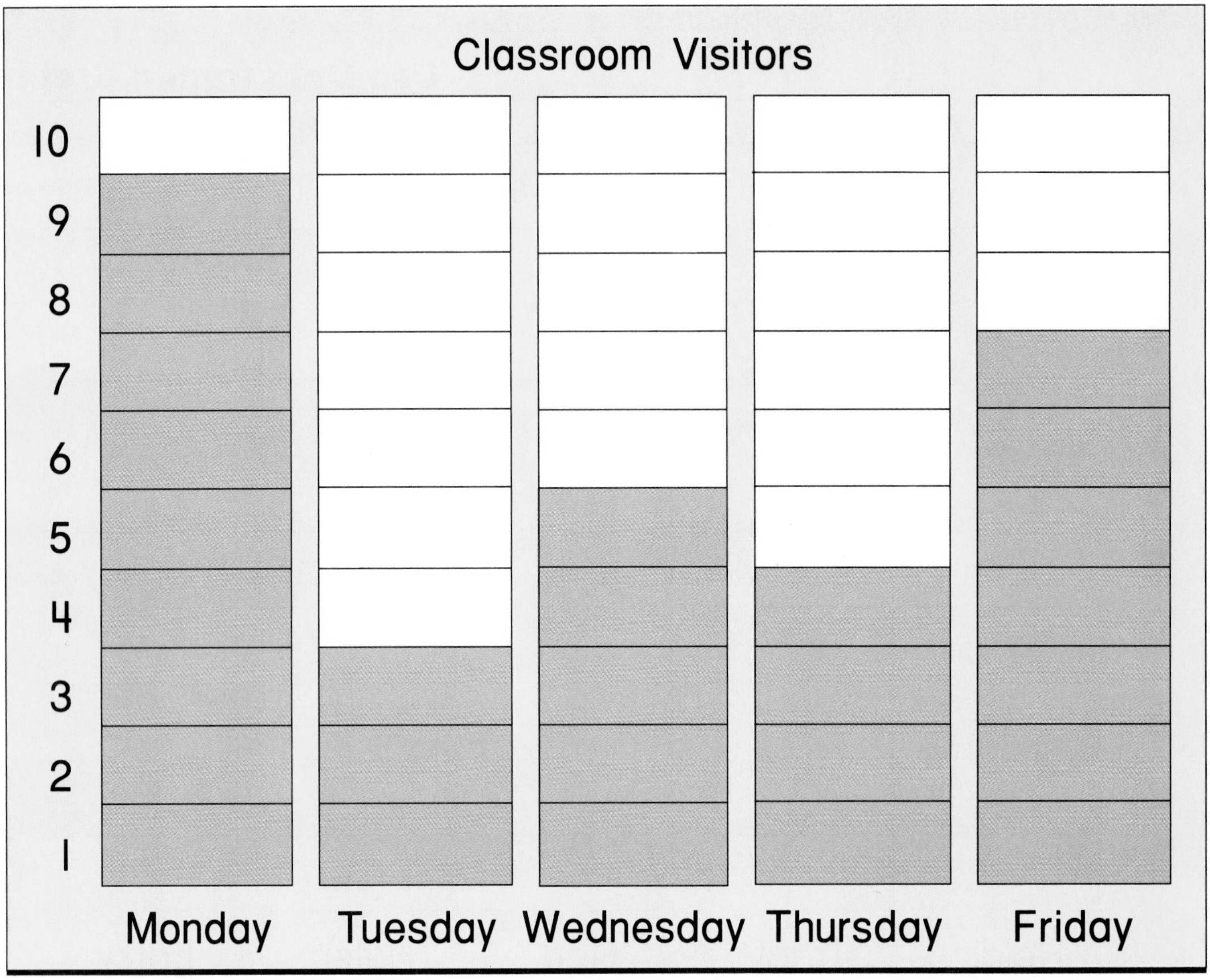

Use the graph.

4. How many visitors were there?

Wednesday 5 ____ Friday ____ Monday ____

Thursday ____ Tuesday ____

5. Which day had the most visitors? ____________

6. Which day had the fewest visitors? ____________

Notes for Home Children learn to solve problems by using a graph.

Name

Number Sense

Solve each group of problems in your head.
Can you tell a pattern for each group?

1.

2.

3.

4.

Let's do some more!

Make up three problems with a pattern.
Ask a friend to find the pattern.

Notes for Home Children develop an understanding for numbers by finding patterns in addition.

Skills Review

Fill in the correct ⬭.

What time is it?

1.

2:00 Ⓐ   12:00 Ⓑ

2.

6:30 Ⓐ   9:30 Ⓑ

3.

4 o'clock Ⓐ   3 o'clock Ⓑ

What number is missing?

4. 37, 38, ____

35 Ⓐ   36 Ⓑ   39 Ⓒ

5. 75, ____ , 77

76 Ⓐ   74 Ⓑ   78 Ⓒ

6. ____, 43, 44

40 Ⓐ   41 Ⓑ   42 Ⓒ

7. 97, ____ , 99

94 Ⓐ   98 Ⓑ   96 Ⓒ

Vocabulary

inch	cups

8. Two ____________ can fill a pint.

9. Use the ____________ ruler to measure.

Notes for Home Children review telling time to the hour and half hour. Then they review before, after, and between. Children review math terms.

Name

Using Doubles to Subtract

I use 6 + 6 = 12 to solve 12 − 6.

6 + 6 = 12 12 − 6 = 6

Add or subtract.

1.

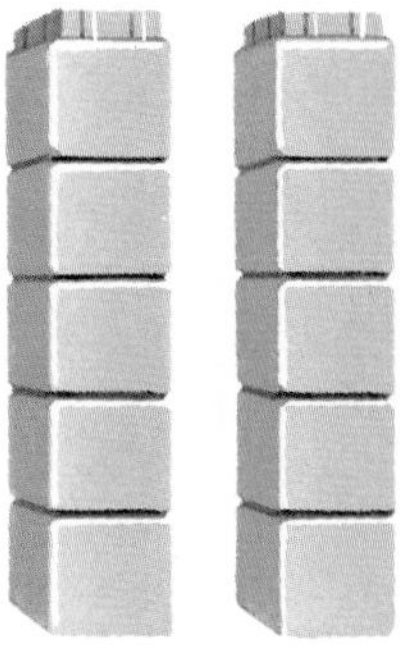

5 + 5 = ____

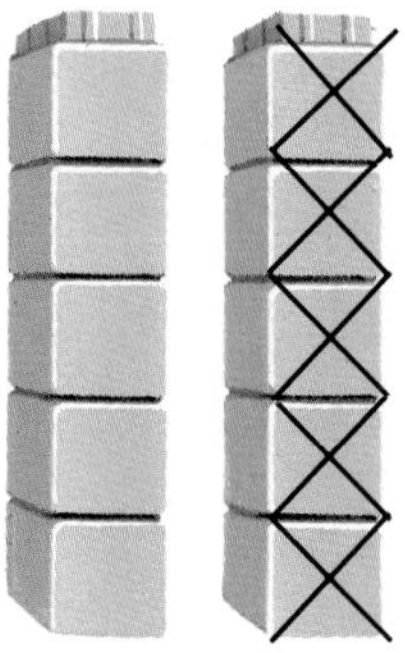

10 − 5 = ____

2.

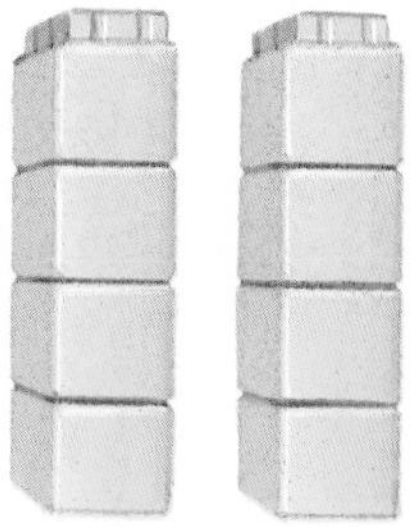

4 + 4 = ____

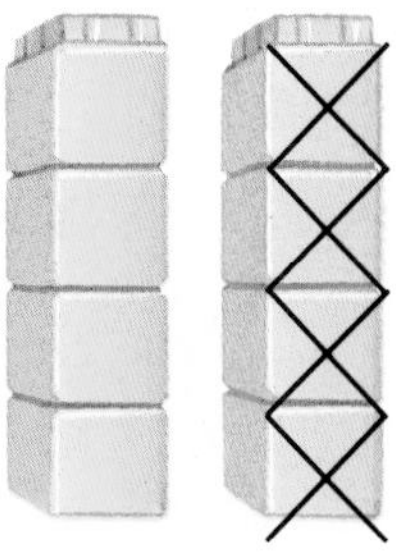

8 − 4 = ____

Notes for Home Children learn subtraction doubles by using addition doubles.

Add or subtract.

3. $\begin{array}{r} 4 \\ +\,4 \\ \hline 8 \end{array}$ $\quad \begin{array}{r} 8 \\ -\,4 \\ \hline \end{array}$

4. $\begin{array}{r} 6 \\ +\,6 \\ \hline \end{array}$ $\quad \begin{array}{r} 12 \\ -\,6 \\ \hline \end{array}$

5. $\begin{array}{r} 5 \\ +\,5 \\ \hline \end{array}$ $\quad \begin{array}{r} 10 \\ -\,5 \\ \hline \end{array}$

6. $\begin{array}{r} 9 \\ -\,8 \\ \hline \end{array}$ $\quad \begin{array}{r} 10 \\ -\,5 \\ \hline \end{array}$ $\quad \begin{array}{r} 9 \\ -\,4 \\ \hline \end{array}$ $\quad \begin{array}{r} 5 \\ -\,3 \\ \hline \end{array}$ $\quad \begin{array}{r} 8 \\ -\,4 \\ \hline \end{array}$ $\quad \begin{array}{r} 7 \\ -\,6 \\ \hline \end{array}$ $\quad \begin{array}{r} 10 \\ -\,7 \\ \hline \end{array}$

7. $\begin{array}{r} 6 \\ -\,3 \\ \hline \end{array}$ $\quad \begin{array}{r} 8 \\ -\,8 \\ \hline \end{array}$ $\quad \begin{array}{r} 12 \\ -\,6 \\ \hline \end{array}$ $\quad \begin{array}{r} 10 \\ -\,3 \\ \hline \end{array}$ $\quad \begin{array}{r} 9 \\ -\,5 \\ \hline \end{array}$ $\quad \begin{array}{r} 10 \\ -\,8 \\ \hline \end{array}$ $\quad \begin{array}{r} 8 \\ -\,3 \\ \hline \end{array}$

8. $\begin{array}{r} 10 \\ -\,6 \\ \hline \end{array}$ $\quad \begin{array}{r} 9 \\ -\,3 \\ \hline \end{array}$ $\quad \begin{array}{r} 7 \\ -\,4 \\ \hline \end{array}$ $\quad \begin{array}{r} 4 \\ -\,2 \\ \hline \end{array}$ $\quad \begin{array}{r} 8 \\ -\,5 \\ \hline \end{array}$ $\quad \begin{array}{r} 2 \\ -\,1 \\ \hline \end{array}$ $\quad \begin{array}{r} 9 \\ -\,2 \\ \hline \end{array}$

9. $\begin{array}{r} 5 \\ -\,2 \\ \hline \end{array}$ $\quad \begin{array}{r} 8 \\ -\,6 \\ \hline \end{array}$ $\quad \begin{array}{r} 9 \\ -\,6 \\ \hline \end{array}$

Notes for Home Children practice subtraction facts.

Name

Related Subtraction Facts for 11

Write how many parts.

Subtract.

1.

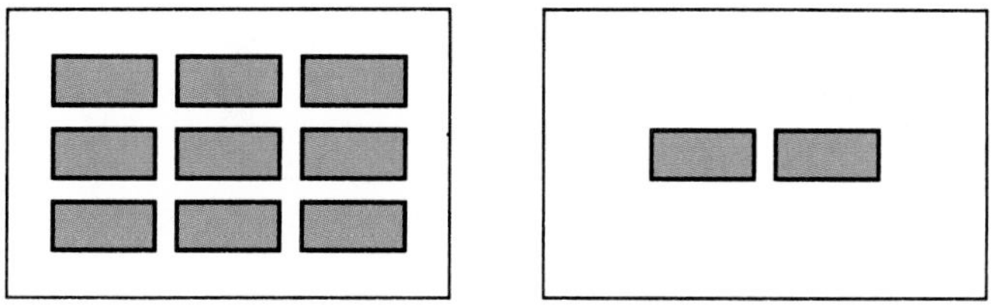

9 ___ 2 ___

11 − 2 = 9 ___

11 − 9 = 2 ___

2.

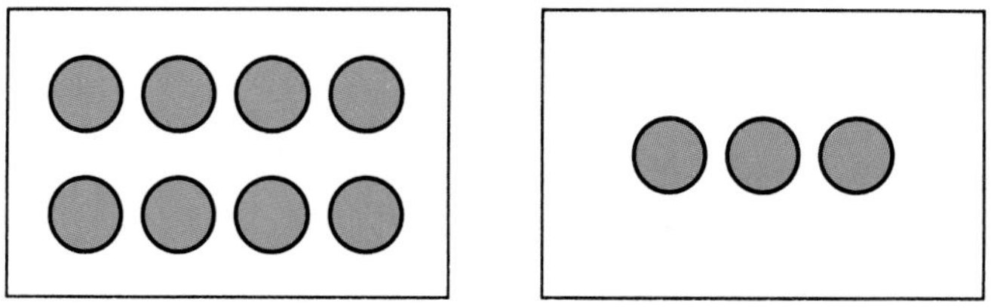

___ ___

11 − 3 = ___

11 − 8 = ___

3.

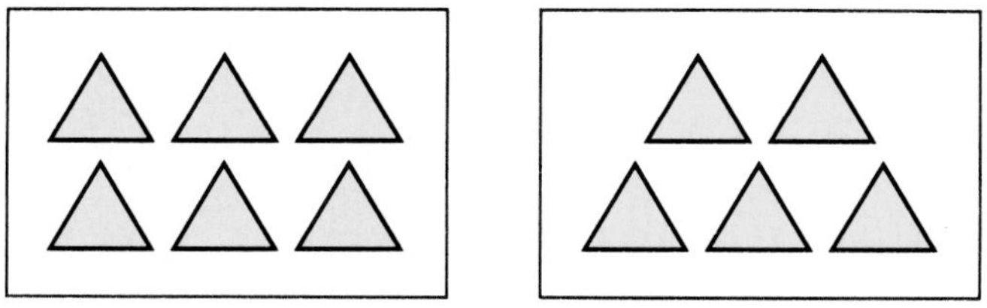

___ ___

11 − 5 = ___

11 − 6 = ___

Notes for Home Children solve subtraction facts for 11 by thinking of related numbers that make 11.

Subtract.

4. $\begin{array}{r} 11 \\ -3 \\ \hline 8 \end{array}$ $\begin{array}{r} 11 \\ -8 \\ \hline \end{array}$
5. $\begin{array}{r} 11 \\ -4 \\ \hline \end{array}$ $\begin{array}{r} 11 \\ -7 \\ \hline \end{array}$
6. $\begin{array}{r} 11 \\ -2 \\ \hline \end{array}$ $\begin{array}{r} 11 \\ -9 \\ \hline \end{array}$

7. $\begin{array}{r} 11 \\ -7 \\ \hline \end{array}$ $\begin{array}{r} 11 \\ -4 \\ \hline \end{array}$
8. $\begin{array}{r} 11 \\ -9 \\ \hline \end{array}$ $\begin{array}{r} 11 \\ -2 \\ \hline \end{array}$
9. $\begin{array}{r} 11 \\ -6 \\ \hline \end{array}$ $\begin{array}{r} 11 \\ -5 \\ \hline \end{array}$

10. $\begin{array}{r} 12 \\ -6 \\ \hline \end{array}$ $\begin{array}{r} 11 \\ -5 \\ \hline \end{array}$ $\begin{array}{r} 10 \\ -7 \\ \hline \end{array}$ $\begin{array}{r} 11 \\ -6 \\ \hline \end{array}$ $\begin{array}{r} 9 \\ -4 \\ \hline \end{array}$ $\begin{array}{r} 10 \\ -6 \\ \hline \end{array}$ $\begin{array}{r} 11 \\ -7 \\ \hline \end{array}$

11. $\begin{array}{r} 10 \\ -8 \\ \hline \end{array}$ $\begin{array}{r} 11 \\ -8 \\ \hline \end{array}$ $\begin{array}{r} 11 \\ -4 \\ \hline \end{array}$ $\begin{array}{r} 9 \\ -5 \\ \hline \end{array}$ $\begin{array}{r} 11 \\ -6 \\ \hline \end{array}$ $\begin{array}{r} 11 \\ -3 \\ \hline \end{array}$ $\begin{array}{r} 10 \\ -9 \\ \hline \end{array}$

Problem Solving

Write a number sentence.

12. Rosa caught 4 fish on Monday.
She caught 7 fish on Wednesday.
How many fish did she catch in all?

____ + ____ = ____ fish

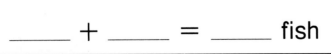

Notes for Home Children practice subtraction facts through 11. Then they solve a problem involving addition.

Name ______

Related Subtraction Facts for 12

7 and 5 are parts of 12.

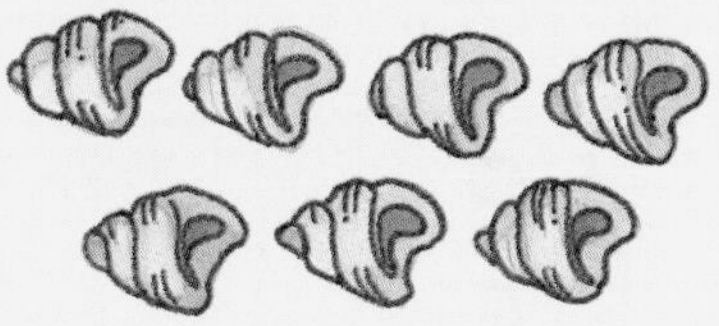

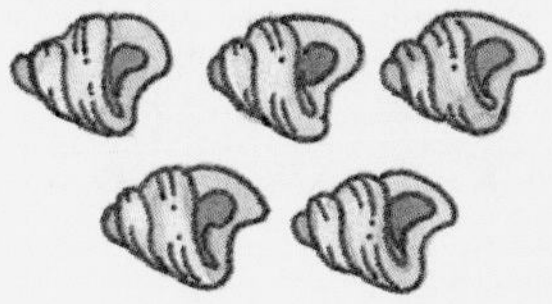

7 5

Write how many parts.

Subtract.

1.

9 3

$12 - 3 =$ 9

$12 - 9 =$ 3

2.

___ ___

$12 - 4 =$ ___

$12 - 8 =$ ___

3.

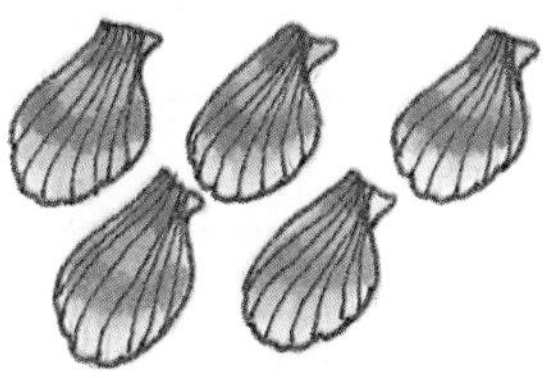

___ ___

$12 - 5 =$ ___

$12 - 7 =$ ___

Notes for Home Children solve subtraction facts for 12 by thinking of related numbers that make 12.

Subtract.

4. $\begin{array}{r} 12 \\ -\ 4 \\ \hline 8 \end{array}$ $\begin{array}{r} 12 \\ -\ 8 \\ \hline \end{array}$

5. $\begin{array}{r} 12 \\ -\ 3 \\ \hline \end{array}$ $\begin{array}{r} 12 \\ -\ 9 \\ \hline \end{array}$

6. $\begin{array}{r} 12 \\ -\ 5 \\ \hline \end{array}$ $\begin{array}{r} 12 \\ -\ 7 \\ \hline \end{array}$

7. $\begin{array}{r} 12 \\ -\ 9 \\ \hline \end{array}$ $\begin{array}{r} 12 \\ -\ 3 \\ \hline \end{array}$

8. $\begin{array}{r} 12 \\ -\ 7 \\ \hline \end{array}$ $\begin{array}{r} 12 \\ -\ 5 \\ \hline \end{array}$

9. $\begin{array}{r} 12 \\ -\ 8 \\ \hline \end{array}$ $\begin{array}{r} 12 \\ -\ 4 \\ \hline \end{array}$

10. $\begin{array}{r} 12 \\ -\ 8 \\ \hline \end{array}$ $\begin{array}{r} 11 \\ -\ 6 \\ \hline \end{array}$ $\begin{array}{r} 12 \\ -\ 4 \\ \hline \end{array}$ $\begin{array}{r} 11 \\ -\ 5 \\ \hline \end{array}$ $\begin{array}{r} 11 \\ -\ 3 \\ \hline \end{array}$ $\begin{array}{r} 12 \\ -\ 7 \\ \hline \end{array}$ $\begin{array}{r} 11 \\ -\ 9 \\ \hline \end{array}$

11. $\begin{array}{r} 12 \\ -\ 9 \\ \hline \end{array}$ $\begin{array}{r} 12 \\ -\ 5 \\ \hline \end{array}$ $\begin{array}{r} 11 \\ -\ 7 \\ \hline \end{array}$ $\begin{array}{r} 12 \\ -\ 6 \\ \hline \end{array}$ $\begin{array}{r} 11 \\ -\ 4 \\ \hline \end{array}$ $\begin{array}{r} 11 \\ -\ 8 \\ \hline \end{array}$ $\begin{array}{r} 12 \\ -\ 3 \\ \hline \end{array}$

Talk About Math

How are these facts the same?
How are they different?

$12 - 4 = 8$

$12 - 8 = 4$

Notes for Home Children practice subtraction facts through 12.

Finding Families of Facts

These facts make a family.

$5 + 6 = 11$	$11 - 6 = 5$
$6 + 5 = 11$	$11 - 5 = 6$

Use counters.
Add or subtract.

1.

$4 + 8 =$ 12

$8 + 4 =$ ____

$12 - 8 =$ ____

$12 - 4 =$ ____

2.

$3 + 8 =$ ____

$8 + 3 =$ ____

$11 - 8 =$ ____

$11 - 3 =$ ____

Notes for Home Children explore at the CONCRETE level using counters to find families of facts.

Use counters.
Add or subtract.

3.
$\begin{array}{r} 2 \\ +\,9 \\ \hline 11 \end{array}$ $\begin{array}{r} 11 \\ -\,9 \\ \hline \end{array}$

$\begin{array}{r} 9 \\ +\,2 \\ \hline \end{array}$ $\begin{array}{r} 11 \\ -\,2 \\ \hline \end{array}$

4.
$\begin{array}{r} 3 \\ +\,9 \\ \hline \end{array}$ $\begin{array}{r} 12 \\ -\,9 \\ \hline \end{array}$

$\begin{array}{r} 9 \\ +\,3 \\ \hline \end{array}$ $\begin{array}{r} 12 \\ -\,3 \\ \hline \end{array}$

5.
$\begin{array}{r} 3 \\ +\,8 \\ \hline \end{array}$ $\begin{array}{r} 11 \\ -\,8 \\ \hline \end{array}$

$\begin{array}{r} 8 \\ +\,3 \\ \hline \end{array}$ $\begin{array}{r} 11 \\ -\,3 \\ \hline \end{array}$

6.
$\begin{array}{r} 5 \\ +\,7 \\ \hline \end{array}$ $\begin{array}{r} 12 \\ -\,7 \\ \hline \end{array}$

$\begin{array}{r} 7 \\ +\,5 \\ \hline \end{array}$ $\begin{array}{r} 12 \\ -\,5 \\ \hline \end{array}$

7.
$\begin{array}{r} 4 \\ +\,7 \\ \hline \end{array}$ $\begin{array}{r} 11 \\ -\,7 \\ \hline \end{array}$

$\begin{array}{r} 7 \\ +\,4 \\ \hline \end{array}$ $\begin{array}{r} 11 \\ -\,4 \\ \hline \end{array}$

8.
$\begin{array}{r} 5 \\ +\,6 \\ \hline \end{array}$ $\begin{array}{r} 11 \\ -\,6 \\ \hline \end{array}$

$\begin{array}{r} 6 \\ +\,5 \\ \hline \end{array}$ $\begin{array}{r} 11 \\ -\,5 \\ \hline \end{array}$

Notes for Home Children explore at the CONCRETE level using counters to find families of facts.

Name

Addition and Subtraction Through 12

Find the sum or difference.

Use yellow for 8.

Use blue for 9.

Use purple for 10.

Use red for 11.

Use orange for 12.

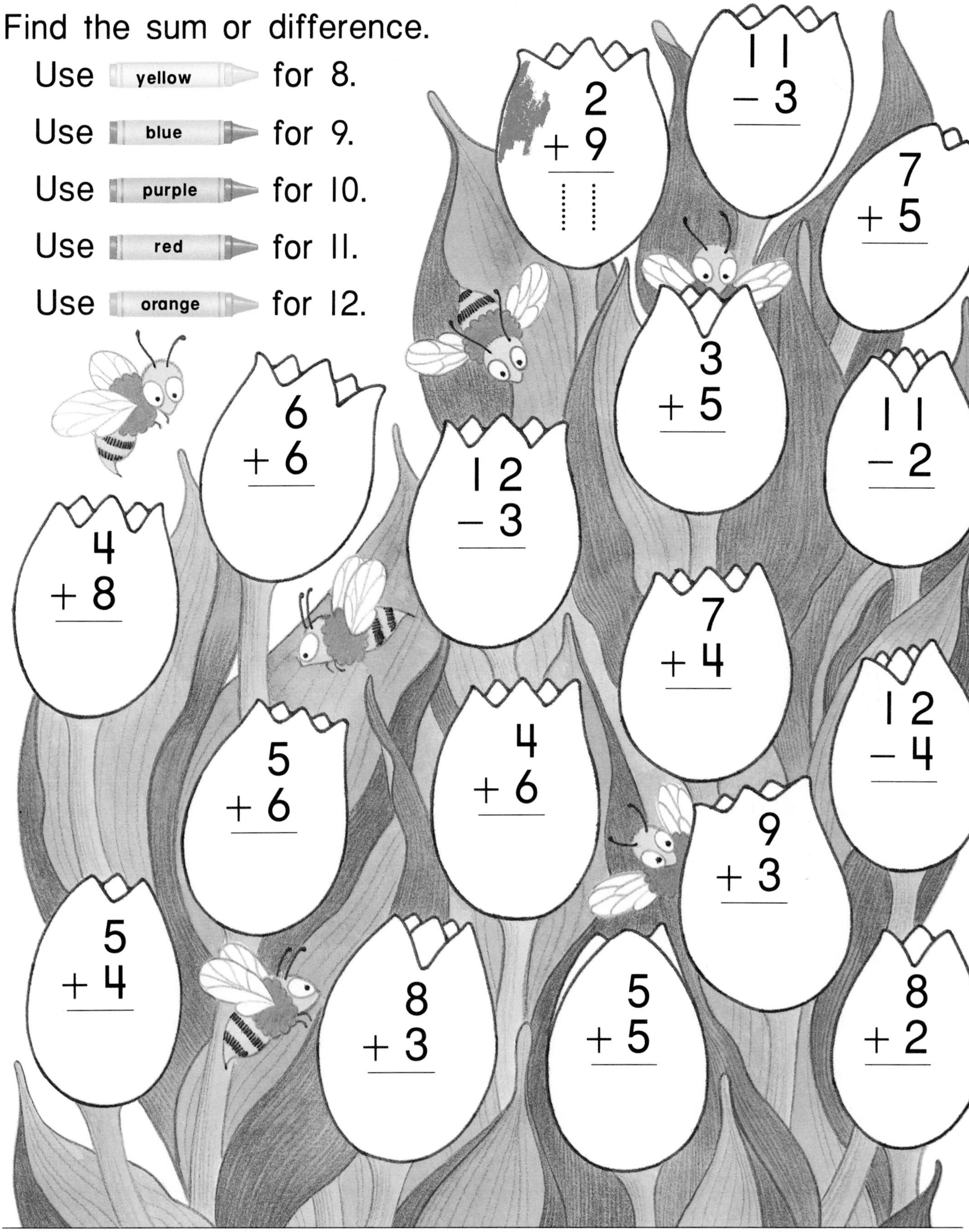

Notes for Home Children practice addition and subtraction facts through 12.

Ring facts for each number.

2. 

9 + 2 8 + 4 5 + 5 8 + 3

---

3. 

6 + 6 5 + 7 3 + 8 6 + 5

---

4. 

11 − 9 11 − 4 12 − 3 12 − 5

---

5. 

12 − 4 11 − 5 11 − 2 11 − 3

---

6. 

11 − 8 12 − 7 12 − 9 11 − 6

Problem Solving

Read the problem.
Write + or − in the □.
Then add or subtract.

7. There are 12 children outside.
7 children go back to class.
How many are still outside?

  12
□ 7
―――

____ children

Notes for Home Children practice addition and subtraction facts through 12. Then they solve a problem by choosing the operation.

See More Practice Set B on page 359.

Using a Problem-Solving Guide

I use a 3-step guide to help me solve problems.

Rosa had 9 dolls.
She gave 5 to her sister.
How many dolls does Rosa have left?

PROBLEM-SOLVING GUIDE

Step 1: **Understand. . . .**	**What is the question?**	How many dolls does Rosa have left?
	What are the facts?	Rosa had 9 dolls. She gave 5 dolls to her sister.
Step 2: **Plan and Solve. .**	**What can you do?**	Subtract. 9 dolls -5 dolls $= 4$ dolls
	How can you find the answer?	Rosa has 4 dolls left.
Step 3: **Look Back. . . . .**	**Does the answer make sense?**	Rosa starts out with 9 dolls. If she gives 5 dolls away, she will have less than 9 dolls.

Notes for Home Children learn to use a three-step problem-solving guide to solve problems.

Think about Step 1, **Understand**.
Ring the facts. Underline the question.

1. There were 12 frogs.
4 frogs jumped away.
How many frogs
were left?

2. Andy saw 9 birds.
Then he saw 3 more.
How many birds did
Andy see?

Think about Step 2, **Plan and Solve**.
Ring + or −.
Use counters or mental math to help solve.

3. There were 12 frogs.
4 frogs jumped away.
How many frogs were left?

+ −

12
− 4
8 frogs

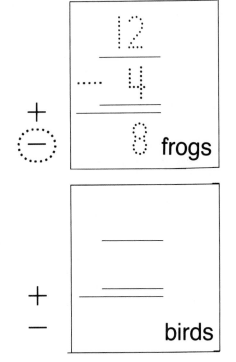

4. Andy saw 9 birds.
Then he saw 3 more.
How many birds did Andy see?

+ −

____
____
birds

Think about Step 3, **Look Back**.
Write the answer in the sentence.
Decide if each answer makes sense. Ring yes or no.

5. There were 8 frogs left.

yes no

6. Andy saw ______ birds.

yes no

Notes for Home Children use a three-step problem-solving guide to solve problems.

Name

Problem-Solving Workshop

Explore as a Team

Work with a partner.
Solve this problem.
Give the number of each floor.

Mary got on the elevator on the fourth floor. ______

She rode down 3 floors. ______

She rode up 8 floors. ______

She rode down 4 floors. ______

She rode up 2 floors. ______

She rode up 1 floor. ______

She rode down 5 floors. ______

She rode up 9 floors. ______

She got off on this floor. ______

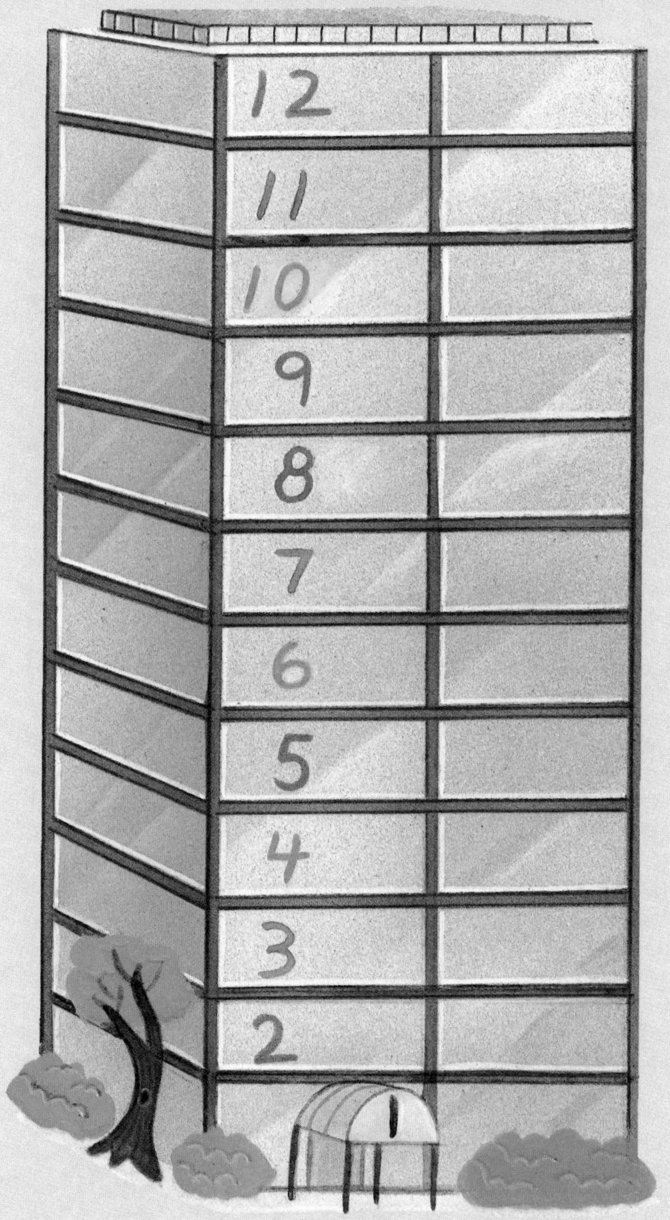

Notes for Home Children explore with a partner to solve a problem involving logical reasoning.

Problem Solving WORKSHOP

Problem-Solving Workshop

Explore with a Calculator

Use a  to solve.

Write + or – in the □.

1.

5	+	2	–	3	=	4
5	–	2	–	3	=	0
5	–	2	+	3	=	6
5	+	2	+	3	=	10

2.

9	□	1	□	2	=	12
9	□	1	□	2	=	8
9	□	1	□	2	=	10
9	□	1	□	2	=	6

3.

6	□	3	□	3	=	0
6	□	3	□	3	=	6
6	□	3	□	3	=	12
6	□	3	□	3	=	6

4.

8	□	2	□	1	=	7
8	□	2	□	1	=	11
8	□	2	□	1	=	9
8	□	2	□	1	=	5

Notes for Home Children explore with a calculator by guessing and checking to solve addition and subtraction problems.

Name ______________________________

More Practice

Set A Use after page 340.

Find the sum.

Use blue for 11.

Use yellow for 12.

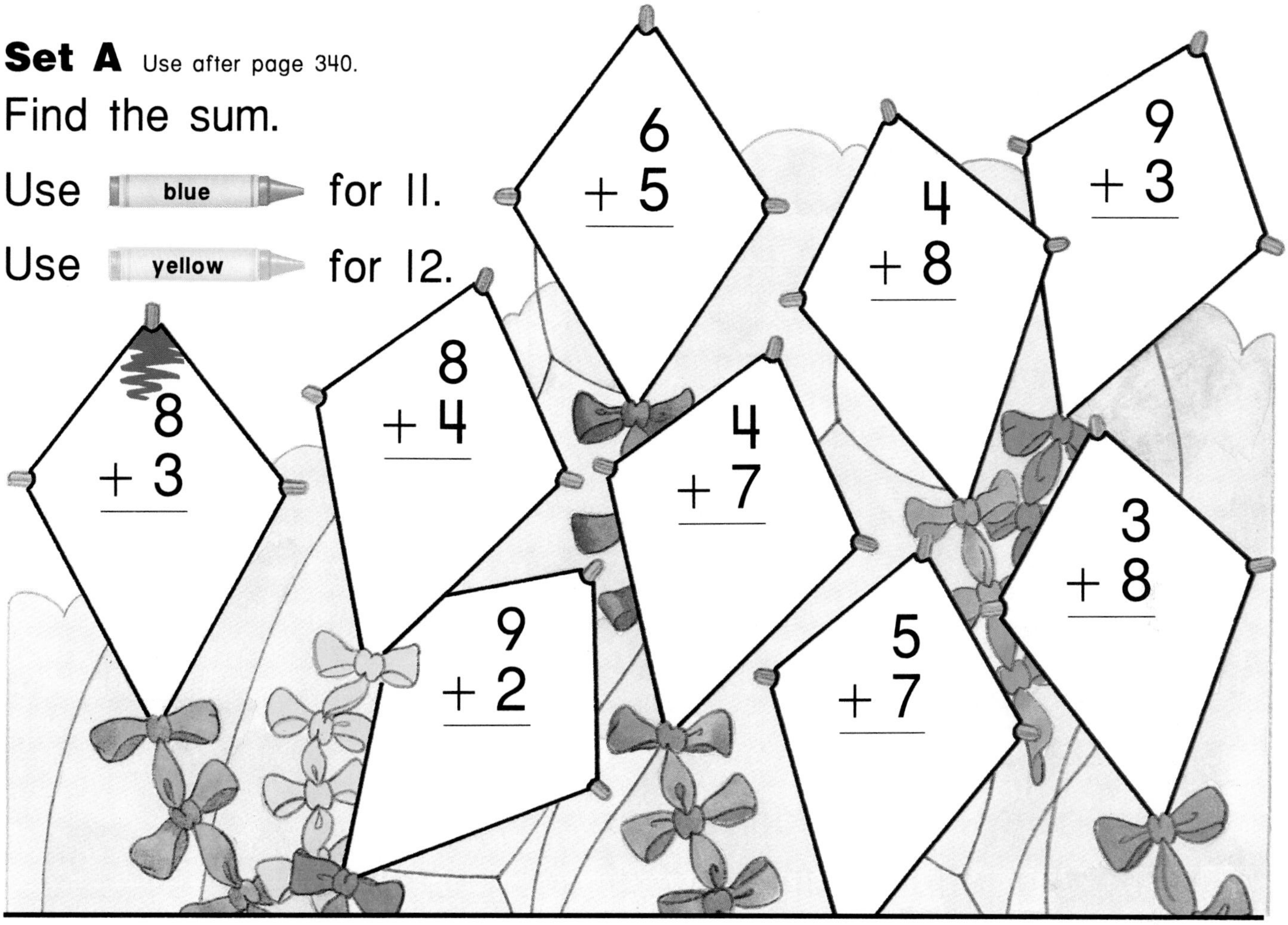

Set B Use after page 354.

Find the sum or difference.

1.	5 + 5 = 10	12 − 4	7 + 5	11 − 2	12 − 7	3 + 9
2.	11 − 4	5 + 6	12 − 9	7 + 4	11 − 8	4 + 6

Notes for Home Set A: Children practice addition facts through 12.
Set B: Children practice addition and subtraction facts through 12.

Enrichment

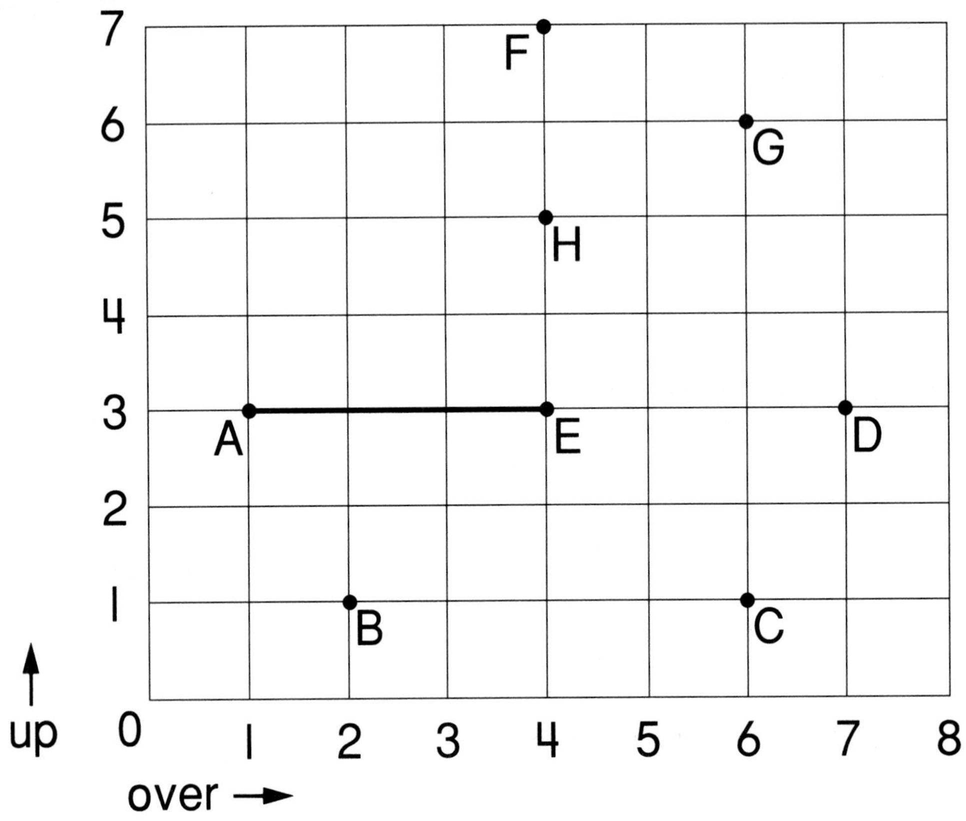

1. Start at 0. Follow each path.
Write the letter at the end of each path.

over →	up ↑	
1	3	A
4	7	
2	1	
7	3	

over →	up ↑	
4	3	
6	1	
4	5	
6	6	

2. Draw a line to connect the letters
in alphabetical order.

Notes for Home Children are challenged to use a coordinate grid to complete a table.

Name ______________________

Chapter 11 Review/Test

Add or subtract.

1.

3	9	3	5	5	6
+ 8	+ 2	+ 9	+ 5	+ 6	+ 5

2.

12	10	11	11	12	12
− 6	− 5	− 3	− 8	− 3	− 9

3. Add or subtract.

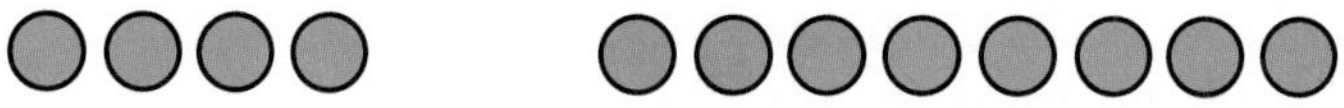

$4 + 8 =$ ____ $12 - 8 =$ ____

$8 + 4 =$ ____ $12 - 4 =$ ____

4. Add.

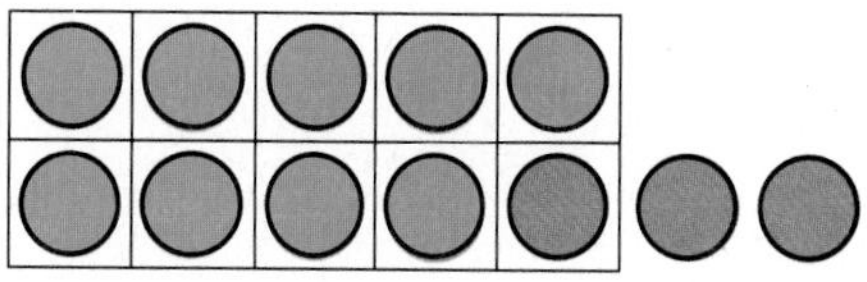

$9 + 3 =$ ____

5. Add.

$\begin{array}{r} 3 \\ 2 \\ +\,7 \\ \hline \end{array}$ $\begin{array}{r} 4 \\ 0 \\ +\,5 \\ \hline \end{array}$

6. Write + or − in the box. Then solve.

There were 12 birds.
5 flew away.
How many were left?

$\begin{array}{r} 12 \\ \square\ \ 5 \\ \hline \end{array}$

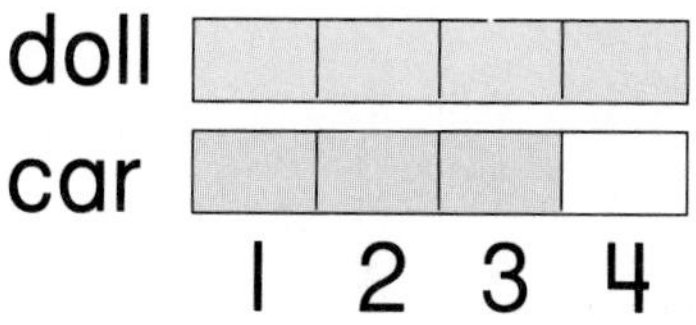

7. Use the graph.
How many? car ____ doll ____

Notes for Home Children are assessed on Chapter 11 concepts, skills, and problem solving.

Exploring Math at Home

Dear Family,

In this chapter I have learned addition and subtraction facts through 12 and how to add three numbers. Please help me with the activities below.

Love, ______________________________

1.

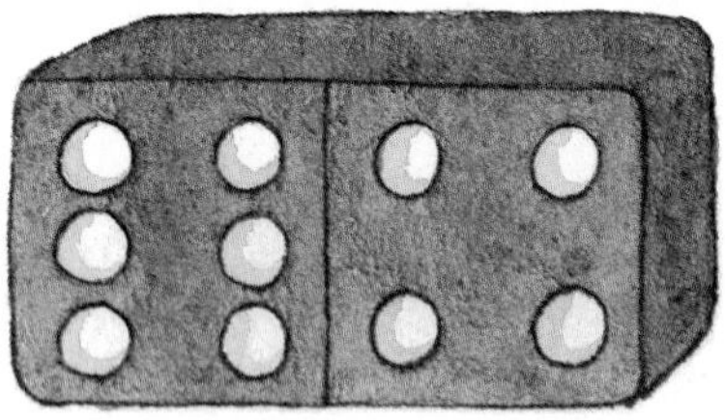

Use dominoes to find sums through 12.

2.

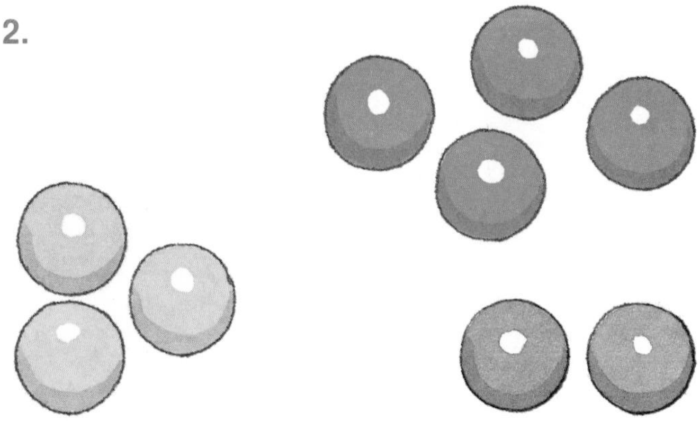

Make three groups of objects to find sums through 12. Combine two of the groups, then add the third to get the sum.

3.

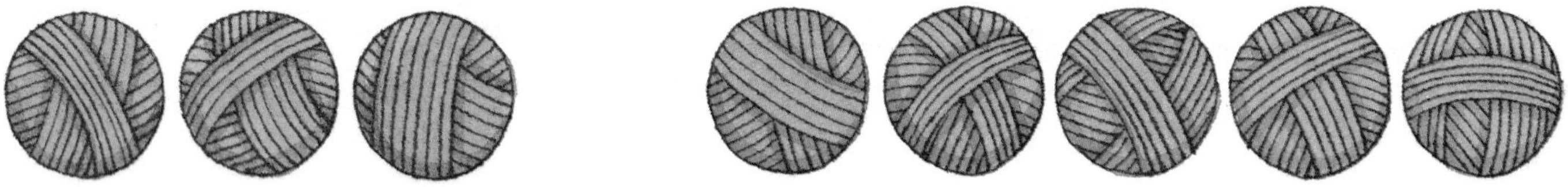

$3 + 5 = 8$ $\quad$ $8 - 5 = 3$

$5 + 3 = 8$ $\quad$ $8 - 3 = 5$

Use two groups of objects whose sum is 2 through 12. Talk about addition and subtraction problems for each family of facts.

Coming Attractions

In the next chapter I will learn about fractions. I will also learn to identify events as sure, unsure, or impossible.

Name

Cumulative Review/Test

Fill in the correct ⬭.
Add or subtract.

1. $11 - 4$

7 Ⓐ 8 Ⓑ 9 Ⓒ

2. $7 + 5$

9 Ⓐ 10 Ⓑ 12 Ⓒ

3. $12 - 9 =$

0 Ⓐ 2 Ⓑ 3 Ⓒ

4. $8 + 3 =$

8 Ⓐ 11 Ⓑ 12 Ⓒ

5. $10 - 6$

2 Ⓐ 4 Ⓑ 5 Ⓒ

6. $3 + 7$

10 Ⓐ 11 Ⓑ 12 Ⓒ

7. $12 - 4$

5 Ⓐ 7 Ⓑ 8 Ⓒ

8. $11 - 5 =$

6 Ⓐ 7 Ⓑ 9 Ⓒ

9. $2 + 1 + 7$

9 Ⓐ 10 Ⓑ 12 Ⓒ

10. Which holds more?

Ⓐ

Ⓑ

11. What time is shown?

3:30 Ⓐ
8:00 Ⓑ
8:30 Ⓒ

Notes for Home Children are assessed on Chapters 1-11 concepts, skills, and problem solving using a multiple-choice format.

Fill in the correct ◯.

12. How many?

54 Ⓐ   56 Ⓑ   57 Ⓒ

13. How much?

51¢ Ⓐ   56¢ Ⓑ   61¢ Ⓒ

14. What number is missing?

78, 79, ____, 81

70 Ⓐ   77 Ⓑ   80 Ⓒ

15. Which is greater?

67 Ⓐ   87 Ⓑ

Solve.

16. John had 8¢.
He earned 3¢ more.
How much does
he have now?

10¢ Ⓐ   11¢ Ⓑ   12¢ Ⓒ

17. Jan had 12¢.
She spent 9¢.
How much does
she have now?

1¢ Ⓐ   2¢ Ⓑ   3¢ Ⓒ

18. What comes next?

3, 6, 9, 3, 6, 9, 3, ____

3 Ⓐ   6 Ⓑ   9 Ⓒ

19. Solve.

Ed started reading at 4:00.
He read for 2 hours.
What time did he stop?

5:00 Ⓐ   6:00 Ⓑ   7:00 Ⓒ

Notes for Home Children are assessed on Chapters 1-11 concepts, skills, and problem solving using a multiple-choice format.

Chapter

12

Fractions and Probability

Listen to the math story, "Half a Heart."
Detective Bones found half a heart.
How did she use it to solve her case?

Notes for Home Children listen to a math story introducing chapter concepts and skills. Then they answer a question about the story.

Equal Parts

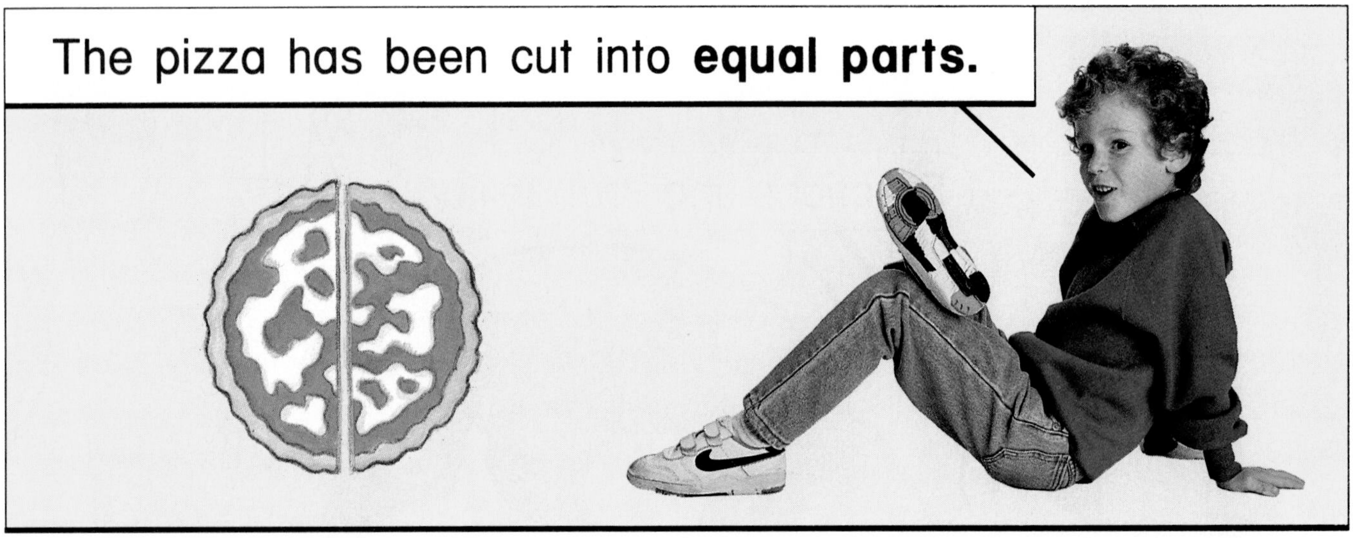

Ring the pizzas that show equal parts.

1.
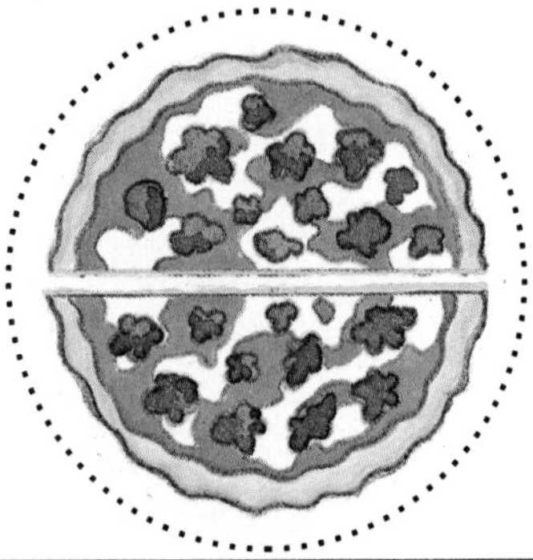

2.
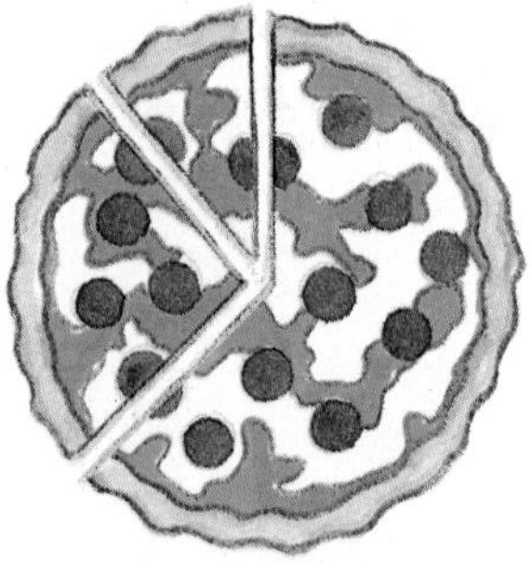

3.
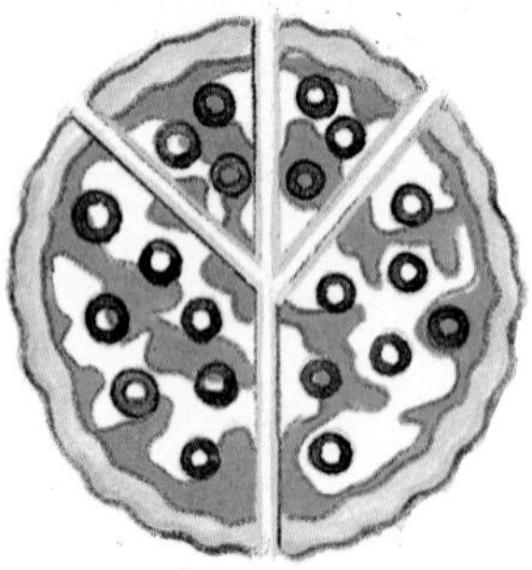

4.
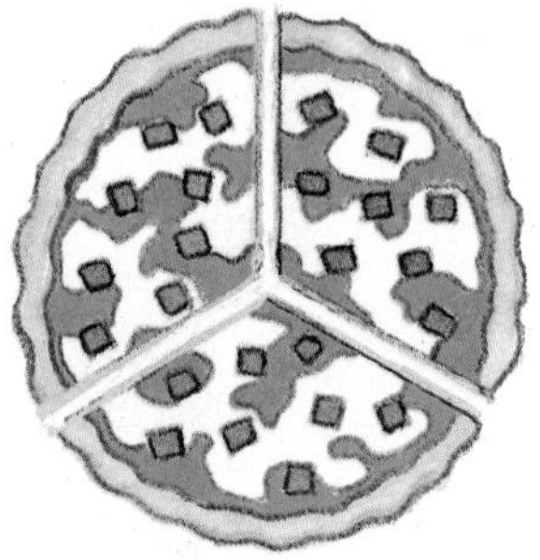

5.

6.
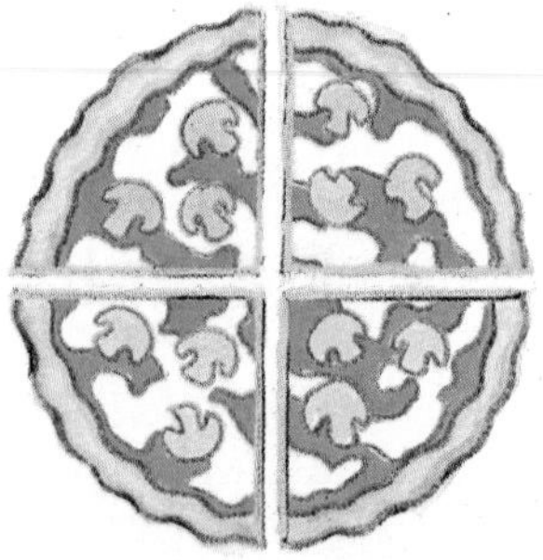

Notes for Home Children identify objects divided into equal parts as readiness for fraction concepts.

Name

Identifying Equal Parts

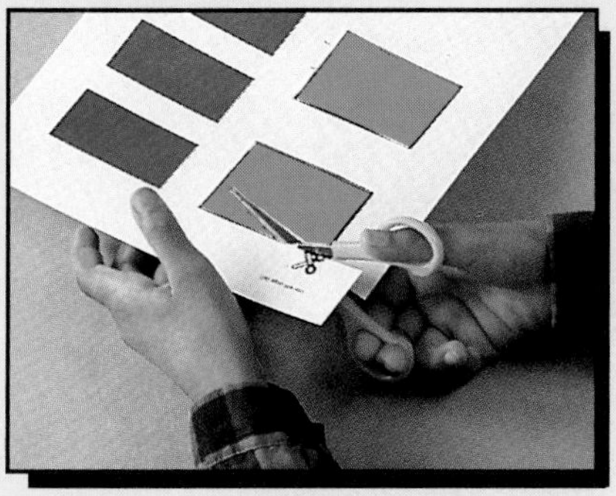

1. Cut out the shapes on page 369.

2. Paste the shapes on the rectangles below.

3. Record how many equal parts.

1. Paste the green shapes to cover this rectangle.

How many equal parts? ____

2. Paste the blue shapes to cover this rectangle.

How many equal parts? ____

Notes for Home Children explore at the CONCRETE level using a cut and paste activity to identify equal parts of a region.

Ring the shape that shows equal parts.

3.

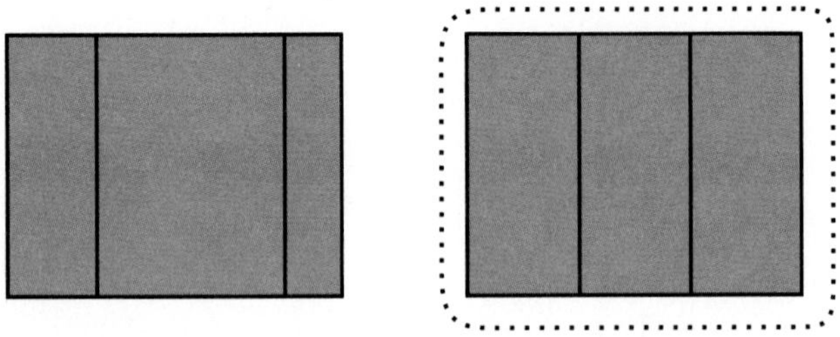

4.

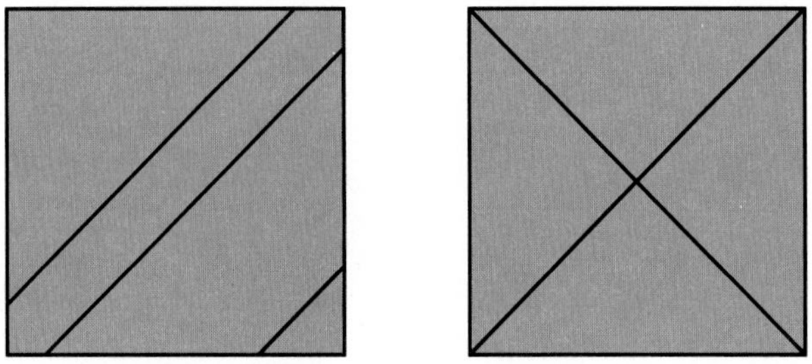

5.

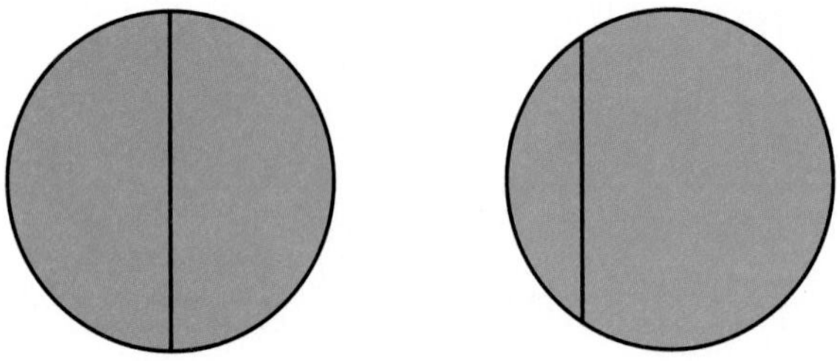

6.

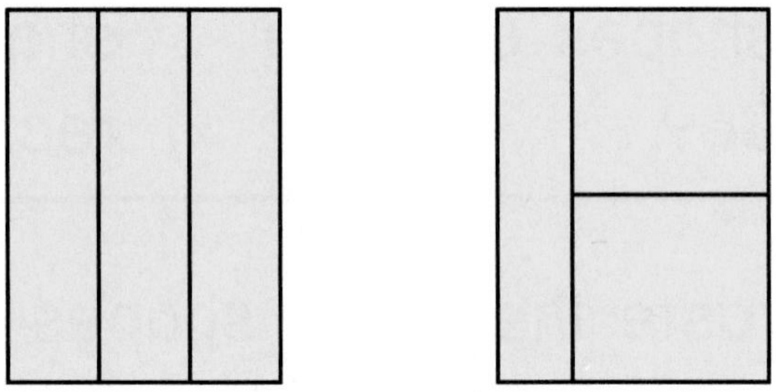

7.

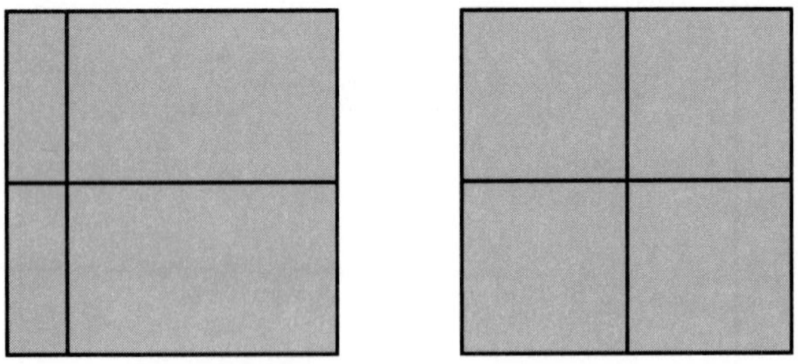

8.

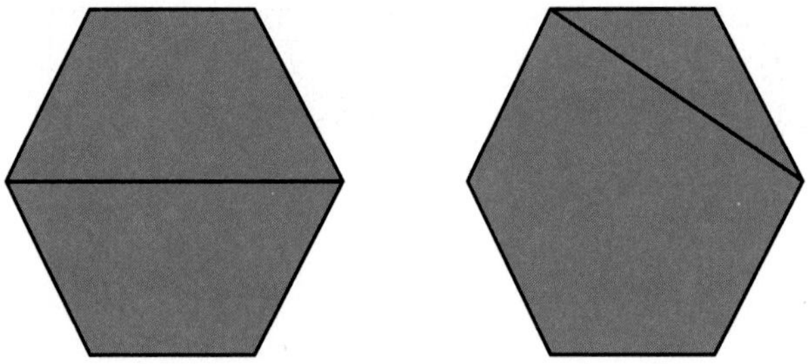

9.

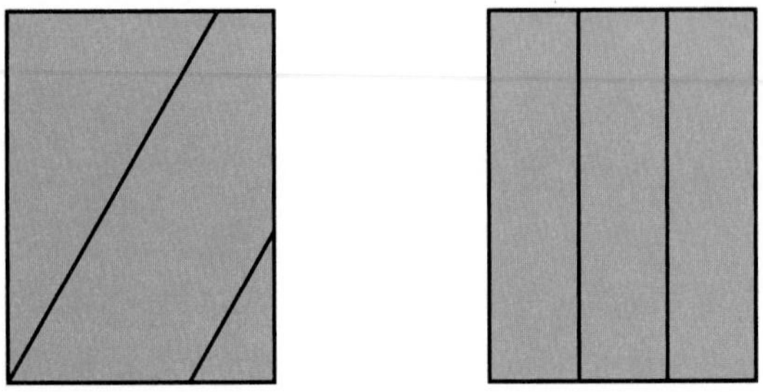

10.

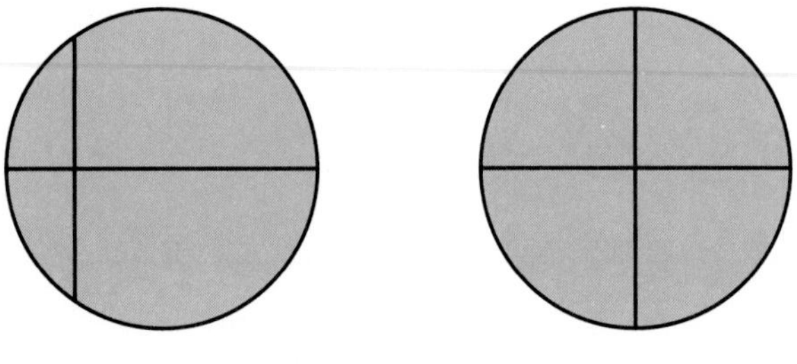

Notes for Home Children identify shapes with equal parts.

Use with page 367.

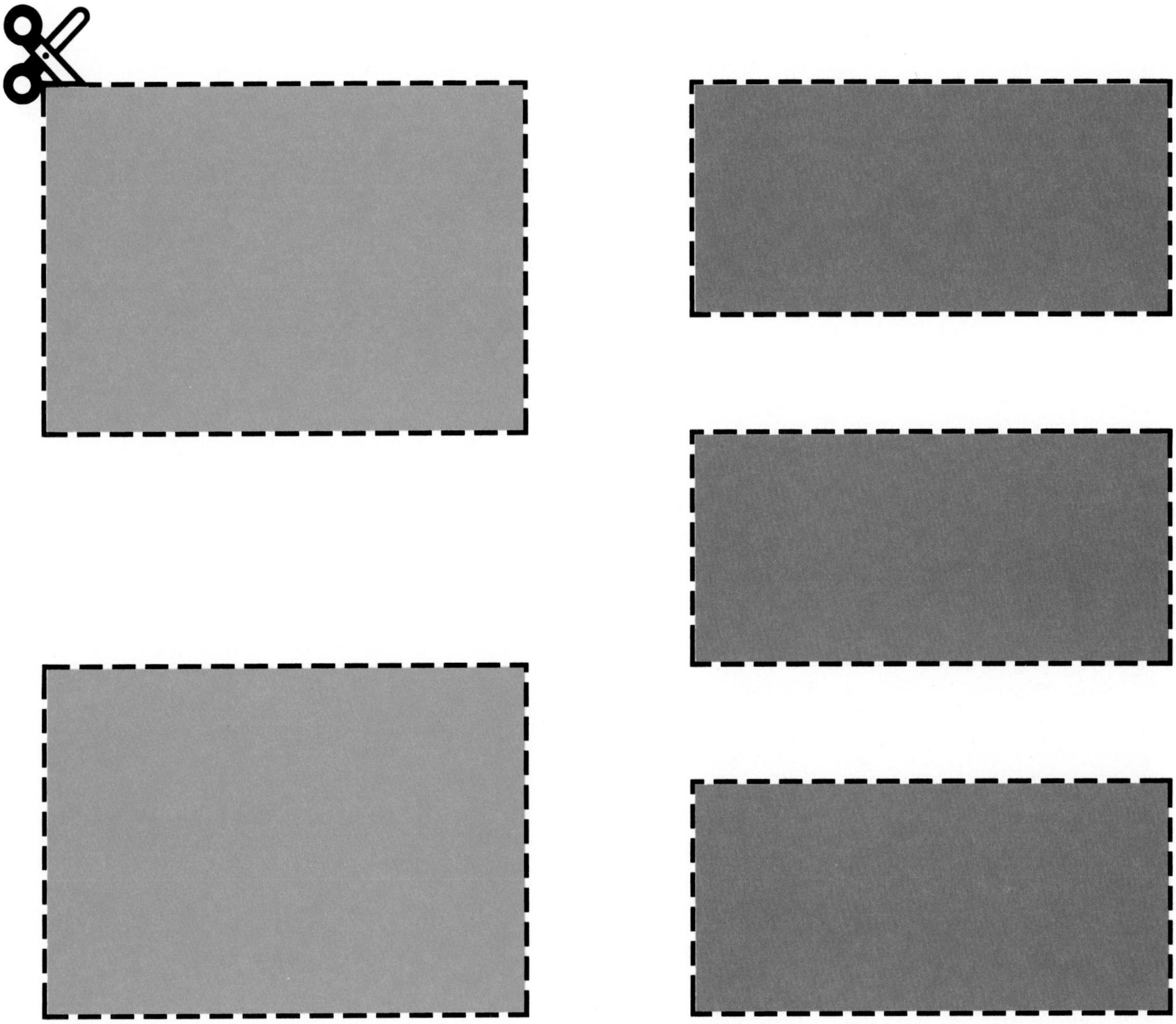

Name

Halves

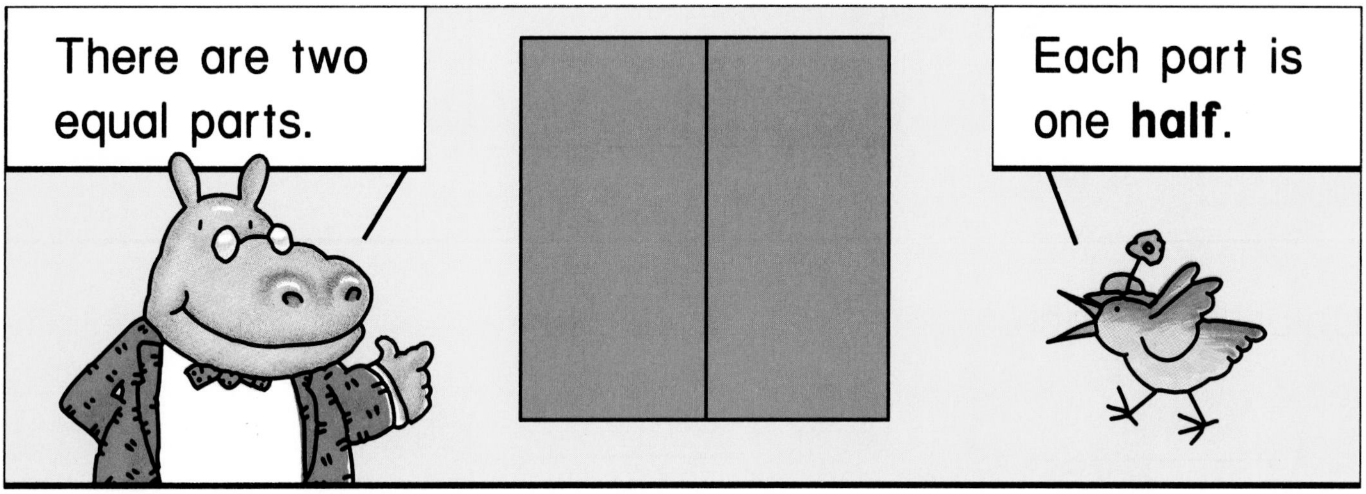
There are two equal parts.
Each part is one **half**.

Ring the shapes that show halves.

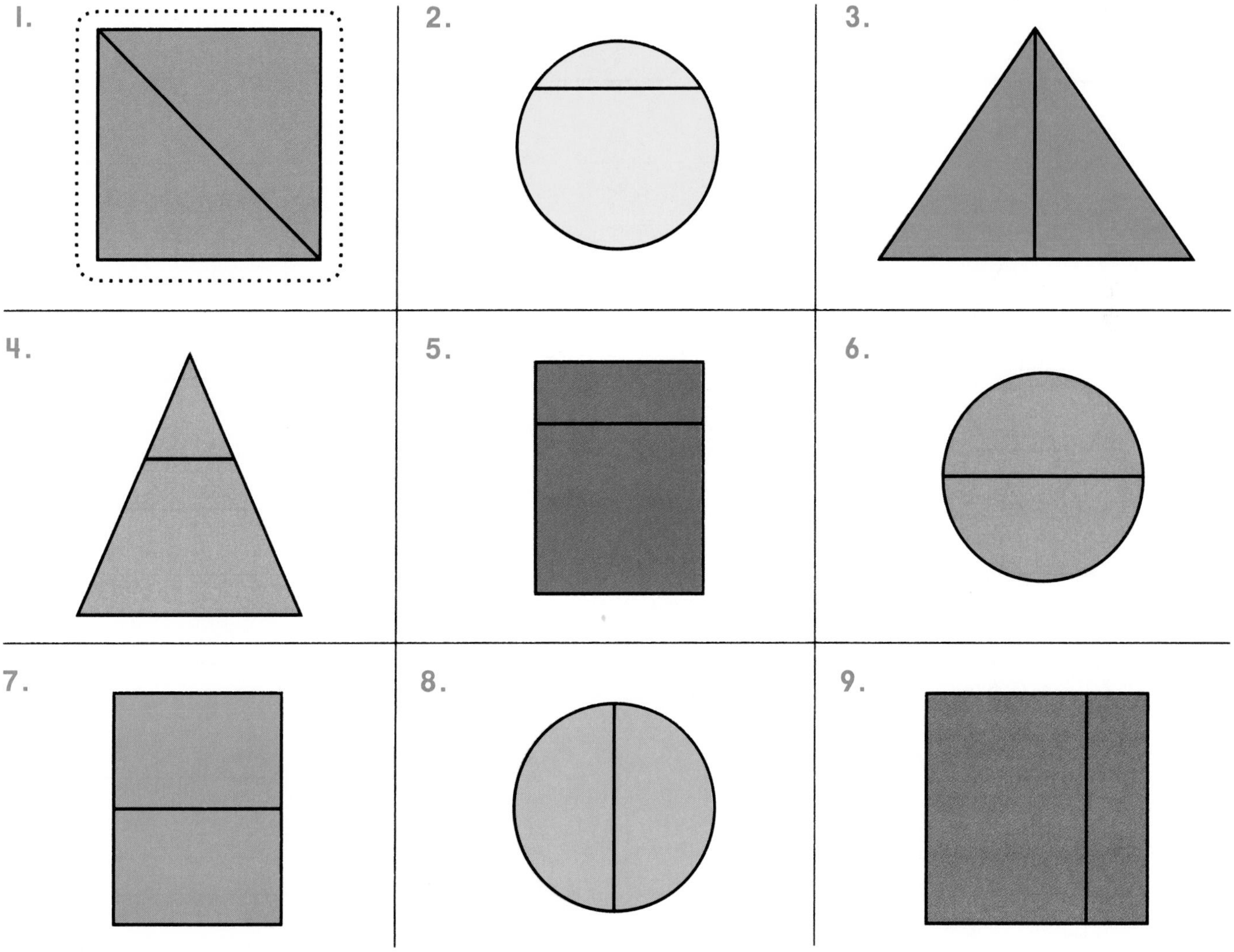
1.
2.
3.
4.
5.
6.
7.
8.
9.

Notes for Home Children identify shapes that show halves.

$\frac{1}{2}$ part red / equal parts

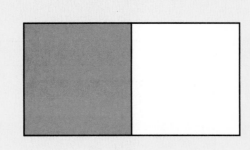

One **half** is red.

$\frac{1}{2}$ is red.

Color $\frac{1}{2}$ of each.

10.

11.

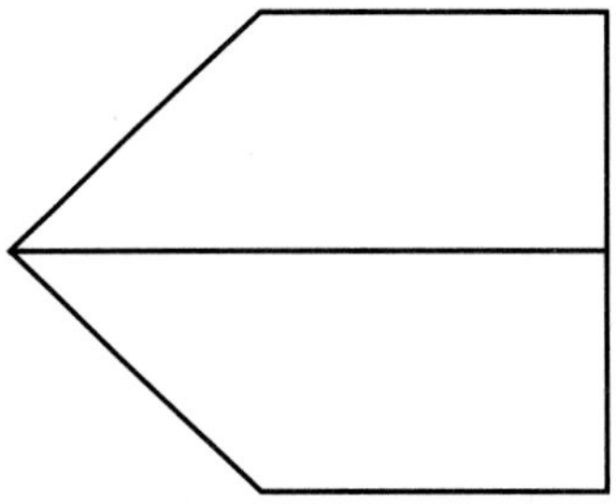

12.

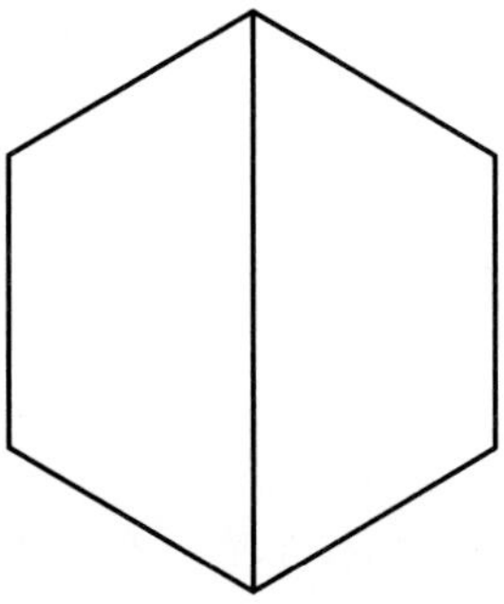

13.

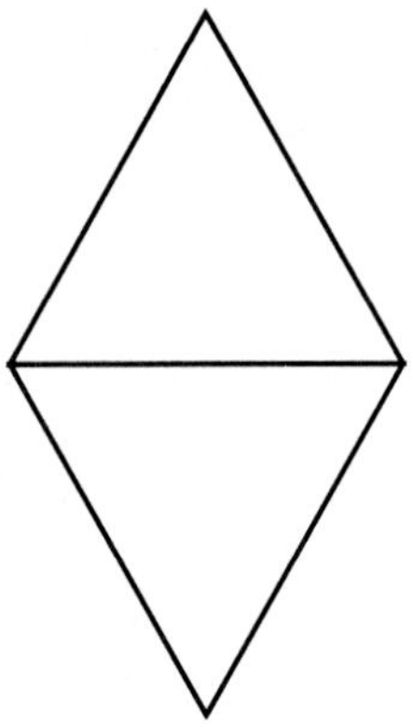

14.

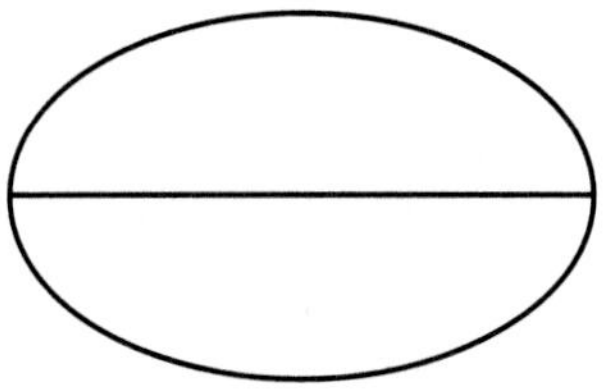

15.

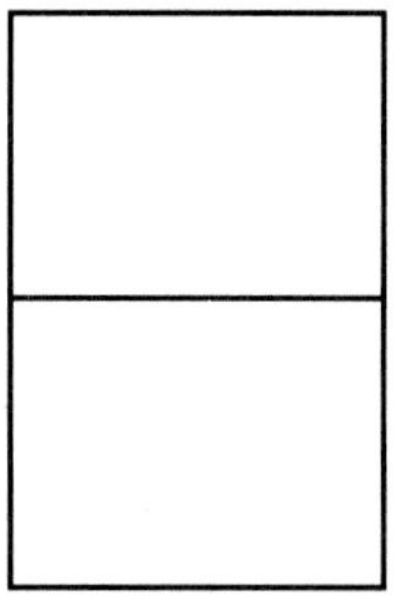

16.

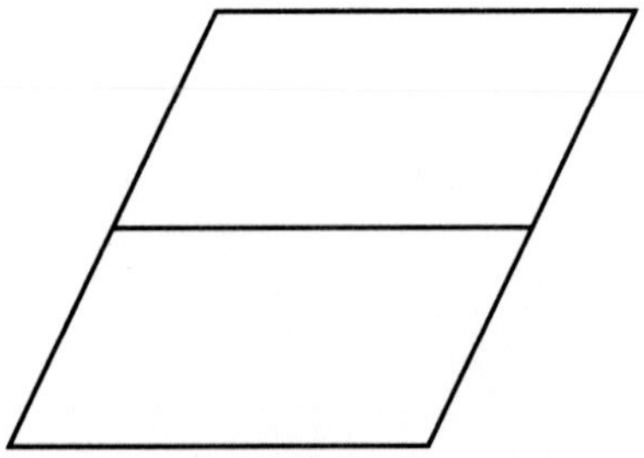

17.

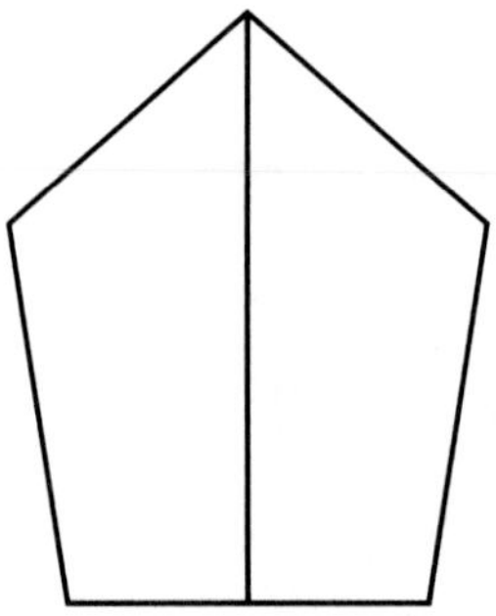

18.

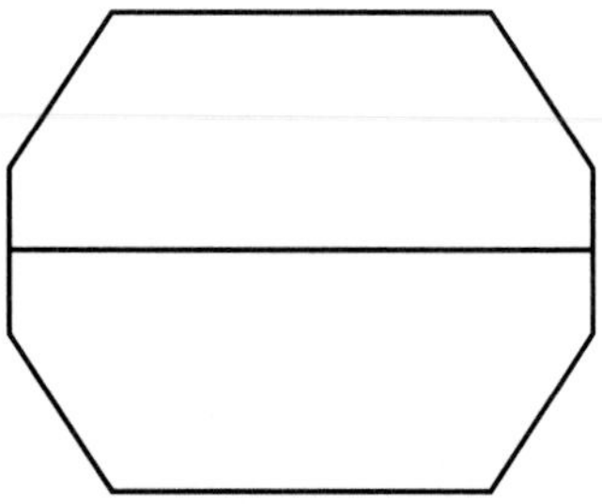

Notes for Home Children practice identifying one half of given shapes.

Name

Thirds

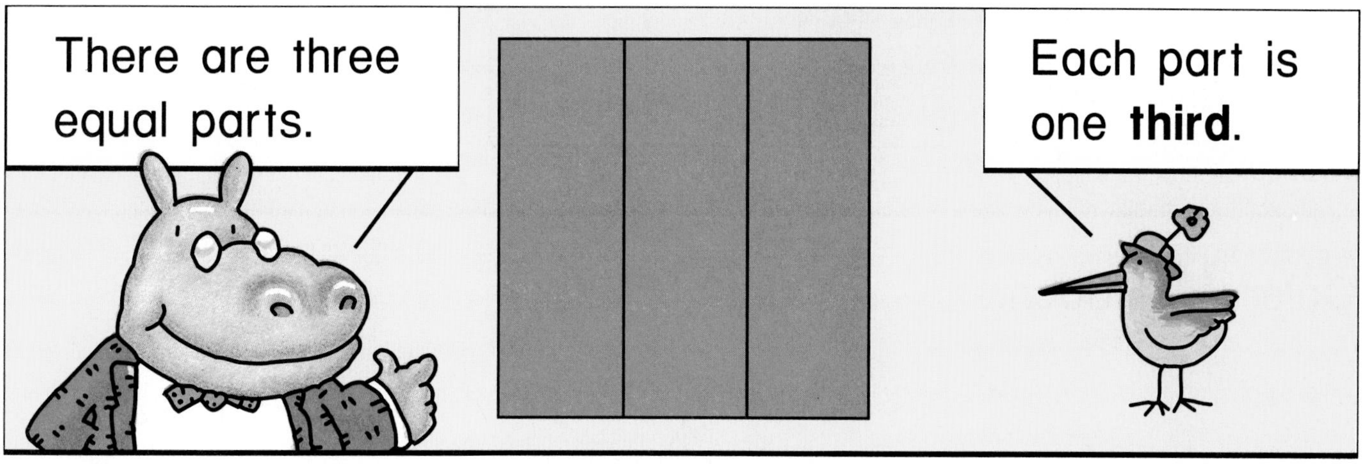
There are three equal parts.
Each part is one **third**.

Ring the shapes that show thirds.

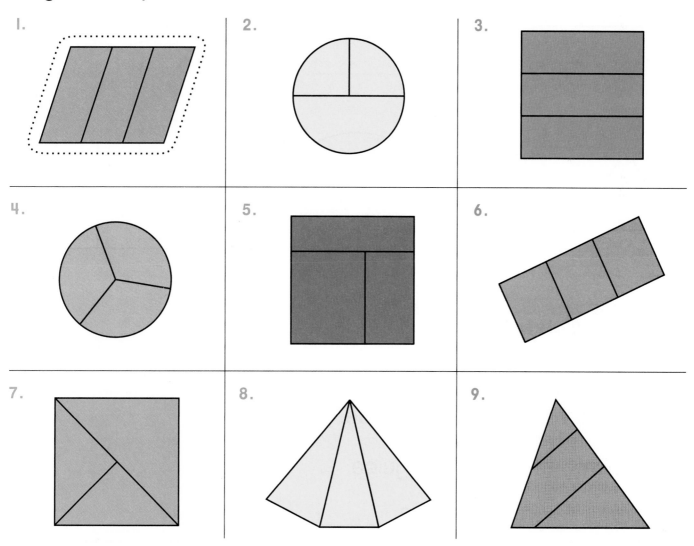

1\. 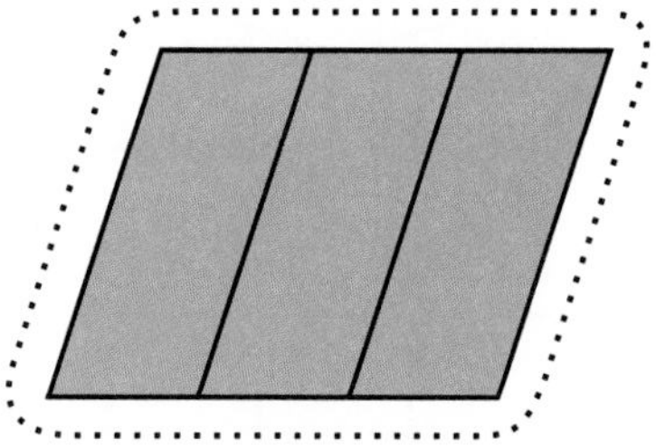

2\. 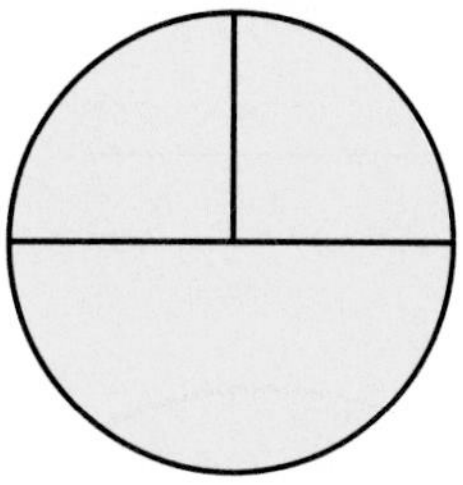

3\. 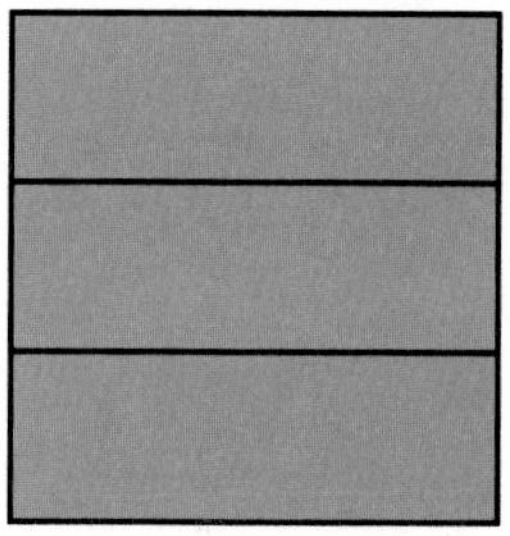

4\. 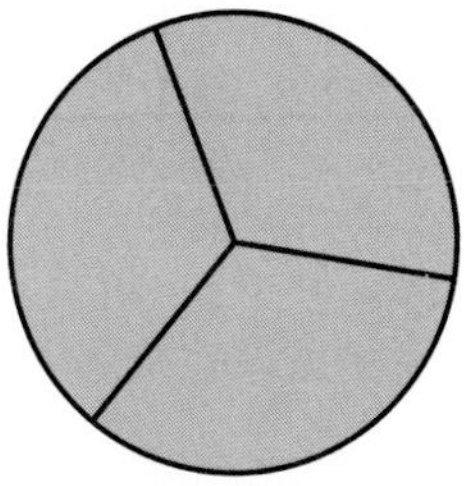

5\. 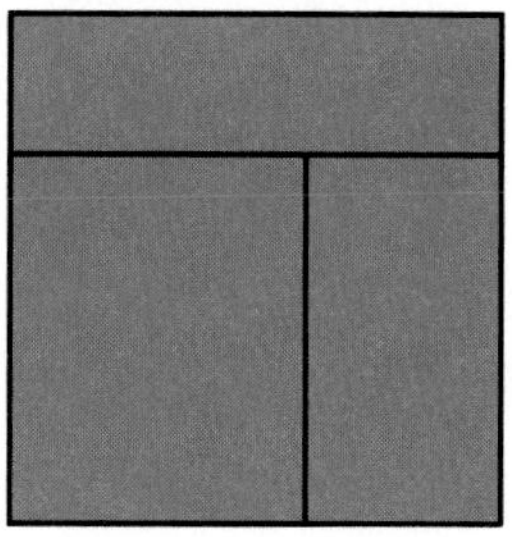

6\. 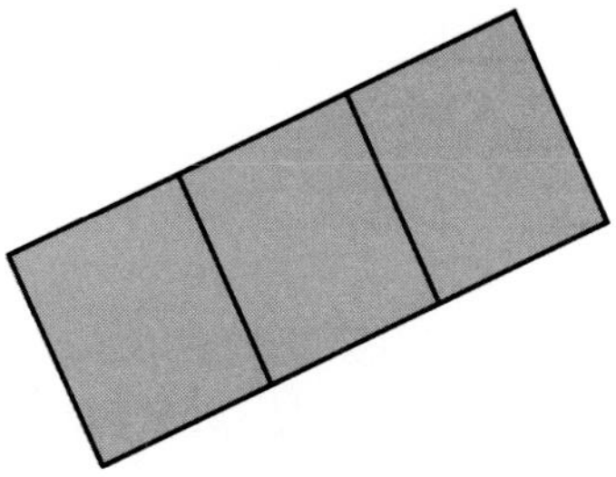

7\. 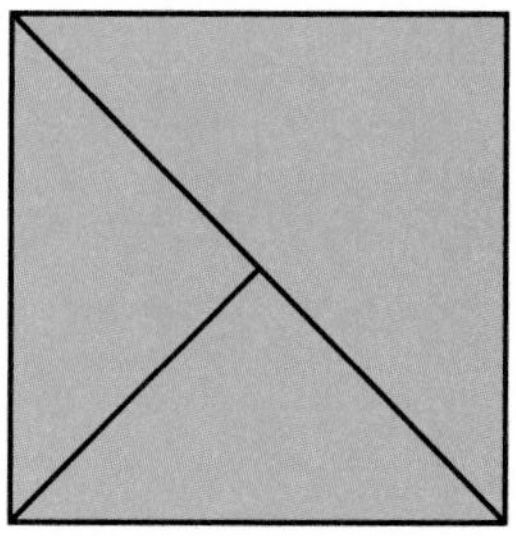

8\. 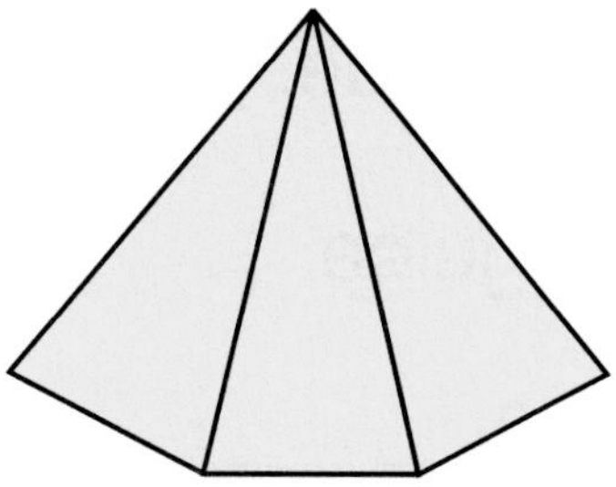

9\. 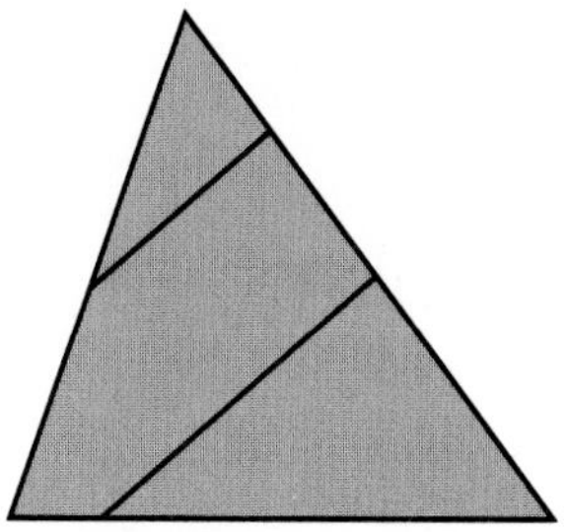

Notes for Home Children identify shapes that show thirds.

$\frac{1}{3}$ 1 part blue / 3 equal parts

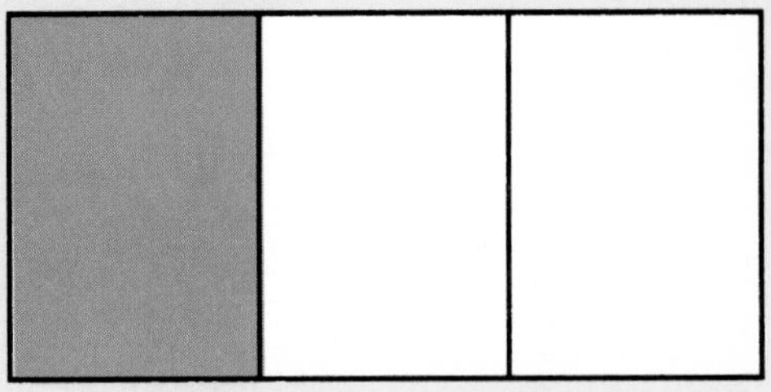

One **third** is blue.
$\frac{1}{3}$ is blue.

Color $\frac{1}{3}$ of each.

10.

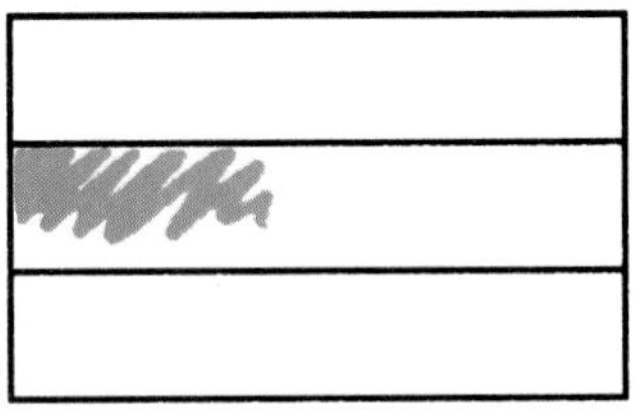

11.

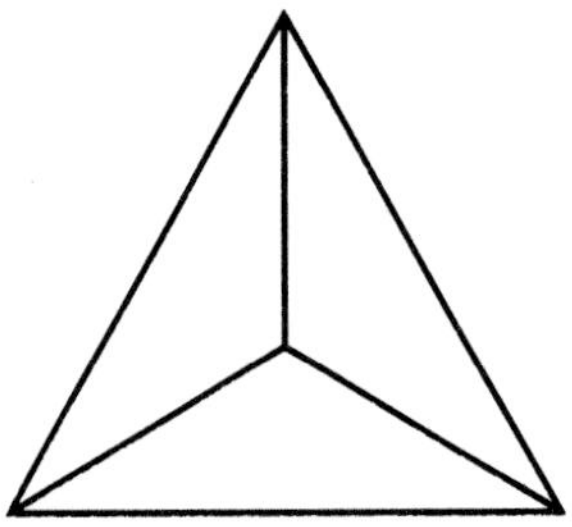

12.

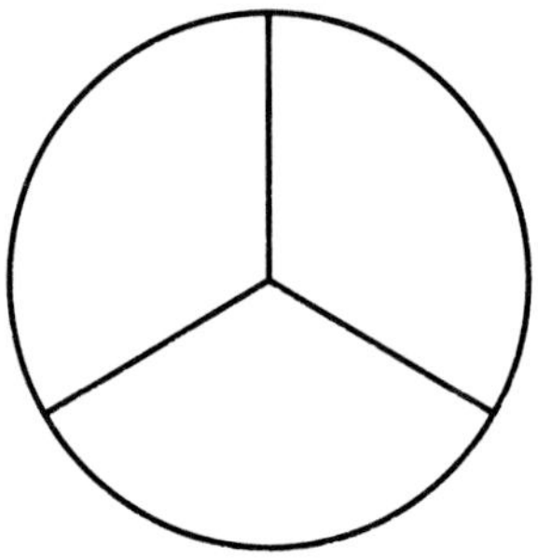

13.

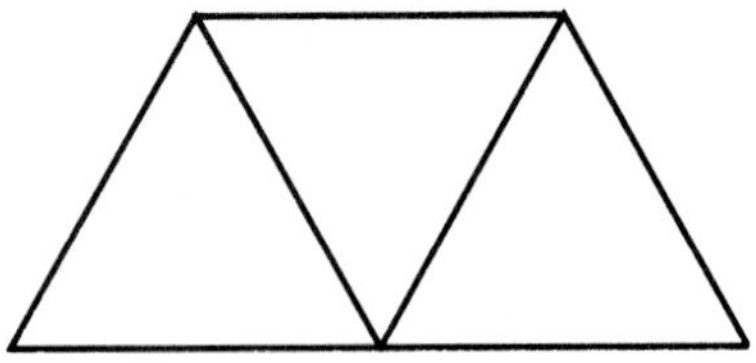

14.

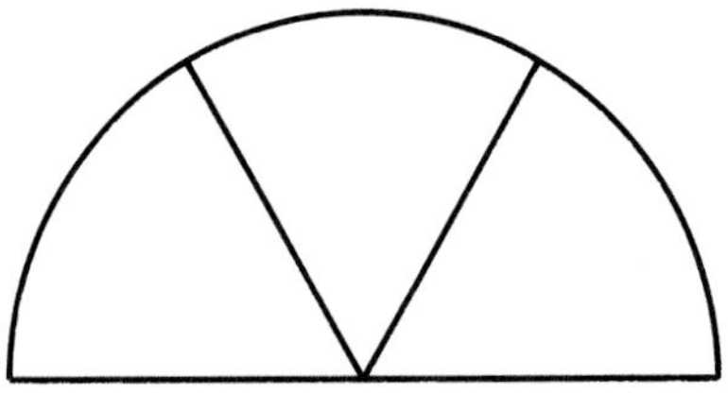

15.

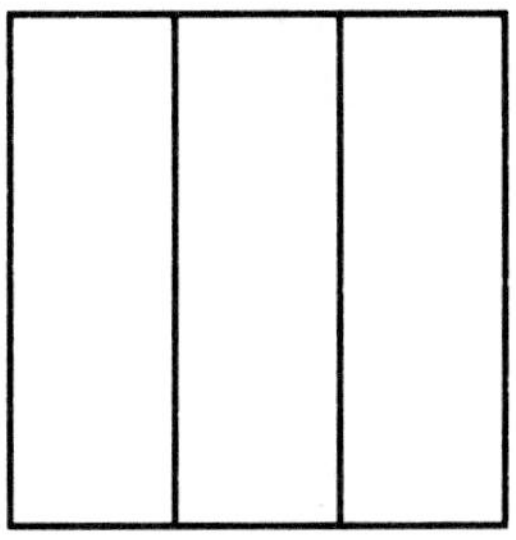

Problem Solving

Solve.

16. Anna has $\frac{1}{3}$ glass of juice.

John has $\frac{1}{2}$ glass of juice.

Who has more juice? ____________

Anna John

Notes for Home Children practice identifying one third of given shapes. Then they solve a problem involving fractions.

Name

Fourths

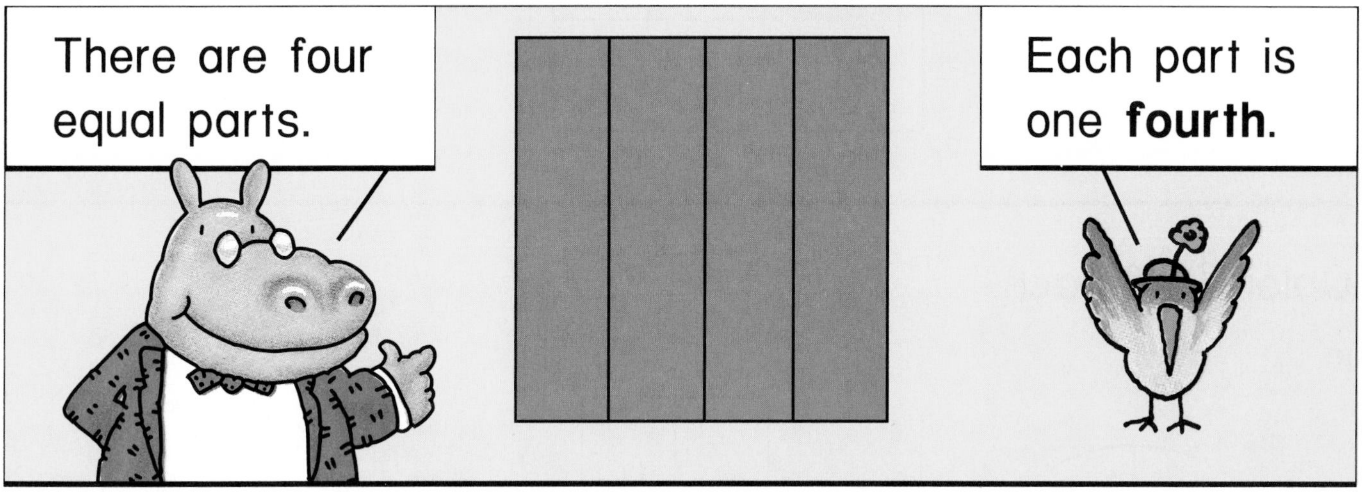

There are four equal parts.

Each part is one **fourth**.

Ring the shapes that show fourths.

1. 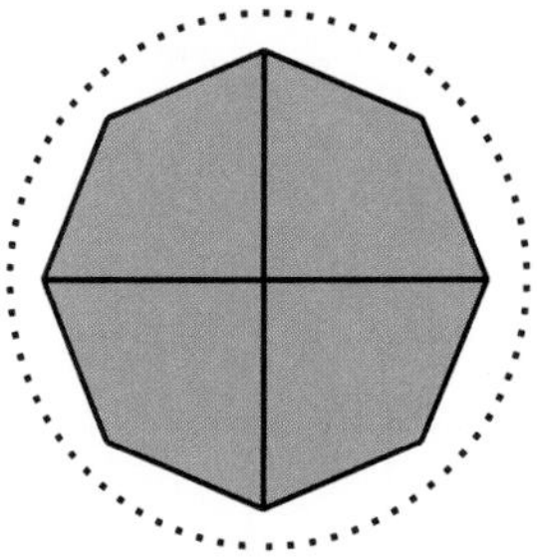

2. 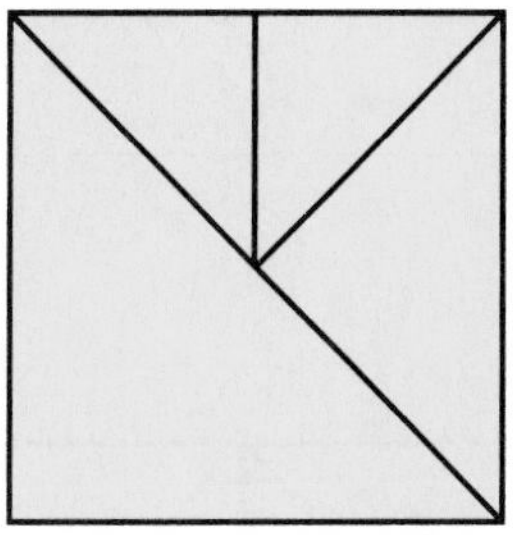

3. 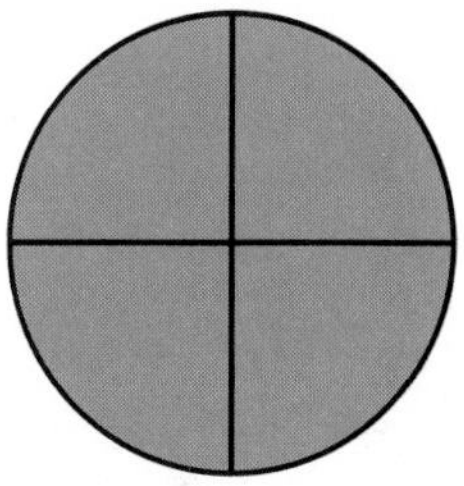

4. 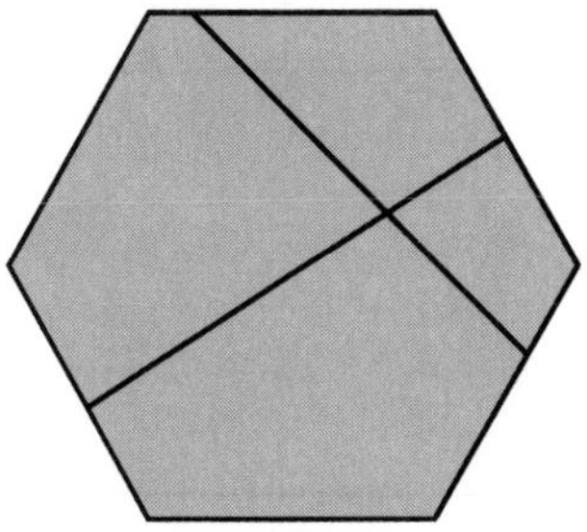

5. 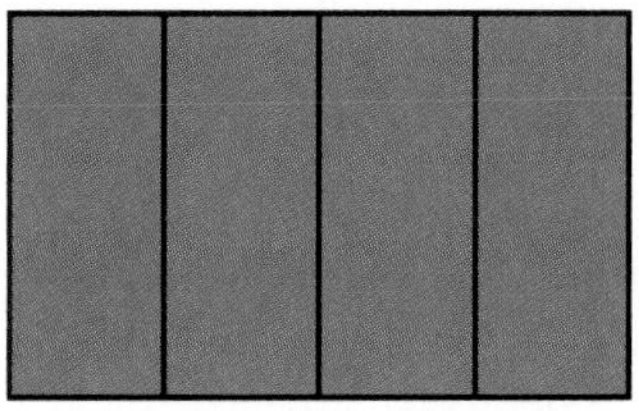

6. 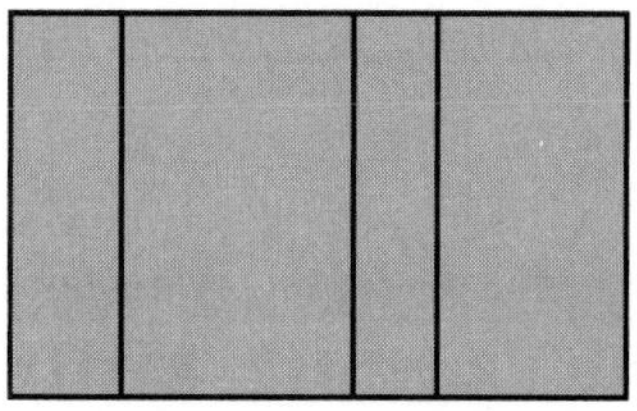

7. 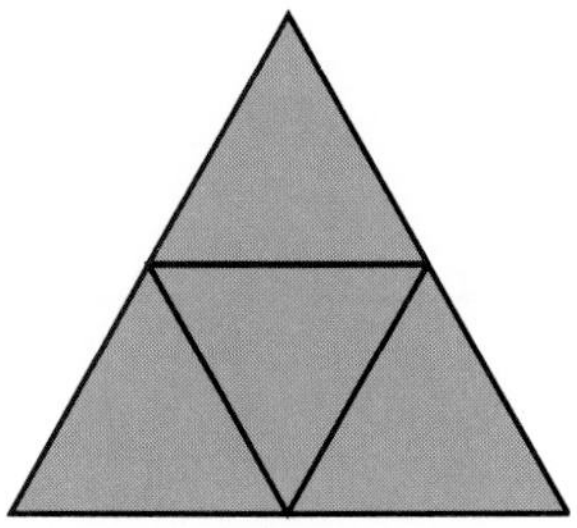

8. 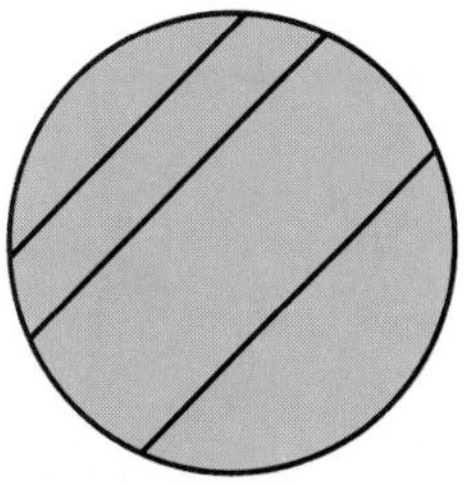

9. 

Notes for Home Children identify shapes that show fourths.

$\frac{1}{4}$ 1 part green, 4 equal parts

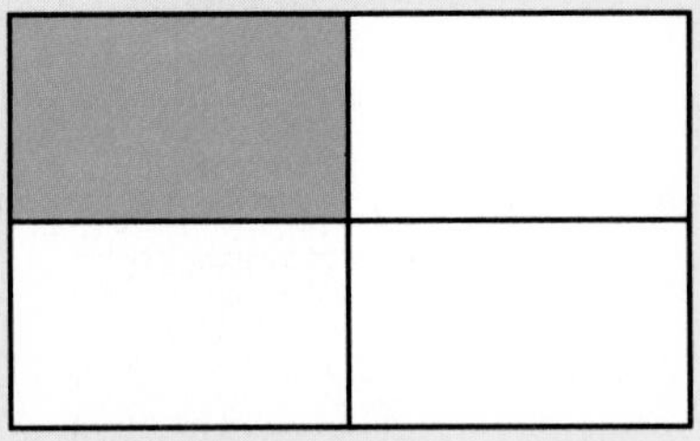

One **fourth** is green.
$\frac{1}{4}$ is green.

Color $\frac{1}{4}$ of each.

10.

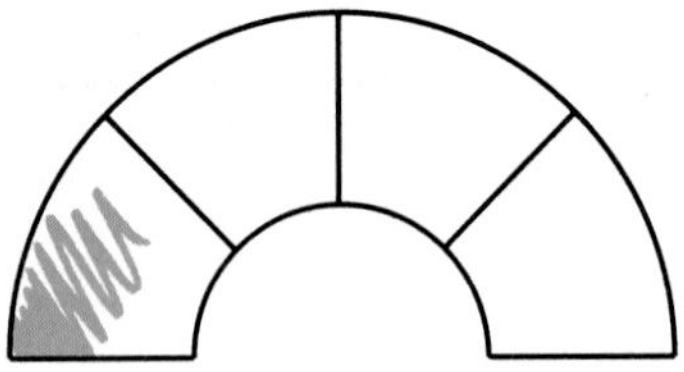

11.

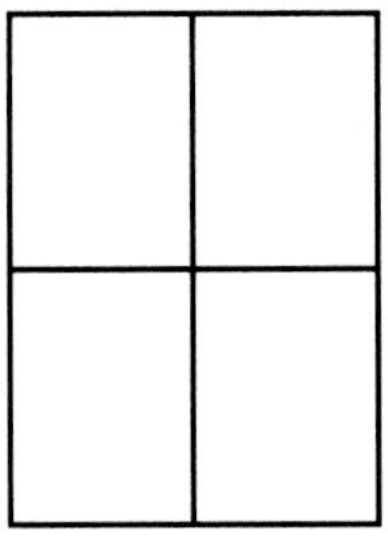

12.

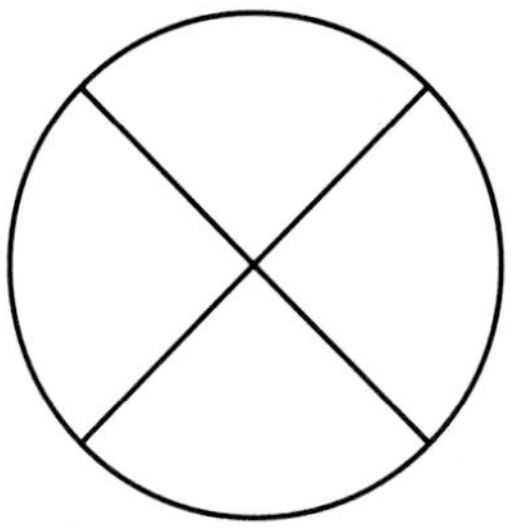

13.

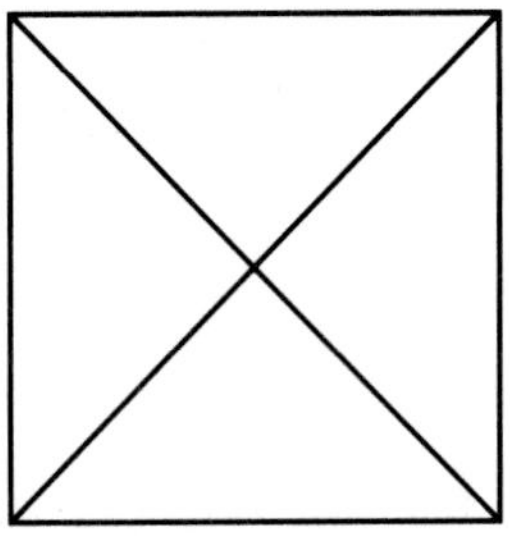

14.

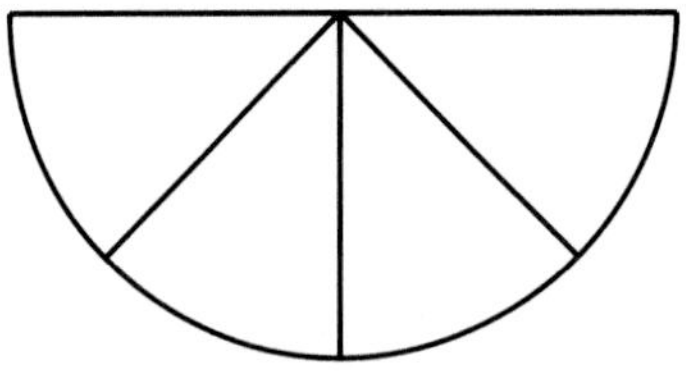

15.

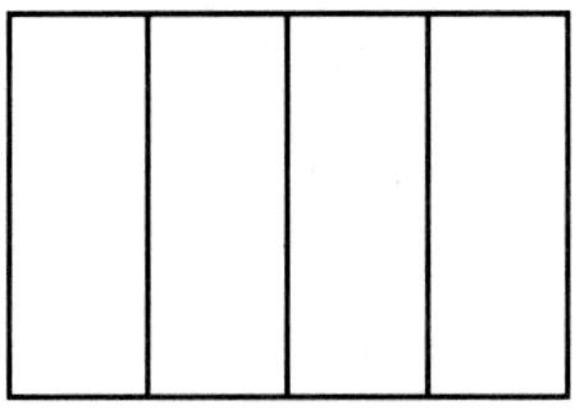

Talk About Math

What does the bottom number name in the fraction $\frac{1}{4}$?

$\frac{1}{4}$

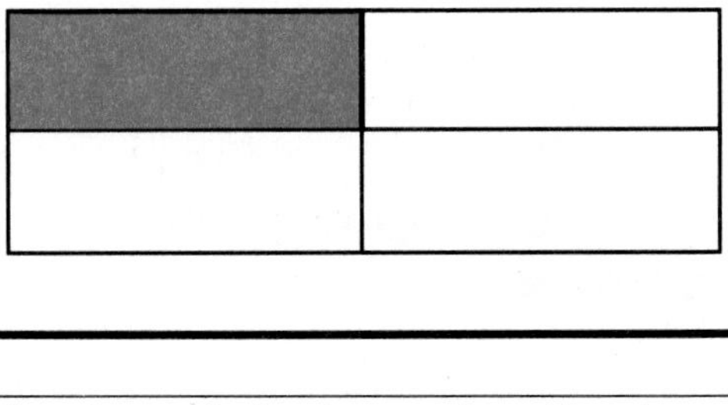

Notes for Home Children practice identifying one fourth of given shapes. Then they verbalize the meaning of fractions.

See More Practice Set A on page 393.

Name

Finding the Fraction of a Set

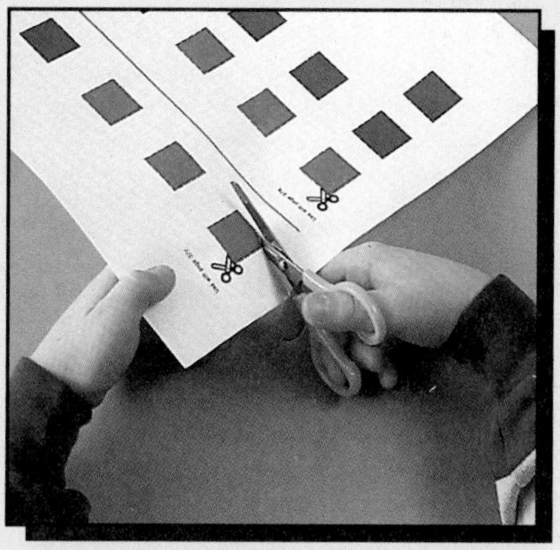

1. Cut out the shapes on page 379.

2. Paste the squares on the mat.

3. Write how many.

1. Paste 1 blue square and 3 red squares on the mat.

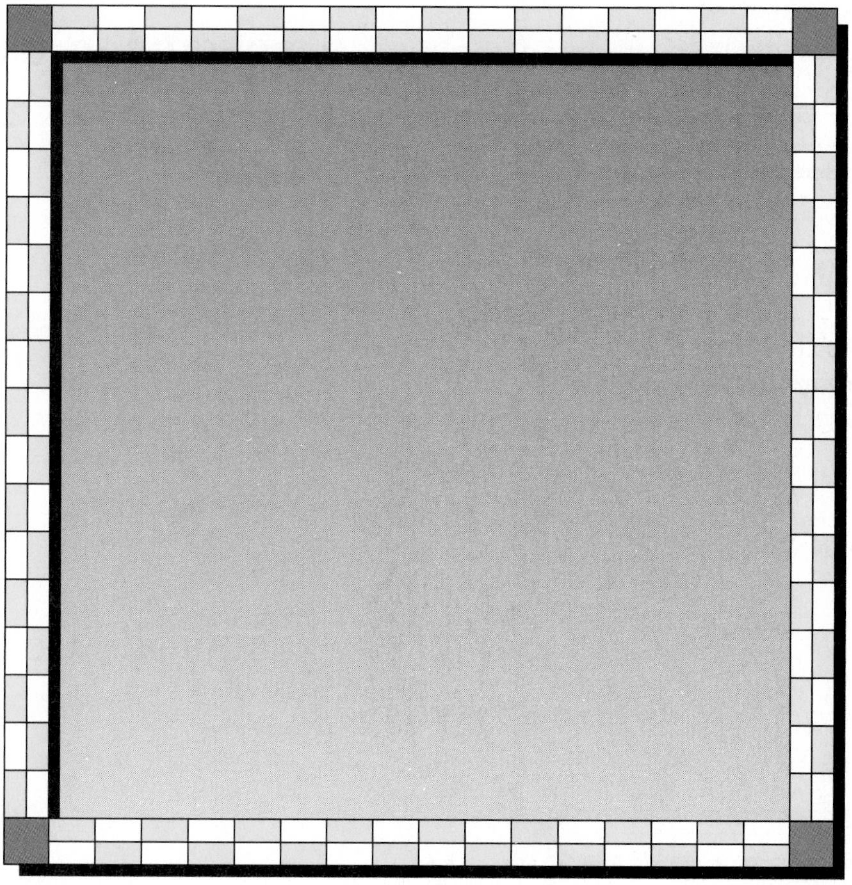

☐ blue square

☐ squares in all

Notes for Home Children explore at the CONCRETE level using a cut and paste activity to investigate fractions of a set.

2. Paste I red square and 2 blue squares on the mat.

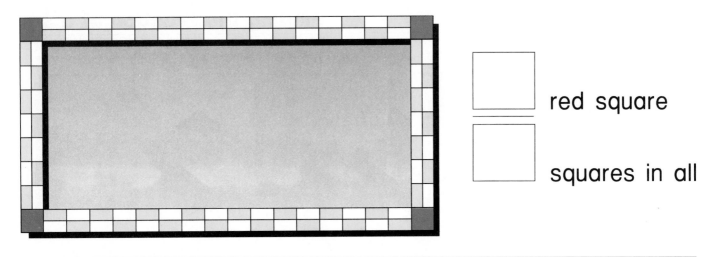

☐ red square

☐ squares in all

3. Paste I blue square and I red square on the mat.

☐ blue square

☐ squares in all

4. Paste I red square and 3 blue squares on the mat.

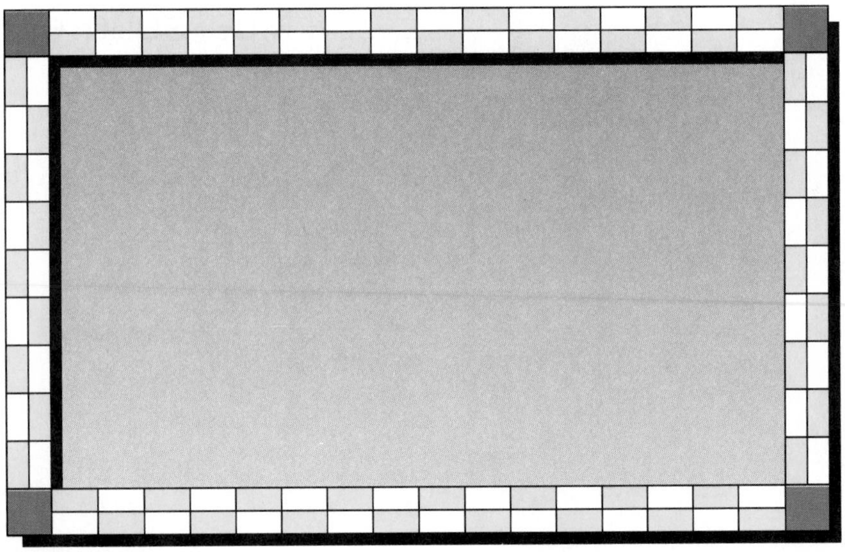

☐ red square

☐ squares in all

Notes for Home Children explore at the CONCRETE level using a cut and paste activity to investigate fractions of a set.

Use with page 377.

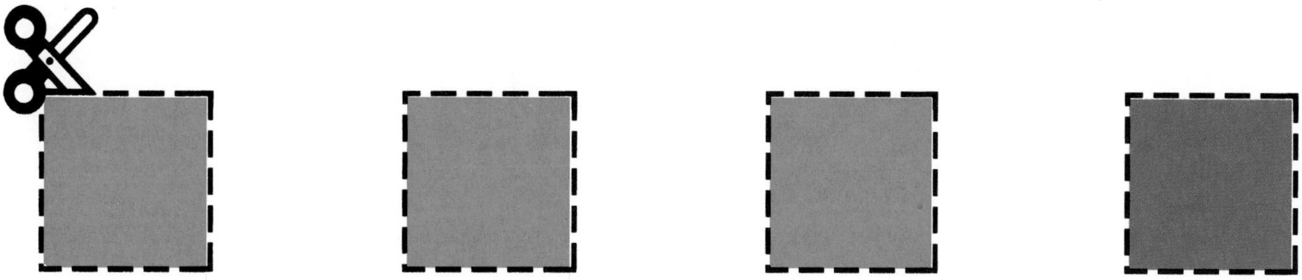

Use with page 378.

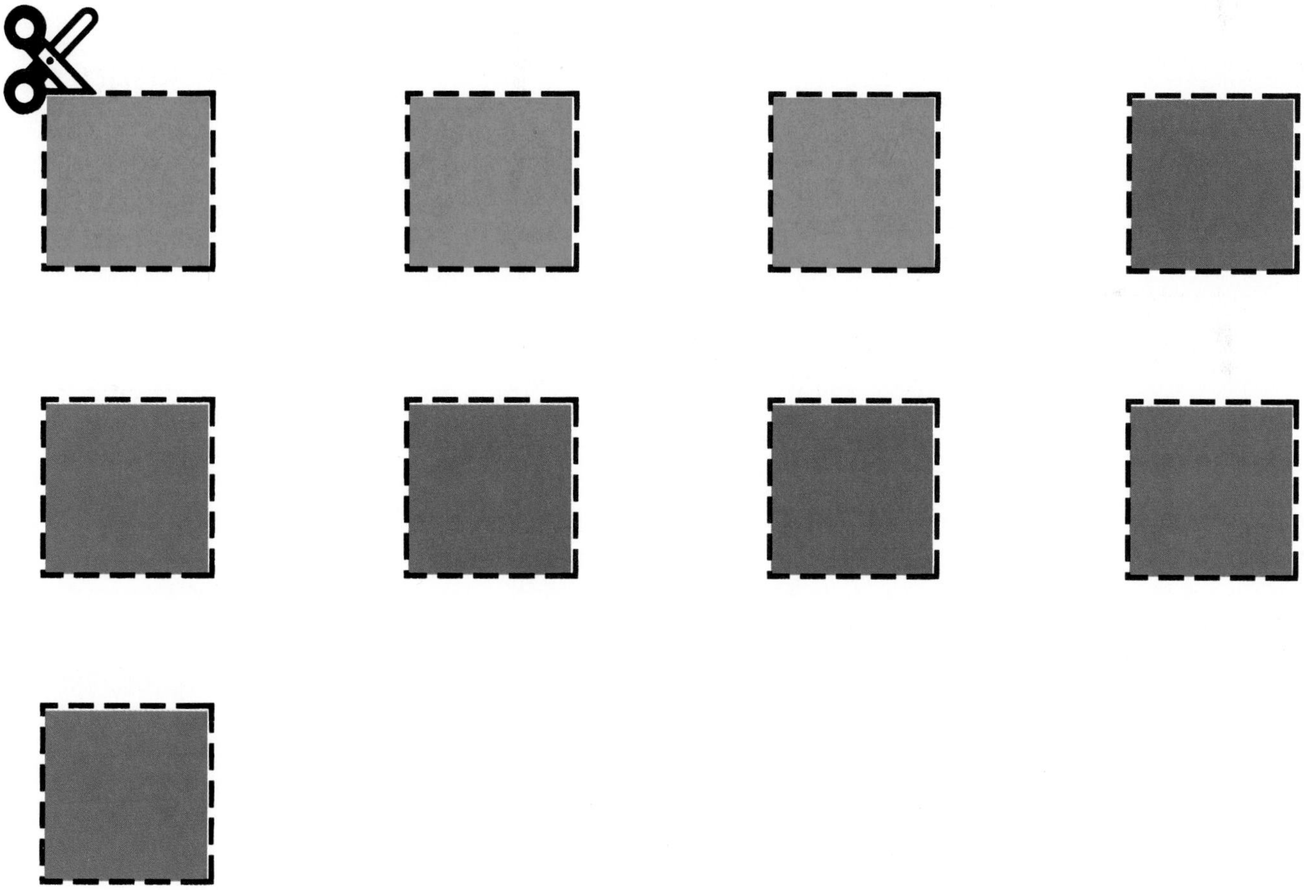

Name ____________________

PROBLEM-SOLVING STRATEGY

Draw a Picture

Two children want to share 6 apples.
Draw the same number of apples for each child.
How many apples does each child get?

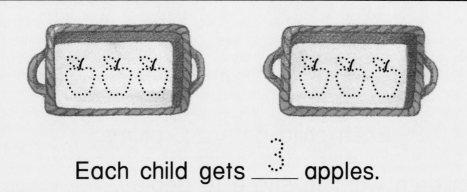

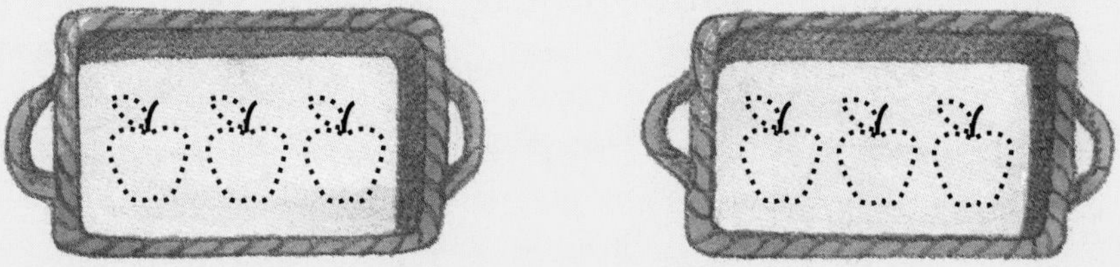

Each child gets 3 apples.

Draw the same number for each child.
How many does each child get?

1. Four children want to share 8 oranges.

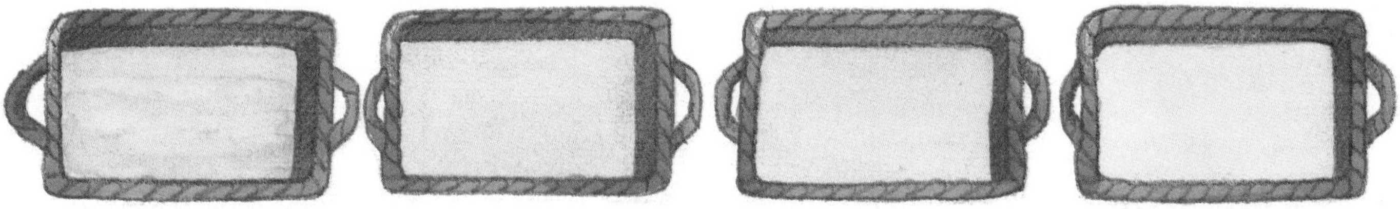

Each child gets ____ oranges.

2. Three children want to share 9 pears.

Each child gets ____ pears.

Notes for Home Children solve problems by drawing pictures to show equal groups.

Draw the same number for each child.
How many does each child get?

3. Three children want to share 6 plums.

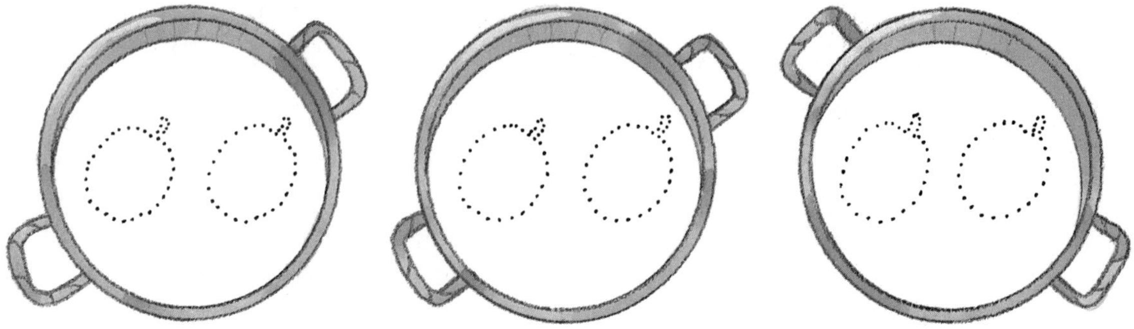

Each child gets 2 plums.

4. Two children want to share 10 apples.

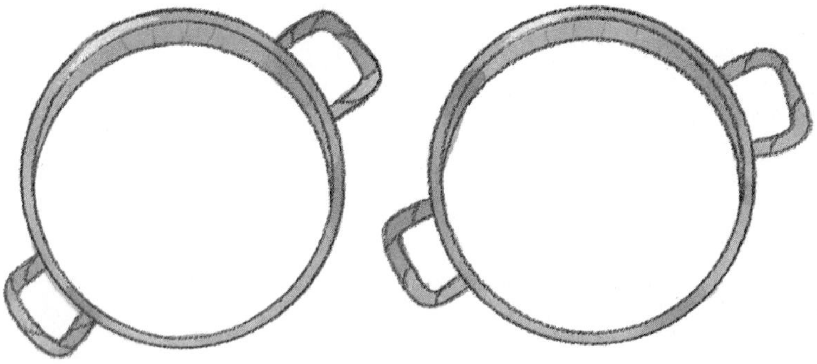

Each child gets ____ apples.

5. Four children want to share 12 peaches.

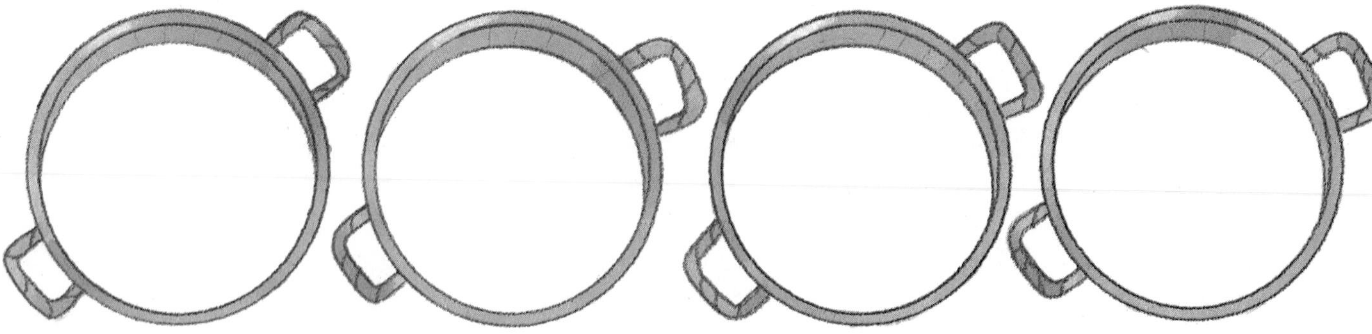

Each child gets ____ peaches.

Notes for Home Children solve problems by drawing pictures to show equal groups.

Number Sense

Show three different ways to cut a sandwich into halves.

Let's do some more!

Show three different ways you can cut a sandwich into fourths.

Notes for Home Children develop an understanding about fractions by showing different ways to divide a shape in half.

Skills Review

Fill in the correct ⬭.

Add.

1. $\begin{array}{r} 1 \\ 4 \\ +\ 6 \\ \hline \end{array}$ Ⓐ 9 Ⓑ 10 Ⓒ 11

2. $\begin{array}{r} 5 \\ 4 \\ +\ 1 \\ \hline \end{array}$ Ⓐ 9 Ⓑ 10 Ⓒ 11

3. $\begin{array}{r} 3 \\ 0 \\ +\ 5 \\ \hline \end{array}$ Ⓐ 3 Ⓑ 5 Ⓒ 8

Find the sum or difference.

4. $9 + 2 =$ Ⓐ 10 Ⓑ 11 Ⓒ 12

5. $\begin{array}{r} 11 \\ -\ 4 \\ \hline \end{array}$ Ⓐ 7 Ⓑ 8 Ⓒ 9

6. $12 - 3 =$ Ⓐ 7 Ⓑ 8 Ⓒ 9

7. $\begin{array}{r} 12 \\ -\ 6 \\ \hline \end{array}$ Ⓐ 6 Ⓑ 7 Ⓒ 8

8. $8 + 3 =$ Ⓐ 9 Ⓑ 10 Ⓒ 11

9. $5 + 7 =$ Ⓐ 10 Ⓑ 11 Ⓒ 12

Vocabulary

10. Use green to color the addition words.

Use yellow to color the subtraction words.

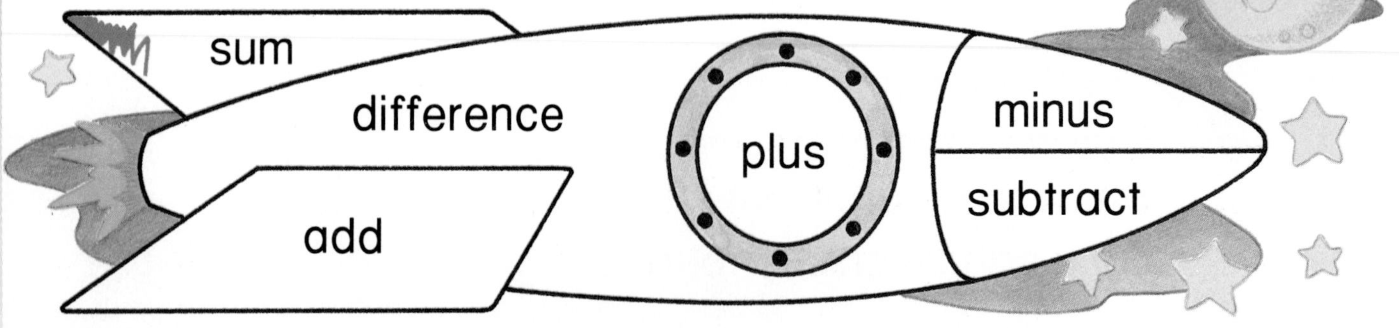

Notes for Home Children review adding three numbers. Then they review addition and subtraction facts through 12. Children review addition and subtraction terms.

Name

Probability

This is sure to happen.

This is sure not to happen.

Ring the picture if it is sure to happen.

1. If you go swimming, you will get wet.

2. Tomorrow you will be 200 years old.

3. The cow will jump over the moon.

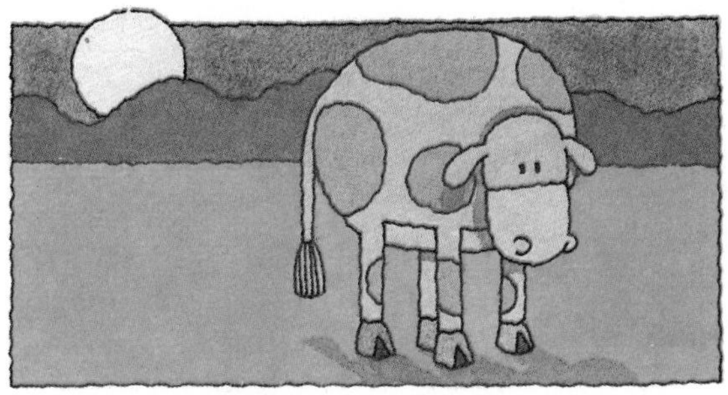

4. If you pick one of these cards, it will show a 3.

Notes for Home Children identify events that are sure to happen.

Ring the picture if it is sure to happen.

5. The spinner will land on blue.

6. If you touch a hot pot, it will feel cold.

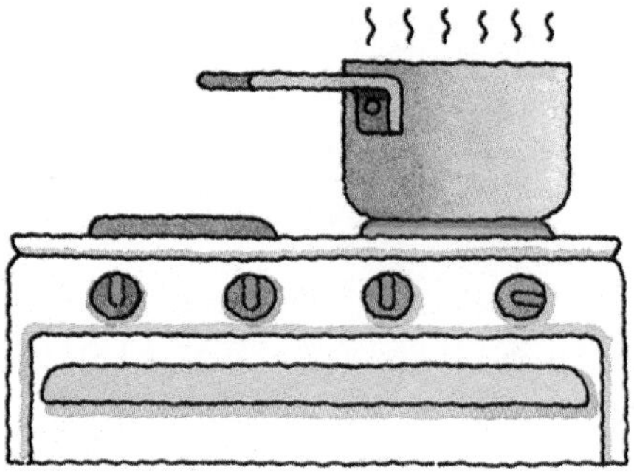

7. The sun will set today.

8. The spinner will land on green.

9. The dog will read you a story.

10. If you drop the toy, it will fall.

Notes for Home Children identify events that are sure to happen.

See More Practice Set B on page 393.

Name

Probability

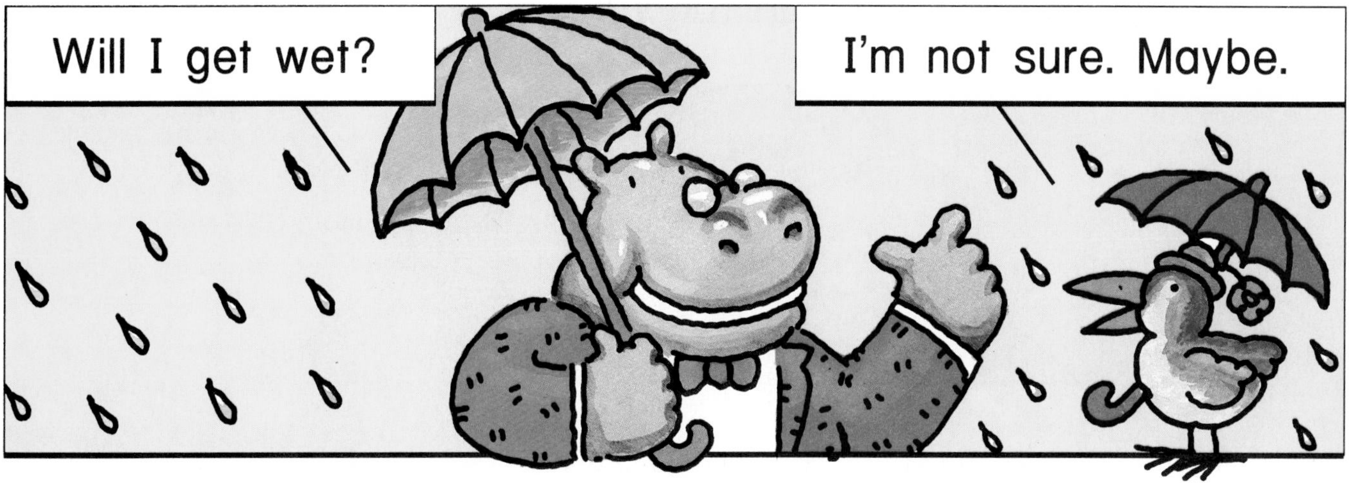

Is this sure to happen?
Ring yes, maybe, or no.

1. You will eat something today.

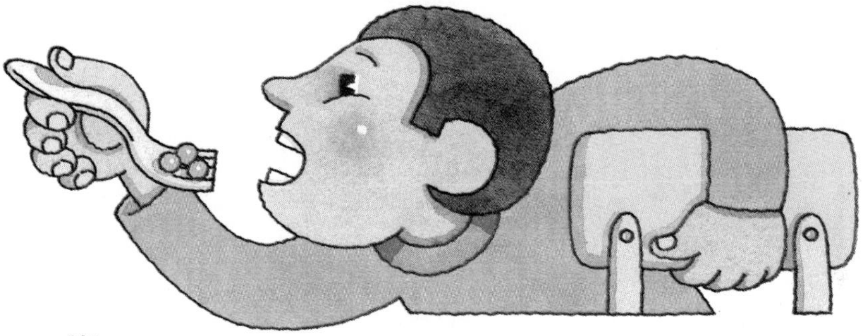

yes   maybe   no

2. If you drop a glass, it will break.

yes   maybe   no

Notes for Home Children identify events as sure to happen, unsure to happen, or sure not to happen.

Is this sure to happen?
Ring yes, maybe, or no.

3. The cat will make lunch for you.

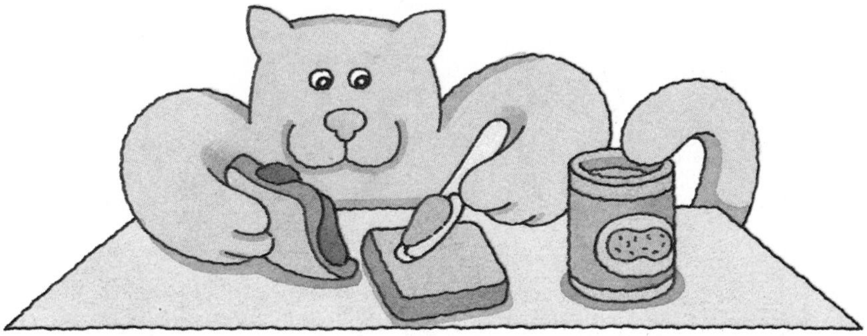

yes maybe no

4. The fish will swim in the water.

yes maybe no

5. It will rain today.

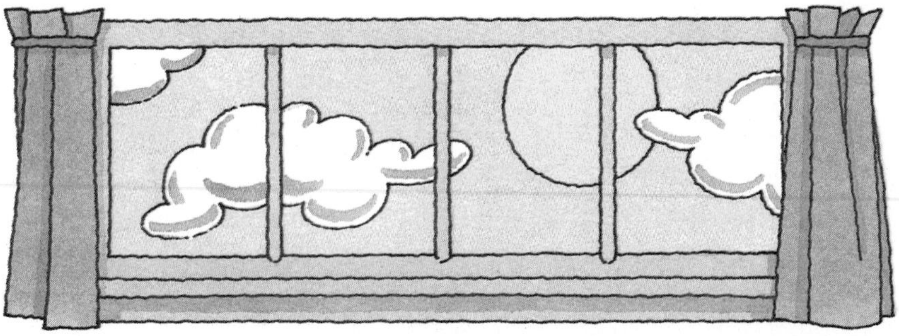

yes maybe no

Notes for Home Children identify events as sure to happen, unsure to happen, or sure not to happen.

Name

Collecting Data

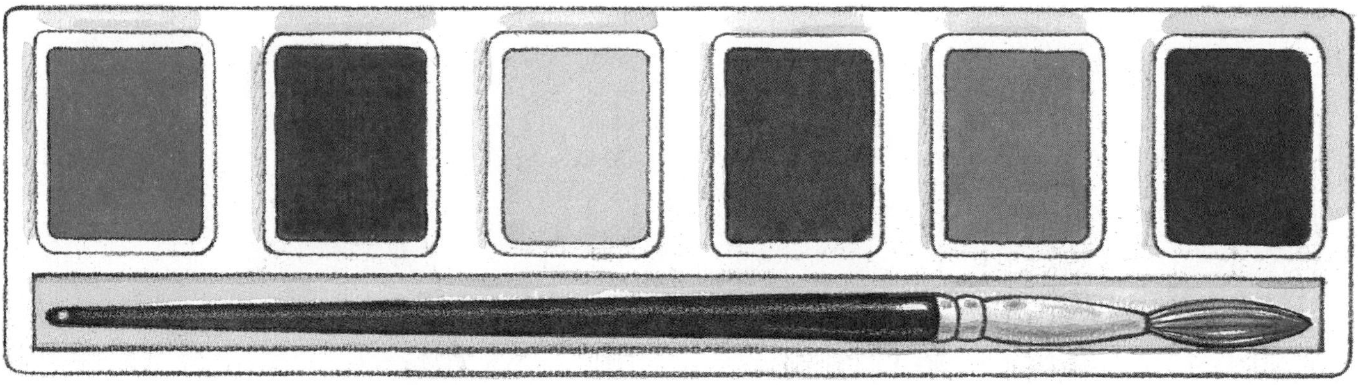

What is the most popular color in your class?

1. Make a tally mark for each child's favorite color.

Color	Tallies	Total
red		
blue		
yellow		
green		
orange		
purple		

2. Which color was chosen most often? ______________

3. Which color was chosen least often? ______________

Notes for Home Children solve a problem by collecting and recording data.

Mr. Chen's class went to the zoo.
After their trip, they made a chart
to show how many animals they saw.

Animal	Tallies
lions	𝍸 |
monkeys	𝍸 𝍸 |
elephants	||||
giraffes	|||
tigers	𝍸
zebras	||

4. Write how many.

elephants 4   tigers ____   giraffes ____

lions ____   zebras ____   monkeys ____

5. Which animal did they see most often? ____________

6. Which animal did they see least often? ____________

Notes for Home Children solve a problem by using collected data.

Name

Problem-Solving Workshop

Explore as a Team

Work with a partner.
Use hippo counters.

1. Have one partner make 4 groups of hippos.
Put 2 counters in each of the groups.
How many hippos in all?

2. Use 12 hippos. Draw two swimming pools.
Put the same number of hippos in each pool. How many hippos did you put in each pool?

3. Have one partner make 2 groups of hippos.
Put 6 counters in each of the groups.
How many hippos in all?

Notes for Home Children explore with a partner at the CONCRETE level to solve problems involving multiplication and division.

Problem-Solving Workshop

Explore with a Computer

Primary Graphing and Probability Project

1. Will Ben pick a blue marble?

yes   maybe   no

2. At the computer, pick a bag of marbles.
Get 10 marbles.

3. Color red the marbles you picked that were red.
Color blue the marbles you picked that were blue.

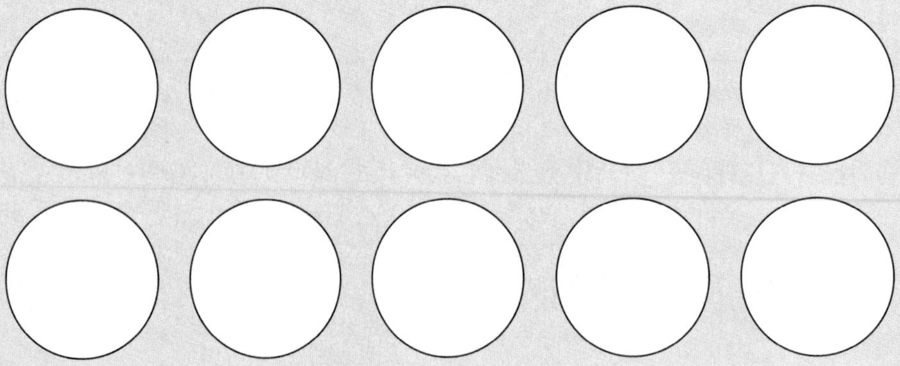

Notes for Home Children identify an event as sure to happen, unsure to happen, or sure not to happen. Then they use the computer for random selection of marbles and record the results.

Name

More Practice

Set A Use after page 376.

Color.

1. $\frac{1}{2}$

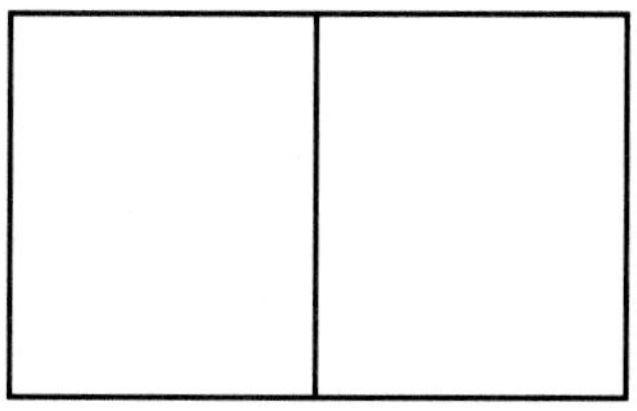

2. $\frac{1}{3}$

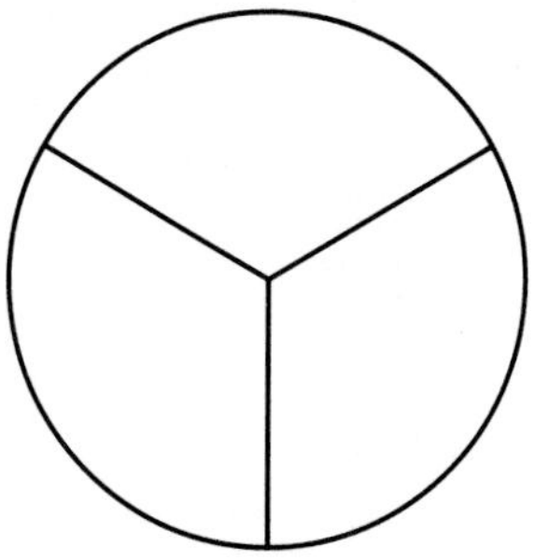

3. $\frac{1}{4}$

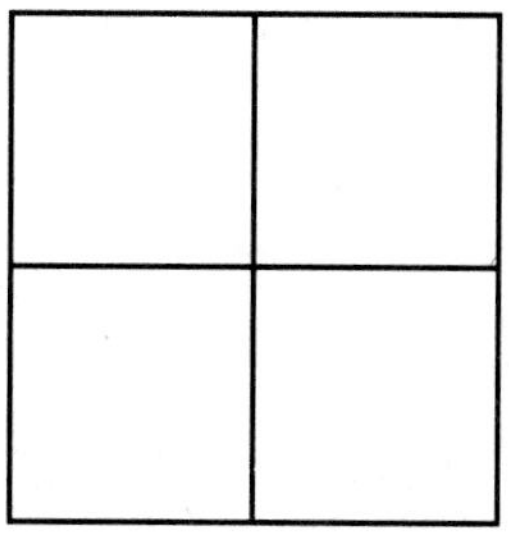

4. $\frac{1}{4}$

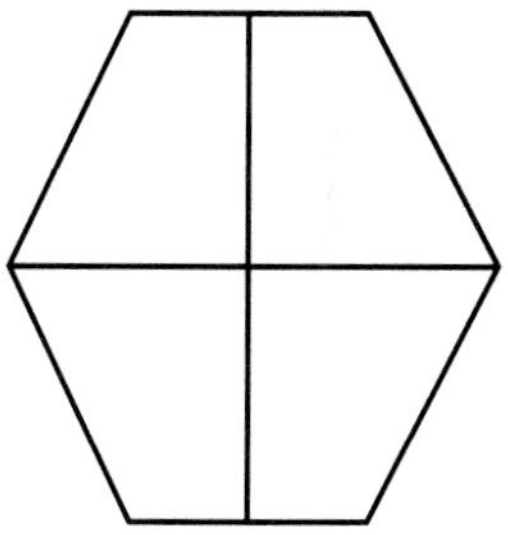

5. $\frac{1}{2}$

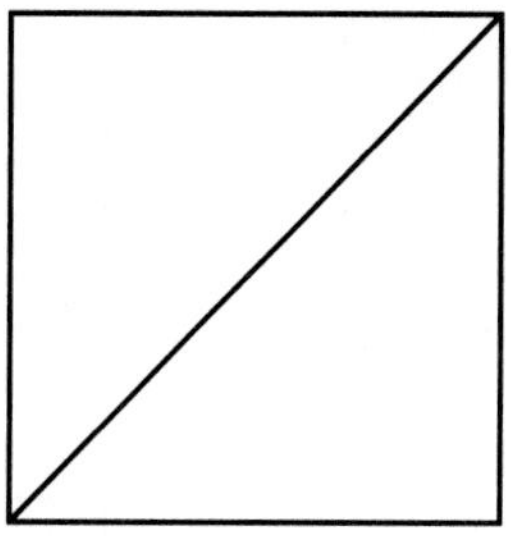

6. $\frac{1}{3}$

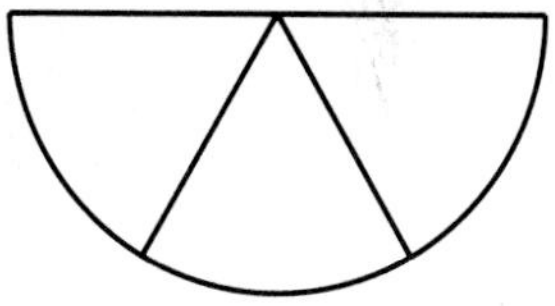

Set B Use after page 386.

Ring the picture if it is sure to happen.

1. If you take a bath, you will get wet.

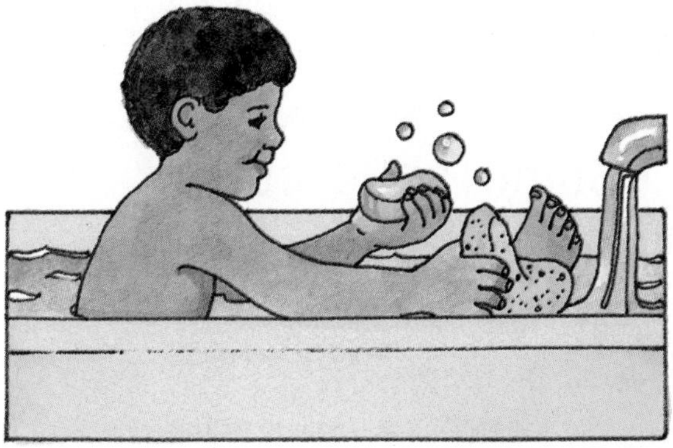

2. The iron will stay cool if you turn it on.

Notes for Home Set A: Children practice coloring fractional parts of a shape.
Set B: Children identify events as sure to happen.

Enrichment

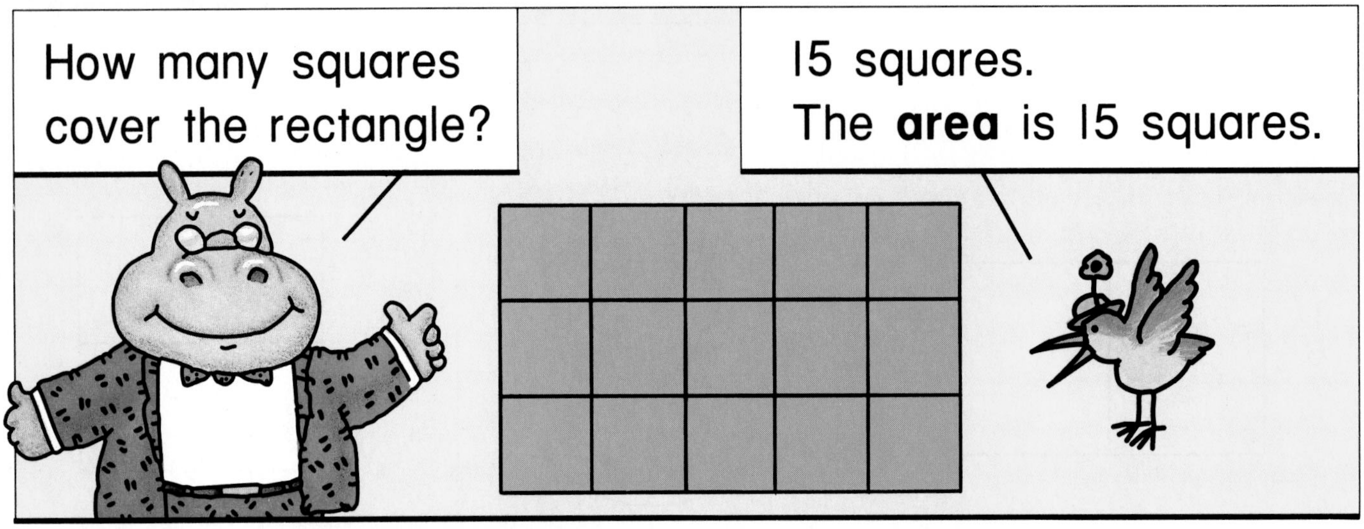

How many squares cover the rectangle?
15 squares.
The **area** is 15 squares.

1. 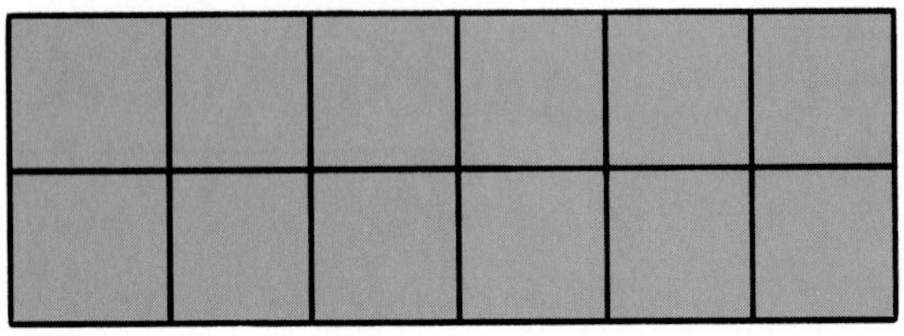

12 squares

2. 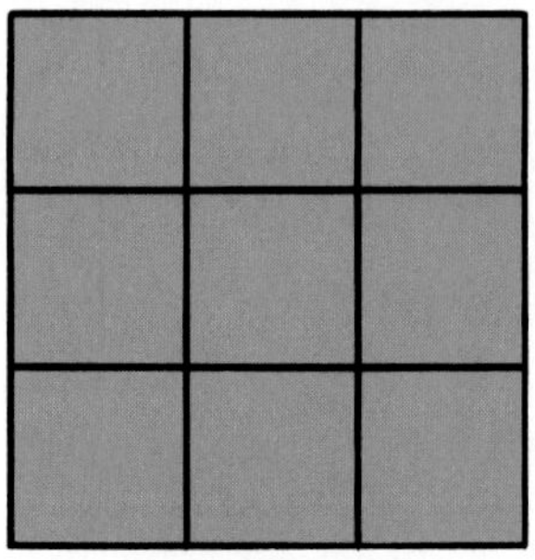

_____ squares

3. 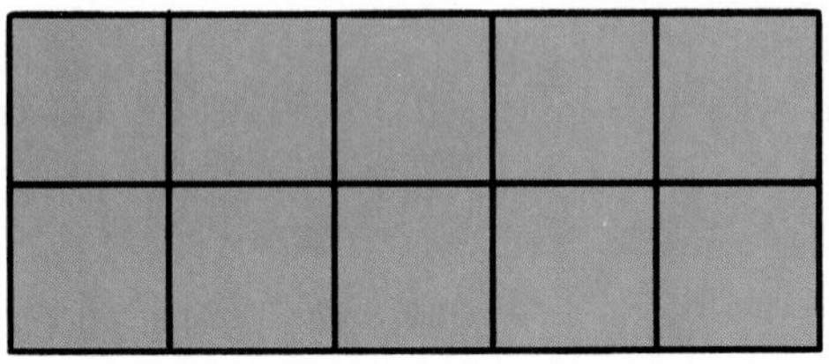

_____ squares

4. 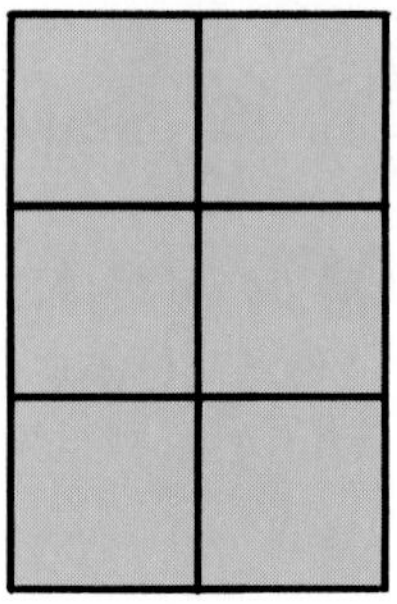

_____ squares

5. 

Some squares are hidden.

_____ squares in all

Notes for Home Children are challenged to find the areas of given shapes.

Name

Chapter 12 Review/Test

1. Ring the shape that shows equal parts.

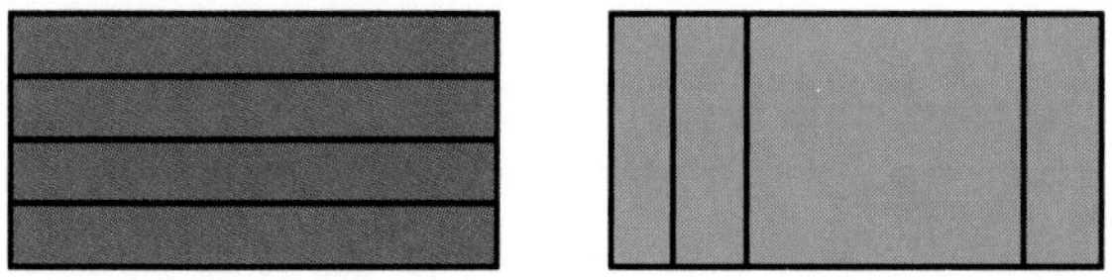

2. Color $\frac{1}{2}$.

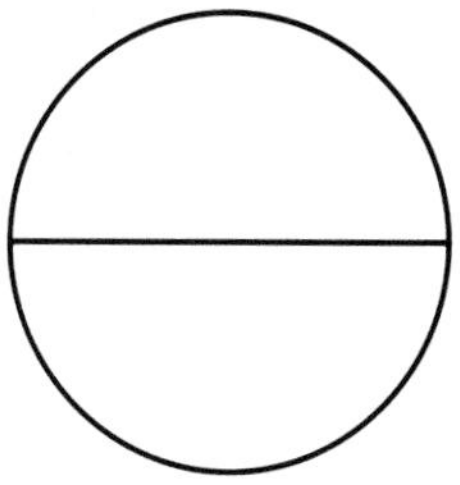

3. Color $\frac{1}{3}$.

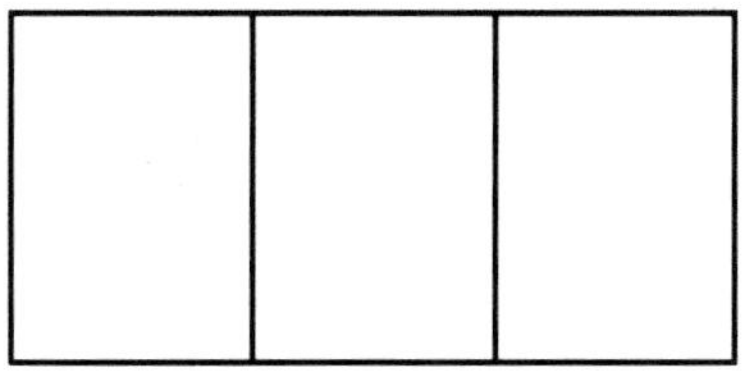

4. Color $\frac{1}{4}$.

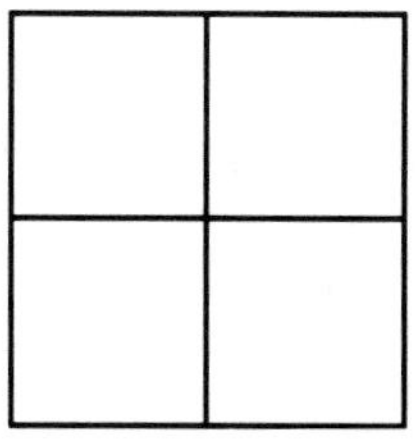

5. Can cows fly?
Ring yes or no.

yes no

6. Will the sun shine today?
Ring yes, maybe, or no.

yes maybe no

7. Write how many.

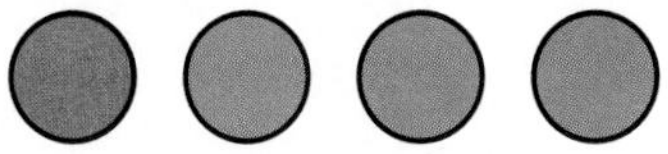

red circles ☐

circles in all ☐

8.

ball	|||| |||| ||
truck	|||| ||

Write how many.

truck ____ ball ____

Draw the same number for each.
How many does each child get?

9. Two children want to share 8 apples.

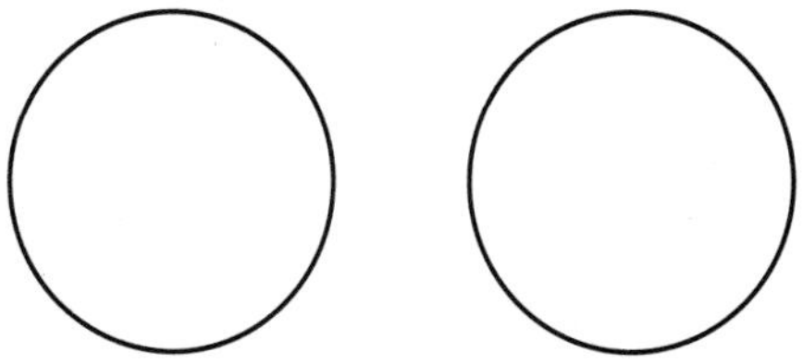

Each child gets ___ apples.

Notes for Home Children are assessed on Chapter 12 concepts, skills, and problem solving.

Addition and Subtraction Through 12

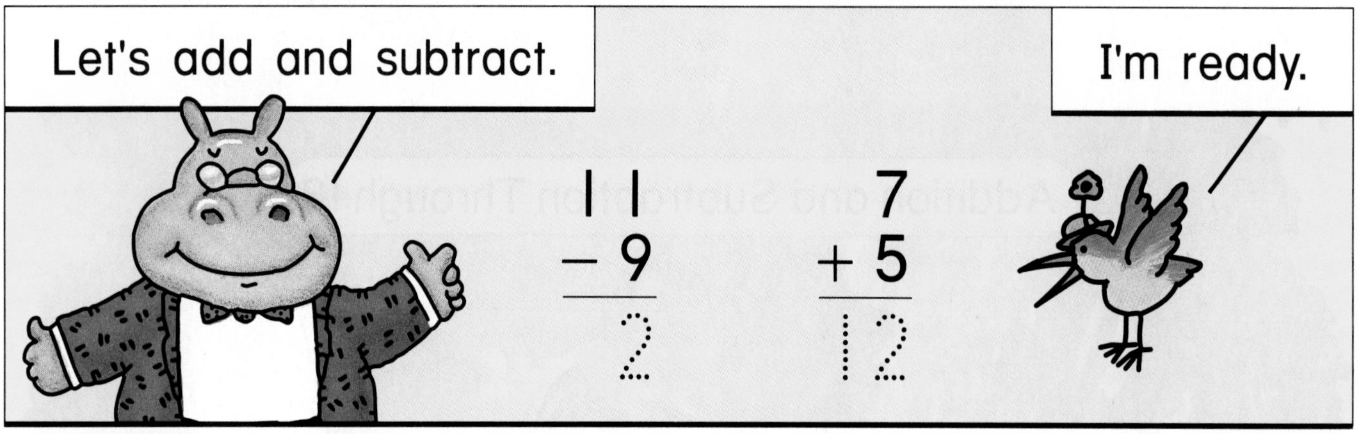

Add or subtract.

1.

5	12	3	8	7	10	9
+ 6	− 4	+ 7	− 3	+ 2	− 2	+ 3

2.

11	1	9	8	7	3	10
− 8	+ 9	− 5	+ 4	− 3	+ 8	− 7

3.

6	11	12	7	10	5	9
+ 6	− 6	− 9	+ 4	− 4	+ 3	− 2

4.

12	6	4	10	5	11	2
− 7	+ 4	+ 5	− 5	+ 7	− 4	+ 9

Notes for Home Children review addition and subtraction facts through 12 as readiness for facts through 18.

Name

Adding with Doubles

This is a new doubles fact.

7 + 7 = 14

Write the sum.

1.

8 + 8 = ____

2.

9 + 9 = ____

3. 9 + 9 = ____ 8 + 8 = ____ 7 + 7 = ____

4. 6 + 6 = ____ 5 + 5 = ____ 4 + 4 = ____

Notes for Home Children learn to use doubles to find sums through 18.

Write the sum.
Ring the doubles.

5.	8 + 8 = 16	4 + 7	9 + 3	2 + 2	6 + 4	7 + 2	8 + 4
6.	5 + 3	2 + 8	7 + 7	6 + 3	5 + 7	9 + 9	4 + 6
7.	2 + 9	3 + 3	6 + 5	6 + 6	3 + 4	4 + 8	9 + 2
8.	4 + 5	2 + 6	5 + 5	8 + 3	4 + 4	7 + 3	5 + 6
9.	1 + 1	3 + 9	1 + 8				

Notes for Home Children practice addition facts through 18 and identify facts that are doubles.

Name ____________________

Adding with Doubles and 1 More

First, think of the double.
Then add 1 more.

$6 + 6 = 12$ $6 + 7 = 13$ $7 + 6 = 13$

Write the sum.

1.

$8 + 8 =$ 16 $8 + 9 =$ ____ $9 + 8 =$ ____

2.

$7 + 7 =$ ____ $7 + 8 =$ ____ $8 + 7 =$ ____

Notes for Home Children learn to use doubles and 1 more to find sums through 18.

Write the sum.

3. $\begin{array}{r} 7 \\ +\,7 \\ \hline 14 \end{array}$ $\begin{array}{r} 7 \\ +\,8 \\ \hline \end{array}$ $\begin{array}{r} 8 \\ +\,7 \\ \hline \end{array}$

4. $\begin{array}{r} 8 \\ +\,8 \\ \hline \end{array}$ $\begin{array}{r} 8 \\ +\,9 \\ \hline \end{array}$ $\begin{array}{r} 9 \\ +\,8 \\ \hline \end{array}$

5. $\begin{array}{r} 6 \\ +\,6 \\ \hline \end{array}$ $\begin{array}{r} 6 \\ +\,7 \\ \hline \end{array}$ $\begin{array}{r} 7 \\ +\,6 \\ \hline \end{array}$

6. $\begin{array}{r} 5 \\ +\,5 \\ \hline \end{array}$ $\begin{array}{r} 5 \\ +\,6 \\ \hline \end{array}$ $\begin{array}{r} 6 \\ +\,5 \\ \hline \end{array}$

7. $\begin{array}{r} 6 \\ +\,6 \\ \hline \end{array}$ $\begin{array}{r} 7 \\ +\,8 \\ \hline \end{array}$ $\begin{array}{r} 9 \\ +\,8 \\ \hline \end{array}$ $\begin{array}{r} 9 \\ +\,9 \\ \hline \end{array}$ $\begin{array}{r} 6 \\ +\,5 \\ \hline \end{array}$ $\begin{array}{r} 6 \\ +\,7 \\ \hline \end{array}$ $\begin{array}{r} 8 \\ +\,9 \\ \hline \end{array}$

8. $\begin{array}{r} 6 \\ +\,7 \\ \hline \end{array}$ $\begin{array}{r} 7 \\ +\,7 \\ \hline \end{array}$ $\begin{array}{r} 5 \\ +\,6 \\ \hline \end{array}$ $\begin{array}{r} 8 \\ +\,8 \\ \hline \end{array}$ $\begin{array}{r} 8 \\ +\,7 \\ \hline \end{array}$ $\begin{array}{r} 7 \\ +\,6 \\ \hline \end{array}$ $\begin{array}{r} 9 \\ +\,8 \\ \hline \end{array}$

Talk About Math

Which facts are 1 more than a double?

6 + 7   9 + 3

9 + 8   8 + 5

Notes for Home Children practice finding sums through 18. Then they are asked to verbalize about doubles.

See More Practice Set A on page 427.

Name

Adding Three Numbers

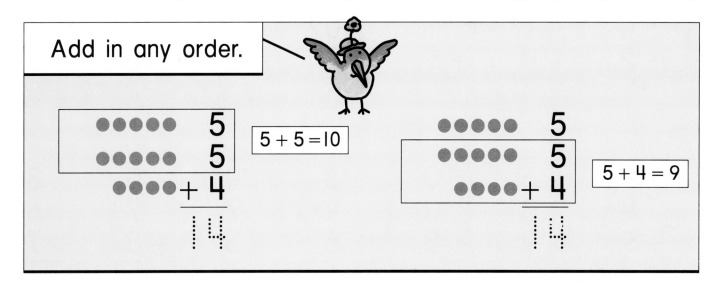

Add in any order.

5 5 + 4 14 (5 + 5 = 10)	5 5 + 4 14 (5 + 4 = 9)

Write the sum.

1.
5 4 + 3 (5 + 4 = 9)	5 4 + 3 (4 + 3 = 7)

2.
6 4 + 2 (6 + 4 = 10)	6 4 + 2 (4 + 2 = 6)

3.
3 7 + 3 (3 + 7 = 10)	3 7 + 3 (7 + 3 = 10)

Notes for Home Children learn to add three numbers in any order to find sums through 18.

Write the sum.

4.	5	3	7	8	5	3	7
	4	1	1	0	4	4	2
	+ 2	+ 4	+ 9	+ 8	+ 9	+ 8	+ 5

5.	4	6	3	6	4	0	3
	4	3	3	4	7	7	6
	+ 9	+ 9	+ 3	+ 6	+ 3	+ 8	+ 7

6.	4	3	3	2	6	1	7
	6	3	5	6	1	8	2
	+ 3	+ 5	+ 9	+ 2	+ 6	+ 9	+ 6

Problem Solving

Solve.

7. Jessica has 6 blue ribbons, 5 red ribbons, and 3 yellow ribbons.

She has _____ ribbons in all.

Notes for Home Children practice adding three numbers to find sums through 18. Then they solve a problem involving addition.

Name

Using 10 to Add

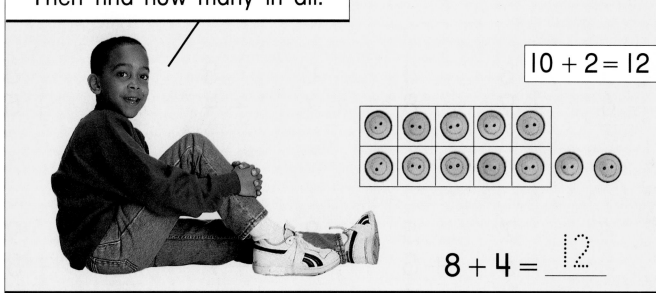

Add to 10.
Then find how many in all.

$10 + 2 = 12$

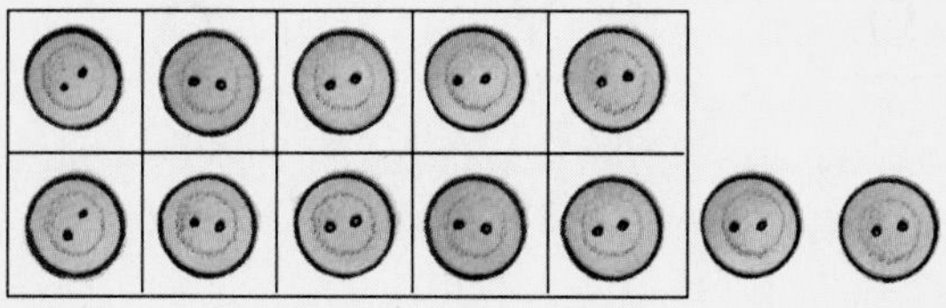

$8 + 4 = $ 12

Draw buttons to solve.
Write the sum.

1.

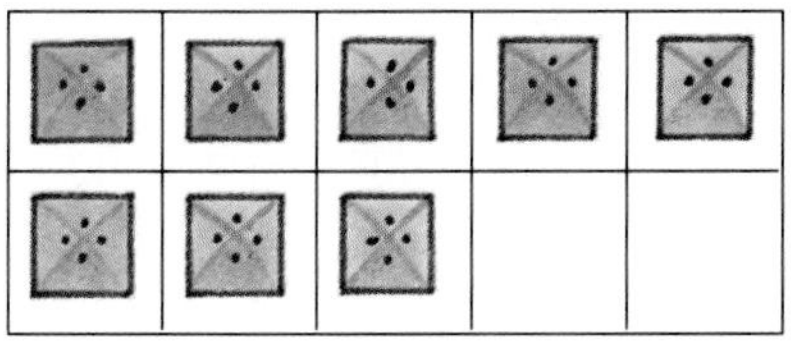

$8 + 5 = $ ____

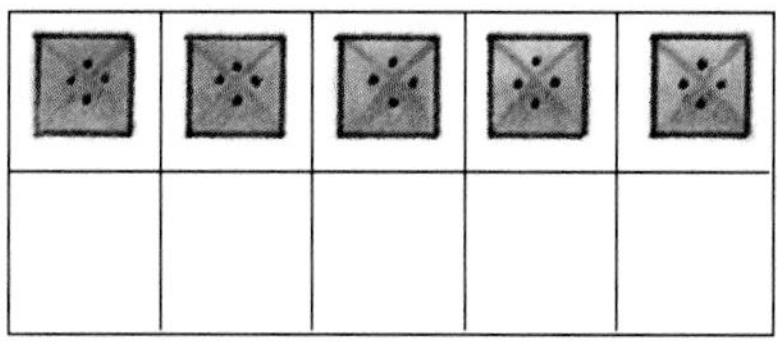

$5 + 8 = $ ____

2.

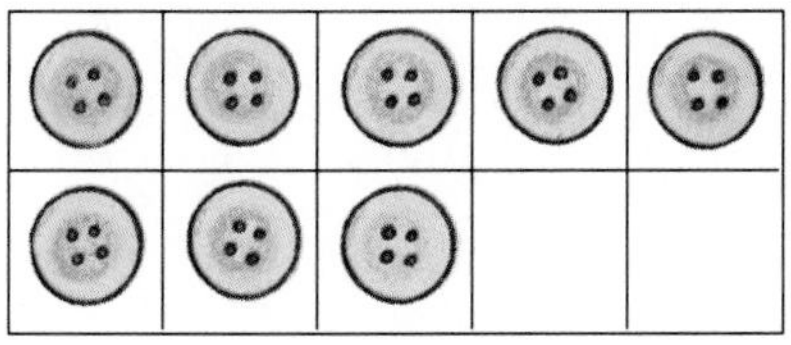

$8 + 6 = $ ____

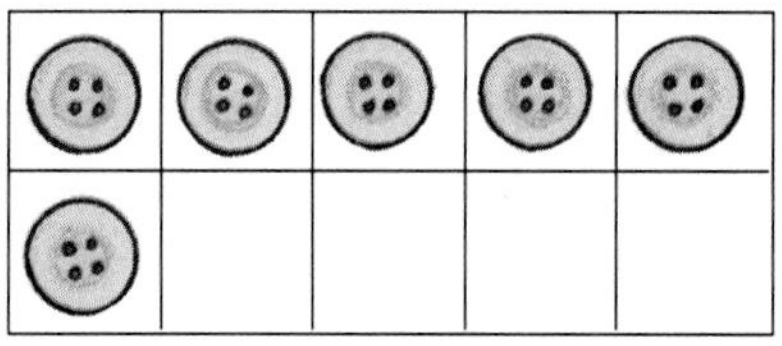

$6 + 8 = $ ____

Notes for Home Children find sums through 18 by adding to 10 and then finding how many in all.

Write the sum.

3.	8	7	5	3	6	9	4
	+ 5	+ 8	+ 8	+ 8	+ 8	+ 8	+ 8
	13						

4.	8	8	8	8	8	8	8
	+ 6	+ 9	+ 8	+ 7	+ 4	+ 3	+ 5

5.	6	7	5	8	6	8	9
	+ 8	+ 6	+ 8	+ 8	+ 7	+ 9	+ 3

6.	7	7	9	9	8	4	6
	+ 6	+ 7	+ 9	+ 8	+ 6	+ 8	+ 5

7.	7	7	8
	+ 5	+ 8	+ 5

Notes for Home Children practice finding sums through 18.

Name ______________________

Using 10 to Add

First, add to 10.
Then find how many in all.

10 + 3 = 13

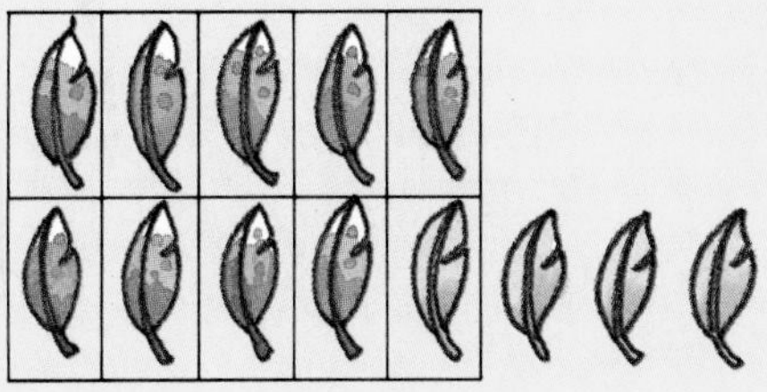

9 + 4 = 13

Write the sum.

1.

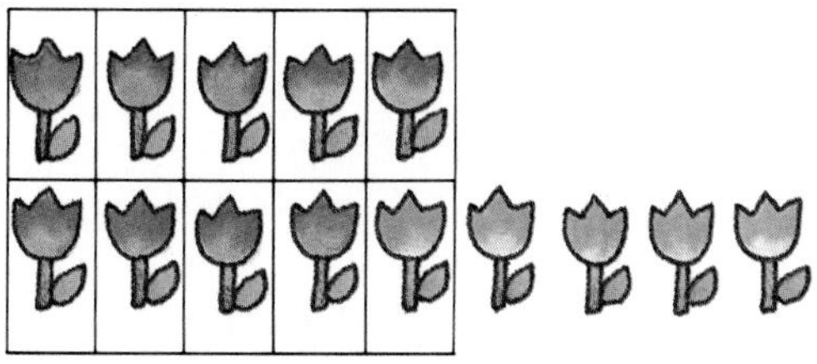

9 + 5 = ____

2.

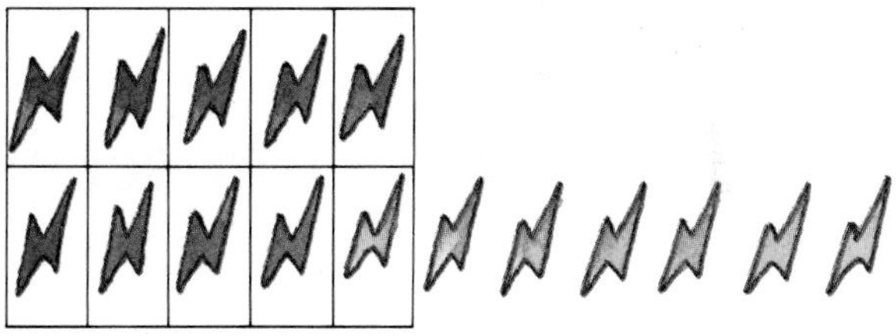

9 + 7 = ____

3.

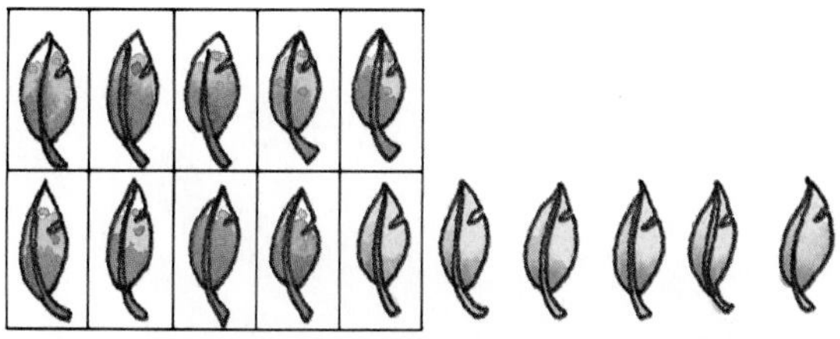

9 + 6 = ____

4.

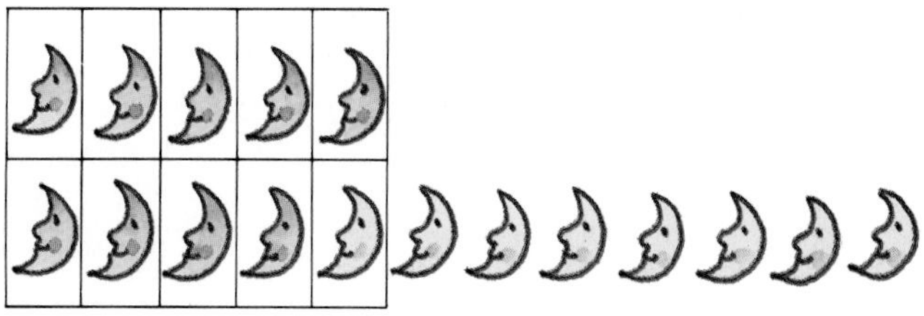

9 + 8 = ____

Notes for Home Children find sums through 18 by adding to 10 and then finding how many in all.

Write the sum.

5.	9	6	5	4	9	9	9
	+ 4	+ 9	+ 9	+ 9	+ 6	+ 7	+ 8
	13						

6.	7	8	9	6	5	8	9
	+ 9	+ 5	+ 5	+ 8	+ 8	+ 6	+ 9

7.	7	8	8	7	8	7	3
	+ 7	+ 9	+ 7	+ 8	+ 8	+ 6	+ 9

Problem Solving

Add or subtract to solve.

8. Susan had 9 stickers. She gave 3 to Amy. How many stickers does she have now?

____ stickers

9. Bob had 7 stickers. He bought 8 more. How many stickers does he have now?

____ stickers

Notes for Home Children practice finding sums through 18. Then they solve problems by choosing the operation.

Name

Too Much Information

Sometimes you don't need all the information in a problem.

Ted saw 8 monkeys.
~~2 monkeys were red.~~
Then Ted saw 6 more monkeys.
How many monkeys did Ted see?

8
+ 6
14 monkeys

Cross out the information you don't need.
Then solve.

1. Sally had 11¢.
Nick had 5¢.
Sally spent 3¢.
How much money does Sally have now?

____ ¢
☐ ____ ¢
____ ¢

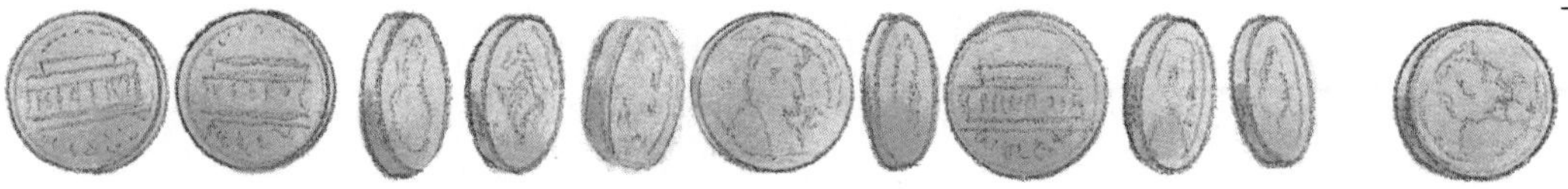

2. Clare had 9 books.
2 of the books were about animals.
Then she bought 4 more books.
How many books does she have now?

____
☐ ____
____ books

Notes for Home Children find and cross out unnecessary information. Then they solve problems.

Cross out information you don't need.
Then solve.

3. Fred saw 9 birds in the tree.
3 birds flew away.
~~All of the birds were blue.~~
How many birds are still in the tree?

9
− 3
6 birds

4. Katra had 4 dogs.
She also had 3 cats.
2 of the dogs ran away.
How many dogs does Katra have now?

____
☐ ____
____ dogs

5. Bea wrote 7 letters.
Jay wrote 9 letters.
Bea had 3 stamps.
How many letters did they write in all?

____
☐ ____
____ letters

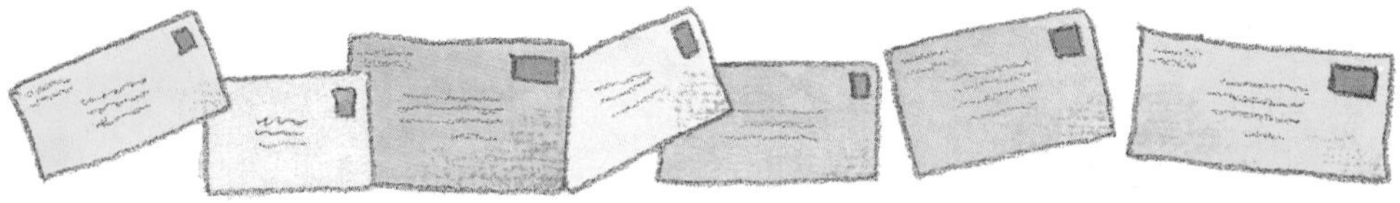

6. Rod had 11¢.
He spent 6¢.
He bought 3 stickers.
How much money does Rod have now?

____¢
☐ ____¢
____¢

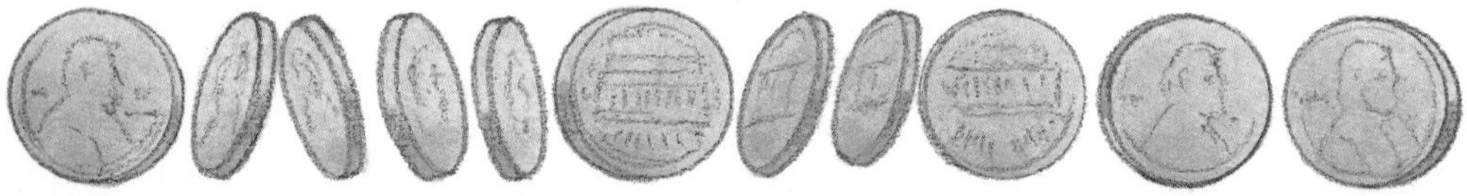

Notes for Home Children find and cross out unnecessary information. Then they solve problems.

Name

Number Sense

Find all the doubles in the picture.

Let's do some more!

Look for doubles in your home.
Make a list of what you find.

Notes for Home Children develop an understanding of numbers by finding doubles.

Skills Review

Fill in the correct ⬭.
Which holds more?

1.

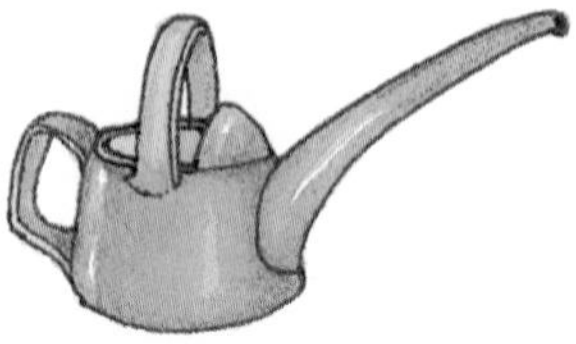

Ⓐ Ⓑ

2.

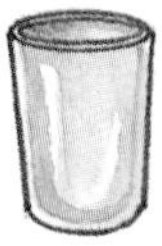

Ⓐ Ⓑ

Which shape shows equal parts?

3.

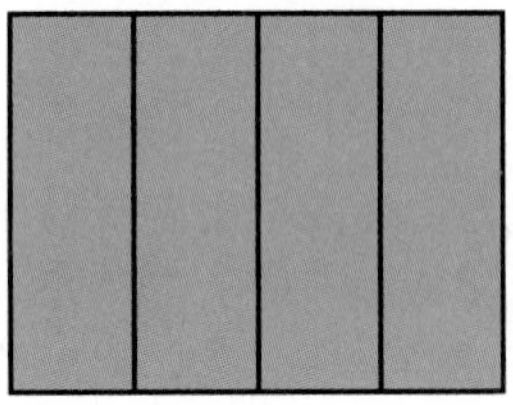
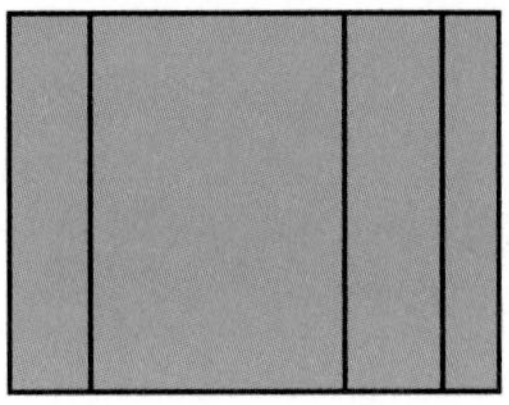

Ⓐ Ⓑ

4.

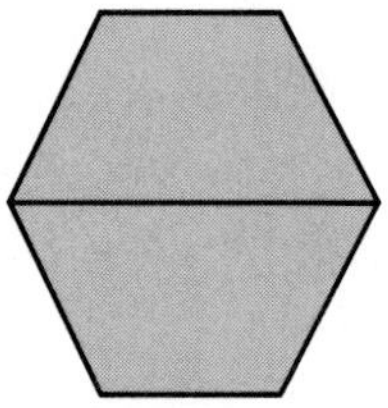
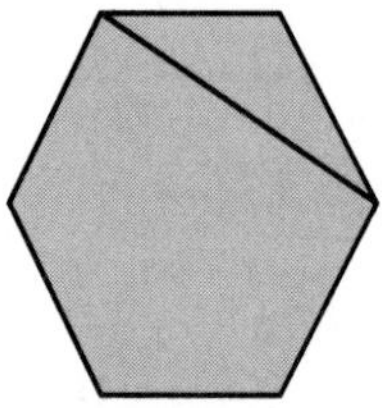

Ⓐ Ⓑ

5.

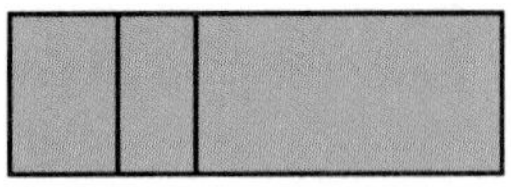
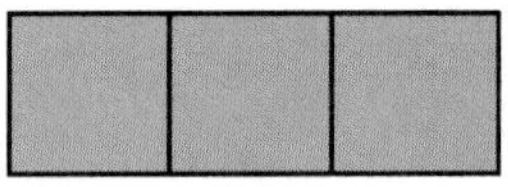

Ⓐ Ⓑ

6.

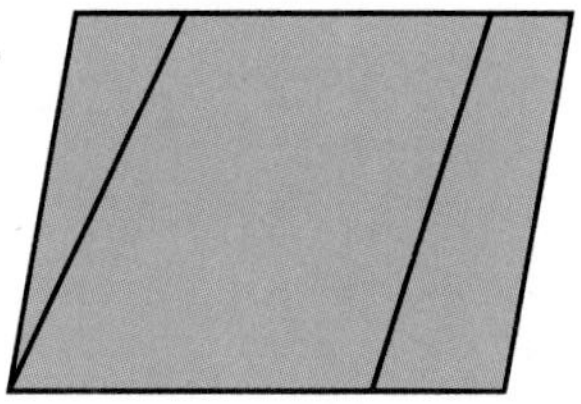
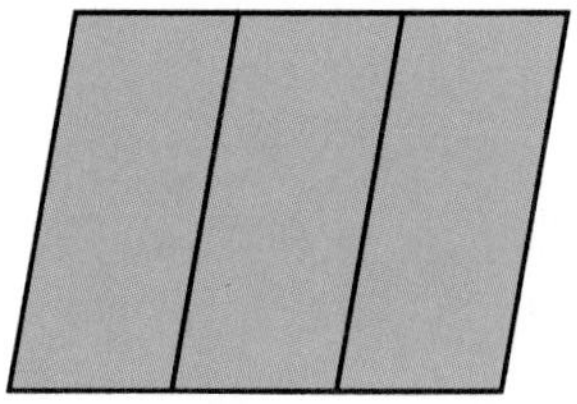

Ⓐ Ⓑ

Vocabulary

7. Match.

halves •

thirds •

fourths •

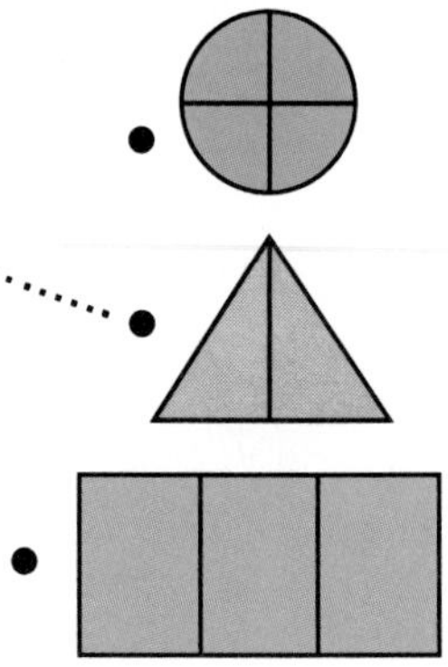

Notes for Home Children review which of two containers holds more. Then they review equal parts of a whole and complete a chart using fraction terms.

Name ______

Using Doubles to Subtract

$7 + 7 = \underline{14}$ $14 - 7 = \underline{7}$

Add or subtract.

1.

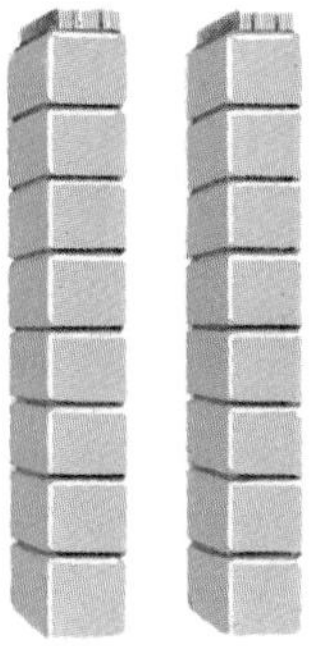

$8 + 8 =$ ______

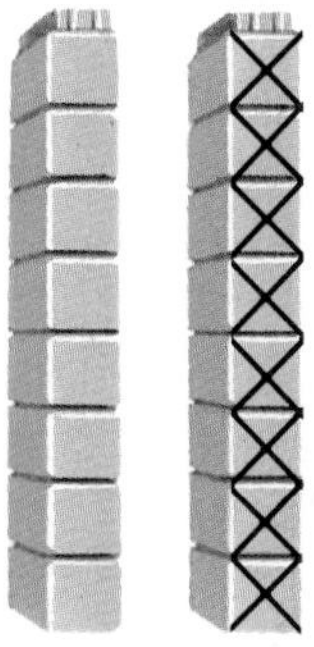

$16 - 8 =$ ______

2.

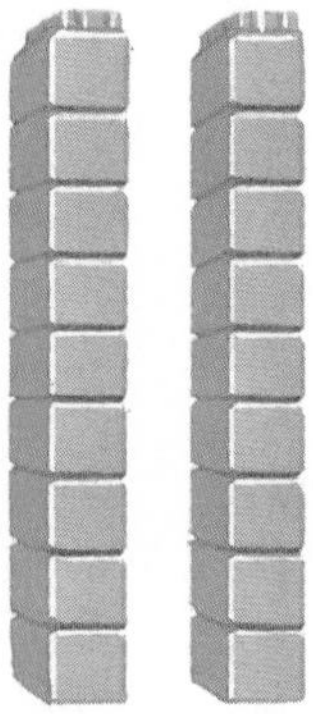

$9 + 9 =$ ______

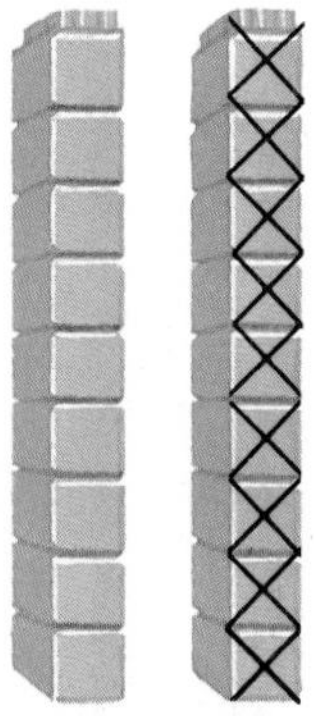

$18 - 9 =$ ______

Notes for Home Children learn subtraction facts by using addition doubles.

Add or subtract.

3.	$\begin{array}{r} 8 \\ +8 \\ \hline 16 \end{array}$	$\begin{array}{r} 16 \\ -8 \\ \hline \end{array}$	4. $\begin{array}{r} 7 \\ +7 \\ \hline \end{array}$	$\begin{array}{r} 14 \\ -7 \\ \hline \end{array}$	5. $\begin{array}{r} 9 \\ +9 \\ \hline \end{array}$ $\begin{array}{r} 18 \\ -9 \\ \hline \end{array}$

6.	$\begin{array}{r} 12 \\ -6 \\ \hline \end{array}$	$\begin{array}{r} 10 \\ -7 \\ \hline \end{array}$	$\begin{array}{r} 11 \\ -8 \\ \hline \end{array}$	$\begin{array}{r} 18 \\ -9 \\ \hline \end{array}$	$\begin{array}{r} 9 \\ -4 \\ \hline \end{array}$	$\begin{array}{r} 10 \\ -5 \\ \hline \end{array}$	$\begin{array}{r} 12 \\ -9 \\ \hline \end{array}$
7.	$\begin{array}{r} 9 \\ -7 \\ \hline \end{array}$	$\begin{array}{r} 11 \\ -4 \\ \hline \end{array}$	$\begin{array}{r} 16 \\ -8 \\ \hline \end{array}$	$\begin{array}{r} 12 \\ -7 \\ \hline \end{array}$	$\begin{array}{r} 10 \\ -6 \\ \hline \end{array}$	$\begin{array}{r} 9 \\ -2 \\ \hline \end{array}$	$\begin{array}{r} 11 \\ -6 \\ \hline \end{array}$
8.	$\begin{array}{r} 11 \\ -5 \\ \hline \end{array}$	$\begin{array}{r} 10 \\ -2 \\ \hline \end{array}$	$\begin{array}{r} 9 \\ -5 \\ \hline \end{array}$	$\begin{array}{r} 12 \\ -4 \\ \hline \end{array}$	$\begin{array}{r} 14 \\ -7 \\ \hline \end{array}$	$\begin{array}{r} 10 \\ -4 \\ \hline \end{array}$	$\begin{array}{r} 12 \\ -5 \\ \hline \end{array}$
9.	$\begin{array}{r} 12 \\ -3 \\ \hline \end{array}$	$\begin{array}{r} 11 \\ -9 \\ \hline \end{array}$	$\begin{array}{r} 9 \\ -6 \\ \hline \end{array}$	$\begin{array}{r} 12 \\ -8 \\ \hline \end{array}$	$\begin{array}{r} 11 \\ -3 \\ \hline \end{array}$		

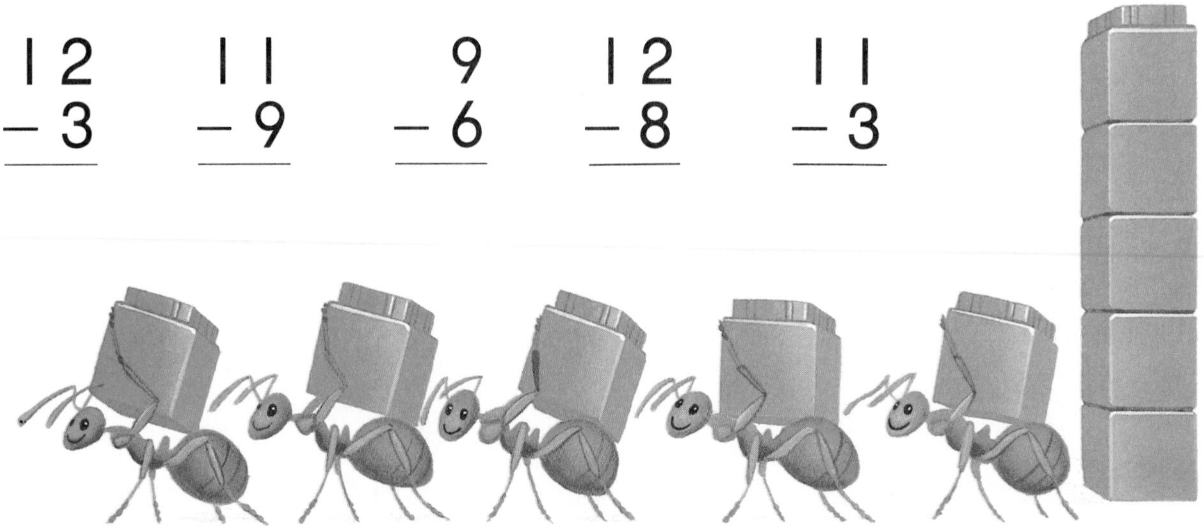

Notes for Home Children practice subtraction facts.

Name ______

Related Subtraction Facts for 13 and 14

9 and 4 are parts of 13.

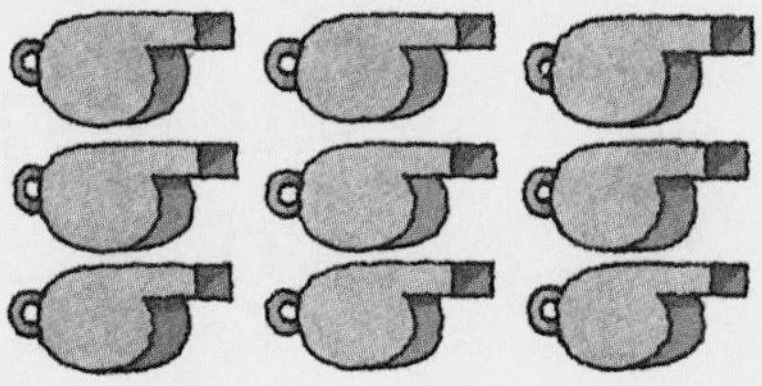

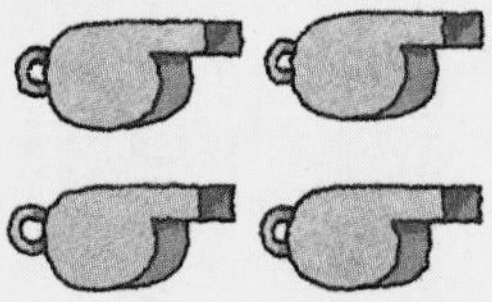

13 − 4 = 9

13 − 9 = 4

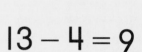

Write the parts. Subtract.

1.

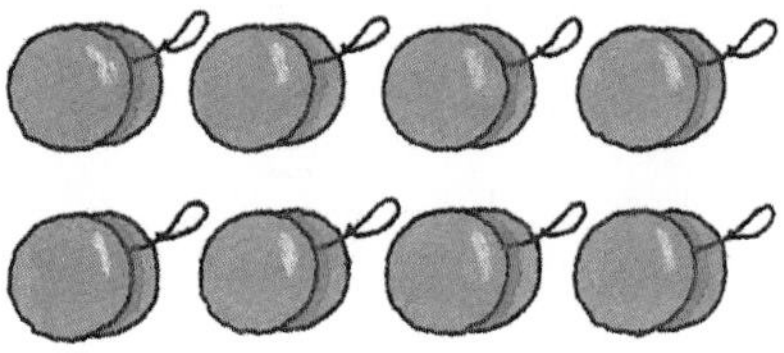

8 5

13 − 5 = 8

13 − 8 = 5

2.

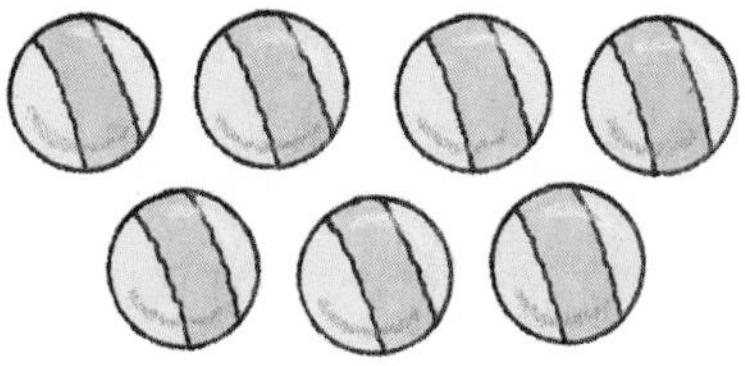

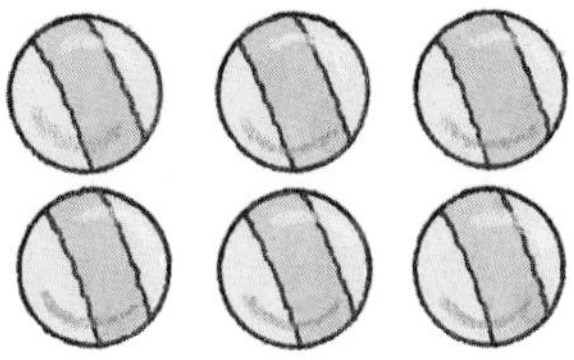

___ ___

13 − 6 = ___

13 − 7 = ___

3.

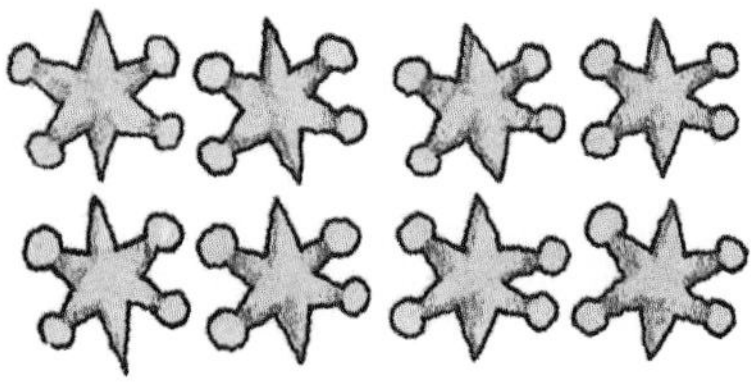

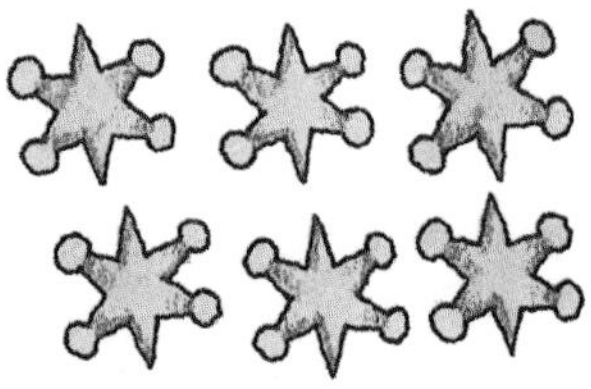

___ ___

14 − 6 = ___

14 − 8 = ___

Notes for Home Children solve subtraction facts for 13 and 14 by thinking of related numbers that make 13 and 14.

Write the difference.

4. $13 - 4$ 9 $13 - 9$

5. $14 - 5$ $14 - 9$

6. $13 - 5$ $13 - 8$

7. $14 - 6$ $14 - 8$

8. $13 - 9$ $13 - 4$

9. $14 - 9$ $14 - 5$

10. $13 - 9$ $16 - 8$ $14 - 9$ $13 - 6$ $18 - 9$ $13 - 7$ $14 - 7$

Problem Solving

Add or subtract to solve.

11. If you had 15¢ and you bought a toy for 7¢, how much would you have?

_____ ¢

12. If you had 8¢ and you earned 5¢, how much would you have?

_____ ¢

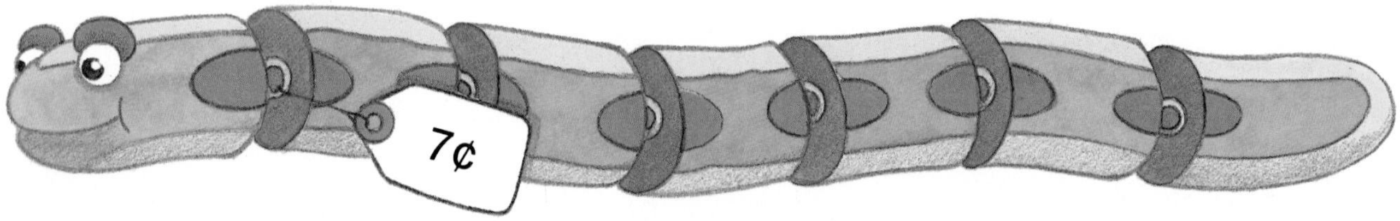

Notes for Home Children practice finding differences from 18 or less. Then they solve problems by choosing the operation.

Name ______________________________

Related Subtraction Facts for 15 Through 18

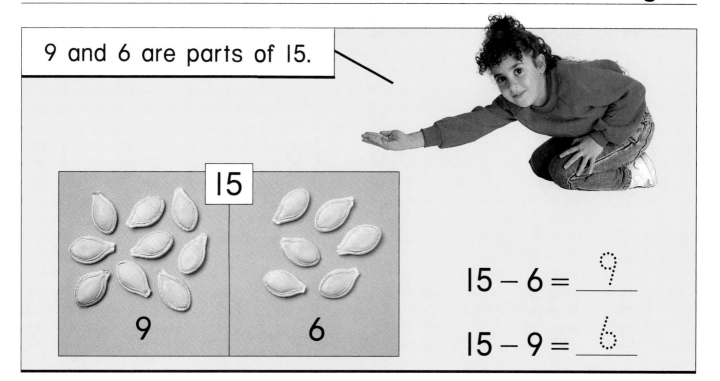

9 and 6 are parts of 15.

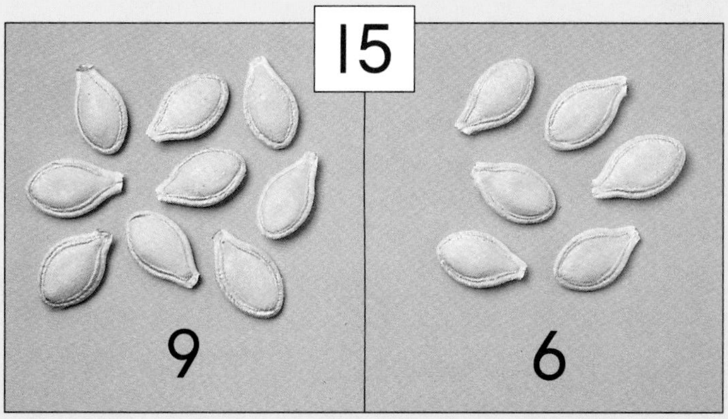

15 − 6 = 9

15 − 9 = 6

Subtract.

1.

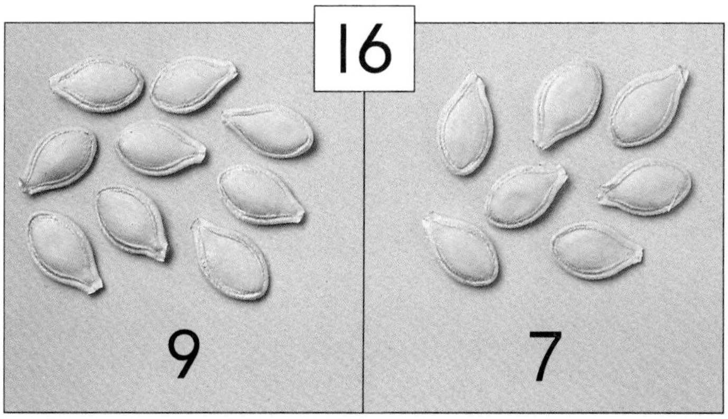

16 − 7 = ____

16 − 9 = ____

2.

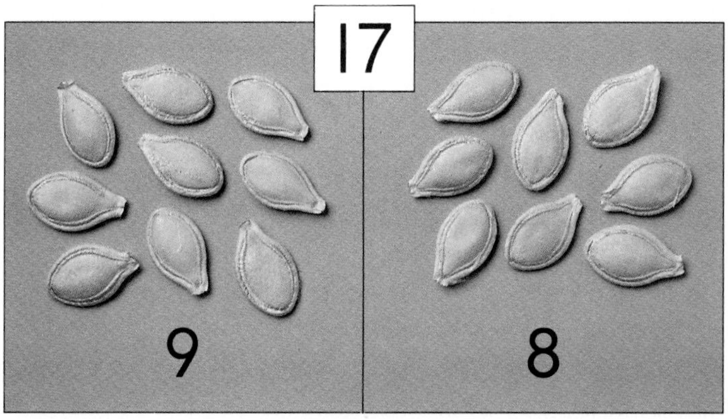

17 − 8 = ____

17 − 9 = ____

Notes for Home Children learn related subtraction facts for 15 through 18.

Subtract.

3.	$\begin{array}{r} 15 \\ -\ 6 \\ \hline 9 \end{array}$	$\begin{array}{r} 15 \\ -\ 9 \\ \hline \end{array}$	4.	$\begin{array}{r} 13 \\ -\ 4 \\ \hline \end{array}$	$\begin{array}{r} 13 \\ -\ 9 \\ \hline \end{array}$	5.	$\begin{array}{r} 17 \\ -\ 8 \\ \hline \end{array}$	$\begin{array}{r} 17 \\ -\ 9 \\ \hline \end{array}$
6.	$\begin{array}{r} 14 \\ -\ 5 \\ \hline \end{array}$	$\begin{array}{r} 14 \\ -\ 9 \\ \hline \end{array}$	7.	$\begin{array}{r} 16 \\ -\ 7 \\ \hline \end{array}$	$\begin{array}{r} 16 \\ -\ 9 \\ \hline \end{array}$	8.	$\begin{array}{r} 15 \\ -\ 7 \\ \hline \end{array}$	$\begin{array}{r} 15 \\ -\ 8 \\ \hline \end{array}$

9.	$\begin{array}{r} 14 \\ -\ 8 \\ \hline \end{array}$	$\begin{array}{r} 18 \\ -\ 9 \\ \hline \end{array}$	$\begin{array}{r} 17 \\ -\ 8 \\ \hline \end{array}$	$\begin{array}{r} 13 \\ -\ 5 \\ \hline \end{array}$	$\begin{array}{r} 15 \\ -\ 8 \\ \hline \end{array}$	$\begin{array}{r} 17 \\ -\ 9 \\ \hline \end{array}$	$\begin{array}{r} 13 \\ -\ 8 \\ \hline \end{array}$
10.	$\begin{array}{r} 16 \\ -\ 8 \\ \hline \end{array}$	$\begin{array}{r} 13 \\ -\ 6 \\ \hline \end{array}$	$\begin{array}{r} 16 \\ -\ 7 \\ \hline \end{array}$	$\begin{array}{r} 15 \\ -\ 7 \\ \hline \end{array}$	$\begin{array}{r} 13 \\ -\ 7 \\ \hline \end{array}$	$\begin{array}{r} 14 \\ -\ 6 \\ \hline \end{array}$	$\begin{array}{r} 16 \\ -\ 9 \\ \hline \end{array}$

Talk About Math

Which fact is related to $15 - 6 = 9$?

$15 - 9 = 6$

$6 + 6 = 12$

$15 - 8 = 7$

Notes for Home Children practice subtraction facts through 18.

Name **Activity**

Families of Facts

These facts make a family.

$7 + 9 = 16$ $16 - 9 = 7$

$9 + 7 = 16$ $16 - 7 = 9$

Use counters.
Add or subtract.

1. $6 + 8 =$ 14

   $8 + 6 =$ ____

   $14 - 8 =$ ____

   $14 - 6 =$ ____

2. $5 + 8 =$ ____

   $8 + 5 =$ ____

   $13 - 8 =$ ____

   $13 - 5 =$ ____

Notes for Home Children explore at the CONCRETE level using counters to find fact families.

Use counters.
Add or subtract.

3.

$\begin{array}{r} 4 \\ +9 \\ \hline 13 \end{array}$	$\begin{array}{r} 9 \\ +4 \\ \hline \end{array}$
$\begin{array}{r} 13 \\ -9 \\ \hline \end{array}$	$\begin{array}{r} 13 \\ -4 \\ \hline \end{array}$

4.

$\begin{array}{r} 8 \\ +9 \\ \hline \end{array}$	$\begin{array}{r} 9 \\ +8 \\ \hline \end{array}$
$\begin{array}{r} 17 \\ -9 \\ \hline \end{array}$	$\begin{array}{r} 17 \\ -8 \\ \hline \end{array}$

5.

$\begin{array}{r} 5 \\ +9 \\ \hline \end{array}$	$\begin{array}{r} 9 \\ +5 \\ \hline \end{array}$
$\begin{array}{r} 14 \\ -9 \\ \hline \end{array}$	$\begin{array}{r} 14 \\ -5 \\ \hline \end{array}$

6.

$\begin{array}{r} 7 \\ +8 \\ \hline \end{array}$	$\begin{array}{r} 8 \\ +7 \\ \hline \end{array}$
$\begin{array}{r} 15 \\ -8 \\ \hline \end{array}$	$\begin{array}{r} 15 \\ -7 \\ \hline \end{array}$

7.

$\begin{array}{r} 7 \\ +9 \\ \hline \end{array}$	$\begin{array}{r} 9 \\ +7 \\ \hline \end{array}$
$\begin{array}{r} 16 \\ -9 \\ \hline \end{array}$	$\begin{array}{r} 16 \\ -7 \\ \hline \end{array}$

8.

$\begin{array}{r} 6 \\ +9 \\ \hline \end{array}$	$\begin{array}{r} 9 \\ +6 \\ \hline \end{array}$
$\begin{array}{r} 15 \\ -9 \\ \hline \end{array}$	$\begin{array}{r} 15 \\ -6 \\ \hline \end{array}$

Notes for Home Children explore at the CONCRETE level using counters to find fact families.

Name

Addition and Subtraction Through 18

We can add and subtract through 18! Congratulations!

Add or subtract.

1.	4	14	9	14	13	5	13
	+ 9	− 9	+ 4	− 6	− 7	+ 9	− 8
	13						
2.	9	16	15	8	5	17	9
	+ 6	− 7	− 9	+ 9	+ 8	− 8	+ 5
3.	14	15	7	8	13	6	17
	− 5	− 6	+ 9	+ 6	− 4	+ 9	− 9

Notes for Home Children practice addition and subtraction facts through 18.

Ring the facts for each number.

5. 7

- 3 + 4
- 15 − 9
- 14 − 7
- 16 − 9

6. 9

- 6 + 5
- 18 − 9
- 14 − 5
- 16 − 7

7. 8

- 14 − 5
- 14 − 6
- 5 + 3
- 17 − 9

8. 13

- 9 + 4
- 8 + 5
- 18 − 9
- 4 + 9

9. 5

- 14 − 9
- 4 + 3
- 13 − 8
- 2 + 4

10. 14

- 7 + 9
- 5 + 9
- 16 − 9
- 6 + 8

Notes for Home Children practice addition and subtraction facts through 18.

See More Practice Set B on page 427.

Too Little Information

Sometimes you don't have enough information to solve a problem.

Steve has 9¢.
Carole has more money than Steve.
How much money does Carole have?

enough   not enough

Is there enough information?
Ring enough or not enough.

1. Mack had 11 apples.
He ate 2 apples.
How many apples does he have now?

enough   not enough

2. William has 9 pears.
His brother has more pears.
How many pears do they have together?

enough   not enough

Notes for Home Children determine if there is enough information to solve problems.

Is there enough information?
Ring enough or not enough.

3. Nina bought 4 cans of beans.
She bought 5 cans of corn.
How many cans did she buy?

enough   not enough

---

4. Amy bought 6 bananas.
She bought some pears.
How many pieces of fruit did Amy buy?

enough   not enough

---

5. Joe had 17¢.
He spent 9¢.
How much money does he have now?

enough   not enough

---

6. Anna had 6 books.
She got 9 more books.
How many books does she have now?

enough   not enough

Notes for Home Children determine if there is enough information to solve problems.

Name

Problem-Solving Workshop

Explore as a Team

Work with a partner.
The weights are in pounds.
Give the missing weights.

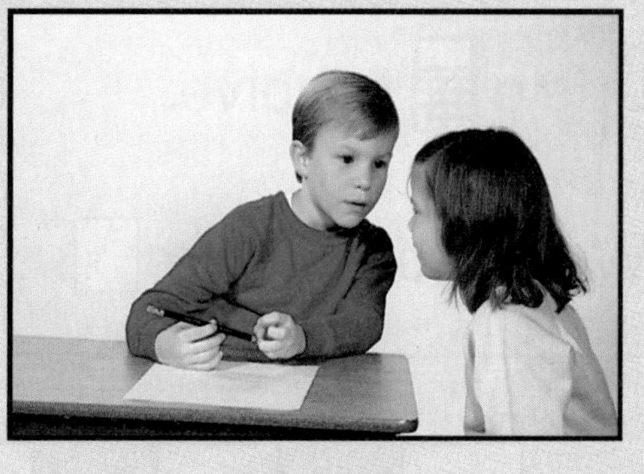

Notes for Home Children explore with a partner to solve a problem using logical reasoning.

Enrichment

Jeff put 18 toys in 3 boxes.
How many toys were in each box?

1. 9 7 2

2. ___ 3 7

3. 5 9 ___

4. 4 ___ 8

5. 3 ___ ___

6. ___ 5 ___

7. ___ ___ ___

Notes for Home Children are challenged to find three numbers that add up to a given sum.

Name

Add or subtract.

1. $\begin{array}{r} 8 \\ +8 \\ \hline \end{array}$ $\begin{array}{r} 8 \\ +9 \\ \hline \end{array}$ $\begin{array}{r} 9 \\ +8 \\ \hline \end{array}$ $\begin{array}{r} 8 \\ +6 \\ \hline \end{array}$ $\begin{array}{r} 6 \\ +9 \\ \hline \end{array}$ $\begin{array}{r} 5 \\ +8 \\ \hline \end{array}$

2. $\begin{array}{r} 9 \\ +9 \\ \hline \end{array}$ $\begin{array}{r} 18 \\ -9 \\ \hline \end{array}$ $\begin{array}{r} 14 \\ -9 \\ \hline \end{array}$ $\begin{array}{r} 14 \\ -5 \\ \hline \end{array}$ $\begin{array}{r} 16 \\ -7 \\ \hline \end{array}$ $\begin{array}{r} 16 \\ -9 \\ \hline \end{array}$

Add.

3. $\begin{array}{r} 5 \\ 7 \\ +3 \\ \hline \end{array}$ $\begin{array}{r} 6 \\ 2 \\ +9 \\ \hline \end{array}$

Add or subtract.

4. 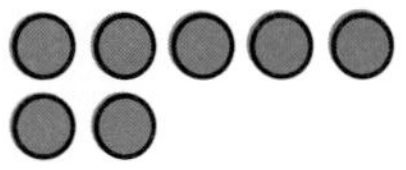 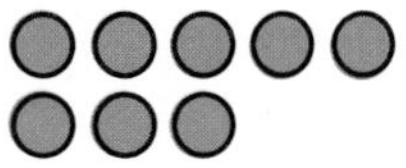

$7 + 8 =$ ____ $15 - 8 =$ ____

$8 + 7 =$ ____ $15 - 7 =$ ____

Cross out the information you don't need. Then solve.

5. Mike had 16¢.
Sally had 9¢.
Mike spent 7¢.
How much money does Mike have now?

____¢
− ____¢
____¢

Is there enough information? Ring enough or not enough.

6. Jim has 8¢. Pam has more money than Jim. How much money does Pam have?

enough not enough

Notes for Home Children are assessed on Chapter 13 concepts, skills, and problem solving.

Exploring Math at Home

Dear Family,

In this chapter I have learned addition and subtraction facts through 18. I have also learned about families of facts. Please help me with the activities below.

Love, ______________________________

1.

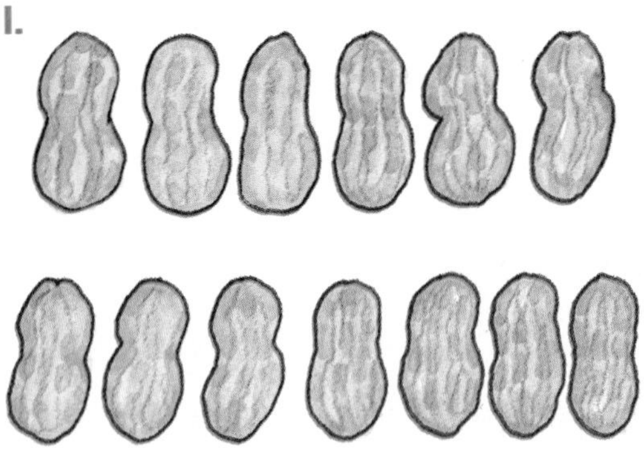

$$\begin{array}{r} 6 \\ +\ 7 \\ \hline 13 \end{array}$$

Use peanuts to create number sentences through 18.

2.

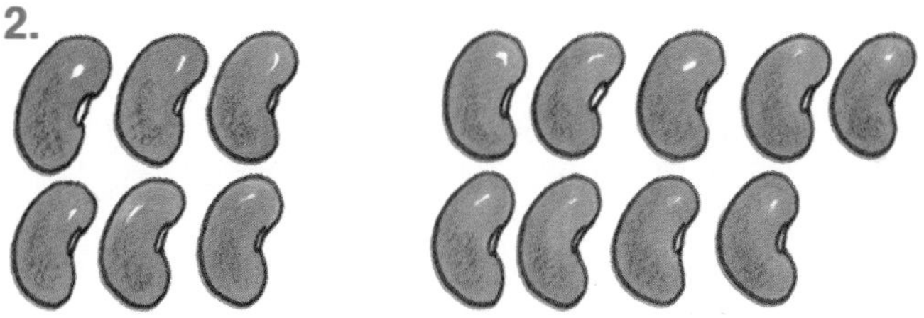

$6 + 9 = 15$ $15 - 9 = 6$

$9 + 6 = 15$ $15 - 6 = 9$

Use dried beans to create families of facts through 18. Try a different family daily.

3.

Practice using addition and subtraction flashcards through 18. Use a timer to see how long it takes to complete the answers. Compare the times from day to day.

Coming Attractions

In the next chapter I will learn to add and subtract two-digit numbers.

Chapter 14

Exploring Larger Numbers

Listen to the math story, "Michael's Recycle Bicycle."
The 3 friends wanted to collect many cans.
How did Michael's idea help them?

Notes for Home Children listen to a math story introducing chapter concepts and skills. Then they answer a question about the story.

Name

Adding a Two-Digit and a One-Digit Number

1. Use tens and ones counters. Show how many.

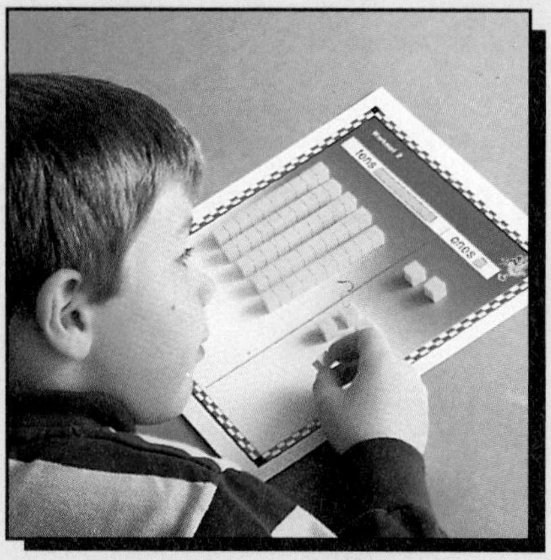

2. Show more tens and ones counters.

3. Write how many in all.

Use Workmat 2.
Use tens and ones counters.

	Show this many.	Show this many more.	Write how many in all.
1.	2 ones	5 tens 4 ones	5 tens 6 ones
2.	3 tens 3 ones	4 ones	____ tens ____ ones
3.	5 ones	2 tens 2 ones	____ tens ____ ones
4.	2 tens 4 ones	4 ones	____ tens ____ ones

Notes for Home Children explore at the CONCRETE level using tens and ones counters and a workmat as readiness for adding a two-digit and a one-digit number.

Name

Adding a Two-Digit and a One-Digit Number

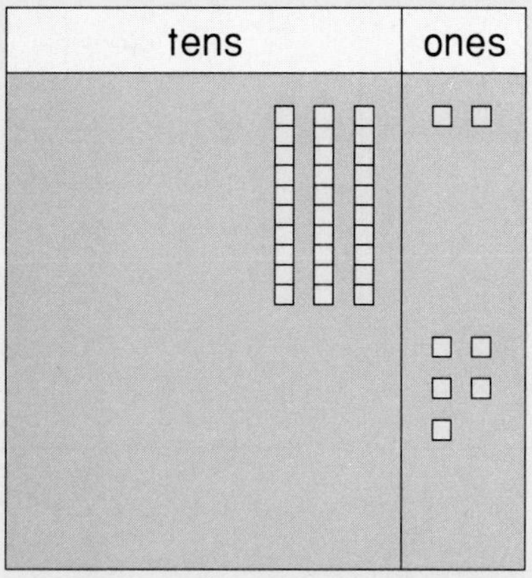

	tens	ones
	3	2
+		5
	3	7

Add.

1.

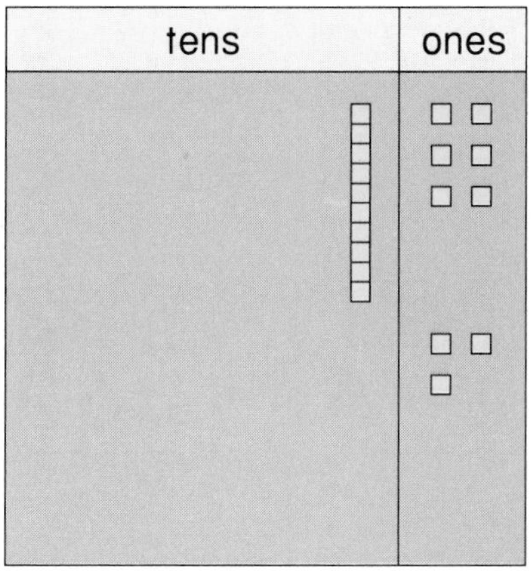

	tens	ones
	1	6
+		3

2.

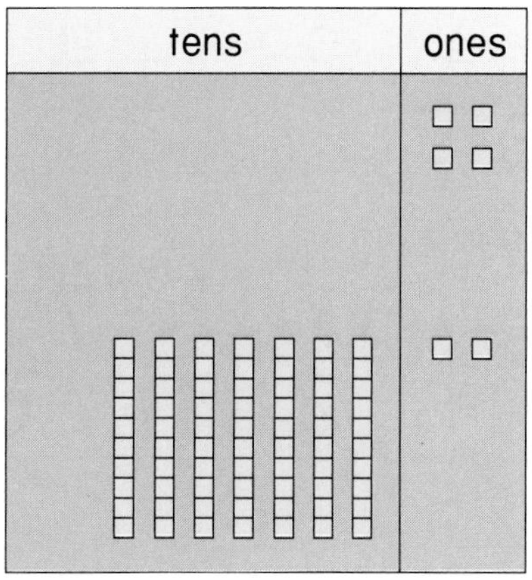

	tens	ones
		4
+	7	2

3.

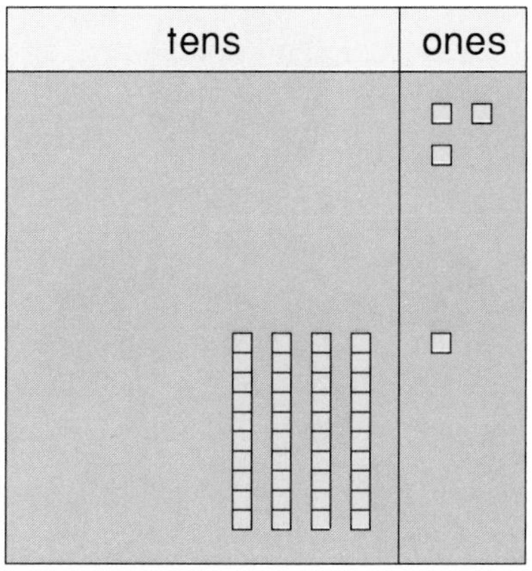

	tens	ones
		3
+	4	1

4.

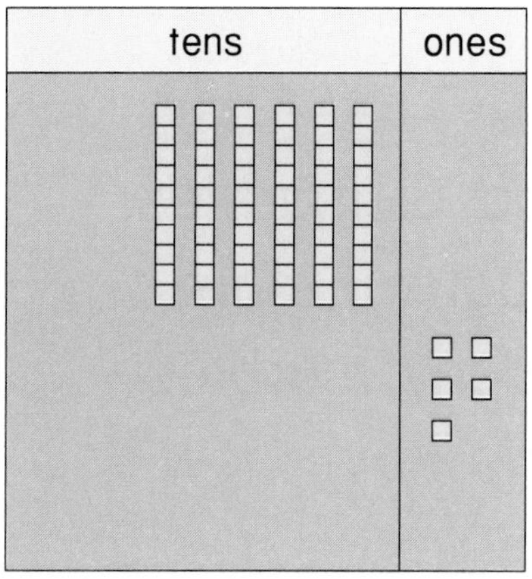

	tens	ones
	6	0
+		5

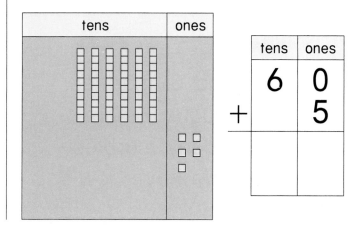

Notes for Home Children learn to find sums for two-digit and one-digit numbers using pictures.

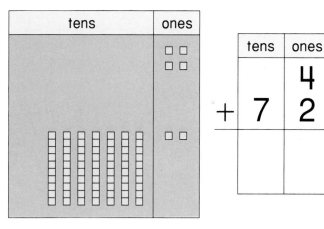

Add.

5.

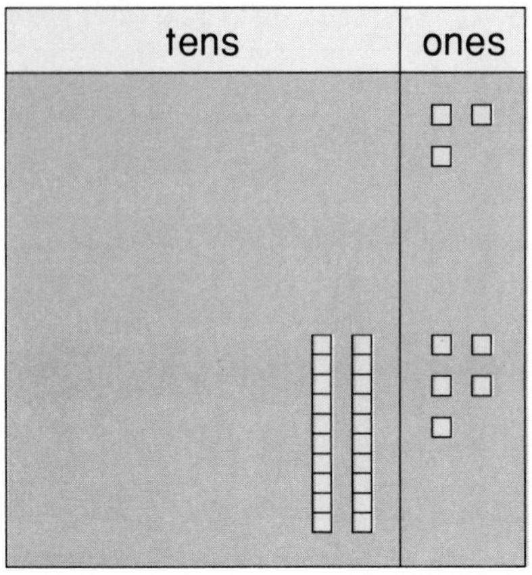

$\begin{array}{r} 3 \\ +25 \\ \hline 28 \end{array}$

6.

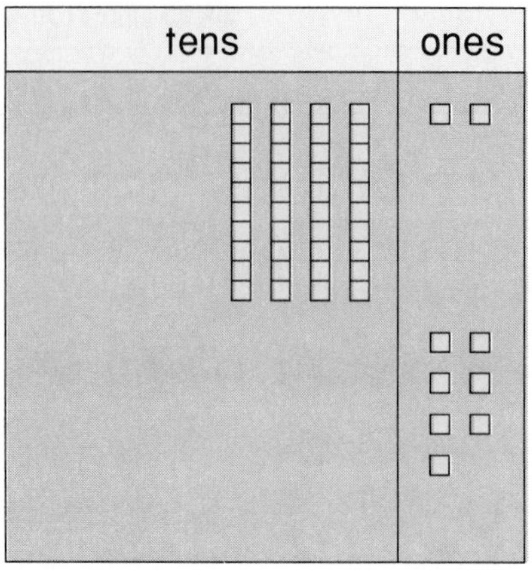

$\begin{array}{r} 42 \\ +\ \ 7 \\ \hline \end{array}$

7. $\begin{array}{r} 13 \\ +\ \ 6 \\ \hline \end{array}$ $\begin{array}{r} 4 \\ +12 \\ \hline \end{array}$ $\begin{array}{r} 8 \\ +11 \\ \hline \end{array}$ $\begin{array}{r} 15 \\ +\ \ 2 \\ \hline \end{array}$ $\begin{array}{r} 14 \\ +\ \ 4 \\ \hline \end{array}$ $\begin{array}{r} 11 \\ +\ \ 3 \\ \hline \end{array}$

8. $\begin{array}{r} 31 \\ +\ \ 7 \\ \hline \end{array}$ $\begin{array}{r} 63 \\ +\ \ 2 \\ \hline \end{array}$ $\begin{array}{r} 2 \\ +41 \\ \hline \end{array}$ $\begin{array}{r} 84 \\ +\ \ 5 \\ \hline \end{array}$ $\begin{array}{r} 3 \\ +73 \\ \hline \end{array}$ $\begin{array}{r} 50 \\ +\ \ 9 \\ \hline \end{array}$

9. $\begin{array}{r} 5 \\ +23 \\ \hline \end{array}$ $\begin{array}{r} 57 \\ +\ \ 2 \\ \hline \end{array}$ $\begin{array}{r} 71 \\ +\ \ 6 \\ \hline \end{array}$ $\begin{array}{r} 6 \\ +32 \\ \hline \end{array}$ $\begin{array}{r} 41 \\ +\ \ 5 \\ \hline \end{array}$ $\begin{array}{r} 2 \\ +62 \\ \hline \end{array}$

Problem Solving

Solve.

10. Jim had 31 marbles.
He bought 8 more.
How many marbles
does he have now?

_____
+ _____

_____ marbles

Notes for Home Children practice two-digit addition. Then they solve a problem involving addition.

Name ______________________________ **Activity**

Adding Two-Digit Numbers

	tens	ones
	3	4
+	1	5
	4	9

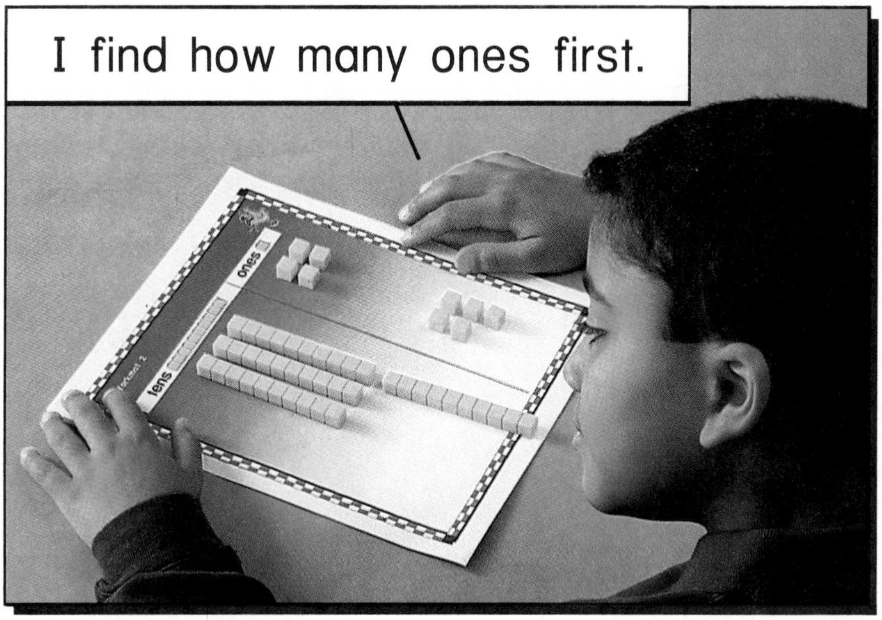

I find how many ones first.
ones
tens

Use Workmat 2.
Use tens and ones counters.
Add and record how many altogether.

1.

	tens	ones
	6	0
+	2	3

2.

	tens	ones
	4	4
+	3	4

3.

	tens	ones
	2	5
+	7	2

4.

	tens	ones
	3	1
+	2	4

5.

	tens	ones
	2	0
+	3	0

6.

	tens	ones
	1	3
+	6	5

Notes for Home Children explore at the CONCRETE level using tens and ones counters and a workmat to find sums of two-digit numbers.

Use Workmat 2.
Use tens and ones counters.
Add and record how many altogether.

7.

	tens	ones
	2	3
+	4	4
	6	7

8.

	tens	ones
	1	7
+	5	2

9.

	tens	ones
	1	2
+	3	1

10.

	tens	ones
	2	5
+	5	3

11.

	tens	ones
	2	7
+	2	1

12.

	tens	ones
	1	1
+	2	8

13.

	tens	ones
	5	3
+	4	6

14.

	tens	ones
	4	5
+	1	1

15.

	tens	ones
	1	4
+	1	2

16.

	tens	ones
	2	6
+	6	3

Notes for Home Children explore at the CONCRETE level using tens and ones counters and a workmat to find sums of two-digit numbers.

Name

Adding Two-Digit Numbers

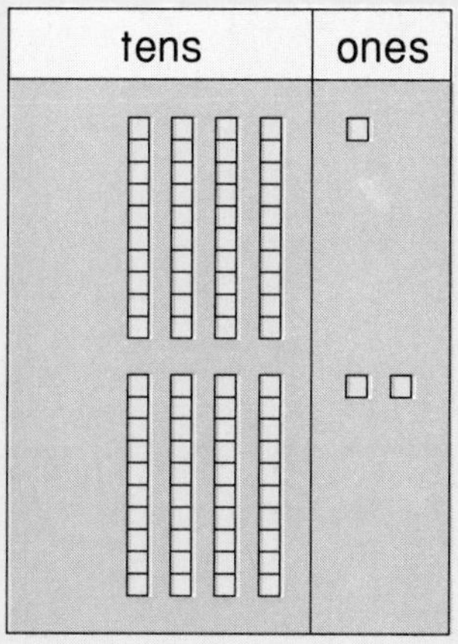

	tens	ones
	4	1
+	4	2
	8	3

Add.

1.

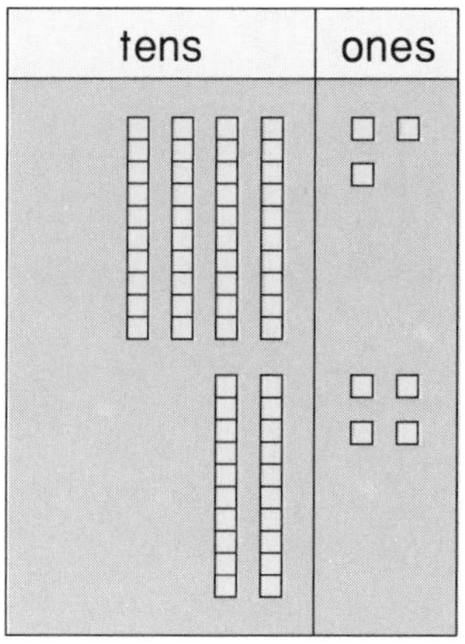

	tens	ones
	4	3
+	2	4

2.

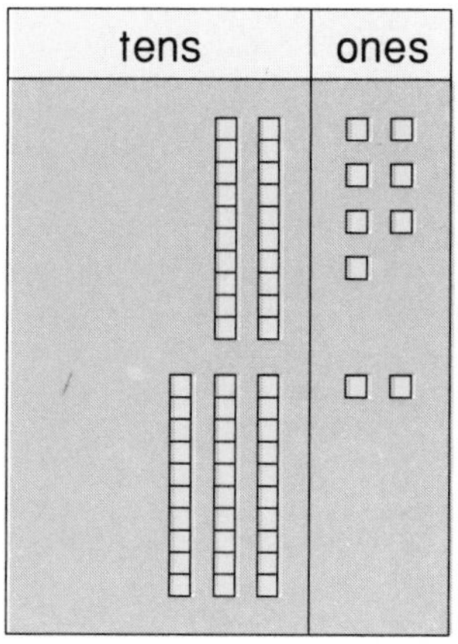

	tens	ones
	2	7
+	3	2

3.

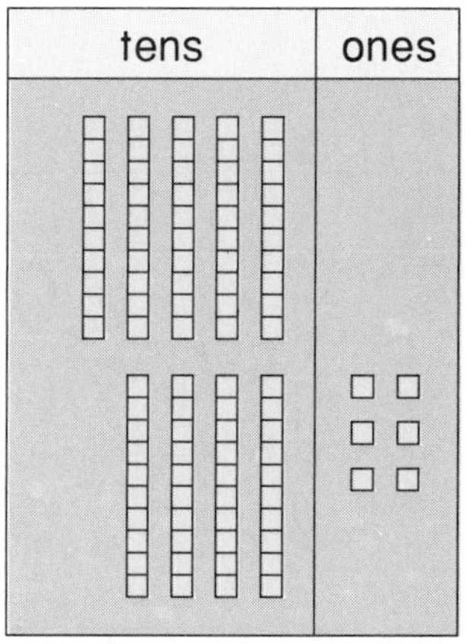

	tens	ones
	5	0
+	4	6

4.

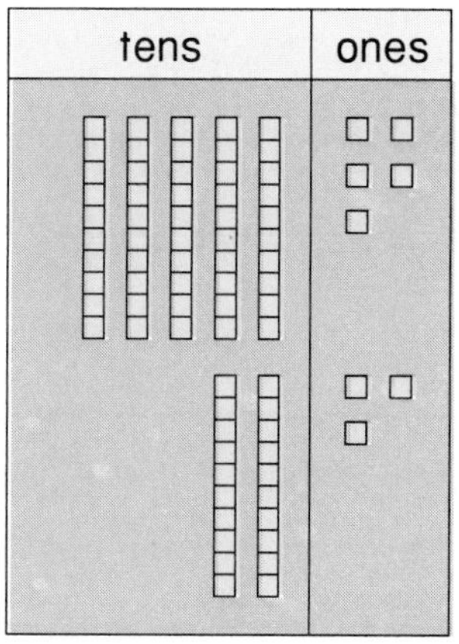

	tens	ones
	5	5
+	2	3

Notes for Home Children learn to find sums for two-digit numbers.

Add.

5.

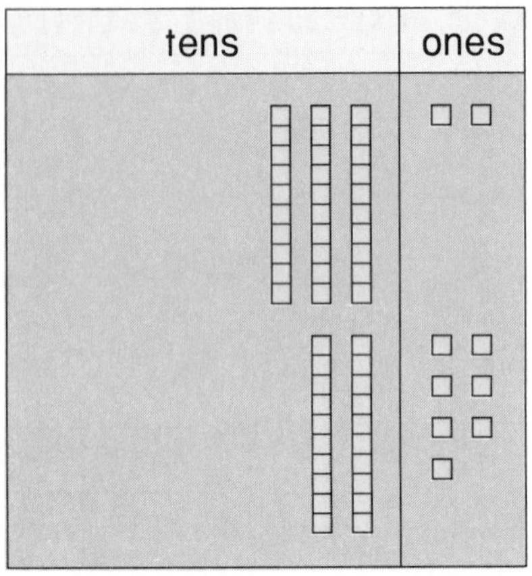

$$\begin{array}{r} 32 \\ +27 \\ \hline 59 \end{array}$$

6.

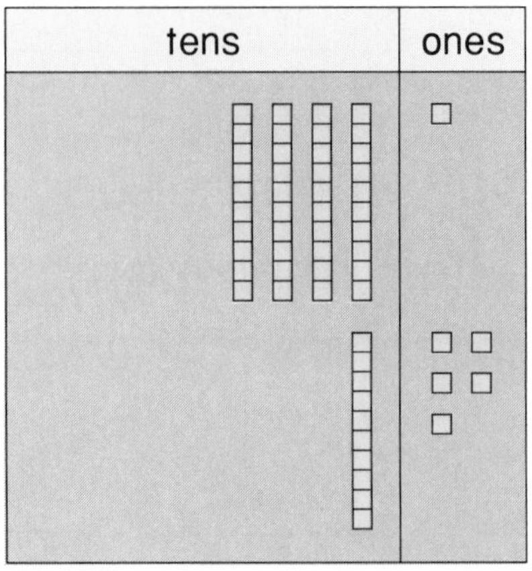

$$\begin{array}{r} 41 \\ +15 \\ \hline \end{array}$$

7. $\begin{array}{r} 64 \\ +13 \\ \hline \end{array}$ $\begin{array}{r} 47 \\ +52 \\ \hline \end{array}$ $\begin{array}{r} 34 \\ +34 \\ \hline \end{array}$ $\begin{array}{r} 25 \\ +61 \\ \hline \end{array}$ $\begin{array}{r} 16 \\ +23 \\ \hline \end{array}$ $\begin{array}{r} 38 \\ +50 \\ \hline \end{array}$

8. $\begin{array}{r} 32 \\ +64 \\ \hline \end{array}$ $\begin{array}{r} 10 \\ +72 \\ \hline \end{array}$ $\begin{array}{r} 12 \\ +16 \\ \hline \end{array}$ $\begin{array}{r} 23 \\ +34 \\ \hline \end{array}$ $\begin{array}{r} 43 \\ +55 \\ \hline \end{array}$ $\begin{array}{r} 62 \\ +22 \\ \hline \end{array}$

9. $\begin{array}{r} 24 \\ +15 \\ \hline \end{array}$ $\begin{array}{r} 36 \\ +21 \\ \hline \end{array}$ $\begin{array}{r} 70 \\ +20 \\ \hline \end{array}$ $\begin{array}{r} 22 \\ +25 \\ \hline \end{array}$ $\begin{array}{r} 47 \\ +21 \\ \hline \end{array}$ $\begin{array}{r} 81 \\ +18 \\ \hline \end{array}$

Talk About Math

Which is easier to add?
Why?

$\begin{array}{r} 26 \\ +43 \\ \hline \end{array}$ or $\begin{array}{r} 20 \\ +70 \\ \hline \end{array}$

Notes for Home Children practice two-digit addition. Then they verbalize about adding.

See More Practice Set A on page 455.

Name

PROBLEM-SOLVING STRATEGY

Try and Check

Each child bought two toys.
Ring what they bought.

1. Adam spent 86¢.

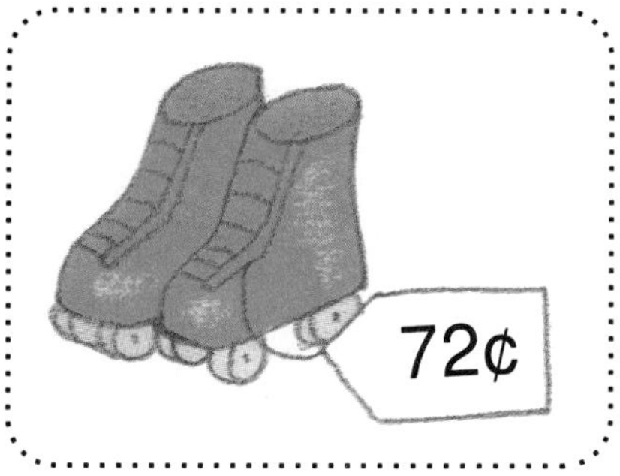

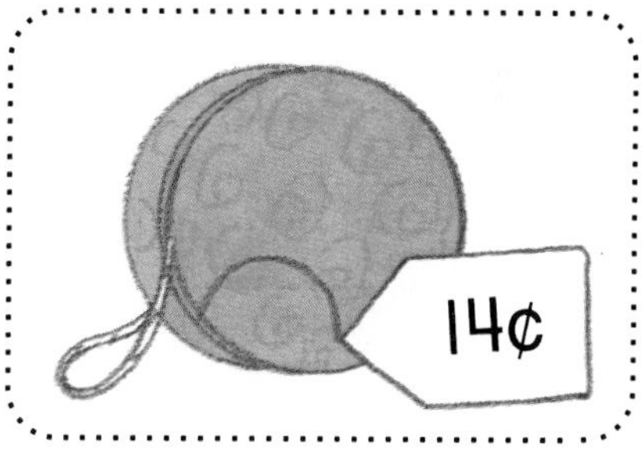

2. Dan spent 99¢.

Notes for Home Children solve problems involving money by trying and checking.

Each child bought two toys.
Ring what they bought.

3. Greg spent 87¢.

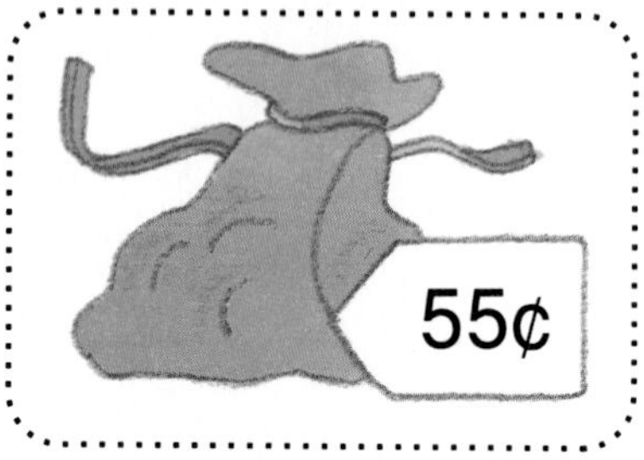

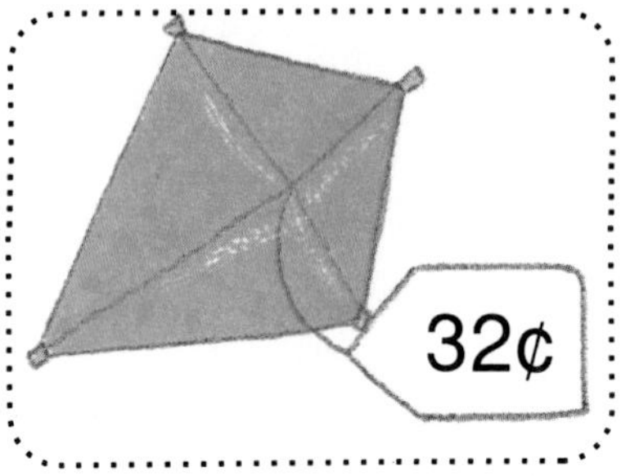

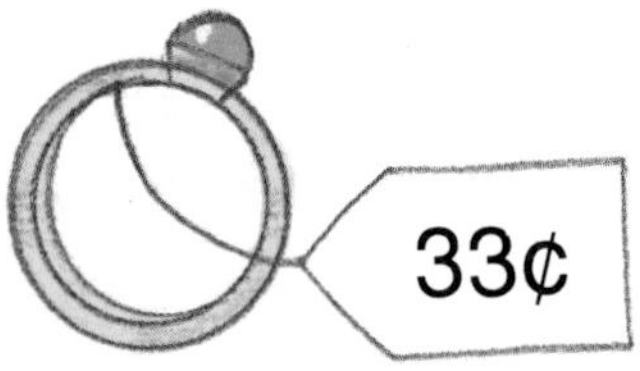

4. Lisa spent 98¢.

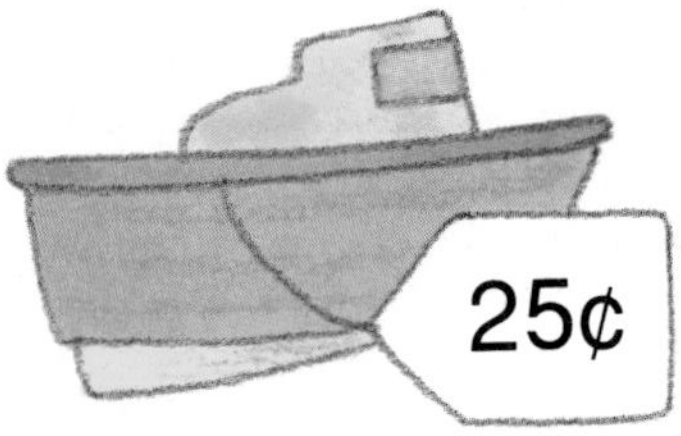

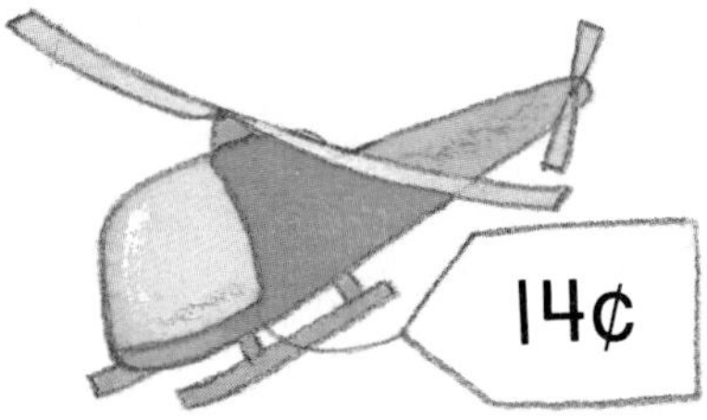

5. Steve spent 75¢.

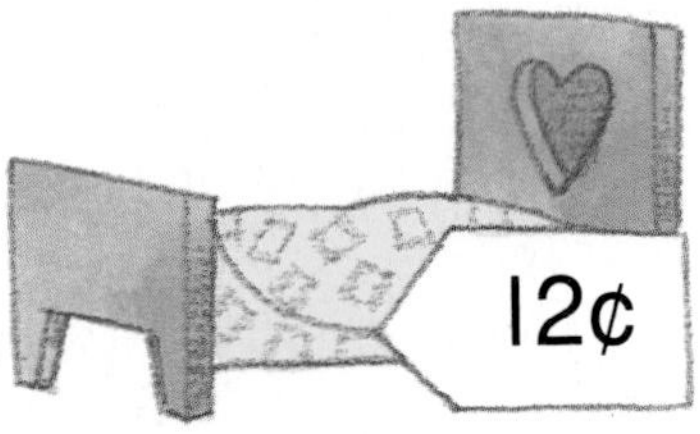

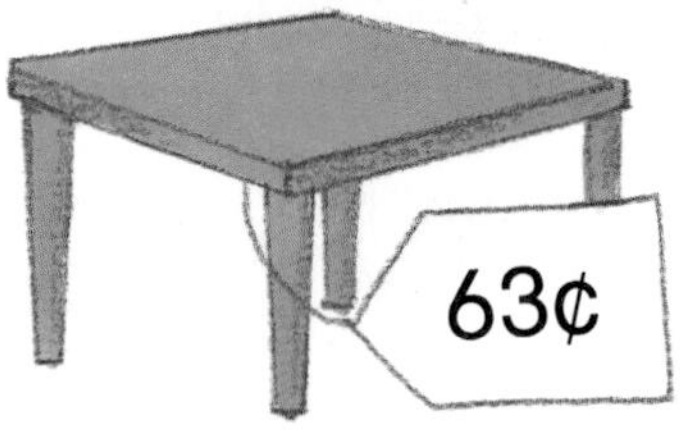

6. Peg spent 68¢.

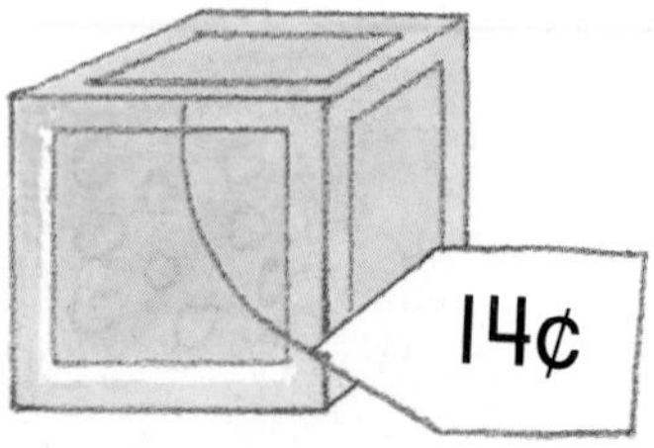

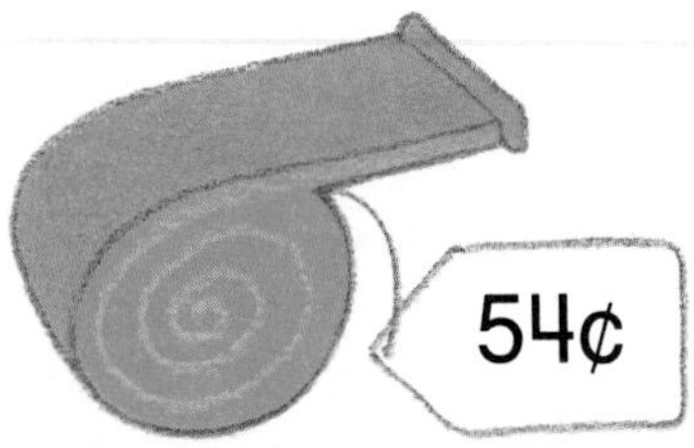

Notes for Home Children solve problems involving money by trying and checking.

Number Sense

Write six pairs of numbers that add up to 50.

1. ______ **2.** ______ **3.** ______

4. ______ **5.** ______ **6.** ______

Let's do some more!

Write six pairs of numbers that add up to 99.

Notes for Home Children develop an understanding of numbers by finding different combinations that make 50.

SKILLS REVIEW

Skills Review

Fill in the correct ◯.
Add or subtract.

1. $\begin{array}{r} 9 \\ +8 \\ \hline \end{array}$ Ⓐ 15 Ⓑ 17 Ⓒ 18	2. $\begin{array}{r} 14 \\ -9 \\ \hline \end{array}$ Ⓐ 8 Ⓑ 7 Ⓒ 5	3. $17 - 8 =$ Ⓐ 9 Ⓑ 8 Ⓒ 7
4. $7 + 6 =$ Ⓐ 11 Ⓑ 12 Ⓒ 13	5. $\begin{array}{r} 16 \\ -7 \\ \hline \end{array}$ Ⓐ 9 Ⓑ 7 Ⓒ 6	6. $\begin{array}{r} 6 \\ +8 \\ \hline \end{array}$ Ⓐ 12 Ⓑ 14 Ⓒ 16
7. $\begin{array}{r} 13 \\ -7 \\ \hline \end{array}$ Ⓐ 6 Ⓑ 7 Ⓒ 8	8. $9 + 7 =$ Ⓐ 14 Ⓑ 15 Ⓒ 16	9. $18 - 9 =$ Ⓐ 7 Ⓑ 8 Ⓒ 9

Vocabulary

Read the riddle. Match.

10. I am a shape.
I have four sides the same length. •

11. Another name for me is one cent. •

12. You use me to measure how long. •

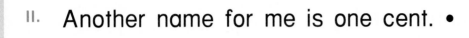

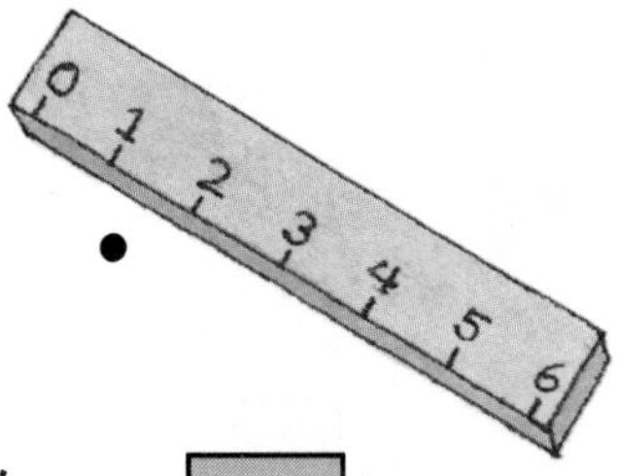

Notes for Home Children review addition and subtraction facts through 18. Then they answer riddles by using math terms.

Name

Subtracting a One-Digit Number from a Two-Digit Number

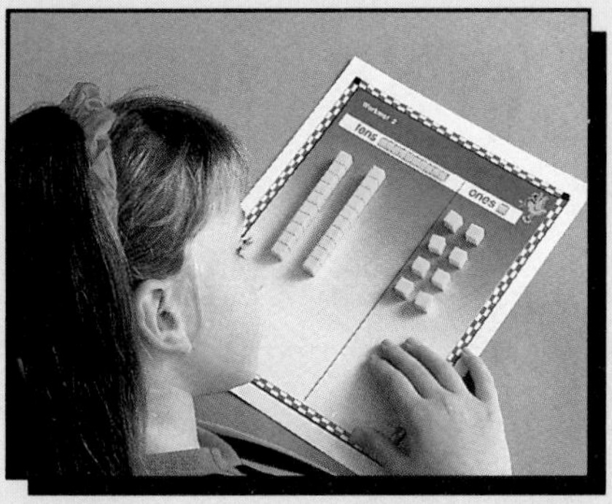

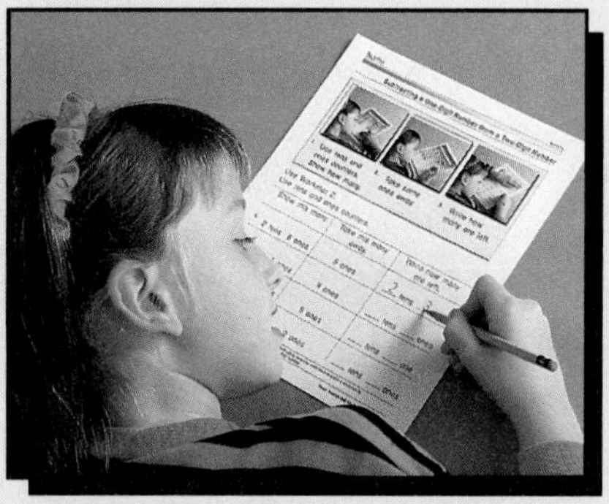

1. Use tens and ones counters. Show how many.
2. Take some ones away.
3. Write how many are left.

Use Workmat 2.
Use tens and ones counters.

Show this many.	Take this many away.	Write how many are left.
1. 2 tens 8 ones	5 ones	2 tens 3 ones
2. 7 tens 6 ones	4 ones	___ tens ___ ones
3. 4 tens 6 ones	5 ones	___ tens ___ one
4. 6 tens 5 ones	2 ones	___ tens ___ ones

Notes for Home Children explore at the CONCRETE level using tens and ones counters and a workmat to subtract a one-digit number from a two-digit number.

Use Workmat 2.

Use tens and ones counters.

	Show this many.	Take this many away.	Write how many are left.
5.	3 tens 5 ones	3 ones	3 tens 2 ones
6.	6 tens 8 ones	6 ones	___ tens ___ ones
7.	5 tens 7 ones	2 ones	___ tens ___ ones
8.	9 tens 9 ones	5 ones	___ tens ___ ones
9.	7 tens 8 ones	4 ones	___ tens ___ ones
10.	4 tens 7 ones	5 ones	___ tens ___ ones
11.	2 tens 9 ones	3 ones	___ tens ___ ones

Notes for Home Children explore at the CONCRETE level using tens and ones counters and a workmat to subtract a one-digit number from a two-digit number.

Name

Subtracting a One-Digit Number from a Two-Digit Number

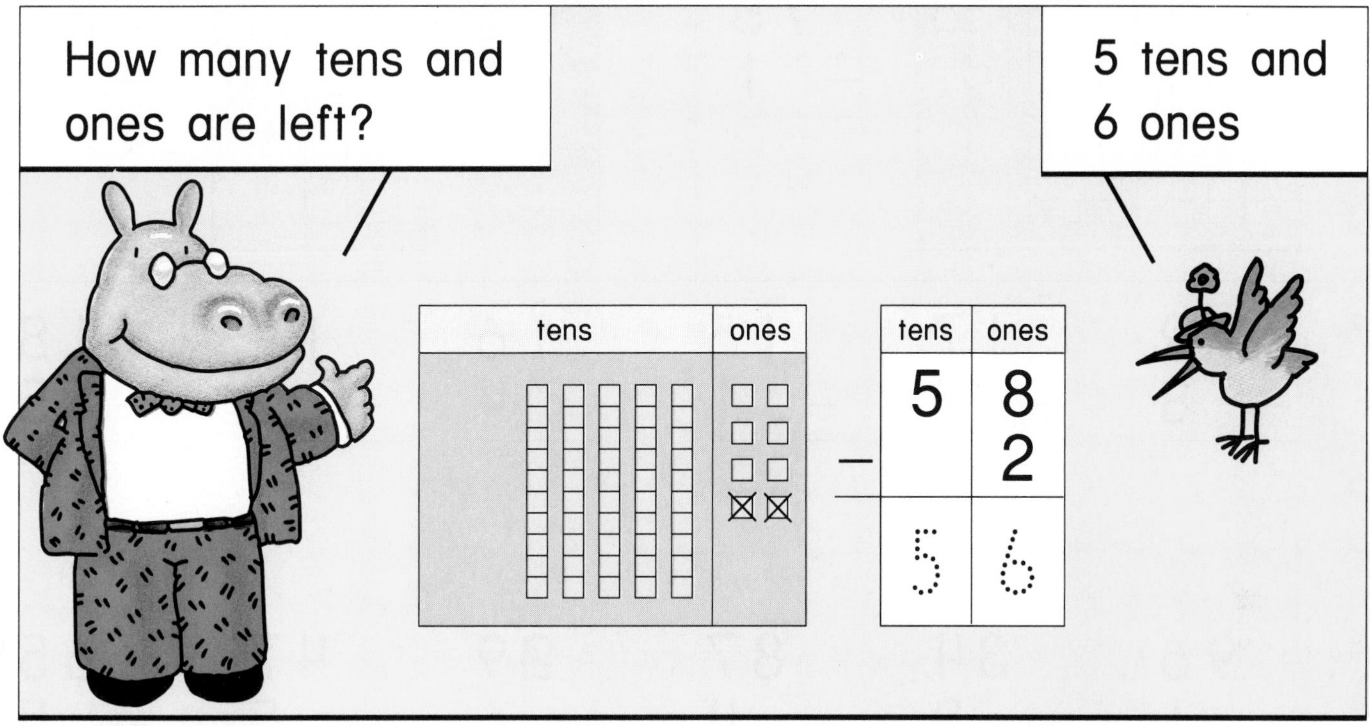
How many tens and ones are left?
5 tens and 6 ones
tens
ones
tens
ones
5
8
−
2
5
6

Subtract.

1.

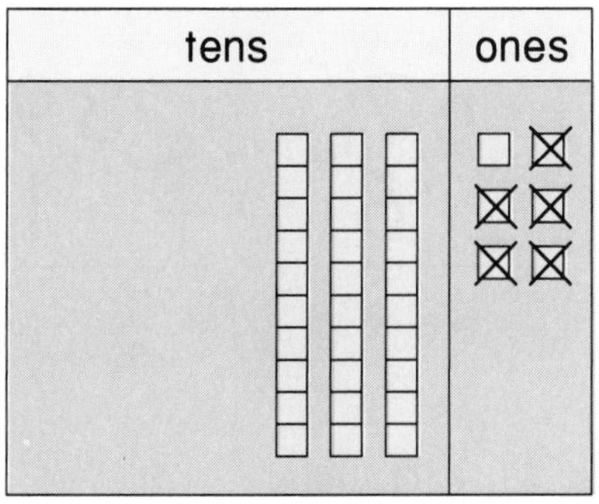

	tens	ones
	3	6
−		5

2.

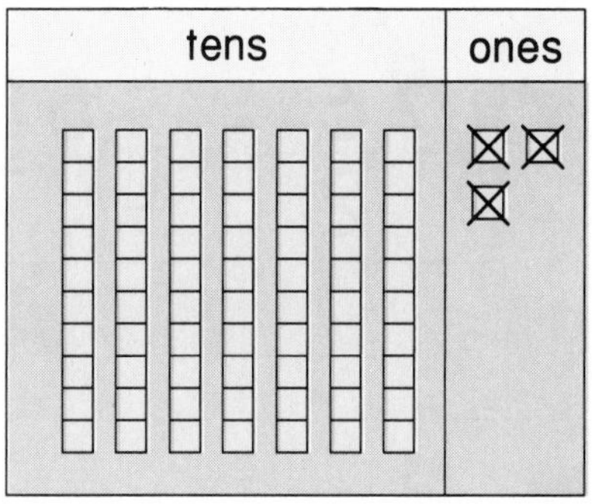

	tens	ones
	7	3
−		3

3.

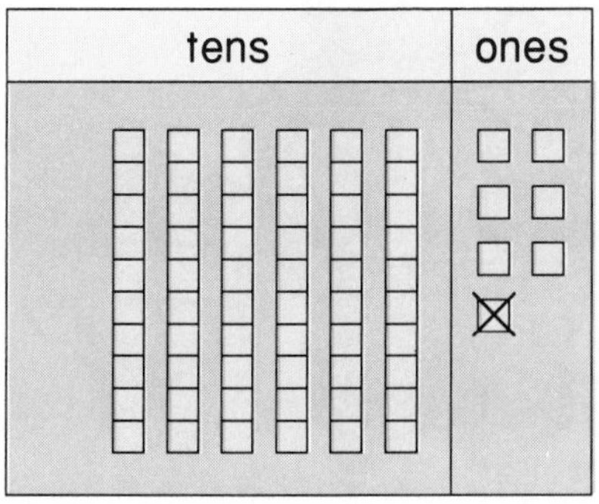

	tens	ones
	6	7
−		1

4.

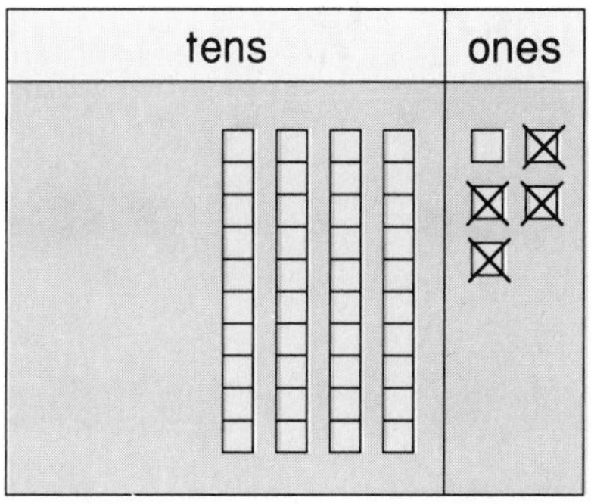

	tens	ones
	4	5
−		4

Notes for Home Children learn to subtract a one-digit number from a two-digit number using pictures.

Subtract.

5. 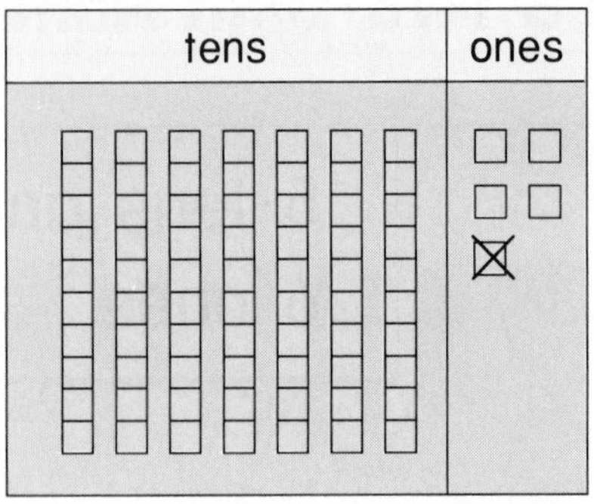

$$\begin{array}{r} 75 \\ -\ 1 \\ \hline 74 \end{array}$$

6. 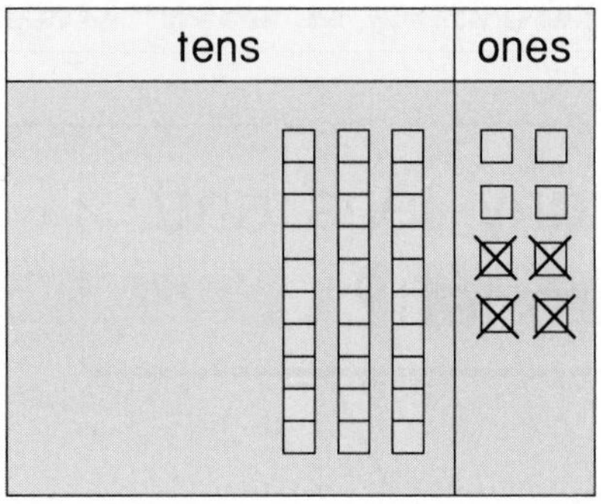

$$\begin{array}{r} 38 \\ -\ 4 \\ \hline \end{array}$$

7.
$\begin{array}{r} 19 \\ -\ 8 \\ \hline \end{array}$ $\begin{array}{r} 17 \\ -\ 7 \\ \hline \end{array}$ $\begin{array}{r} 15 \\ -\ 1 \\ \hline \end{array}$ $\begin{array}{r} 16 \\ -\ 4 \\ \hline \end{array}$ $\begin{array}{r} 19 \\ -\ 2 \\ \hline \end{array}$ $\begin{array}{r} 18 \\ -\ 5 \\ \hline \end{array}$

8.
$\begin{array}{r} 96 \\ -\ 1 \\ \hline \end{array}$ $\begin{array}{r} 34 \\ -\ 3 \\ \hline \end{array}$ $\begin{array}{r} 87 \\ -\ 4 \\ \hline \end{array}$ $\begin{array}{r} 29 \\ -\ 6 \\ \hline \end{array}$ $\begin{array}{r} 47 \\ -\ 5 \\ \hline \end{array}$ $\begin{array}{r} 65 \\ -\ 5 \\ \hline \end{array}$

9.
$\begin{array}{r} 29 \\ -\ 4 \\ \hline \end{array}$ $\begin{array}{r} 76 \\ -\ 2 \\ \hline \end{array}$ $\begin{array}{r} 58 \\ -\ 7 \\ \hline \end{array}$ $\begin{array}{r} 95 \\ -\ 3 \\ \hline \end{array}$ $\begin{array}{r} 67 \\ -\ 6 \\ \hline \end{array}$ $\begin{array}{r} 39 \\ -\ 1 \\ \hline \end{array}$

10.
$\begin{array}{r} 68 \\ -\ 2 \\ \hline \end{array}$ $\begin{array}{r} 49 \\ -\ 9 \\ \hline \end{array}$ $\begin{array}{r} 36 \\ -\ 4 \\ \hline \end{array}$

Notes for Home Children practice two-digit subtraction.

Name

Subtracting Two-Digit Numbers

	tens	ones
	5	6
−	4	3
	1	3

I find how many ones are left first.

Use Workmat 2.
Use tens and ones counters.
Subtract and record how many are left.

1.

	tens	ones
	3	9
−	1	2

2.

	tens	ones
	7	0
−	3	0

3.

	tens	ones
	6	4
−	1	3

4.

	tens	ones
	9	8
−	4	5

5.

	tens	ones
	8	9
−	3	5

6.

	tens	ones
	4	7
−	2	0

Notes for Home Children explore at the CONCRETE level using tens and ones counters and a workmat to find differences of two-digit numbers.

Use Workmat 2.
Use tens and ones counters.
Subtract and record how many are left.

7.

tens	ones
8	5
− 6	1
2	4

8.

tens	ones
9	3
− 7	2

9.

tens	ones
4	8
− 1	4

10.

tens	ones
7	7
− 4	5

11.

tens	ones
8	9
− 1	3

12.

tens	ones
6	5
− 5	0

13.

tens	ones
9	2
− 6	1

14.

tens	ones
7	4
− 1	4

15.

tens	ones
5	7
− 2	2

16.

tens	ones
6	8
− 4	3

Notes for Home Children explore at the CONCRETE level using tens and ones counters and a workmat to find differences of two-digit numbers.

Name

Subtracting Two-Digit Numbers

I find how many ones are left.
Then I find how many tens are left.

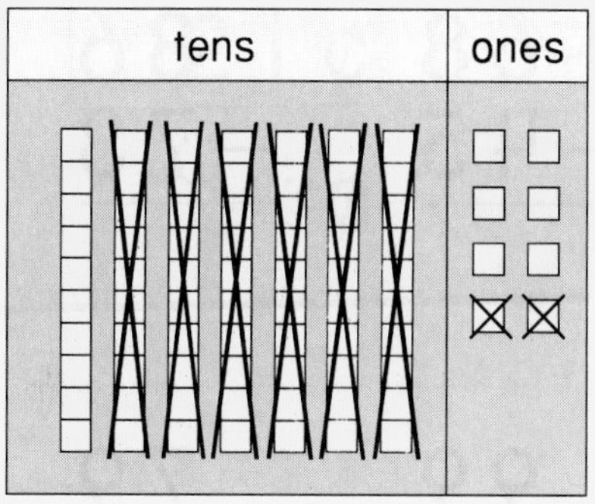

	tens	ones
	7	8
−	6	2
	1	6

Subtract.

1.

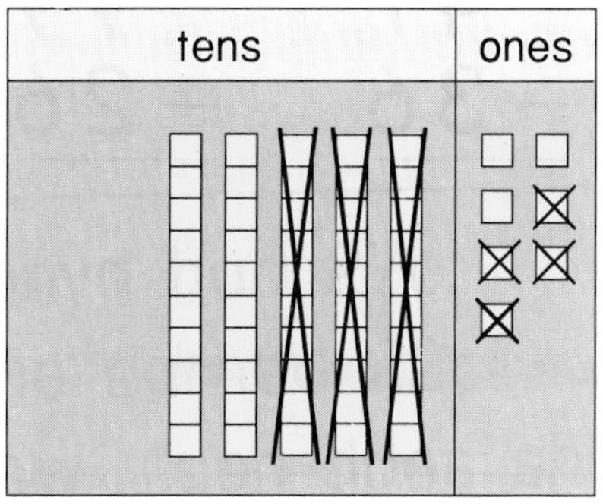

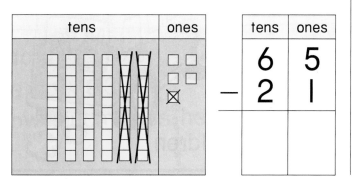

	tens	ones
	5	7
−	3	4

2.

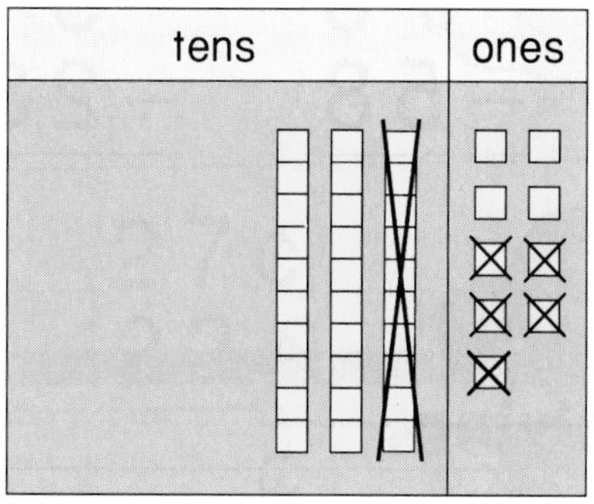

	tens	ones
	3	9
−	1	5

3.

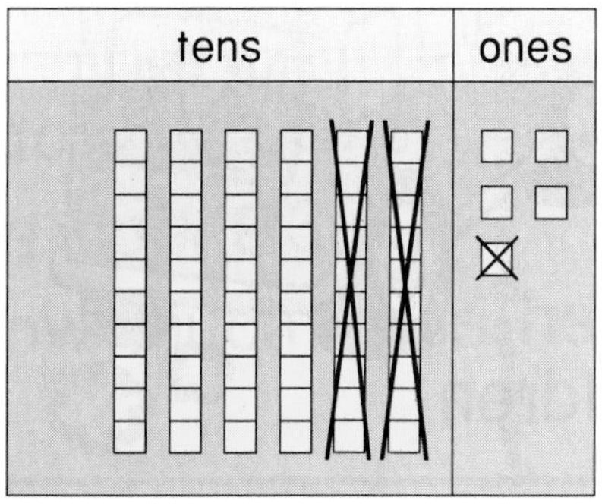

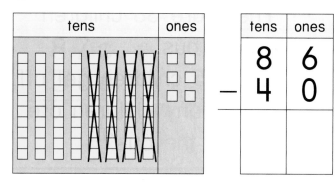

	tens	ones
	6	5
−	2	1

4.

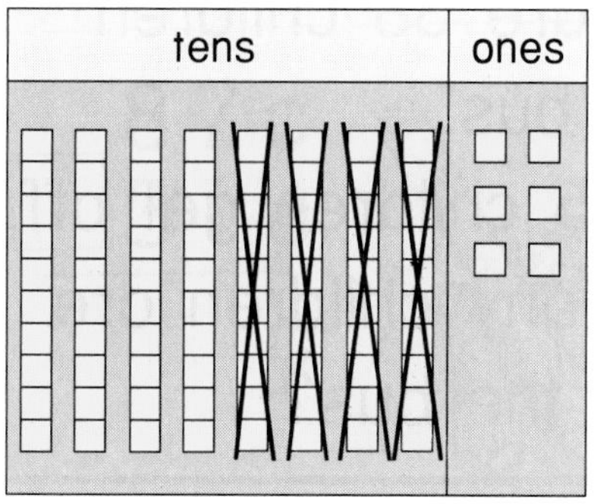

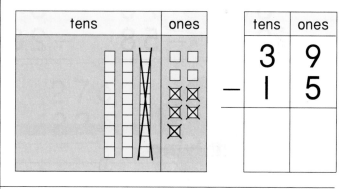

	tens	ones
	8	6
−	4	0

Notes for Home Children learn to subtract two-digit numbers.

Problem-Solving Workshop

Explore with a Calculator

Use a 🖩 to solve.

1. Tony had 97¢. He bought the ball. How much does he have now?

71 ¢

2. Ann bought the boat and the skates. How much did she spend?

___ ¢

3. Gina had 89¢. She bought the doll. How much does she have now?

___ ¢

4. Jim bought the truck and the teddy bear. How much did he spend?

___ ¢

5. Steve bought the ball and the boat. How much did he spend?

___ ¢

6. Diane had 76¢. She bought the skates. How much does she have now?

___ ¢

Notes for Home Children explore with a calculator to solve addition and subtraction problems.

Name ______________________

More Practice

Set A Use after page 438.

Add.

1.

32	41	46	12	28	9
+ 26	+ 6	+ 52	+ 74	+ 11	+ 70
58					

2.

71	20	51	26	52	21
+ 21	+ 30	+ 14	+ 3	+ 32	+ 54

Set B Use after page 450.

Subtract.

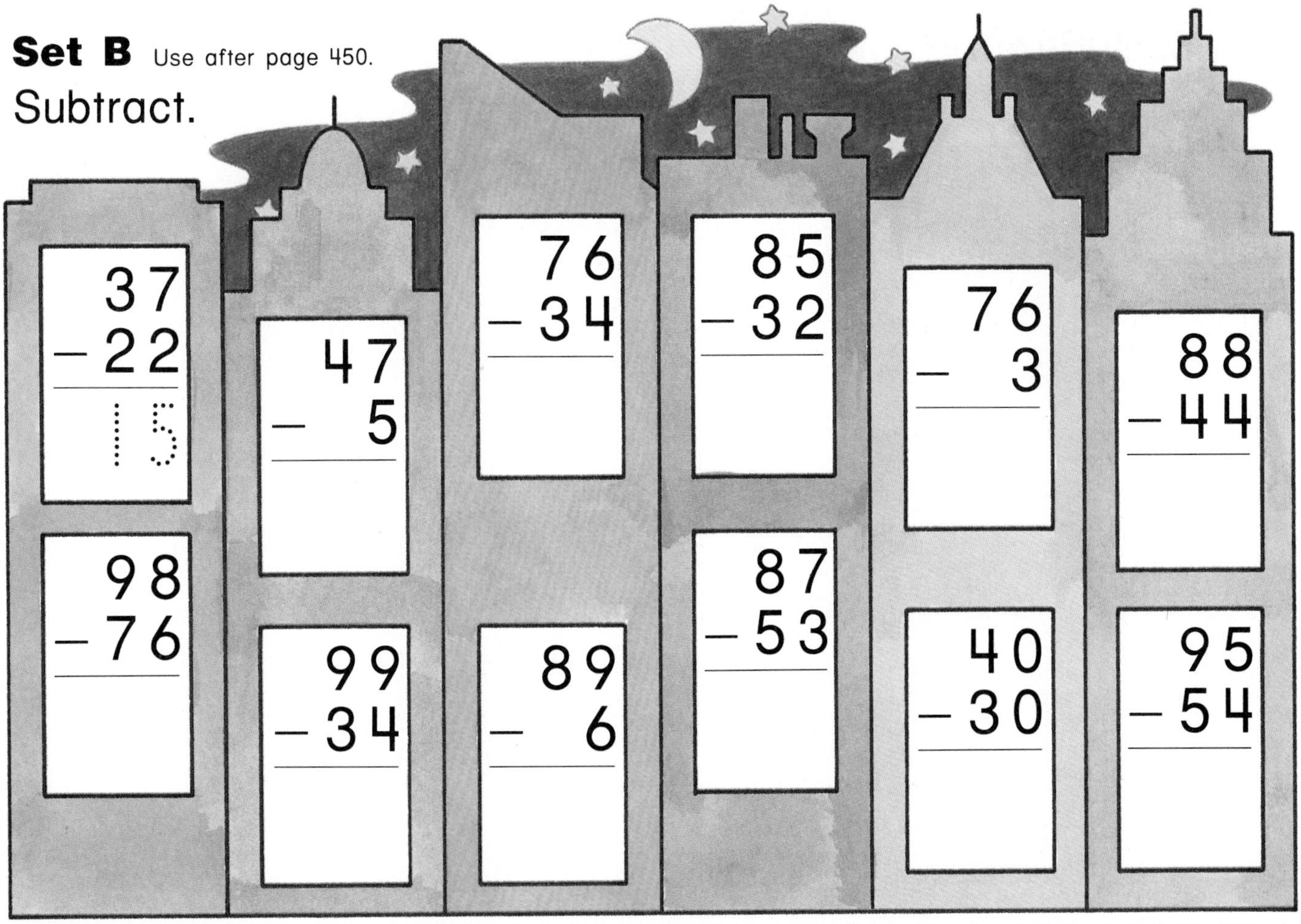

37	47	76	85	76	88
− 22	− 5	− 34	− 32	− 3	− 44
15					
98	99	89	87	40	95
− 76	− 34	− 6	− 53	− 30	− 54

Notes for Home Set A: Children practice two-digit addition.
Set B: Children practice two-digit subtraction.

Enrichment

I need to trade 10 ones for 1 ten. Then I add.

I need to trade 1 ten for 10 ones. Then I subtract.

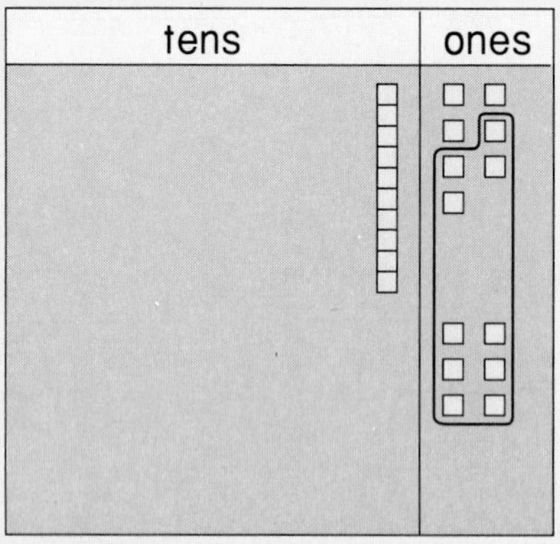

$$\begin{array}{r} 17 \\ +\ 6 \\ \hline 23 \end{array}$$

$$\begin{array}{r} 25 \\ -\ 9 \\ \hline 16 \end{array}$$

Add or subtract.

1.

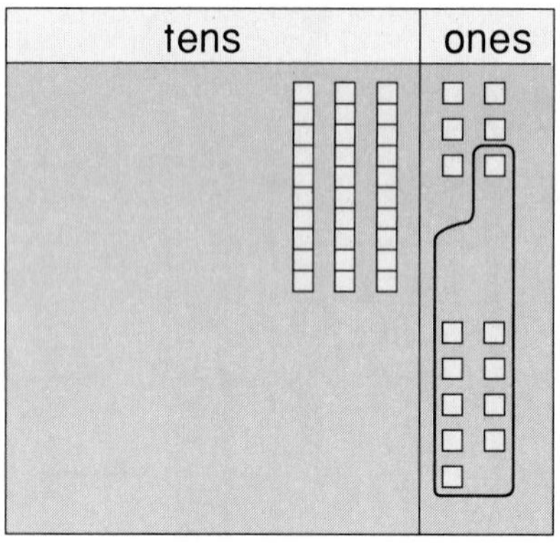

$$\begin{array}{r} 36 \\ +\ 9 \\ \hline \end{array}$$

2.

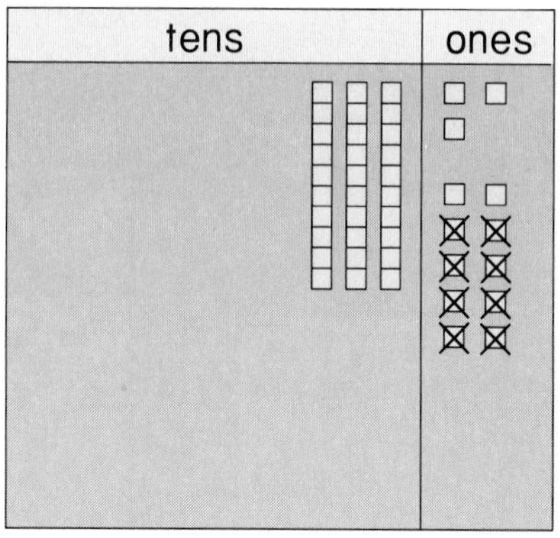

$$\begin{array}{r} 43 \\ -\ 8 \\ \hline \end{array}$$

3.

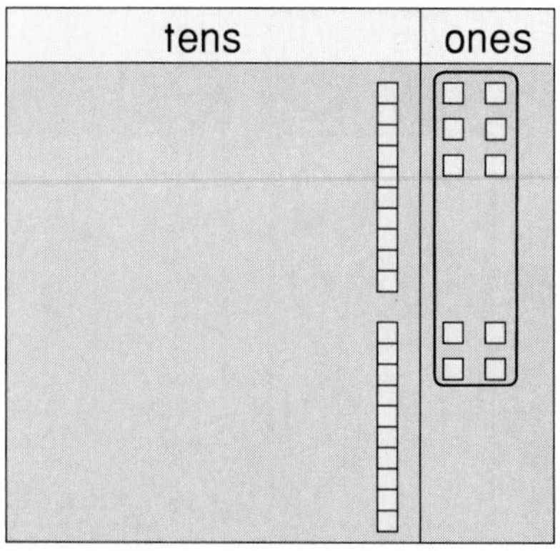

$$\begin{array}{r} 16 \\ +14 \\ \hline \end{array}$$

4.

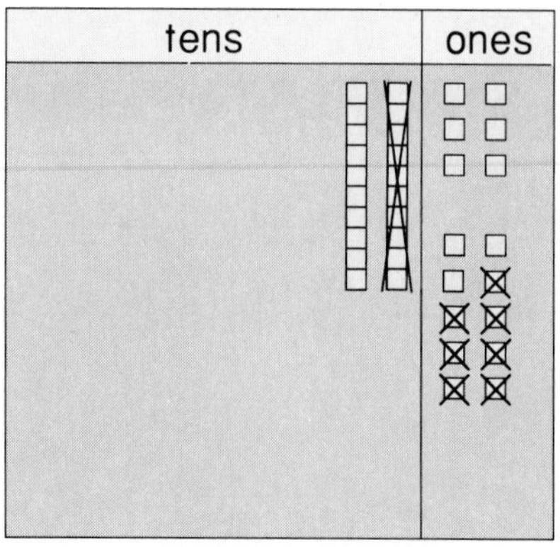

$$\begin{array}{r} 36 \\ -17 \\ \hline \end{array}$$

Notes for Home Children are challenged to find answers for addition and subtraction exercises.

Name

Chapter 14 Review/Test

Add or subtract.

1.

53	45	37	79	94	87
+ 5	+ 20	+ 22	− 6	− 52	− 24

Add.

2.

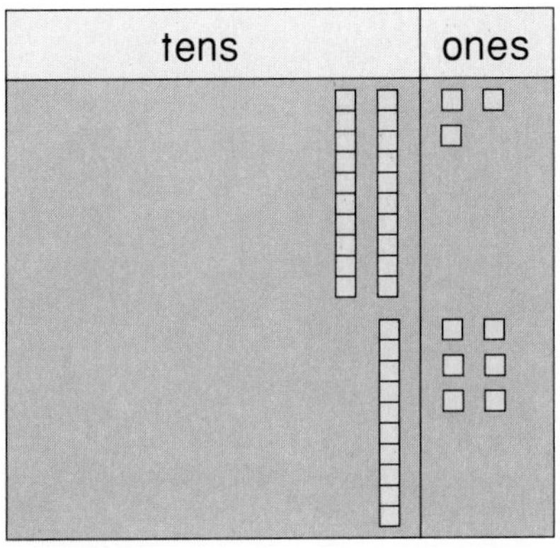

$$\begin{array}{r} 23 \\ +16 \\ \hline \end{array}$$

Write + or − in the box.
Then solve.

3. Sue had 76¢.
She spent 24¢.
How much does
she have now?

$$\begin{array}{r} 76¢ \\ \square\ 24¢ \\ \hline ¢ \end{array}$$

Subtract.

4.

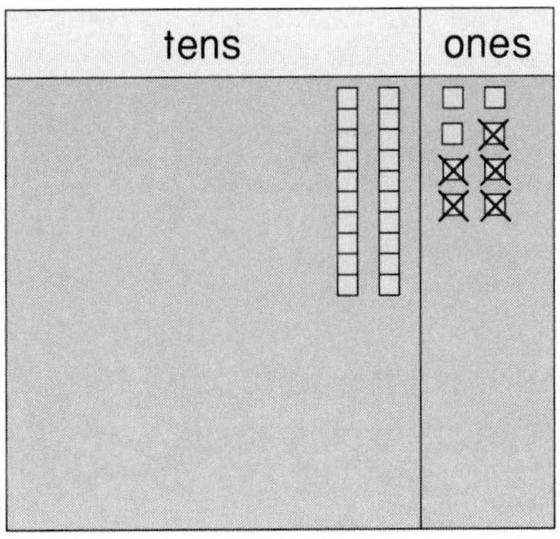

$$\begin{array}{r} 28 \\ -\ \ 5 \\ \hline \end{array}$$

5.

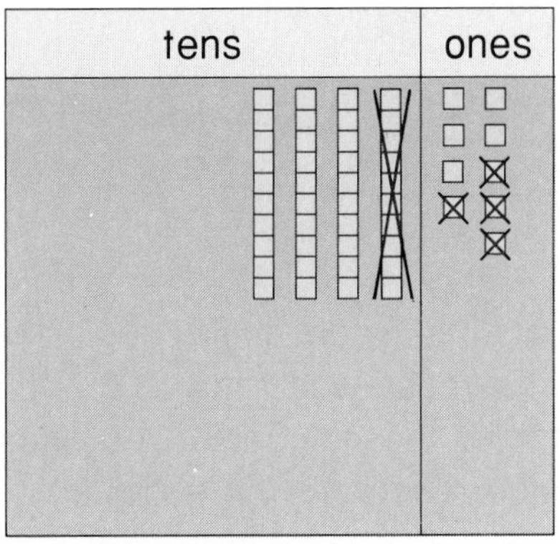

$$\begin{array}{r} 49 \\ -14 \\ \hline \end{array}$$

Ring two items.

6. Cliff spent 98¢.
What did he buy?

Notes for Home Children are assessed on Chapter 14 concepts, skills, and problem solving.

Exploring MATH AT HOME

Exploring Math at Home

Dear Family,

In this chapter I have learned to add and subtract two-digit numbers. Please help me with the activities below.

Love, ______________________________

1.

Go grocery shopping. Look at the register tape of items that cost less than $1.00. Put a circle around the number in the ones place. Put a square around the number in the tens place.

2.

Use bundles of ten straws and loose ones to add and subtract tens and ones through 99. Practice some problems daily.

Please continue to review math skills and concepts your child has learned this year. It is helpful to review skills and concepts by using objects from home.

Name ____________________

Cumulative Review/Test

Fill in the correct ⬭.
Add or subtract.

1. $\begin{array}{r} 12 \\ -\ 5 \\ \hline \end{array}$

4 Ⓐ 7 Ⓑ 9 Ⓒ

2. $14 - 8 =$

6 Ⓐ 8 Ⓑ 9 Ⓒ

3. $\begin{array}{r} 9 \\ +\ 7 \\ \hline \end{array}$

13 Ⓐ 14 Ⓑ 16 Ⓒ

4. $8 + 9 =$

12 Ⓐ 16 Ⓑ 17 Ⓒ

5. $\begin{array}{r} 2 \\ +\ 8 \\ \hline \end{array}$

7 Ⓐ 9 Ⓑ 10 Ⓒ

6. $\begin{array}{r} 15 \\ -\ 6 \\ \hline \end{array}$

6 Ⓐ 9 Ⓑ 10 Ⓒ

7. $11 - 8 =$

1 Ⓐ 3 Ⓑ 5 Ⓒ

8. $\begin{array}{r} 4 \\ +\ 9 \\ \hline \end{array}$

13 Ⓐ 15 Ⓑ 16 Ⓒ

9. $\begin{array}{r} 75 \\ -\ 40 \\ \hline \end{array}$

30 Ⓐ 35 Ⓑ 45 Ⓒ

10. $\begin{array}{r} 89 \\ -\ 42 \\ \hline \end{array}$

47 Ⓐ 49 Ⓑ 57 Ⓒ

11. $\begin{array}{r} 32 \\ +\ 54 \\ \hline \end{array}$

78 Ⓐ 86 Ⓑ 89 Ⓒ

12. $\begin{array}{r} 6 \\ 4 \\ +\ 7 \\ \hline \end{array}$

14 Ⓐ 15 Ⓑ 17 Ⓒ

Notes for Home Children are assessed on Chapters 1-14 concepts, skills, and problem solving using a multiple-choice format.

Fill in the correct ⬭.

13. Which shows equal parts?

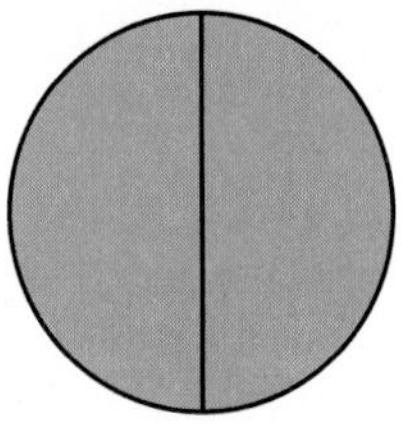

Ⓐ

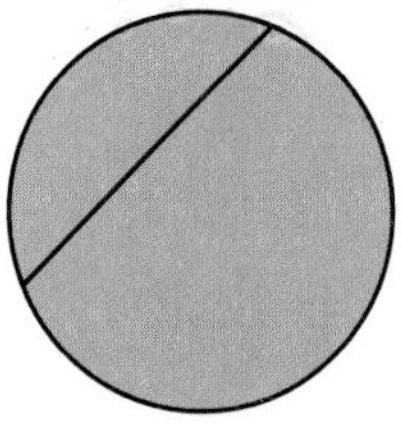

Ⓑ

14. How much money?

36¢ Ⓐ 46¢ Ⓑ 56¢ Ⓒ

15. How many?

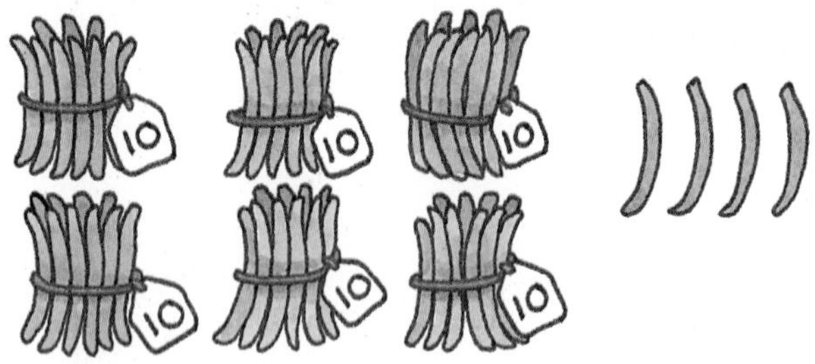

54 Ⓐ 60 Ⓑ 64 Ⓒ

16. What time is shown?

1:00 Ⓐ 1:30 Ⓑ 10:30 Ⓒ

17. What comes next?

L M N L M N L ____

L Ⓐ M Ⓑ N Ⓒ

18. Solve.

Ed started working at 2:00.
He worked for 1 hour.
What time did he stop?

3:00 Ⓐ 4:00 Ⓑ 5:00 Ⓒ

19. James had 12¢.
He spent 4¢.
How much does
he have now?

5¢ Ⓐ 6¢ Ⓑ 8¢ Ⓒ

20. Amy had 7¢.
She found 4¢ more.
How much does
she have now?

1¢ Ⓐ 10¢ Ⓑ 11¢ Ⓒ

Notes for Home Children are assessed on Chapters 1-14 concepts, skills, and problem solving using a multiple-choice format.

add

$2 + 3 = 5$

after

1, 2, 3, 4, 5

4 comes **after** 3.

amount

The **amount** is 6 cents.

before

1, 2, 3, 4, 5

2 comes **before** 3.

between

1, 2, 3, 4, 5

3 comes **between** 2 and 4.

cent (¢)

1¢

centimeter (cm)

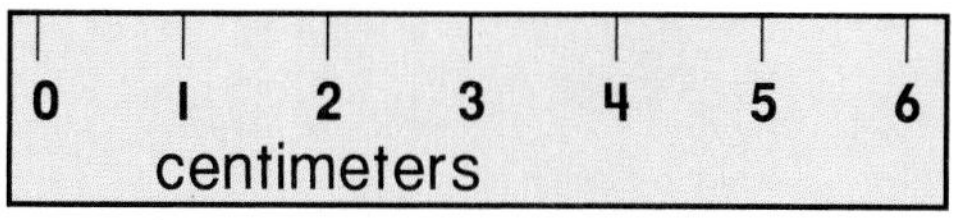

circle

cone

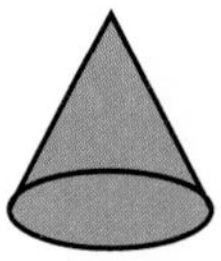

cube

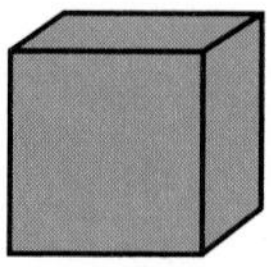

cup

cylinder

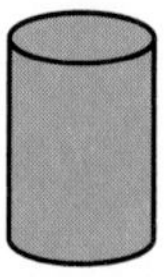

difference

$7 - 1 = 6$

$$\begin{array}{r} 7 \\ -\ 1 \\ \hline 6 \end{array}$$

difference

Notes for Home Children use a picture glossary for Grade One math vocabulary development.

dime

10¢

doubles

$$4 + 4 = 8$$
$$8 - 4 = 4$$

equal parts

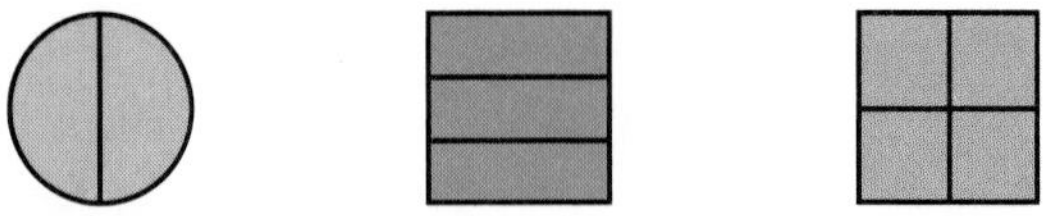

halves **thirds** **fourths**

family of facts

$3 + 5 = 8$ $8 - 5 = 3$

$5 + 3 = 8$ $8 - 3 = 5$

greater than

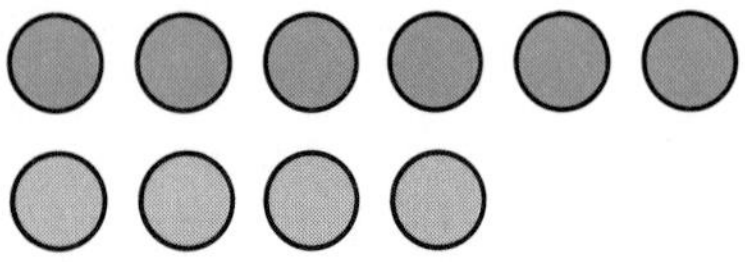

6 is **greater than** 4.

heavier

hour hand

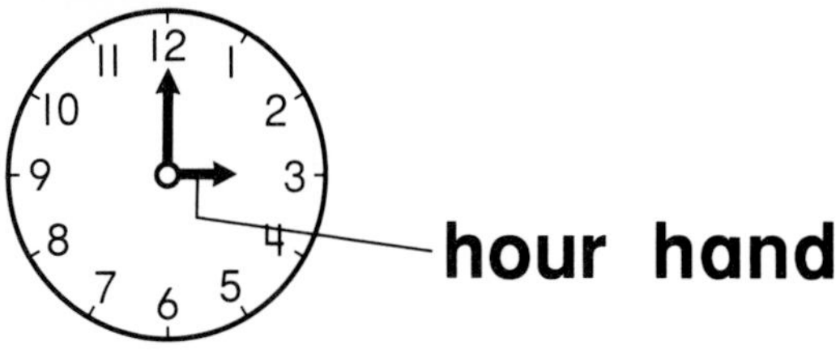

inch

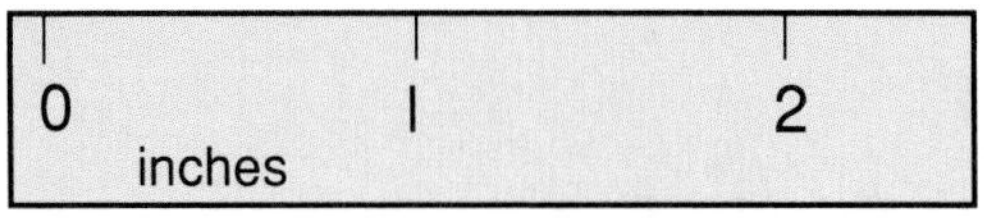

inside

The pear is **inside** the bowl.

kilogram

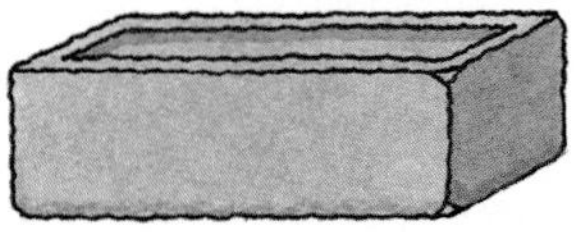

The brick is about as heavy as 1 **kilogram**.

less than

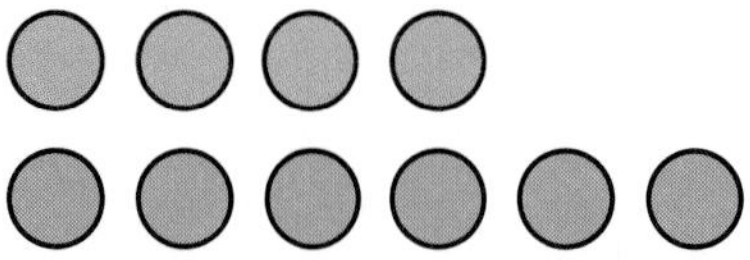

4 is **less than** 6.

lighter

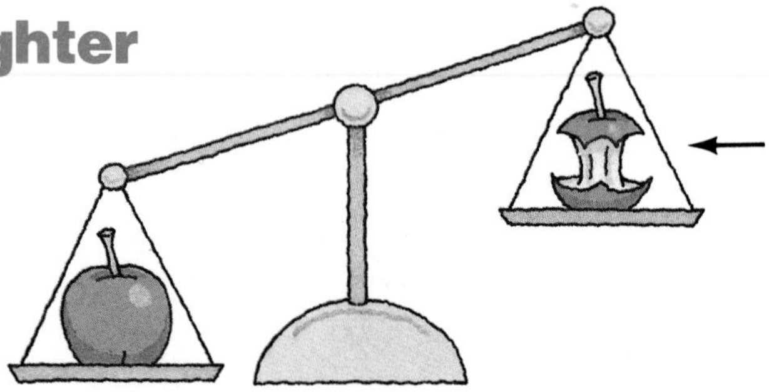

Notes for Home Children use a picture glossary for Grade One math vocabulary development.

liter

longer

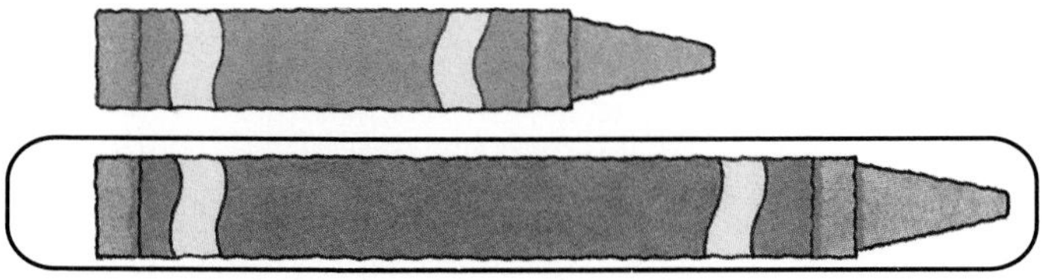

longest

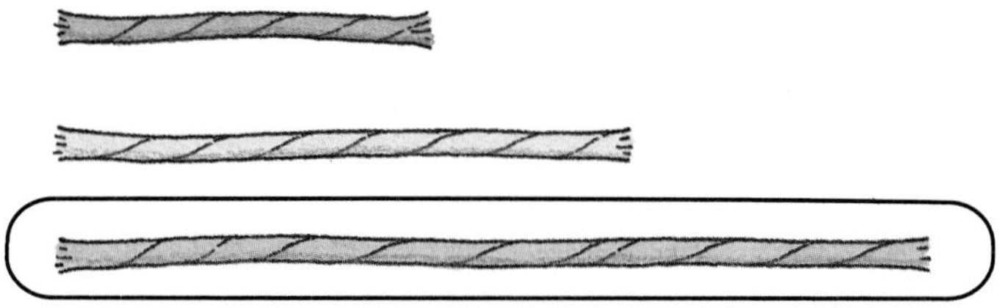

minute hand

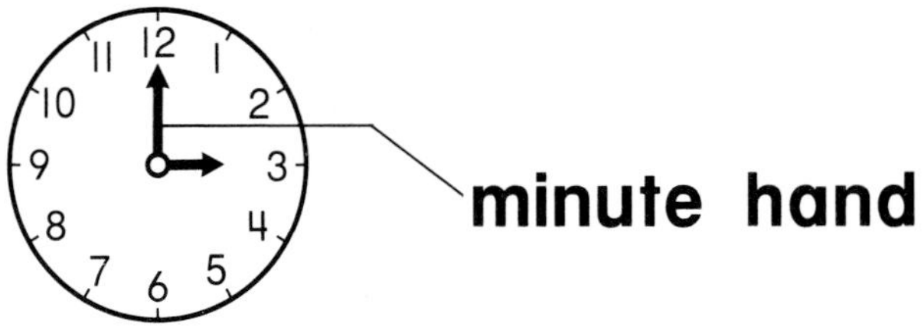

money

nickel

5¢

number sentence

$1 + 4 = 5$

$6 - 2 = 4$

ones

5 ones

ordinal

first second third fourth

outside

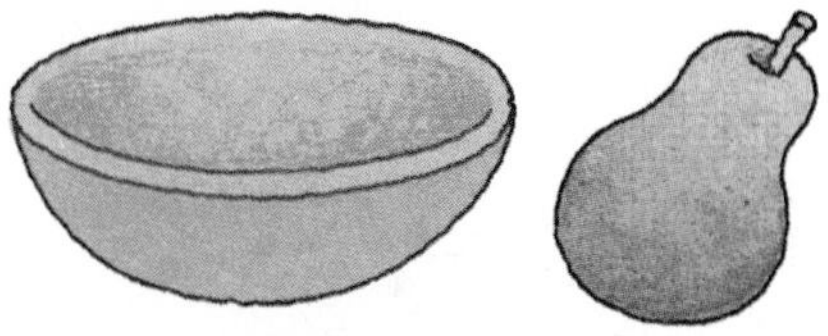

The pear is **outside** the bowl.

penny

1¢

pint

Notes for Home Children use a picture glossary for Grade One math vocabulary development.

pound

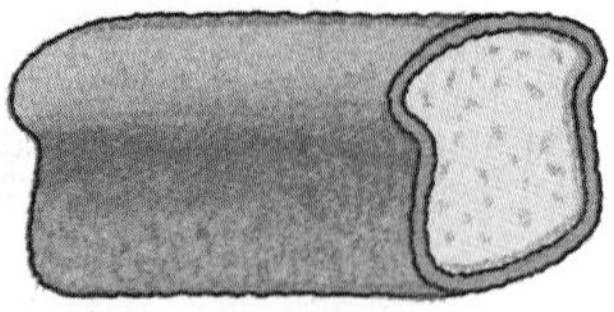

The bread weighs about 1 **pound**.

quart

quarter

25¢

rectangle

shorter

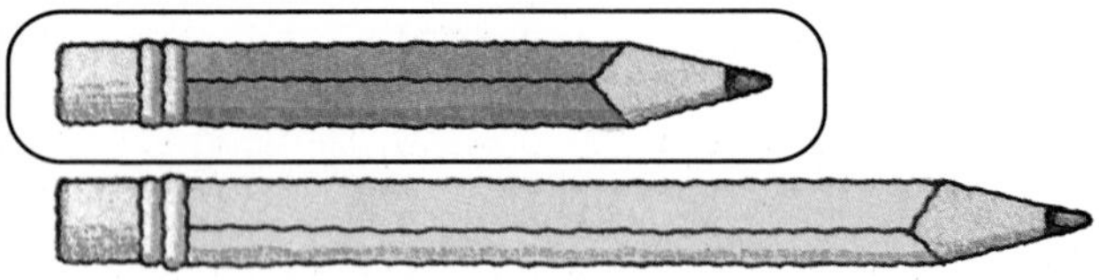

shortest

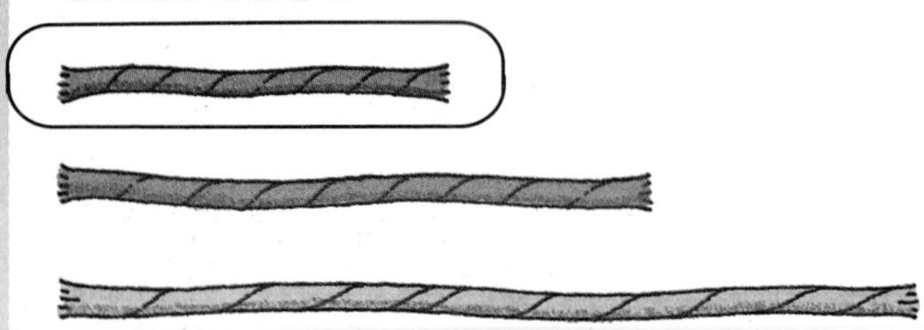

sphere

square

subtract

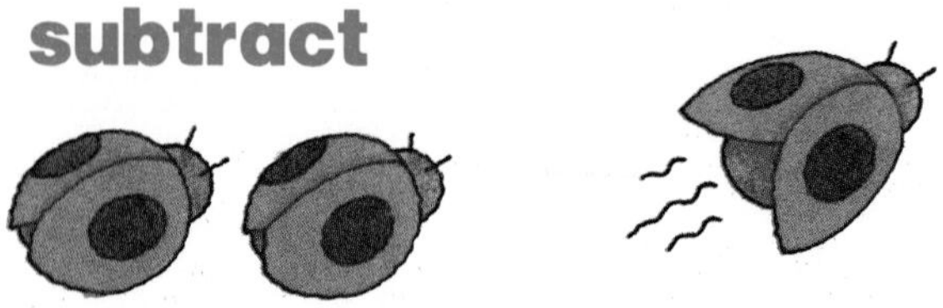

$3 - 1 = 2$

sum

$2 + 3 = 5$

$$\begin{array}{r} 2 \\ +\,3 \\ \hline 5 \end{array}$$

↑ **sum** ↑

taller

tallest

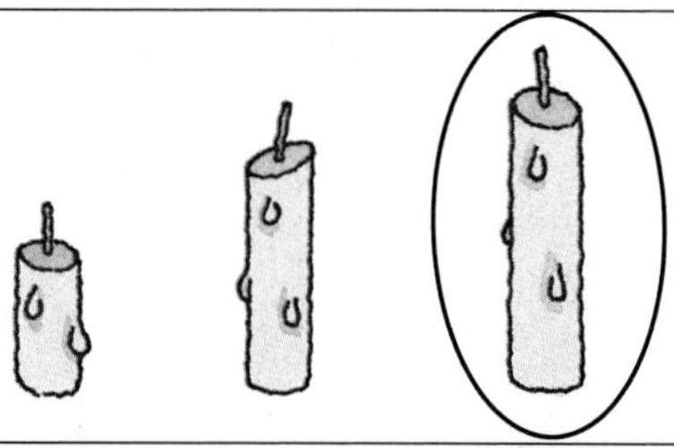

tens

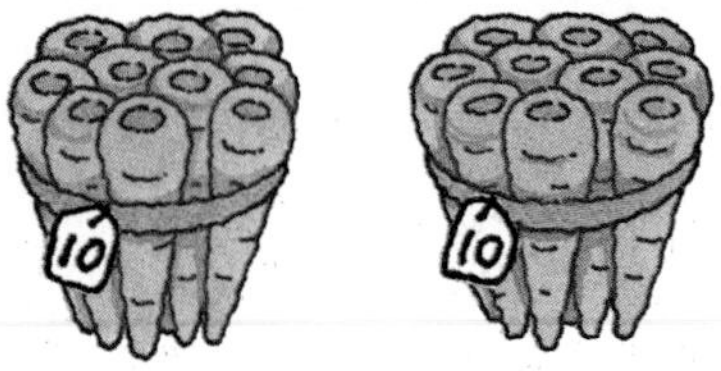

triangle

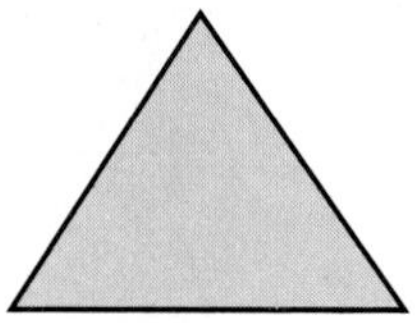

Notes for Home Children use a picture glossary for Grade One math vocabulary development.

REVIEW FOR

TEXAS ASSESSMENT OF ACADEMIC SKILLS

You can use these pages to prepare
for the Texas Assessment of Academic Skills test.

Lesson	Pages	Domain	TAAS Mathematics Objective	Topic
1	3-8	Concepts	1	Number concepts
2	9-12		2	Relations, functions, and other algebraic concepts
3	13-16		3	Geometric properties and relationships
4	17-22		4	Measurement concepts using metric and customary units
5	23-24		5	Probability and statistics
6	25-26	Operations	6	Use of addition to solve problems
7	27-28		7	Use of subtraction to solve problems
8	29-30	Problem Solving	11	Solution strategies and problem solving
9	31-32		12	Expressing or solving problems using mathematical representations

Name

Practice Test Lesson

1. How many crayons?
Mark your answer.

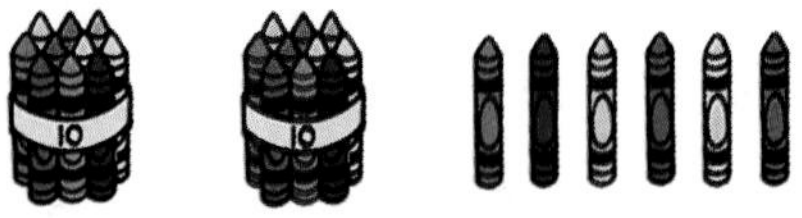

◯ 8 ◯ 26
◯ 27 ◯ 36

2. Find a shape that has $\frac{1}{4}$ shaded. Mark your answer.

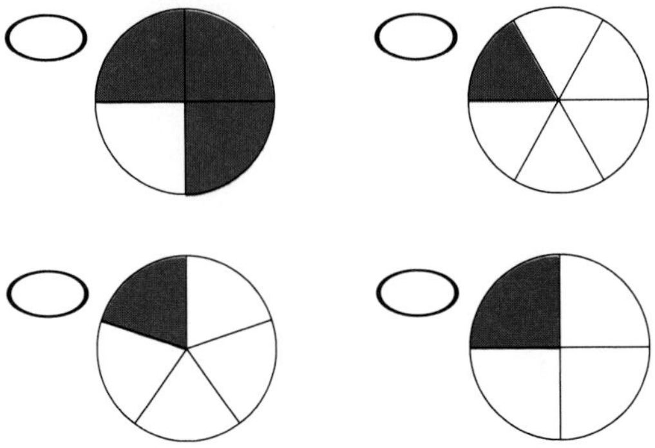

3. 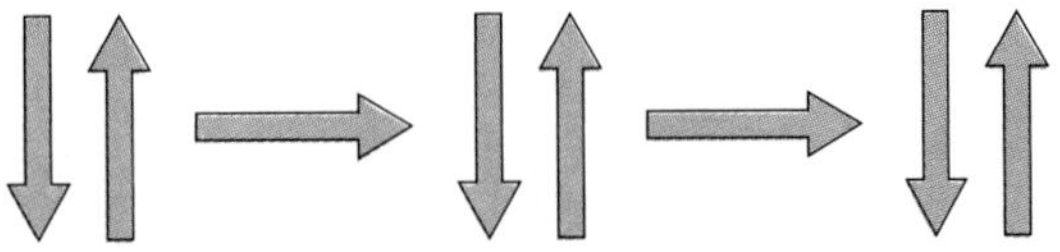

Which comes next?
Mark your answer.

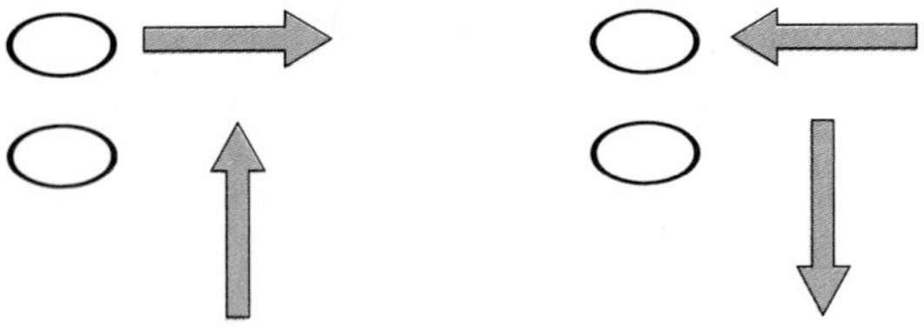

4. 

How many sides?
Mark your answer.

◯ 2 ◯ 3
◯ 4 ◯ 5

5. About how many inches long is the row of hearts?
Mark your answer.

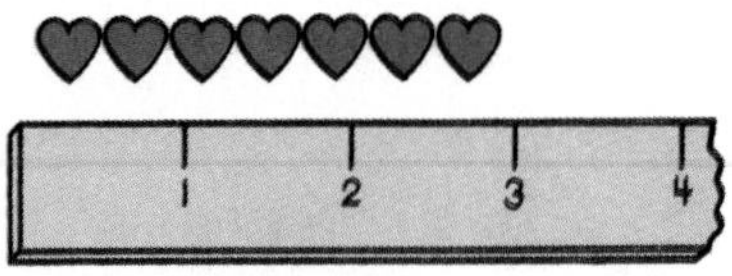

◯ 3 inches ◯ 4 inches
◯ 7 inches ◯ 8 inches

6. Amy had 14 pencils. She lost 6 of them. How can you find out how many pencils Amy has left?
Mark your answer.

◯ $14 + 6 = \square$
◯ $14 - 6 = \square$

Name ______

LESSON 1

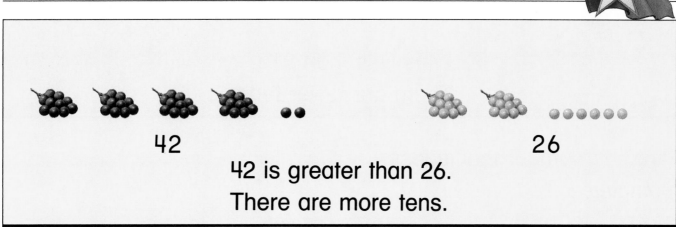

42   26

42 is greater than 26.
There are more tens.

Ring the number that is greater.
Complete.

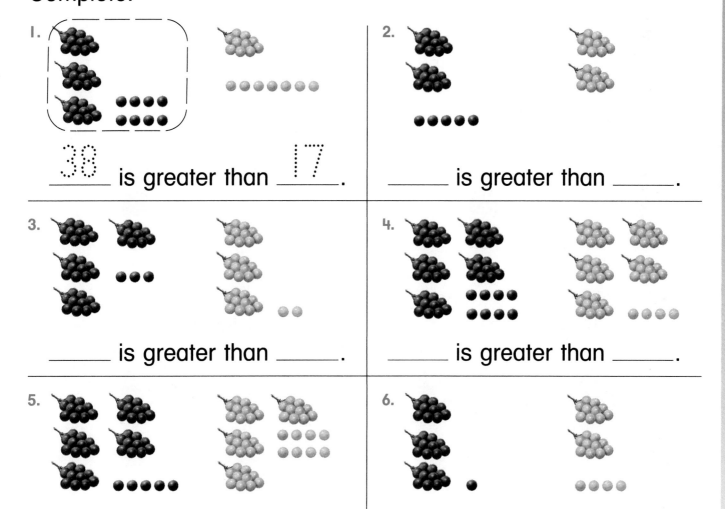

1. 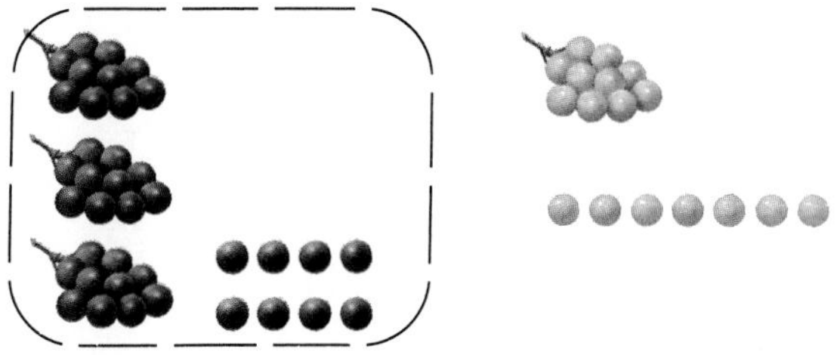

38 is greater than 17.

2. 

______ is greater than ______.

3. 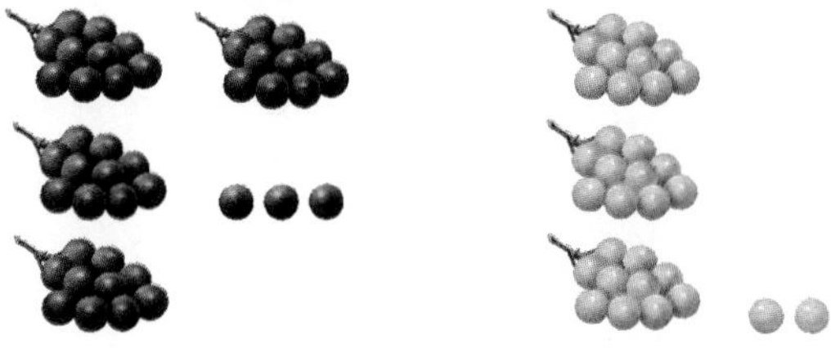

______ is greater than ______.

4. 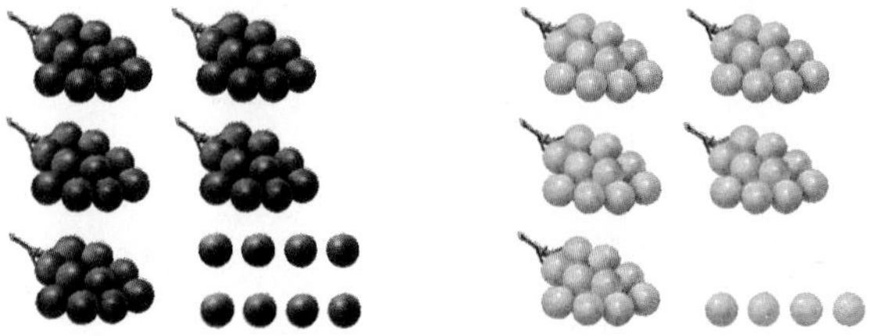

______ is greater than ______.

5. 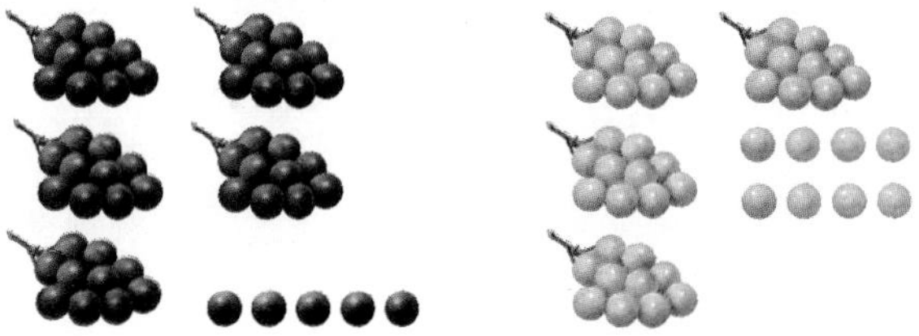

______ is greater than ______.

6. 

______ is greater than ______.

Notes for Home Children practice for the Grade 3 TAAS test by reviewing the comparison of whole numbers.

24

31

24 is less than 31.
There are fewer tens.

Ring the number that is less.
Complete.

7.

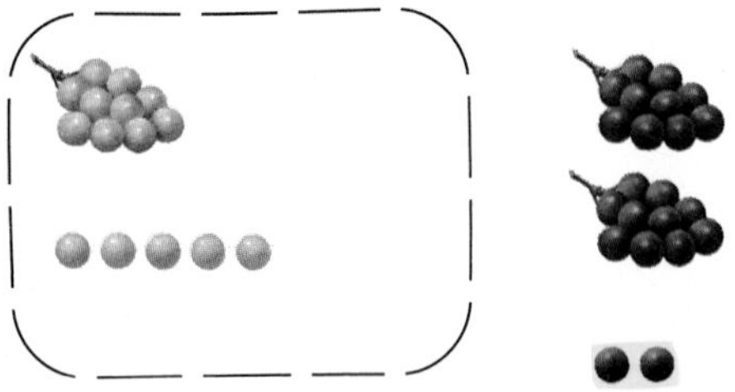

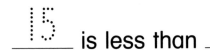

15 is less than 22.

8.

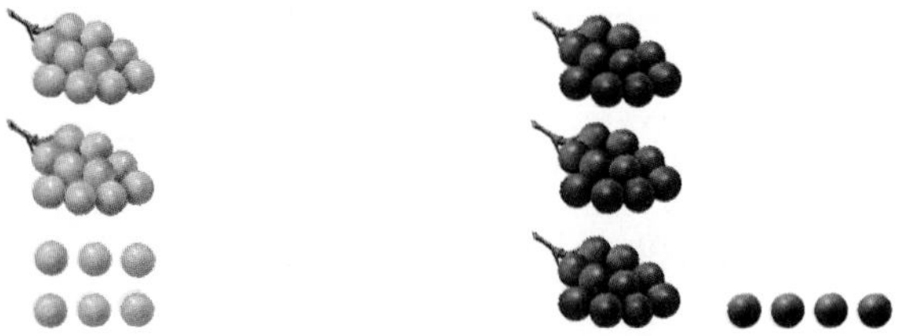

_____ is less than _____.

9.

_____ is less than _____.

10.

_____ is less than _____.

11.

_____ is less than _____.

12.

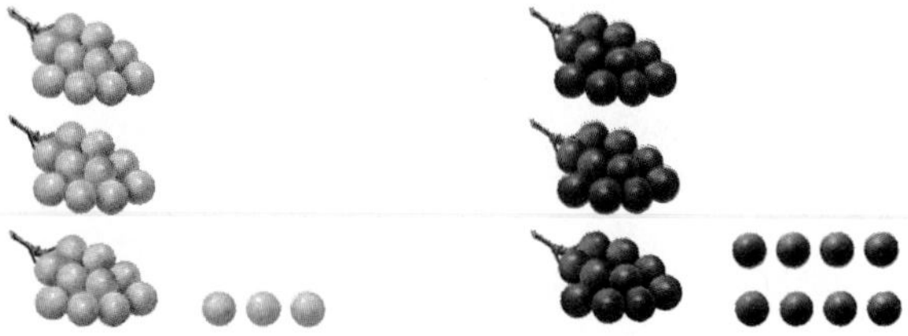

_____ is less than _____.

Notes for Home Children practice for the Grade 3 TAAS test by reviewing the comparison of whole numbers.

Name

Lesson 1

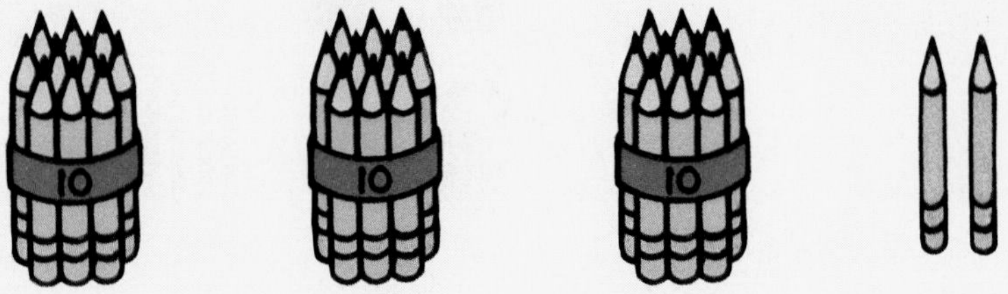

tens	ones
3	2

32

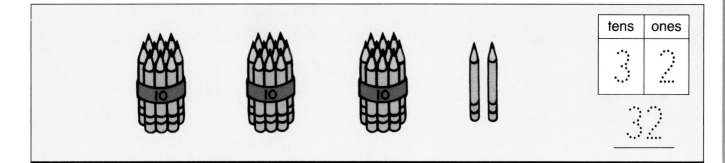

Write the number of tens and ones.
Then write the number.

1.

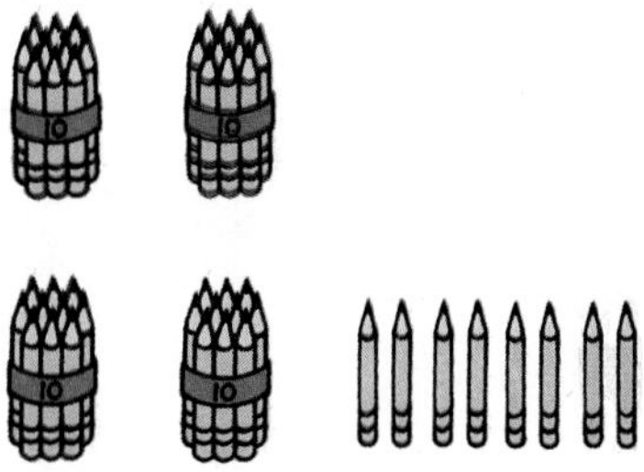

tens	ones

______

2.

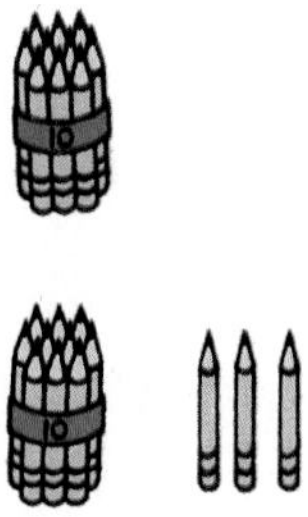

tens	ones

______

3.

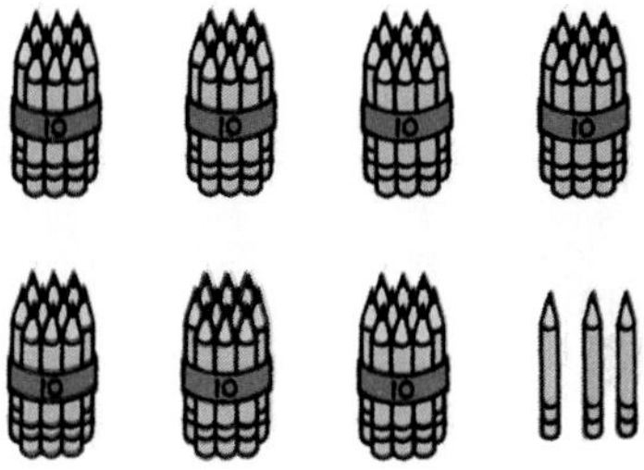

tens	ones

______

4.

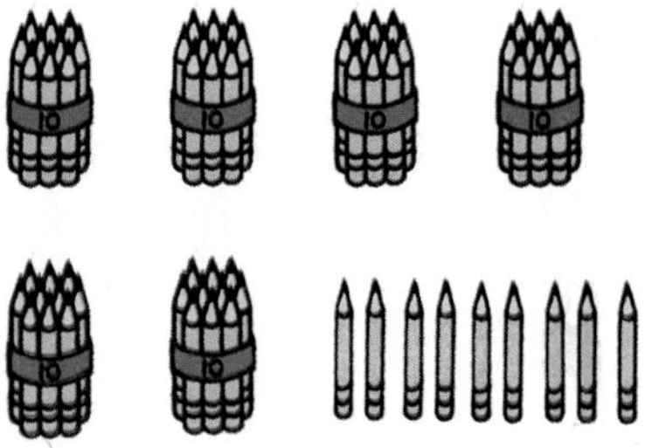

tens	ones

______

5.

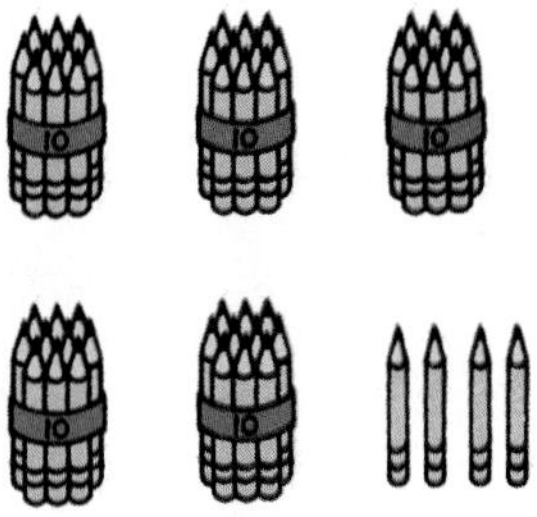

tens	ones

______

6.

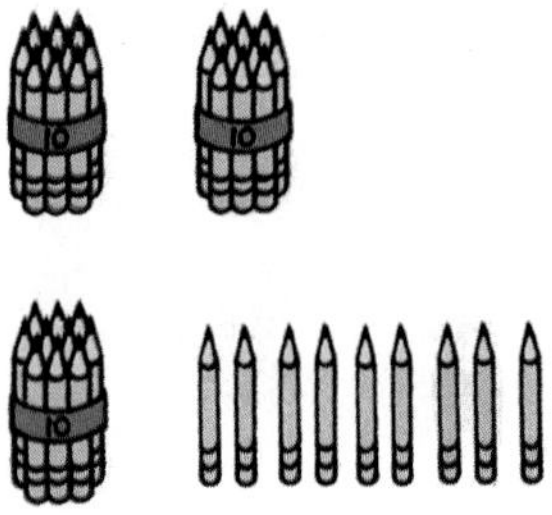

tens	ones

______

Notes for Home Children practice for the Grade 3 TAAS test by reviewing tens and ones.

Write the number.

7.

24 ______

8.

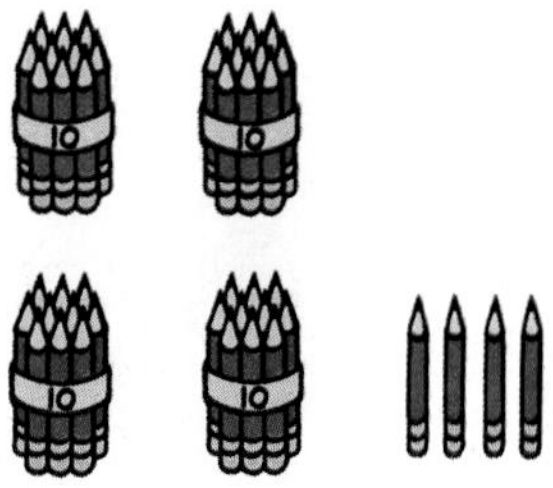

______

9.

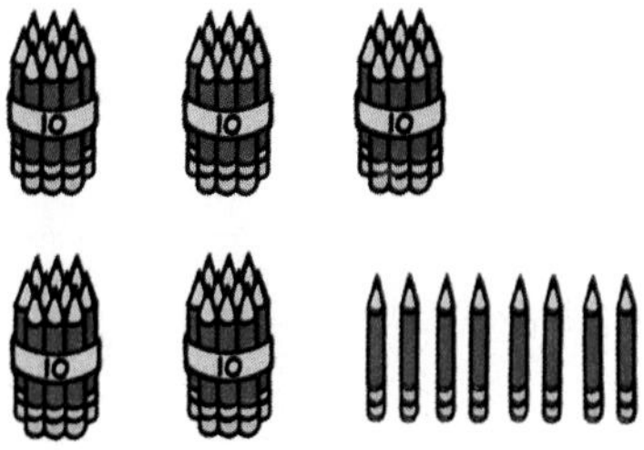

______

10.

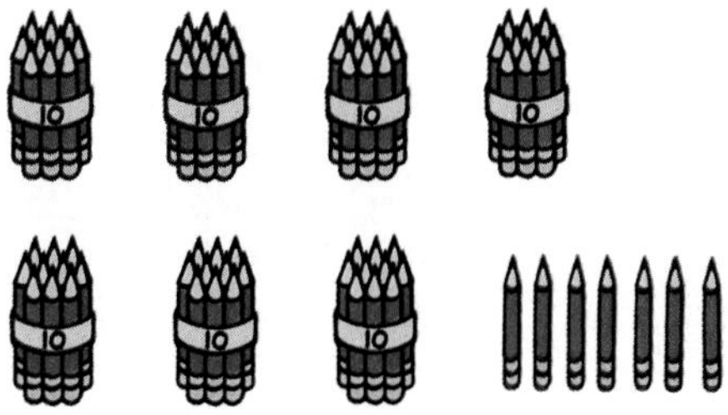

______

11.

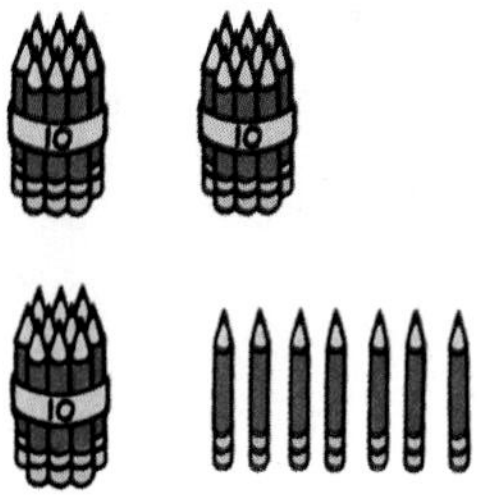

______

12.

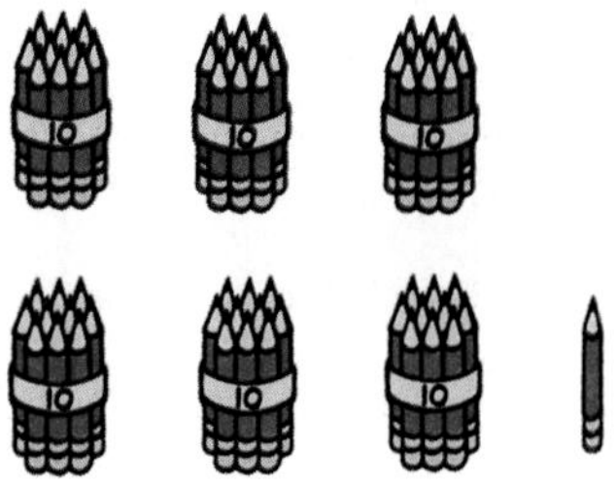

______

13.

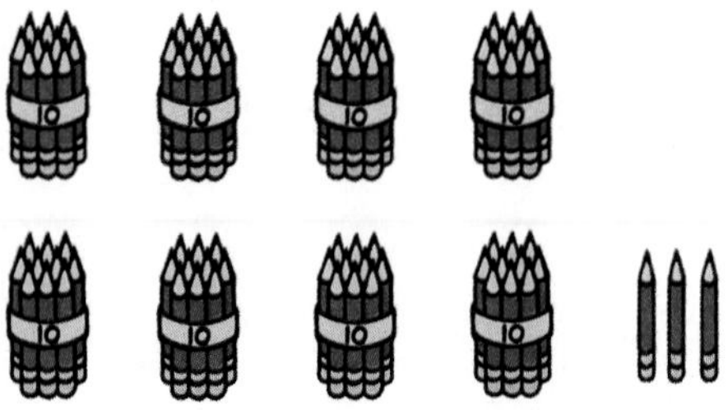

______

14.

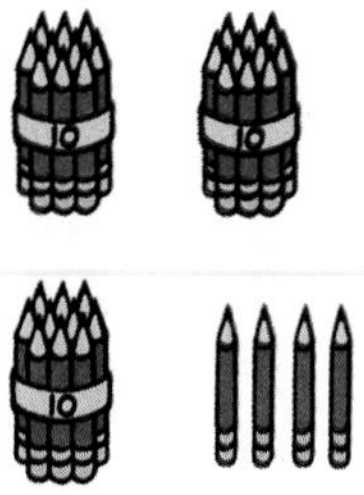

______

Notes for Home Children practice for the Grade 3 TAAS test by reviewing tens and ones.

Name

Lesson 1

$\frac{1 \text{ part blue}}{2 \text{ equal parts}}$

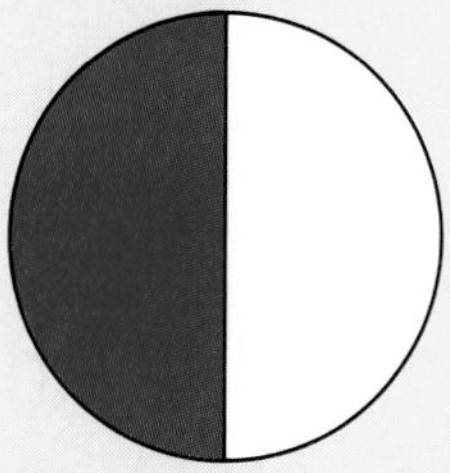

One half is blue.

$\frac{1}{2}$ is blue.

Color $\frac{1}{2}$ of each.

1.

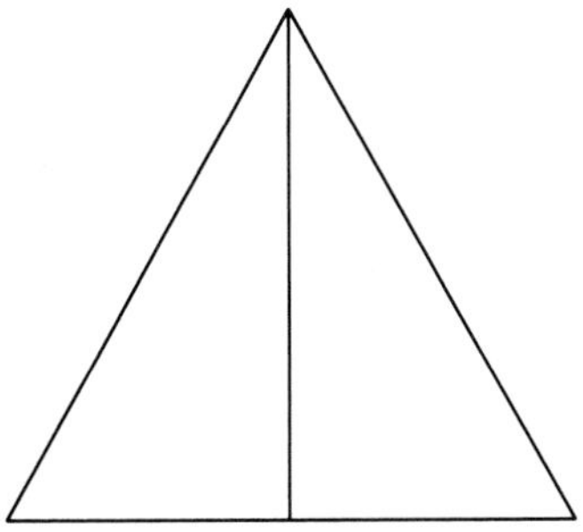

2.

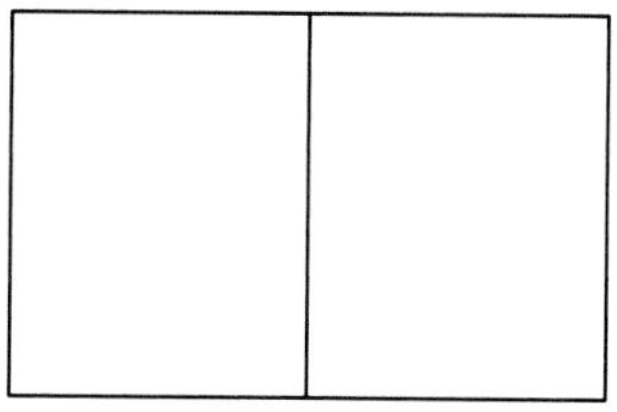

3.

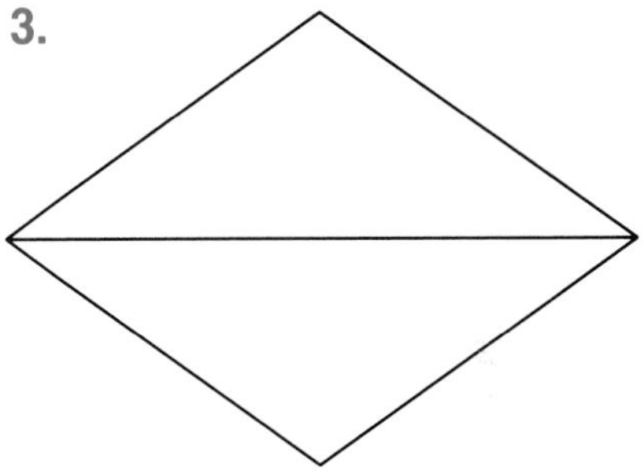

4.

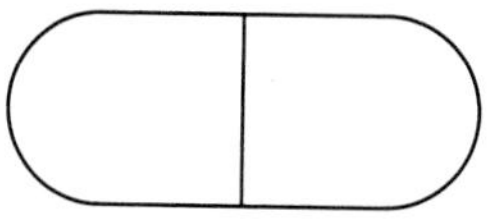

5.

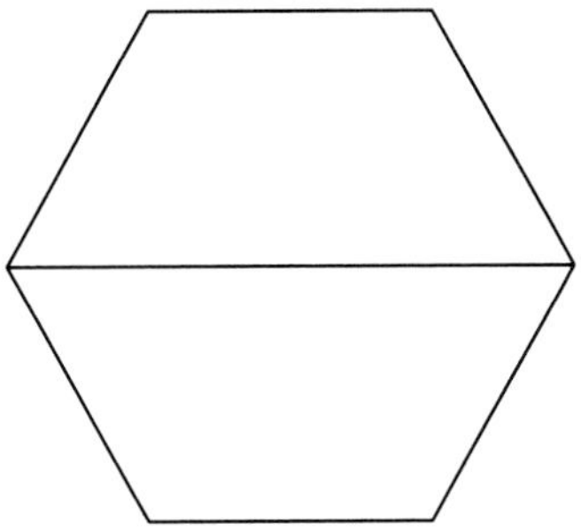

6.

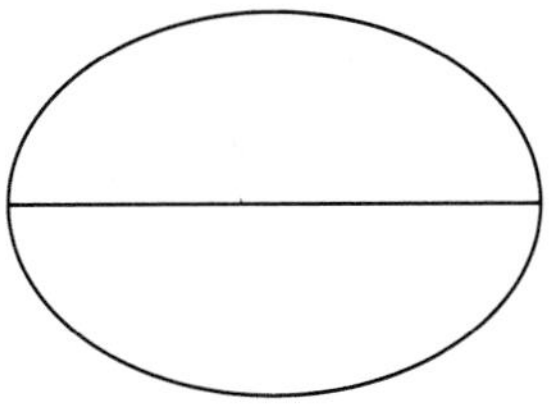

7.

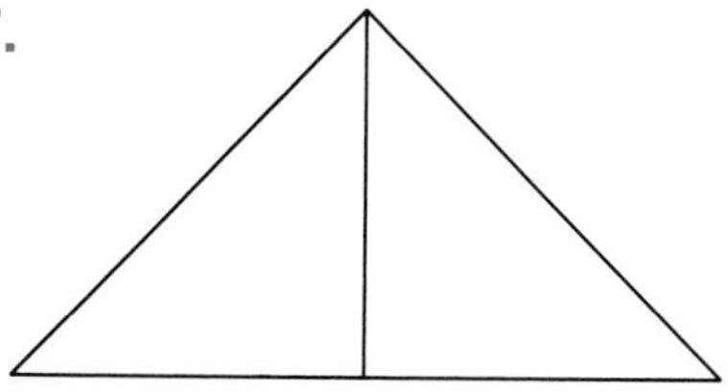

8.

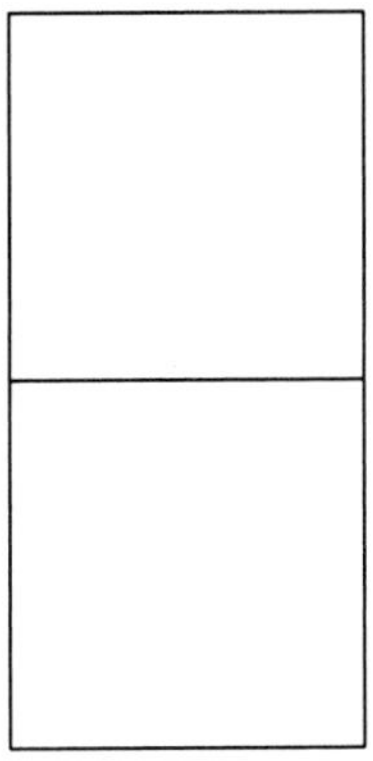

9.

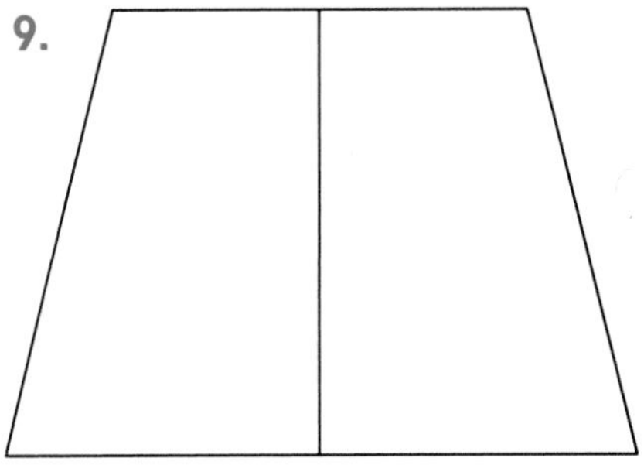

Notes for Home Children practice for the Grade 3 TAAS test by reviewing fractional halves.

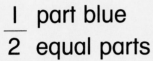

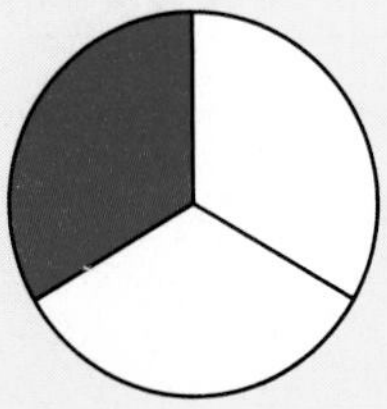

One third is green.

$\frac{1}{3}$ is green.

$\frac{1}{3}$ part green / equal parts

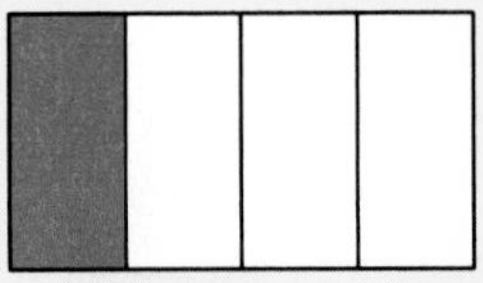

One fourth is red.

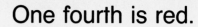

$\frac{1}{4}$ is red.

$\frac{1}{4}$ part red / equal parts

Color $\frac{1}{3}$ of each.

10. 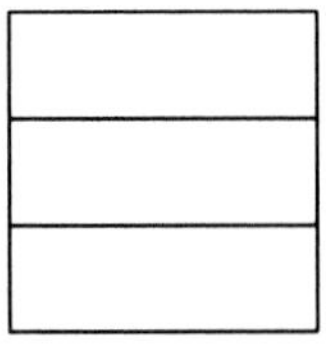

11. 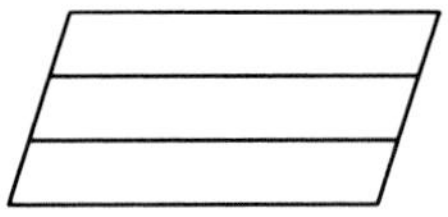

12. 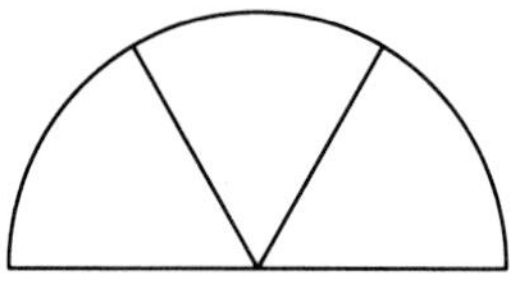

13. 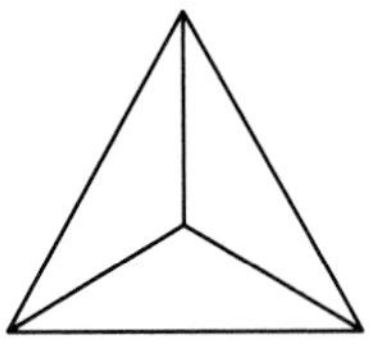

14. 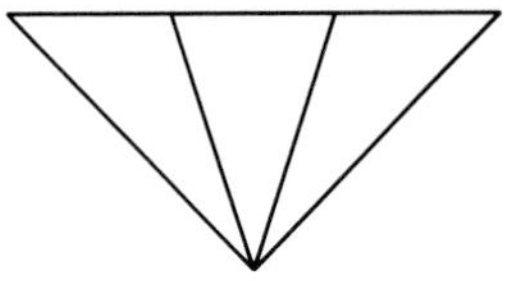

15. 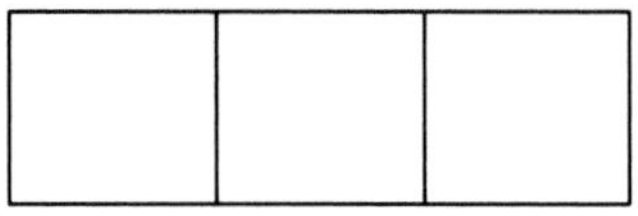

Color $\frac{1}{4}$ of each.

16. 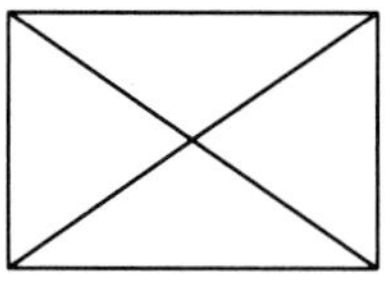

17. 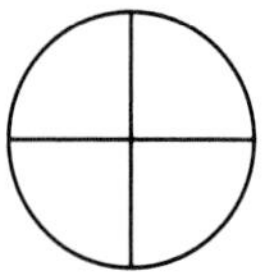

18. 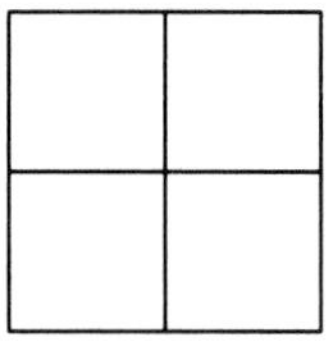

19. 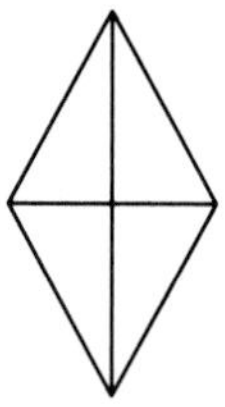

20. 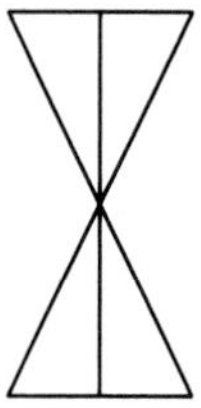

21. 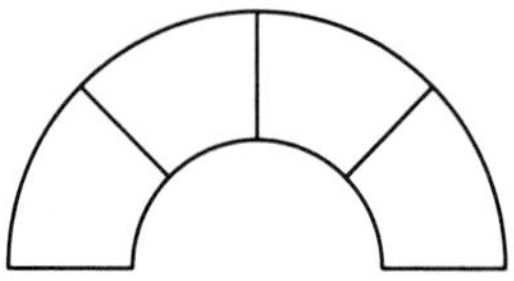

Notes for Home Children practice for the Grade 3 TAAS test by reviewing fractional thirds and fourths.

Name ______

LESSON 2

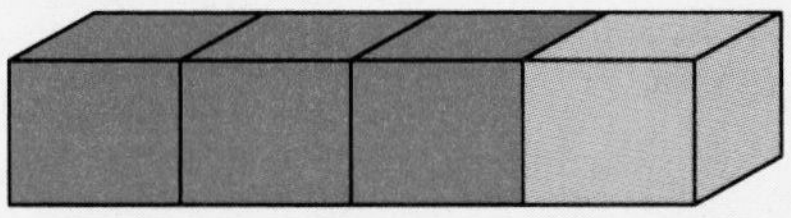

$3 + 1 = 4$

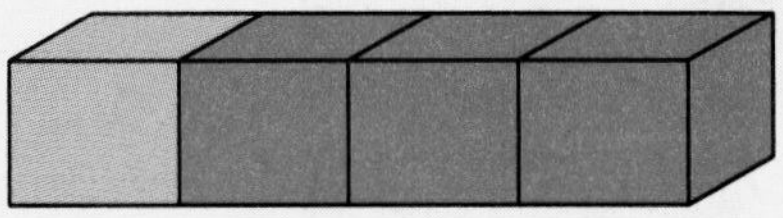

$1 + 3 = 4$

Write the sum.

1\.

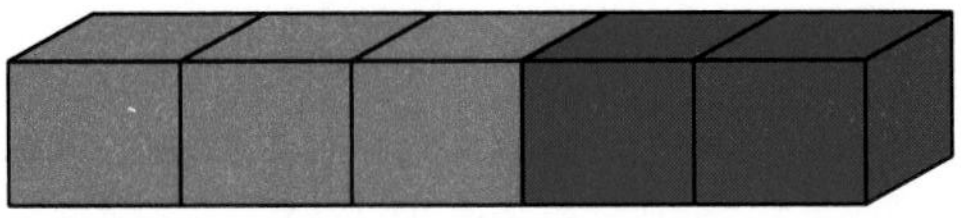

$3 + 2 =$ ___

2\.

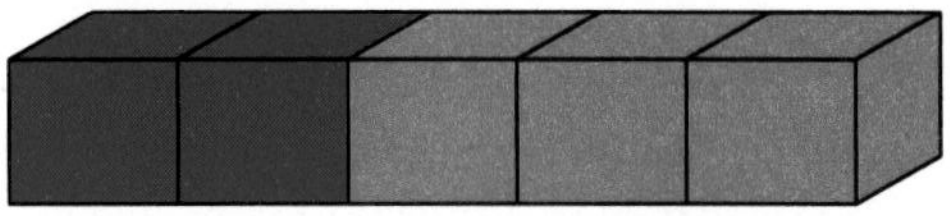

$2 + 3 =$ ___

3\.

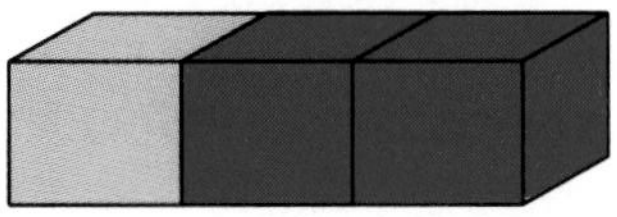

$1 + 2 =$ ___

4\.

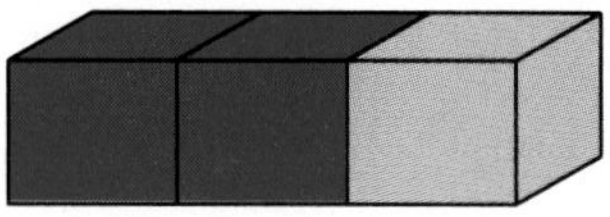

$2 + 1 =$ ___

5\.

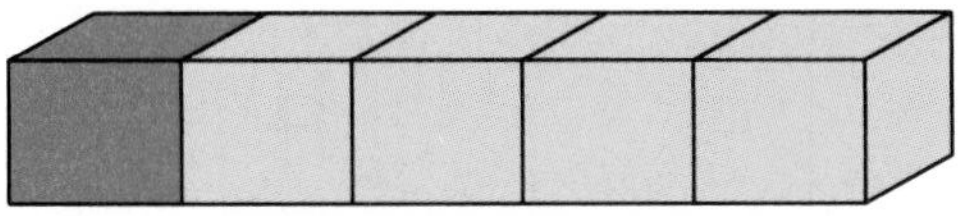

$1 + 4 =$ ___

6\.

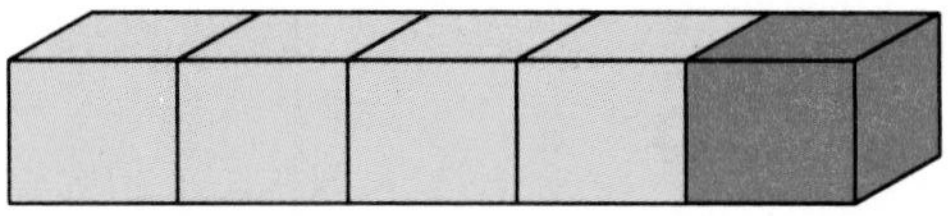

$4 + 1 =$ ___

7\.

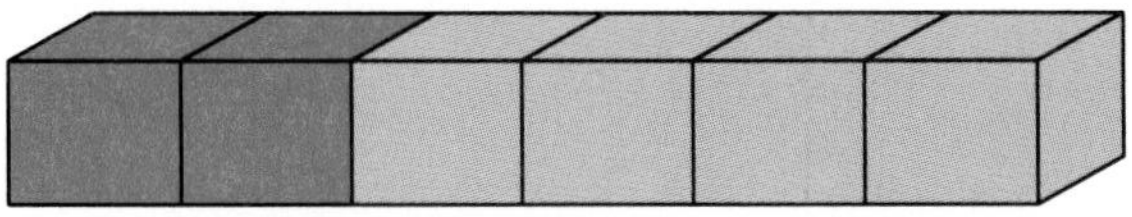

$2 + 4 =$ ___

8\.

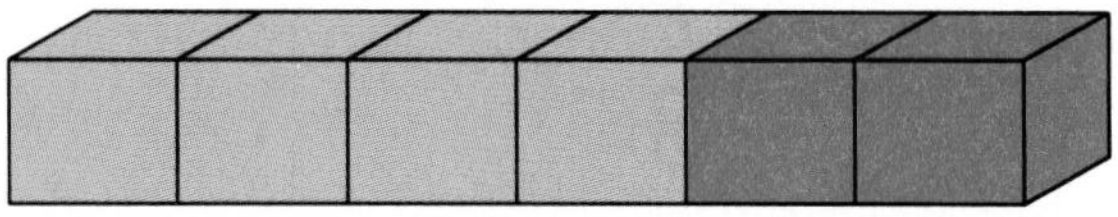

$4 + 2 =$ ___

Notes for Home Children practice for the Grade 3 TAAS test by reviewing addition of two numbers in any order.

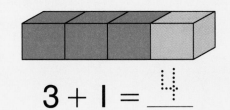

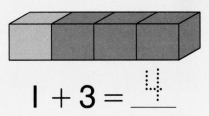

Add in any order.

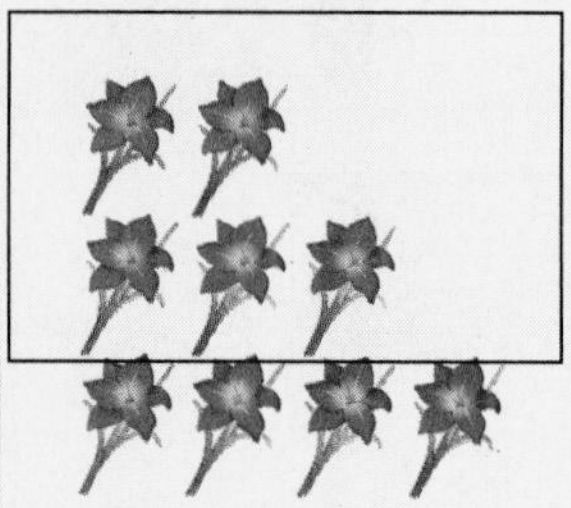

$$\begin{array}{r} 2 \\ 3 \\ +\ 4 \\ \hline 9 \end{array}$$

2 + 3 = 5

$$\begin{array}{r} 2 \\ 3 \\ +\ 4 \\ \hline 9 \end{array}$$

3 + 4 = 7

Write the sum.

9. $\begin{array}{r} 2 \\ 3 \\ +\ 1 \\ \hline 6 \end{array}$

10. $\begin{array}{r} 3 \\ 3 \\ +\ 3 \\ \hline \end{array}$

11. $\begin{array}{r} 4 \\ 4 \\ +\ 0 \\ \hline \end{array}$

12. $\begin{array}{r} 5 \\ 2 \\ +\ 1 \\ \hline \end{array}$

13. $\begin{array}{r} 6 \\ 1 \\ +\ 9 \\ \hline \end{array}$

14. $\begin{array}{r} 5 \\ 7 \\ +\ 1 \\ \hline \end{array}$

15. $\begin{array}{r} 1 \\ 5 \\ +\ 6 \\ \hline \end{array}$

16. $\begin{array}{r} 4 \\ 6 \\ +\ 1 \\ \hline \end{array}$

17. $\begin{array}{r} 7 \\ 4 \\ +\ 2 \\ \hline \end{array}$

18. $\begin{array}{r} 7 \\ 8 \\ +\ 1 \\ \hline \end{array}$

19. $\begin{array}{r} 4 \\ 2 \\ +\ 9 \\ \hline \end{array}$

20. $\begin{array}{r} 6 \\ 2 \\ +\ 4 \\ \hline \end{array}$

Notes for Home Children practice for the Grade 3 TAAS test by reviewing addition of three numbers in any order.

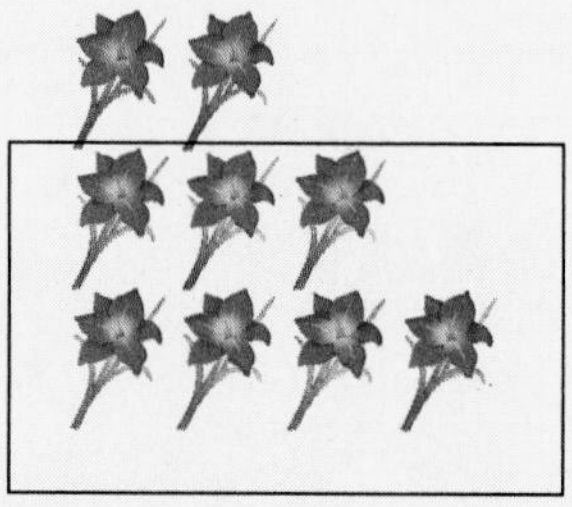

Name

Lesson 2

What is the pattern?
Ring what comes next.

1.

2.

3.

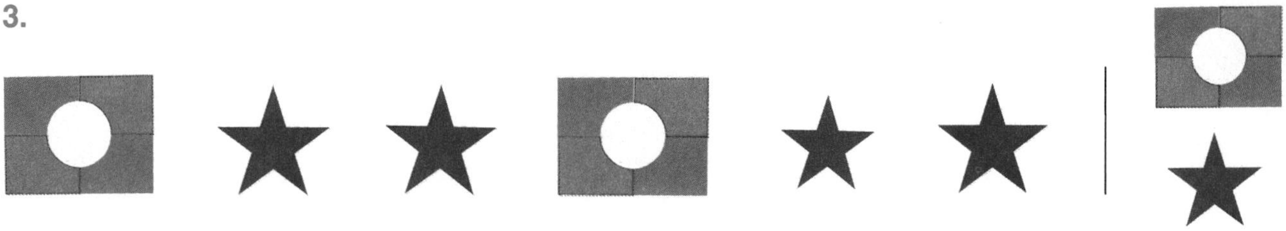

4.

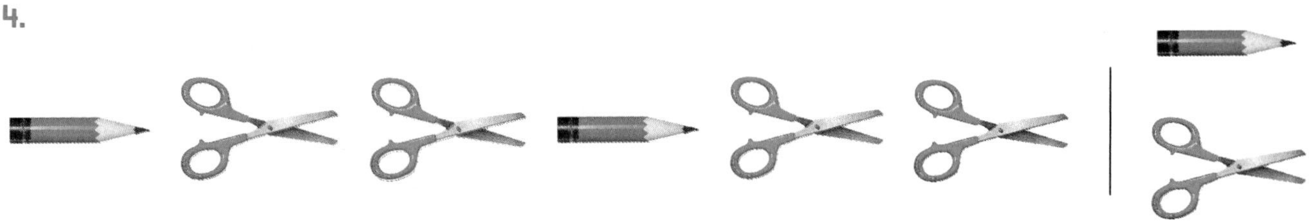

Notes for Home Children practice for the Grade 3 TAAS test by reviewing missing elements in patterns.

What is the pattern?
Ring what comes next.

5.

6.

7.

8.

9.

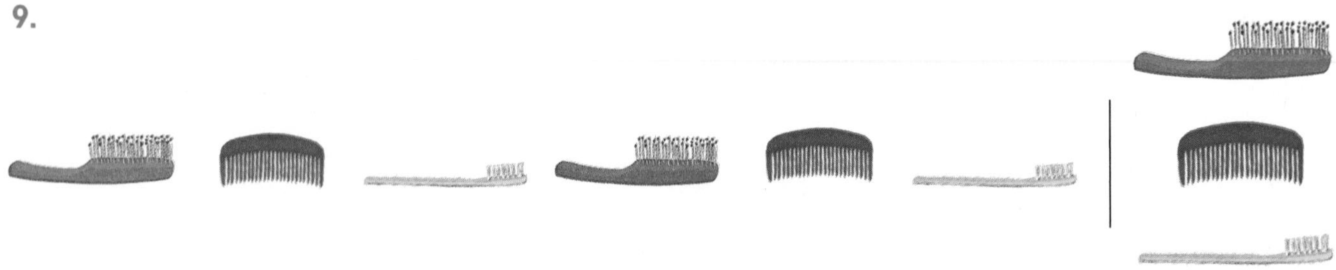

Notes for Home Children practice for the Grade 3 TAAS test by reviewing missing elements in patterns.

Name

LESSON 3

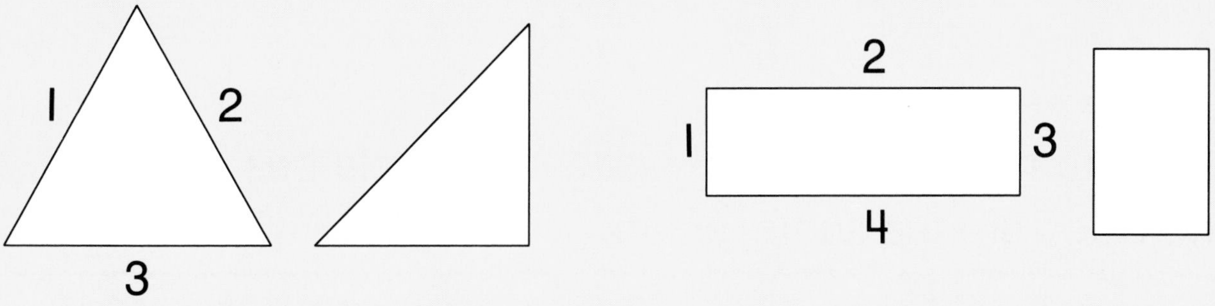

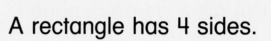

A triangle has 3 sides.

A rectangle has 4 sides.

1. Put an X on each triangle.

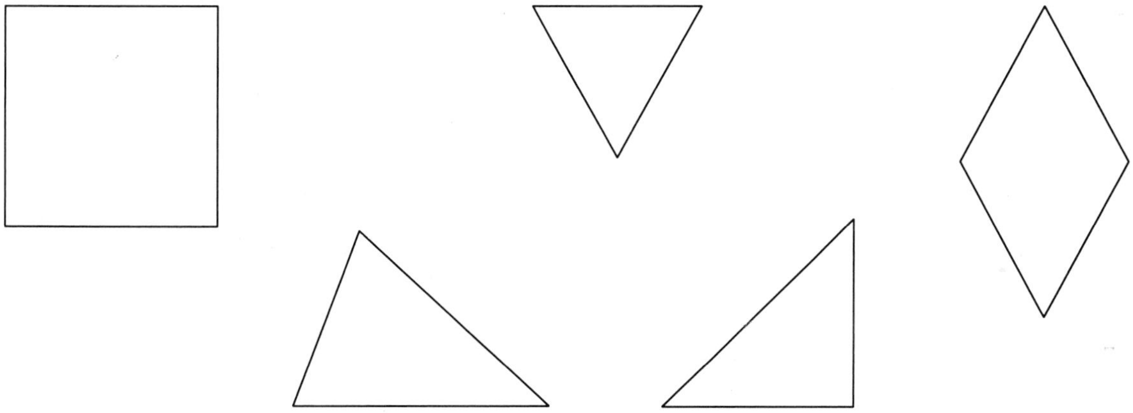

2. Put an X on each rectangle.

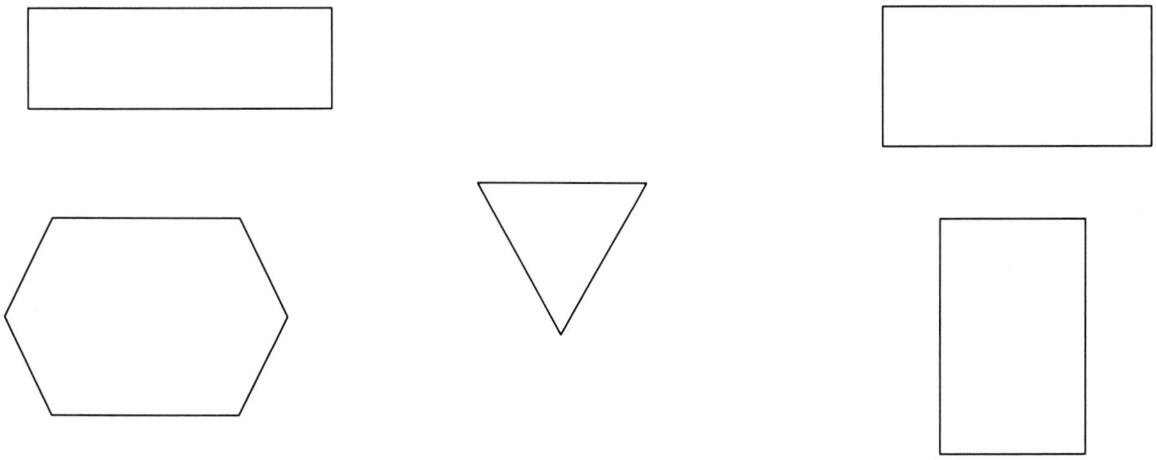

Notes for Home Children practice for the Grade 3 TAAS test by reviewing two-dimensional shapes.

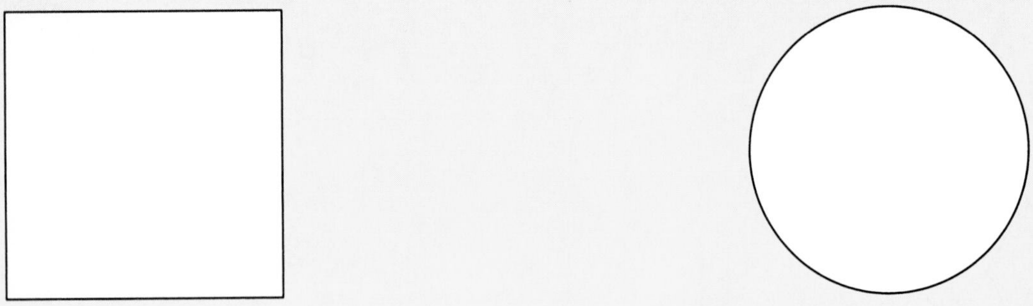

A square has 4 sides.
The sides are the same length.

A circle has no sides.

3. Put an X on each square.

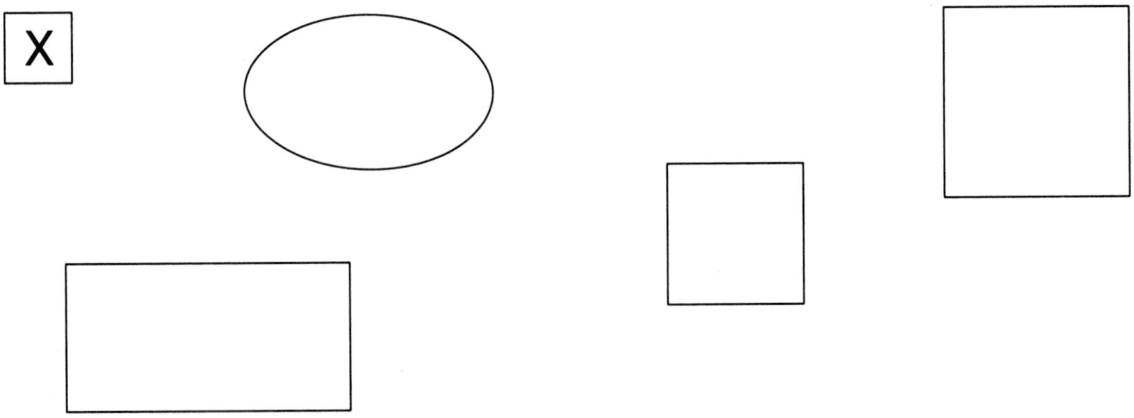

4. Put an X on each circle.

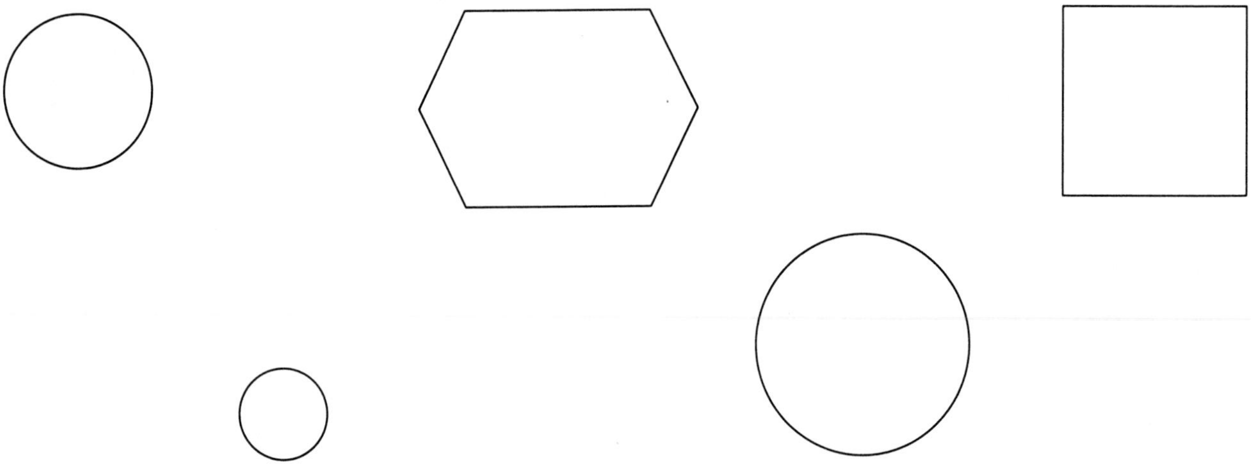

Notes for Home Children practice for the Grade 3 TAAS test by reviewing two-dimensional shapes.

Name

Lesson 3

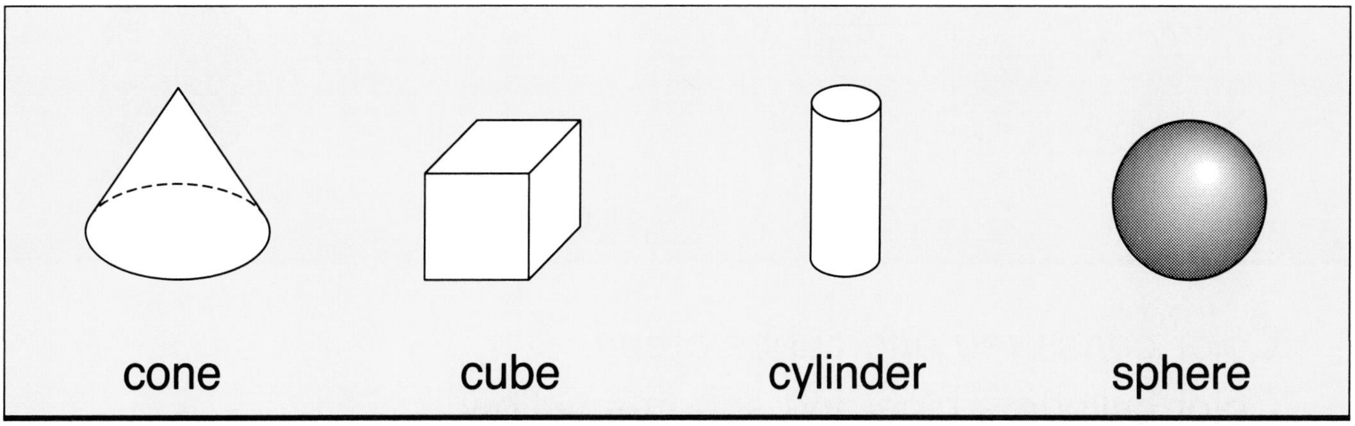

1. Color cones red and cubes green.
Color cylinders blue and spheres yellow.

Notes for Home Children practice for the Grade 3 TAAS test by reviewing three-dimensional shapes.

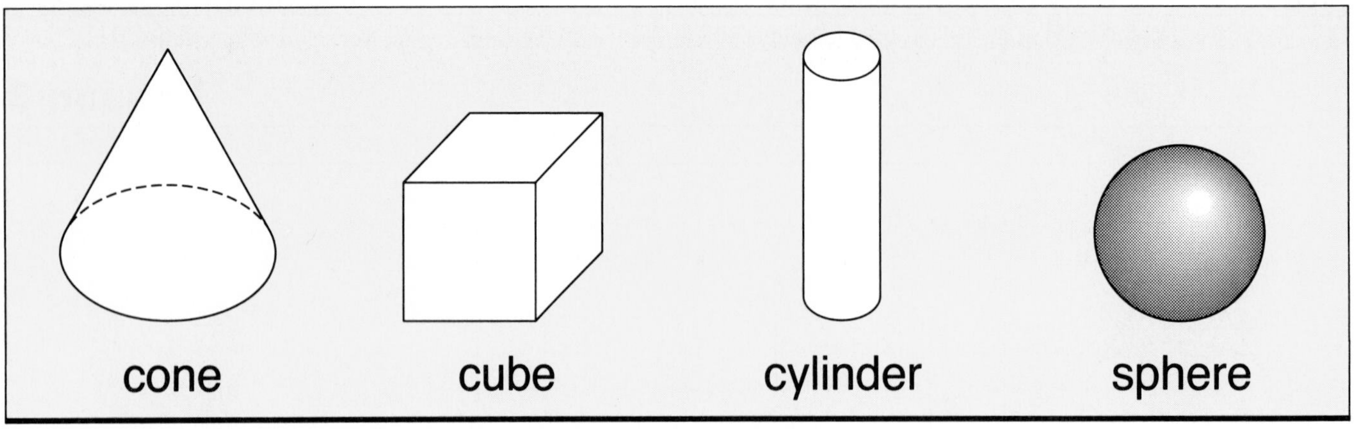

2. Color cones red and cubes green.
Color cylinders blue and spheres yellow.

Notes for Home Children practice for the Grade 3 TAAS test by reviewing three-dimensional shapes.

Name ______________________________

LESSON 4

5:30

Circle the time.

1.

1:00 1:30

2.

5:30 6:30

3.

4:00 4:30

4.

9:00 10:00

5.

3:00 3:30

6.

1:30 12:30

Notes for Home Children practice for the Grade 3 TAAS test by reviewing units of time.

Write the time.

7.

4:00

8.

9.

10.

11.

12.

13.

14.

15.

16.

17.

18.

Notes for Home Children practice for the Grade 3 TAAS test by reviewing units of time.

Name ______________________

Lesson 4

The paintbrush is about 4 inches long.

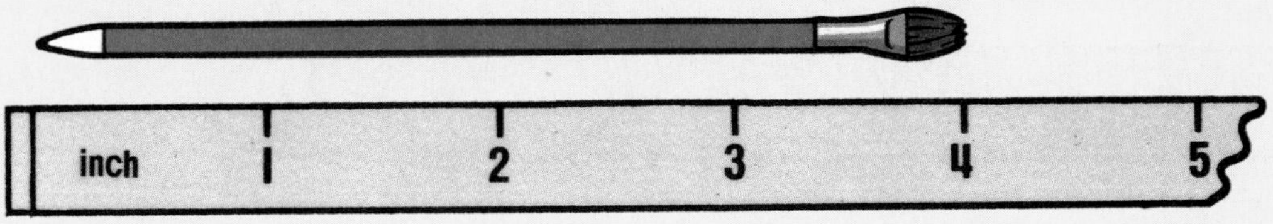

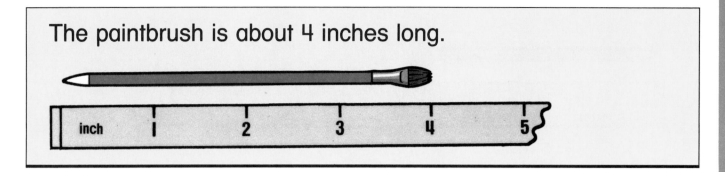

Use an inch ruler.
About how long is each brush?

1.

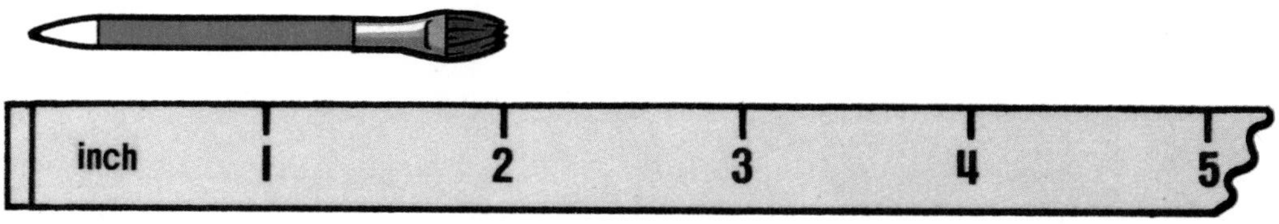

2 inches

2.

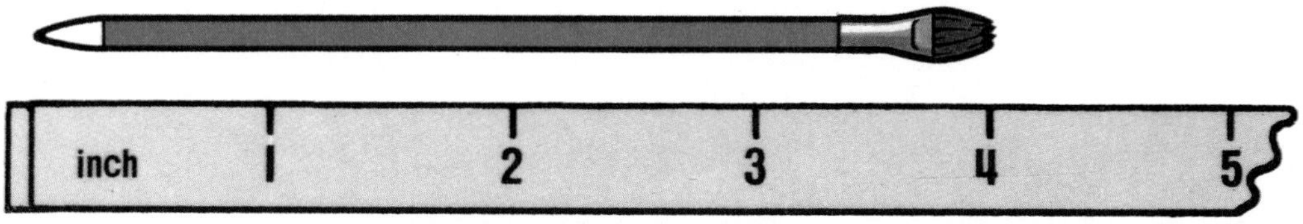

____ inches

3.

____ inches

4.

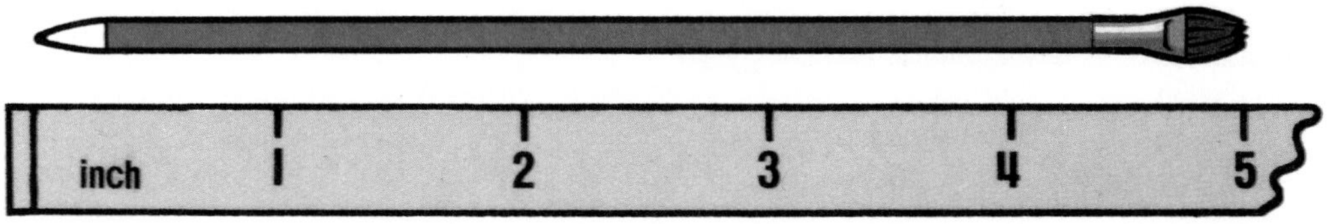

____ inches

Notes for Home Children practice for the Grade 3 TAAS test by measuring length using an inch ruler.

The paintbrush is about 6 cm long.
Cm is short for centimeters.

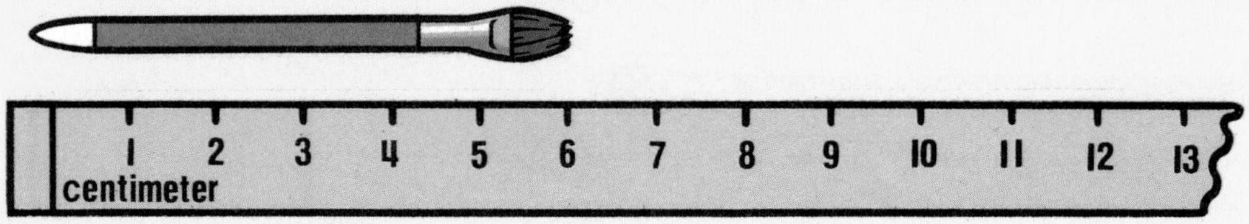

Use a centimeter ruler.
About how long is each brush?

5.

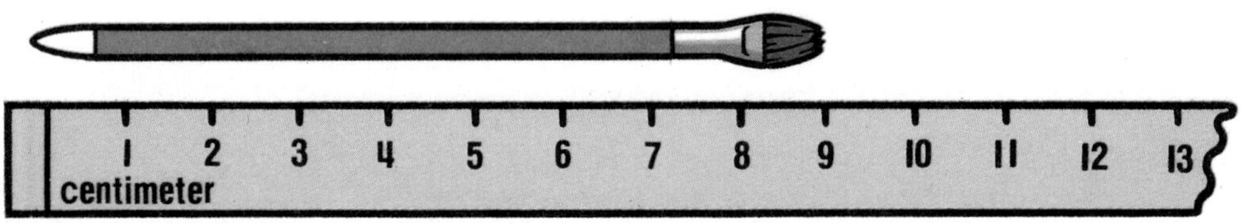

9 cm

6.

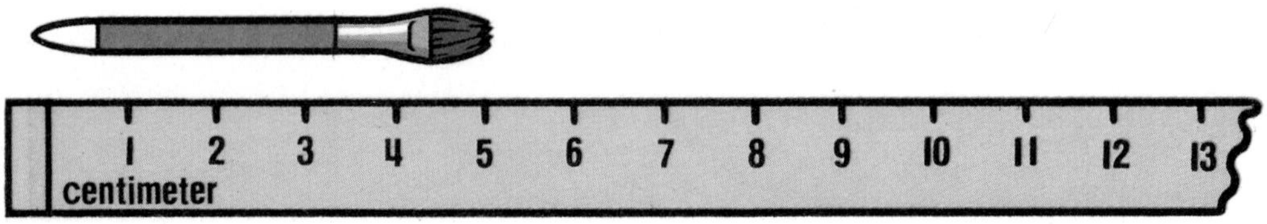

____ cm

7.

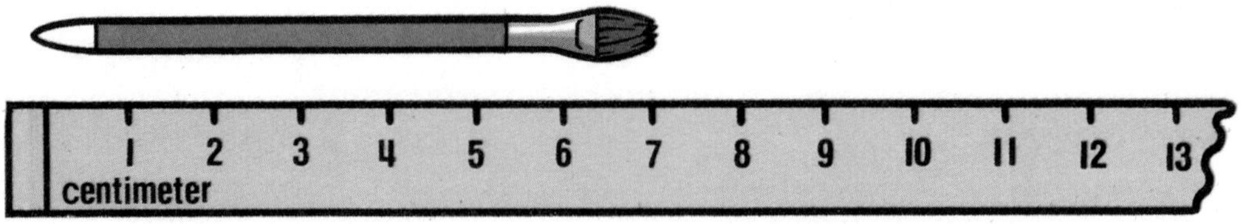

____ cm

8.

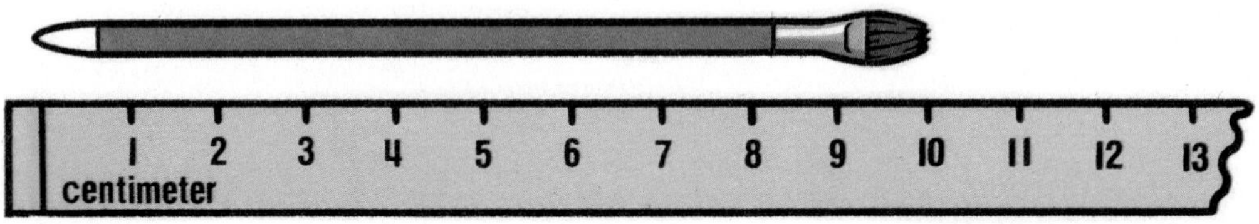

____ cm

Notes for Home Children practice for the Grade 3 TAAS test by measuring length using a centimeter ruler.

Name ______________________

Lesson 4

I unit

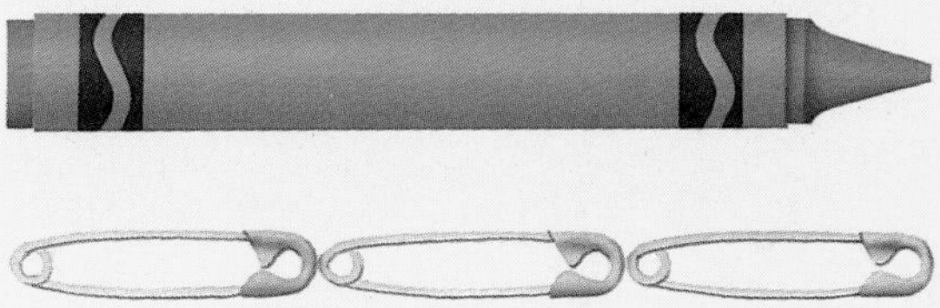

about 3 units long

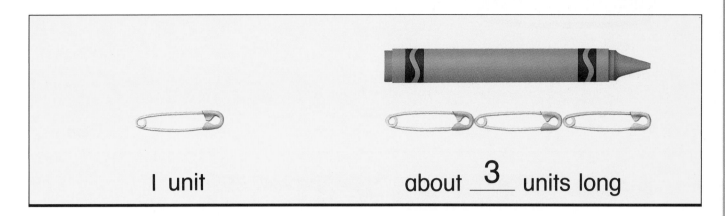

About how long is each object?

I.

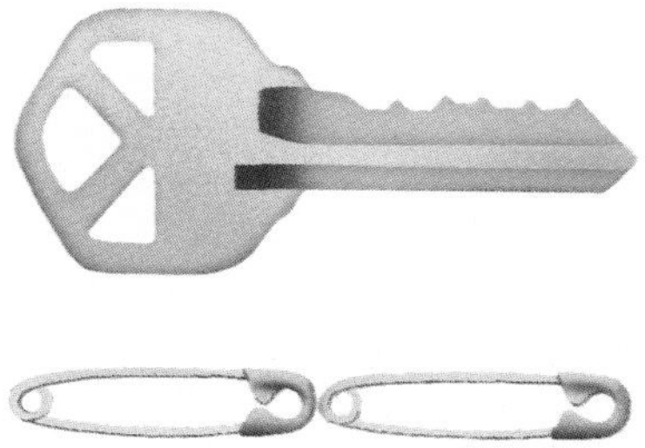

2 units

2.

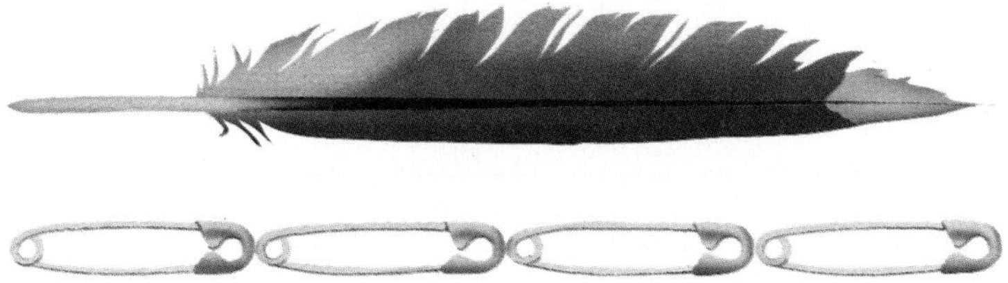

____ units

3.

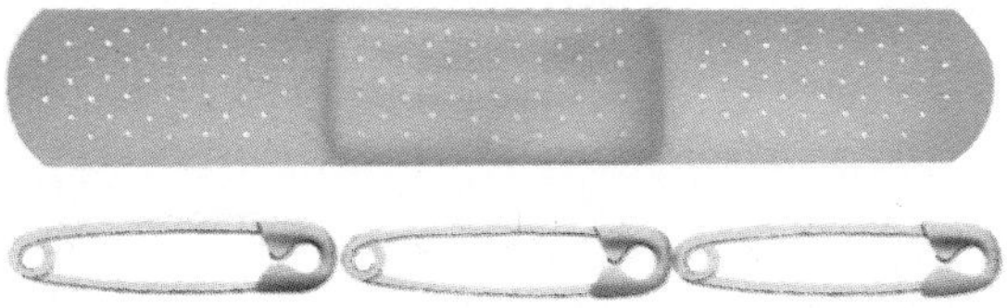

____ units

4.

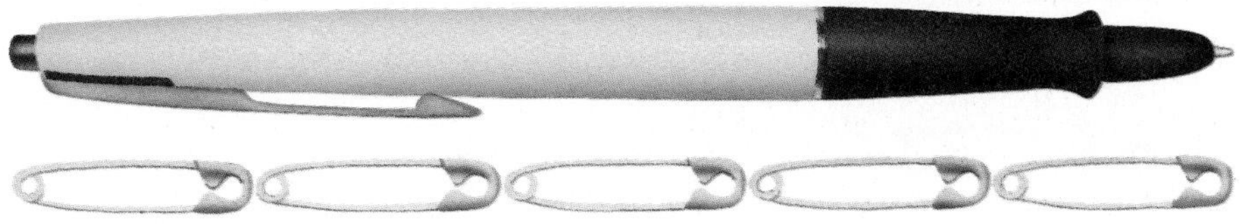

____ units

Notes for Home Children practice for the Grade 3 TAAS test by measuring length using nonstandard units.

Texas TAAS REVIEW

About how long is each object?

5.

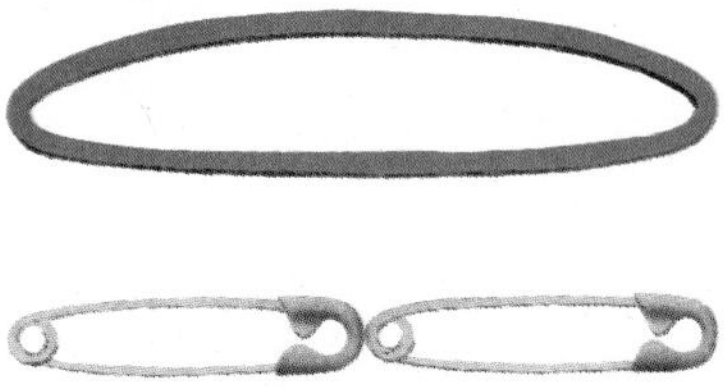

2 units

6.

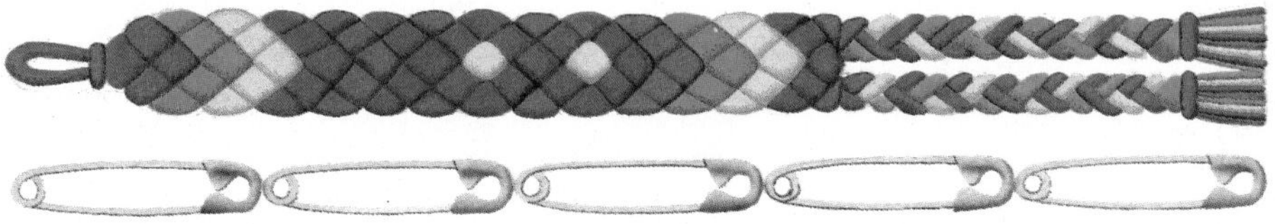

_____ units

7.

_____ units

8.

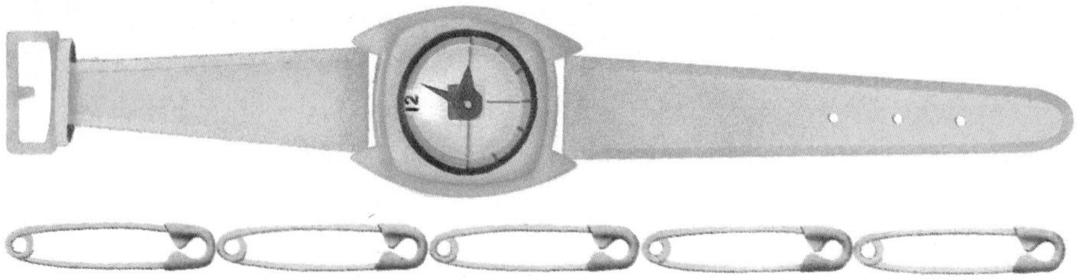

_____ units

9.

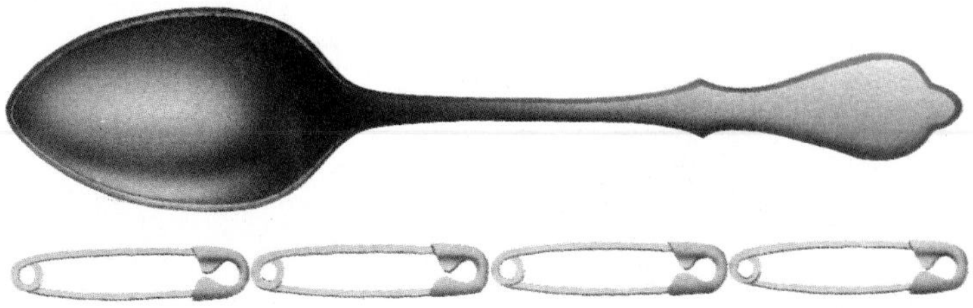

_____ units

Notes for Home Children practice for the Grade 3 TAAS test by measuring length using nonstandard units.

Name ____________________

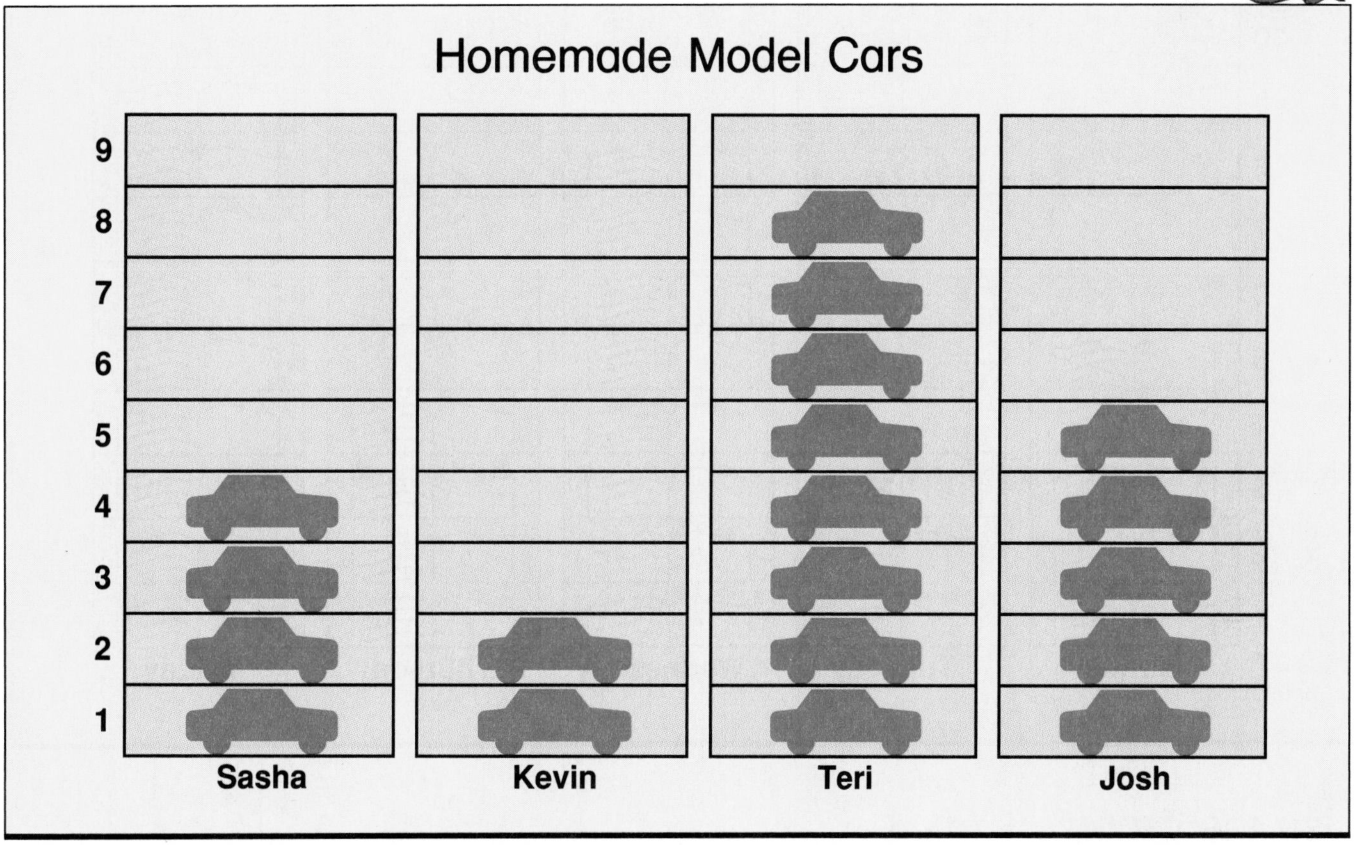

Use the graph.

1. How many model cars were made?

Kevin 2   Sasha ___

Teri ___   Josh ___

2. Who made the most models? ____________________

3. Who made the fewest models? ____________________

Notes for Home Children practice for the Grade 3 TAAS test by reviewing bar graphs.

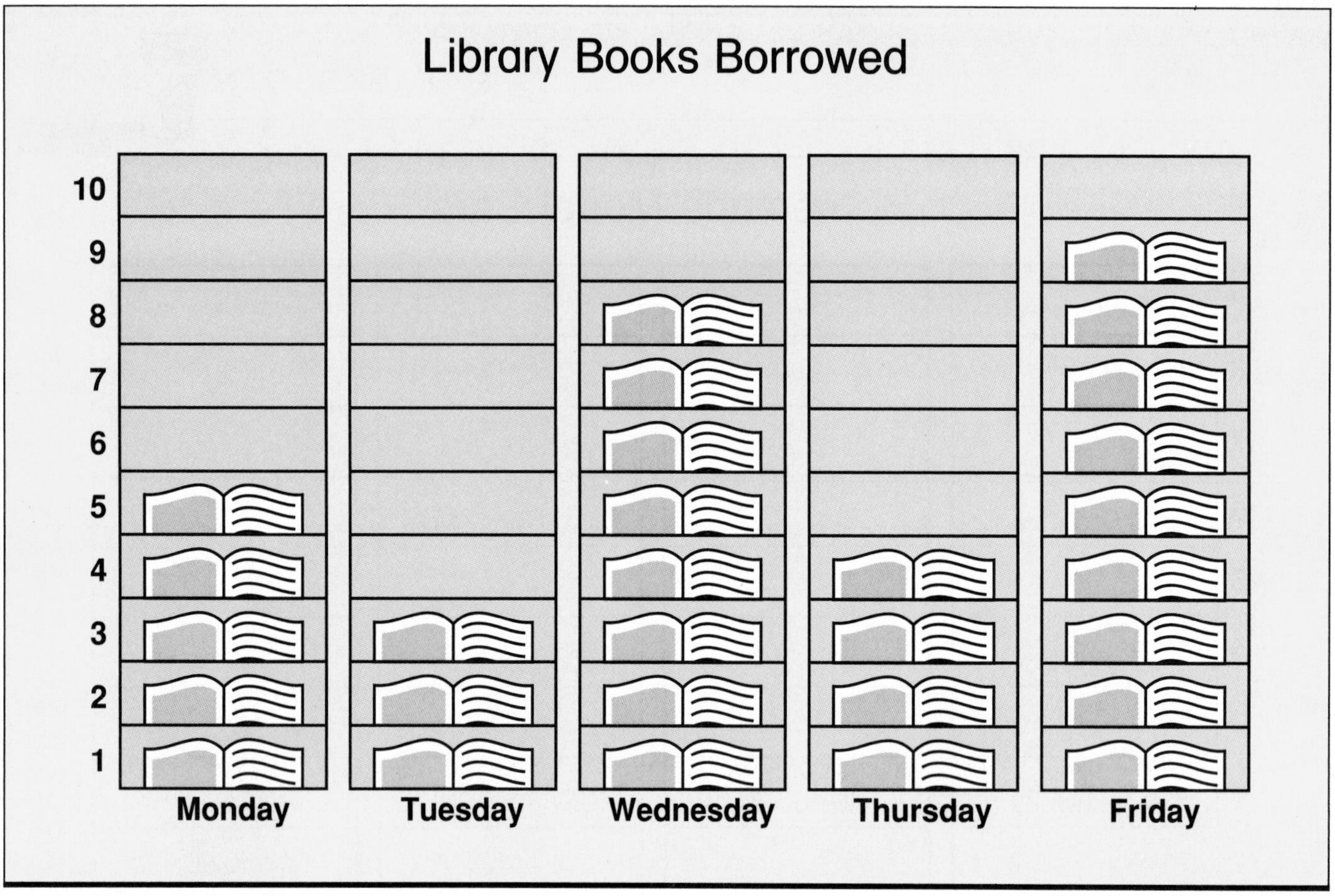

Use the graph.

4. How many library books were borrowed?

Wednesday 8 Thursday ____ Monday ____

Friday ____ Tuesday ____

5. On which day were the most books borrowed?

____

6. On which day were the fewest books borrowed?

____

Notes for Home Children practice for the Grade 3 TAAS test by reviewing bar graphs.

Name

LESSON 6

$4 + 1 = 5$

Add.

1.

$5 + 3 = \underline{8}$

2.

$2 + 2 = \underline{\quad}$

3. $\begin{array}{r} 4 \\ +\ 3 \\ \hline \end{array}$

4. $\begin{array}{r} 2 \\ +\ 9 \\ \hline \end{array}$

5. $\begin{array}{r} 4 \\ +\ 8 \\ \hline \end{array}$

6. $\begin{array}{r} 6 \\ +\ 7 \\ \hline \end{array}$

7. $\begin{array}{r} 6 \\ +\ 8 \\ \hline \end{array}$

8. $\begin{array}{r} 7 \\ +\ 2 \\ \hline \end{array}$

9. $\begin{array}{r} 9 \\ +\ 9 \\ \hline \end{array}$

10. $\begin{array}{r} 9 \\ +\ 5 \\ \hline \end{array}$

11. $\begin{array}{r} 8 \\ +\ 7 \\ \hline \end{array}$

12. $\begin{array}{r} 4 \\ +\ 6 \\ \hline \end{array}$

Notes for Home Children practice for the Grade 3 TAAS test by reviewing addition of whole numbers.

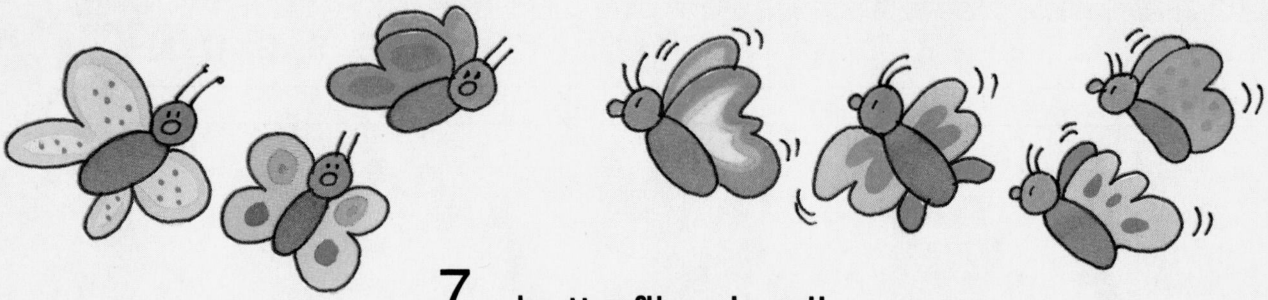

7 butterflies in all

Tell an addition story.
How many are there in all?

13.

10 ladybugs in all

14.

____ crickets in all

15.

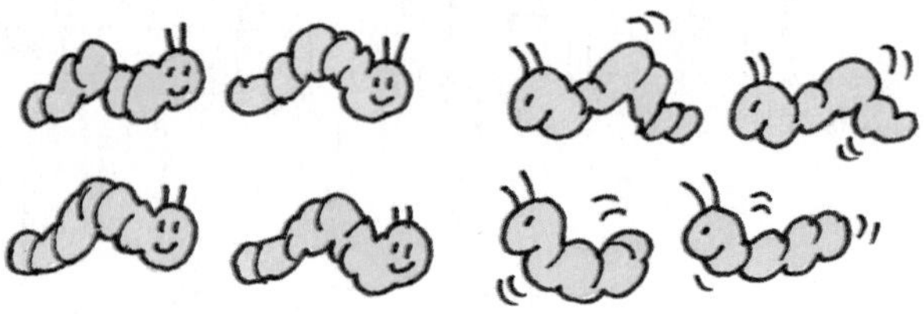

____ caterpillars in all

16.

____ flies in all

17.

____ bees in all

18.

____ ants in all

Notes for Home Children practice for the Grade 3 TAAS test by reviewing addition of whole numbers.

Name

LESSON 7

$12 - 4 = 8$

Write how many are left.

1.

$4 - 1 = 3$

2.

$10 - 3 = \_\_\_$

Subtract.

3. $\begin{array}{r} 8 \\ -\ 3 \\ \hline \end{array}$

4. $\begin{array}{r} 12 \\ -\ 6 \\ \hline \end{array}$

5. $\begin{array}{r} 17 \\ -\ 8 \\ \hline \end{array}$

6. $\begin{array}{r} 5 \\ -\ 3 \\ \hline \end{array}$

7. $\begin{array}{r} 11 \\ -\ 3 \\ \hline \end{array}$

8. $\begin{array}{r} 18 \\ -\ 9 \\ \hline \end{array}$

9. $\begin{array}{r} 9 \\ -\ 4 \\ \hline \end{array}$

10. $\begin{array}{r} 6 \\ -\ 2 \\ \hline \end{array}$

11. $\begin{array}{r} 16 \\ -\ 9 \\ \hline \end{array}$

12. $\begin{array}{r} 15 \\ -\ 7 \\ \hline \end{array}$

Notes for Home Children practice for the Grade 3 TAAS test by reviewing subtraction of whole numbers.

$5 - 2 = 3$ 3 cats are left.

Tell a subtraction story.
Write how many are left.

13.

$18 - 9 =$ ____

____ bugs are left.

14.

$10 - 6 =$ ____

____ elephants are left.

15.

$12 - 7 =$ ____

____ dogs are left.

16.

$15 - 6 =$ ____

____ bears are left.

Notes for Home Children practice for the Grade 3 TAAS test by reviewing subtraction of whole numbers.

Name ______________________________

LESSON 8

Jamal saw 6 birds in a tree.
2 flew away.
How many birds were left?

$$\begin{array}{r} 6 \\ \boxed{-}\ 2 \\ \hline 4 \end{array}$$ birds

Write + or − in the ☐.
Then add or subtract.

1. Maria saw 9 rabbits in the field.
4 hopped away.
How many rabbits were left?

$$\begin{array}{r} 9 \\ \square\ 4 \\ \hline \end{array}$$ ____ rabbits

2. Beth saw 7 kites.
She saw 3 more.
How many kites did she see in all?

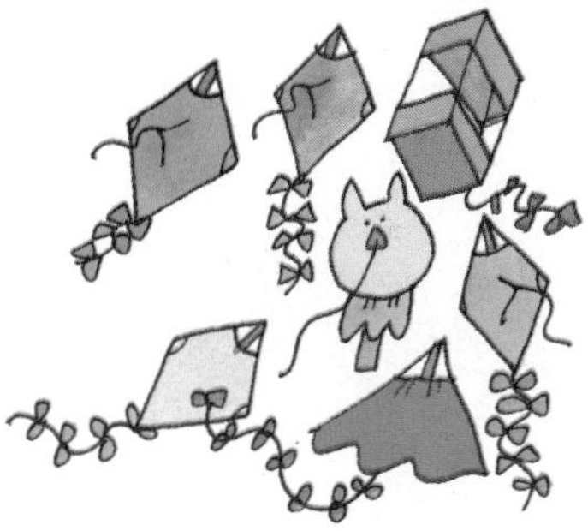

$$\begin{array}{r} 7 \\ \square\ 3 \\ \hline \end{array}$$ ____ kites

3. Andy had 12 frogs.
7 frogs jumped away.
How many were left?

$$\begin{array}{r} 12 \\ \square\ 7 \\ \hline \end{array}$$ ____ frogs

Notes for Home Children practice for the Grade 3 TAAS test by reviewing addition and subtraction problems with whole numbers.

Texas TAAS REVIEW

Write + or − in the □.
Then add or subtract.

4. Jason saw 5 cats on the step.
He saw 6 more cats in the tree.
How many cats did he see?

$$\begin{array}{r} 5 \\ \boxed{+}\ 6 \\ \hline 11 \end{array}$$

11 cats

5. There were 16 fish.
8 swam away.
How many fish were left?

$$\begin{array}{r} 16 \\ \square\ 8 \\ \hline \end{array}$$

____ fish

6. Kevin saw 6 cars.
He saw 8 more.
How many cars did Kevin see?

$$\begin{array}{r} 6 \\ \square\ 8 \\ \hline \end{array}$$

____ cars

7. Willa had 17 apples.
9 were eaten.
How many apples were left?

$$\begin{array}{r} 17 \\ \square\ 9 \\ \hline \end{array}$$

____ apples

Notes for Home Children practice for the Grade 3 TAAS test by reviewing addition and subtraction problems with whole numbers.

Name ______________________________

This pictograph shows the favorite pets of the class.

Favorite Pets

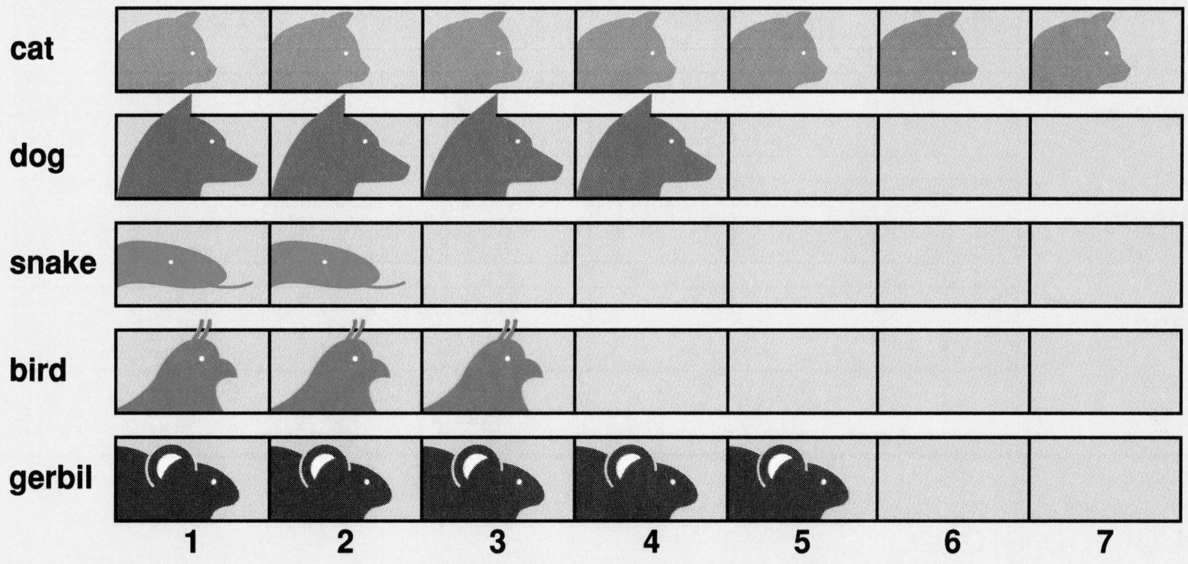

Look at the graph.

1. How many of each pet are there?

cats 7 ___ birds ___ gerbils ___

dogs ___ snakes ___

2. Ring the most favorite pet.

cats or birds dogs or gerbils

3. Ring the least favorite pet.

snakes or gerbils cats or dogs

Notes for Home Children practice for the Grade 3 TAAS test by reviewing a pictograph.

This pictograph shows what the children ate for lunch.

Lunch Food

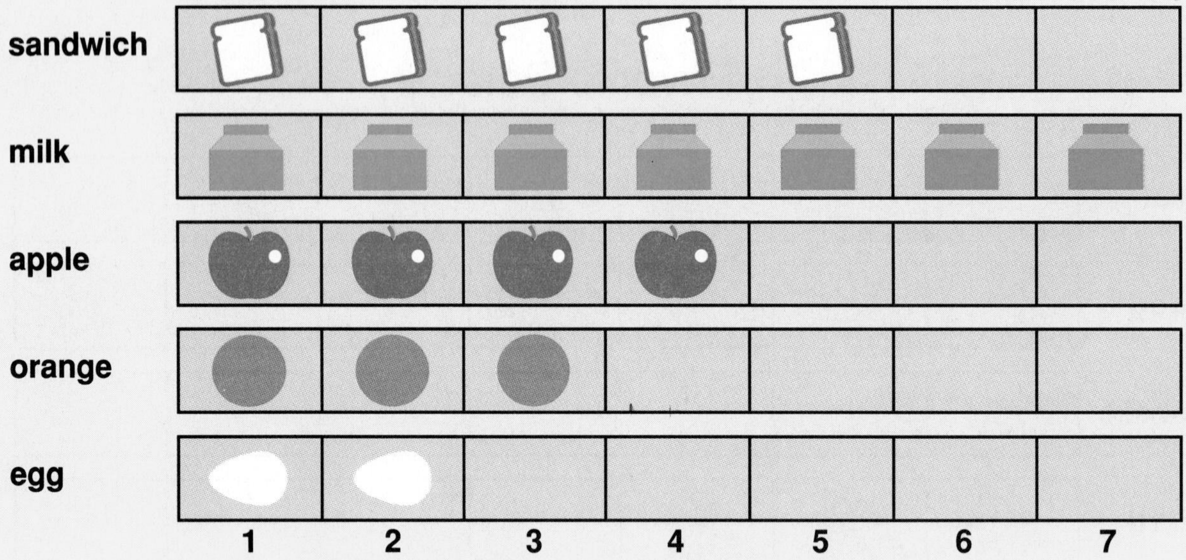

Look at the graph.

4. How many of each food did the children eat?

oranges 3 sandwiches ____ apples ____

eggs ____ milks ____

5. Ring the food that was eaten the most.

eggs or milks sandwiches or apples

6. Ring the food that was eaten the least.

apples or oranges eggs or sandwiches

Notes for Home Children practice for the Grade 3 TAAS test by reviewing a pictograph.

Use with page 46.

Use with pages 47-48.

Use with page 49.

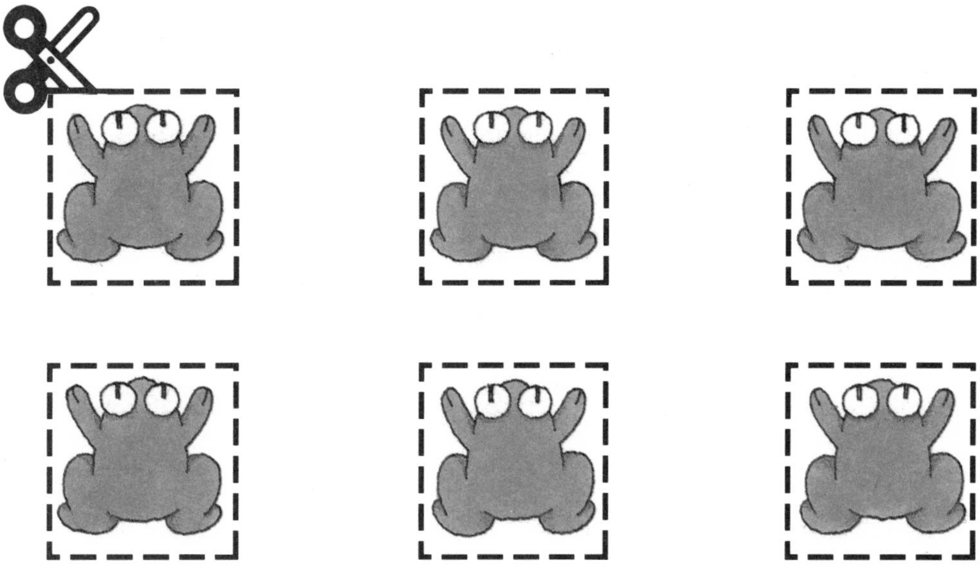

Use with page 106.

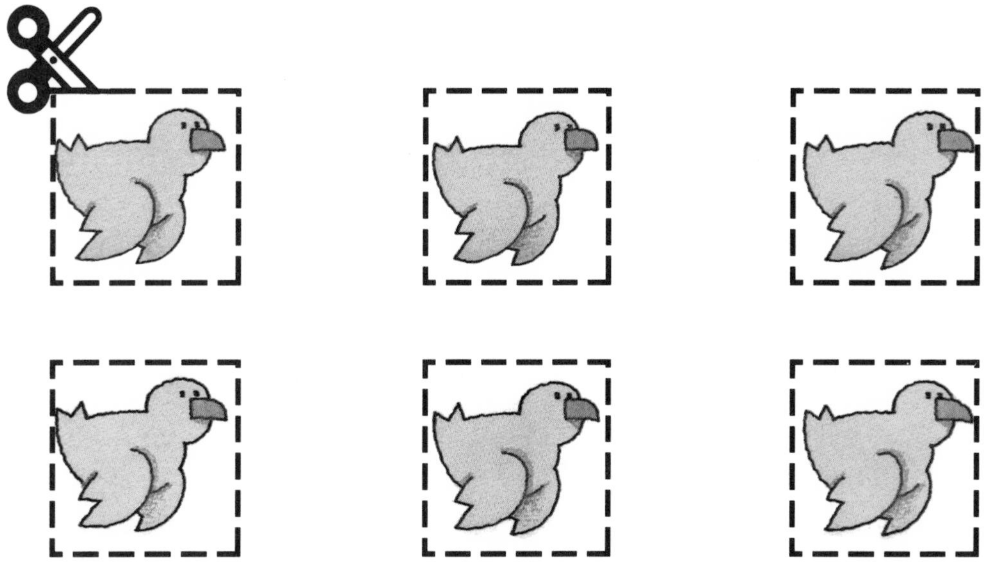

Use with pages 107-108.

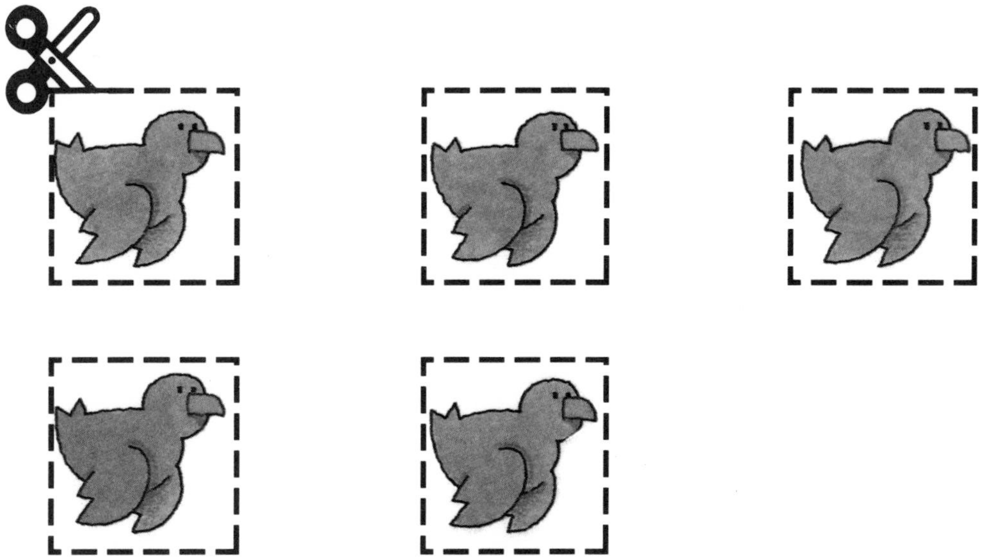

Use with page 109.

Use with pages 187-188.

Use with pages 189-190.

Use with pages 185-186.

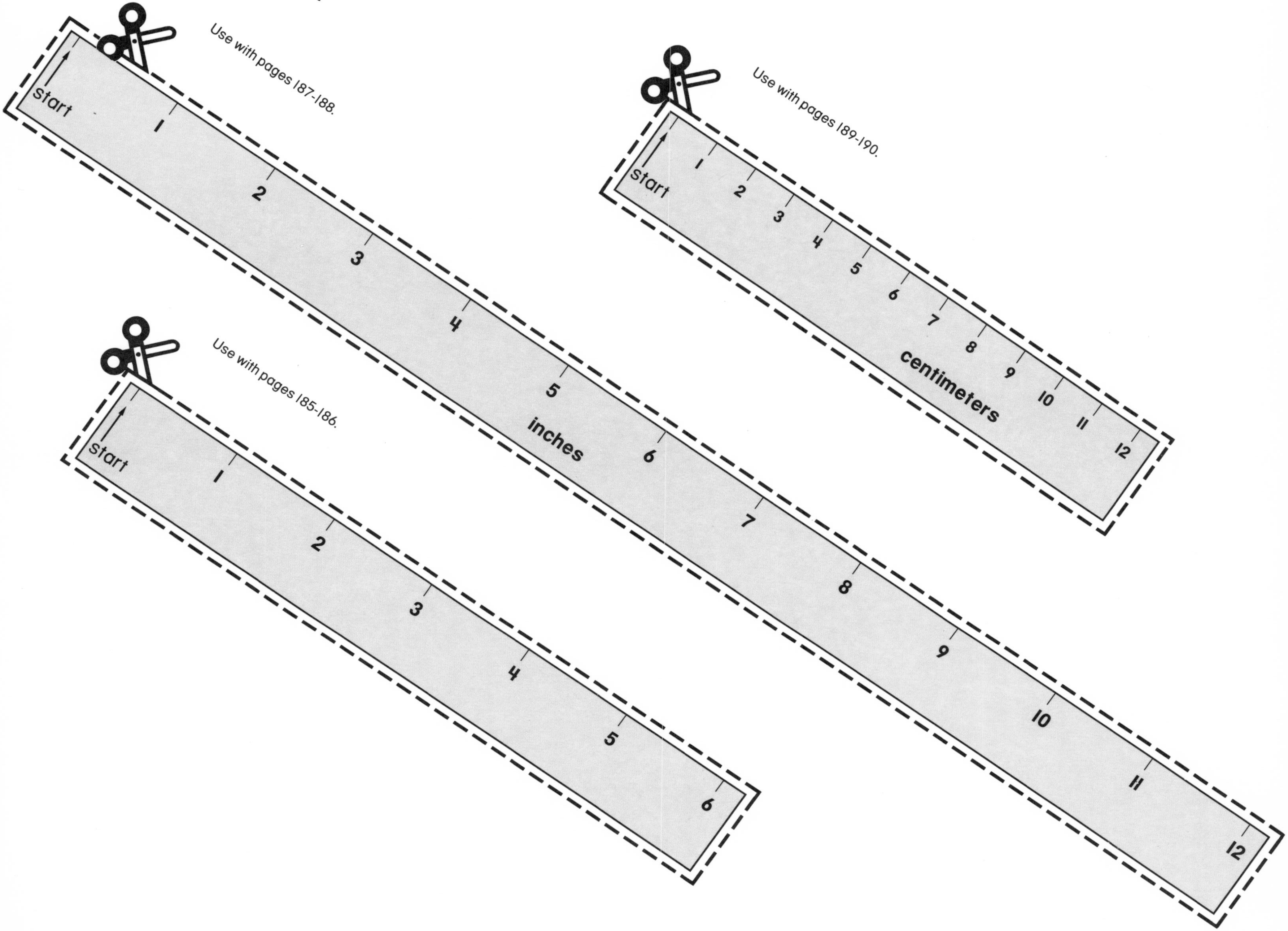